Anglo-Saxon England 1

Her mon mæg giet gesion hiora swæð

ANGLO-SAXON ENGLAND

I

Edited by
PETER CLEMOES

MARTIN BIDDLE

RENÉ DEROLEZ

STANLEY GREENFIELD

PETER HUNTER BLAIR

PAUL MEYVAERT

RAYMOND PAGE

JULIAN BROWN

HELMUT GNEUSS

LARS-GUNNAR HALLANDER

JOHN LEYERLE

BRUCE MITCHELL

FRED ROBINSON

CAMBRIDGE
At the University Press
1972

Published by the Syndics of the Cambridge University Press
Bentley House, 200 Euston Road, London NW1 2DB
American Branch: 32 East 57th Street, New York, NY10022

© Cambridge University Press 1972

Library of Congress Catalogue Card Number: 78-190423

ISBN: 0 521 08557 8

Printed in Great Britain
at the University Printing House, Cambridge
(Brooke Crutchley, University Printer)

Contents

Contents

*Abbreviations listed before the bibliography (pp. 309–10) are used throughout
the volume without other explanation*

Illustrations

Illustrations

Preface

This new periodical, to be published annually, expresses the growing sense of community among scholars working in the various branches of Anglo-Saxon studies in many parts of the world. It reflects their increasing realization that the different disciplines they represent aid each other and are but aspects of a common interest. This is all the more so because the surviving source materials of any one kind are inevitably limited. One type of evidence needs to be studied in relation to another if the connections they had originally are to be understood today. No other periodical meets this need comprehensively. This is the only regular publication devoted solely to Anglo-Saxon studies and to fostering cooperation between them all. The editors want to stimulate investigation of the less commonly considered forms of evidence – Anglo-Latin literature for example. In this way and by bringing related specializations into direct communication we hope to promote fresh areas of knowledge and to invigorate growth in new directions. In all fields we intend to encourage new thinking which is aware of the potential of evidence, while respecting its limitations, and which is supported by technical skill, rational argument and expressive writing.

The present volume, it is hoped, makes a worthwhile start. The span of ecclesiastical history that it represents begins early in the seventh century with the conversion of East Anglia and ends in fourteenth-century Iceland with material from a late-twelfth-century service-book from England supplying information on Edward the Confessor. Its contributions to intellectual history increase our understanding of two important schools: the Old English Orosius is examined afresh as a unique witness to the geographical knowledge in King Alfred's court, and the leading part played by Bishop Æthelwold's school at Winchester in the period of monastic reform is revealed more clearly both as regards the systematic training it gave in vernacular usage and as regards the composition of Latin poetry it encouraged and the Latin authors, such as Horace, that it knew. Allegory in Old English literature is a topic explored by several contributors – its roots in patristic thought, its subordination to an inclusive visionary image, its use for homiletic purposes, and the contrast between its relatively schematized, consistent method and the less conceptualized, less defined movement of thought in *Beowulfian* epic. Two articles deal with the relationship between the Old English poem *The Phoenix* and Lactantius's *De Ave Phoenice*: in treating *The*

Phoenix as a visionary poem one author emphasizes its differences from Lactantius, while the other elucidates three readings in the Old English by reference to Lactantius's Latin and (as a slightly different contribution to lexical studies) identifies some previously unrecognized Lactantian material in the Cleopatra Glossary. Indeed, Anglo-Saxon relations with the continent in their many-sidedness form a constantly recurring theme: the new conclusion that the Leiden Riddle was copied at Fleury in the tenth century and the first publication of a poem on free will composed by a foreigner in Bishop Æthelwold's Winchester are examples of only two of the several kinds of attention that these all-pervading connections with Europe receive in this volume; another kind – to mention no more than one – lies behind an account of the revolution in our ideas of Anglo-Saxon domestic buildings fomented during the last two decades by the excavation of comparable buildings on the continent and also gives rise to an appeal to follow recent continental precedent (in suitable cases) by using archaeology to assist the study of the fabric of Anglo-Saxon churches above ground. Concerning the relations between the Anglo-Saxons and the other peoples in the British Isles, a new answer is given to a major, basic question when, on the grounds of a Northumbrian palaeographical ancestry and affinities with Pictish sculpture, it is argued that the Book of Kells is likely to have been produced in a great insular centre in eastern Scotland during the second half of the eighth century. Another sort of synthesis is represented by a formulation of the principles that should govern the study of surviving Anglo-Saxon buildings; and a survey of our present knowledge of the Anglo-Saxon house – intended to be the first of a series of review articles – sums up a rapidly changing subject that is of great interest not only to archaeologists but also to those concerned with related evidence in documents, literature and the arts. The bibliography, which covers publications in all branches of Anglo-Saxon studies in 1971 and which is to be continued annually, is meant to help a reader to keep in touch with current work in specializations other than his own and, perhaps, to save him from overlooking a piece of work in his own specialization which has been published in an out-of-the-way place. There is to be an index to *Anglo-Saxon England* after five issues.

The contributors link the generations as the well as disciplines, for early writings by some accompany the work of others with long experience, including the last article for a periodical by the late Kemp Malone. It is fitting that there should be this sign of continuity as Malone's long-sustained and influential contribution draws to its close. May the future of our studies be worthy of their past.

My thanks go to the contributors (including the compilers of the bibliography), to my fellow editors and to the Cambridge University Press and members of its staff for actively supporting this venture at its outset. I am grateful to Mrs Janet Godden for help in preparing the typescript for the press and in checking the proofs.

PETER CLEMOES

for the editors

Material may be submitted to any of the editors, but it would be appreciated if the one most convenient regionally were chosen (Australasian contributions should be submitted to Bruce Mitchell) unless an article deals mainly with archaeology, palaeography, art, history or Viking studies, in which case the most suitable editor would be Martin Biddle (archaeology), Julian Brown (palaeography and art), Peter Hunter Blair (history) or Raymond Page (Viking studies). A potential contributor is asked to get in touch with the editor concerned as early as possible to obtain a copy of the style sheet and to have any necessary discussion. Articles must be in English.

The editors' addresses are

Mr M. Biddle, Winchester Research Unit, 13 Parchment Street, Winchester, Hampshire (England)

Professor T. J. Brown, Department of Palaeography, King's College, University of London, Strand, London WC2R 2LS (England)

Professor P. A. M. Clemoes, Emmanuel College, Cambridge CB2 3AP (England)

Professor R. Derolez, Rozier 44, 9000 Gent (Belgium)

Professor H. Gneuss, Englisches Seminar, Universität München, 8 München 13, Schellingstrasse 3 (Germany)

Professor S. B. Greenfield, Department of English, College of Liberal Arts, University of Oregon, Eugene, Oregon 97403 (USA)

Dr L.-G. Hallander, Lövångersgatan 16, 162 21 Vällingby (Sweden)

Mr P. Hunter Blair, Emmanuel College, Cambridge CB2 3AP (England)

Professor J. Leyerle, Centre for Medieval Studies, University of Toronto, Toronto 181 (Canada)

Mr P. Meyvaert, Mediaeval Academy of America, 1430 Massachusetts Avenue, Cambridge, Massachusetts 02138 (USA)

Dr B. Mitchell, St Edmund Hall, Oxford OX1 4AR (England)

Dr R. I. Page, Corpus Christi College, Cambridge CB2 1RH (England)

Professor F. C. Robinson, Department of English, Yale University, New Haven, Connecticut 06520 (USA)

The pre-Viking age church in East Anglia

DOROTHY WHITELOCK

It is well known that sources for the Anglo-Saxon period are unevenly distributed, and that we are particularly badly off for reliable evidence relating to East Anglia, especially in the period before the Viking raids and settlements. The main reason for this lies in the effects of those raids and settlements, for not only were the monasteries destroyed, but the two East Anglian sees of *Dommoc* and Elmham ceased to exist, and only Elmham was restored, and not, as far as our evidence goes, much before 955.[1] Henceforward there was only one bishop for the whole of East Anglia, though at times it appears to have had a centre for Suffolk at Hoxne[2] as well as one at Elmham. The East Anglian see was transferred to Thetford in 1071–2, and eventually about 1095 to Norwich.[3] With such breaks in continuity it is not to be wondered that no pre-Viking age manuscripts or charters have come down by preservation in East Anglian churches, and it is doubtful how far any information in post-Conquest writers is likely to go back on genuine tradition.[4] What we know about the early church in East Anglia comes from evidence preserved elsewhere, except in as far as the finds at Sutton Hoo have implications concerning the conversion of this kingdom.[5] Our main

---

[1] The profession of Athulf, bishop of Elmham, to Oda, archbishop of Canterbury from 941 to 958, is extant, though the name is wrongly given as *Eadulf* (*BCS* 918). His first recorded attestation is in 955 (*BCS* 917). Previously part, at least, of East Anglia had been administered by Theodred, bishop of London, whose signatures occur from 926 to 951. See *Anglo-Saxon Wills*, ed. D. Whitelock (Cambridge, 1930), p. 99.   [2] *Ibid.* p. 102.

[3] See B. Dodwell, 'The Foundation of Norwich Cathedral', *TRHS* 5th ser. 7 (1957), 1–18.

[4] On the unreliability of post-Conquest writers about East Anglia, see below, p. 11, n. 1, and D. Whitelock, 'Fact and Fiction in the Legend of St Edmund', *Proc. of the Suffolk Inst. of Archaeology* 31 (1969), 217–33. It is possible that the twelfth-century *Liber Eliensis* may occasionally preserve a correct tradition, but one cannot be certain, and some of its information is contrary to earlier sources. Seeing that some reliable early documents were available at Peterborough after the Conquest (see below, p. 15) one cannot pronounce it impossible for any to have survived at other destroyed houses, such as Ely; but nothing is quoted with the detail which allowed the Peterborough information to be accepted as genuine. Hence it seems best to use only pre-Conquest evidence in the body of this article, and to relegate to footnotes later claims. These have too often been repeated without indication of their sources as if they were established fact.

[5] Since numismatists no longer maintain that this richly furnished heathen burial must be dated after the middle of the seventh century, but allow a date much earlier, perhaps in the time of Rædwald, the presence of some Christian objects in heathen surroundings presents no great difficulty.

Architectural remains tell us practically nothing about early East Anglia. It is suggested that the ruins of South Elmham may be a little before the Danish Conquest, and that there may be

                                           CAS

source is Bede's *Historia Ecclesiastica,* but this can be supplemented by some pieces of evidence from other sources, and it may be worth while to assemble these and study their implications.[1]

In his preface, Bede mentions as his authorities for the church in East Anglia first Albinus, abbot of the monastery of St Peter and St Paul in Canterbury, who had encouraged him to write the *Historia Ecclesiastica* and had sent him by Nothhelm, priest of the church of London, information on the names of the kings and bishops under whom the English provinces, including East Anglia, were converted; secondly, he says: 'What things concerning the church occurred in the province of the East Angles we discovered partly from the writings and tradition of those before us, partly from the account of the most reverend Abbot Esi.' One of the writings would be the *Vita Fursei;* others may have been documents sent by Albinus. It is possible that in the 'tradition of those before us' was included information from his own abbot, Ceolfrith, who, as we shall see,[2] had visited as a young man the monastery of St Botulf in East Anglia; but Ceolfrith left Jarrow in 716, and as early as this Bede may not have availed himself of this opportunity. He never mentions Botulf. But he does refer to an aged brother of his monastery, still living, who said that a very truthful and religious man told him that he had seen Fursa in East Anglia, and heard his vision from his own lips.[3] There may also have been unrecorded contacts between East Anglian and Northumbrian ecclesiastics: as we shall see,[4] Bede had seen a manuscript which had been brought from Rome to East Anglia.

Some traditions about East Anglia may have been current in Northumbria from contacts between the royal families of the two kingdoms, and have reached Bede: Hereswith, sister of St Hild, and kinswoman of Edwin of Northumbria, was married to Æthelric, brother of Anna of East Anglia, and mother of Aldwulf of East Anglia,[5] whom Bede is able to quote as

---

evidence that those at North Elmham were of a church rebuilt on one dating from the seventh century (see H. M. Taylor and Joan Taylor, *Anglo-Saxon Architecture* (Cambridge, 1965), pp. 228–33). But excavation is in progress at North Elmham, and an interim report by P. Wade-Martins is published in *Norfolk Archaeology* 34 (1969), 352–97.

[1] The following abbreviations are used: *BCS* = *Cartularium Saxonicum,* ed. W. de G. Birch (London, 1885–93); *Councils* = *Councils and Ecclesiastical Documents relating to Great Britain and Ireland,* ed. A. W. Haddan and W. Stubbs (Oxford, 1869–78); *EHD* = *English Historical Documents* c. *500–1042,* ed. D. Whitelock (London, 1955); *FW* = *Florentii Wigorniensis Monachi Chronicon ex Chronicis,* ed. B. Thorpe (London, 1848–9); *HE* = Bede's *Historia Ecclesiastica Gentis Anglorum,* quoted by book and chapter; *LE* = *Liber Eliensis,* ed. E. O. Blake (London, 1962); *MGH* = Monumenta Germaniae Historica; *WM* = William of Malmesbury: *GP* = *De Gestis Pontificum Anglorum,* ed. N. E. S. A. Hamilton, Rolls Series (1870); *GR* = *De Gestis Regum Anglorum,* ed. W. Stubbs, RS (1887–9).

[2] Below, pp. 10–11.   [3] *HE* III. 19.   [4] Below, p. 9.

[5] *HE* IV. 23. On her husband's name, see F. M. Stenton, 'The East Anglian Kings of the Seventh Century', *The Anglo-Saxons: Studies in some Aspects of their History and Culture presented to Bruce Dickins,* ed. P. Clemoes (London, 1959), pp. 48–9; repr. *Preparatory to Anglo-Saxon England,* ed. D. M. Stenton (Oxford, 1970), pp. 398–9.

claiming to have seen Rædwald's temple still standing in his boyhood;[1] Hild herself spent a year in East Anglia in 647, intending to follow her sister Hereswith to Chelles, where she had become a nun, but Aidan recalled Hild to Northumbria;[2] a later royal marriage was that of King Anna's daughter Æthelthryth to Ecgfrith of Northumbria,[3] and she brought with her her chief thegn, Owine, who then entered religion at Lastingham,[4] a house with which Bede was in contact. All this was some way in the past when Bede was writing, but knowledge about East Anglia may have been handed down.

From the *Historia Ecclesiastica* we learn that Rædwald of East Anglia came into contact with Christianity before 616 at the court of his overlord Æthelberht of Kent, and was 'initiated into the mysteries of the Christian faith'.[5] He abandoned it on his return, under the influence of his wife and others, but compromised by erecting an altar for the Christian sacrifice in the same temple as an *arula* (the diminutive is probably contemptuous) to offer victims to idols. It was this temple which King Aldwulf, who lived until about 713, testified to having seen. One should note also that the monk of Whitby who wrote the Life of St Gregory, says that the mysterious visitor who appeared to Edwin when he was an exile staying at Rædwald's court was said to be Bishop Paulinus.[6] One cannot accept this as fact, seeing that Bede either was ignorant of it or rejected it; yet it is certainly probable that Æthelberht would send some ecclesiastics back with Rædwald to East Anglia after his conversion.[7]

We next learn that Earpwald, Rædwald's son, was persuaded by his overlord, Edwin of Northumbria, who had been baptized in 627, to accept the Christian faith with all his people; but he was killed soon afterwards by a heathen called Ricberht, and the province remained heathen for three years.[8] Meanwhile Earpwald's brother[9] Sigeberht had fled from Rædwald's hostility and was living in exile in Gaul, where he became converted. As soon as he came to the throne, in 630 or 631, he was eager to convert his people, and was supported by Bishop Felix, who had been born and ordained in Burgundy, had come to Archbishop Honorius at Canterbury, and been sent by him to

---

[1] *HE* II. 15.   [2] *HE* IV. 23.   [3] *HE* IV. 19.

[4] *HE* IV. 3. But Imma, a thegn of Ælfwine, King Ecgfrith's brother, who had previously been a thegn of Æthelthryth, could not have come with her from East Anglia, for he was a youth at the time of his capture at the battle of the Trent in 678 (*HE* IV. 22).   [5] *HE* II. 15.

[6] *The Earliest Life of Gregory the Great*, ed. B. Colgrave (Lawrence, 1968), p. 100.

[7] *LE* (p. 4) even brings Augustine himself into these regions. It repeats a tradition that there had been a villa at *Cratendun* about a mile from Ely, where utensils of iron and coins of kings were often found. It says that Æthelthryth first chose a dwelling there, but moved to a higher site, and that there was a monastery, founded by St Augustine and dedicated to St Mary, which was destroyed by Penda's army. On p. 33 it says that Æthelthryth laboured to restore it, adorning it with monastic buildings.

[8] *HE* II. 15.

[9] FW (1, 260) and WM (*GR* 1, 97) make Sigeberht Earpwald's half-brother, on the mother's side, but this is not in Bede.

convert the East Angles.[1] He was given a see at *Dommoc*, Dunwich or Felixstowe.[2] Sigeberht was eager to imitate the things which he had seen well arranged in Gaul, and established a school[3] where boys could be taught letters, with the help of Felix, who provided him with teachers and masters as in the Kentish school. Later Sigeberht resigned his throne to his kinsman Ecgric, and entered a monastery which he had himself founded.[4] A considerable time after, he was unwillingly dragged from the monastery to accompany the army against an attack by Penda of Mercia, and rode unarmed, carrying only a staff. He was killed and along with him his successor Ecgric.[5] Anna then came to the throne.

[1] *HE* ii. 15 and iii. 18.

[2] *Dommoc*, as in the Leningrad and Tiberius C. ii manuscripts of Bede, and in the Old English version, is the best recorded form. It used confidently to be identified as Dunwich, but S. E. Rigold, in 'The Supposed See of Dunwich', *JBAA* 3rd ser. 14 (1961), 55–9, makes a case for Felixstowe, with which it was identified in 1298 by Bartholomew Cotton, a Suffolk man. Since in Bede and the record of the synod of *Clofeshoh* of 803 (*BCS* 312) it is called a *civitas*, it must have been on a Roman site, and Rigold suggests that this was Walton Castle, a Saxon Shore fort about half a mile from Felixstowe, destroyed by the sea in the eighteenth century. *Dommoc* does not easily become *Dun*. Rigold says that, apart from one twelfth-century manuscript of William of Malmesbury's *Gesta Pontificum*, Thomas of Elmham in the fifteenth century is the first to equate it with Dunwich. But one should also pay attention to the tradition preserved at the priory of Eye. This was founded in the reign of William I, and its foundation charter gives it 'all the churches which then existed or might subsequently be erected in the town of *Donewic* . . . and also the schools there' (Dugdale, *Monasticon* iii, 404–6). The priory established a cell at Dunwich, which was destroyed by the sea. Leland, who equates Dunwich with Felix's see at *Dunmoc*, says that in his day the priory of Eye had a gospel book, known as the Red Book of Eye, on which people took oaths, and that the monks affirmed that it had belonged to Felix, which suggests that they connected the cell they had had in Dunwich with Felix's see. Leland thinks the claim probable: 'Nam præterquam quod sit scriptus litteris majusculis Longobardicis, refert vetustatem mire venerandum' (*De Rebus Britannicis Collectanea*, ed. T. Hearne (London, 1770) iv, 26–7). The identification of this manuscript with fragmentary gospels in Cambridge, Corpus Christi College 197, based on a statement by Bishop Tanner in *Bibliotheca Britannica*, *s.v. Faelix*, has been shown improbable by M. R. James, *The Sources of Archbishop Parker's Collection of Manuscripts at Corpus Christi College, Cambridge* (Cambridge, 1899), pp. 6–9. The seal of Æthelwald, bishop of *Dommoc* (see below, p. 18) was found near the priory of Eye. Another argument in favour of Dunwich, which I owe to Mr D. Charman, is the fact that the *Quo Warranto Inquest Roll* speaks of carrying services owed by sokemen of South Elmham, which was a manor of the bishops of East Anglia from pre-Conquest times, to Dunwich.

[3] WM (*GP*, p. 147) says that Felix founded schools. He says that he died at *Dommoc* and was translated to *Seham*, where there were in William's day traces of a church burnt by the Danes, and later (p. 153) he calls it an episcopal see. *LE* (p. 17) agrees in the place of burial, saying that there was a great and famous monastery there, founded by a venerable *clito* called Lutting, under Abbot Wereferd. The author claims an English source, which has not come down, when he says that Felix founded a monastery at *Seham* and a church at *Redham* (probably Reedham, Norfolk); *Seham* was destroyed by the Danes along with Ely after the martyrdom of King Edmund. Their description shows that both WM and *LE* mean by *Seham* the Cambridgeshire Soham; A. Jessopp ('Norwich', *Diocesan Histories* (London, 1884), p. 11, n. 1) mentions 'traditions of a later age' that Felix established a school at Saham Tony, Norfolk. *Chronicon Abbatiæ Rameseiensis* (ed. W. D. Macray, RS (1886), p. 127) describes the translation of the bones of St Felix from Soham to Ramsey.

[4] *LE* (p. 11), in an entry interlined in the oldest manuscript, says this monastery was at *Betrichesworde* (later Bury St Edmund's). This, if true, would help to explain the choice of this place for the translation of St Edmund's body later on.   [5] *HE* iii. 18.

It is sometimes categorically stated that Felix came from one of the monasteries established in Burgundy by the Irish missionary Columbanus. There is no support for this in Bede, but recently Mr James Campbell has examined the continental background at this era and shown how likely this is.[1] It is also possible that Sigeberht's conversion in Gaul was at a place under Irish influence, but it is only late authorities that make him know Felix there and bring him to East Anglia with him, which is contrary to Bede's account.[2] Even if Felix did come from a Columban monastery, it does not follow that he observed Celtic practices to the extent of keeping the Celtic Easter, for this was given up by some of Columbanus's followers in Gaul. At this early date, some amount of difference of usage might easily be tolerated by Archbishop Honorius, who, Bede says, held the Celtic missionary from Iona to Northumbria, St Aidan, in high regard some years later, as also did Felix.[3]

However, the Irish connections of Felix are at most a probability, not a certainty. There was, however, a certain Celtic strain in the conversion of East Anglia. In Sigeberht's reign there came an Irishman called Fursa from Ireland and he was given by the king a Roman fort, *Cnobheresburg*, almost certainly to be identified with Burgh Castle,[4] in which to found a monastery for himself and his companions.[5] Bede's long chapter on Fursa[6] is mainly concerned with his vision of the other world, taken from the *Vita Fursei*, but he adds to his source the information that Fursa converted many people by his preaching.[7] The monastery which he founded, and which he left in charge of his half-brother Foillan and two Irish priests Gobban and Dicuil, when he left, first to join his brother Ultan as a hermit, and then to go to Gaul, was adorned by King Anna and the nobles of the province with statelier buildings and gifts. What made Fursa leave East Anglia for Gaul was that 'he saw the province disturbed by the invasions of the heathens and foresaw that danger also threatened the monasteries'. The plural is of interest. Besides Burgh Castle, we know that Sigeberht had founded the monastery into which he retired. There may have been others. Fursa built a monastery

---

[1] 'The First Century of Christianity in England', *Ampleforth Jnl* 76 (1971), 16–29.

[2] FW I, 17; WM, *GP*, p. 147.   [3] *HE* III. 25.

[4] Excavations at Burgh Castle have revealed a Christian cemetery and some early plaster and post-holes of a wooden building; see Taylor and Taylor, *Anglo-Saxon Architecture*, p. 118.

[5] An apocryphal story in an Irish source, probably of the ninth century, *The Monastery of Tallaght* (ed. E. J. Gwynn and W. J. Purton, *Proc. of the R. Irish Acad.* 29 (1911–12), 134), says that Fursa was given land by the daughter of 'the king of the eastern country'. She asked him: 'What manner of man art thou?' 'Like an old smith', he said, 'with his anvil on his shoulder.' 'The anvil of devotion', said she. 'Perseverance in holiness', said he. 'A question', said she: 'if God should give thee a block where thine anvil might be planted, wouldst thou abide there?' 'It would be likely indeed', said he. Then she bestowed on him the spot where he was.

[6] *HE* III. 19. The version of the *Vita Fursei* used by Bede was very similar to that edited by B. Krusch, MGH, Script. Rer. Merov. 4, 434–40.

[7] A ninth-century work, *Virtutes Fursei* (ed. B. Krusch, *ibid.* p. 441) makes the claim that Fursa constructed monasteries and churches and established monks and virgins for the service of the Lord.

at Lagny, on the Marne, but after his death his remains were translated by the patrician Erchinvald to Péronne.[1]

At this point one can supplement Bede's account from a source[2] which Father Grosjean showed in 1960 to be worth more consideration than it had received. He showed that an account of Foillan, Fursa's half-brother, was written not later than 655–6, at Nivelles. It tells us that after Fursa's death (*c.* 649–50) the tempest which he had foreseen raged; the most Christian king, Anna, was expelled and the monastery (*Cnobheresburg*) despoiled, the monks and all its goods scattered. Abbot Foillan would have been led away to death but for divine intervention: the heathens heard of the approach of King Anna and were afraid. The monks were redeemed from captivity and the holy relics were found. The equipment of the altar and books were laden on a ship, and Foillan and his followers went across to the Frankish kingdom and were received by the patrician Erchinvald at the place where Fursa lay buried (Péronne). Not much later, however, these *peregrini* were expelled by Erchinvald and came to Nivelles, where they were well received by Iduberge (Itte) and her daughter St Gertrude. Foillan founded a monastery at Fosse by the River Biesme. It is known that Itte died on 8 May 652, and the account appears to have been written while Gertrude was still alive. Later Foillan and three companions were murdered by brigands.

This text allows us to add a little to the political history of East Anglia. Bede was not writing political history, but he does tell us of an attack by Penda of Mercia in which the kings Sigeberht and Ecgric were killed.[3] He does not date it, but Penda was hardly likely to be strong enough to attack the East Angles until after he had defeated Oswald of Northumbria in 641.[4] This attack may well have been the disturbance which caused Fursa to go to Gaul. Bede also tells us that Penda attacked and killed King Anna. This is dated 654 by manuscripts A, B and C of the *Anglo-Saxon Chronicle*, 653 by manuscript E. From the Nivelles account one can add an attack by heathens (presumably Mercians) in between the two mentioned by Bede, a serious attack which temporarily drove out Anna; but this time he was able to return. It can be dated between Fursa's death, 649–50, and that of St Itte in May 652, probably some time before this, to allow of Foillan's journey to Péronne and his stay there. The interest of the Nivelles account for ecclesiastical history is that it suggests that the monastery of *Cnobheresburg* came to an end by *c.* 651, or at least that it was then deserted by its Celtic inmates. There is no further evidence of Celtic influence in the East Anglian church.

---

[1] According to the *Virtutes Fursei* (p. 445) Fursa died at Mézerolles in Ponthieu, on his way to revisit his brothers Foillan and Ultan in England.

[2] *Additamentum Nivialense de Foillano*, discussed by P. Grosjean in *AB* 78 (1960), 365–9.

[3] *HE* III. 18.

[4] The date 637 given by *LE* (p. 11) is certainly too early.

From Bede, we learn that Felix was succeeded after an episcopate of seventeen years by his deacon, Thomas, a man of the Gyrwe,[1] i.e. the people immediately west of East Anglia, in the fenlands. The extent of their territory is uncertain. We know from Bede that it included Peterborough,[2] and from *The Resting-Places of the English Saints* that it included Crowland.[3] The *Tribal Hidage*[4] divides it into the South and North Gyrwe, with 600 hides each. Æthelthryth was married to a *princeps* (ealdorman) of the South Gyrwe.[5] The author of the *Liber Eliensis*, who claims to have a written source for this information, says that he gave her the Isle of Ely as her dower;[6] and since Bede says that the Isle contained 600 families,[7] it is natural that it should sometimes have been identified as the area of the South Gyrwe. But Bede says that Ely is in the province of the East Angles, and that it was because Æthelthryth came from that province that she wished to have a monastery in Ely.[8] If we accept recent suggestions for identifying the names which follow the North Gyrwe in the *Tribal Hidage*, the area of the Gyrwe did not come as far south as Ely.[9] By the early eighth century, Crowland was in the diocese of the Middle Angles,[10] who came under Mercian control in the mid seventh century; but it is likely that previously the Gyrwe were subordinate to East Anglia.[11]

---

[1] *HE* III. 20. [2] *HE* IV. 6.

[3] F. Liebermann, *Die Heiligen Englands* (Hannover, 1889), p. 11. This tract seems first to have been compiled in the late tenth century.

[4] *BCS* 297, 297A and 297B. This list was drawn up in the time of one of the Mercian overlords, Wulfhere, Æthelbald or Offa, and survives in Old English in BM Harley 3271, of the first half of the eleventh century, and in Latin in some post-Conquest manuscripts. Many of the names are corrupt. See F. M. Stenton, *Anglo-Saxon England*, 3rd ed. (Oxford, 1971), p. 296, and C. Hart, 'The Tribal Hidage', *TRHS* 5th ser. 21 (1971), 133–57.

[5] *HE* IV. 19. [6] *LE*, pp. 4, 15 and 32. [7] *HE* IV. 19.

[8] See the discussion by H. M. Chadwick, *The Origin of the English Nation* (Cambridge, 1907), pp. 7–8 and by E. Miller, *The Abbey and Bishopric of Ely* (Cambridge, 1951), p. 11. *LE* (p. 3) says: 'Girvii sunt omnes Australes Angli in magna palude habitantes, in qua est insula de Ely, sed verius secundum Bede attestationem de provincia est Orientalium Anglorum in eiusdem ingressu provincie sita.'

[9] The South and North Gyrwe are mentioned after the people of Lindsey, with Hatfield Chase. They are followed by the East and West *Wixna*, whom Hart would identify with the *provincia Wissa* mentioned in the Life of Guthlac by Felix, a name which can be connected with Wisbech, Cambridgeshire, and the river names Wissey and Ouse. Next come the *Spalda*, normally connected with Spalding, Lincolnshire, the *Wigesta*, the *Herefinna* and the *Sweord ora*, of whom the last two were tentatively connected by Stenton with the later Hurstingstone hundred in Huntingdonshire and Sword Point on the edge of Whittlesey Mere. Then, with the *Gifle* and the *Hicce*, the area near the River Ivel and Hitchin is reached.

[10] *Felix's Life of St Guthlac* (ed. B. Colgrave (Cambridge, 1956), pp. 142–7) depicts Headda, bishop of Mercia and Middle Anglia, coming on an episcopal visitation, and ordaining Guthlac priest and consecrating his church. In later times, Ely also was in the Middle Anglian diocese, with its see at Dorchester on Thames and later at Lincoln. The abbey of Ely, which claimed independence of diocesan control, used to invite the bishops of East Anglia to perform episcopal functions for them, rather than the bishop of the diocese.

[11] Certainly they would be part of the *imperium* exercised by Rædwald. Presumably Penda absorbed them before he attacked East Anglia, but after his death in 654 Wulfhere may not have at once recovered all that his father had held.

They were probably converted from East Anglia, for, though the presence of a man of this people in Felix's household need not mean that the Gyrwe as a whole had been converted, surely Thomas, when he became bishop, if not before, would wish to spread the faith among his own people.[1] Thomas, who must have adopted this name in religion, was ordained bishop by Archbishop Honorius. At that time, East Anglia was the only kingdom outside Kent which acknowledged the authority of Canterbury. East Anglian contact with Canterbury was never broken. Five years later, Thomas's successor Boniface, whose original name was Berhtgils, and who came from Kent, was consecrated by Archbishop Honorius.[2] He held the see for seventeen years, and then Archbishop Theodore consecrated Bisi.[3] He attended the synod of Hertford in 672, but became infirm, and Theodore took the opportunity to divide the see into two, consecrating Æcci and Beaduwine in place of Bisi.[4] Bede does not name the second see, which later evidence shows to have been at Elmham.[5] Some writers when assessing the influence of the church of Canterbury established by Augustine tend to ignore its permanent influence in East Anglia. Bede had no occasion to refer to subsequent bishops of East Anglia until he describes the state of the English church in 731, when Aldberht and Heathulac were bishops.[6]

Bede tells us also that King Anna was a good man, especially when referring to his saintly daughters,[7] Æthelthryth, wife of Ecgfrith of Northumbria, who founded Ely, Seaxburg, wife of Earconberht of Kent, who succeeded Æthelthryth as abbess of Ely, and Æthelberg, who became abbess of Faremoutiers-en-Brie, as also did Anna's stepdaughter, Sæthryth.[8] The fact that these last two ladies went to a nunnery abroad, like Hereswith, widow of Anna's brother Æthelric, who went to Chelles some time before 647,[9] suggests that there were at that time no nunneries in or near East Anglia. The first may have been Æthelthryth's foundation at Ely about 673. We learn also of Anna that he was generous to Fursa's monastery,[10] and it is unlikely that his

---

[1] If one could accept the stories in *LE* of Augustine's monastery at *Cratendun* (see above, p. 3, n. 7), and Felix's activity at Soham (see above, p. 4, n. 3), we should have evidence for activity in the Cambridge area before the conversion of the midlands by the Celtic missionaries was begun.

[2] *HE* III. 20.   [3] *HE* IV. 5.   [4] *Ibid*.

[5] It is now generally accepted that this is North Elmham, Norfolk, not South Elmham, Suffolk. It was normal for Anglo-Saxon sees to follow tribal divisions, and Theodore would be likely to wish to give a see to each of the East Anglian 'folks'. Both North Elmham and South Elmham became important manors of the bishops of East Anglia. See B. Dodwell, 'The Honour of the Bishop of Thetford/Norwich in the Later Eleventh and Early Twelfth Centuries', *Norfolk Archaeology* 33 (1963–5), 185–99 and Derek Charman, *South Elmham in the Thirteenth Century* (Suffolk Records Society, 1971).

[6] *HE* v. 23.   [7] *HE* III. 8 and IV. 19.

[8] Bede does not mention Wihtburg, claimed as a daughter of Anna in *The Resting-Places of the English Saints* (Liebermann, *Die Heiligen Englands*, p. 5). Her body was then at Ely, to which it had been translated in Edgar's reign from Dereham, where, according to *LE* (pp. 13 and 120–3), she had been a solitary.   [9] Above, p. 3.   [10] *HE* III. 19.

gifts were confined to this one house. It was at his court, under his influence, that Cenwalh of Wessex was converted to Christianity.[1] His brother Æthelwald, who succeeded after their brother Æthelhere had fallen at the battle of the *Winwæd* in 654, stood sponsor to King Swithhelm of Essex when he was baptized by Bishop Cedd.[2] It is of interest that, though the East Anglian church was aligned with Canterbury, whereas Cedd was Celtic by training and had been consecrated by Bishop Finan in Northumbria, this baptism took place at the East Anglian royal vill of Rendlesham.

Nothing more can be learnt about the church of East Anglia from the *Historia Ecclesiastica*, but in another work Bede has a very interesting notice of a bishop who can be identified with one in the episcopal list for *Dommoc*. The genuineness of a little work known as the *Eight Questions* was established by Paul Lehmann in 1919;[3] in it Bede answers questions on theological points asked by Nothhelm, the priest of London mentioned in Bede's preface to the *Historia Ecclesiastica* and in his work called *Thirty Questions*. Bede says that he has seen a volume with many pictures representing the *passiones siue labores* of St Paul which had been brought from Rome by *Cuduini*, bishop of the East Angles. He must be the Cuthwine entered in the list of bishops of *Dommoc* between Eardred, who attended a synod in 716, and Aldberht, whom Bede says was bishop in 731. So at least one East Anglian bishop visited Rome. The bringing of a manuscript with pictorial representations from Rome at this period is in itself exciting enough, but this entry enables one to identify the subscription *Cuduuini* on a ninth-century illuminated manuscript of Sedulius's *Carmen Paschale*, now in Antwerp,[4] which is a copy of an insular manuscript, itself derived from an Italian exemplar. Possibly Cuthwine brought this back with him from Rome; at any rate, he would appear to have collected illuminated manuscripts. Moreover, since Bede saw the manuscript of the *passiones siue labores* of St Paul, it must have reached Northumbria, perhaps by the good offices of the Abbot Esi whom Bede mentions as an informant of the affairs of the East Anglian church.

---

[1] *LE* (p. 18) adds that he was baptized by Felix, Anna standing as sponsor, and that he recovered his kingdom with Anna's help.

    LE gives extra information on Anna: it mentions (pp. 281–2) a church built by him on the borders of the Britons and the English (see below, p. 12, n. 3) and it says (p. 18) that he was buried at Blythburgh and venerated there 'until this day', and that his son *Iurminus* was also buried there, but afterwards translated to *Betricheswrde*. There is no early evidence for the existence of this son. WM (*GP*, p. 156) calls him *Germanus* and says he was buried at Bury St Edmund's. On his translation in 1095, see below, p. 10, n. 3. *LE* (p. 13) mistakenly makes Anna the husband of Hereswith and hence the father of King Aldwulf.

[2] *HE* III. 22. *LE* (p. 19) attributes Swithhelm's conversion to the persuasion of Æthelwald, whom he often visited.

[3] 'Wert und Echtheit einer Beda abgesprochenen Schrift', *Sitzungsberichte der Bayerischen Akademie der Wissenschaften* (München), *Philos.-philol. und hist. Klasse*, 1919, Abhandlung 4.

[4] Museum Plantin-Moretus no. 126. See W. Levison, *England and the Continent in the Eighth Century* (Oxford, 1946), pp. 133–4.

Bishop Cuthwine of *Dommoc*, who journeyed to Rome and collected illuminated manuscripts, may have been an isolated figure among East Anglian churchmen, but we are not forced to assume this. The Antwerp manuscript shows that either the Italian original or an insular copy of it had reached the continent by the ninth century, and the most likely period for this to happen would be during the English missions to the continent in the eighth century, for these were followed with interest by the English at home. Quite a number of manuscripts and works from England have come down to us because they were taken abroad and thus found a safer home before the Viking ravages. If Cuthwine's *Sedulius* had not reached the continent, we might never have known of its existence. Moreover, it would be a coincidence if the only manuscript ever sent from East Anglia happened to survive. If one wonders why more manuscripts from East Anglia have not been preserved on the continent, the answer may be that perhaps they have, but we have no means of identifying them; in the case of the *Sedulius*, it was the subscription *Cuduuini* which provided a clue. At any rate it would seem reasonable to assume that the East Angles would not have sent manuscripts abroad if such were a great rarity at home[1] – not unless the church had lost all interest in learning, and there is evidence to show that this was not the case.

Though Bede never mentions St Botulf, he was familiar with a work which does, the anonymous *Vita Ceolfridi*, written in Jarrow or Wearmouth, after 717, probably by one of Bede's pupils. Ceolfrith, who was born in 642 or 643, entered the monastery of Gilling in 659 or 660, but not long afterwards the abbot and some of the monks, including Ceolfrith, withdrew to Ripon, at the invitation of Wilfrid, the great opponent of Celtic practices. In, or soon after, 669, Ceolfrith went to Kent to study more fully the practices of the monastic life. Then 'he came also to East Anglia to see the monastic practices of Abbot Botulf, whom report had proclaimed on all sides to be a man of unparalleled life and learning and full of the grace of the Holy Spirit'.[2] The *Anglo-Saxon Chronicle* (654A, B and C; 653E), in the same annal in which it records the death of King Anna, says: 'Botulf began to build the minster at *Icanho*.' This used to be identified as Boston (*Botulfes stan*), but Boston is not in East Anglia.[3] If we accept the chronicler's date, Botulf's monastery had

---

[1] On an ancient text of the gospels which survived until the sixteenth century and was held to have belonged to Bishop Felix, see above, p. 4, n. 2.

[2] *Venerabilis Baedae Opera Historica*, ed. C. Plummer (Oxford, 1896) I, 389; trans. *EHD*, p. 698.

[3] Iken, Suffolk, has been suggested, e.g. by J. C. Cox, in *Victoria County History of Suffolk* II, 7, by F. S. Stevenson, 'St Botolph (Botwulf) and Iken', *Proc. of the Suffolk Inst. of Archaeology* 18 (1924), 29–52, and by W. T. Whitley, 'Ycean-ho', *JBAA* n.s. 36 (1931), 233–8, but these use uncritically the late Lives of St Botulf. A twelfth-century charter of Nigel, bishop of Ely (*LE*, p. 336), granting Hadstock to Ely, says: 'locus ille antique religioni sub beato Botulfo abbate ibidem quiescente fuerat consecratus.' Hadstock is in Essex, but near the boundaries of Cambridgeshire

been going some fifteen years when Ceolfrith visited it. We can thus add another to the list of East Anglian houses, and see its fame and influence extending beyond the bounds of that kingdom. It is doubtful whether one can accept anything on the authority of the Life of St Botulf written by Folcard in the late eleventh century,[1] not earlier than 1070, which makes Botulf study at a continental house before coming to England and founding *Icanho*. But, wherever he was trained, one can be sure that the practices in his monastery would not be of a Celtic type, for Ceolfrith, who had left Gilling in dissatisfaction with Celtic usages, would hardly have gone to East Anglia to study at another house of this type.

and Suffolk. Its older name was *Cadenho*, and it is dedicated to St Botulf. It looks as if Nigel thought that Botulf had had a monastery there, but whether rightly or not cannot be ascertained. Other places were claiming his relics long before this time: *The Resting-Places of the English Saints* says in one place that he 'rests in Thorney', and in another that he is buried in *Medeshamstede* (Liebermann, *Die Heiligen Englands*, pp. 11 and 15); the version of this tract in *The Chronicle of Hugh Candidus* (ed. W. T. Mellows (London, 1949), p. 63) includes 'St Botulf the abbot' among saints at Thorney, but on p. 60 puts 'St Botulf the bishop' at Bury St Edmunds; WM (*GP*, p. 156) says he is buried at Bury, along with St Germanus, and that nothing is known about him except that he is said to have been a bishop. His remains and those of St Jurmin are said to have been translated at Bury in 1095 (*Memorials of St Edmund's Abbey*, ed. T. Arnold, RS (1890), 1, 352). It may be these conflicting claims that gave rise to the story that St Æthelwold asked for the bodies of saints lying in destroyed places, and that the king had the relics of Botulf from *Icanho* divided into three, giving the head to Ely, the middle parts to Thorney, and keeping the rest in the royal shrine. These were eventually given to Westminster (*Acta Sanctorum*, 3rd ed. (1867), June, IV, 324 and 330). *LE* (p. 222) claims that Ely had the head and larger bones but that these were robbed and taken to Winchester soon after 1093. This is hard to reconcile with Bishop Nigel's charter on Hadstock. Botulf became a very popular saint, and dedications to him are wide-spread; his name occurs, besides in Boston, first recorded in 1130, in Botesdale, Suffolk, recorded in 1275.

[1] The printed versions of the Life, *Acta Sanctorum ordinis S. Benedicti*, ed. J. Mabillon (Paris, 1668–1701) III, 1–7, and *Acta Sanctorum*, 3rd ed., June, IV, 326–9, do not include the preface which shows the author to be Folcard; this is given in T. D. Hardy, *Descriptive Catalogue of Materials relating to the History of Great Britain and Ireland*, RS (1862), 1, 373–4. Folcard makes Botulf meet at a continental house the sisters of a king of the 'South Angles', Edelmund, who, with his mother, Sywara, is unknown to history. Folcard may have had in mind Bede's mention of English royal ladies at continental houses. Nor does it inspire confidence that he sends Botulf with his brother Adulph to the ancient Saxon stock in *Saxonia* (as yet unconverted) to learn further about the Christian faith, and makes Adulph become bishop of Utrecht in the days before the mission to Frisia. The kings Adelherus and Adelwoldus, whom he calls kinsmen of Edelmund, are willing to give estates to Botulf, but he will only accept waste or ownerless lands, not wishing anyone to be expelled by royal violence. After founding *Ykanno* in a desert spot, he (like St Guthlac) is troubled by demons. He was loved by all, including the Scots, the neighbours of his country. The one correct thing in this account is that Æthelhere and Æthelwald were kings of East Anglia at the required time; but Folcard could have seen from the *Anglo-Saxon Chronicle* that Anna was killed in the year in which Botulf began to build *Icanho*, and Æthelhere in the next year. He could have got the name of Æthelwald from Bede or some regnal list. Further absurdities occur in the Slesvig Breviary (*Acta Sanctorum*, 3rd ed., June, IV, 329): Botulf is of the line of the kings of the Scots, and comes to England from the Scots, to be received by Edmund, king of England; after seven years he receives a beautiful spot and builds a church, but is troubled by unclean spirits, and leaves to found a church dedicated to St Martin by the Thames. Thirteen years later he asks for another place, and builds in a solitude far from the sea two churches in honour of St Peter and St Paul. Then he goes to Rome, returning with many relics.

The reference to Botulf's monastery is given additional significance by some material to which Dr C. T. Talbot called attention in 1955,[1] and which was published and discussed by Professor Finberg in 1961.[2] A Life of St Mildburg, foundress of the double monastery of Wenlock, Shropshire, by Goscelin, contains a record of transactions relating to the foundation, which Professor Finberg calls 'St Mildburg's Testament'. This quotes some early documents shown by their formulae to be authentic. One is a charter issued between the accession of Æthelred of Mercia in 674 and the death of Archbishop Theodore in 690, in which *Edelheg* (i.e. Æthelheah), abbot of the monastery called *Icheanog*, gives with the consent of the whole *familia* of Abbot Botulf of revered memory to Mildburg ninety-seven hides at Wenlock and twelve by the River Monnow, and five at Maund and thirty in the district of *Lydas* (Lyde ?): 'in propriam perpetualiter ... potestatem, ut secundum regularis vite normam cuicumque voluerit vivens sive moriens integram habeat facultatem condonare; ita tamen ut sub jurisdicionibus ecclesie venerabilis Botulfi abbatis idem locus non coacte sed spontanee secundum Deum immobiliter perduret, quia eiusdem ecclesie pecunia emitur a rege qui cognominatur Merwaldus'. According to a paragraph preceding this document, which is perhaps based on another charter, Mildburg had given in exchange to Abbot Edelheg and Abbess Liobsynde sixty hides at *Homtun*, a place which cannot be identified. Nothing is known of this abbess, whose name appears to be continental. From this source we can see that the monastery of *Icanho* continued to flourish after Botulf's death, and had influence as far away as Shropshire.[3]

The position of *Icanho* in this respect should be compared with another monastery in eastern England, *Medeshamstede* (later called Peterborough), in

[1] 'The *Liber Confortatorius* of Goscelin of St Bertin', *Studia Anselmiana* 37 (1955), p. 8, n. 42 and p. 18, n. 89, where attention is called to the BM Additional MS 34633.

[2] *The Early Charters of the West Midlands* (Leicester, 1961), pp. 197–216. I am not convinced that the narrative embodying the charters is authentic.

[3] In a letter to the monks of Ely (*LE*, pp. 281–2; *The Letters of Osbert of Clare*, ed. E. W. Williamson (Oxford, 1929), no. 33) Osbert of Clare relates a vision of St Æthelthryth seen at a church dedicated to her on the borders of the Britons and the English. He claims that a little wooden church was built there, in the province of the Mercians, by Anna, king of the East Angles. He tells the story on the authority of Osbert, prior of Daventry, a monk of Cluny, who had then become a canon of *Brommiensis campi ecclesia*, and who was wont to relate it when he was distributing alms in the congregation of clerics of St Mildburg, as he had learnt it from those who witnessed it. As an Osbert attests a document of 1115 as prior of Bromfield, Shropshire (R. W. Eyton, *Antiquities of Shropshire* (London, 1854–60) v, 210), and there is evidence that Wenlock Priory had rights to a share of the income of Bromfield church (*ibid.* v, 216), it is clear that *Brommiensis campi* is Bromfield, not Bromholm, Norfolk, as hitherto supposed. While it is impossible that Anna should found a church on the far side of heathen Mercia, it is of interest that there was a belief in the neighbourhood of Wenlock in the early twelfth century that East Anglia had played a part in the early history of the church in this area. It shows also that a dedication to St Æthelthryth on the Welsh borders was at least as early as this account. Williamson notes that Hyssington, Shropshire, has a dedication to her.

the region of the Gyrwe. Sir Frank Stenton showed in 1933[1] that certain genuine early documents relating to this house survived the Viking invasions. It possessed lands at Shifnal, the Lizard and Wattlesborough in Shropshire. It was instrumental in founding colonies far from the mother house. Between 674 and 691 Friduric, a *princeps* of Æthelred of Mercia, gave to the *familia* of *Medeshamstede* twenty hides at Breedon-on-the-Hill, Leicestershire, 'so that they should found a monastery there and appoint a priest of good repute to minister baptism and teaching to the people assigned to him'. Headda was sent, and the house prospered; it was increased by a grant of thirty-one hides at *Hrepingas* from Friduric, and by a purchase of fifteen hides at *Cedenac*. Headda was probably also the founder of the monasteries of Woking and Bermondsey, Surrey, for which he obtained a privilege from Pope Constantine between 708 and 715. In 731, Breedon supplied an archbishop of Canterbury,[2] Tatwine, the author of a set of Latin riddles.[3] The surviving remains of a sculptured frieze show that it had an impressive church in the eighth century.[4] As Sir Frank says, the *Medeshamstede* documents 'reveal something of the way in which Christianity and the monastic order which was a chief agent in its expansion, were spread in the midlands a generation after the death of the last of the heathen Mercian kings'. Hugh Candidus, the twelfth-century Peterborough historian, may have had a good source for his claim that the second abbot of *Medeshamstede*, Cuthbald, who succeeded in 673 or 674, founded the monastery of Brixworth,[5] the church of which has been called 'the greatest English building of the pre-Danish period'.[6] The Wenlock evidence now allows us to add the East Anglian monastery of *Icanho* to the influences which spread the Christian faith in the areas under Mercian domination.[7]

[1] 'Medeshamstede and its Colonies', *Historical Essays in Honour of James Tait* (Manchester, 1933), pp. 313–26; repr. *Preparatory to Anglo-Saxon England*, ed. D. M. Stenton, pp. 179–92.

[2] *HE* v. 23.

[3] Ed. Thomas Wright, *Anglo-Latin Satirical Poets and Epigrammatists of the Twelfth Century*, RS (1872), II, 525–34.

[4] See A. W. Clapham, 'The Carved Stones at Breedon-on-the-Hill', *Archaeologia* 77 (1928), 219–40, and T. D. Kendrick, *Anglo-Saxon Art* (London, 1938), pp. 171–8.

[5] Ed. W. T. Mellows, p. 15. There is no need to suppose that this Cuthbald is the same as the Cuthbald (*HE* v. 19, where the Moore manuscript reads *Cudualdi* and Leningrad and Tiberius C. ii read *Cudbaldi*) who was abbot of Wilfrid's monastery in Oundle in 709. The name is not uncommon. Mellows's suggestion (p. 22 n.) that Wilfrid's monastery in the province of Oundle was actually Peterborough is very improbable.

[6] F. M. Stenton, *Anglo-Saxon England*, 3rd ed., pp. 111–12.

[7] Another important influence was that of Wilfrid, who, though a Northumbrian, was a passionate opponent of Celtic practices. He founded several monasteries in Mercian territory about 665, and he administered the diocese of Middle Anglia from 691 to 702. We know the names of four of his abbots in 709, but the name of only one foundation, Oundle. He had much influence over Æthelthryth. *LE* (p. 37) claims that he stayed with her before going to Rome in 677, and Bede (*HE* IV. 19) implies that he was at Ely some time after 695. The influence of Ely must have spread into the midlands if the Ely tradition (*LE*, pp. 32, 35, 42 and 52) is correct in making

In view of the importance of *Medeshamstede* – and there is evidence that it was also connected with the foundation of Bardney in Lincolnshire and Hoo in Kent – it is a pity that Bede says so little about its founder, Seaxwulf. We can place no reliance on the terms in which Hugo Candidus speaks of him, e.g.: 'virum strenuissimum et religiosissimum et tam mundanis quam ecclesiasticis rebus doctissimum',[1] for they are a commonplace. Bede's reference to him as *constructor*[2] makes it difficult to accept the post-Conquest Peterborough claim that this house was founded by Peada of Mercia and his father-in-law Oswiu of Northumbria in 654,[3] for Bede would hardly have been silent about this royal foundation, which would make *Medeshamstede* the earliest recorded foundation in the midlands. Since Seaxwulf seems to have founded this monastery some time before he became bishop of the Mercians in 673 or 674, he can hardly have received his early education in Middle Anglia, seeing that the conversion of this area did not begin until Peada brought four priests from Northumbria in 652. It is more probable that he was trained by the East Anglian church, not by the Celtic mission. Sir Frank Stenton has remarked: 'There is no discernible Celtic strain in the early history of *Medeshamstede*.'[4] It has been suggested above that the district of the Gyrwe, in which *Medeshamstede* lay, was converted from East Anglia. When Æthelthryth, daughter of Anna of East Anglia, was married to Tondberht, *princeps* of the South Gyrwe, he was presumably Christian, for Bede would not have passed over her marriage to a heathen without comment.[5] If we could trust the *Liber Eliensis*, which dates her marriage two years before Anna's death,[6] and hence in 652, we could be confident that the Gyrwe did not owe their conversion to the priests brought by Peada in that very year; but even if we confine ourselves to the indications in Bede, that she was consort of Ecgfrith for twelve years, and spent a year at Coldingham before founding Ely,[7] in 673 according to the *Anglo-Saxon Chronicle*, and allow her the minimum period of one year of widowhood after Tondberht, who Bede says lived only a short time after the marriage, this first marriage cannot have been later than 659, only a few years after Peada's missionaries arrived. Certainty cannot be reached, but it is at least a possibility that the Gyrwe were converted and Seaxwulf educated by the church of East Anglia.

Werburg, daughter of Wulfhere of Mercia and Eormenhild, become a nun at Ely. She left to rule many monasteries, including Hanbury in Staffordshire and Threckingham in Kesteven. *LE* (p. 52) says she returned to succeed her mother as abbess of Ely.

[1] Ed. W. T. Mellows, p. 9.   [2] *HE* iv. 6.

[3] On the spurious accounts of the foundation of Peterborough, see Hugh Candidus, ed. W. T. Mellows, pp. 7–22, and the twelfth-century additions to the Peterborough manuscript of the *Anglo-Saxon Chronicle* (Laud Misc. 636) *s.aa.* 654, 656 and 675.

[4] *Anglo-Saxon England*, 3rd ed., p. 125.   [5] *HE* iv. 19.

[6] *LE*, pp. 14–15.   [7] *HE* iv. 19.

After the time of Bede we have no early narrative sources for the East Anglian church.[1] The episcopal lists of its two sees have survived, because they were inserted into a Mercian compilation, drawn up in the last decade of the eighth century, to which later entries were added.[2] They can be supplemented to some extent by an entry of the consecration of Æthelfrith (of Elmham) in 736 in the annals available to Symeon of Durham,[3] by three surviving episcopal professions to the archbishop of Canterbury,[4] by an entry of the death of Ælfhun of *Dommoc* in 798 in the F version of the *Anglo-Saxon Chronicle*, and by charters, for the East Anglian bishops attended synods and also the courts of their Mercian overlords. No East Anglian charters have survived. The succession of the bishops of the two sees is set out in an appendix to this article.

One eighth-century work written in East Anglia has come down, presumably because copies of it had spread to parts of England which suffered less severely by the Viking ravages,[5] namely, the *Vita Sancti Guthlaci* written by Felix.[6] He dedicated it to 'my lord King Ælfwald, beloved by me beyond any other of royal rank, who rules by right over the realm of the East Angles'. Ælfwald reigned from about 713 to 749;[7] Felix was writing after Æthelbald of Mercia had become overlord of southern England, a position which he held in 731 and is unlikely to have acquired before the death of Wihtred of Kent in 725 and the abdication of Ine of Wessex in 726. Felix tells us nothing about himself, but he says that King Ælfwald had commanded him to write, and he mentions the king's sister, Ecgburg, an abbess, presumably of an East Anglian nunnery or double monastery.[8] The Life supplies little about East

---

[1] If the papal letter given by WM (*GP*, pp. 52–3) can be accepted, it shows an East Anglian king, Aldwulf, being addressed along with Æthelred (of Mercia) and Aldfrith (of Northumbria) by Pope Sergius in about 693, asking them to receive Berhtwald as primate. Stubbs regarded it as questionable; see *Councils* III, 229–31. The absence of any king of Kent might show uncertainty as to who was effective king, for after a period of 'doubtful or foreign kings', Wihtred and Swæfheard were sharing the rule (*HE* IV. 26 and V. 8); Ine of Wessex may have been excluded because he was at war with Kent about that time.

[2] See below, pp. 19–20.

[3] *Symeoni Monachi Opera Omnia*, ed. T. Arnold, RS (1882–5), II, 31–2.

[4] See below, p. 18.

[5] Guthlac's cult spread rapidly. One of the two Old English poems on him, *Guthlac A*, assigned to the eighth century, seems the work of a poet unfamiliar with fenland scenery.

[6] The best edition is that of B. Colgrave, *Felix's Life of St Guthlac* (Cambridge, 1956), whose work on the sources has been drawn on in what follows.

[7] The date 747, sometimes given for his accession, comes from a mistake in the *Chronicle of Melrose*, which calls Selred, whom the *Anglo-Saxon Chronicle* records as killed in 746, *estanglorum rex*. He was a king of the East Saxons.

[8] Ed. B. Colgrave, pp. 70, 146 and 156. *LE* (p. 19) calls her abbess of Repton, possibly from a memory that an abbess of this house is mentioned by Felix. It is sometimes stated, without any reference given, that she had two sisters, Æthelburg and Hwætburg, who became abbesses of Hackness, Yorkshire. This goes no further back than 1875, when D. H. Haigh published in the *Yorkshire Archaeol. Jnl* 3, 349–91, a theory based partly on his own highly conjectural interpretation of an inscription at Hackness and partly on a series of improbable identifications.

Anglia, but it shows that Crowland was by the early eighth century in the diocese of Middle Anglia,[1] and hence that the Gyrwe of this area were under Mercian control. Felix made use of both the verse and the prose versions of Bede's Life of Cuthbert, of the Life of St Martin by Sulpicius Severus, of Jerome's Life of Paul, of Athanasius's Life of St Anthony in the translation by Evagrius, of the *Dialogues* of Gregory the Great and his *Exposition on Job*, of Aldhelm's *De Metris* and his verse and prose works *De Laude Virginitatis*, and of a Life of St Fursa. He has a phrase which he could have got either from Gildas's *De Excidio*, or from Rufinus's *Historia Ecclesiastica*. He quotes the scriptures frequently, and his style has Vergilian echoes. We thus get some insight into what books were available in East Anglia. In his preface, Felix refers to other English scholars in their midst who could have written the work better, and, without our laying too much stress on this use of the modesty convention, one can assume that he could not have said this if he were the only learned man in East Anglia.

The king who commissioned this work, Ælfwald, wrote along with 'all the *abbatia* [higher clergy] with the whole congregation of the servants of God' in his province to the missionary, St Boniface, between 742 and 749.[2] Boniface had written to ask for their prayers, and the letter says that masses and prayers are said for him in their seven monasteries, and it asks for prayers in return and for the mutual exchange of the names of those who die, that prayers may be offered for them. The seven monasteries may have included *Icanho*; the earlier foundation to which King Sigeberht retired; the nunnery or double monastery presided over by the king's sister, Abbess Ecgburg; perhaps also the double monastery of Ely, since Bede says this was in East Anglia;[3] and the monastery of which Bede's informant, Abbot Esi, had been head, unless he was abbot of one previously mentioned. But there may have been monasteries unrecorded in our sources. It seems unlikely that the letter would exclude the episcopal churches of *Dommoc* and Elmham. If they are reckoned among the seven *monasteria*, this need not imply that they were monastic in organization; like its Old English equivalent, *mynster*, *monasterium* may have borne the more general meaning of a large church. The Elmham contingent to the synod of *Clofeshoh* of 803 consisted of the bishop, four priests and two deacons, whereas the bishop of *Dommoc* took with him two abbots and four priests,[4] which may

---

[1] See above, p. 7, n. 10.

[2] *Die Briefe des heiligen Bonifatius und Lullus*, ed. M. Tangl, MGH, Epist. Sel. 1, 181–2. Tangl notes two quotations from Latin poems sent to Aldhelm. See *Aldelmi Opera*, ed. R. Ehwald, MGH, Auct. Ant. 15, p. 524, line 3 and p. 533, lines 183–4.

[3] Ely preserved no memory of abbesses after Werburg (see above, p. 13, n. 7). Possibly it was Ecgburg's nunnery, for if so, this would continue the practice of keeping it in the family; she was daughter of Æthelthryth's cousin, King Aldwulf, who helped in the foundation.

[4] *BCS* 312.

suggest that the two most important monasteries were in the diocese of *Dommoc*.

The East Anglian bishops were constant in their attendance at synods,[1] including the important one at *Clofeshoh* in 747 which issued a comprehensive set of statutes;[2] but here only Heardwulf of *Dommoc* was present. His colleague Eanfrith of Elmham may have been prevented by illness. Alhheard of Elmham and Heardred of *Dommoc* attended the legatine synod of 786, which also issued statutes.[3] The record of the synod of *Clofeshoh* of 803,[4] which among other business finally abolished the short-lived archiepiscopate of Lichfield, is unusual in giving the names of the clergy who accompanied the bishops on this important occasion. Alhheard, bishop of the church of Elmham, brought the priests Folcberht, Freothoberht, Eadberht and Wulflaf, and the deacons Hunferth, perhaps the later bishop of this name, and Beorn-helm, while Tidfrith, bishop of the *civitas* of *Dommoc*, was accompanied by the abbots Wulfheard and Lull, and the priests Ceolhelm, Cynulf, Tilberht and Eadberht. Another synod from which statutes are extant, that at Chelsea in 816,[5] was attended by Tidfrith of *Dommoc* and Sibba of Elmham. During the period of the overlordship of the Mercian kings, bishops of East Anglia attest their charters even when it is not clear that these were issued at synods.

Three of the East Anglian ecclesiastics who attended the synod of *Clofeshoh* in 803 are mentioned in a letter written by Alcuin between 798 and 804.[6] It is addressed to the two bishops, Alhheard and Tidfrith, and Alcuin says he has heard of their good way of life from Abbot Lull, no doubt the one who accompanied Tidfrith to *Clofeshoh*. The letter consists merely of general exhortations and a request that his name be remembered in their prayers, but it shows that one East Anglian abbot visited Alcuin on the continent. In another of his letters Alcuin shows that Lull had spoken in praise of an illustrious man called Ardberht, but we know nothing about him.[7]

Synods under the presidency of the kings of Mercia were held also at *Clofeshoh* on 30 October 824, attended by Wermund of *Dommoc* and Hunberht of Elmham,[8] and two at the same place in 825,[9] when Hunberht was accompanied by Wilred, who signs once as *electus*. But this practice seems to have come to an end after Egbert of Wessex conquered Kent and annexed Surrey, Sussex and Essex in 825, and the East Anglians killed Beornwulf of Mercia in 825 and his successor Ludeca in 827. Henceforward, no East

[1] See Appendix, below, pp. 19–22. [2] *Councils* III, 362–76.
[3] *Councils* III, 447–62; there is a better edition by E. Dümmler, MGH, Epist. 4, no. 3; trans. *EHD*, no. 191.
[4] *BCS* 312. [5] *BCS* 358; *Councils* III, 579–85.
[6] Ed. E. Dümmler, no. 301. [7] *Ibid.* no. 302.
[8] *BCS* 379. [9] *BCS* 384 and 386.

Anglian bishops attest the charters of Mercian kings.[1] They appear at the only two recorded later synods, Hunberht and Wilred appearing both at one held *æt Astran* in 839[2] and at one held at London on 8 November 845,[3] and on neither of these occasions was any king present. Since no later records of synods are found, we cannot tell how long Hunberht and Wilred remained in office. The episcopal lists end with their names.

But the list for *Dommoc* can be shown to be incomplete. Canterbury preserved the professions of faith of three East Anglian bishops: that of Tidfrith of *Dommoc* to Archbishop Æthelheard about 798,[4] that of Hunferth of Elmham to Archbishop Wulfred between 816 and 824,[5] and that of a Bishop Æthelwald of *Dommoc* to Archbishop Ceolnoth, some time between 845 and 870.[6] His name is not on the list, and he is clearly later than Wilred.[7] He was the owner of a seal now in the British Museum, inscribed SIG EÐILVVALDI: EP, found at Eye.[8]

Seeing that the *Dommoc* list is incomplete, so also may the Elmham list be. Its last name is Hunberht, and one cannot tell how long, after 845, he held the see. The twelfth-century *Annals of St Neots* make him anoint Edmund king in 856,[9] but it is uncertain whether they had good evidence for this statement. Other post-Conquest writers[10] assume that he is the bishop mentioned, but without name, by Abbo as present with King Edmund in 869,[11] and Symeon of Durham even makes him share his martyrdom.[12] As he was bishop by 824, at the latest, this would make him hold his see for at least forty-five years, and, while this is not impossible, the martyrdom of so aged a bishop would surely not have been unnoted by Abbo and forgotten in Bury tradition. These later writers probably gave the name Hunberht to the bishop unnamed in Abbo's account merely because his was the last name in the Elmham list.

---

[1] At first sight, two charters in the name of Beorhtwulf of Mercia appear to contradict this; *BCS* 450, issued at Tamworth on Christmas Day 845 (by which 844 is intended, the year beginning at Christmas), is attested by *Hunberht episcopus*, and *Wihtred episcopus*; but Hunberht is probably an error for Tunberht of Lichfield, which see would otherwise be unrepresented, and Wihtred, the last of the episcopal attestations, is far more probably an error for *Wihtred abbas* than for *Willred episcopus*. Abbot Wihtred attests frequently Mercian charters from 816 on, and in several texts, including three of 841, he heads the list of abbots. *BCS* 428 is an undated charter almost identical with *BCS* 450, and shares these errors in the witness-list. Both texts are from the same cartulary.

[2] *BCS* 421. [3] *BCS* 448. [4] *BCS* 286.

[5] *BCS* 375. [6] *BCS* 528.

[7] See below, p. 21, n. 6.

[8] See D. M. Wilson, *Anglo-Saxon Ornamental Metalwork 700–1100 in the British Museum* (London, 1964), pl. xvii and pp. 79–81 and 131.

[9] See *Asser's Life of King Alfred*, ed. W. H. Stevenson (Oxford, 1904; repr. 1959 with contr. by D. Whitelock), p. 131.

[10] E.g. *Rogeri de Wendover Chronica*, ed. H. O. Coxe (London, 1841) I, 308.

[11] *Passio Sancti Eadmundi*, in *Memorials of St Edmund's Abbey* I, 11.

[12] *Symeoni Monachi Opera Omnia* I, 55 and II, 107.

William of Malmesbury, who had lists ending with Wilred and Hunberht, and was probably familiar with Florence's statement that these bishops held their sees in the reigns of Ludeca of Mercia (825–7) and Egbert of Wessex (802–39), says that in the time of Ludeca and his predecessor Burgred (an error for Beornwulf), the bishops became impoverished by the ravages of these kings, and so *Dommoc* was suppressed and the two sees united into one, with its centre at Elmham.[1] Charter evidence shows, however, that there were still two bishops as late as 845, and it seems probable that we have here only a theory on the reason for the disappearance of *Dommoc*. It is usually assumed that both sees ceased together after the Danish invasions, and were not combined as the see of Elmham until the mid tenth century.

In conclusion, one can claim that, even when one ignores the material in late sources,[2] the scattered references in early sources imply that the church in East Anglia was not behind that of most other kingdoms, and that it was influential outside its borders in the late seventh century.

APPENDIX

EPISCOPAL SUCCESSION IN EARLY EAST ANGLIA

The episcopal lists divide into two columns after the division of the see by Archbishop Theodore, but it is not until one comes to those in Florence of Worcester[3] and William of Malmesbury[4] that the columns are assigned to a named see; neither does Bede tell us to which see the bishops after the division belonged. We can, however, see that Florence and William were correct in their assignment of the columns, because the record of the synod of *Clofeshoh* of 803 (*BCS* 312) allots Alhheard to Elmham and Tidfrith to *Dommoc*; the F version of the *Anglo-Saxon Chronicle*, *s.a.* 798, says Bishop Ælfhun was buried at *Dommoc*; and the extant profession of Hunferth makes him refer to his see as *Helmamensis ecclesiam*.

The earliest surviving list is found in BM Cotton Vespasian B. vi, of the early ninth century, but based on a collection drawn up in the last decade of the eighth century.[5] This manuscript originally took the Elmham list to Alhheard and the *Dommoc* list to Tidfrith; then a later hand added two names, *Uuermund* and *Uuilred*, to the Elmham list, and *Hunberht* to the *Dommoc* list. It would appear from the later

---

[1] *GP*, p. 148.

[2] To those already mentioned one can add the story in John of Brompton that before the Danes came a chapel in honour of St Benedict had been built by a hermit called Suneman, on the site of the later abbey of Holme, Norfolk, and had attracted other persons to it (Dugdale, *Monasticon* III, 61); or the claim that Seaxwulf founded a community of hermits in *Ancarig* (later Thorney) (Hugh Candidus, ed. W. T. Mellows, pp. 12 and 42; cf. the spurious Thorney foundation charter, *BCS* 1297).   [3] FW, I, 233.   [4] *GP*, pp. 147–8.

[5] See K. Sisam, 'Anglo-Saxon Royal Genealogies', *Proc. of the Brit. Acad.* 39 (1953), 289, 291, 308–9, 323–4 and 328; and, for the episcopal lists in this manuscript and in Cambridge, Corpus Christi College 183 and BM Cotton Tiberius B. v, see R. I. Page, 'Anglo-Saxon Episcopal Lists', *Nottingham Med. Stud.* 9 (1965), 71–95 and 10 (1966), 2–17.

lists that these names have been added to the wrong columns; moreover, the Vespasian manuscript lacks two names, Sibba and Hunferth, before Hunberht. Charter evidence shows the later lists correct in adding Sibba, and Hunferth's profession survives and shows that he is in the proper column (Elmham).[1] The Vespasian list has another omission, in this case shared by the later versions, and so going back to a common source: Heardwulf, who attended the synod of *Clofeshoh* in 747, does not appear. His name should have come before that of Heardred in the *Dommoc* list, and the error is due to both names beginning with the same element.

Because of the errors in Vespasian, I take the lists in Cambridge, Corpus Christi College 183 and BM Cotton Tiberius B. v, as the basis of my account, and I ignore mere differences in spelling or miscopyings.[2]

The undivided see

Felix. In Bede and all lists; held see for seventeen years (Bede), 630/1–47/8.

Thomas. In Bede and all lists; consecrated by Archbishop Honorius; held see for five years (Bede), 647/8–52/3.

Berhtgils. In Bede and all lists; also called Boniface (Bede and FW, called only Boniface by WM); consecrated by Archbishop Honorius; held see for seventeen years (Bede), 652/3–69/70.

Bisi. In Bede and all lists; consecrated by Archbishop Theodore; attended council of Hertford on 24 September 672 (called 673 by Bede); the see divided in his lifetime, because of his ill-health, and Æcci and Beaduwine consecrated (Bede).

The see of 'Dommoc' after the division

Æcci. In Bede and all lists.[3]

Æscwulf. In all lists.

Eardred. In all lists; perhaps at synod of *Clofeshoh* in 716.[4]

Cuthwine. In all lists; mentioned by Bede in *Eight Questions*.[5]

Aldberht. In Bede and all lists; was holding the see in 731 (Bede).

Ecglaf. In all lists, interlined in Vespasian B. vi; attests a dubious charter (*BCS* 162) dated 742.[6]

---

[1] A Crowland forgery, *BCS* 409, allegedly of 833, which calls Hunberht *Helm' episcopus* and Wilred *Dommocensis episcopus*, may have used FW's lists.

[2] FW agrees with these lists except that in the Elmham list he puts Hunferth instead of Alhheard, thus having two bishops of this name, one before and one after Sibba. WM, who arranges the bishops in contemporary pairs, tries to remedy this error, but it is the second, instead of the first, Hunferth, whom he replaces by Alhheard. He writes *Sigga* for Sibba and *Edredus* for Eardred.

[3] An *Acca episcopus* appears at a synod alleged in *BCS* 91 to have met at *Clofeshoh* in 716, but he is probably Acca of Hexham, since in 716 Northumbria was not a separate province. If so, *Dommoc* may be represented by *Hærdred* (for Eardred); Nothberht of Elmham was present. The charter is not free from suspicion, and the list includes two successive bishops of Lichfield, Headda and Wor; yet it is possible that Headda had retired.

[4] See preceding note.   [5] See above, p. 9.

[6] It has too many episcopal signatories, fifteen for eleven sees. If we allot Eanfrith to Elmham and Ecglaf, who follows immediately, to *Dommoc*, we are left with the following unidentified bishops: *Huetlac*, whom Stubbs (*Councils* III, 342) took as the Heathulac who held Elmham in

Heardwulf. Omitted from the lists; attended synod of *Clofeshoh* in 747 as 'bishop of the East Angles';[1] possibly attests a dubious charter (*BCS* 162) dated 742.[2]

Heardred. In all lists; attests in 781 (*BCS* 241, synod of Brentford); also in 785 (*BCS* 247), 786 (*BCS* 248), 788 (*BCS* 254) and 789 (*BCS* 255, 256 and 257), all issued at synods at Chelsea; attended the Legatine synod of 786.[3]

Ælfhun. In all lists; attests in 790 or 793 (*BCS* 265, dubious), 793–5 (*BCS* 274, synod of *Clofeshoh*), 793 (*BCS* 267, spurious) and 796 (*BCS* 280 and 281, both spurious); died at Sudbury in 798 and was buried in *Dommoc* (*ASC* F).

Tidfrith. In all lists; made his profession to Archbishop Æthelheard (*BCS* 286) about 798; received, along with Alhheard of Elmham, a letter from Alcuin;[4] attests in 798 (*BCS* 289 and 290, spurious, where he signs as *Dammoce episcopus*), 799 (*BCS* 293 and 295, council at Coleshill), 801 (endorsement to *BCS* 201, synod of Chelsea), 803 (*BCS* 308, at *Clofeshoh* on 6 October, and *BCS* 309, 310 and 312, all at synod of *Clofeshoh* on 12 October, the last with his attestation *Dummucæ civitatis episcopus*), 805 (*BCS* 321, at *Aclaeh*, and *BCS* 322, at the same place on 26 July), 805–7 (*BCS* 318), 814 (*BCS* 343) and 816 (*BCS* 357); attended the synod of Chelsea on 27 July 816 (*BCS* 358); succeeded in 798 (*ASC* F).

Wermund. In all lists, but in wrong column in Vespasian B. vi; attests one charter (*BCS* 379) issued at synod of *Clofeshoh* on 30 October 824.

Wilred. In all lists, but in wrong column in Vespasian B. vi; attests as *electus* in 825 (*BCS* 384, synod of *Clofeshoh*) and as *episcopus* in the same year (*BCS* 386);[5] attended the council of all bishops south of the Humber *æt Astran* in 839 (*BCS* 421) and a meeting in London under Archbishop Ceolnoth on 8 November 845 (*BCS* 448).

Æthelwald. Not in any list; made his profession to Ceolnoth, archbishop of Canterbury, between 845 and 870 (*BCS* 528), referring to *officium Dommuciæ civitatis*; he may be the *ðelwald* (for *Eðelwald*) *episcopus* who witnessed a Kentish deed of 859–70.[6] On his seal, see above, p. 18.

731; *Eðelfrid*, whom he identifies as Heathulac's successor in 736, and *Redwulf*, which he suggests is meant for *Eardwulf* (i.e. Heardwulf) of *Dommoc*, who attended the synod of *Clofeshoh* in 747. Though most of the signatories are correct for 742, it appears that this list must either have been compiled from lists of different dates, or, if it is genuine, the ninth-century copy in which it survives includes some interpolated names.

[1] *Councils* III, 362.

[2] See above, p. 20, n. 6.

[3] *Councils* III, 447–61 or MGH, Epist., ed. E. Dümmler, no. 3 (a better text). On the possibility that he appears in *BCS* 162, see above, p. 20, n. 6.

[4] See above, p. 17.

[5] He appears also in the Crowland forgery, *BCS* 409, on which see above, p. 20, n. 1. He should not be identified with the *Wihtred episcopus* in *BCS* 428 and 450, on which see above, p. 18, n. 1.

[6] *BCS* 404; *Select English Historical Documents of the Ninth and Tenth Centuries*, ed. F. E. Harmer (Cambridge, 1914), no. 7. It is strange that this document should be witnessed by a bishop from East Anglia, but no other bishop of this name is recorded. Yet by this date the lists for several sees are incomplete, and there would be room for an Æthelwald at London or Selsey; the only other bishop in this deed is called *Whelm* (*sic*), and cannot be identified. As Miss Harmer points out, the transaction is not earlier than 863, if the *Seferth presbyter* is the *Sefreth subdiaconus* of *BCS* 507 of that year.

The see of Elmham

Beaduwine. In Bede and all lists; attests as *Beduuin* (*BCS* 85, undated, but the witnesses belong to 693).

Nothberht. In all lists; attests in 706 (*BCS* 116) and 716 (*BCS* 91, synod of *Clofeshoh*).[1]

Heathulac. In Bede and all lists; was holding the see in 731 (Bede).[2]

Æthelfrith. In all lists; consecrated by Archbishop Nothhelm in 736 (Symeon of Durham).

Eanfrith. In all lists. Attests a charter dated 742[3] (*BCS* 162, dubious) and one of about 758 (*BCS* 327).[4]

Æthelwulf. In all lists; attests in 781 (*BCS* 241, synod of Brentford).

Alhheard. In all lists except FW, who replaces him by Hunberht; received, along with Tidfrith, a letter from Alcuin;[5] attests in 785 (*BCS* 247), 786 (*BCS* 248), 788 (*BCS* 254) and 789 (*BCS* 255 and 257) – all issued at synods at Chelsea; also in 790 or 793 (*BCS* 265, dubious), 793 (*BCS* 267, spurious), 793–5 (*BCS* 274, synod of *Clofeshoh*), 798 (*BCS* 289), 799 (*BCS* 293, at Tamworth, and *BCS* 295, at Coleshill), 801 (endorsement to *BCS* 201, synod of Chelsea), 803 (*BCS* 308, at *Clofeshoh* on 6 October, and *BCS* 309, 310 and 312, all at synod of *Clofeshoh* on 12 October, the last with his attestation *Elmhamis ecclesiæ episcopus*), 805 (*BCS* 321, at *Aclaeh*, and *BCS* 322 at the same place on 26 July), and 805–7 (*BCS* 318); attended the Legatine synod of 786.[6].

Sibba. Omitted by Vespasian B. vi; in other lists (*Sigga* in WM); attests in 814 (*BCS* 343) and 816 (*BCS* 357); attended the synod of Chelsea on 27 July 816 (*BCS* 358).

Hunferth. Omitted by Vespasian B. vi; in other lists;[7] made his profession to Archbishop Wulfred between 816 and 824 (*BCS* 375), calling himself *ad suscipiendam ac dispensandam Helmamensis ecclesiam electus atque constitutus*; he may be the *Hunfrið diaconus* who accompanied Bishop Alhheard to *Clofeshoh* in 803 (*BCS* 312).

Hunberht. In all lists, but in wrong column in Vespasian B. vi; attests in 824 (*BCS* 379, synod of *Clofeshoh* on 30 October), 825 (*BCS* 384, synod of *Clofeshoh*, and *BCS* 386, synod of *Clofeshoh* later in the year); attended the council of all bishops south of the Humber *æt Astran* in 839 (*BCS* 421) and a meeting in London under Archbishop Ceolnoth on 8 November 845 (*BCS* 448);[8] said to have anointed Edmund king of East Anglia in 856; post-Conquest writers identify him with the bishop present with King Edmund in 869, and Symeon of Durham makes him share his martyrdom.[9]

---

[1] See above, p. 20, n. 3.

[2] He may be intended by the *Huetlac* in *BCS* 162; see above, p. 20, n. 6.

[3] See above, p. 20, n. 6.

[4] This charter is wrongly dated 803 because Cynewulf of Wessex has been confused with Cenwulf of Mercia.   [5] See above, p. 17.   [6] See above, p. 21, n. 3.

[7] On the duplication of his name by FW see above, p. 20, n. 2.

[8] The name *Hunberht* in *BCS* 428 and 450 is probably an error for Tunberht (of Lichfield); see above, p. 18, n. 1.   [9] See above, p. 18.

An interim revision of
episcopal dates for the province of Canterbury,
850–950: part I

MARY ANNE O'DONOVAN

This paper is offered in the hope that it will provide reliable evidence for those wishing to make use of episcopal dates during the century 850–950. The original editors of the *Handbook of British Chronology* were assured by experts that 'until all the available charter-evidence had been critically sifted, it would be useless to try and revise the available lists of Anglo-Saxon bishops', so they used for their lists the information available in W. Stubbs's *Registrum Sacrum Anglicanum*, 2nd ed. (Oxford, 1897) and W. G. Searle's *Anglo-Saxon Bishops, Kings and Nobles* (Cambridge, 1899). We are still far from the desired state of charter study, but a good deal has been done on this and related studies in the last few decades, and perhaps the time has come to look again at the bishops' dates. In many cases the episcopal witnesses can corroborate or impugn the genuineness of a charter, and it is sometimes the misfortune of the Anglo-Saxon historian, in using the appearance of a certain bishop to strengthen the validity of a charter, to find that the date of the bishop's episcopate is determined by the very charter in question. So the critical sifting of all the available charter evidence must include a study of episcopal dates – one cannot take place without the other.

The episcopal successions have been for the most part provided by the episcopal lists, several of which have been recently discussed and edited by Dr R. I. Page. In some places, where there were lacunae, the charters have supplied possible names. These can only be suggestions, because throughout the century under review there were undoubtedly men who bore the title of bishop, but who did not hold any known see. They may have been appointed to help an ageing incumbent, although not necessarily to become his successor, or they may have been given part of a large diocese to administer, as Asser very probably was given part of Sherborne. But generally we have only their names and – without further evidence – can only guess at their positions.

In the late ninth and early tenth centuries there were several interrupted episcopal lists, most probably resulting from the disorganization caused by the Viking irruptions. It is difficult to assign bishops to the affected sees with any assurance. The lack of charter material for Alfred's reign and for the period 904–24 complicates the question further. The episcopal dates for the whole century (except for those of Canterbury) have been largely adduced from the charter evidence and the gaps to which I have referred account for much of the uncertainty in the middle of the dating lists. Use of the charters has been much facilitated by the recent publication of P. H. Sawyer's *Anglo-Saxon Charters*. I have discussed in detail only those charters which are particularly important from the point of view of episcopal dating, and very often my dating criteria have been the dating apparatus and witnesses rather than the diplomatic formulae.

As its title indicates, this paper is not meant to be any final statement on episcopal dates for the period: it is an attempt to assemble the work already done by various scholars and to combine this with some discussion of the evidence offered by the charters. In addition to the printed material which is acknowledged in the notes, I am gratefully indebted to Mr T. A. M. Bishop for his advice on some palaeographical points; to Miss Ann Hamlin and Professor Frank Barlow for their advice and patience in reading the manuscript and typescript respectively; and above all to Professor Dorothy Whitelock. This paper was originally written for her *festschrift* at the invitation of the editors. It proved too long for inclusion, and so I offer it to her now with affection and gratitude for her constant encouragement, criticism and help.

The lists have been arranged as in the *Handbook*, alphabetically under dioceses, followed by notes in the same order. The notes for the last ten dioceses, beginning with Lichfield, form a concluding part II of the article and will be in the next issue of *Anglo-Saxon England*. Episcopal names have been given in their most familiar form: variants are given in the notes. The printing of a name in italic in the lists indicates some uncertainty as to the bishop's existence or his assignation to that particular see, the reason for which should be sought in the notes. Likewise, a date printed in italic is not completely reliable, but usually gives a more precise dating than its more dependable alternative in roman type, and again an explanation will be given in the notes. I have tried to indicate in the notes the evidence for each date given in the lists. Where the episcopal succession seems to be fairly secure I have not cited the episcopal lists in detail, but where there is some doubt the question has been discussed, though I have not in most cases gone beyond the material afforded by the lists, William of Malmesbury's *Gesta Pontificum* and the chronicle attributed to Florence of Worcester and the lists appended to it. (I have treated FW *Chron* and FW *Lists* as two separate authorities.) Where I have argued for the dating of a particular charter, further use of that dating will be made with a reference back to the original discussion under the see and bishop where it occurs, e.g. *BCS* 716 (937; see above, *Cornwall, Conan*). In the lists of dates the mark ' × ' between two dates serves to indicate that the event under review took place anywhere between those two dates inclusively. The mark '–' between two dates indicates that they come from a single source – usually a charter – which cannot be dated more closely.

The following abbreviations are used in parts I and II of this article:

ADL	*Annales Domitiani Latini*, ed. F. P. Magoun, Jr, *MS* 9 (1947), 235–95
AngSac	*Anglia Sacra*, ed. H. Wharton (London, 1691)
Asser	*Asser's Life of King Alfred*, ed. W. H. Stevenson (Oxford, 1904; repr. 1959 with contr. by D. Whitelock)
BCS	*Cartularium Saxonicum*, ed. W. de G. Birch (London, 1885–93)
Councils	*Councils and Ecclesiastical Documents relating to Great Britain and Ireland*, ed. A. W. Haddan and W. Stubbs (Oxford, 1869–78)
Crawford Charters	*The Crawford Collection of Early Charters and Documents*, ed. A. S. Napier and W. H. Stevenson (Oxford, 1895)
Dart	J. Dart, *The History and Antiquities of the Cathedral Church of Canterbury* (London, 1726), Appendix
Earle and Plummer, *Chronicles*	*Two of the Saxon Chronicles Parallel . . .*, ed. C. Plummer on the basis of an ed. by J. Earle (Oxford, 1892; repr. 1952 with contr. by D. Whitelock)
ECW	H. P. R. Finberg, *The Early Charters of Wessex* (Leicester, 1964)
ECWM	H. P. R. Finberg, *The Early Charters of the West Midlands* (Leicester, 1961)
EHD	*English Historical Documents* c. *500–1042*, ed. D. Whitelock (London, 1955)
FW *Chron*	*Florentii Wigorniensis Monachi Chronicon ex Chronicis*, ed. B. Thorpe (London, 1848–9)
FW *Lists*	The episcopal lists appended to Florence of Worcester
GP	William of Malmesbury, *De Gestis Pontificum Anglorum*, ed. N. E. S. A. Hamilton, Rolls Series (1870)
GR	William of Malmesbury, *De Gestis Regum Anglorum*, ed. W. Stubbs, RS (1887–9)
Handbook	*Handbook of British Chronology*, ed. F. M. Powicke and E. B. Fryde, 2nd ed. (London, 1961)
Harmer, *SelEHD*	*Select English Historical Documents of the Ninth and Tenth Centuries*, ed. F. E. Harmer (Cambridge, 1914)

Heming	*Hemingi Chartularium Ecclesiae Wigorniensis*, ed. T. Hearne (Oxford, 1723)
Ker, *Catalogue*	N. R. Ker, *Catalogue of Manuscripts containing Anglo-Saxon* (Oxford, 1957)
Memorials	*Memorials of Saint Dunstan*, ed. W. Stubbs, RS (1874)
Page, *EpLists*	'Anglo-Saxon Episcopal Lists', *Nottingham Med. Stud.* 9 (1965), 71–95 and 10 (1966), 2–24
Robinson, *Saxon Bishops*	J. Armitage Robinson, *The Saxon Bishops of Wells*, British Academy Supplemental Papers 4 (1918)
Robinson, *St Oswald*	J. Armitage Robinson, *St Oswald and the Church of Worcester*, British Academy Supplemental Papers 5 (1919)
Sawyer	P. H. Sawyer, *Anglo-Saxon Charters* (London, 1968)
Stenton, *Abingdon*	F. M. Stenton, *The Early History of the Abbey of Abingdon* (Reading, 1913)
Stenton, *A-S England*	F. M. Stenton, *Anglo-Saxon England*, 3rd ed. (Oxford, 1971)
Stenton, *EHR*	F. M. Stenton, 'The Supremacy of the Mercian Kings', *EHR* 33 (1918), 433–52
Stubbs	W. Stubbs, *Registrum Sacrum Anglicanum*, 2nd ed. (Oxford, 1897)
Textus Roffensis	*Textus Roffensis*, ed. P. Sawyer, EEMF 7 (1957) and 11 (1962)
Whitelock, *Æthelgifu*	*The Will of Æthelgifu*, ed. and trans. D. Whitelock (Oxford, 1968)
Whitelock, *ASC*	*The Anglo-Saxon Chronicle*, trans. D. Whitelock with D. C. Douglas and S. I. Tucker (London, 1961)

THE LISTS

Bishop	*Accession*	*Death or translation*
	CANTERBURY	
Ceolnoth	833 elected 29 June, consecrated 27 Aug.	870 (*ob.* 4 Feb.)
Æthelred	870 trans. fr. Wiltshire	888 (*ob.* 30 June)
Plegmund	890	923 (*ob.* 2 Aug.)
Athelm	Aug. 923 × Sept. 925 trans. fr. Wells	926 (*ob.* 8 Jan.)
Wulfhelm	926 trans. fr. Wells	941 (*ob.* 12 Feb.)
Oda	941 trans. fr. Ramsbury	958 or *959* (*ob.* 2 June)

Episcopal dates for the province of Canterbury, 850–950

Bishop	Accession	Death or translation
	CORNWALL	
Kenstec	823 × 870	before 888 × 893
Asser	888 × 893	909
	diocese returned to Sherborne during his episcopate	
Conan	July 924 × 931	946 or *953* × Nov. 955
	CREDITON	
Eadwulf	*c.* 909	June 934 × *Dec. 934* or 937
Æthelgar	June 934 × *Dec. 934* or 937	*952* or 953
	DORCHESTER	
Alhheard	869 or *871–4* × 888	893 × 896
Wigmund or *Wilferth*	893 × 900	903 × 909
Cenwulf	*c.* 909	909 × 925
Wynsige	909 × 925	934 or *937 × 939* or 945
Æthelwald	934 or *937 × 939* or 945	949 × 950
Osketel	949 × 950	971 (*ob.* 1 Nov.)
	DUNWICH	
Wilred	825	845 × 870
Æthelwald	845 × 870	?
	ELMHAM	
Hunberht	816 × 824	845 or *856* × ? or *Nov. 869*
	HEREFORD	
Cuthwulf	836 × 839	857 × 866
Mucel	857 × 866	857 × 866
Deorlaf	857 × 866	884 × 888
Cynemund	888 elected	888 × 900
Edgar	888 × 900	*930* or 930 × 931
Tidhelm	*930* or 930 × 931	934 or *937* × 940
Wulfhelm	934 or *937* × 940	934 or *937* × 940
Ælfric	934 or *937* × 940	949 × *958* or 971
	LEICESTER	
Ræthhun	814 × 816	839 × Dec. 840
Ealdred	839 × Dec. 840	Dec. 840 × 843–4
Ceolred	Dec. 840 × 843–4	869 or *871–4* × 888

See Dorchester for later succession

Bishop	Accession	Death or translation
	LICHFIELD	
Tunberht	843 × Nov. 845	857 × 862
Wulfsige	857 × 862	866 × 869
Burgheard	866 × 869	869 × 883
or *Eadberht*	866 × 869	875 × 883
Wulfred	869 or 875 × 883	889 × 900
Wigmund or *Wilferth*	889 × 900	903 × 915
Ælfwine (Ælle)	903 × 915	935 × 941
Wulfgar	935 × 941	946 × 949
Cynesige	946 × 949	963 × *Dec. 963* or 964

Bishop	Accession	Death or translation
	LINDSEY	
Beorhtred	836 × 839	862 × *866* or ?
Eadbald	862 × 866	866 × 869
Burgheard	866 × 869	869 × ?
or *Eadberht*	866 × 869	875 × ?

Apparent vacancy until Leofwine's appearance in 953

Bishop	Accession	Death or translation
	LONDON	
Ceolberht	816 × 824	Nov. 845 × 860–July 863
Deorwulf	Nov. 845 × 860–July 863	867 × 890–96
Swithwulf	867 × 890–96	867 × 890–96
Heahstan	867 × 890–96	897
Wulfsige	897 × 900	909 × 926
Æthelweard	909 × 926	909 × 926
Leofstan	909 × 926	909 × 926
Theodred	909 × 926	951 × 953

Bishop	Accession	Death or translation
	RAMSBURY	
Athelstan	*c.* 909	*c.* 909 or *924 × 927* or 928
Oda	*c.* 909 or *924 × 927* or 928	941
		trans. to Canterbury
Ælfric	941 × 949	949 × 951

Bishop	Accession	Death or translation
	ROCHESTER	
Tatnoth	844	845 × 868
	elected	
Badenoth	845 × 868	845 × 868
Wærmund	845 × 868	845 × 868
Cuthwulf	845 × 868	868 × 880

Bishop	Accession	Death or translation
Swithwulf	868 × 880	893 × 896
Ceolmund	893 × 900	909 × 926
Cyneferth	909 × 926	Jan. 933 × May 934
Burgric	Jan. 933 × May 934	946 × 964
Beorhtsige	946 × 949	955 × 964

SELSEY

Guthheard	839 × Nov. 845	860–July 863 × ?
Wighelm	860–July 863 × 900	*c. 909* or 909 × 925
Beornheah	? or *909* or 909 × 925	930 × 931
Wulfhun	930 × 931	940 × 943
Alfred	940 × 943	953 × 956

SHERBORNE

Ealhstan	816 × 817–18 or *824*	867
Heahmund	867 × 868	871
Æthelheah	871 × 877	879 × 889
Wulfsige	879 × 889	890–96 × 900
Asser	890–96 × 900	909
Æthelweard	*c.* 909	*c.* 909
Wærstan	*c.* 909	*918* or *c.* 909 × 925
Æthelbald	*c.* 909 or *918* × 925	*c.* 909 or *918* × 925
Sigehelm	*c.* 909 or *918* × 925	932 × 934
Alfred	932 × 934	939 × 943
Wulfsige	939 × 943	958 × 963–4

WELLS

Athelm	*c.* 909	923 × Sept. 925 trans. to Canterbury
Wulfhelm	923 × Sept. 925	Jan. 926 × *927* or 928 trans. to Canterbury
Ælfheah	Jan. 926 × *927* or 928	*937* or 937 × 938
Wulfhelm	*937* or 937 × 938	956

WINCHESTER

Helmstan	838 × 839	844 × 852 or *853*
Swithhun	Oct. 852 or *Oct. 853*	862 or 863 (*ob.* 2 July)
Ealhferth	862 or 863 × 867	871 × 877
Tunberht	871 × 877	878 × 879
Denewulf	878 × 879	908
Frithestan	909	932 × 933
Byrnstan	May 931	934 (*ob.* 1 Nov.)
Ælfheah	935	951 (*ob.* 12 March)

Bishop	Accession	Death or translation
WORCESTER		
Alhhun	843 or *Dec. 844* × Nov. 845	869 × 872
Wærferth	*872* or 869 × 872	*915* or 907 × 915
Æthelhun	*915* or 907 × 915	*922* or 915 × 922
Wilferth	*922* or 915 × 922	928 × 929
Cenwald	928 × 929	957 or *958*

NOTES

Canterbury

Ceolnoth

The year of his election and consecration is given in *ASC* (all versions) *s.a* 830, *recte* 833 (the correction is made by analogy with the preceding and following annals). *ADL*, also *s.a.* 830, gives the dates of his election and consecration as 29 June and 27 August (III Kal. Iul. and VI Kal. Sept.). However in 833 27 August was not a Sunday; 24 August would be the nearest. Ceolnoth's first reliable appearance is in 835 as the beneficiary of *BCS* 414 and he is a witness in 836 (*BCS* 416). *BCS* 405 and *BCS* 406, both original charters witnessed by Ceolnoth, are given their dates of 832 and 831 respectively only by much later endorsements, so his appearances here do not discredit the *Chronicle* evidence. Nor does his mention in *BCS* 408, which is dated 832. This is an abbreviated, cartulary version of *BCS* 407, which has a rubric dating it to 841, although internal evidence dates it to 825–39. Finally Ceolnoth witnesses *BCS* 411 (773) which F. M. Stenton (see Sawyer 270) regards as suspect, being perhaps the result of a scribal confusion between Egbert II of Kent and Egbert of Wessex, leading to a witness-list of the latter being combined with a grant of the former, certainly not reliable evidence for Ceolnoth's archiepiscopate.

The year of Ceolnoth's death is given in *ASC* as 870 in all versions except C, which is a year ahead; D by mistake has 'go to Rome' for 'die'. Stubbs gives 4 February as the day of his death, from a post-Conquest Canterbury calendar (*AngSac* I, 53). *ADL* and William of Malmesbury (*GP*, p. 20) both say that Ceolnoth died in the forty-first year of his archiepiscopate. Calculated from the dates 830 and 870 which would be available from the *Chronicle*, this is reasonable, but it must have been worked out by someone ignorant of consecration day or *obit*, or both. Of the charter material, Ceolnoth's latest acceptable signature occurs in *BCS* 519 (888 for 867; see part II, *Sherborne, Heahmund*), and his successor Æthelred appears first as the donor of *BCS* 536, dated 873, but with the indiction 7, which fits 874. Ceolnoth also appears as a witness to this charter, as the scribe added witness-lists of the mid ninth century to the body of the text, probably because his exemplar was deficient here. Both archbishops appear in consecutive witness-lists to *BCS* 538, which is dated 874 but belongs in part to the reign of Æthelwulf (839–58). Ceolnoth also witnesses *BCS* 535, which in Birch's version is dated in error 872, but which actually belongs to 862 (see *ECWM* 79 and pp. 153–7).

Æthelred

Succeeded to Canterbury in 870 according to *ADL* and *ASC* F and according to the addition made to the Parker manuscript (*ASC* A) under this year by the scribe of *ADL* (T. A. M. Bishop, personal comment; cf. Ker, *Catalogue*, p. 187). These entries record that Æthelred was bishop of Wiltshire before his appointment to Canterbury, and *ADL* continues with a long (spurious) account of how Æthelred replaced clerics with monks at Canterbury. Æthelred's first closely dateable signature occurs in *BCS* 536 (873 or 874; see above, *Ceolnoth*).

He died in 888 according to *ADL* and all the Chronicle versions except C which is a year in advance. His *obit* is recorded as 30 June in Oxford, Bodleian Library, Add. C. 260 (ref. fr. *AngSac*). Æthelred last witnesses in 882 (*BCS* 550).

Plegmund

Succeeded in 890 according to *ASC* F, *ADL* and Canterbury additions to *ASC* A and in E. He signs first a spurious charter of 895 (*BCS* 571) and makes a grant in the same year (*BCS* 572), which may however be a misdated abbreviation of *BCS* 638 (see Sawyer 1288 and 1627). Plegmund is named as archbishop in a letter from Pope Formosus (*BCS* 573), dated by his pontificate to 891–6. This letter contains some spurious material on the primacy of Canterbury, but it may well have a genuine base. Plegmund's death is recorded under 923 by the Canterbury annotator of *ASC* A though he has not entered the event in F or *ADL*. In A, the date 922 has been altered to 923, but this was done before the manuscript reached Canterbury as is witnessed by *ASC* G. See Robinson, *Saxon Bishops*, pp. 56–8 for the redating of Plegmund's death from 914. His *obit* is given as 2 August (*AngSac* I, 53).

Athelm (Æthelhelm)

Translated from the bishopric of Wells to succeed Plegmund. The exact date of his succession is not known, but he was in office by 4 September 925 (*BCS* 641, the only charter he witnesses). A Canterbury manuscript, BM Cotton Galba E. iv, records no gap between the two archbishops, but is not reliable evidence (it gives Athelm a span of nine years at Canterbury). His *obit* is recorded as 8 January (BM Cotton Nero C. ix. i, ref. fr. Dart) and as his successor appears as archbishop in 926 (see below), this ties Athelm's death to 8 January 926 (see Robinson, *Saxon Bishops*).

Wulfhelm

Followed Athelm from Wells. It seems clear from the evidence cited above that Wulfhelm could not have succeeded Athelm before 926, although *ASC* E and F, *ADL* and a Canterbury addition to A give the date of his consecration as 925. One of these references is probably the model for the others, though it is difficult to tell which is the original source. The indications are that the archetype of E is the source. This version contains two records of Edward's death, under 924 and 925, the later being combined with the notice of Wulfhelm's consecration. Professor Whitelock suggests (Whitelock, *ASC*, p. 68) that the 924 entry was copied into E's archetype and into F from A at Canterbury, which makes it probable that the 925 entry was native to E, from which the information about Wulfhelm was transferred to the other chronicles at Canterbury. However this does not cast any light on the source of E's information or its reliability.

The charters offer no conclusive evidence on the side either of the *obit* or of the *ASC* 925 date. *Pace* the *obit*, Athelm could have died between 4 September 925 (*BCS* 641, which is also witnessed by Wulfhelm as a bishop) and the end of the year. Wulfhelm signs as archbishop in two reputable charters of 926 (*BCS* 658 and *BCS* 659). He also signs *BCS* 635, dated 921 but belonging in style to Athelstan's reign and with a witness-list suitable to the years 931–4. Wulfhelm also appears as archbishop in a memorandum dated 923 (*BCS* 637), which again is not reliable (see Sawyer 1629). On the whole 926 is the most acceptable date for the changeover from Athelm to Wulfhelm.

None of the *Chronicle* versions records Wulfhelm's death, though his *obit* is given as 12 February by Canterbury tradition (*AngSac* i, 53). His death can be assigned to 941 or 942 from the charter evidence. Wulfhelm signs as archbishop several times in 940, four times in 941 (*BCS* 765, *BCS* 766, *BCS* 768 and *BCS* 770) and once in 943 (*BCS* 785). His successor Oda signs frequently as bishop (of Ramsbury) in 940 and twice in 941 (*BCS* 767 and *BCS* 770). Oda appears as archbishop once in 940 (*BCS* 761), once in 941 (*BCS* 769) and frequently from 942 onwards. Of the charters for Wulfhelm as archbishop in 941, *BCS* 766 is at least tampered with, for it names Oda as bishop of Sherborne – the sees of lesser bishops were not named in charters of this period, and anyway Oda belonged to Ramsbury; *BCS* 768 is acceptable; *BCS* 770 is less reliable (Professor Whitelock, personal comment): it shares much of its text with another charter from the same cartulary,

BCS 763, but can still be taken into consideration here. *BCS* 765 is less easy to assess. It is dated 24 July 960, but the indiction, regnal year and concurrent belong to the year 941, and the epact unfortunately to 939. Otherwise the charter is undistinguished except for the low positions of bishops Ælfheah and Theodred in the witness-list. If the charter belongs to Edmund's reign (October 939–46), these can only be the bishops of Winchester and London, who together almost invariably head the episcopal witnesses. However, if one could accept the evidence of this charter for Wulfhelm's appearance in 941 after 12 February (his *obit*), then his death must be placed in 942. *BCS* 785, dated 943, cannot be reliable evidence for that year, as it purports to be issued by Athelstan, in the sixth year of his reign (930–1) and is witnessed by three archbishops. Wulfhelm's appearance here can therefore be discounted.

Oda's appearance at Canterbury in 940 (*BCS* 761) seems impossible, although there is nothing suspicious about the charter except the combination of year and archbishop, and the lack of an indiction figure, which indicates careless copying at some stage. F. M. Stenton (*Abingdon*, p. 42) treats it as reliable, so perhaps the date may be adjusted to 941/2 as the simplest solution. *BCS* 769 (941) also bears Oda's witness as archbishop, and H. P. R. Finberg (*ECW* 255) argues from this against 942 as the date of Oda's succession.

The question rests therefore on the *obit* of 12 February, the 24 July 941 of *BCS* 765 and the evidence of *BCS* 769. The acceptance of the first two dates means that Wulfhelm died in 942, and that *BCS* 769 must be discredited. The acceptance of the *obit* and *BCS* 769 implies that Wulfhelm died in 941 and that *BCS* 765 must be ignored. Finally the two charters can be reconciled by ignoring the *obit*, which places Wulfhelm's death in 941 after 24 July. Onc is, however, reluctant to discard the *obit*, which has the merit of coming from an unbiassed, though late, Canterbury source. Of the two contradictory charters *BCS* 769 is probably to be preferred as the more consistent. This leaves 12 February 941 as the most probable date for Wulfhelm's death.

Oda

Succeeded to Canterbury in 941 after 12 February (see above). Oda's *obit* was recorded at Canterbury as 2 June (*AngSac* I, 54) and he is generally accepted as having died in 958, the date given by Florence of Worcester. Oda signs up to 957, and appears twice in 958 (*BCS* 1021 and *BCS* 1032). *BCS* 1021 is not really acceptable – it is issued by Eadred (955) – but there seems to be nothing suspicious about *BCS* 1032. Oda appears at Eadwig's court after the latter's split with Edgar, also once in 957 (*BCS* 998). He also witnesses *BCS* 1046, dated 17 May 959. This does not clash with the archbishop's *obit*, if it is assumed that he did not die until 959. The charter has been viewed with suspicion by W. H. Stevenson (see Sawyer 658) and Professor Whitelock (personal comment), and does not accord with F. M. Stenton's view of Eadwig's attitude towards the reformers (*Abingdon*, p. 49). Eric John has however argued recently (*Orbis Britanniae* (Leicester, 1966), pp. 188–94) for its acceptance. But the attestation of the queen-mother raises doubts, as does the great number of events which would need to be placed between Oda's death on 2 June 959 and Eadwig's death on 1 October. Ælfsige of Winchester was appointed as Oda's successor, but died of cold in the Alps while journeying to Rome to fetch his *pallium*. He was replaced at Canterbury by Beorhthelm (probably of Wells) before the king died. Eric John argues that Ælfsige might well have died of cold – or something attributable to cold – during the summer or early autumn of 959, but the account of Ælfsige's death in the Life of Dunstan by 'B', who was writing at less than fifty years' remove from these events, fits much better with a winter journey: 'obfuit illi in Alpinis montibus maxima nivis difficultas, quae tanto eum gelu rigoris obstrinxerat, ut in moriendo deficeret...' (*Memorials*, p. 38). Quite apart from this, which can be criticized as subjective evidence, placing Oda's death in June 959 necessitates a dangerously compressed sequence of events. Charter evidence shows that Beorhthelm was witnessing as the holder of Canterbury before Eadwig's death: he testifies as 'bishop of the church of Canterbury' in *BCS* 1045 (959). He also appears with this title in the Athelney charter (*ECW* 483) which is witnessed by Eadwig and dated 958. This might have resolved the question, except that the indiction is given as 2, which could fit 958, but much more probably belongs to 959. Considering the evidence as a whole, the possibility of 959 as the year of Oda's death cannot be excluded, but 958 has a much stronger claim on that event.

Cornwall

Kenstec

Appears only in his profession of obedience to Archbishop Ceolnoth of Canterbury (*BCS* 527; *Councils* I, 674) as bishop elect to the people of Cornwall. His succession cannot be dated more closely than 833–70 (Ceolnoth's archiepiscopate). H. P. R. Finberg has suggested (*Lucerna: Studies in some Problems in the Early History of England* (London, 1964), p. 105) that Kenstec was already bishop of Cornwall and made his profession to Ceolnoth under compulsion, after Egbert's triumphant campaigns against the British. If so, his calling himself 'electus' requires explanation. Only the last of Egbert's recorded campaigns, that of 838, would fit with Kenstec's profession. Egbert was also victorious in 815 and 825 (*ASC*, correcting the two-year dislocation) and his donation of three Cornish estates to Sherborne could belong to one of these occasions (see *Crawford Charters* VII and Robinson, *Saxon Bishops*, pp. 18–28) and need have no connection with Kenstec's profession. A late-tenth-century writer, who gives as the motive for the donation of these estates that it was to enable an annual visitation of the people of Cornwall to suppress their errors, is referring to the gift of them to Crediton in the reign of Edward the Elder (*BCS* 614). Hence it is only a surmise that Kenstec's profession belongs to Egbert's time.

Kenstec must almost certainly have died before Asser received 'Exeter, with all the diocese belonging to it in Saxon territory and in Cornwall' (Asser, ch. 81); see below.

Asser

Although there are other explanations, it seems likely that the gift quoted above laid on Asser the episcopal charge of Cornwall and part or all of Devon (see Finberg, *Lucerna*, pp. 109–10). This gift must have been made after 888 because P. Grierson ('Grimbald of St Bertins', *EHR* 55 (1940), 529–61) calculated that Asser's first long visit to Alfred occurred in 887 and lasted until Christmas, and Asser states that the gift of Exeter came later. Asser was writing in 893, so the gift had been made by then. The area concerned was originally included in the diocese of Sherborne, and when Asser became bishop of Sherborne he would have taken both parts under his control. Asser died in 909; see part II, *Sherborne*, *Asser*.

Conan (Cunan)

According to a tenth-century letter (cf. *Crawford Charters* VII and pp. 104–6), Conan was appointed to Cornwall by Athelstan, which would place his succession in the years between Athelstan's accession in 924 and Conan's first signatures which occur in 931 (*BCS* 674, *BCS* 675 and *BCS* 677). The antiquarian John Leland reported 'Ex charta Donat: Æthelstani. Erexit in ecclesia S. Germani quendam Conanum episcopum anno Di. 936 Nonis Decembris' (*De Rebus Britannicis Collectanea*, ed. T. Hearne (Oxford, 1770) I, 75; *Councils* I, 676). The editors of *Councils* note that Leland wavers between 936 and 926, and H. P. R. Finberg (*Lucerna*, p. 112 and n.) argues that this extract refers to the founding of the see of St German's and Conan's appointment, and must be assigned to the year 926, since Conan was signing as bishop several years before 936. However, it seems that the editors of *Councils* were in error: Leland (as edited by Hearne) does not waver in dating the St German's charter, he gives it as 936 without qualification. The uncertainty between 926 and 936 occurs in Leland's next entry, which concerns a donation of Athelstan to St Petroc's, Bodmin. It is possible to understand the St German's extract as referring, not to Conan's appointment as bishop, but to the transfer of his see to St German's, perhaps from the mysterious *Dinnurrin* of Kenstec's profession. But it would be wiser not to place too much reliance on the wording of the extract which is after all only Leland's précis of a document which may not even have been authentic. Leland himself may have assumed that a donation to this bishop implied the creation of a see in this year.

Conan continues to sign until 934. He also appears in 936 in the St German's charter discussed above, and perhaps in 937, if one can accept the testimony of *BCS* 716, a suspect charter dated to that year. Its secular witnesses look more suitable to the years 931–4, but the ecclesiastical witnesses as a group can belong only to 937. Conan is probably intended by the *Caynan* who witnesses *BCS* 738, a poor charter of Athelstan dated 843, but belonging in intention to the period 931–4. He also witnesses the suspect *BCS* 785, dated 943, but probably based on material from 931 (see above, *Canterbury*, *Wulfhelm*). The year of Conan's death is unknown, the limit being Daniel's appearance in a charter of 955 (*BCS* 917, a charter of Eadwig). The Old English letter (*Crawford Charters* VII) states that Daniel was appointed to Cornwall by Eadred (946–23 November 955), but it also implies that Daniel did not take office until after Æthelgar of Crediton's death in 952 or 953, thus suggesting that Daniel's appointment took place between 952 and late in 955. We do not know if the see fell vacant for any length of time between the occupancies of Conan and Daniel.

Crediton

Eadwulf

Named as the first bishop of Crediton in episcopal lists and in the Plegmund narratives (e.g. *Crawford Charters* VII; Robinson, *Saxon Bishops*, pp. 7–24). See part II, *Winchester, Frithestan*, for discussion of the division of the West Saxon bishoprics *c.* 909. No charters survive from the years 909–24 (*BCS* 635, dated 921, has a witness-list belonging to 931–4), but Eadwulf witnesses frequently in Athelstan's charters, his latest appearance being in *BCS* 702, an original charter dated 28 May 934, and in *BCS* 703, a charter bearing the date 7 June 930 and a corresponding regnal year, but with indiction, concurrent and epact for 934. Professor Whitelock (*EHD*, p. 505) accepts *BCS* 703 as authentic for 934. Florence of Worcester records Eadwulf's death under the year 931, but his evidence is not acceptable in the face of strong charter evidence to the contrary. Eadwulf, then, died after 7 June 934, and before his successor's appearance, for which see below.

Æthelgar

Named as Eadwulf's successor in the episcopal lists and in *Crawford Charters* VII. He witnesses a variety of apparently early charters: *BCS* 393, dated 826, but with witnesses from *c.* 939 (Sawyer 446); *BCS* 667, dated 930, but with later witnesses (Professor Whitelock has suggested that much of the witness-list has been supplied from another Abingdon charter, *BCS* 883 of 949); and *BCS* 670 and 671, a pair of suspect charters dated 931, but with witnesses belonging to 934 or *937* × 939. *Crawford Charters* (p. 137, n. 1) says 941 for the two charters, but this seems untenable. *ECW* 435 gives 934–9. The presence of Ælfric of Hereford would give a closer dating if his predecessor signs in 937 (see below, *Hereford, Tidhelm*). *BCS* 705 and its Anglo-Saxon version *BCS* 706 are more difficult. They are dated 16 December 934, with the indiction for 934, although strictly speaking it should have been changed to the indiction for 935 after September. The text is somewhat suspicious, but the witness-list is particularly full, the key signature being that of Ælfheah of Winchester (Ælfheah of Wells also signs, so there is no danger of confusion). Ælfheah's predecessor died on 1 November 934, so there was just time for Ælfheah to have been elected and consecrated by 16 December 934. However one also has to take into account *BCS* 707, dated 935 but with the indiction for 934, in which Ælfheah signs as 'previsor in electione sua'. It is possible that Ælfheah was only bishop elect when he witnessed *BCS* 705, though this is often stated in charters. *BCS* 705's evidence should probably be regarded as suspect. Æthelgar next appears in a reputable charter for 937 (*BCS* 714) as well as in several less reputable documents for that year (*BCS* 716, *BCS* 721 and *BCS* 722). Eadwulf's death and Æthelgar's succession therefore fall between 7 June and 16 December 934 if one accepts *BCS* 705, and between 7 June 934 and 937 if *BCS* 705 is rejected.

Æthelgar's death can also be calculated from the charters, although there is again a slight discrepancy in the evidence available. Æthelgar signs frequently up to and including 951; he then signs twice in 953 (*BCS* 898 and *BCS* 899). His successor Ælfwold signs once in 952 (*BCS* 895), once in 953 (*BCS* 900) and frequently from 955 on. The year 953 would be suitable for the changeover were it not for Ælfwold's witness of *BCS* 895 in 952, a charter which looks unexceptionable (Professor Whitelock, personal comment; it is a copy of a lost Abingdon original). Of Æthelgar's latest appearances, *BCS* 898 survives in an unsatisfactory form but *BCS* 899 is accepted by F. M. Stenton (*Abingdon*, p. 42). It is possible that the date of one of these charters has been miscopied, perhaps that of *BCS* 895, since it is in the minority.

Dorchester

Bishopric transferred from Leicester because of Danish invasions (*c.* 874?; cf. *Councils* III, 129; I cannot find any primary authority for this information). The last bishop of Leicester, Ceolred, signs his latest charter in 869 (*BCS* 524). FW *Lists* says that Ceolred was bishop in the time of Kings Alfred and Burgred, which would extend his known episcopate to 871–4, but it might be a mistake to rely heavily on this.

Alhheard (Ealhheard)

Witnesses in 888 (*BCS* 557) and 889 (*BCS* 561). He is assigned to Dorchester in *ASC* (896), 'biscop æt Dorceceastre', and Plummer (Earle and Plummer, *Chronicles* II, 111) draws attention to the wording 'biscop æt', suggesting that the see was thought to be only temporarily at Dorchester. In *ASC* Alhheard is recorded as having died during the three years preceding the entry, which may mean 893–5 or 894–6.

(Wigmund or Wilferth)

One or other of these bishops, both of whom sign between 900 and 903, may belong to Dorchester; see part II, *Lichfield, the Viking period*.

Cenwulf

Named as one of the seven bishops consecrated by Plegmund in BM Add. 7138, and in the Leofric Missal. In these Cenwulf is assigned to a Mercian province seated at Dorchester. His consecration is probably to be placed *c.* 909 (see part II, *Winchester, Frithestan*). He does not appear elsewhere.

(Wynsige)

Though not in any list, Wynsige witnesses several charters from 925 to 934, and also *BCS* 716 (937, see above, *Cornwall, Conan*), and is entered in the *Liber S. Galli* (Stubbs, p. 26). *BCS* 719 (937) names his see Leicester, but this is a text concocted from Malmesbury charters, perhaps by William of Malmesbury, who assigned the union of Leicester and Dorchester to Oscytel's successor Leofwine (*GP*, p. 312). He may have put Wynsige there because there seems no other vacant see. Wynsige's death is unrecorded.

(Æthelwald)

A bishop of this name appears in charters for 945 (*BCS* 808), 946 (*BCS* 815) and 949 (*BCS* 876 and *BCS* 883). He also appears in *BCS* 740, dated 939 but very suspect, *BCS* 667, dated 930 with witnesses from *c.* 949 (see above, *Crediton, Æthelgar*), and *BCS* 812, the attached witness-list being from 943–7, perhaps late 946 (Whitelock, *Æthelgifu*, p. 43). Professor Whitelock suggests that Æthelwald may belong to Dorchester, as he has no known provenance (*Æthelgifu*, p. 44). If *ASC*'s mention of the length of Osketel's episcopate *s.a.* 971 is correct, Æthelwald must have died very shortly after his signatures in 949. If Æthelwald did not belong to Dorchester, the bishopric may have fallen vacant for a while, as there is a gap of at least ten years between Wynsige's last signature and Osketel's appearance.

Osketel (Oscytel)

Referred to as bishop of Dorchester, whence he was advanced to York, in *ASC* B and C under the year of his death 971 (where his *obit* also is given, as 1 November). The length of his episcopate including that at Dorchester is given as twenty-two years, which would place his ordination in 949–50. His first signatures appear in 951 (*BCS* 890 and *BCS* 891). The evidence for the circumstances and date of Osketel's elevation to York, which lie outside the scope of this paper, has been discussed by Professor Whitelock ('The Dealings of the Kings of England with Northumbria', *The Anglo-Saxons: Studies in some Aspects of their History and Culture presented to Bruce Dickins*, ed. P. Clemoes (London, 1959), pp. 73–5).

Dunwich

Wilred

Appears last in the episcopal lists for Dunwich. William of Malmesbury (*GP*) gives the explanation that the see proved too poor and was amalgamated with Elmham. However this more probably belongs to the tenth century, and the break after the next bishop should be assigned to the Danish invasions (see above, p. 19). Wilred signs as bishop elect (*BCS* 384) and as bishop (*BCS* 386) in 825 – perhaps his consecration took place at the synod of *Clofeshoh* of that year. His last signature appears in 845 (*BCS* 448), and his death-date is limited only by the profession of his successor. See above, p. 21.

In the *Handbook* Husa and Cunda are inserted in the Dunwich and Elmham lists at this point on the strength of *BCS* 416 (836), but there seems no reason why they should be put here rather than in any other list.

Æthelwald

Known from his profession, 845–70, to Archbishop Ceolnoth (*Councils* III, 659) and from his seal (see above, p. 18). The date of his death is unknown. The see was not revived.

Elmham

Hunberht

Last bishop of Elmham in FW *Lists*, in Cambridge, Corpus Christi College 183 and in BM Cotton Tiberius B. v (see Page, *EpLists*). He was consecrated between 816, when his predecessor-once-removed witnesses, and 824, when he witnesses in *BCS* 379. His signatures appear until 845 (*BCS* 448; on *BCS* 450 see above, p. 18, n. 1). The *Annals of St Neots, s.a.* 856 (Asser. pp. 131–2), record that Hunberht crowned King Edmund of East Anglia. Edmund's accession is placed *s.a.* 855, which agrees with FW *Chron.* If these post-Conquest sources can be relied upon, this brings Hunberht's known episcopate up to 856. The date of his death is sometimes given as 20 November 870 (*recte* 869) on the strength of Symeon of Durham's statement that he was martyred with King Edmund of East Anglia. This appears to be based on Abbo of Fleury's *Vita* of the king, which contains the story of how one of Edmund's bishops tried to persuade him to flee from the advancing Vikings. Though Symeon may have had other sources, and bishops have been known to remain in office for fifty years, it is odd that Bury tradition knows nothing of this martyrdom. Apart from Symeon's story, we have no indication of Hunberht's death. See above, p. 18.

For Husa and Cunda, see above, *Dunwich*. By the mid tenth century part, if not all, of the diocese of East Anglia was under the care of the bishop of London (see *Anglo-Saxon Wills*, ed. D. Whitelock (Cambridge, 1930), no. 1).

Hereford

Cuthwulf

Last name in episcopal list for Hereford in CCCC 183; also in *GP* and FW *Lists*. Cuthwulf signs first in 839 (*BCS* 421), his predecessor having last appeared in 836 (*BCS* 416). His last signature occurs in 857 (*BCS* 492).

(*Mucel*)

In the twelfth-century lists, Cuthwulf's name is followed by that of Mucel, who does not appear anywhere else. The editors of *Councils* suggest that his name should be omitted from the lists, because in the profession of the next bishop of Hereford, Deorlaf, Mucel is not included in the list of Deorlaf's immediate predecessors. But it would be unwise to assume from this that he did not occupy the episcopate, if only for a few weeks. His possible dates are indicated only by those of Cuthwulf and Deorlaf.

Deorlaf

First appears in *BCS* 452, a charter which seems to belong to 843–5, long before Cuthwulf disappears. Apart from *BCS* 452, Deorlaf does not sign until 866 (*BCS* 513). *BCS* 452 is written in the vernacular on a single-sheet parchment in a ninth-century hand (T. A. M. Bishop, personal comment; Sawyer 204) and is generally accepted as genuine. It contains no date, but should belong to the years 843–5, since it is witnessed by Alhhun of Worcester who cannot sign before 843–4, and probably not before December 844 (see part II, *Worcester, Alhhun*), and by Cyneferth of Lichfield, whose successor signs first in 845. F. Harmer (*SelEHD* III), who accepts the charter, does not identify the Deorlaf of *BCS* 452 with the bishop of Hereford, but assigns him to an unknown see. The only feature which can be counted against the charter, apart from Deorlaf's appearance, is that it is not written on one side of the parchment only, but runs on to the reverse. This is not unique to *BCS* 452 – *BCS* 449 (845) also continues on to the back of the sheet – but in this case the charter actually refers to the fact that the witnesses are inscribed 'verte folium'.

There is no easy explanation for Deorlaf's presence: he may be an unknown suffragan bishop (there were no vacant sees at this date) who perhaps later succeeded to Hereford, or, if one postulates that *BCS* 452 is a slightly later copy of an original, the copyist might have inserted his name by mistake. In any case, it is safest to keep to the dates offered by the majority of charters, that is 857 × 866 for the beginning of his episcopate. Deorlaf continues signing until 884 (*BCS* 552).

Cynemund

Follows Deorlaf in *GP* and FW *Lists*. He signs *BCS* 557 (888) as bishop elect, his only appearance.

Edgar

Follows Cynemund in the catalogues as above. He signs first in 900 (*BCS* 596, not a very convincing document – see Sawyer 360) and also in *BCS* 607, dated 900 with indiction for 904, and perhaps belonging to late 900, with the indiction IIII misread for VII. His latest signature appears in 930 (*BCS* 669; *Crawford Charters* iv).

Tidhelm

Follows Edgar in the catalogues. His first reputable signature comes in 931 (*BCS* 677) although he also signs *BCS* 700, which is dated 930, with the regnal year 6 (929–30), but with indiction and epact for 934. The text of *BCS* 700 is generally condemned (Sawyer 406), but the witness-list looks consistent with the date 930 and would not fit 934 (Hrothweard of York witnesses, who was replaced by Wulfstan in 931). Tidhelm's signatures continue until 934 (*BCS* 702 and *BCS* 705) and possibly until 937 (*BCS* 716, see above, *Cornwall, Conan*), and his death must occur after his latest appearance and before the first signature of his successor Ælfric.

(Wulfhelm)

Included here in the catalogues, but appears nowhere else, unless he can be identified with the bishop Wulfhelm who witnesses occasionally between 931 and 943–7 (see part II, *Wells, Wulfhelm*) and is assignable to no known see. It is possible that this Wulfhelm was a suffragan bishop under Tidhelm and later Ælfric, whose name was inserted into the episcopal list by later historians who did not know his real position. There are no signatures from any Wulfhelm other than the archbishop for the years between Tidhelm and Ælfric. The identification of the bishop of Hereford with the other Wulfhelm can be only hypothetical.

Ælfric

Follows Wulfhelm in the catalogues. His signatures should not appear before those of Tidhelm cease, but at first sight there are several charters which bear his witness before 937, and even before 934. *BCS* 667 in which Ælfric signs, has the date 930, but its witness-list is much later, belonging probably to 949, in which case Ælfric could be bishop either of Hereford or of Ramsbury, while the witnesses of *BCS* 670 and *BCS* 671 (dated 931) belong to 934 or *937–9* (for all three charters see above, *Crediton, Æthelgar*). Ælfric's witness of *BCS* 689 (932) is a different matter, for the charter is reputable and generally accepted, with an excellent dating apparatus (the indiction has been miscopied, II for V, but this is unimportant when the date, regnal year, epact and concurrent all agree). The witness-list also is very full, like several of Athelstan's charters of the years 931–4, and a bishop Ælfric signs at the end of the list of bishops. However, although it is possible that this is Ælfric of Hereford acting as a suffragan, or another unidentified bishop, it is much more likely that this Ælfric belongs at the head of the list of abbots rather than among the bishops. There is an Abbot Ælfric who appears in this position in several charters of 931–4, and may even be the future bishop of Hereford.

Otherwise, Ælfric appears first in *BCS* 746, a charter of Athelstan which bears the date 850 and indiction 13. The charter itself is acceptable (Professor Whitelock, personal comment; Sawyer 392), although the date has been miscopied. Birch suggests 940 as the original date, which would fit the indiction. He was working on the assumption that Athelstan died in 940, but the charter could still belong to the autumn of 939, between 24 September, when the indiction would change from 12 to 13, and 27 October, when Athelstan died, if one could rely on the indiction being correct. However, the indiction 13 corresponds with 850 as well as 940, which undermines its usefulness. The witness-list gives a fairly close date to the charter with the appearance of Bishop Wulfhelm of Wells, whose episcopate begins in 937/8 (see part II, *Wells*), and the king's death in late 939. Ælfric then signs several times in 940 and 941, after which his signatures are indistinguishable from those of his namesake at Ramsbury until 949, when both witness *BCS* 885. One Bishop Ælfric continues to sign into 951, but one cannot tell which, since Ælfric of Ramsbury's successor does not appear until 951, while the next bishop of Hereford, Althulf, does not certainly sign until 971 (*BCS* 1270); earlier signatures may belong to Athulf of Elmham. A Wulfric, not in the list, who signs 958–70, may belong to Hereford.

Leicester
Ræthhun, Ealdred and Ceolred

Ræthhun and Ealdred are really outside the scope of this article, but since they have a bearing on Ceolred's dates, they have been included. Ræthhun signs first in 816 (*BCS* 356), his predecessor having last signed in 814 (*BCS* 343 and *BCS* 351). Ræthhun's last generally accepted appearance is in 839 (*BCS* 421), but his name is included in the earlier version of *BCS* 432, issued on Christmas Day 841, in modern reckoning 25 December 840. Ræthhun is followed in the episcopal lists that cover this period (CCCC 183, BM Cotton Tiberius B. v, FW *Lists* and *GP*) by Ealdred and then Ceolred. Ealdred makes only one charter appearance in *BCS* 434, unfortunately also dated Christmas 841, and is followed within a few years by Ceolred. Roger of Wendover says, *s.a.* 873, that Ealdred was deposed from the bishopric. The date is obviously wrong, but if a sound tradition lies behind the statement, it would explain the brevity of Ealdred's episcopate.

The appearance of both Ræthhun and Ealdred on Christmas Day 840 must discredit one of the two charters involved. At first *BCS* 432, which Ræthhun signs, looks the more reliable. Its evidence is accepted by F. M. Stenton (*A-S England*, p. 44). But there is something wrong with the dating clause. The indiction is given as III, which is correct for 840, but should have been changed to IIII on 24 September, as has been done in *BCS* 433 and *BCS* 434, both of which bear the same date as *BCS* 432. Furthermore, in *BCS* 432 the regnal year is given as III. King Beorhtwulf's dates are usually taken as 840–52. His death is given in FW *Chron s.a.* 852, in a section where the dates of other annals correspond to those of *ASC*, and elsewhere Florence says that Beorhtwulf died in the thirteenth year of his reign. William of Malmesbury (*GR* I, 96) gives the length of his reign as thirteen years, as does the list of Mercian regnal lengths in Heming (I, 242). This would place the beginning of his reign in 839–40, and the third year of his reign would be 841–2. Here also *BCS* 432's dating looks incorrect, unless one disregards the received tradition about the length of Beorhtwulf's reign.

In contrast, *BCS* 434 (and its shorter version *BCS* 435) is at first unpromising, and F. M. Stenton (*EHR*, p. 445, n. 57) has condemned it as spurious. But although the charter is elaborately worded, it does not bear any obvious marks of forgery, and the concession recorded in the grant, that of not having to entertain the king's *fæstingmen*, is found in other Mercian charters of the early ninth century, one of which survives in the original (*BCS* 370).

BCS 434's indiction is correct for Christmas 840, and the signature of Bishop Ealdred is also in its favour, since it is his only (surviving) appearance, and he would therefore be an unusual choice for a forger to include.

On balance, and taking into account that Ræthhun appears in only one version of *BCS* 432, I would prefer to accept Ealdred as the bishop who represented Leicester at Beorhtwulf's Christmas court in 840. It is therefore Ealdred's appearance there that limits the beginning of Ceolred's episcopate.

Ceolred makes one earlier appearance, in *BCS* 428, which Birch dates to 'before 840'. The charter is in any case suspect (Sawyer 205), but the date must be later than this. P. H. Sawyer (Sawyer 205) and H. P. R. Finberg (*ECWM* 250) give a date 840–8. If the arguments for Ealdred are accepted, the early limit must be December 840; the later limit can be narrowed down by the signature of Heahberht of Worcester, since his successor witnesses in November 845 (*BCS* 448; see part II, *Worcester, Alhhun*).

Otherwise Ceolred first witnesses in *BCS* 443, a charter generally accepted as genuine (Sawyer 1271). It has the date 844, with an indiction for 843, and the regnal year for 842–3, so it cannot be given a more precise date than 843–4. Ceolred's signatures continue until 869 (*BCS* 524). FW *Lists* says that Ceolred was bishop in the time of Kings Alfred and Burgred, which would extend his known episcopate to 871–4, but it might be a mistake to rely heavily on this. His successor at Dorchester – whither the see had been transferred – appears first in 888. The succession in the Viking period is discussed under that heading in part II, *Lichfield*.

To be concluded

The relationship between geographical information in the Old English Orosius and Latin texts other than Orosius

JANET M. BATELY

A great deal has been written about the geographical first chapter of the Old English Orosius[1] since it attracted the attention of scholars in the sixteenth century. Not only has this chapter been a valuable source of information for historians and historical geographers, but also it has proved a fertile subject for speculation, particularly as regards the origins and accuracy of the modifications made in it to its Latin original. Most discussions have been concerned exclusively with the apparently independent section on the geography of *Germania*. Recently, however, a theory has gained favour which requires all the 'new' geographical information in this work to be taken into consideration: the theory that, to help him in his translation and adaptation, the author[2] may have used a *mappa mundi*, a traditional map portraying the *orbis terrarum* of classical geographers.[3] Thus Professor Labuda considers the source of certain additional details, such as the association of the Sabaei with Arabia Eudaemon and the location of the legendary Land of Women and Riphaean mountains north of the ninth-century Croats of Bohemia, to be a *mappa mundi* on which the author marked the positions of Germanic, Slav and Baltic countries.[4] Dr Havlík and Professor Derolez suggest that the apparent clockwise deviation of a number of directions in Or. may similarly be due to the use of an enlarged *mappa mundi*. According to them, the author of Or. would seem to have described the relative posi-

---

[1] For the Old English version, cited henceforth as Or., cf. *King Alfred's Orosius*, ed. Henry Sweet, Early English Text Society o.s. 79 (London, 1883), my references being to page and line. For the Latin, cited henceforth as OH, cf. *Pauli Orosii Historiarum adversum Paganos Libri VII*, ed. Carolus Zangemeister, Corpus Scriptorum Ecclesiasticorum Latinorum 5.

[2] I do not propose to consider here the suggestion that Or. may be the work of more than one man: cf. Elizabeth M. Liggins, 'The Authorship of the Old English Orosius', *Anglia* 88 (1970), 289–322.

[3] For a most useful study of medieval *mappae mundi* cf. Marcel Destombes, *Mappemondes A.D. 1200–1500*, Monumenta Cartographica Vetustioris Aevi 1 (Amsterdam, 1964).

[4] Cf. G. Labuda, *Źródła, sagi i legendy do najdawniejszych dziejów Polski* (Warsaw, 1960), pp. 13–90, esp. pp. 38 ff., and *Źródła skandynawskie i anglosaskie do dziejów Słowiańszczyzny* (Warsaw, 1961), esp. pp. 12–14 and commentary, nn. 12, 27, 38, 75, 76, 172, 173, 199 and 216.

tions of peoples and countries from the standpoint not of astrological north, south, east and west, but of cartographic *oriens*[1] (near the mouth of the Ganges), *meridies* (south of the Nile), *occidens* (near the Pillars of Hercules) and *septentrio* (in the region of the river Tanais).[2] Thus, for instance, the Abodriti, whose 'centre', Mecklenburg, was true north-east of the Old Saxons, are cartographic north of them, by virtue of their location on an imaginary line between Saxonia and *septentrio*.[3] Finally, Dr Linderski, on the basis of possible classical sources that he has found for Or.'s siting of Dacia east of the Vistula and placing of an unnamed waste-land between Carentania and Bulgaria, has suggested that if the author did indeed use such a map – an alternative being a 'description' – it was almost certainly a late offspring of the *Commentarii* of Agrippa and his now lost *mappa mundi*.[4]

This theory is a most attractive one. However, its proponents have not attempted to examine more than a handful of the modifications to the Latin text, nor have they fully explored the alternative possible explanations for the phenomena that they have perceived. I propose, therefore, to reopen the question of the sources of the geographical additions and alterations in Or. as a whole,[5] and to pay special attention to the possibility of a written rather than a cartographic origin for details other than those involving contemporary information. Since the nature of this information varies according to where it occurs – in the parts of the first chapter dealing with the world except the continent of Europe, or in the parts of the first chapter dealing with the continent of Europe, or in the remainder of the translation – this survey can be conveniently divided into three sections.

THE GEOGRAPHY OF THE WORLD OTHER THAN CONTINENTAL EUROPE (OR. 8,1 – 14,25 AND 24,12 – 28,24)

Here 'new' material is of two types, the first offering modifications of information provided by OH, the second giving additional information about such matters as boundaries and the relative positions of countries and of natural phenomena, and about a handful of other topics of general interest.

[1] In *mappae mundi* the east is normally put at the top.

[2] Cf. L. Havlík, 'Slované v anglosaské chorografii Alfréda velikého', *Vznik a počátky Slovanů* 5 (1964), 53–85, and R. Derolez, 'The Orientation System in the Old English Orosius', *England Before the Conquest: Studies in Primary Sources presented to Dorothy Whitelock*, ed. Peter Clemoes and Kathleen Hughes (Cambridge, 1971), pp. 253–68.   [3] Cf. Havlík, p. 67.

[4] Cf. Jerzy Linderski, 'Alfred the Great and the Tradition of Ancient Geography', *Speculum* 39 (1964), 434–9.

[5] I exclude from this study a number of details which could be derived from OH, either direct or via a plan made by the translator himself, or which seem to be mere slips of the pen. Cf., e.g., Or. 8, 7–8: 'suþan ⁊ norþan ⁊ eastan', OH i. ii. 2: 'tribus partibus'; Or. 10, 30: 'west from Tigres þære ie', OH i. ii. 20: 'a flumine Tigri'; Or. 26, 2: 'be westan', OH i. ii. 89: 'ab oriente'; and Kemp Malone, 'King Alfred's North', *Speculum* 5 (1930), 145, 149, 163, 164, 165 and 166.

Almost all of it could have been derived from Latin texts current in the early Middle Ages.

Of the modifications, the largest group seems to involve 'correction' on the part of the translator. Thus, whereas OH puts *mare Creticum* west of Crete, Or. asserts that the Sicilian Sea is in this position.[1] Whereas OH describes the Cyclades as bounded 'ab oriente . . . litoribus Asiae, ab occidente mari Icario, a septentrione mari Aegaeo, a meridie mari Carpathio', Or. claims that 'be eastan him is se Risca sæ, 7 be suðan se Cretisca, 7 be norðan se Egisca, 7 be westan Addriaticum'.[2] Whereas OH refers to *Gades insulae*, *Fortunatae insulae* and *Orcades insulae* (the last named said to be thirty-three in number), Or. uses in each instance the singular 'þæt igland'.[3] Whereas OH puts *Syria Palaestina* east of *Aegyptus inferior* and *mare Nostrum* north, Or. shifts Palestine to the north and introduces *Sarracene þæt land* as the eastern boundary.[4] And whereas OH describes Paraetonium as the boundary of Egypt and Africa, Or. names the Nile as separating these two countries.[5] For all these alterations Or. has the support of Latin texts. Thus the much plagiarized *Etymologies* of Isidore of Seville refer to a sea called *Siculus*, 'qui a Sicilia usque ad Cretam vadit',[6] and also, in common with a number of other authorities, have a singular *Gadis insula*,[7] while singular Fortunate and Orcades islands are reported by Jordanes and the Ravenna Geographer respectively.[8] That the Nile forms the boundary of Egypt and Africa[9] is information found in writers such as Mela, Solinus and Bede,[10]

[1] OH I. ii. 97: 'ab occasu et septentrione mari Cretico, a meridie mari Libyco, quod et Hadriaticum uocant'; Or. 26, 33–4: 'westan 7 be norðan Creticum se sæ, 7 be westan Sicilium, þe man oðre naman hæt Addriaticum'. The omission of a southern boundary may be due to the fact that both western and southern seas are called Adriatic.

[2] OH I. ii. 98; Or. 26, 36 – 28, 2. *Risca* is an error for *Icarisca*.

[3] OH I. ii. 7, 11, 72 and 78; Or. 8, 25 and 24, 4; 10, 2; and 24, 16.

[4] OH I. ii. 27; Or. 12, 16–17. That Syria is north could have been deduced from OH I. ii. 23.

[5] OH I. ii. 88; Or. 24, 33. Or. elsewhere describes the boundary as west of Alexandria (cf. 8, 12) possibly following OH I. ii. 8, though a source other than OH cannot be ruled out. Cf., e.g., *Pomponii Melae de Chorographia Libri Tres*, ed. Carolus Frick (Leipzig, 1880) I. ix. 60 and *Liber Nominum Locorum ex Actis*, Migne, Patrologia Latina 23, col. 1298.

[6] *Isidori Hispalensis Episcopi Etymologiarum sive Originum Libri XX*, ed. W. M. Lindsay (Oxford, 1911) XIII. xvi. 2; *Anonymi de Situ Orbis Libri Duo*, ed. Maximilianus Manitius (Stuttgart, 1884) 13, 8–9; etc. For the alternative name Adriatic, cf. OH I. ii. 100.

[7] *Etymologies* XIV. vi. 7; cf. also Mela II. vii. 97, *De Situ Orbis* 8, 12 and the version of OH found in the *Cosmographia* II. 2, for which cf. *Geographi Latini Minores*, ed. Alexander Riese (Heilbronn, 1878). I have found no instances of the singular in the manuscripts of OH most closely related to Or.

Cf., e.g., Jordanes, *De Gothorum Origine*, PL 69, col. 1251, with its reference to two islands, 'una Beata, et alia quae dicitur Fortunata', and *Ravennatis Anonymi Cosmographia*, ed. M. Pinder and G. Parthey (Berlin, 1860) 439, 6–7: 'insulam Dorcadas'.

[9] Africa was considered in medieval as in classical times to be part of Asia. It is therefore surprising to find elsewhere in Or. reference to the Ptolemies as rulers of Africa. Cf. 58, 29–30, rendering an allusion in OH II. i. 4 to the African kingdom of the Carthaginians.

[10] Cf. Mela I. i. 8; *C. Iulii Solini Collectanea Rerum Memorabilium*, ed. Th. Mommsen (Berlin, 1895) 40. 1; Bede, *De Natura Rerum*, PL 90, col. 276; etc.

while the account of the Cyclades appears to be based on Pliny's description of 'Cyclades et Sporades ab oriente litoribus Icariis Asiae, ab occidente Myrtois Atticae, a septentrione Aegaeo mari, a meridie Cretico et Carpathio inclusae'.[1] As for the 'correction' to OH's account of Aegyptus inferior, this could have had its origin in a statement such as the 'Aegyptus inferior finitur ab oriente Scenitarum Arabia Trogodite' of Dicuil and of the *Divisio Orbis Terrarum*,[2] with *Scenitae Arabes* identified with the Saracens, as in writers such as Ammianus Marcellinus.[3]

A second group of modifications shows not correction but simplification, the name of the part being replaced by the name of the whole. With one exception it is sea-names that are involved. Thus, when OH refers to the constituent parts of *mare Rubrum* as *sinus Persicus* and *sinus Arabicus*, Or. uses the term *se Reada Sæ*.[4] Where OH refers to seas called *Tyrrhenum, Hadriaticum, Myrtoum, Creticum* and *Ionium*, to *mare Cimmericum* and to *Pontus Euxinus*, Or. generally substitutes or adds the term *Wendelsæ*, the word with which it habitually renders OH *mare magnum* or *mare nostrum*.[5] Where OH distinguishes between an *oceanus Indicus* and an *oceanus Eous*, Or. has only the 'garsecg' called *Indisc*.[6] And when OH alludes to an area composed of *Albania* and *regio Amazonum*, Or. introduces the designation *Sciþþia lond*.[7] These modifications too all have the support of Latin texts. Thus the translator could have obtained a complete list of the constituent parts of *mare magnum* from a text such as Isidore's *Etymologies*[8] and could have derived the

---

[1] *C. Plini Secundi Naturalis Historiae Libri XXXVII*, ed. Carolus Mayhoff (Leipzig, 1906 etc.) IV. xii. 71.

[2] *Dicuili Liber de Mensura Orbis Terrae*, ed. J. J. Tierney (Dublin, 1967) IV. 1; *Divisio Orbis Terrarum* (*Geographi*, ed. Riese) 20. *Divisio* is apparently Dicuil's source here.

[3] Cf. *Ammianus Marcellinus*, ed. John C. Rolfe (London, 1935–7) XXII. xv. 2: 'Scenitas . . . Arabas, quos Sarracenos nunc appellamus.'

[4] Cf. OH I. ii. 18: 'mare Rubrum et sinum Persicum', Or. 10, 27: 'se Reada Sæ'; and OH I. ii. 34, Or. 14, 2. Sweet punctuates incorrectly here.

[5] OH I. ii. 7, 58, 59, 90, 99, 102, 49 and 52; Or. 8, 25; 22, 11; 22, 14; 26, 7; 28, 9; 28, 10; 28, 11; and 28, 15. Exceptions are Or. 28, 2; 26, 34; and 26, 33 and five references to the Euxine. The strange allusion to a *Wendelsæ* called *Libia Æthiopicum* (Or. 26, 1–2) is perhaps best explained as due to scribal error, with an original *Libicum written Libia Æthiopicum under the influence of the 'correct' *Libia Æthiopicum* (OH I. ii. 88: 'gentes Libyoaethiopum') that occurs only eight words later in the text.

[6] OH I. ii. 13; Or. 10, 6–14. Cf. Or. 10, 16–17, where an unnamed ocean is made eastern boundary of India and 'seo Reade Sæ' its southern boundary; OH I. ii. 15: 'reliqua . . . Eoo et Indico oceano terminatur'. [7] OH I. ii. 50; Or. 14, 22.

[8] Cf. *Etymologies* XIII. xvi, Mela I. i. 7 etc., where *mare magnum* is said to stretch from the Straits of Gibraltar not merely to the Aegean, as in OH, but through the Black Sea to the Sea of Azov. This extent may be reflected in Or. 8, 11–12: 'Ond þonne of þære ilcan ie Danai suþ andlang Wendelsæs, 7 þonne wiþ westan Alexandria þære byrig Asia 7 Affrica togædre licgeað', which could be derived from OH, but which it is tempting to associate with references such as Mela I. ii. 9: 'Dein cum iam in suum finem aliarumque terrarum confinia devenit media nostris aequoribus excipitur, reliqua altero cornu pergit ad Nilum altero ad Tanain', or *Remigii Autissiodorensis Commentum in Martianum Capellam*, ed. Cora E. Lutz (Leiden, 1962) VI. 304. 6: 'Per maria: id est in Meroe intrat Nilus ad terraneum mare, inde per Danaum ad septentrionem.'

knowledge that *sinus Arabicus* and *sinus Persicus* were part of *mare Rubrum* from the same source.[1] As for the Indian ocean, this is identified with *Eoum mare* by Remigius in his commentaries on Martianus Capella,[2] while the Albanians and Amazons are linked as Scythians by writers such as Mela and Isidore.[3]

Finally, there is a third, small group whose function may be described as 'particularizing'. The portion of the Nile that flows from the 'great lake' through 'Aethiopica deserta' is given the name *Ion*; Scythia east of the Caspian sea is described as '*þa ealdan Sciþþian*', presumably to distinguish it from a second Scythia, west of the Caspian; the Albania of OH is identified with a people or place called *Liubene*.[4] Here only limited support is provided by Latin texts. *Ion* is a variant of *Geon*, the name of one of the four rivers of Paradise, which is frequently identified with the Nile in Christian Latin writings and is, moreover, described by Isidore as 'universam Aethiopiam cingens'.[5] The designation '*þa ealdan Sciþþian*' may be connected with the 'eremosa et antiqua Scythia' of the Ravenna Geographer or with Isidore's description of the Scythians east of the Caspian sea as 'gens antiquissima'.[6] For the name *Liubene*, however, I know of no Latin parallel, unless it is based on a corrupt manuscript reading such as the *Libani*, for *Albani*, of the corresponding passage of the *Cosmographia*.[7]

The completely new material in this section of Or. can be similarly sub-divided. A number of additions are apparently aimed at clarifying the

---

[1] Cf. *Etymologies* XIII. xvii. 4 and Bede, *De Natura Rerum*, col. 262.

[2] Cf. Remigius VI. 303, 1: 'ab Eoo mari: id est Indico'.

[3] Cf. Mela III. v. 36 and 39, *Etymologies* XIV. iii. 31 and 34 etc. According to these and other authorities, Scythia extended to Sarmatia and the Tanais. Mela could also have influenced the translator in his description of the chain of mountains running east–west across Asia to end in Cilicia (Or. 14, 6–12): cf. 'Taurus ipse ab Eois litoribus exsurgens vaste satis attollitur, dein dextro latere ad septentrionem, sinistro ad meridiem versus it in occidentem rectus et perpetuo iugo' (I. xv. 81); see also *De Situ Orbis* 72, 3–4: 'Cilicia, qua incipit mons Taurus'. However, in this instance dependence solely on OH I. ii. 36–46 cannot be ruled out.

[4] Or. 12, 25–7, OH I. ii. 30: 'Fluuium Nilum . . . aliqui auctores ferunt . . . orientem uersus per Aethiopica deserta prolabi'; Or. 14, 17, OH I. ii. 47: 'Scytharum gentes'; and Or. 14, 23–5: '*þa lond . . . Albani hi sint genemde in Latina, 7 we hie hataþ nu Liubene*', OH I. ii. 50: 'regio . . . Albania'.   [5] *Etymologies* XIII. xxi. 7.

[6] Cf. *Ravennatis Anonymi Cosmographia* 30, 9 (also 29, 10 and 422, 1, where, however, the reference is to *Scanza*) and *Etymologies* IX. ii. 62. It is not impossible, however, that Or.'s usage here has been influenced by OH I. xv, where it is stated that the Amazons' husbands had been driven from their homeland. Cf. OE *Ealdseaxan*, 'old (i.e. continental) Saxons'.

[7] *Cosmographia* II. 19 (temporarily deserting its source, OH): 'sed generaliter in regione proxima Libani (MS L; MS V, *Albani*) morantur'. The *u* could have originated as an alternative to *b*: cf. *Fauius* for *Fabius* etc. However, the possibility that the name was a genuine one, known to the Anglo-Saxons or other Germanic peoples, cannot be ruled out, particularly if wrong identification is allowed. Cf. Adam of Bremen's placing of the *Albani* (equated with the *Wizzi*) in the Baltic area (*Gesta Pontificum Hammaburgensis Ecclesiae*, PL 146, col. 635). Suitable candidates might be the people of Livland, the Livonians, who, according to Saxo Grammaticus, were present at the battle of Bravalla in the eighth century (cf. *Saxonis Gesta Danorum*, ed. J. Olrik and H. Ræder (Hauniae, 1931) VIII. iv. 1).

geographical situation as expressed in OH and again have the support of Latin texts. Thus the Tanais is said to flow 'suðryhte' and to pass Alexander's altars 'on westhealfe',[1] information which the translator could have derived from authorities such as Mela in the first instance[2] and Solinus and Capella in the second.[3] The flood of water from the Palus Maeotidis is described as flowing 'wið eastan' when it enters the Euxine, possibly as an echo of the observation in Priscian's *Periegesis*,

> Panditur hinc Ponti pelagus Titanis ad ortus;
> Quod petit obliquo boream solemque meatu.[4]

Cappadocia, put by OH 'in capite Syriae', is said to be north of that country, an interpretation found also in the *Liber Nominum*.[5] The placing of Arabia Eudaemon 'ondlong þæs Readan Sæs, þæs dæles þe þær norþ scyt' recalls Bede's statement that *sinus Persicus* 'Aquilonem . . . petit',[6] while the inclusion of *Coelle*, *Damascena* and *Iudea* (Coele Syria, Damascene and Iudaea) in Syria and the addition of *Sabei* to the wrongly split Arabia Eudaemon have the support of a number of writers including Mela.[7] Even the unexpected addition of the names *Moab*, *Amon* and *Idumei* to the list of Syrian provinces could be the result of their association with the Saracens in a Latin text such as the *Liber Nominum*.[8]

A second group of additions takes the form of entirely new information

[1] Or. 8, 17; OH I. ii. 4–5: 'Europa incipit . . . sub plaga septentrionis, a flumine Tanai, qua Riphaei montes Sarmatico auersi oceano Tanaim fluuium fundunt, qui praeteriens aras ac terminos Alexandri Magni in Rhobascorum finibus sitos Maeotidas auget paludes.'

[2] Cf. Mela I. i. 8; *De Situ Orbis* 41, 8–9; etc.

[3] Cf. Solinus 49.5 and 52.7; *De Situ Orbis* 78, 13–14 and 80, 3–4; and *Martianus Capella*, ed. Adolfus Dick (Leipzig, 1925) VI. 692 and 694.

[4] Or. 8, 20; OH I. ii. 5: 'late'. Cf. *La Periégèse de Priscien*, ed. P. van de Woestijne (Brugge, 1953), lines 138–9. The mouth of the Palus was considered by Pliny (IV. xii. 76) to be in the centre of the northern curve of the Pontus Euxinus. For another possibility – that Or. may merely be putting the mouth of the Palus to the east of Theodosia – cf. Kemp Malone, 'King Alfred's North', p. 140. Knowledge that Theodosia was in Europe and thus had the sea to its east could have been derived from a number of Latin texts, including Pliny IV. xii. 87 and Mela II. i. 3.

[5] Or. 12, 5–7, OH I. ii. 25; cf. *Liber Nominum*, col. 1299: 'Cappadocia regio in capite Syriae, id est, ad septentrionem'.

[6] Or. 10, 34–6, OH I. ii. 21; cf. Bede, *De Natura Rerum*, col. 262. For *aquilo*, 'north', see below, p. 52; for the identification of *sinus Arabicus* and *sinus Persicus* with *mare Rubrum*, see above, p. 49. According to both Bede and OH I. ii. 24, the *sinus Arabicus* extends westward, i.e. in the general direction of the *mare Rubrum* up to that point; cf. Dicuil VI. 18, where it is *sinus Arabicus* that extends 'longe in septentrionalem partem'.

[7] Or. 12, 3–4 and 10, 35–6; OH I. ii. 24 and 21. Cf. Mela I. xi. 62, Capella VI. 678 etc. and below, p. 59, n. 5; also *Servii Grammatici qui Feruntur in Vergilii Carmina Commentarii*, ed. Georgius Thilo and Hermannus Hagen (Leipzig, 1881), *Aeneid* I. 416: 'Sabaeo: Arabico. Arabiae autem tres sunt: inferior, petrodes, eudemon, in qua populi sunt Sabaei', Mela III. viii. 79; Isidore, *Etymologies* IX. ii. 14 etc.

[8] Or. 12, 4; OH I. ii. 24: 'prouincias Commagenam Phoeniciam et Palaestinam, absque Saracenis et Nabatheis, quorum gentes sunt xii'. Cf. *Liber Nominum*, col. 1297 (of Arabia): 'habet gentes multas, Moabitas, Ammonitas, Idumaeos, Saracenos, aliosque quamplurimos'.

about the position of the country or countries or of the natural phenomenon under discussion. Thus, in the course of its rewriting of OH I. ii. 20–2, Or. names the *Reada Sæ* as southern boundary of the complex Babylonia, Chaldaea and Mesopotamia, a departure from the text of OH in which it has the support of Dicuil.[1] In reorganizing the account of the western boundary of Europe, it introduces 'Scotland' (i.e. Ireland) as the country 'hire on westende', not only recognizing its true position, but also reflecting the views of writers such as the Ravenna Geographer.[2] In its account of *Thila* it adds the comment that this is 'þæt ytemeste land', obviously influenced by the commonplace description of that island as *Ultima Thyle* in Latin texts.[3] Similarly with the backing of Latin texts are the siting of Armenia north of the Taurus range[4] and the substitution of the Tiber for OH's 'portum urbis Romae',[5] while, although the placing of *Tuscania* north of Corsica could be explained in terms of contemporary misinformation, even here a written source cannot be ruled out.[6]

All these additions and modifications serve to define or clarify geographical positions. Occasionally, however, we find in this section comments of a more general nature. Thus Mount Olympus in Asia Minor is described as 'se hehsta beorg', presumably as a result of confusion between this and the Greek mountain of the same name, which is frequently described in Latin writings as of exceptional height.[7] The *fretum Hadriaticum* of OH appears as a sea that 'ægþer is ge nearo ge hreoh', an echo of definitions of *fretum* such as Isidore, *Etymologies* XIII. xviii. 2: 'Fretum autem appellatum quod ibi semper mare ferveat; nam fretum est angustum et quasi fervens mare, ubi undarum fervore nominatum, ut Gaditanum vel Siculum.'[8] Also falling into this category are the observation that Ireland's climate is superior to Britain's

---

[1] Or. 10, 33–4; cf. Dicuil II. 6: 'Mesopotamia, Babillonia, Chaldea finiuntur . . . a meridie mari Persico'. *Divisio* 22 and *Dimensuratio* (*Geographi*, ed. Riese) 3 name only Mesopotamia in this context. For the equation *sinus Persicus: mare Rubrum* see above, p. 49.

[2] Or. 8, 27, *Ravennatis Anonymi Cosmographia* 9, 13–17. Cf. also Or. 24, 15, where Or. corrects OH I. ii. 80 by putting Ireland west of Britain, not between Britain and Spain.

[3] Or. 24, 20; OH I. ii. 79: 'insula Thyle'. Cf. Isidore, *Etymologies* XIV. vi. 4 etc.

[4] Or. 12, 6–7. Cf. Dicuil I. 19, *Dimensuratio* 6, *Divisio* 18 and *Agrippae Fragmenta* (*Geographi*, ed. Riese) 30.

[5] Or. 28, 16; OH I. ii. 102. Cf. Isidore, *Etymologies* XV. i. 56 and *Cosmographia* II. 25.

[6] Or. 28, 20; OH I. ii. 103: 'a circio et septentrione Ligusticum sinum'. Cf. Mela II. vii. 122 and p. xi, n. 20, where a scribe(?) makes Corsica 'Etrusco litori propior', and, for the (incorrect) identification of Liguria with Etruria, see below, p. 57 and n. 2. *Tuscania* is the medieval name for Etruria; cf. *Glossarium Ansileubi*, in *Glossaria Latina*, ed. W. M. Lindsay *et al.* (Paris, 1926–31) I, TU 171.

[7] Or. 12, 15; OH I. ii. 26. Cf. Isidore, *Etymologies* XIV. iv. 13 and viii. 9: 'Olympus . . . nimium praecelsus'; Remigius II. 52.3: 'Olympus autem mons est ultra omnes nubes et pene ad ipsum confinium aetheris pertingens'; etc. For the location of the world's highest mountain in Asia, cf. *Wonders of the East*, in *Three Old English Prose Texts*, ed. Stanley Rypins, Early English Text Society o.s. 161 (London, 1921), pp. 64 and 105.

[8] Or. 28, 11–12; OH I. ii. 100. Cf. also Mela II. vii. 115; *Glossarium Ansileubi*, FR 140; etc.

'for ðon þe sio sunne þær gæð near on setl þonne on oðrum lande' – quite possibly the result of the misapplication of a comment on Ireland that 'propinquus sol collocatur'[1] – and the surprising claim that the floods of the Nile occur in winter and are caused by north winds.[2] This last must surely owe its origin to a statement such as Isidore, *Etymologies* XIII. xxi. 7, 'Nilus ... Aquilonis flatibus repercussus aquis retroluctantibus intumescit, et inundationem Aegypti facit', interpreted in the context of an association *aquilo*/'winter', as in Servius's gloss on *Aeneid* IV. 310: 'Mediis Aquilonibus media hieme, ut per Aquilones "hiemem" significet.'[3] The equation *aquilo*/ 'north wind' is a common one in Latin texts;[4] however, since Or. habitually translates the *aquilo*, 'north-east', of his original as 'north',[5] there is no need to look for a specific source for this detail here.

THE GEOGRAPHY OF CONTINENTAL EUROPE (OR. 14,26 – 24,11)

Here changes are so radical that it is possible to consider the whole section as rewritten to conform, with certain exceptions, to the ninth-century situation as known to the author of Or. or his immediate source.[6] 'Contemporary' information could have reached the author in a variety of ways, one of which must have been via Latin or vernacular texts. That the reports of Ohthere and Wulfstan are based on notes made at the time seems obvious enough.[7] Likewise it is theoretically possible that the author owed to a written source the details of the relative positions of the various coun-tries and provinces of Europe which he gives in addition to, or in place of, information provided by OH.[8] Unfortunately evidence for or against such a 'contemporary' written source is virtually non-existent. However, even in

[1] Or. 24, 17–19; OH I. ii. 81: 'Hibernia . . . caeli solique temperie magis utilis'. Cf. *Ravennatis Anonymi Cosmographia* 12, 6–11: 'ad quos dicimus quomodo verbi gratia stat homo in Scotia, ubi iam terra ultra nullo modo invenitur apud humanos oculos, ei comparet quod certissime duo-decim horas diei expleat et propinquus sol collocetur'.

[2] Or. 12, 33–6: 'Þonne on þæm wintregum tidum wyrþ se muþa fordrifen foran from þæm nor-þernum windum þæt seo ea bið flowende ofer eal Ægypta land'; OH I. ii. 28: 'tempestiuis auctus incrementis plana Aegypti rigat'. Or.'s explanation is completely contrary to that of extant Latin texts, where the flooding is said to take place in summer. Cf. Isidore, *De Natura Rerum*, PL 83, col. 1013; Pliny V. x. 55; Bede, *De Natura Rerum*, col. 262; etc.

[3] Cf. also *Glossarium Ansileubi*, ME 102 and GE 233 and Remigius VI. 345.4.

[4] Cf., e.g., Servius, *Aeneid* I. 114 and Remigius VIII. 440. 11.

[5] Or.'s 'north-east' translates OH *boreas*.

[6] This rewriting need not be the work of the translator. For instance, although Or. 22, 10–11, 'be westan suðan Corinton is Achie', seems to be based on OH I. ii. 58, 'Achaia . . . habet . . . ab aquilone angustum terrae dorsum . . . ubi est Corinthus', the apparently correct interpretation of *aquilo* as 'north-east', not, as elsewhere in Or., 'north', suggests an intermediary of some kind. For ninth-century features not mentioned here but appearing elsewhere in Or., see below, p. 57 f.

[7] Cf. my 'King Alfred and the Old English Translation of Orosius', *Anglia* 88 (1970), 439.

[8] There is in existence, for instance, an account of central Europe by the so-called Bavarian Geographer; cf. *Descriptio Civitatum ad Septentrionalem Plagam Danubii*, ed. B. Horák and D. Tráv-niček, *Rozpravy Československé Akademie Věd* 66 (1956).

this section there are certain details for which a 'traditional' source may have been ultimately responsible. Thus, when Or. expands OH's allusion to the Rhine and the Danube as boundaries of Germania by describing the river Rhine as flowing from its source in the Alps 'norþryhte on þæs garsecges earm þe þæt lond uton ymblið þe mon Bryttania hætt' and by describing the Danube as having its source near the banks of the Rhine,[1] in the first instance it could possibly be following a text such as Isidore, *Etymologies* XIII. xxi. 30, 'Rhenus ... a iugo Alpium usque in Oceani profunda cursus suos dirigit',[2] or be sharing a common source with the highly derivative twelfth-century *De Imagine Mundi*, which claims in terms very close to those of Or. that 'Rhenus ab Alpibus nascitur, et contra aquilonem vergens, sinu Oceani excipitur',[3] and in the second instance it could be reflecting either contemporary knowledge of an important water-way or acquaintance with a statement such as *Periegesis* 288: 'Hunc (i.e. the Rhine) prope consurgit fons Histri flumine longo.' Again, the 'strikingly inaccurate localization Moravia-Wisle-Dacia' may be based on a combination of the knowledge that the Vistula was 'east' of Moravian territory with knowledge of the ancient tradition that the Vistula constituted the western boundary of Dacia.[4] This tradition Linderski cites from three Latin works, all based on Agrippa's *Commentarii*, namely the *Natural History* of Pliny, the *Dimensuratio Provinciarum* and the *Divisio Orbis Terrarum*, to which may be added a fourth, Dicuil's *Cosmographia*.[5]

A second detail which may go back to Pliny and the *Dimensuratio* is the locating of a 'westen' between Carentania and Bulgaria. Both these accounts put the *deserta Boiorum* east of Noricum – 'and this is exactly the same area where [Or.'s] wilderness lay – east of Carinthia'.[6] However, Linderski's argument in this instance seems to me less convincing than the arguments of earlier writers, that the 'westen' was the land devastated by the incursions of the Avars and especially as a result of the destruction of the Avar state by Charlemagne.[7] One way in which the knowledge of this 'westen' could have

[1] Or. 14, 28–32; OH I. ii. 52.
[2] Cf. also Mela III. ii. 24, Dicuil VI. 48 etc.
[3] Cf. *De Imagine Mundi*, PL 172, col. 129. For *aquilo*, 'north', see above, p. 52.
[4] Or. 16, 16–17; cf. Linderski, 'Alfred the Great and the Tradition of Ancient Geography', pp. 434–9.
[5] Cf. Pliny IV. xii. 81 (though Dacia is not mentioned by name), *Dimensuratio* 8, *Divisio* 14 and Dicuil I. 16. According to *Divisio*, Dacia 'finitur ab oriente deserto Sarmatiae, ab occidente flumine Vistla'.
[6] Linderski, pp. 438–9. Cf. Or. 16, 14–15 and 22, 16; Pliny III. xxiv. 146: 'Noricis iunguntur lacus Pelso, deserta Boiorum'; and *Dimensuratio* 18: 'Illyricum et Pannonia ... ab occidente desertis, in quibus habitabant Boi et Carni'.
[7] Cf. J. T. Dekan, 'Príspevok k otázke politických hraníc Vel'kej Moravy', *Historica Slovaca* 5 (1948), 209. I have not seen the article by P. Ratkoš in *Historický Časopis* 3 (1955), which, according to Linderski (p. 437), agrees with Dekan in identifying the *westen* with 'a waste-land on the border between Moravia and Bulgaria, somewhere in the region of the river Theiss'.

reached the author of Or. is via a written source such as Einhard's *Life of Charlemagne* or the Annals of Fulda or the Chronicle of Regino of Prum.[1]

Finally, a written source cannot be ruled out for the location of *Mægþa land* in the extreme north-east of Europe.[2] If *mægþa* is to be identified with the genitive plural of OE *mægþ*, 'maiden, virgin, girl, woman, wife', then it is possible that Or.'s source here is a reference such as Paulus Diaconus, *De Gestis Langobardorum* I. xv: '... ego referri a quibusdam audivi, usque hodie in intimis Germaniae finibus gentem harum existere feminarum.'[3]

OTHER GEOGRAPHICAL MATERIAL (OR. 28,25–298,9)

In the main body of Or., where the translator, like his source, passes from world geography to world history, geographical additions are not surprisingly fewer in number and consist mainly of either the labelling of proper names as towns, lands and so on, or the assignation of them to specific countries, though occasionally substitution of one proper name for another is found and sometimes details of more general interest are added. Once again these contributions almost invariably have the support of Latin texts.

'Labels' that fall into this category are the descriptions 'town' attached to Ariminum, Lugdunum, Nicomedia and Tarsus, 'land' attached to Pontus, 'river' attached to Ticinum, and *dun* 'high ground, mountain', attached to Marathon and Dyrrachium.[4] In the cases of the labels 'town' and 'land', conjecture on the part of the translator is a possibility that cannot be ignored.[5] Indeed guess-work seems to have been responsible for a number of incorrect labels[6] – for instance, 'land' applied to the towns of Placentia and Cremona, Argos, Arpi, and Massilia, and, most surprisingly, on one occasion to

[1] Cf. *Einhard's Life of Charlemagne*, ed. H. W. Garrod and R. B. Mowat (Oxford, 1915) 13. 2: 'Quot proelia in eo gesta, quantum sanguinis effusum sit, testatur vacua omni habitatore Pannonia et locus in quo regia Kagani erat ita desertus ut ne vestigium quidem in eo humanae habitationis appareat'; *Annalium Fuldensium Pars Tertia*, Monumenta Germaniae Historica, Script. 1, *s.a.* 884: 'Pannonia de Hraba flumine ad orientem tota deleta est'; and *Reginonis Chronicon, ibid. s.a.* 889: 'Pannoniorum et Avarum solitudines'.

[2] Or. 16, 20–2. For reasons of space, I do not question here the identification *Mægþa land*, 'Land of Women'.   [3] *De Gestis Langobardorum*, PL 95, col. 454.

[4] Or. 184, 23; 284, 25; 280, 23; 284, 11; 124, 28; 128, 2; 282, 28; 278, 3; 186, 22–3; 78, 25; 80, 18–19; 240, 14–15; and 240, 22–3; OH IV. xiii. 12, VII. xxix. 13, VII. xxv. 14, VII. xxviii. 31, III. xvi. 5, III. xvii. 1, VII. xxviii. 17, VII. xxiv. 1, IV. xiv. 6, II. viii. 8, II. ix. 4 and VI. xv. 4 and 18. For variant readings from the manuscripts of OH apparently most closely related to Or., cf. Janet M. Bately, 'King Alfred and the Latin Manuscripts of Orosius's History', *Classica et Mediaevalia* 22 (1961), 69–105.

[5] All five instances, however, have the backing of Latin texts. Cf., e.g., Isidore, *Etymologies* XIV. iii. 39 and 45; *Iulii Honorii Cosmographia* (*Geographi*, ed. Riese) 19; and *Dimensuratio* 9 and 11.

[6] The most striking of these is the labelling as *folc* of a people whose very existence appears to be due to textual corruption or misunderstanding. Thus, Or. 274, 18, 'mid Emilitum þæm folce', OH VII. xxii. 1, 'ab exercitu', could well have arisen from a gloss or comment *a militibus*. Cf. Bately, 'Classical Additions', p. 250.

Tarsus,[1] and 'island' applied to *Libeum* and Clipea and to the home of Gesonae and Sibi and that of Madri and Subagrae.[2] However, guess-work can be ruled out in the cases of the labels 'river' and *dun*. With regard to the first it is tempting to suppose that Or.'s identification of the Ticinus as a river shows acquaintance with an account of Scipio's battle against Hannibal in 218 B.C. such as is provided by Valerius Maximus, especially as there are other details added in Or. that could have been taken from this source.[3] As for *dun* applied to Marathon and Dyrrachium, this is supported by the use of *mons* in connection with these names in several Latin texts,[4] while in the contexts of the battle of the Arusian Plains and the eruption in the Calenian Field the term would seem to be derived from a misunderstanding of Frontinus in the first instance[5] and the reading *agger* for *ager* in the second.[6] The only labels for which I am unable to account with any degree of certainty are a further instance of *dun*, applied to the 'turre ferrata' at Sirmium,[7] and a single instance of *wudu*, applied to the province of Picenum – unless this last reflects knowledge of the fact that Picenum in classical times was famed for its apples and olives.[8]

In assigning place-names to their countries of origin, Or. is again generally correct and generally gives information of a kind that could easily be gleaned from Latin texts. To this category belong the accurate designation as

[1] Or. 204, 13; 40, 17; 188, 24; 240, 18 (*Marisiam*; Cotton MS, *Samariam*); and 278, 5; OH IV. xx. 4, I. xi. 1, IV. xv. 1 and VI. xv. 6. Cf. Or. 158, 32: 'Argus þa burg', OH IV. ii. 7: 'Argos . . . urbem'.

[2] Or. 176, 34; 178, 27; 178, 33; 4, 11; 176, 10; 134, 2–3; and 134, 5; OH IV. ix. 14, IV. x. 2 and 3 (*Lilybaeum*; 'related' MSS, *Libeum*), IV. ix. 5 and III. xix. 6. In each case the context is a sea-journey.

[3] Cf. *Valerii Maximi Factorum et Dictorum Memorabilium Libri IX*, ed. Carolus Kempf (Leipzig, 1888) V. iv. 2 and Bately, 'Classical Additions', p. 248, n. 3. Livy and Silius Italicus also specify the river Ticinus as site of the battle; cf. *Titi Livi ab Urbe Condita Libri*, ed. Guilelmus Weissenborn and Mauritius Müller (Leipzig, 1902 etc.) XXI. xxxix. 10 and *Sili Italici Punica*, ed. Ludovicus Bauer (Leipzig, 1890–2) IV. 81.

[4] Cf. *Lactantii Placidi Commentarii in Statii Thebaida* V. 431, in *P. Papinius Statius* III, ed. Ricardus Jahnke (Leipzig, 1898): 'Marathon mons'; *Cornelii Nepotis Vitae*, ed. Carolus Halm (Leipzig, 1881), *Miltiades* I. 5. 3: 'sub montis radicibus acie regione instructa' (see further Bately, 'Classical Additions', p. 247, n. 5); and Vibius Sequester, *Geographi*, ed. Riese, p. 156: 'Petrae Dyrrachii castra Pompei Magni', under the heading *Montes*, Or.'s allusion likewise being to Pompey's camp.

[5] Or. 158, 23, OH IV. ii. 3; cf. *Iuli Frontini Strategematon Libri IV*, ed. Gottholdus Gundermann (Leipzig, 1888) IV. i. 14, referring to this episode: 'Pyrrhus . . . primus totum exercitum sub eodem uallo continere instituit.' Is Or. 230, 14–15, 'hiora gemitting wæs on sondihtre dune', due to a similar misunderstanding or misreading of OH V. xv. 14, 'e uallo'?

[6] Or. 160, 23: 'anre dune neah Romebyrig'; OH IV. iv. 4: 'agrum Calenum'. Cf., e.g., *Glossarium Ansileubi*, AG 34: 'Agger: monticulis uel aceruus'.

[7] Or. 278, 11–12; OH VII. xxiv. 3. Could the dual meaning of OE *torr*, 'mountain, tower', possibly be responsible for this?

[8] Or. 184, 21; OH IV. xiii. 12. Cf. *Q. Horati Flacci Opera*, ed. Fridericus Klingner (Leipzig, 1959), Sermonum Liber II, 3. 272 and 4. 70; *D. Iunii Iuvenalis Satirarum Libri V*, ed. Carolus Fridericus Hermannus (Leipzig, 1888) XI. 74; Pliny XV. iii. 4; and *M. Valerii Martialis Epigrammaton Libri*, ed. Walther Gilbert (Leipzig, 1896) V. lxxviii. 20.

'Greek' of the Peloponnenses, Lacedaemonians and Messenians, Cherronesi, Ionians, Boeotium, Thebes, Illyricum, and Thessalia[1] – though the last named is wrongly labelled 'town' – and the correct siting of Phrygia in Asia, Ephesus in Asia Minor, Olynthus in Macedonia, Tarsus in Cilicia and the Picentes in Italy.[2] Incorrect assignments, on the other hand, appear, with one exception, to be the result of guess-work. These include the identification of the Triballe with the Scythians mentioned shortly before in OH, of the Greek city of Atalante with the African Atlas of the geographical chapter, and of Mothona in Macedonia with the kingdom of the Thebans in whose context it is referred to, and, somewhat surprisingly, the description of Troy as *Creca burg*.[3] The one exception is the placing of the Molvian Bridge 'binnan Rome', and this could well have had its origin in a misunderstood or misquoted gloss such as the 'Ponte Moluio: propter pontis iuxta Rome' of the Leiden Glossary.[4]

As for the third group of geographical modifications in this section of Or., involving substitution, these can be subdivided according to whether the name substituted is classical or medieval in form. Of the classical substitutions a few are due merely to errors in transmission or of understanding of the Latin text. Thus, for instance, for OH II. v. 9 *Veientes*, Or. has *Sabini* and for OH III. iii. 5 *Praenestinos* it has *Suttrian*, in both cases substituting a proper name that had occurred immediately before in its exemplar.[5] For OH IV. xiii. 12 *Tuscos* it has *Tracio*, for OH IV. xxi. 1 *Macedoniam* it has *Asia*[6] and for OH IV. xvi. 20 *Sardinia* it reads *Capadotia*.[7] However, others have the backing of a wide range of Latin texts. These are the use of *Perse* for *Parthos*, *Læcedemonia* for *Spartanorum*, *Italia* for *Latinos* and *Asirie* for *Syria* and the

---

[1] Or. 56, 7; 56, 14; 80, 1; 80, 13; 94, 21–2; 116, 17–18; 78, 20; 82, 9; 84, 18; 100, 13–14; 96, 4; 276, 14; and 36, 8. Cf. Isidore, *Etymologies* XIV. iv. 7, 10, 11 and 15 and IX. ii. 28; Mela II. iii; *De Situ Orbis* 51, 15, 19, 20 and 21; 52, 20; 55, 17; etc. For *Lacedemonia* as a town-name, see below, p. 57, n. 1. Some of these identifications may be contextual.

[2] Or. 124, 22; 46, 19; 114, 10–11; 124, 28; and 160, 27; OH III. xvi. 5, I. xv. 5, III. xii. 20, III. xvi. 5 and IV. iv. 5. Cf. Isidore, *Etymologies* XIV. iii. 38 and 45; Mela II. iv. 65; and *Liber Nominum*, cols. 1297, 1300 and 1305.

[3] Or. 1–2; 90, 19; 112, 14 (MS L, *Thona*; MS C, *Othono*); and 64, 20–1; OH III. xiii. 8, II. xviii. 7 (*Atalante*; 'related' MSS, *Athlante*), III. xii. 9 (*Mothonam*; 'related' MSS, *Othonam*) and II. iv. 1. There was a second city called Mothona on the Peloponnesian Gulf (cf. OH VI. xix. 6); however, the contextual explanation is probably the most satisfactory one, particularly in view of the textual history of Or.'s form.

[4] Or. 282, 25–6; OH VII. xxviii. 16. Cf. *A Late Eighth-Century Latin–Anglo-Saxon Glossary preserved in the Library of the Leiden University*, ed. J. H. Hessels (Cambridge, 1906) XXXV. 242.

[5] Or. 72, 16–17; and 100, 30; cf. also Or. 142, 3: *Bryti*, OH III. xxii. 13: *Etruscis* and Or. 234, 18: *Marse*, OH V. xviii. 11: *Samnitium*, both apparently contextual errors, and slips such as Or. 110, 22, *Læcedemonia*, for expected *Macedonia*.

[6] Or. 184, 22 and 208, 28. Could the latter reflect knowledge that one of the Scipios campaigned in Asia?

[7] Or. 192, 30. OH says that the battle was in Sardinia, 'contra Sardos'. Is it possible that *Sardos* was incorrectly identified with *Sardis*, a town in Asia, though unfortunately not in Cappadocia?

interchange of *Tusci* and *Etrusci*.[1] Misunderstanding of a Latin text may be responsible for the identification of the Ligures with the Etruscans.[2]

Of the medieval substitutions, the majority are straightforward replacements of the type *Swæfas* for *Alamanni*, *Eforwicceastre* for *Eboracum* and *Mægelan* for *Mediolanum*,[3] of which the most that one can say is that they could, but need not, have had a written source. A few are of special interest in that they provide details about Europe that might have been expected in the geographical section and yet are not to be found there. Thus, firstly, although the geographical section gives no information about Italy other than that provided by OH – if we except the allusion to *Tuscania* as being north of Corsica[4] – elsewhere the translator shows knowledge of the existence of a region called Beneventum in southern Italy, and of a Langobard kingdom in the north.[5] He is also acquainted with the name of an Italian mountain, *Mons Bardo*, which he identifies with the Appennines.[6] Secondly, although the geographical section describes the Spanish peninsula as it was in Orosius's time, elsewhere the (incorrect) description of Carthago Nova as the town 'þe mon nu Cordofa hætt' suggests some awareness of the fact that by the ninth century the capital of the southern part of that area was the city of Cordova.[7] All these identifications could have had a written source, though I have found support for only three of the four in Latin texts.[8]

[1] Or. 106, 22; 286, 9; 80, 13; 60, 18; 128, 26; and 68, 13; OH III. viii. 5, VII. xxx. 4, II. ix. 3, II. ii. 3, III. xvii. 9 and II. v. 3. Cf. *Glossaria Latina*, *Abba*, LA 2, PA 66, ET 5; Freculph, *Chronicon*, PL 106, col. 979: 'Spartham, quam et Lacedaemoniam civitatem'; Acron, in *Acronis et Porphyrionis Commentarii in Q. Horatium Flaccum*, ed. Ferdinandus Hauthal (Berlin, 1864–6), *Carmina*, liber I, 194; Servius, *Aeneid* x. 164; etc. *Tusci* is a possible Latin manuscript variant.

[2] Or. 206, 9: 'Etusci'; OH IV. xx. 24: 'Liguribus'. Is this derived (as a result of misunderstanding or miscopying) from a comment such as Capella VI. 637: 'cuius principium Ligures tenent, dehincque ubertatem soli sacrata occupauit Etruria regio' or Servius, *Aeneid* x. 709: 'Liguria cohaeret Tusciae'? For Or.'s use of *Tuscania* where OH refers to the Ligurian gulf, see above, p. 51 and n. 6.

[3] Or. 276, 3; 270, 14; 294, 30; and 184, 31 (for which cf. Janet M. Bately, 'The Old English Orosius: the Question of Dictation', *Anglia* 84 (1966), 267–70); OH VII. xxii. 7, VII. xvii. 8, VII. xxxv. 23 and IV. xiii. 15. Cf. also Or. 278, 8: 'Hunas', OH VII. xxiv. 2: 'barbaris' etc.

[4] See above, p. 51.

[5] Or. 104, 15 and 192, 5, both referring to Hannibal's main centre of activities in Italy; OH III. vii. 3: 'in Italiam', and IV. xvi. 10: 'Campania'; and Or. 180, 24–5: 'Gallie . . . þe mon nu hæt Longbeardas' and similarly 192, 8–9; OH IV. xii. 1: 'Galli Cisalpini' and IV. xvi. 11: 'Gallos'.

[6] Or. 186, 33: 'Bardan þone beorg'; OH IV. xiv. 8: 'in summo Appennino'.

[7] Or. 196, 23–4; OH IV. xviii. 1.

[8] Cf. *Ravennatis Anonymi Cosmographia* 248, 11–13: 'ab antiquis dicitur Campania, quae nunc Beneventanorum dicitur patria'; *Marci Annaei Lucani Pharsalia*, ed. H. Grotius and C. F. Weber III, Scholiastas (Leipzig, 1831) I. 442: '[Gallia] Togata, quae dicitur Longobardia'; and *ibid*. I. 183: 'gelidas Alpes: vocat montem nivis, respectu montis Pardonis'. Cf. also *Die althochdeutschen Glossen*, ed. Elias Steinmeyer and Eduard Sievers (Berlin, 1879–98) IV. 352: 'Appenninicolę: bardtenberc'. At a later date, Matthew Paris includes *Munt Bardun* in his itinerary to Apulia (cf. Konrad Miller, *Mappaemundi, die ältesten Weltkarten* (Stuttgart, 1895–8) III, 88), while Otto of Freising refers to 'Apenninum, qui modo mutato nomine mons Bardonis uulgo dicitur' (*Gesta Friderici*, ed. G. Waitz (Hanover, 1884) II. xiii etc.).

Thirdly, while the equation of the Illyrii with the *Pulgare* merely adds to and supports the geographical section's account of eastern Europe,[1] another identification in this area has far-reaching implications, both as regards the geographical knowledge of the author of Or. and as regards the date of that work. This is the surprising identification of the Basternae with no less a people than the Hungarians.[2] Now the reason for this identification is fairly easy to guess. The Basternae are said by OH to be 'gens ferocissima' and are mentioned as attempting to cross the Danube, while the Hungarians too are described as 'gens ferocissima' in at least one Latin annal and are likewise associated with the Danube area in the ninth century. However, there is no reference at all to the Hungarians in the geographical section of Or. – the inference generally drawn from this being that Or.'s source at this point either did not know of their existence or dated from the period before the Hungarian migrations – while, even more significantly, the Hungarians do not seem to have arrived at the mouth of the Danube before the year 889.[3]

Lastly, there are a few pieces of additional information of what may be called general interest. All of these have the support of extant Latin texts. Thus Hannibal is said to have crossed the Alps via Mount Jove, a route already known to Mela.[4] The *Gandes* (Gyndes)[5] is said to be nine miles broad in flood – possibly a misapplication of a comment on the Ganges such as is found in Capella or Solinus.[6] Etna is described as the gate of hell and is said to emit sulphurous fumes – a commonplace in medieval texts[7] – while the

---

[1] Or. 110, 32–3; OH III. xii. 5. In the first chapter the *Pulgare* are located between the *westen* (Pannonia?) and the Byzantine Empire.

[2] Or. 206, 34–6: 'seo strengeste þeod . . . þe mon þa het Basterne, 7 nu hie mon hæt Hungerre'; OH IV. xx. 34.

[3] Cf. Regino, *s.a.* 889: 'gens Hungarorum ferocissima et omni belua crudelior, retro ante seculis ideo inaudita quia nec nominata, a Scythicis regnis et a paludibus quas Thanais sua refusione in immensum porrigit, egressa est'. 889 is the date generally accepted by modern historians for the arrival of the Hungarians in the lowlands between the Carpathians and lower Danube; cf., e.g., Andrew B. Urbansky, *Byzantium and the Danube Frontier* (New York, 1968), p. 11. However, the Annals of Hincmar of Rheims, continuation 861–82 (MGH, Script. 1), refer to what was probably an isolated appearance on the borders of the Frankish Empire as early as 862. I hope to discuss the implications of Or.'s reference to the *Hungerre* in my edition.

[4] Or. 186, 18: 'munt Iof'. Cf. Mela II. vi. 89: 'tum mons Iovis, cuius partem occidenti adversam, eminentia cautium quae inter exigua spatia ut gradus subinde consurgunt, Scalas Hannibalis adpellant'; *King Alfred's Old English Version of Boethius De Consolatione Philosophiae*, ed. Walter John Sedgefield (Oxford, 1899), met. 1. 8 and 14: 'Muntgiop' (prose version, *muntum*) and the gloss from BM Cotton Cleopatra A. iii, in *Anglo-Saxon and Old English Vocabularies*, ed. Thomas Wright and Richard Paul Wülcker (London, 1884) 340, 27, 'Alpium: munt geofa' etc.

[5] Or. 72, 26: 'Gandes'; OH II. vi. 2: 'Gyndes' ('related' MSS, *Gandes*, occasionally *Ganges*). *Gandes* also occurs for *Ganges* in some manuscripts of OH.

[6] Cf. Solinus 52.7 (followed by *De Situ Orbis* 80, 5–6 etc.): 'minima Gangis latitudo per octo milia passuum, maxima per viginti patet'; and Capella VI. 694: 'latitudo Gangis ubi diffusior uiginti milia passuum'. Confusion between *viii* and *viiii* is very common in Latin manuscripts.

[7] Or. 88, 30–1; cf. Bede, *De Natura Rerum*, col. 276 and Isidore, *Etymologies* XIV. viii. 14.

Red Sea is said to have dried up into twelve paths, a tradition recorded in patristic writings.[1] The only additions of this type for which I am unable to find precedents are the assertion that the river Jordan floods annually to the depth of one foot[2] and the ludicrous comment that the outside wall of Babylon was two ells high.[3]

From this survey, then, it would appear that the author of Or. must have had access to a considerable body of geographical material other than that to be found in his primary source. Almost all his modifications, apart from those concerning continental Europe, have the support of extant Latin texts, and even for his 'contemporary' information he could have had a written source or sources. However, this does not necessarily mean that the author himself consulted a wide range of texts. Some of the information could have reached him in the form of a *mappa mundi* or commentary; some he could have acquired orally from an informant or informants.

Certainly, the author of Or. could have been aided by a *mappa mundi*: there might even have been one in the manuscript of OH that he (supposedly) translated.[4] From such a source he could have obtained information about the relative positions of countries and of natural phenomena, about the direction of rivers, seas and mountain ranges, and about details such as whether there were one or more Gades or Fortunate islands.[5] From such a source he could have learned of the 'labels' to be applied to certain proper names and the identity of the country to which a place belonged.[6] If the *mappa mundi* was of the type incorporating legends, then from it he could perhaps even have derived a few pieces of general information, such as the cause of the Nile floods or the 'fact' that Olympus is the highest mountain.[7] However, this hypothetical map would need to have been far more detailed – and, incidentally, more accurate – than any *mappa mundi* still extant, for the translator to have derived from it more than a fraction of his new information.

[1] Or. 38, 29. Cf. Jerome, *Tractatus LIX in Librum Psalmorum*, PL suppl. II, p. 124; *Beati Rabani Mauri Commentariorum in Exodum Libri IV*, PL 108, col. 66; etc.

[2] Or. 32, 5–6. Annual flooding of the Jordan is alluded to in I Chronicles XII. 15 and Joshua III. 15; however, there is no reference to the depth of the water.

[3] Or. 74, 19.

[4] *Mappae mundi* are surprisingly rare in extant manuscripts of OH; however, there are two surviving from the eighth and ninth centuries: Albi, B. Rochegude, 29, 487r, and St Gallen, Stiftsbibliothek, 621, p. 35, neither, unfortunately, of any special significance to this study.

[5] There seems to be little to be gained from listing here all the features for which parallels can be found on surviving *mappae mundi*. However, it is perhaps worth noting that a twelfth-century Jerome map, BM Add. 10049, 64v, refers to Idumea as *regio Sirie* (see above, p. 50, n. 8), while the St Sever Beatus map of *c.* 1030, Paris, BN Lat. 8878, 7r, has the legend 'Arabia . . . eodemon. Ipsa est et Saba appellata.'

[6] Some *mappae mundi* indicate towns and mountains pictorially.

[7] I have found no legend relevant to this study, apart from that referred to above, p. 59, n. 5. However, some *mappae mundi* depict the Asian Olympus, without comment, as a large mountain.

Moreover, although in theory a *mappa mundi* may seem a likely source for certain details, there is no feature that actually requires us to suppose that one was used by the translator.[1] Invariably there are reasonable alternative sources. Thus, for instance, the inclusion of *Mægþa land*, *Sermende* and Riphaean mountains in an account of ninth-century Europe could be due, as Labuda suggests, to the author's possession of a *mappa mundi* containing these traditional details and his insertion on it of 'contemporary' information with which he had been provided.[2] On the other hand, it could, as we have seen, be due to the author's consultation of, or familiarity with, Latin texts;[3] while a third possible explanation is that it formed part of the author's contemporary information. As late as the twelfth century a writer of the stature of Adam of Bremen could not only accept the existence of a northern Land of Women as fact[4] but also believe in the reality of the Riphaean mountains, which he locates on the borders of Sweden and Norway.[5] As for the Sarmatae, their name continues to appear in geographical treatises of the medieval period, and is sometimes applied to the Slavs.[6] Similarly, the curious replacement of OH *Arabia Eudaemon* by *Arabia 7 Sabei 7 Eudomane* could be due to the translator chancing to notice the word *Sab(a)ei* in close proximity to the words *Arabia Eudaemon* on his hypothetical *mappa mundi*; on the other hand, it is perhaps more convincingly explained as arising from a gloss or comment *Ubi Sab(a)ei* or *Et Sab(a)ei*, incorrectly incorporated in either the original Latin or the translation.[7]

Finally, the apparent clockwise shift affecting certain directions given in the section on *Germania*[8] could be due to interpretation – by the author or an intermediary – of 'contemporary' information on a *mappa mundi* in terms not of astrological but of cartographical north, south, east and west. However, here again the evidence is far from conclusive. As Professor Derolez has

[1] For only one feature have I found a parallel in a *mappa mundi* but not in a Latin text: the misplacing of *Cilia* (i.e. Cilicia) and *Issaurio* between Cappadocia and Asia Minor; cf. Or. 12, 10–11 and the St Sever Beatus map, where Isauria and Cilicia (as represented by Tarsus) are sited between Asia Minor and Cappadocia, one to the north and the other to the south. However, the translator or an intermediary may have been puzzled by OH 1. ii. 25, 'Cappadocia ... habet ... a meridie Taurum montem, cui subiacet Cilicia et Isauria usque ad Cilicium sinum', and supposed *cui subiacet* to have Cappadocia as its antecedent.

[2] Cf. Labuda, *Źródła skandynawskie*, p. 48 and commentary, nn. 75 and 76.

[3] See above, p. 54. OH itself (1. ii. 4) refers to the Riphaean mountains and Sarmatian ocean as on the north-east borders of Europe. For the possible implications of the forms *Sermende* and *Riffen*, see my projected edition.

[4] Adam of Bremen, col. 630, claims that the Swedes' rule extends 'usque ad terram feminarum'. Cf. also col. 569, where an eleventh-century Swedish expedition is said to have perished in this land.   [5] Adam of Bremen, cols. 641 and 647.

[6] Cf., e.g., Remigius VI. 325.4: 'Sarmatae: Sclaui' and VI. 303.15: 'Sarmatorum id est Guinedorum' (i.e. Wends).   [7] See above, p. 50 and n. 7.

[8] For reasons of space, I do not consider here the 'shifted' directions in the accounts of Ohthere and Wulfstan and the various theories put forward to account for them. Suffice it to say that they do not require explanation involving use of a *mappa mundi*.

pointed out, a number of apparent deviations are the result of modern methods of calculation, involving a mechanical choice of pivotal centres, which it probably never entered the head of a medieval geographer to use;[1] at least one seems to be the result of modern error.[2] Others in their turn may have arisen from medieval methods of calculation[3] and presentation,[4] or from mistaken beliefs,[5] or even from errors made by the author of Or. or by his informants.[6] Once again there are realistic alternatives to a *mappa mundi* source.

[1] Cf. Derolez, 'Orientation System', p. 259. The mouth of the Elbe, for instance, may be true north-west, not west, of the geographical centre of the Old Saxons, but it is certainly part of their western boundary. Similarly, the *Sysyle*, though true south-east, are also on the eastern boundary of the Saxons, while to a native of, say, Quedlinburg or Halberstadt, Or.'s claim (16, 8–10) that the *Afdrede* live north, the *Hæfeldan* north-east and the *Sysyle* east would seem perfectly correct.

[2] Cf. R. Ekblom, 'Alfred the Great as Geographer', *SN* 14 (1941–2), 131, where it is claimed that the *Afdrede* were in fact not north of the Saxons, as stated by Or. 16, 8, but north-east of them, since they lived in Mecklenburg, with their geographical centre the district round Wismar and Schwerin. In the ninth and tenth centuries, however, the name *Abodriti* seems to have been used for a complex of tribes inhabiting not only Mecklenburg but also modern Schleswig-Holstein, where they would indeed be north of Saxon territory. Cf. Wolfgang Fritze, 'Probleme der abodritische Stammes- und Reichsverfassung', in H. Ludat, *Siedlung und Verfassung der Slawen zwischen Elbe, Saale, und Oder* (Giessen, 1960), pp. 141–217.

[3] In some cases the apparent shift may be due to the use of directions worked out on the basis of travellers' routes, perhaps with deductions of the type 'x is north of y, and z is west of x; therefore z must be north-west of y'. In the ninth century, for instance, an important trade-route ran from Lüneburg to Lübeck and then passed along the West Jutland coast; cf. H. Jankuhn, 'Der frankisch–friesische Handel zur Ostsee im frühen Mittelalter', *Vierteljahrschrift für social- und Wirtschaftgeschichte* 40 (1953), 197. Travellers from Saxonia following this route would have first the *Abodriti* to their north and then Danish territory to their north-west, and might well think of 'þæt lond þe mon Ongle hæt, 7 Sillende 7 sumne dæl Denc' (Or. 16, 7–8) as north-west, not north, of the Saxons. Again, for most of his journey across Burgundy, a traveller following the *Grande Route d'Italie* would have Provence to his south-east (cf. Or. 22, 34) rather than to his south.

[4] For instance, when the author of Or. says (16, 8–9) that the 'Wilte, þe mon Hæfeldan hætt' are north-east, rather than east, of the Saxons, he may merely be reporting the information that the great complex of tribes known as *Wilti* were generally north-east of the Saxons, and that one branch of these – named, perhaps, because they were the nearest or the most important – were called *Hæfeldan*. Similarly, when he groups together Frisians and the mouth of the Elbe, he need not be referring – as Ekblom would maintain that he is – merely to one small section of the Frisians; cf. Derolez, 'Orientation System', p. 259.

[5] It is tempting to suppose that the author of Or. or his informant(s) not only believed the Danes of the Jutland peninsula to live north-west of the Saxons (see above, n. 3), but also considered the Jutland peninsula to extend in a north-westerly direction. Indisputably erroneous is the information that Vasconia was south-east, rather than south-west, of Aquitania; cf. Or. 22, 32 and 34–5.

[6] For instance, if the identification of *Osti* with *Wostroze* is correct, Or.'s reference to Wends living north of them (16, 29–30) could be the result not of knowledge that the island of Rügen was roughly in this position, but of a combination of two pieces of information: that the Wostroze had the Baltic to their north and that Wends inhabited the southern shore of the Baltic as far as the Vistula. Again, the comment (Or. 16, 24–5) that the South Danes had the North Danes on their north and east (for which there are several possible explanations) could be due to attempted rationalization of an original statement that the South Danes had the North Danes on their east.

On the other hand, there does appear to be evidence in support of the theory that the author of Or. may have derived some at least of his geographical information from a gloss or commentary on his Latin original. In the body of the translation there is quite a large amount of additional material which can be traced back to classical sources, and the works from which this material may have come include a number mentioned above in connection with the geographical additions – Pliny, Livy, Frontinus, Valerius Maximus, Servius, Mela, Isidore's *Etymologies* or a work drawing on this, Jordanes, Remigius, Lactantius Placidus, Acron, Silius Italicus, the *Liber Nominum* and Lucan scholia.[1] Occasionally this material is presented in a way that suggests that the translator cannot have been acquainted with the context to which it belongs. Thus, for instance, he knows of a connection between the names Cinna and Smyrna; however, he is unaware that Smyrna is the name of a poem, written by the poet Cinna, and accordingly he attaches it to the consul Cinna and identifies it as the place of that consul's death.[2] Similarly there is geographical material that seems to have been derived at second hand, notably the reference to Ireland's climate, the interpolation of the name *Sabei*, the description of Thessalia as a Greek town, and possibly also the addition of Moab, Amon and Idumei to the list of Syrian provinces and the identification of Galli Cisalpini, Carthago Nova and Basternae with the Langobards, Cordova and the Hungarians respectively.[3] It is tempting to suppose that some of these too are based on a commentary or gloss.[4]

The translator of Or., then, may have had at his disposal a *mappa mundi*, though there is no evidence that this was actually the case. He was quite possibly aided by an annotated or glossed Latin manuscript or by a (Latin?) commentary on OH, though this too is a matter of conjecture. What is certain is that he has incorporated in his translation of OH not only the information about contemporary Europe for which he is renowned but also a great deal of other geographical material derived – directly or indirectly – from a wide variety of Latin sources.

---

[1] Some of these are alternatives. Cf. Bately, 'Classical Additions', pp. 240–1 and 250.

[2] *Ibid.* p. 241.

[3] See above, pp. 50, 52, 56, 57 and 58. In the third instance, Or.'s source may merely have glossed *Thessalia* as *Gr(a)eciae* and the translator himself have drawn the conclusion that the place was a town.

[4] In addition to the occasional lightly glossed manuscript of OH there still exist collections of Orosian glosses (cf., e.g., St Gallen, Stiftsbibliothek, 905) and a fragment of a commentary on OH (cf. Rome, Vatican Library, Reginenses Latini, 1650). However, there is no evidence that these were actually used by the translator.

The origin of
Standard Old English and Æthelwold's school at Winchester

HELMUT GNEUSS

'In literary culture', Sir James Murray has said, 'the Normans were about as far behind the people whom they conquered as the Romans were when they made themselves masters of Greece.'[1] Indeed when the Normans set foot on English soil Anglo-Saxon England was in possession not only of a remarkable literature but also of a highly developed written standard language, known and used in all regions of the country.[2] Most of our Old English manuscripts were written in the late tenth century and in the eleventh in a form of English – although not always quite pure – which the grammarians call late West Saxon. This form of the language is by no means just a dialect, any more than its literature is merely the literary product of a dialect. This fact is first brought home to us when we examine the negative evidence – the rareness before the end of the tenth century of texts in dialects other than West Saxon and their almost complete absence after this time, a state of affairs for which various explanations might be found, historical factors among others. Considerably more important, however, is a positive criterion: texts in this late West Saxon were written and read in other parts of the country too, in Kent (Canterbury), in Mercia (Worcester) and indeed even in Northumbria (York).[3] Moreover, texts which had originally been written in Anglian were transcribed into late West Saxon, as was a large part of Old English poetry. There can be no doubt: in our Old English texts of the eleventh century we are dealing with a standard literary language which, although based on a dialectal foundation, had extended its domain beyond the borders of this dialect.

[1] J. A. H. Murray, *The Evolution of English Lexicography* (Oxford, 1900), p. 14.
[2] Nothing comparable is to be found at this time or earlier in other Germanic dialects; for Old High German see W. Braune, K. Helm and W. Mitzka, *Althochdeutsche Grammatik* 12th ed. (Tübingen, 1967), p. 11, and S. Sonderegger in *Kurzer Grundriss der germanischen Philologie bis 1500*, ed. L. E. Schmitt 1 (Berlin, 1970), 302–3.
[3] Cf. Kenneth Sisam, *Studies in the History of Old English Literature* (Oxford, 1953), p. 153, and *Sermo Lupi ad Anglos*, ed. Dorothy Whitelock, 3rd ed. (London, 1963), pp. 41–2. See also René Derolez, 'Norm and Practice in late Old English', *Proceedings of the Eighth International Congress of Linguists*, ed. Eva Sivertsen (Oslo, 1958), pp. 415–17, and Randolph Quirk, *ibid.* p. 417.

How did this first Standard English come into being, where are its origins to be found, what circumstances fostered its expansion and what brought about its end? Of these questions, the final one is the most easily answered. In the course of the twelfth century various dialects once more replaced the old standard language, and this situation remained unchanged for three centuries. What the country needed, but did not then have, was an English-speaking political or ecclesiastical centre which might have been active in preserving and developing an established form of the language.[1] It was perhaps partly due to this lack that a tendency towards major linguistic changes and innovations prevailed in early Middle English, both in its written and in its spoken forms and varying according to the dialect. The part played at this time by Anglo-Norman, in other words French literature in England, should not be forgotten either.

But if the disappearance of Standard Old English may thus appear as a well-nigh inevitable consequence of historical events, it is by no means easy to explain its origins. We start our search for them within West Saxon territory, because it is in the dialect of this region that we recognize the basis of the Old English literary language. The number and diffusion of Old English manuscripts point to the fact that it was a relatively late form of West Saxon which constituted this basis: of 189 significant manuscripts, 160 date from *c.* 1000 or later.[2] However, we must guard against features of language which belong to the composition of a text at an earlier date and which have been retained in a late copy. We must therefore take into account the entire linguistic and literary development of the West Saxon kingdom.

Our attention is drawn first of all to King Alfred and his literary circle at the end of the ninth century. Alfred is famous, if not as the founder, at least as a vital promoter of Old English prose in West Saxon territory. Further, his political skill and military successes have made of him a popular national figure, whose aura has still not faded today. Even some German schoolchildren know the story of the burnt cakes. Why should we not suppose that a king such as this, a king of such historical and literary stature, was in some way instrumental in bringing a literary language into being? Additional weight is added to this speculation by the fortunate circumstance that we possess three manuscripts which date from Alfred's time or the period shortly after his death and which display certain phonological similarities, although not always consistently. The most important of these is the Oxford manuscript, Bodleian Library, Hatton 20, of Alfred's translation of Gregory the Great's *Cura Pastoralis*, which originated between 890 and 897 in a

[1] But see J. R. Hulbert, 'A Thirteenth Century English Literary Standard', *JEGP* 45 (1946), 411–14.
[2] Cf. N. R. Ker, *Catalogue of Manuscripts Containing Anglo-Saxon* (Oxford, 1957), pp. xv–xix.

scriptorium working for the king. Henry Sweet published the text of this manuscript in 1871 and pointed out the significance of its early form of West Saxon.[1] This was the starting-point of something approaching a revolution in English philology; until then late West Saxon forms had been regarded as standard, whereas thenceforth the early West Saxon used in this work was introduced as norm into nearly all our dictionaries and grammars. In anthologies and editions later texts were even brought into line with its requirements.[2] This was not only a question of convenience; it was also a sign that at least some scholars wanted to see in Alfred the initiator of a standard literary language. Sweet himself, for instance, claimed that West Saxon was 'fixed and regulated by the literary labours of Alfred and his successors',[3] the implication being that the Old English literary language took its origin from Alfred and that late West Saxon was merely its continuation, although this theory leaves unanswered the question as to when the process of geographical extension beyond West Saxon borders began. R. W. Chambers, as one further example, also regarded Alfred's prose as representing 'the national official and literary language'.[4] The idea is positively seductive: King Alfred, the man who battled victoriously against the Danes, the man who put a stop to the decay of learning and who was the founder of English prose, was also the man who created the first English standard language. However, the facts do not bear this view out. Nearly forty years ago Professor Wrenn gave a lecture before the Philological Society,[5] in which he proved not only that the three surviving early West Saxon manuscripts are not in complete agreement with one another in their phonological features but even that each manuscript is not consistent in its own usage. Thus some doubt is cast on the normative character of Alfred's language and of early West Saxon in general.

At this stage I should like to make some points on questions of method. It would seem that linguistic problems in Old English (and surely not only in Old English) have often been dealt with in the past, and occasionally even in the very recent past, from too narrow a point of view and with inadequate means. The shortcomings appear to be twofold. In the first place

---

[1] *King Alfred's West-Saxon Version of Gregory's Pastoral Care*, ed. Henry Sweet, Early English Text Society o.s. 45 and 50 (London, 1871) I, v–vi.

[2] For some recent examples, see the texts edited in The Harvard Old English Series by Francis P. Magoun and Jess B. Bessinger. Professor Magoun explains his principles of normalizing Old English orthography in *The Anglo-Saxon Poems in Bright's Anglo-Saxon Reader done in a Normalized Orthography* (Cambridge, Mass., 1956), pp. iii–iv. Cf. also John C. Pope, *Seven Old English Poems* (Indianapolis, 1966), pp. vii–viii.

[3] *Pastoral Care* I, xxxii–xxxiii.

[4] R. W. Chambers, *On the Continuity of English Prose*, EETS o.s. 191a (London, 1932), p. lxxvii.

[5] C. L. Wrenn, 'Standard Old English', *TPS* 1933, 65–88. See also Randolph Quirk and C. L. Wrenn, *An Old English Grammar*, 2nd ed. (London, 1957), pp. 5–6.

English philology has unfortunately only too often relied on its own resources and possibilities. That the historical background and cultural background and the findings of palaeographers, art historians and many others have to be borne in mind, seems so obvious an axiom that one is almost embarrassed to mention it; yet it is easy to show how, time and again, this principle has been violated. In the second place the linguistic methods themselves have been inadequate. Even editions of Anglo-Saxon texts published quite recently deal in their introductions under the heading 'Language' only with phonology and accidence. Far be it from me to question the value of phonology and accidence, although one might add that every student of philology knows, even in his first terms, that it is possible to transcribe a text from one dialect into another, thus, as it were, masking its real identity. This point, for example, could be of vital importance in locating the origin of Standard Old English. Above all, however, a language does not consist merely of sounds and inflexions. Admittedly research on Old English syntax has a wide field yet to cover and the examination of vocabulary is still in its infancy, but in the future, I think, one may confidently expect significant findings from these disciplines, and particularly from the study of word usage and word geography; the project of a new, comprehensive Old English dictionary, to be based on computer-made concordances of all Old English texts and now well beyond the planning stage, is a decisive step in this direction.[1] In fact a stage may be reached in which it will be scarcely possible to commit oneself to any far-reaching philological opinion without taking the study of vocabulary into consideration. In this connection it is as well to keep in mind that a text that has been transcribed, whether to be modernized or to be brought into line with another dialect, often changes its phonological character but less often its vocabulary. The many thousand lines of Old English poetry, in which the vocabulary could scarcely have been changed for metrical reasons, are not the only evidence to support this view.[2]

If we turn from these thoughts to their practical application in the case of King Alfred, first of all let us ask ourselves whether the circumstances make it appear likely that Alfred wanted to, or indeed was even in a position to, create a standard language. He reigned as king from 871 to 899. It was a

[1] See *Computers and Old English Concordances*, ed. Angus Cameron, Roberta Frank and John Leyerle (Toronto, 1970) and John Leyerle, '"The Dictionary of Old English": a Progress Report', *Computers and the Humanities* 5 (1971), 279–83.
[2] This is not to deny, however, that in some revisions of Old English prose texts changes in the vocabulary were actually made, although less systematically than one would expect. This is what happened in two manuscripts of the Old English Bede and in the Hatton manuscript of Bishop Werferth's translation of Gregory's *Dialogues*; cf. J. J. Campbell, 'The Dialect Vocabulary of the Old English Bede', *JEGP* 50 (1951), 349–72, and H. Schabram, *Superbia: Studien zum altenglischen Wortschatz* 1 (Munich, 1965), 43–4 and 47–8, and see below, p. 81, n. 1.

period of warfare against the Scandinavians and of unremitting fear of renewed attacks. It is true that in 878, after a decisive battle, Alfred succeeded in forcing the Danish army to agree to a peace treaty, but this by no means eliminated the constant threat to that part of England in the south and west which had remained Anglo-Saxon. In his oft-quoted preface to the *Cura Pastoralis* Alfred paints a picture of the catastrophic decline in learning throughout the country. We know that in the whole of England there was scarcely one regular monastery left. The region of Mercia seems to have been the only place where any remnant of the great old Anglo-Saxon culture and scholarship was still to be found. From here and from the continent Alfred fetched teachers and helpers for his educational programme, which consisted of the translation and dissemination of certain important medieval books. All this he carried out in the last seven years of his life, after having himself only shortly beforehand learned Latin.[1] In view of these facts it seems highly unlikely that Alfred consciously aimed at, or achieved, the fostering of a standard language. Be this as it may, the philological facts speak for themselves. The king had some of the books translated by helpers; Bishop Werferth of Worcester rendered the *Dialogues* of Gregory the Great into the dialect of Mercia, and not into any standardized form of West Saxon, as is indicated by the vocabulary. The translation of Bede, which may have been ordered by Alfred too, was likewise in Mercian.[2] In two recent papers it has been convincingly demonstrated that the Old English Orosius was not the work of Alfred himself.[3] For the composition of those books that we can be certain were by the king he must have had a considerable amount of help from scholars and secretaries. Contemporary manuscripts of Alfred's own translations exhibit, as mentioned above, a lack of uniformity in their phonological characteristics. Non-West Saxon dialects were doubtless partly responsible for this – principally, one presumes, Mercian, which was still of literary importance at that time and which was the language of several of the king's collaborators. Others had Welsh, Old Saxon and perhaps some West Frankish dialect as their mother tongue. Incidentally, the king would scarcely have been able to impose a uniform type of spelling either. By a stroke of fortune we are in possession of evidence pertaining to the early textual history of the translation of the *Cura Pastoralis*, interpreted in an

[1] Cf. *Asser's Life of King Alfred*, ed. W. H. Stevenson (Oxford, 1904; repr. 1959 with contr. by D. Whitelock), chs. 87–9; trans. Dorothy Whitelock, *English Historical Documents c. 500–1042* (London, 1955), pp. 271–2.
[2] Cf. Dorothy Whitelock, 'The Old English Bede', *Proc. of the Brit. Acad.* 48 (1962), 57 and n. 5, and Schabram, *Superbia*, pp. 45–8 and n. 50.
[3] Elizabeth M. Liggins, 'The Authorship of the Old English Orosius', *Anglia* 88 (1970), 289–322, and Janet M. Bately, 'King Alfred and the Old English Translation of Orosius', *ibid.* pp. 433–60. Cf. also Günter Büchner, 'Vier altenglische Bezeichnungen für Vergehen und Verbrechen (*Fyren, Gylt, Man, Scyld*)' (Ph.D. thesis, Berlin, 1968), pp. 184–5.

admirable article by Dr Sisam.[1] At least each of the ten Anglo-Saxon bishops was to receive a copy of the work. A scriptorium capable of mastering this kind of book production within a short time must have been rare in the early Middle Ages; Alfred certainly did not have one. What he did therefore was to send the first copies to other scriptoria, where they were copied in turn. Then the first copies and their transcripts were sent back to him, the preface which he had in the meantime composed was added to each of them and finally they were sent to their destinations. The whole procedure was obviously carried out in a great hurry and undoubtedly in places so far away from each other that there could be no question of achieving any uniformity of language. The only important criterion which remains is Alfred's vocabulary. If we were to assume that the Old English literary language originated with Alfred and his circle we would expect his vocabulary not to differ substantially from that of the numerous late West Saxon texts. But here we are confronted with the same picture as Professor Wrenn presented in his examination of the phonological features: the differences are quite considerable. A number of dialectal and semantic studies have shown that there can be no question of a more or less uniform West Saxon vocabulary, and that King Alfred's use of words deviates, in many cases quite appreciably, from that of Ælfric, the chief representative of late West Saxon prose.[2]

In view of these realities, the belief that King Alfred was the founder or at any rate the harbinger of standard Old English becomes not only dubious but downright unlikely. Neither the given situation nor the existing linguistic evidence found in texts dating from before the tenth century points to the existence of a language form, obeying certain norms, which was continued and developed in the late Old English period. Moreover it seems certain that there were hardly any schools or scriptoria which would have adopted and would have helped to spread some kind of standard which King Alfred might have envisaged. His achievement is not a whit the less great for that. With his translations and his cultural policy, as one is tempted to call it, he attained considerable results. His books were read right up to the early thirteenth century. Nevertheless there is no proof that they raised West Saxon above the status of a dialect.

Our task, we must conclude, is to look for the origin of standard Old English elsewhere. Since we know that the West Saxon dialect served as its groundwork, and yet Alfred's time is too early for its genesis, there remain only the tenth and eleventh centuries, the late West Saxon period. And, in point of fact, late West Saxon is simply equated with Standard Old English in some handbooks. But when, and how, did a mere dialect come to achieve

[1] Kenneth Sisam, 'The Publication of Alfred's Pastoral Care', *Studies*, pp. 140–7.
[2] See below, p. 75, n. 4.

such widespread diffusion and recognition? Was it political factors which gave it its impetus or did church organization exert an influence? Did someone somewhere consciously work towards the fixation and diffusion of certain linguistic norms? How do we account for the astonishing uniformity of the phonological and morphological system, or at least of the orthography, in Old English manuscripts of the late tenth century and the eleventh?

There are no indications in the first half of the tenth century of any linguistic process such as might be expected preliminary to the formation of a literary language. The decades after Alfred's death are characterized politically by the consolidation of West Saxon dominion and the recovery of territories settled by the Scandinavians. But intellectual and spiritual life seems to have been in a state of stagnation; there was nobody to take over where Alfred left off. There were still scarcely any regular monasteries. Not one work of even second-rate standing in Anglo-Saxon literature can be shown to date from this time. King Athelstan presented Latin books to ecclesiastical institutions; but we do not find a single mention of him, or of any other English king, taking an interest in works of literature written in English. Our attention is thus directed to the great Benedictine reform in the second half of the tenth century. It was only then that English monastic life was finally restored and that English culture and scholarship regained something of the brilliance which had once emanated from the Northumbrian monasteries, and only then that the conditions were created for the composition of the great Anglo-Saxon prose works at the end of the tenth century. It seems a logical step to presume further that this reform movement was also a driving force in the evolution and diffusion of a literary language. But one should not rest satisfied with seeing here just possibilities and general tendencies towards a linguistic development. One should at least make the attempt to discover some source of conscious language manipulation; one should ask oneself if there was not more involved in the beginnings of the Anglo-Saxon literary language than just the gradual expansion of West Saxon into other dialect regions.

In order to realize the significance of the reform movement for our subject it may be appropriate to recall a few facts and names – names which would perhaps be as well-known today as those of Alfred and Chaucer if the Norman Conquest had not put an end to a literary development so full of promise. Dunstan, an Anglo-Saxon of noble descent, became abbot of Glastonbury in the year 940. Here he introduced monastic practices according to the Benedictine Rule, and so did his pupil Æthelwold when he became abbot of Abingdon around 954. They found their models on the continent: Dunstan was forced to spend some years as an exile in the reformed monastery of St

Peter in Ghent; Æthelwold summoned monks from Corbie to instruct the monks at Abingdon in plain chant and sent one of his own monks to Fleury to study the observances there. However, a real reform movement did not get going in England until the young and energetic King Edgar came to the throne in 959. Now the prime movers in the reform began to move up into key positions in the church. In 960 Dunstan was made archbishop of Canterbury and in 963 Æthelwold became bishop of Winchester. They had the cooperation of Oswald, who had become bishop of Worcester in 961 and had himself lived in Fleury for a long time. It was under these three men, and with vigorous support from the king, that from 960 onwards monasteries, such as Malmesbury, Westminster, Sherborne, Winchester, Peterborough, Ely and Ramsey, to mention but a few, were founded or restored, and cathedrals were transformed into monastic cathedrals, as in Canterbury, Winchester and Worcester. These foundations were confined to the south and Midlands, it is true; but here a new golden age of monastic life in England dawned and brought in its train a renaissance of culture, literature and art: in this connection one need only think of English manuscript illumination.

The Benedictine reform in England had its origin in the West Saxon region. Dunstan and Æthelwold came from there; Glastonbury and Abingdon were situated there. The chancellery of the English kings, which, however, would scarcely have exercised much influence on the language of Old English literature, must also have been West Saxon.[1] So it is not really surprising that the standard literary language, common to all of England in the eleventh century, was also marked by West Saxon features. What is remarkable, however, is its linguistic uniformity, and what strikes us particularly is the relative consistency with which its exponents spelled their sounds and inflexional endings, a conformity which extends to and partly includes the use of vocabulary. No other Old English dialect exhibits a comparable regularity, and even late West Saxon must have been spoken in such a large area that we should not expect to find complete uniformity in the use of language. Finally, Standard Old English conceals from us the progress of certain developments in speech – such as the levelling of unstressed vowels in inflexional syllables – which were at quite an advanced stage in the eleventh century, as we can observe from occasional spellings.

If one takes all these aspects into consideration, it is difficult to go on believing in a process of gradual growth in the influence of a dialect, due simply to the prevailing circumstances. On the contrary, a regulative and organizing element makes itself felt here, for which we should, as I have suggested above, try to find some explanation. It seems that there must have been some leading scriptorium, some influential school behind Standard

---

[1] But see below, p. 82, n. 4.

Old English,[1] and it is my opinion that this can only have been Æthelwold's school at the Old Minster in Winchester. There are many factors which support this view: Winchester was a royal residence; it was one of the centres of the reform movement, the seat of three reformed monasteries, one of which was also a cathedral; and it was situated right in the heart of the West Saxon kingdom. It would thus seem quite feasible that this might have been the centre of a language reform too, and indeed with more likelihood than any other place in the Anglo-Saxon domain. But we must now seek to prove this by exact methods. After all, Dunstan's Canterbury is another possible candidate; and in Canterbury we find not only the oldest cathedral and the oldest monastery in England but also the seat of the primate of the English church. This primate, Dunstan, came from the West Saxon region himself, had close connections with the West Saxon court and had promoted the Benedictine reform for fifteen years from a West Saxon monastery.

What, then, are the factors which speak in favour of Æthelwold, bishop of Winchester, and his school? We possess two different, but closely connected, accounts of Æthelwold's life, one written by Ælfric and the other, in all probability, by Wulfstan, the precentor at the Old Minster, Winchester, who, like Ælfric, was a personal disciple of the bishop.[2] Æthelwold was evidently of noble birth. His parents lived at Winchester; as a young man he spent some time in King Athelstan's retinue, was later ordained priest by Ælfheah, bishop of Winchester, and entered Dunstan's monastery as a monk. When Æthelwold expressed his intention of leaving England to study monastic life in the reformed monasteries on the continent, King Eadred held him back and in 954 made him abbot of the then deserted and ruined monastery at Abingdon. He carried out his office there until the year 963 when he was entrusted by Edgar with the episcopacy of Winchester, a ministry which he held up to his death in 984. Æthelwold was thus a native of the West Saxon kingdom and, with the exception of some short trips (and perhaps a longer stay at Thorney late in his life?), he never seems to have left it during his lifetime. Winchester was his native place and he very probably spent the greater part of his life there. Where the monks in the cathedral

---

[1] Cf. Robert P. Stockwell and C. Westbrook Barritt ('Scribal Practice: some Assumptions', *Language* 37 (1961), 75–82), who even maintain 'that the England of the eighth through the tenth centuries . . . could not have had anything but a reasonably thorough system of instruction for its scribes' (p. 77); they do not deal, however, with the specific question of the origin of the late Old English customs of spelling.

[2] Cf. Dorothy Whitelock, *EHD*, pp. 831–2. More recently, R. N. Quirk has suggested the possibility that Ælfric was the author of both Lives; the ascription of the longer (and earlier?) *Vita* to Wulfstan is in any case not absolutely certain. See R. N. Quirk, 'Winchester Cathedral in the Tenth Century', *ArchJ* 114 (1957), 35–7. There is also a short account of Æthelwold's life by William of Malmesbury, *De Gestis Pontificum Anglorum*, ed. N. E. S. A. Hamilton, Rolls Series (1870), pp. 165–9.

monastery at Winchester, the Old Minster as it was called, came from is not known with certainty, and perhaps it is not so important for our line of inquiry. At any rate, Æthelwold initially brought monks with him from Abingdon to Winchester, and in Abingdon – which was also situated in West Saxon territory – most, if not all, of the religious were presumably natives of those parts. Unfortunately we know as good as nothing about the places from which the numerous monks came who peopled the newly founded or restored monasteries during the time of the Benedictine reform. Still, the few clues that we do have indicate that the members of any particular house mostly came from the neighbourhood.

This question of the origin of the monks is of some importance in English philology, because our Old English manuscripts afford only insufficient evidence on the dialects of the Anglo-Saxon period. But there are two other kinds of evidence for determining and differentiating between these, namely place-names and Middle English dialects, for which the material is richer. Neither of these, however, is absolutely reliable. There may, for instance, be shifts in the demarcation lines between dialects. Let me here cite, as an example, the claim that our only manuscript of the Old English *Apollonius of Tyre* – or at least the scribe who wrote it – must have come from Essex or Middlesex, because of the numerous examples of *æ* for the *i*-umlaut of *a* before nasals which it contains. The origin and transmission of this text, which holds an important place in the history of Old English literature seeing that it is the first known English translation of a narrative prose work from the late classical period, are of some interest to us. The criterion which is used to locate the dialect is reasonably trustworthy with regard to Middle English; but it fails in the case of Old English, a fact which can be proved by a number of texts and manuscripts, which, although they display this very same phonological or orthographic feature, quite definitely come from other parts of England – Kent, for example.[1] So much for the method of determining Old English dialects by means of a comparison with Middle English or with place-names. Another method consists quite simply of taking the language of some manuscripts whose places of origin have been located with certainty by means of non-linguistic criteria and using this as a starting-point for one's investigations. However, even here we still have to contend with the source of error mentioned above: the scribe (or author) of a text may come from the region in which the manuscript has been written, but again this is not necessarily always the case. He may have adapted himself to the current usage prevalent in his scriptorium, but there is no guarantee of this either, and

---

[1] Cf. *Die alt- und mittelenglischen Apollonius-Bruchstücke*, ed. J. Raith (Munich, 1956), pp. 8–16; *The Old English Apollonius of Tyre*, ed. P. Goolden (Oxford, 1958), p. xxxiv; and H. Gneuss, *Hymnar und Hymnen im englischen Mittelalter* (Tübingen, 1968), pp. 160–1 and nn. 4 and 5. See also E. G. Stanley, *ASNSL* 206 (1969), 137.

Professor Campbell is probably right when he believes that 'consistent writing of a dialect could be achieved only by a scribe trained in a monastery where the dialect in question was the official language'.[1]

Let us return to Æthelwold. We may safely assume that he and his associates used the West Saxon dialect. But what was the situation as regards Old English language and literature? Was anybody actively, or even passively, occupied with them at the time of the reform movement? In chronicles, lives of saints and other documents we find quite detailed accounts of the activities of Dunstan, Æthelwold, Oswald and their assistants, of the support they received from King Edgar, of the foundation of new monasteries and the purchasing of land property for these, and of the expulsion of clerics who refused to become monks. Particular emphasis was always laid on the fact that the reformers were scholarly men of wide reading, but only in one instance do documents testify to an interest in the English language on the part of any of these men – namely in the case of Æthelwold. His two biographers relate of him: 'He always took great pleasure in instructing the young men and boys, in explaining Latin books to them in the English language, in teaching them the rules of grammar and metre, and exhorting them gently to strive for greater things. And so it was that many of his pupils became abbots, bishops and even archbishops in England.'[2] Nor did he stop at simply explaining books in English. King Edgar and his wife called upon him to translate the Benedictine Rule into English. The king may have known that Æthelwold was the right man for the translation, or perhaps Æthelwold offered to undertake it himself, for the king rewarded him with land, which Æthelwold in turn gave to the monastery he had restored at Ely. In his translation of the Rule he shows himself to be a capable translator and, both in sentence structure and in the use of words, a skilful master of Old English prose. His style is lucid and easily comprehensible; and he seldom has to experiment in his choice of vocabulary. Where he found no suitable word in English, he either used a loan-word or created a new word himself. All this points to the fact that he had devoted many years to the study not only of Latin but also of English usage.[3] It is worth mentioning too that the manuscripts of Æthelwold's translation show the form

---

[1] *The Vespasian Psalter*, ed. D. H. Wright and A. Campbell, EEMF 14 (Copenhagen, 1967), p. 82.

[2] Translated from the version of the *Vita* ascribed to Wulfstan, ch. XXXI, Migne, Patrologia Latina 137, col. 95.

[3] Cf. H. Gneuss, 'Die Benediktinerregel in England und ihre altenglische Übersetzung', in *Die angelsächsischen Prosabearbeitungen der Benediktinerregel*, ed. A. Schröer, Bibl. d. ags. Prosa 2, 2nd ed. (Darmstadt, 1964). Ælfric, Wulfstan of Winchester and William of Malmesbury do not mention Æthelwold as the translator of the Rule (although William of Malmesbury knew the Old English version; cf. *Memorials of Saint Dunstan*, ed. W. Stubbs, RS (1874), p. 290). The translation was first attributed to Æthelwold by the twelfth-century *Liber Eliensis*. Leland, Bale and Pits do not seem to have known of this. The relevant section of the *Liber Eliensis* was quoted by Wanley,

of spelling which was usual in late Old English writings and which was based on the phonology of the West Saxon dialect region, and thus also of Winchester, in the tenth century. But too much attention should not be attached to this point, as the earliest copy which has come down to us of the Old English Benedictine Rule, Oxford, Corpus Christi College 197, was made about one or two decades after the completion of the original version; while all other copies are eleventh century or even later. This translation of the Benedictine Rule was not Æthelwold's only opus. In an account of the Benedictine reform in England, of which unfortunately only a fragment is extant, he shows that he was capable of writing good original Old English prose.[1] He is also regarded as the author, or one of the authors, of the *Regularis Concordia*, a monastic rule for England, drawn up in Latin. Furthermore it has been suggested recently that he may have introduced a new type of charter in Old English and that he may have had something to do with a revival of the *Anglo-Saxon Chronicle*.[2]

What was the position as regards his school and the achievements of his pupils at the monastery? Some of these may have carried on his work as a translator anonymously – we possess many examples of Old English translations bearing no name – and some relevant texts are discussed below. However, we do know the names of two of his pupils: Wulfstan, who later became the precentor at the Old Minster in Winchester, and Ælfric, who went to the monastery at Cerne as master of novices soon after 987 and became abbot of Eynsham in 1005. Wulfstan is known to us as the author of Latin prose and verse.[3] Ælfric, the most important writer of Old English prose, expressly acknowledges that he was a pupil of Æthelwold – and surely not without a certain amount of pride; among other places, he mentions this in the preface

together with his description of the Old English Rule in Cambridge, Corpus Christi College 178 (*Librorum Vett. Septentrionalium Catalogus* (Oxford, 1705), pp. 122–3); an abbreviated version of this section was printed, somewhat earlier, by Henry Wharton (*Anglia Sacra* (London, 1691) I, 604) and again, from Wharton, by Thomas Tanner, *Bibliotheca Britannico-Hibernica* (London, 1748), p. 269n., and Thomas Wright, *Biographia Britannica Literaria* (London, 1842–6) I, 440n. Wright takes it for granted that Æthelwold was the translator of the Rule, and as far as I can see the attribution has never been seriously questioned since his day. (Æthelwold did not, of course, translate the *Regularis Concordia* into English, as William Hunt will have it (*DNB* VI, 904).)

[1] Dorothy Whitelock has demonstrated that there can no longer be any doubt about the attribution of this piece to Æthelwold: 'The Authorship of the Account of King Edgar's Establishment of Monasteries', *Philological Essays: Studies in Old and Middle English Language and Literature in Honour of Herbert Dean Meritt*, ed. James L. Rosier (The Hague, 1970), pp. 125–36.

[2] Cf. Eric John, 'The Sources of the English Monastic Reformation', *RB* 70 (1960), 197–203, and 'The Beginning of the Benedictine Reform in England', *RB* 73 (1963), 83 and n. 3. According to Leland, Æthelwold was also a skilled mathematician and the author of a scientific work; see Quirk, 'Winchester Cathedral in the Tenth Century', p. 30 and n. 1. Other, theological and historical, works are ascribed to Æthelwold by Bale and Pits.

[3] See Gneuss, *Hymnar und Hymnen*, p. 246.

to his Grammar where he declares that it may be used as a basic primer for both Latin *and* English.[1] Ælfric's significance for the history of English prose is universally recognized nowadays. His stylistic skill and his efforts to achieve a certain linguistic norm[2] are inconceivable without a thorough schooling – and this even more so in the case of his Grammar. His very first work, the *Catholic Homilies*, exhibits a language form which exemplifies in every respect the late Old English standard language. It was written during his first years at Cerne, that is to say directly after his move there which took place only three years after Æthelwold's death. With this evidence in mind we cannot fail to recognize the importance which the school at Winchester had for the first English literary language.[3]

But there is a further and still more convincing argument to support the claim that Æthelwold's school aspired, or at least contributed substantially, to a standard usage in language. A very restricted group of texts, which date from the end of the tenth century and the beginning of the eleventh and which were written in close connection with Winchester, display – as opposed to other West Saxon and non-West Saxon texts – a remarkable uniformity in the choice of expression within certain groups of synonyms. It is, of course, not possible to give a detailed analysis of this material within the limits of an article such as this, but the relevant evidence can be found in a number of recent or forthcoming works. These include Hans Schabram's study of the Old English terminology for Latin *superbia* (1965), a Berlin Ph.D. thesis on the Old English words for 'guilt' by G. Büchner (1968), a Munich Ph.D. thesis – not yet finished – on the Old English words for 'crown' and 'wreath', another Munich thesis – just finished – on the Old English Benedictine Rule, my study of the Old English hymn glosses (1968) and some earlier studies on Old English semantic fields, word geography and linguistic borrowing, among them the theses by Hilding Bäck and Hans Käsmann.[4]

---

[1] *Ælfrics Grammatik und Glossar*, ed. J. Zupitza, 2nd ed. with contr. by H. Gneuss (Berlin, 1966), p. 3: 'ac heo byð swa ðeah sum angyn to ægðrum gereorde'.

[2] Cf. Peter Clemoes, 'Ælfric', *Continuations and Beginnings: Studies in Old English Literature*, ed. E. G. Stanley (London, 1966), pp. 176–209, and John C. Pope, Introduction to *Homilies of Ælfric: a Supplementary Collection* I, EETS 259 (London, 1967).

[3] Numerous small revisions to the *Catholic Homilies* show how painstakingly and systematically Ælfric sought to regularize his use of English; see Sisam, *Studies*, pp. 183–5, and Peter Clemoes, *Ælfric's First Series of Catholic Homilies: BM Royal 7 C. xii*, ed. Norman Eliason and Peter Clemoes, EEMF 13 (Copenhagen, 1966), p. 33.

[4] See above, p. 66, n. 2, p. 67, n. 3 and p. 72, n. 1; Hilding Bäck, *The Synonyms for 'Child', 'Boy', 'Girl' in Old English* (Lund, 1934); and Hans Käsmann, 'Tugend und Laster im Alt- und Mittelenglischen' (unpub. Ph.D. thesis, Berlin, 1951). A considerable number of studies of Old English semantic fields and dialect words are listed by F. Holthausen, *Altenglisches etymologisches Wörterbuch*, 2nd ed. with new bibl. H. C. Matthes (Heidelberg, 1963), pp. xxiii–xxvii; A. Campbell, *Old English Grammar* (Oxford, 1959), pp. 366–8; and O. Funke, 'Altenglische Wortgeographie', *Anglistische Studien: Festschrift zum 70. Geburtstag von Friedrich*

This much can be said briefly: as is to be expected, the typical 'Winchester words' represent only a small fraction of the entire vocabulary, but once a definitive Old English dictionary has been compiled they may well turn out to be more extensive than at present imagined. Further, they consist only of those words of which it can be proved from similar contexts in other contemporary texts – West Saxon ones too – that they could have been replaced by synonyms. In this case, it seems, we are justified in disregarding to a certain extent the linguistic and non-linguistic characteristics which usually differentiate the members of any pair or group of so-called 'synonyms'. There is very little that can be said about the reasons which prompted the choice of one word rather than another in the various instances. We find some expressions from church usage, such as the translation for *ecclesia* and expressions for 'altar', 'martyr' and 'disciple'; here the religious terminology may still have been in the process of formation, or rather, re-formation. In the main, however, the words are taken from a great variety of spheres, as, for example, the words for 'son' and 'stranger', 'guilt', 'vice' and 'pride', 'crown' and 'path'. Verbal concepts, such as 'to drive away', 'to burn' and 'to cleanse', are also to be found. So we see that it was not a case of some sort of new 'technical' vocabulary being laid down; stylistic considerations, rather, must have been the chief concern in choosing the individual words. Thus our group of texts, which I shall call 'the Winchester group' from now on, has *gelaðung* instead of *cyrice*, where the people, not the buildings, are meant; for Latin *discipulus* it prefers *leorningcniht* to other loan formations and semantic loans; it employs *cyðere*, but not *þrowere* and not normally the loan-word *martyr*; it retains the old (pagan?) word *weofod* and has neither *alter* nor *altare*; it prefers *sunu* to *bearn* and replaces *cniht* in the sense of 'boy' by *cnapa*; and it almost always has *gylt* while Alfred and some late Old English texts usually have *scyld*. The words for *superbus* and *superbia* are almost exclusively *modig* and *modignes* and occasionally the recent French loan *pryte*, but never *ofermod* and *ofermodignes* as in earlier West Saxon prose (and in Wulfstan!), nor *oferhygdig* and *oferhygd*, the words of Anglian prose and of poetry. The word for 'vice' is *leahtor* and rarely *unþeaw*, which is used by Alfred and in some late West Saxon texts. The increasing use of *miht* instead of *mægen*, 'virtue', may go back to Winchester practice too. The Winchester group employs *wuldorbeag* for *corona*, especially in a religious sense ('crown of life'), and in a concrete, secular sense *cynehelm*, but never Alfred's *beag* and hardly ever any of the other words for *corona* found in late Old

Wild, ed. K. Brunner, H. Koziol and S. Korninger, Wiener Beiträge zur englischen Philologie 66 (Vienna, 1958), pp. 39–51.

I have to thank Miss M. Gretsch and Mr J. Kirschner for making available to me material and results of their work in progress on the Old English Benedictine Rule and the Old English words for 'crown' and 'wreath' respectively.

English texts. For 'path' the preferred word seems *pæð*, as opposed to *stig* and *siðfæt*; instead of *fremde*, *ælðeodig* or *elfremed* is used; *werod* is preferred to *swete* and *myrig*, *(ge)blissian* to *(ge)fægnian*, *utanydan* to *adræfan*, *adrifan* (and possibly *afeormian* to *(ge)clænsian* and *forswælan* to *forbærnan?*). Other words that may belong in the Winchester vocabulary are *gedyrstlæcan*, 'to dare'; *gerihtlæcan*, 'to correct, to mend one's ways' (but not in the sense 'to lead, to direct'); *geefenlæcan*, 'to emulate'; *hæfen*, *hæfenleas* and *hæfenleast*, 'possession', 'poor' and 'poverty'; and *onhrop*, 'importunity'.

We find a vocabulary, regulated in this way, used in a number of Old English texts or groups of texts with a degree of consistency unparalleled in any other Old English writings. First, there are the works of Ælfric; here, of course, personal style may have something to do with it.[1] Another text that belongs here is the Old English interlinear version in the Lambeth Psalter, Lambeth Palace Library 427, written in the first half of the eleventh century. The points of agreement which it has with Ælfric's usage, and the points of disagreement which set it apart from eleven other Old English interlinear versions of the psalter, cannot be overlooked. It seems significant that the glossator of the Lambeth Psalter appears to have deliberately rejected words from the earlier psalter glosses he may have utilized when such words did not agree with the usage of the Winchester group, while in many other cases he has combined a word from the earlier psalter glosses with a 'modern' or 'Winchester' word, thus producing numerous double or multiple glosses.[2] Unfortunately the origin of this manuscript is not known; however, it is quite possible that it was connected with one or more Winchester manuscripts.[3] The third text which displays the same characteristic choice of words is in BM Cotton Julius A. vi and Vespasian D. xii and was unpublished until recently. It consists of glosses on the prototype of a schoolbook, which was extremely popular in the later Middle Ages, the

[1] For Ælfric's usage, see especially Pope, *Homilies of Ælfric* I, 99 ff. and the literature quoted there.
[2] The manuscript was edited by Uno Lindelöf, *Der Lambeth-Psalter*, Acta Societatis Scientiarum Fennicae 35, no. 1 and 43, no. 3 (Helsingfors, 1909–14). Lindelöf (II, 56) lists a number of rare words, which Ælfric and the Lambeth Psalter have in common; he also lists (II, 41–2) words which are characteristic of our Winchester group. In connection with correspondences of usage between the Lambeth Psalter and the Spelman Psalter, C. and K. Sisam are thinking of 'some influential monastic school in which these standard equivalents were taught', *The Salisbury Psalter*, EETS 242 (London, 1959), p. 74. For the dependence of the Lambeth glossator on earlier models see Schabram, *Superbia*, p. 27. J. R. Stracke, 'Studies in the Vocabulary of the Lambeth Psalter Glosses' (unpub. Ph.D. thesis, University of Pennsylvania, 1970), who deals with the double glosses, does not seem to recognize the real significance of many of these (esp. pp. 134 ff.).
[3] The only Old English glossed psalter which shows a number of definite links with the Lambeth Psalter is BM Stowe 2, the Spelman Psalter, written about the middle of the eleventh century. D. H. Turner thinks that Stowe 2 and Le Havre 330, an eleventh-century missal from New Minster, Winchester, 'seem to have a scribe or scribes in common'. See *The Missal of the New Minster, Winchester*, ed. D. H. Turner, Henry Bradshaw Society 93 (1962), pp. xi–xiii. Turner's discovery might indicate where we have to look for the 'influential monastic school' mentioned by C. and K. Sisam (see above, preceding note).

Expositio Hymnorum. It is difficult to pin-point the place where these two manuscripts were written; they probably have some connection with Canterbury. However, an examination of the Latin *Expositio* soon makes it clear that – because of differences in liturgical observance – there can be no question of its having originated in Canterbury; its composition must be connected with Winchester, since it gives so exact an account of the practice, introduced there by Æthelwold and described by Ælfric.[1] The fourth of the texts we are interested in here was located by Max Förster. It is a translation of the Rule of Canons by Bishop Chrodegang of Metz, containing an additional section in chapter two. This section explains, with the help of examples, how the religious in monasteries should be addressed with titles. All the names mentioned in the examples are to be found in a list of the monks at the Old Minster, Winchester, dating from the time of Æthelwold's successor. Particularly interesting for us, however, is the fact that among them there is mention of a *Wulfstan cantor*; this can only be that same Wulfstan of Winchester who was a pupil of Æthelwold's and who has been referred to above. There can be little doubt that the translation of Chrodegang's Rule was carried out at the Old Minster in Winchester, and this is of importance to us for its vocabulary is fairly close to that of the three texts, or groups of texts, already mentioned.[2]

The fitting in of this last piece of evidence shows us where to look for the source of this standardized Old English vocabulary. We can also show that it was a specific and planned vocabulary, prevalent in one school and restricted to a certain area, and not just a modern trend in general usage. Even in Æthelwold's own translation of the Benedictine Rule we find divergences; however, this translation was doubtless carried out at an early stage of his career as a teacher in Winchester, and the vocabulary which we have been dealing with here probably only crystallized gradually within his school. This would explain why Æthelwold's usage in many respects seems rather 'modern' and often corresponds to that of the Winchester group or that of late West Saxon texts in general; he has, for example, *ælþeodig*, *cnapa* and *wuldorbeag* and he uses *leahtor*, not *unþeaw*, and *gylt* but never *scyld*, while out of seventeen Old English words for *superbia* and its relations fourteen belong to the *modig* family (*modigness*, *modig*, *modigian*). But the remaining three point back to earlier usage – *ofermettu* (twice) and *ofermod*.[3] Another example of a

[1] For text and introduction see Gneuss, *Hymnar und Hymnen*, esp. pp. 69–74 and 91–101.

[2] *The Old English Rule of Bishop Chrodegang and the Capitula of Bishop Theodulf*, ed. A. S. Napier, EETS o.s. 150 (London, 1916); Max Förster, 'Lokalisierung und Datierung der altenglischen Version der Chrodegang-Regel', *Sitzungsberichte der Bayer. Akademie der Wissenschaften, Phil.-hist. Abt.*, Jg. 1933, Schlussheft, pp. 7–8.

[3] See Schabram, *Superbia*, pp. 55–8. However, of the two instances of *ofermettu*, one does not translate *superbia* but *exaltatio* (Schröer's ed., 23.9) while the other occurs only in BM Cotton Faustina A. x, in a chapter which is not part of the actual Rule (Schröer, 138.30).

less 'modern' expression is *mægen*, 'virtue', whereas *miht* is not used in this sense. Also Æthelwold has not yet settled on a translation word for *discipulus*: he tries six different ones, none of which occurs more than three times. Furthermore, whereas the Winchester group prefers *sunu*, he uses almost exclusively *bearn*.[1] The Old English Benedictine Rule thus clearly represents an intermediate, but rather advanced, stage between an older, partly unsettled usage and that of the Winchester group. There is another manuscript which seems to hold a similar position in the development of vocabulary usage; this is BM Royal 2. B. v, a Latin psalter with an Old English interlinear gloss, written about the middle of the tenth century, perhaps at the New Minster, Winchester, or at the Nunnaminster. The Regius Psalter, as it was called by its editor,[2] shows some striking correspondences with the 'modern' vocabulary of the Old English Benedictine Rule and with the Winchester group; it has *ælþeodig* once, *ælfremed* twice (besides *fremðe*) and *cnapa*; among the words it shares with other late West Saxon texts are *eornostlice*, *gedeorf*, *mese* and *scrudnian*, while the loan-word *chor* first appears in this psalter and the Old English Benedictine Rule. There are other close links between these two texts: they have *forbrytan*, whereas the Winchester group seems to prefer *tobrytan*; and they are the first Old English prose texts to employ *cantic*, while the Winchester group has *lofsang* (e.g. eleven times in the Lambeth Psalter as against only one *cantic*, in a double gloss together with *lofsang*). Wildhagen thought that the Regius gloss was the first fruit of the Benedictine reform, but this fact seems to be obscured by the considerable number of early West Saxon and Anglian words in this translation, which may – or may not – point back to an Anglian exemplar. A detailed investigation of the Regius gloss is badly needed; it might tell us more about its rôle in the history of Old English vocabulary.

What seems particularly important for our argument is the fact that even those contemporaries of Ælfric who otherwise kept to Standard Old English felt themselves at liberty, in their choice of words, to follow their own inclinations or other models. This is the case with Wulfstan, archbishop of York and bishop of Worcester, who corresponded with Ælfric and yet used a vocabulary which was not that of Æthelwold's school. Other cases in point are the widely read first English prose translation of the gospels, dating from

---

[1] There will be a much fuller treatment of the vocabulary of the Old English Benedictine Rule in the forthcoming thesis by M. Gretsch. It is interesting to note that the 'Account of King Edgar's Establishment of Monasteries' (see above, p. 74 and n. 1) holds about the same place as the Old English Rule in the development of word usage.

[2] *Der altenglische Regius-Psalter*, ed. Fritz Roeder, Studien zur englischen Philologie 18 (Halle, 1904). See also Karl Wildhagen, 'Studien zum Psalterium Romanum in England und zu seinen Glossierungen', *Festschrift für Lorenz Morsbach*, ed. F. Holthausen and H. Spies, Studien zur englischen Philologie 50 (Halle, 1913), pp. 448–53; C. and K. Sisam, *The Salisbury Psalter*, pp. 52–6; and Ker, *Catalogue*, no. 249.

the turn of the tenth century,[1] and the interlinear glosses to the *Regularis Concordia*, to the Rule of St Benedict, to the Canterbury hymnal (Durham, Cathedral Library, B. III. 32) and to Defensor's *Liber Scintillarum*. Thus Wulfstan uses *ofermodigness*, *ofermettu* and *pryte*, instead of *modigness* in the Winchester group; he has *unþeaw* besides *leahtor*, employs *cyrice* (and *for-bærnan*) and does not have *gylt*. Similarly the West Saxon Gospels have *weofod* as well as *altare*; they have *cyrice* and *geferræden*, but not *gelaðung*; *afeormian* is rare, but *clænsian* (*geclænsian*, *aclænsian*) is frequent; *fremed* appears side by side with *ælfremed* and *elðeodisc*; and the words for the *superbia* field are *ofermod* and *ofermodigness*.

The present unsatisfactory state of Old English lexicography[2] does not yet permit us to draw up a more or less complete list of genuine 'Winchester' words. The main problem we are facing is that a considerable number of characteristic late West Saxon words are widely used in many texts of the period including those of the Winchester group. They are expressions like *angsum*, 'narrow, anxious' (and *angsumnys*); *behreowsung*, 'penitence'; *bepæcan*, 'deceive'; *besargian*, 'lament'; *eornostlice*, 'ergo'; *gedeorf*, 'labour'; *heordræden*, 'custody, care'; *mærsian*, 'praise'; *mese*, 'table'; *scrudnian*, 'to examine, consider'; *teart* or *teartlic*, 'sharp, severe'; *þæslic*, 'suitable'; and *wæfels*, 'dress, cloak'. How are we to draw a line between these words and the 'Winchester' words defined above? Similarly most of the Winchester words also occur elsewhere, more or less frequently, in late Old English texts, for example in glossaries, in interlinear glosses, in Wulfstan's genuine works etc. In view of this overlapping of usages it might seem somewhat hazardous to try to establish something like our Winchester group. But there are some fairly reliable criteria which we can apply when utilizing and interpreting studies like those mentioned above,[3] namely the consistency with which a particular expression is employed in certain texts, the fact that these texts share quite a number of words consistently used, the fact that they avoid certain other synonymous words and the fact that they use some very rare words, which occur only or mainly in their group.

Finally, convincing evidence for the existence – and significance – of the group or school here postulated can be found in the revision of Bishop Werferth's translation of Gregory's *Dialogues*, preserved in Oxford, Bodleian Library, Hatton 76. The text of this manuscript, written in the first half of the eleventh century, differs considerably in the use of individual words from that of the two other copies still extant, which, although approximately

[1] A recent attempt to see in the West Saxon Gospels a product of the Alfredian movement which in turn goes back to an Anglian gloss has not convinced me: M. Grünberg, *The West-Saxon Gospels: a Study of the Gospel of St Matthew with Text of the Four Gospels* (Amsterdam, 1967), pp. 366–71.

[2] Cf., e.g., Hans Schabram, *Anglia* 84 (1966), 83–8.   [3] P. 75 and n. 4.

contemporary with the Hatton manuscript, offer the original text. The correspondences between the vocabulary of the Winchester group and that of the Hatton manuscript of Gregory's *Dialogues* are so close and remarkable that, more than sixty years ago, Hans Hecht did not hesitate to call the reviser of Werferth's work a member of Æthelwold's school.[1]

Everything therefore seems to point to the conclusion that the school at Winchester, represented by the texts mentioned above, was marked by a decided concern for language and style. But what about other centres which could possibly have been active in spreading a literary language after the Benedictine reform? When we survey the entire organization of the church in England there seem to be only two other possible candidates – the monastic cathedrals of Canterbury and Worcester, the seats of Dunstan and Oswald. We can eliminate Worcester for various reasons, but principally because it was situated in the dialect region of Mercia. Important points in favour of Canterbury would seem to be the personality of Dunstan, who was a brilliant organizer and scholar, and, as has been mentioned above, the fact that the primate of the English church had his residence there. But as in the case of Worcester, differences between the dialects make it almost impossible for us to assume that Canterbury was the cradle of the Old English literary language. Kentish had phonological characteristics which in Canterbury, even in the eleventh century – as can be seen from the manuscripts written there – were not always successfully suppressed in favour of the standard language imported from the West Saxon region, at least in spelling; Canterbury may even have had certain features of vocabulary peculiar to itself, which will have to be examined more closely.[2]

It is obvious that what I have said so far about the Winchester origin of Standard Old English is, and may remain, a hypothesis. Above all I am well aware that far more work will have to be done on various aspects of the problem, and that some details of what I have said about the use of individual words may have to be modified in the light of future research and of new dictionaries, concordances, special glossaries and editions of Old English texts as yet unpublished. But more evidence for deliberate standardization may also be forthcoming. Why, for example, should most Old English scribes (from the tenth century onwards) carefully observe the distinction

---

[1] 'entsprechend dem Sprachgebrauch der Schule Æthelwolds, der er angehört, ersetzt er eine sehr beträchtliche Anzahl von Wörtern des älteren Textes durch andere . . .', *Bischof Wærferths von Worcester Übersetzung der Dialoge Gregors des Grossen*, Bibl. d. ags. Prosa 5 (Leipzig und Hamburg, 1900–7) II, 131. See also Hecht's 'Wortlisten' II, 136–70, and Günther Scherer, 'Zur Geographie und Chronologie des angelsächsischen Wortschatzes im Anschluss an Bischof Waerferth's Übersetzung der Dialoge Gregors' (Ph.D. thesis, Berlin, 1928); and cf. Schabram, *Superbia*, p. 44, n. 41.

[2] For some notes on the vocabulary of the Old English glosses in the Canterbury hymnal (Durham, Cathedral Library, B. III. 32) see Gneuss, *Hymnar und Hymnen*, pp. 188–9.

between two types of script – one for Old English and one for Latin – although one set of letter forms would have been quite enough (as is shown by earlier Old English and by Middle English manuscripts)?[1] Possible standardization in late Old English syntactic usage will have to be investigated also.[2] The fact that some normative features of the language – spelling and inflexion – seem to be followed by authors and scribes all over the country, whereas other features, such as the vocabulary, were not, need not invalidate our hypothesis. It is well known that dialectal and individual word usage differs within languages that are spelt everywhere and by everybody according to strict rules. It may, of course, seem somewhat rash to attribute the spread of Standard Old English to one monastic school merely on account of that school's demonstrable interest in the vocabulary, but, in view of what we now know about the complexity of the dialectal structure of a language, we are forced to assume that some kind of spiritual and intellectual centre was responsible, and no other institution seems to have a better claim than the Old Minster at Winchester.

Let us review our findings briefly. In the eleventh century there was a widespread diffusion in all parts of England of a standard literary language, which must have developed from a West Saxon basis. We cannot prove, nor does it seem likely, that its beginnings were earlier than the Benedictine reform. On the contrary, Mercian or, as some have thought, a Mercian–Kentish church language[3] seems to have had – at least up to the end of the ninth century – quite as good a prospect of becoming the standard written language of England. The Benedictine reform paved the way for the process of language unification. Two hubs of the reform – Canterbury and Worcester – can be eliminated as the original centres of diffusion for the gradually emerging literary language. In Winchester, on the other hand, an entire school is engaged in what one might term the study of language. Here they translate from Latin and try even to regulate the use of vocabulary. Here, then, could be the starting-point for the systematic diffusion of the new standard. Many factors may have contributed to this, notable among them the key position which Winchester enjoyed within the English church, the royal chancellery, if there was one at this time,[4] the comparatively large

---

[1] Cf. Ker, *Catalogue*, pp. xxv–xxvii.

[2] Many of Ælfric's emendations referred to above, p. 75, n. 3, regularize syntax.

[3] Karl Wildhagen, who coined this term ('Studien zum Psalterium Romanum in England', p. 437), seems to have been thinking of a kind of *Mischsprache*, but see A. Campbell, *The Vespasian Psalter*, EEMF 14, pp. 82–3. For the importance of Mercian as a pre-Alfredian 'literary dialect' see *The Life of St Chad*, ed. R. Vleeskruyer (Amsterdam, 1953), pp. 39–62.

[4] Pierre Chaplais has shown that before the time of Edward the Confessor, no central royal secretariat seems to have been in existence in England. His findings about the production of charters in Anglo-Saxon England strengthen the case for a monastic, or at least ecclesiastical origin of Standard Old English. Cf. P. Chaplais, 'The Origin and Authenticity of the Royal

number of reformed monasteries on West Saxon territory and the popularity of Ælfric's writings. But it seems inconceivable that the late Old English standard language could have had such a success without having been consciously regulated and cultivated: the source of this cultivation and care may well have been Æthelwold and his circle in Winchester – England's first English philologists.[1]

Anglo-Saxon Diploma', *Jnl of the Soc. of Archivists* III, no. 2 (1965), 48–61, and 'The Anglo-Saxon Chancery: from the Diploma to the Writ', *ibid.* III, no. 4 (1966), 160–76. I owe the knowledge of these papers to Mr Peter Hunter Blair. For earlier views on the question of an Anglo-Saxon secretariat, see R. Drögereit, 'Gab es eine angelsächsische Königskanzlei?', *Archiv für Urkundenforschung* 13 (1935), esp. 335–41 and 418, and Dorothy Whitelock, *EHD*, p. 345. For the rôle played by the Abingdon and Winchester scriptoria in the development of handwriting in tenth-century England, see now T. A. M. Bishop, *English Caroline Minuscule* (Oxford, 1971), pp. xxi–xxii.

[1] This paper was first delivered in 1966 as an *Antrittsvorlesung* in the University of Munich. It was subsequently revised in the light of recent work dealing with the vocabulary of Old English. In the summer of 1970, when I held a Visiting Fellowship at Emmanuel College, Cambridge, I was given the opportunity to present the revision to expert audiences in the Universities of Cambridge and London, and the version here printed owes a number of valuable suggestions to colleagues in these universities, in particular to Professor Peter Clemoes.

Three Latin poems from Æthelwold's school at Winchester

MICHAEL LAPIDGE

I present here an edition of three Anglo-Latin poems from a Cambridge University Library manuscript, Kk.5.34, 71r–80r.[1] In addition to these three poems the manuscript contains important recensions of the *Aetna*, the *Culex*, Ausonius's *Technopaegnion* and the late Latin *Carmen de ponderibus*. These recensions have occupied the interest of previous editors and almost no attention has been given to the Anglo-Latin poems. These Anglo-Latin poems are nevertheless of considerable interest to the study of Anglo Latinity and of medieval Latin in general. I have named them the *Altercatio magistri et discipuli*, the *Responsio discipuli* and the *Carmen de libero arbitrio*[2] respectively, for reasons which will become clear in the following discussion.

THE STYLE AND COMPOSITION OF THE POEMS

I shall postpone discussion of the manuscript for the present, because I believe that evidence in the Anglo-Latin poems themselves is decisive in dating it and indicating its probable place of origin. Nothing has been written about these three poems. The Cambridge University Library catalogue suggests that they are eighth-century, for the perfectly incredible reason that 'the eighth century, according to Mr Wright, produced most of the Anglo-Latin poets'. H. A. J. Munro, in attempting to date the manuscript in the preface to his *Aetna*,[3] reports the opinion of Henry Bradshaw that the poem (edited here below as the *Altercatio*) with the rubric *uersus .L. de quodam superbo* is by Lantfridus, a disciple of Æthelwold at Winchester in the late tenth century. (Munro, by the way, doubts this report and argues that the manuscript is earlier.) How Bradshaw arrived at what seems such a remarkable piece of divination is not clear, and his posthumously collected papers contain no further thoughts on the subject.

[1] I should like to acknowledge the kindness of Peter Dronke and Alistair Campbell, who read this article in typescript and made numerous valuable suggestions.
[2] This poem is listed in H. Walther, *Initia Carminum ac Versuum Medii Aevi Posterioris Latinorum* (Göttingen, 1959), no. 3883. For some reason the other two poems (which are listed on the same page of the Cambridge University Library catalogue) are omitted by Walther.
[3] *Aetna*, ed. H. A. J. Munro (Cambridge, 1867), p. 29.

Internal evidence is sufficient to establish that the poems are indeed Anglo-Latin (see *Altercatio* 23 and *de libero arbitrio* 179). One must first examine their Latinity within the larger context of Anglo-Latinity. (By 'Anglo-Latin' I understand literature written in England in Latin before the Norman Conquest.) The Oxford scholar, Professor Alistair Campbell, has done more for the study of Anglo-Latin than anyone,[1] but much work remains. There are numerous poems in manuscript still unpublished. No study has been published on the style or grammar of Anglo-Latin poetry in general. Campbell has observed, however, that there are two broad traditions of Anglo-Latinity: the one called hermeneutic and having its principal proponent in Aldhelm; the other, the classical, having its principal proponent in Bede.[2] Since it will be seen at once that the three poems printed here, in their predilection for bizarre and Greek vocabulary, belong to the so-called hermeneutic tradition, I shall consider them together with poetry which belongs to this tradition: the poems of Aldhelm, Æthelwulf's *de abbatibus* (written between 803 and 821), Frithegodus's *Breuiloquium vitae Wilfredi* (written *c.* 950), and Wulfstan the Cantor's *Narratio de S. Swithuno* (written between 992 and 994). The following features are of interest; I do not pretend that they are exclusive to Anglo-Latin but rather that they are found in more intensive concentration there than elsewhere:[3]

1. The use of distributive numerals and multiplicative circumlocutions.[4] This is a poetic device invented by classical poets to meet the problem that numbers such as *duodecim* and *quattuordecim* would not scan.[5] It is a device used with restraint by classical poets but exaggerated and abused by Aldhelm and later Anglo-Latin poets. Frithegodus in particular enjoys stuffing his hexameters with such numerals, e.g. 'quis duoquindecies denos pariter quoque quinos' (1212) and 'octonis etenim bis forte quaterque uigenis' (1240); cf. *Altercatio* 100–4.

2. The abuse of *ast*. In archaic Latin *ast* meant 'if' and was generally used in simple protases. Horace, it seems, first used *ast* to mean *at* (*epod.* 15.24, *serm.* 1.6.125 etc.) in positions where a long syllable was required and *at* would not meet this metrical requirement.[6] This usage was followed by Vergil and hence was

---

[1] For example, his editions of *Frithegodi monachi Breuiloquium vitae beati Wilfredi et Wulfstani cantoris Narratio metrica de sancto Swithuno*, Thesaurus Mundi 1 (Zürich, 1950); *Chronicon Æthelweardi* (London, 1962) and *Æthelwulf, de abbatibus* (Oxford, 1967); also his paper entitled 'Some Linguistic Features of Early Anglo-Latin Verse and its use of Classical Models', *TPS* (1953), pp. 1–20.

[2] *Chronicon Æthelweardi*, p. xlv; 'Linguistic Features of Early Anglo-Latin Verse', p. 11.

[3] Nor is the following list meant to be exhaustive. Campbell has drawn my attention, for example, to the use of the abl. sg. of the gerund (with -ō) as a participle-equivalent in Anglo-Latin poetry. I have been directly concerned with features well attested in the poems printed here.

[4] See B. Löfstedt, 'Zum Gebrauch der lateinischen distributiven Zahlwörter', *Eranos* 56 (1958), 71–117 and 188–223. Löfstedt's treatment of medieval Latin prose (pp. 87–9) is excellent; it is perhaps regrettable that he considers medieval Latin poetry only briefly (p. 95).

[5] B. Axelson, *Unpoetische Wörter* (Lund, 1945), p. 96.

[6] See A. Klotz, *Hermes* 61 (1926), 33–4 and F. Skutsch, *Kleine Schriften* (Leipzig, 1914), p. 160, n. 1.

widely used in late Latin (by Juvencus for example). Anglo-Latin poets in turn adopt this practice but carry it to absurd extremes: *ast* meaning *at* occurs more frequently in Æthelwulf's *de abbatibus* (a poem of some 800 lines) than in the entire *Aeneid*. It is also used frequently in the post-positive position by Anglo-Latin poets, a practice for which there are few antecedents (excepting Valerius Flaccus 5.548, 6.197 and 8.255). So often is it used that its meaning becomes blurred; consider *Altercatio* 5–6, where *ast* must mean 'and' or 'or':

> scammate si regem pauidus quoque damma leonem
> prouocet ast aquilam si parua columba cruentam . . .

See the note to this passage (line 6), below, p. 108.

3. The use of compound adjectives terminating in *-dicus, -loquus* or *-loquax*, such as *ueridicus, falsidicus, ueriloquus, falsiloquus, sanctiloquus, blandiloquus, stultiloquus, multi-loquus* and *stultiloquax*. Examples of these words in Anglo-Latin poetry are too numerous to be conveniently listed here.

4. The extreme tendency to use nouns in *-amen*[1] declined in the ablative singular or accusative plural to fill the requirement of the dactyl in the fifth foot of a hexameter. Only two classical poets exhibit a tendency to coin words for this purpose: Lucretius and Ovid. In Lucretius we find four such words in the fifth foot: *conamina* (6.1041), *frustraminis* (4.817) followed by a vowel, *lateramina* (6.233) and *vexamine* (5.340). But it was Ovid who first used this device on a large scale. Ovid very frequently closes hexameters with *-amina* or *-amine* in the fifth foot; the most remarkable instances are *respiramina* (*Met.* 2.828), *renovamine* (*Met.* 8.729), *caelamina* (*Met.* 13.291), *curvamine* (*Met.* 2.130, 3.66, 3.672, 6.64, 8.194, 9.450, 11.590 and 12.95), *firmamina* (*Met.* 10.491), *simulamina* (*Met.* 10.727), *imitamina* (*Met.* 4.445 and 15.200 and *Fast.* 4.211), *irritamina* (*Met.* 12.103), *oblectamina* (*Met.* 9.342 and 11.412), *piamina* (*Fast.* 2.19 and 3.333) and *hortamine* (*Met.* 1.277). Other Latin poets studiously avoided this tendency, and the line of Vergil's *Aeneid*, 'nauticus exoritur vario certamine clamor' (3.128), has few fellows in that poem. But the tendency is widespread in Anglo-Latin poetry. One is inclined to suspect that the Anglo-Latin poets learned this device from their study of Ovid. The tendency is already widely attested in Aldhelm,[2] who frequently fills the fourth and fifth feet of his hexameters in the *Carmen de virginitate* with nouns such as *certamine* (140, 197, 276, 870, 1258, 1548, 1552 and 2486), *fundamina* (3, 1385 and 2657), *vibramine* (27 and 216), *modul-amine* (69 and 831), *conamine* (89), *generamina* (143), *velamine* (211, 237, 628, 1146, 1515 and 2557), *praesagmina* (304), *spiramine* (396), *fragmine* (864 and 1758), *medic-amine* (1090), *ligamina* (1213), *peccamina* (1317), *oramina* (1348, 1536 and 2872) and *solamina* (2517). Nor does this list include the frequent and tiring cadences in more common words such as *flamine, famine, gramine* etc. Subsequent Anglo-Latin poets

---

[1] The only study of such nouns is by E. Norden, *Ennius und Vergilius* (Leipzig, 1915), pp. 27–9. Norden is concerned with the use of nouns in *-amen* as against those in *-mentum* and does not study the use of terminations in *-amine* in dactylic feet.

[2] Bede's *Vita Cuthberti* (ed. W. Jaager, Palaestra 198 (Leipzig, 1935)) is distinctly Anglo-Latin in this respect. Bede closes his hexameters with *solamine* (161, 465 and 760), *medicamine* (157 and 906), *fundamina* (34 and 459), *luctamine* (48), *examine* (98), *tutamine* (135), *fragmina* (197), *iuvamine* (264), *precamina* (340) and *modulamine* (798).

energetically pursue the course set by Ovid and Aldhelm. In addition to the nouns used by Aldhelm, Frithegodus fills the fifth feet of his hexameters with *luctamine* (405), *tutamine* (704), *rogitamine* (419), *frustramine* (1111), *oculamina* (1072), *miseramina* (1011), *iuuamina* (583), *gestamine* (1234), *fraglamine* (1241), *moderamine* (476), *hortamine* (308) and *examine* (173). By far the worst offender in this respect is Wulfstan who, in addition to all those nouns used by Aldhelm and Frithegodus, uses *meditamine* (1.96, 282 and 384), *lustramine* (1.622 and 1035 and 2.351), *uocitamine* (1.1227), *vegetamine* (1.1403), *sinuamine* (2.292 and 1133) and *decoramine* (2.955). In fact the cadence of hexameters in *-amine* (and in *medicamine* in particular) in Wulfstan makes plainly tedious reading. For some reason, Æthelwulf is entirely free of this vice, but for one occurrence of a cadence in *solamina* (200). The poems edited below reflect this English technique to some degree: the *Altercatio* has *uocitamine* (108) and the *de libero arbitrio*, *conamine* (171).

5. The use of the archaic passive present infinitive ending in *-ier*, invariably in the fifth dactylic foot of a hexameter and invariably followed by a word beginning with a vowel. The reason for this is simple. If the correct form (ending in *-i*) were used, the resulting elision would destroy the metre. This device was used sparingly by classical Latin poets, in particular by Lucretius,[1] Catullus, Vergil and Horace. A fairly complete list of this form in classical Latin poetry is found in Kühner–Holzweissig;[2] this list, however, does not extend beyond the fourth century and the incompleteness of the list has misled subsequent scholarship.[3] In fact the use of *-ier* endings of the passive present infinitive is found often in late Latin poetry (e.g. *de providentia divina* 45: *popularier*). But nowhere to my knowledge is this poetic helpmeet used as frequently as by Anglo-Latin poets.[4] The practice was established by both Bede and Aldhelm. Bede's *Vita Cuthberti* has *tutarier* (147), *benedicier* (231), *munirier* (376), *famularier* (451), *condier* (524), *cogier* (605), *plectier* (606), *firmarier* (630) and *pulsarier* (684). Aldhelm's *Carmen de virginitate* has *venerarier* (371), *famularier* (549, 759, 945 and 2072), *effarier* (1746), *adsciscier* (1785) and *conversarier* (2053). There is one instance of this form in Æthelwulf, *inmergier* (164); several in Frithegodus, *famularier* (57), *uescier* (128), *scrutarier* (174) and *sternier* (220); and one in Wulfstan, *deducier* (1.645). The *Altercatio* has *profiterier* (27).

6. The use of *necne* for *necnon*.[5] The synonymy of these two words is not commonly

---

[1] C. Bailey (*T. Lucreti Cari de rerum natura* (Oxford, 1947) 1, 84) observes that there are forty-eight occurrences of the *-ier* form in Lucretius as against 468 occurrences of the normal *-i* form.

[2] Kühner-Holzweissig, *Ausführliche Grammatik der lateinischen Sprache* 1, 691–3. Of classical poets the list omits Varro Atacinus, *torquerier* (*Fragmenta Poetarum Latinorum*, ed. W. Morel, p. 97) and Julius Montanus, *spargier* (*FPL*, p. 120).

[3] E.g. A. S. Pease (*P. Vergili Maronis Aeneidos Liber Quartus* (Cambridge, Mass., 1935), p. 407 *ad* 4.493), who observes that this form is 'apparently disappearing only after Ausonius'.

[4] I do not argue that this poetic helpmeet was used in the Middle Ages exclusively by Anglo-Latin poets; the *Ecbasis Captivi* once has *scrutarier* (735) and Radbod once *perflarier* (Monumenta Germaniae Historica, Poetae 4, 169), to choose two random examples from approximately contemporary poetry.

[5] On this question see D. Norberg, *Beiträge zur spätlateinischen Syntax* (Uppsala, 1944), p. 115. Norberg gives a few examples from early medieval Latin prose as well as three examples from Carolingian poetry. He is concerned with demonstrating that confusions such as *necne* for *necnon* arose in a period when Latin was no longer a living language. For the Anglo-Latin poets at least there was no confusion: *necnon* was used when a long, *necne* when a short syllable was needed.

found, and although it occurs quite often in the Anglo-Latin prose of Lantfridus of Winchester[1] it is most frequently found in poetry, invariably in those positions where the long syllable of *necnon* would have been metrically intolerable. For example, Frithegodus writes 'indulgent proceres, magnates, necne calones' (332) and Wulfstan 'te cherubin laudant, seraphin tibi necne resultant' (1.988; see also 1.942, 2.10 and 227 *et passim*). The Anglo-Latin poems presented here use *necne* in this way: see for example *Altercatio* 18, *Responsio* 3 and 34 and *de libero arbitrio* 119.

It will be seen that each of these features is in some way a device to facilitate the writing of quantitative verse; they are devices employed in large measure by poets to whom Latin versification did not come easily. In the absence of a detailed study of Anglo-Latin poetic technique, these impressions are enough to demonstrate that the three poems edited here pertain evidently to an Anglo-Latin poetic tradition that spans three centuries, but are not enough to date or localize them within this tradition.

A step towards this objective may be taken by considering certain internal evidence in the poems. First, the extremely rare phrase *caelica Tempe* which occurs in two of the poems printed here. To my knowledge there are only four occurrences of this phrase: in Frithegodus's *Breuiloquium* 980, in Lantfridus's *Translatio et miracula S. Swithuni* c. 51,[2] in *Altercatio* 45 and in *de libero arbitrio* 53. The rarity of this phrase may therefore draw attention to the tenth century, and more specifically to either Winchester (Lantfridus) or Canterbury (Frithegodus). A further piece of internal evidence is even more telling. Wulfstan in his *Narratio de S. Swithuno* is at one point in book 1 discussing the miracles effected by the remains of St Swithhun when he suddenly and for no apparent reason adopts a personal tone: 'if you had been there, you would have seen the sick healed' ('si praesens stares, aegros remanere uideres', 1.1103). He then proceeds to refute an imaginary and doubting interlocutor with this direct outburst:

> inuida qua propter resecandaque lingua sileto,
> et reticendo tuum iam foedum claude labellum;
> conticeant reprobi peruerso corde maligni . . . (1.1104–6)

This outburst is identical in spirit and diction to one in the *Altercatio*. There the student interrupts the master's eloquent warning with 'conquinisce, precor; foedum iam claude labellum' 68. That there is some connection

---

[1] *Translatio et miracula S. Swithuni*, ed. E. P. Sauvage, *AB* 4 (1885), 367–410. For the interchange of *necne* and *necnon* see e.g. pp. 375.18, 382.21, 385.14, 388.15, 391.15, 392.20 and 393.25.

[2] *Ibid.* p. 406.30. The possibility that this phrase was expanded from Aldhelm's 'sed manet in tempis paradisi hactenus heros' (*Carm. de virg.* 272) is remote. Instead see my note to *Altercatio* 45, below, p. 114.

between these two virtually identical lines is undeniable. And it is virtually certain that it was the *Altercatio* which inspired the *Narratio*, not *vice versa*. For such an outburst of indignant rebuke is in the *Narratio* a strange and isolated phenomenon; it is the very essence of the *Altercatio*. From this it may be concluded that Wulfstan knew the *Altercatio* when he composed his *Narratio*. Since this work was written between 992 and 994, we have a *terminus ante quem* for the composition of the *Altercatio*. Furthermore, since Wulfstan was the precentor at Winchester, may it not be surmised that it is most likely that he gained his knowledge of the *Altercatio* there? He may have known the *de libero arbitrio* as well. One of the opening dedicatory lines of the *Narratio de S. Swithuno* mentions the church of St Peter at Winchester: 'basilica Petri, reserat qui limen Olimpi'. The *de libero arbitrio* too speaks of St Peter as 'clauibus inmensi reserat qui limen Olimphi' 163. But this phrase has the air of a cliché and may be a commonly known expansion of Aldhelm's cadence *limen Olimpi (Carm. de virg.* 1307). In any case attention is once again drawn to late-tenth-century Winchester.

These associations may be confirmed by consideration of the closing lines of the *de libero arbitrio*, which are addressed to a certain unnamed *praesul*. This *praesul* is praised as follows:

> pontificemque pium meritis et honore colendum
>   insignemque humilem protege, Christe, libens,
> quem deus omnipotens cathedra subuexit in alta,
>   dogmate mellifluo uerteret ut scelera.
> gentes Anglorum felices praesule tanto
>   ritus qui prauos corrigit ut genitor,
> extorres superuenientes uosque beati:
>   cunctis his tribuit quicquid opus fuerit.
> quis numerare queat bona nobis quae bonus ille
>   contulit hanc postquam uenimus ad patriam? (175–84)

There are several salient features here which may serve to identify this *praesul*: that he was a bishop and a highly esteemed teacher, that he corrected the corrupt practices of the church and that he welcomed foreigners from abroad. I suggest that the bishop in question is none other than Æthelwold, who became bishop of Winchester in 963.

Æthelwold must by any reckoning be regarded as one of the outstanding men of the later Anglo-Saxon period. That he was a pre-eminent teacher could scarcely be disputed; indeed much of the credit for the intellectual revival of the tenth century in England must go to him. Ælfric gives us a clear picture of Æthelwold's stern invigilation of literary studies at Winchester: 'circuitque Atheluuoldus singula monasteria, mores instituens, obedientes admonendo et stultos verberibus corrigendo: erat terribilis ut leo

inobedientibus seu discolis, mitibus vero et humilibus mitior columba'.[1]
Wulfstan notes in praising Æthelwold that he first *did* before he taught:

> Adeluuoldus uenerabilis heros
> inculcat precepta sagax, quae more paterno
> iam prius instituit, nobis rituque magistro
> obseruanda dedit. . . (*Narratio de S. Swithuno* 1.1306–9)

It is noteworthy that the *de libero arbitrio* makes the identical observation concerning its *praesul*: 'dogmate quodque mones claris prius actibus imples' 63. Æthelwold's own literary activities were very considerable: he almost certainly wrote the *Regularis Concordia*;[2] he translated the Benedictine Rule into English;[3] he wrote an account in English of the revival of the monasteries.[4] As Professor Helmut Gneuss shows elsewhere in this periodical, Æthelwold's interest in English usage was a principal reason for the establishment of what might be called standard literary Old English in England at this time.[5] But the most incontestable proof of Æthelwold's intellectual activity and excellence is to be seen in the work of his two most eminent disciples: Ælfric and Wulfstan the Cantor.[6] It is to the great period of literary enthusiasm under the patronage of Æthelwold that the poems edited here belong.[7]

[1] Ælfric's *Life of Æthelwold* is found in *Chronicon Monasterii de Abingdon*, ed. J. Stevenson, Rolls Series (1858) II, 255–66; the excerpt quoted is found on pp. 262–3; cf. also 'quam benignus extitit erga studiosos . . . .' (p. 265).

[2] See Ælfric's letter to the monks of Eynsham, ed. M. Bateson, *Compotus Rolls of the Obedientiaries of St Swithun's Priory, Winchester*, ed. G. W. Kitchin (Hampshire Record Society, 1892), p. 175: 'liber consuetudinum quem sanctus atheluuoldus uuintoniensis episcopus cum coepiscopis et abbatibus . . . undique collegit ac monachis instituit obseruandum'.

[3] Ptd A. Schröer, *Die angelsächsischen Prosabearbeitung der Benedictinerregel* (Kassel, 1888; repr. with contr. by H. Gneuss, Darmstadt, 1964).

[4] This piece is printed in O. Cockayne, *Leechdoms, Wortcunning and Starcraft*, RS (1866) III, 432–44. That this piece is incontestably by Æthelwold has been demonstrated recently by Professor D. Whitelock, 'The Authorship of the Account of King Edgar's Establishment of the Monasteries', *Philological Essays: Studies in Old and Middle English Language and Literature in Honour of Herbert Dean Meritt*, ed. J. L. Rosier (The Hague, 1970), pp. 125–36.

[5] The reader may conveniently be directed to the evidence and bibliographical information pertaining to Æthelwold's literary activity which Professor Gneuss has assembled. See above, pp. 73–4.

[6] The works of Ælfric are well known, but those of Wulfstan deserve to be collected and studied. There is the *Narratio de S. Swithuno*. There are the three poems to Winchester saints edited by C. Blume in the *Sitzungsberichte d. k. Akad. d. Wiss. in Wien* 146, 3 (Vienna, 1903), pp. 1 ff. Finally, it has been suggested that the *Vita Æthelwoldi* is not a late Norman copy of Ælfric's *Vita Æthelwoldi*, but may have antedated it and may have been its source; it is in all likelihood by Wulfstan (see D. J. V. Fisher, 'The Early Biographers of St Æthelwold', *EHR* 67 (1952), 381–91).

[7] One interesting piece of information: the *Altercatio* was drawn among other things from a bestiary (see lines 1–10); like much Anglo-Latin verse of the time it is charged with Greek words. It is remarkable then that Æthelwold sent to his foundation at Peterborough both a 'liber bestiarum' and a 'liber de litteris grecorum' (*Cartularium Saxonicum*, ed. W. de Gray Birch (London, 1885–99), no. 1128). Apparently Æthelwold considered that such books were essential to literary study; the *Altercatio* would seem to be the product of such study.

In the attempt to identify the prelate who 'corrects the depraved practices of the church like a father', 'ritus qui prauos corrigit ut genitor', no stronger candidate could be found than Æthelwold. In the opinion of some modern historians, Æthelwold was the principal motivating force in the thoroughgoing English monastic reform movement of the tenth century.[1] For Æthelwold had himself had much experience as a monk charged with the business of reform. He had been given charge of the ruined abbey of Abingdon in 954; under his direction Abingdon became one of the principal English abbeys. When elevated to the bishopric of Winchester in 963 he had straightway expelled all dissolute clerks from the Winchester abbeys and had replaced them with monks from Abingdon. As a man of business Æthelwold energetically sought endowments for his bishopric.[2] His energy is reflected in the list of English monasteries which he either founded or restored: Abingdon, the two Winchester abbeys, Peterborough, Ely, Thorney and Crowland, and also probably St Albans, Chertsey and St Neots. Under Æthelwold the reconstruction of the Old Minster at Winchester was undertaken on a magnificent scale; when standing, the Old Minster must have been the most impressive church in England.[3] The document which provided the pattern of the reformed English monasticism, the *Regularis Concordia*, was almost certainly written by Æthelwold. In short, the designation 'ritus qui prauos corrigit ut genitor' is highly appropriate to Æthelwold.

The *praesul* of the poem is said to have welcomed foreigners from abroad: 'extorres superuenientes'. Because the Benedictine practice in England was largely modelled on that of the continent, relations between England and the continent were particularly intimate at this period. Oda, archbishop of Canterbury (942–58), had been tonsured in Fleury in 936; Dunstan had been exiled briefly at Saint-Pierre-au-Mont-Blandin, Ghent, during Eadwig's

---

[1] In the traditional view, Æthelwold was seen as subordinate to Dunstan in this movement. See T. Symons, 'The English Monastic Reform of the Tenth Century', *Downside Review* 60 (1942), 1–22, 196–222 and 268–79; J. A. Robinson, *The Times of St Dunstan* (Oxford, 1923; repr. 1969), pp. 104–22; and D. Knowles, *The Monastic Order in England* (Cambridge, 1940; repr. 1963), pp. 39–42. This view has most recently been upheld by H. Dauphin, 'Le Renouveau Monastique en Angleterre au Xe Siècle et ses Rapports avec la Réforme de S. Gérard de Brogne', *RB* 70 (1960), 185–6. This traditional view has been challenged notably by E. John, 'The King and the Monks in the Tenth-Century Reformation', *Bull. of the John Rylands Lib.* 42 (1959–60), 61–87; *idem*, 'The Sources of the English Monastic Reformation', *RB* 70 (1960), 197–203; and M. Deanesly, *The Pre-Conquest Church in England*, 2nd ed. (London, 1963), pp. 304–5 and 312–16.

[2] See E. John, 'Some Latin Charters of the Tenth-Century Reformation in England', *RB* 70 (1960), 333–59, and especially F. Chaplais, 'The Origin and Authenticity of the Royal Anglo-Saxon Diploma', *Jnl of the Soc. of Archivists* 3, 2 (1965), 48–61.

[3] Some idea of what Winchester cathedral might have looked like may be gathered from R. N. Quirk's exhaustive examination of the extant written sources ('Winchester Cathedral in the Tenth Century', *ArchJ* 114 (1957), 28–68; see esp. pp. 29–30 concerning Æthelwold's accomplishments). More recently, excavation has been begun at Winchester (and is still under way) under the direction of M. Biddle. Since 1964 reports of this excavation have been published in *AntJ*, the most recent report being published in 1971.

reign; Oswald had been sent to Fleury by Oda his uncle and had spent several years there before returning to England in 959. Æthelwold in particular seems to have had close continental connections. He himself had wished to go to Fleury but had been prevented by royal intervention; he had later sent his disciple Osgar to Fleury.[1] Osgar returned to England in 963 to replace Æthelwold as abbot of Abingdon when Æthelwold was elevated to Winchester. Æthelwold imported monks from Corbie to teach his monks at Winchester the rules of psalmody and plain-chant.[2] Monks were imported from Ghent and Fleury to advise in the preparation of the *Regularis Concordia* at Winchester, as the proemium of that work tells us.[3] Lantfridus, who became Æthelwold's secretary at Winchester and who wrote the *Translatio et miracula S. Swithuni*, was from the continent.[4] There is, then, abundant evidence that Æthelwold welcomed foreigners at Winchester; I suggest that the author of the *de libero arbitrio* was one such: 'postquam uenimus ad patriam' 184.

Æthelwold became bishop of Winchester in 963; he died there in 984. Hence the identification of the *praesul* of the *de libero arbitrio* as Æthelwold carries with it the implication that the poem was written sometime between 963 and 984. Some earlier lines of the poem may possibly indicate that it was composed after 975. These lines contain another address to the *praesul*:

> praesul et insigni clarissime dignus honore,
>   uates clariuidens, doctor et egregie,
> augustam regi sedem qui corde parasti
>   expertem neui, criminis ac uitii,
> rex quia quem celsi nequeunt concludere caeli
>   mentibus in sanctis is manet ac nitidis. (57–62)

This passage is difficult, but perhaps not impossible. The renowned *praesul* is said to have 'prepared a mighty seat for the king with [his] heart free of blemish, sin and vice'. An ambiguous phrase, but one which would indicate that the prelate was responsible for the religious education of the king. It is likely that Æthelwold was tutor of King Edgar from 954 to 955; he certainly was from 955 to 957, the date at which Edgar was chosen as king by the Mercians.[5] The *de libero arbitrio* would seem to indicate also that the king

---

[1] Ælfric's *Life of Æthelwold*, ed. Stevenson II, 259: 'misit Osgarum monachum trans mare ad monasterium Sancti Benedicti Floriacense, ut mores regulares illic disceret'.   [2] *Ibid.* I, 129.
[3] *Regularis Concordia*, ed. T. Symons (London, 1953), p. 3.
[4] Ælfric calls him *se ofersæwisca* ('the foreigner'); *Ælfric's Lives of the Saints*, ed. W. W. Skeat, Early English Text Society o.s. 76, 82, 94 and 114 (London, 1881–1900), I, 466, line 402.
[5] Æthelwold is without doubt the 'certain abbot' whom the *Regularis Concordia* mentions in connection with King Edgar's religious education: 'attamen respectu diuino attactus, abbate quodam assiduo monente ac regiam catholicae fidei uiam demonstrante, coepit magnopere Deum timere, diligere ac uenerari' (*Regularis Concordia*, ed. Symons, p. 1). See D. Knowles, *The Monastic Order in England*, p. 40, n. 5 and E. John, 'The King and the Monks in the Tenth-Century Reformation', who rightly conjectures that the tutelage must have taken place at Abingdon.

was dead: 'the king, since the high heavens could not contain him, yet remains in our holy and shining minds'. Edgar died in 975. The obliquity of the reference precludes certainty here, but it may tentatively be suggested that the poem was composed between 975 and 984.

At this point a brief summary of the foregoing conclusions may be helpful. The *de libero arbitrio* was in all likelihood addressed to Æthelwold, bishop of Winchester 963–84. It may possibly have been composed after 975 (and certainly before 984), probably by a foreigner invited to Winchester by Æthelwold. The *Altercatio* was composed no later than 994, by which time it was known to one of Æthelwold's disciples at Winchester, Wulfstan. The *Responsio* was clearly written in conjunction with the *Altercatio*: both poems are addressed to the same 'Ioruert' and both contain a stock of common idioms. It may therefore be reasonably concluded that all three poems were composed at Winchester during the time of Æthelwold or, in the case of the *Altercatio* and *Responsio*, within the decade immediately after his death.

THE MANUSCRIPT

To review what is known of the manuscript:[1] the Cambridge University Library catalogue notes that it is written in 'a very early half-Saxon hand . . . which perhaps may be assigned to the ninth or tenth century'. Later scholarship has followed this tentative proposal without reserve. Baehrens alone among editors doubted the dating of ninth–tenth centuries and assigned the manuscript instead to the tenth–eleventh centuries.[2] There has been little attempt either to verify or to dispute the vague assignation made by the catalogue. Vollmer drew attention to two *probationes pennae* found on 111v:[3]

> Sæwine est frater noster et Byrtgyt soror nostra
> Sawin est frater noster. Sægyt soror nostra.

Sægyt is deleted by points and *Godguð* written above. Vollmer noted that the names are Anglo-Saxon (since they could be located in Searle's *Onomasticon Anglo-Saxonicum*) and that the name *Sæwine leuita* is found in the *Liber Vitae of Hyde Abbey*[4] in an entry which he thought to be of about the year 1000; on these grounds he suggested that the manuscript is perhaps of that date. That the names are Anglo-Saxon need not be disputed. The occurrence

---

[1] The manuscript is discussed by T. Öhler, *Rheinisches Museum für Philologie* n.s. 1 (1842), 135–6; H. A. J. Munro, *Aetna* (1867), p. 29; R. Peiper, *Fleckeisens Jahrbücher f. klass. Philologie, Suppl. bd.* 11 (1880), 283; E. Baehrens, *Poetae Latini Minores* (Leipzig, 1880) 11, 11; and R. Ellis, *Aetna* (1901), pp. vii, xii and liii–liv.

[2] 'C, Cantabrigiensis, saeculi X–XI (huic enim aetati ego attribuo) . . .' (*PLM* 11, 11).

[3] F. Vollmer, 'P. Virgili Maronis iuvenalis ludi libellus', *Sitzungsberichte d. k. Akad. d. Wiss. zu München* (Munich, 1908) 11, p. 34.

[4] *Liber Vitae: Register and Martyrology of New Minster and Hyde Abbey, Winchester*, ed. W. de Gray Birch (London, 1892).

of one name does not prove much by itself; a collocation of these names would be far more useful. Vollmer knew no Anglo-Saxon (he confuses the letter wynn with *p*, for example) and did not realize that Anglo-Saxon names might be spelled in a variety of ways. In fact the name *Godgyð* is found twice in the *Liber Vitae* (pp. 57 and 123), *Sægit* twice (pp. 53 and 137) and *Brytgyð* twice (pp. 30 and 64); in addition the names *Godgið* and *Birhtgyþ* are found together at the end of a list of Winchester devotees in various handwritings of the eleventh and twelfth centuries (p. 30). But in any case Vollmer's dating to the year 1000 is not to be trusted: he did not notice that the first layer of names in the *Liber Vitae* is *c.* 1020 and that *Saewine leuita* is added in a still later hand.[1] One further fact which was disregarded by Vollmer: the *probationes pennae* in our manuscript are not in the main hand but are in a (Norman) hand of *c.* 1120. In short, these *probationes pennae* may be of some help in discovering the provenance of the manuscript, but they are of no help in dating it.

The evidence which I have assembled above indicates that the three Anglo-Latin poems edited here were composed in Æthelwold's school at Winchester, at least one of them not before 963. If that is so, the manuscript in which these poems are found cannot be ninth–tenth century as the catalogue states and all recent editors assume; it must be no earlier than the late tenth century and perhaps even early eleventh, as Baehrens conjectured. Mr T. A. M. Bishop is of the opinion that it 'could have been written at Winchester or Hyde in the late tenth century'.[2] If this were the case, it is likely that the Anglo-Saxon names found in the *probationes pennae* on 111v in a hand of the early twelfth century are identical with those found in the *Liber Vitae* of Hyde Abbey, Winchester.

THE 'ALTERCATIO MAGISTRI ET DISCIPULI' AND THE 'RESPONSIO DISCIPULI'

Although there is no indication of speakers in the manuscript, it is evident that these two poems form one continuous dialogue. The poem which I have called *Altercatio magistri et discipuli* is a series of interchanges between a disgruntled student and a pompous teacher; since there is no indication in the manuscript, I have indicated changes of speaker by means of the rubrics *magister* and *discipulus* in my printed text. The poem I have called *Responsio*

---

[1] *Liber Vitae*, p. 35, line 8 (not line 6, as Vollmer reports).

[2] I am very grateful to Mr Bishop for re-examining this manuscript for me and for placing his knowledge of English manuscripts at my disposal. It is unfortunate that very few manuscripts in Winchester literary script (as distinct from (say) the script of the Winchester *Benedictional*) have survived; the best known surviving example is the manuscript of Bede's *Historia Ecclesiastica* at Winchester (see S. Potter, 'The Winchester Bede', *Wessex* 3, 2 (1935), 39–49 for a facsimile of one folio of this manuscript). The script of Kk.5.34 is strikingly similar to (but not identical with) that of the Winchester Bede.

discipuli would seem to be a statement by the student, and is patently a continuation of the heated debate that was the matter of the *Altercatio*.

It may be helpful to consider briefly the *Altercatio* and the *Responsio* against the background of medieval dialogue and debate literature. The dialogue was very common in classical literature – in Plato and Xenophon, in Varro and Cicero, in Tacitus, Plutarch and Lucian – and has been exhaustively studied by Rudolf Hirzel.[1] Hirzel's study of antiquity as well as his more cursory treatment of the Renaissance and the eighteenth century is exceedingly useful; but it is regrettable that he devoted no more than four pages out of a work of some thousand pages to the Middle Ages. For it was during the Middle Ages that the classical dialogue form was adapted and expanded to embrace countless varieties of form: historical and literary, poetic and prose, didactic and bellelettristic. Already during late antiquity the dialogue was used by Christian writers as a framework within which to expound Christian doctrine: Justin Martyr's *Dialogus cum Tryphone Judaeo*,[2] Minucius Felix's *Octavius* and Evagrius's *Altercatio Simonis Iudaei et Theophili Christiani*[3] are the most noteworthy examples of this intention.[4] Later Christian authors use the dialogue to frame biographical accounts of outstanding Christians; for example, Sulpicius Severus (*Dialogus* concerning St Martin of Tours), Cassian (the *Collationes*), Gregory the Great (*Dialogi sanctorum*) and Palladius Helenopolitanus (*Dialogus de vita S. Chrysostomi*).[5] In the early Middle Ages the dialogue is used for biographical purposes by Ermenrich of Ellwangen (*Vita Hariolfi*)[6] and by Arnold of St Emmeram (*de memoria beati Emmerami*);[7] the form culminates perhaps in the *Dialogus miraculorum* of Caesarius of Heisterbach.[8] In estimating the contribution of Christianity to medieval debate and dialogue literature rudimentary catechistic works as well as the exegetic *quaestiones* must be considered.[9] In a different way too the form of interchange common in the classical (and particularly the Vergilian) eclogue

[1] R. Hirzel, *Der Dialog: ein literarhistorischer Versuch*, 2 vols. (Leipzig, 1895).
[2] Migne, Patrologia Graeca 6, cols. 471–800.
[3] Ed. E. Bratke, Corpus Scriptorum Ecclesiasticorum Latinorum 45. This work is thought to be based on a lost work of Ariston of Pella.
[4] See Hirzel, *Der Dialog* II, 368–9. Three works of Augustine should be included here: the *contra Academicos*, the *de vita beata* and the *de ordine*. The pseudo-Augustinian *Altercatio ecclesiae et synagogae* (Migne, Patrologia Latina 42, cols. 1131–40) is unquestionably later.
[5] PG 47, cols. 5–82; cf. P. R. Coleman-Norton, 'The Use of Dialogue in the Vita Sanctorum', *JTS* 27 (1926), 388–95, and more recently, M. Hoffmann, *Der Dialog bei den christlichen Schriftstellern der ersten vier Jahrhunderte*, Texte und Untersuchungen zur Gesch. d. altchr. Literatur (Berlin, 1966).
[6] MGH, Script. 10, 11–15.
[7] Migne, Patrologia Latina 141, cols. 1026–90.
[8] See M. Plezia, 'L'Histoire Dialoguée: Procédé d'Origine Patristique dans l'Historiographie Médiévale', *Studia Patristica* 4 (1961), 490–6.
[9] See G. Bardy, 'La Littérature Patristique des Quaestiones et Responsiones sur l'Écriture Sainte', *Revue Biblique* 41 (1932), 211–36, 341–69 and 515–37; and 42 (1933), 11–30, 211–29 and 328–52.

spawns a genre of literature which becomes well known in the Middle Ages – the eclogue turned to Christian purpose to frame a debate between Christian and pagan attitudes. The earliest of such christianizing eclogues are by Damasus and Severus Endelechius; the best known in the Middle Ages is the so-called *Ecloga Theoduli*. The fact that the *Ecloga Theoduli* was widely known as a school-text is perhaps a reason for the development of the countless varieties of debate poems in the high Middle Ages – the debates of winter and spring, of the love of knights and the love of clerks, of the love of men and the love of women, of the body and soul, of wine and water, to name only the best known examples.[1]

More important for the present discussion is the wide range of dialogue literature whose purpose is plainly didactic and pedagogic. The interchange in such works consists in pertinent questions posed by *discipuli* followed by extensive expositions by the *magister*. This form of exposition seems to have originated in late antiquity; the earliest examples are the *Ars minor* of Donatus,[2] the *Instructiones* of Eucherius,[3] the *de partibus divinae legis* of Junillus[4] and the *Antikeimenon* of Julian of Toledo.[5] Anglo-Latin authors use this dialogue form for their grammatical writings; so Aldhelm in his *de metris*[6] and Bede in his *Cunabula grammaticae*;[7] it is also used by an approximately contemporary Irish author.[8] Likewise the grammatical works of the Carolingian renaissance: Paulus Diaconus is said to have written a commentary on Donatus in question and answer form, and the *Ars grammatica* of Clemens Scottus is in this form.[9] And the great didactic works of Alcuin are in the form of questions from *discipuli* and *responsiones* from the *magister*.[10] Closely related to this didactic form of dialogue are the so-called *altercationes* or *disputationes* whose purpose again is largely didactic; these include the

---

[1] See the brief comments by P. Dronke, *Poetic Individuality in the Middle Ages* (Oxford, 1970), pp. 84–7, and the extensive discussion in H. Walther, *Das Streitgedicht in der lateinischen Literatur des Mittelalters* (Munich, 1920), esp. pp. 34ff. and 93ff.

[2] Keil, *Grammatici Latini* 4, 355–66. Works in this form are generally concerned with expounding grammar, but there is also the medical work of Caelius Aurelianus and the rhetorical work of Chirius Fortunatianus in this form.

[3] Ed. C. Wotke, CSEL 31, 63–161. A dialogue of similar form by Salonius, Eucherius's son, is found in PL 53, cols. 967–1012.

[4] PL 68, cols. 15–42.

[5] PL 96, cols. 595–704. It has been argued that the earliest such didactic dialogue was to be found in a manuscript at Schlettstadt dated *c.* 700; see M. Förster, 'Das älteste mittellateinische Gesprächbüchlein', *Romanische Forschungen* 27 (1910), 342–8.

[6] Ed. R. Ehwald, MGH, Auct. Antiq. 15, 150–204.   [7] PL 90, cols. 613–32.

[8] Ed. G. Calder, *Auraicept na N-Eces* (Edinburgh, 1917). This so-called 'scholar's primer' is a grammatical treatise derived largely from Isidore and Vergilius the Grammarian.

[9] Ed. J. Tolkien, *Philologus Suppl. bd.* 20, 3.

[10] These works are found in PL 101: *Grammatica* (cols. 849–902), *de orthographia* (cols. 903–20), *Dialogus de rhetorica et virtutibus* (cols. 919–50) and *de dialectica* (cols. 951–76). These four are in the form of dialogues between Alcuin the master and Charlemagne the pupil. The *Disputatio puerorum per interrogationes et responsiones* (PL 101, cols. 1097–144) is not certainly by Alcuin.

disputatio between Alcuin and Pippin (Charlemagne's son)[1] and the *Altercatio Hadriani et Epicteti*, a work perhaps of the second or third century that was frequently copied in the Middle Ages.[2]

The didactic dialogue gives birth in turn to a form which is generally called the colloquy.[3] The colloquy is still an interchange between master and student, but in the colloquy the master's reply becomes a vehicle with which to convey new and difficult (and often bizarre and hermeneutic) vocabulary to the student. In simple form the colloquy may be a medieval equivalent to the twentieth-century 'traveller's phrase book,' in which the travelling monk is provided with the necessary phrases and vocabulary to introduce himself to a foreign monastery.[4] Or the colloquy may be an uncomplicated record of conversation between student and master (with pedagogic intent) such as the colloquy of Ælfric.[5] Most often, as in the case of the colloquies of Ælfric Bata, the colloquy becomes a showpiece of excessively obscure vocabulary.[6]

One final form of medieval dialogue must be mentioned, which is attested far more widely in the vernacular literatures (particularly Norse and Irish) than in medieval Latin, namely the flyting. The vernacular flytings consist in exchanges of personal abuse and invective, often with the intention of provoking mortal combat. Of such a pitch is the exchange between Ced and Conall in the Middle Irish *Scela Mucce Meic Dathó* or in the confrontation of Oðinn and Þórr in the Old Norse *Hárbarzljóð*, or again, the confrontation of Loki and the assembly of Norse gods in the *Lokasenna*.[7] Of a slightly different order is the flyting of Oðinn and Vafþrúðnir in the Norse *Vafþruð-*

---

[1] PL 101, cols. 975–80; also ed. W. Wilmanns, *ZDA* 14 (1869), 530–55.

[2] Ed. W. Suchier, with introduction and commentary by L. W. Daly, Illinois Stud. in Lang. and Lit. 24 (1939), pp. 1–168. Daly's introduction to this work is by far the most extensive treatment of question-and-answer dialogue literature.

[3] See G. N. Garmonsway, 'The Development of the Colloquy', *The Anglo-Saxons: Studies in some Aspects of their History and Culture presented to Bruce Dickins*, ed. P. Clemoes (London, 1959), pp. 248–61.

[4] E.g. the third colloquy in *Early Scholastic Colloquies*, ed. W. H. Stevenson (Oxford, 1929), pp. 21–6, which contains phrases such as 'quanam in parte uultis properare uel pergere?' and the (suggested) reply, 'Romam uolumus ire, et uisitare reliquias Sancti Petri Apostoli . . .' etc.

[5] *Ælfric's Colloquy*, ed. G. N. Garmonsway (London, 1939). In English one might compare the *Dialogues of Solomon and Saturn*, ed. R. J. Menner (New York, 1941), and the Middle English 'Questiones by-twene the Maister of Oxenford and his Clerke', ed. C. Horstmann, *EStn* 8 (1885), 284–7. See also E. Merrill, *The Dialogue in English Literature*, Yale Studies in English (New York, 1911).

[6] This is most evident in the second, fifth, sixth and seventh colloquies printed in Stevenson, *Early Scholastic Colloquies*.

[7] There are also flytings preserved in the Eddaic *Helgakviða Hundingsbana II*, st. 24–9 (between Guðmundr and Sinfjǫtli) and the *Helgakviða Hjǫrvarðssonar*, st. 12–30 (between Atli and Hrimgerðr). See B. Phillpotts, *The Elder Edda and Ancient Scandinavian Drama* (Cambridge, 1920), pp. 156–9. In Anglo-Saxon, the exchange between Unferth and Beowulf might be considered a flyting. Saxo Grammaticus, *Gesta Danorum*, records three flytings: between Fridleif and the giant (6.178), between Grep and Erik (5.132 ff.) and between Gotvar and Erik (5.139).

nismál.[1] There is also a series of flytings between rival poets preserved in the Irish 'contentions of the bards' (*iomarbhaigh na bhfileadh*); although these contentions as they are preserved are of the seventeenth century, they would seem to stem from a very ancient tradition.[2] All these vernacular flytings have a violence and intensity that is not found anywhere in Latin literature.

The *Altercatio* and the *Responsio* which are presented here belong to a little known genre of medieval Latin poetry which may be seen to derive from the latter two classes of dialogue literature discussed above: it combines the form of interchange between *magister* and *discipulus* found in the didactic dialogues with the violence of invective found in the vernacular flytings.[3] There are few surviving examples of such *magister–discipulus* flytings in medieval Latin. Perhaps the best known one is that found in the *Hisperica Famina*. This work, as Damon has conclusively demonstrated by recourse to the indentations in the manuscript,[4] is a dialogue. It opens with a formal address (1–22) by the *magister* (or *faminator* – Robinson Ellis's word) in which he expresses his joy as he sees the assembly of scholars before him: 'cum insignes sophie speculator arcatores' (4).[5] The *magister* straightway invites a debate: 'hinc lectorum sollertem inuito obello certatorem' (22). After some preamble a student speaks (53–60): he has attempted to acquire proficiency in Hisperic speech: 'hispericum arripere tonui sceptrum' (54), but right now only a thin trickle seeps from his lips 'ac exiguus serpit per ora riuus' (56). The *magister* interrupts at once (61–86), asks indignantly what trade the student practises, and then advises the student to go back to the farm. But the student is unperturbed and continues (87ff.), this time producing a torrent of 'Ausonian' rhetoric: 'pari ausonicum exubero pululamine fluuium' (92). Again the *magister* interrupts, this time using a series of *adynata*, 'sooner will you touch the heavens, sooner will fish dwell on land and terrestrial animals in the sea' etc., to point out that the student will never succeed in producing Hisperic speech: 'haud hispericum propinabis auido gutture tollum' (109). By contrast the *magister* praises his own Hisperic eloquence. He concludes with a magisterial discussion of the twelve common faults which mar Hisperic speech.

[1] The exchange between Oðinn and Vafþruðnir is concerned with the revelation of secret lore; as such it is a member of a huge corpus of riddle literature common in Norse and Anglo-Saxon as well as Irish. For example, Heiðrek in the Old Norse *Hervarar saga* forfeits his life because he is unable to answer Oðinn's questions. In Irish literature one might compare the exchange between Cuchulainn and Emer in the *Tochmarc Emire* or that between the two scholars in the *Immacallam in dá Thuarad* (ed. W. Stokes, *Revue Celtique* 26 (1905), 4–64).

[2] The 'bardic contentions' are edited by L. McKenna, Irish Texts Society 20–1 (London, 1918). See also E. Knott and G. Murphy, *Early Irish Literature* (London, 1966), pp. 88–92.

[3] In a consideration of the development of this genre, the comments by Walther (*Das Streitgedicht*, pp. 17ff.) concerning the importance of the diatribe in rhetorical education are very relevant.

[4] P. W. Damon, 'The Meaning of the *Hisperica Famina*', *Amer. Jnl of Philol.* 74 (1953), 398–406.

[5] Ed. F. J. H. Jenkinson (Cambridge, 1908). A new edition of the *Hisperica Famina* by M. Herren is soon to be published by the Pontifical Institute of Mediaeval Studies, Toronto.

One is reluctant to introduce the *Hisperica Famina* and their concomitant morass of interpretational problems into any discussion of literary form. I should stress at once that there are virtually no stylistic similarities between the *Hisperica Famina* and the much later *Altercatio* presented here; the Anglo-Latin diction of the *Altercatio* and the *Responsio* is a distinct idiom worked out by generations of English writers, as I have noted above.[1] And yet there are striking similarities in form: the list of *adynata* used by the student to delineate his master's monstrous arrogance in the *Altercatio* (1–13) is reminiscent of that used by the Hisperic *magister* to illustrate his student's ineptness. The boasting of the Hisperic *magister* is no less aggravating than that of the Welsh one in the *Altercatio*. The very nature of the exchange – in each case the paternal contempt of the *magister* (HF 74–7; *Altercatio* 57–67) balanced against the student's vigour and exuberance – is remarkably alike. In the absence, however, of any exact verbal parallels it is impossible to postulate a certain relationship between the two works; their similarity would rather seem to attest to the vitality of a class-room tradition of Latin flyting poetry.

Another very similar exchange between *magister* and *discipulus* is found in a German manuscript from Würzburg of the ninth century, preserved in the Bodleian Library, Oxford (Laud Misc. 252).[2] It has been edited by Wilhelm Meyer[3] and again by Karl Strecker.[4] Meyer did not realize that the poem was a dialogue (and hence could not understand how lines 1–26 and lines 27–36 were related), but Strecker rightly prints it as a dialogue. As transmitted, the poem is a fragment of what would have been a longer exchange. The *magister* of this dialogue, speaking apparently of proficiency in rhetoric or in poetic composition, observes that one would be secure provided one knew how to interpret the behaviour of winds: 'ventorum rabidos discernere mores/si scit: tutus erit pelagi luctantibus undis' (MGH, Poetae 4, 1086, lines 20–1). But if one were ignorant of the ways of the sea and did not know how to hold the sails against the wind, he would without doubt be caught up in the raging waters and, cast headlong from the poop, would drown:

> ast ignarus aquas qui vult transire feroces
> huc illucque vagas discurrens nauta per undas,
> si non vela sapit ventum distendere contra,
> haut dubium, capietur aquis turgentibus atque
> pronus ab arce ratis fundum mergetur in imum. (22–6)

---

1 See, however, the comments by P. Grosjean, 'Confusa caligo: Remarques sur les Hisperica Famina', *Celtica* 3 (1956), 64.

2 B. Bischoff and J. Hofmann, *Libri Sancti Kyliani*, Quellen und Forschungen zur Geschichte des Bistums und Hochstifts Würzburg 6 (Würzburg, 1952), 38 and 130. (Mr Malcolm Parkes very kindly supplied me with this reference.)

3 'Bruckstück eines Gedichtes aus der Karolinger-Zeit', *Nachrichten d. k. Gesells. d. Wiss. z. Göttingen, phil.-hist. Kl.* (1917), pp. 589–93. 4 MGH, Poetae 4, 1086.

So in the *Altercatio*, after the discipulus has upbraided the master for pretending to omniscience and for praising his own poetry excessively, the master replies in a calm and grandiloquent tone: 'you are not borne on the high seas by a lofty trireme but by a tiny skiff full of leaks; already the elements are preparing a storm. Beware lest you be shipwrecked and drowned in the deep' (61–7). The student who replies to the master of the first poem is weary of the exchange: 'iam pectore et ore fatigor./verba latent sensusque fugit' (29–33). He begs for a remission: 'desine quapropter forti me tangere versu' (33).[1] But the student of the *Altercatio* has far more energy; he advises his *magister* to stop abusing the ancient poets (56) and continues the attack.

Approximately contemporary with the *Altercatio* are two satires by Warner of Rouen which were written between 996 and 1026. One of these poems is an attack on a certain Scot called Moriuht (*Satire I*);[2] the other is a dialogue between Warner himself and one Franbaldus, a monk who had recently abandoned Mont St Michel (*Satire II*).[3] Though neither of these poems is properly a *magister–discipulus* debate, they each bear a remarkable resemblance to the *Altercatio*. In *Satire II*, for example, Warner and Franbaldus insult each other's knowledge of the quadrivium. Franbaldus charges that Warner may well know the rules of Donatus but that he is ignorant of music (ed. Musset, p. 262, line 75); Warner replies that Franbaldus is learned in music but a dolt in grammar: 'musicus es doctus, grammatica uacuus' (78). And so the flyting ensues, until at length Franbaldus gives a magisterial exposition of musical theory (103–26), well stuffed with technical vocabulary – *diatesseron, diapente, epitritus, epogdous* etc. (an exposition, I assume, very much like that demanded by the student of the *Altercatio* (77–83)). In the *Altercatio* the *magister*, after his learning has been thoroughly impugned by the student, ends by giving a magisterial exposition of computation. In *Satire I* Warner derides Moriuht for the very reason that the *discipulus* derides his master in the *Altercatio*. Moriuht has dared to state that he is a great grammarian; he prefers his own poetry to that of the great classical poets; what is more, he

---

[1] Cf. the request made by the student in the *Responsio*: 'desine iam nos/rodere uerbis' (72–3). The debate between Terentius and his *delusor* (MGH, Poetae 4, 1088–90) assumes a form similar to these debates between master and student. In this poem the *delusor* taunts Terentius to demonstrate the utility of his verse ('dic, vetus auctor, in hoc quae iacet utilitas?'). In the face of an extremely virulent attack Terentius is led to ask, 'cur, furiose, tuis lacerasti carmina verbis' (p. 1090, line 48)? So the student in the *Responsio* had been led to ask of his *magister*, 'cur mea falso/carmina blasmas' (12–13)?

[2] Ed. H. Omont, 'Satire de Garnier de Rouen contre le Poète Moriuht', *Annuaire-Bulletin de la Société de l'Histoire de France* 31 (1894), 193–210.

[3] Ed. L. Musset, 'Le Satiriste Garnier de Rouen et son Milieu', *Revue du Moyen Âge Latin* 10 (1954), 237–66. The poem is certainly a dialogue but Musset's designations of speakers are not always certain.

belches his trivial poetry (worthy to be consigned to the garbage heap) throughout the courtyard:

> ausus se magnum dicere grammaticum;
> coepit doctiloquos semet preferre poetis,
> Homero magno, Virgilio, Statio;
> per totam cortem versus ructabat oberrans
> dignos confectis stercore paginulis. (334–8)[1]

Likewise the student of the *Altercatio* charges that the *magister* has 'dared to profess himself the greatest of philosophers, accomplished in all learning': 'summum profiterier audet/se fore philosophum cunctoque sophismate comptum' (27–8). What is more, he does not fear to call himself 'master in all arts': 'insuper haud metuit sese uocitare "magistrum/artibus in cunctis"' (31–2). And he does not cease praising his own poetry – poetry of such quality that schoolboys do not deign to look at it: 'desinit haud talem nobis laudare poesim/qualem nec pueri dignantur cernere scolis' (35–6).

The similarities among these various poems are too close to be coincidental. Yet in the absence of any direct and unmistakable verbal reminiscences it is impossible to conjecture what might have been the relationship between them. We are dealing, it seems, with a distinct genre of medieval Latin school poetry which has left very few descendants. It is to be hoped that subsequent research will uncover more of them.

THE 'CARMEN DE LIBERO ARBITRIO'

The *Carmen de libero arbitrio* presents fewer interpretational difficulties than the *Altercatio* and the *Responsio*. It is a poetic attempt, through exploration of the notions of providence and predestination, to understand the relationship of human striving and choice to divine grace. It proceeds from a conception of the universe that is found abundantly in late Latin poetry – in Dracontius's *de laudibus dei*, for example – and which derives ultimately from Manilius: namely, that the universe is bound together temporally and spatially by cosmic bonds (*cosmica nexa*); the universe is thus unified and is one with God (*est natura deus*); and all events are bound to each other in a cosmic chain (*fatalis series*) from which no deviation is possible. It should be noted that such a conception of universal order is not essentially Christian, but rather derives from that widely diffused and originally Stoic cosmology which was current in late antiquity. In any case the poet's problem was to explain how man could conceivably have free will if all events in the cosmos were ordained and foreseen by providence. He makes his explanation by

---

[1] Omont, 'Satire de Garnier', p. 206; *doctiloquos* (335) should be emended to *doctiloquis*.

resort to an elaborate and apparently original simile (he calls it a 'paradigm'): a certain wise king sits on a lofty watch-tower (*specula*) surrounded by soldiers and elders; he orders that one hundred purple robes and an equal number of crowns be placed in front of him, and addresses soldiers who are in a race-course below, telling them that in the race which will be run under his surveillance the speedy runner will win a crown and become one of the king's select soldiers, but the slow and lazy runner will be whipped, bound and cast in prison (69–86). This illustration, transparent though it is, is explained in detail: the king represents God the Father, whose wisdom (variously called Christ or the Holy Ghost) is the watch-tower. The will or mercy of the king which grants rewards to the winners represents God's grace (*gratia*); the running of the race (*scammata*) signifies free will (89–108).

The basic problem of the *de libero arbitrio* – how to resolve the apparent contradiction between human free will and the unalterable chain of fate – is common enough in Latin literature. Perhaps the best known and most trenchant investigation of this problem is that in books 4 and 5 of Boethius's *de consolatione philosophiae*. There is no need to argue that this work was widely read in the tenth century;[1] it may be demonstrated that a reading of the *de consolatione philosophiae* was the inspiration of the questioning of the *de libero arbitrio*. The entire *Problemstellung* of the Anglo-Latin poem is exactly anticipated by Boethius. After Philosophia in the *de consolatione* has expounded the notion of a fatal series of causes, Boethius asks, can there be any free will left in such a series, or are men's minds also bound by the chain: 'sed in hac haerentium sibi serie causarum estne ulla nostri arbitrii libertas an ipsos quoque humanorum motus animorum fatalis catena constringit' (5, pr. 2)? The resolution of this contradiction proceeds from the discussion of providence in book 4. It is remarkable that much of the vocabulary used in Boethius's discussion of providence is also found in the Anglo-Latin poem. So, for example, the striking collocation of words *stabilis simplicitas*. Boethius states that the moving series of fate is related to the stable simplicity of providence as the circumference of a circle to the still point at its centre – 'ita est fati series mobilis ad prouidentiae stabilem simplicitatem' (4, pr. 6). The expression is used to distinguish the turmoil of human affairs from the stable simplicity of God by the author of *de libero arbitrio*: 'sed quantum res periturae/distant a stabili simplicitate dei' (113–14)! For Boethius the *intuitus* of providence sees all things and awards whatever is predestined

[1] There are abundant manuscripts of the ninth and tenth centuries and also abundant commentaries. In the ninth century there is the anonymous St Gall commentary and the Vat.Lat. 3363 commentary, not to mention the Anglo-Saxon translation by Alfred and the Old High German glosses by Notker. In the tenth century there are the commentaries by Remigius of Auxerre and the anonymous Parisinus lat. 10400, those by Bovo of Corvey and Adalbold of Utrecht, as well as several others. See discussion by P. Courcelle, *La Consolation de Philosophie dans la Tradition Littéraire* (Paris, 1967), pp. 241–74.

according to merit: 'quae tamen ille ab aeterno cuncta prospiciens prouidentiae cernit intuitus et suis quaeque meritis praedestinata disponit' (5, pr. 2). The author of the *de libero arbitrio* also speaks of the *intuitus* of the divine mind and for him too predestination grants rewards and acceptance into the kingdom of heaven according to merit: 'praedestiuenatio: caelo/promittit sanctis quae bona pro meritis' (105–6). At the very end of the *de consolatione* Philosophia explains that God remains as a spectator (with foreknowledge of all things) of our actions, and that he dispenses rewards to the good, punishments to the evil: 'manet etiam spectator desuper cunctorum praescius deus uisionisque eius praesens semper aeternitas cum nostrorum actuum futura qualitate concurrit bonis praemia malis supplicia dispensans' (5, pr. 6). We are here very close indeed to the Anglo-Latin poet's conception of God watching over all things and granting rewards; in the poem God is called *prescius auctor* (17), and at one point he awards *pretia* and *supplicia*: 'uictus supplicium, uictor adit pretium' (102). So closely does the Anglo-Latin poet appear to have followed Boethius that the dominant image of the *de libero arbitrio* – that of the king on the watch-tower – is derived from Boethius as well. For at one point Boethius observes that God looks down from 'the high watch-tower of providence' and recognizes what is appropriate for everyone: 'qui [*scil.* deus] cum ex alta prouidentiae specula respexit, quid unicuique conueniat agnoscit et quod conuenire nouit accommodat . . .' (4, pr. 6). The latter part of Boethius's sentence may be reflected in the Anglo-Latin poet's 'quos nouit [*scil.* auctor] iustos conuocat ad superos' (18); it is in any case evident that the Anglo-Latin poet simply expanded the metaphor of the watch-tower as he had found it in Boethius.[1]

In its concern with predestination, the *de libero arbitrio* may well be seen in the context of the doctrinal debate on predestination which had been waged in France about a century earlier. This debate had as its principal point of departure the theology of Augustine; the two most important contributors to the debate, Gottschalk of Orbais and John Scotus Eriugena, each concerned himself with a different aspect of Augustine's doctrine – Gottschalk with the notion of the two *civitates* (hence his two *praedestinationes*), and John with the notion of evil as the absence of good.[2] There were also contributions to the debate by Hincmar of Reims, Prudentius of

---

[1] Although the author of the *de libero arbitrio* was from the continent, one should not overlook the fact that there was an established tradition of Boethian interpretation in England, most fully attested by Alfred's translation. In particular, the notion of God rewarding the good and punishing the evil is germane to both Alfred's *Boethius* and to the *de libero arbitrio*. On the other hand, the poem's literal fidelity to Boethius's conception of the chain of fate (*fatalis series*) has no parallel in Alfred. See K. Otten, *König Alfreds Boethius* (Tübingen, 1964), pp. 54–5 and 58–60.

[2] Gottschalk, *de praedestinatione, Oeuvres Théologiques et Grammaticales de Godescalc d'Orbais*, ed. D. C. Lambot (Louvain, 1945), pp. 180–258; John Scotus Eriugena, *de praedestinatione*, PL 122, cols. 355–440.

Troyes and Ratramnus of Corbie.[1] There is little point in rehearsing all the intricacies of that debate here, since it will be seen at once that the *de libero arbitrio*, because of its Boethian orientation, views the problem of free will and predestination from a different standpoint from that of the earlier theologians. Yet it is probable that the poet was familiar to some degree with the debate; in particular he seems to have known Ratramnus, whose approach to these problems most closely resembles his own.[2] Ratramnus (like the poet and unlike the other contributors) begins by explaining that God fixes all events of the cosmos into an immutable order: 'ita in aeterna dispositione consistunt immobiliter fixa qualiter creaturarum ordo per successiones temporum . . .'[3] With this compare *de libero arbitrio* 9–16, where the poet explains that a *fatalis series* orders everything. Similarly Ratramnus states that God knows all events past, present and future: 'ergo omnia novit [*scil.* deus] et omnia concludit, continet atque disponit, praeterita, praesentia et futura nequaquam eum latent . . .'[4] All events are inspected by God: 'quaecunque sunt, et fuerunt, et futura sunt, uno intuitu contuetur'.[5] These expressions call to mind that of the poet: 'actus praeteritos, praesentes, necne futuros/auctor sic hominum prospicit intuitu' (119–20). But although God thus has foreknowledge of all events, both Ratramnus and the poet argue that no man is compelled to damnation by God's foreknowledge. Each man by his own choice and own deeds is either rewarded or punished, as Ratramnus explains: 'Dei praescientia neminem compellit ad peccatum . . . sed unusquisque proprio actu, vel remuneratur, vel condemnatur.'[6] And it is this point, expressed here in theological terms by Ratramnus, that is made by the poet in his elaborate similes of the racecourse and of the two paths (see especially 100–8 and 123–8).

AUTHORSHIP

One may now raise the question of the authorship of the three poems. At this point we are in a position to see how remarkably close was the opinion of the Cambridge librarian Bradshaw over a hundred years ago that the .L. in the epigraph to the *Altercatio – uersus .L. de quodam superbo –* stood for Lantfridus of Winchester.[7] For several reasons the hint (I cannot consider it more than that) offered by Bradshaw is worth pursuing. The *Altercatio* was, I believe, written in the Winchester circle to which Lantfridus belonged.

[1] Hincmar, *de praedestinatione dei et libero arbitrio*, PL 125, cols. 65–474; Prudentius, *de praedestinatione contra J. Scottum*, PL 115, cols. 1009–366; Ratramnus, *de praedestinatione dei*, PL 121, cols. 11–80.

[2] It is well known that Æthelwold imported monks from Corbie to instruct the Winchester monks in plain-chant (see above, p. 93). Could it have been a monk from Corbie, familiar there with the writings of Ratramnus, who had come to England and written the *de libero arbitrio*?

[3] PL 121, col. 15.   [4] *Ibid.*   [5] *Ibid.*

[6] *Ibid.* col. 68.   [7] See above, p. 85.

The very rare phrase *caelica Tempe* is found in the *Altercatio* (and in the *de libero arbitrio*) as well as in Lantfridus's *Translatio et miracula S. Swithuni*. At several points in this rather arid account of the removal of the Winchester saint's remains Lantfridus essays poetry; conceivably it may not have been beyond his powers to write the *Altercatio*. But as none of these circumstances may be counted as definitive evidence, I can see no means of deciding the case either way.

One other possibility must be considered. We have seen that Wulfstan knew the *Altercatio* intimately enough to be able to produce one of its lines verbatim ('foedum iam claude labellum' (68)) and also to repeat one of its curious expressions (*cuneis supernis*) in his hymn to Æthelwold.[1] It might reasonably be asked if he was the author of the *Altercatio*. This author had some specialized knowledge of musical theory (77–82). Wulfstan was the precentor at Winchester and it is known from William of Malmesbury that he composed a work *de tonorum harmonia*[2] (which is no longer extant). However, the survival of two manuscripts of a Winchester troper[3] and our knowledge of the existence of the famous Winchester cathedral organ are sufficient to indicate that specialized knowledge of musical theory was not the privileged possession of Wulfstan alone. And a very important stylistic feature of Wulfstan's verse weighs against the hypothesis. Wulfstan has a remarkable predilection for elision in his hexameters (a most rare predilection among Anglo-Latin poets); the author of the *Altercatio* studiously avoids elision and even allows himself two hiatus (38 and 71). This is a serious difference, and the possibility that (say) the *Altercatio* is a work of youth whereas the *Narratio de S. Swithuno* is a work of old age is not worth entertaining. I take it then that Wulfstan is not the author of the *Altercatio*. Nor can he have been the author of the *de libero arbitrio*, for that poem is by a foreigner and 'Wulfstan' is an English name.

Finally, beside the open question whether Lantfridus was the author of the *Altercatio* (and hence of the *Responsio*) there is another possibility worth considering. Since the *de libero arbitrio* was written by a foreigner who, like Lantfridus, had come from abroad and since this poem shares the rare phrase *caelica Tempe* with Lantfridus's known work, just as the *Altercatio* does, it is possible that Lantfridus wrote the *de libero arbitrio*. I consider it unlikely, however, that he or anyone else wrote all three poems. The *Altercatio* is a

---

[1] See my note to *Altercatio* 120, below, pp. 120–1.

[2] William of Malmesbury, *de gestis regum Anglorum*, ed. W. Stubbs, RS (1887) I, 167: 'fecit et aliud opus De Tonorum Harmonia valde utile'.

[3] These two manuscripts (Cambridge, Corpus Christi College 473 and Oxford, Bodleian Library 775) are edited by W. H. Frere, *The Winchester Troper*, Henry Bradshaw Society (London, 1894). J. Handschin, however, has argued that both manuscripts are eleventh-century ('The Two Winchester Tropers', *JTS* 37 (1936), 34–49 and 156–72).

brilliantly spirited piece by a poet of considerable learning and imagination. There is a palpable difference between the buoyancy of the *Altercatio* and the more pedestrian and didactic tone of the *de libero arbitrio*, even when allowance has been made for the difference of genre of the two works. The poet of the *Altercatio* is very frequently careless with regard to quantity (see the tentative list of false quantities in my note to line 13, below, p. 109). On the other hand, the poet of the *de libero arbitrio* is scrupulously careful in this regard; I have noted only a couple of examples of false quantity (see my note to line 174, below, p. 136). What is more, he goes to considerable lengths to accommodate words which would naturally be unmetrical: he adds a syllable each to *praedestinatio* and to *prouidentia*, for example. In spite of the similarities which the poems share and which make them unquestionably the productions of one school, I doubt whether they are the production of one author. But this is only an impression; I could not pretend that such impressions ever amount to proof.

Editor's Note: I have expanded silently the very few abbreviations found in the manuscript. I have not followed the erratic and incomplete punctuation of the manuscript but have repunctuated in accord with modern principles. No indentations are found in the manuscript. Each line in it begins with a majuscule, but I have not thought it necessary to reproduce these. I have not modernized the spelling nor altered it at all, except where a spelling is patently wrong (e.g. *de libero arbitrio* 90 *spendida* and 120 *autor* MS); in those few cases I have noted the erroneous spellings in the apparatus. On the very few occasions that ę is found in the manuscript I have printed *ae* (e.g. *Altercatio* 71 *normę dialecticę* MS).

C: Cantabrigiensis bibl. univ. Kk.5.34, 71r–80r

Altercatio magistri et discipuli

⟨*discipulus*⟩

71r   Si torpens celeri tigrem superare fugacem
       cursu testudo desideret ac feritate;
       si lepus atque canem temptet laniare ferocem,
       scorpius exilis tunicatum si crocodrillum;
       scammate si regem pauidus quoque damma leonem   5
       prouocet ast aquilam si parua columba cruentam;
       scandere sique polum pinnis myirmica supernum
       appet*a*t atque tetrum deuincere mole camelum;
       sique ferae siluas, piscesque marina fluenta
       destituant, seriem propriamque creata relinquant: 10
       mundanas uariare uices natura stupebit
       cunctaque disponens proprias laxabit habenas;
71v   moxque soluta ruent perituri climata cosmi.
       porten*t*o simile paradigma gerit uafer atqu*e*

Readings in C: 8 appetit   14 portendo, atqui

This poem is written in hexameters.

Title. I propose this title. The rubricator has written *uersus .L. de quodam superbo* at the beginning of the poem. Whoever wrote this had not read the poem carefully. The poem is not a diatribe but a dialogue. I have indicated changes of speaker; there is no such indication in the manuscript.

6   *ast* here, if retained, would have to mean 'and' or 'or', a far remove from its normal meaning. In support of this meaning one might consider 80: 'quid epogdous atque emiolius est epytritus?' where the scribe has written *uel ast* above *est*. For the scribe, apparently, *ast* was equivalent to *atque*. These two readings, as well as the favour which *ast* enjoyed at the hands of Anglo-Latin poets, weigh strongly against the inclination to emend to *aut*.

7   *myirmica*. A glossary word, deriving ultimately from Greek μύρμηξ, 'ant'. Hence it is glossed as *formica*; see Goetz, *Corpus Glossariorum Latinorum* (abbreviated hereafter as *CGL*) v, 222.28 and 621.35; and cf. Servius on *Aen.* 4.402. In the glossaries the word is spelled *mirmica*; the extra syllable could have been added by the Anglo-Latin poet *metri gratia*.

12   *disponens* ('setting in order', 'arranging') is not a happy expression here, though it may be that *cuncta disponens* is a noun-phrase (almost a kenning) for *natura* – 'the all-disposer'. Perhaps the poet wrote *deponens*.

13   *climata*. A false quantity here (*clĭmata*) as often with Greek words in this poem. It would appear that the false quantity of this word is common to Anglo-Latin poetry; cf. Frithegodus, *Breuiloquium* 25: 'huc ades, o formose, Dei per

Three Latin poems from Æthelwold's school at Winchester

Altercatio magistri et discipuli

⟨discipulus⟩

If the sluggish tortoise wished to excel the fleet tiger in racing and in ferocity; and if the hare tried to rend the fierce hunting-dog [and] the feeble scorpion the armoured crocodile; if also the timorous deer provoked the lion, king [of the beasts], to mortal combat, or the small dove provoked the bloody eagle; if the ant sought to climb the lofty sky on feathered wings and to exceed the hideous camel in bulk; if wild beasts deserted the woods and fish the flowing seas, and all creatures abandoned their position in the scheme of things (10): nature would be [too] dumbfounded to mete out positions in the cosmos, and she [who normally] arranges all things would release her own reins; at once the four corners of the dying cosmos would collapse (13).

---

climata testis'. Nevertheless, the poet of the *Altercatio* makes many such errors which have no parallel in other Anglo-Latin verse. The most striking examples of false quantity in the poem are as follows: *simĭlĕ* (14), *sȳcophanta* (15), *mĕro* (25), *hȳdromello* (25), *phĭlŏsŏphus* (29 and 30), *Tempē* (45), *stătim* (49), *dialecticāē* (71 plus hiatus!), *hēmĭŏlĭus* (80), *ēpĭtrĭtus* (80), *sŭam* (86), *ŭtique* (96) and *ȳmeras* (97). On errors in the scansion of Greek words in Anglo-Latin see the brief comments by A. Campbell, 'Linguistic Features of Early Anglo-Latin Verse', p. 14.

14 *paradigma*. A glossary word from Greek παράδειγμα, glossed as *similitudo*. *exemplum* (CGL II, 588.51) and *similitudo.fabula* (CGL IV, 267.3); also found occasionally in patristic Latin (e.g., Tertullian, *de anima* 43).

14–18 It is remarkable that nearly all the words in this torrent of abuse are to be found in Horace's *Satires*: *uafer* (I. 3.130, II. 3.21, II. 4.55 and II. 5.24), *furcifer* (II. 7.22), *cerritus* (II. 3.278), *balatro* (I. 2.2), *spurcus* (II. 5.18), *agaso* (II. 8.72), *garrulus* (I. 4.12, I. 9.33 and II. 5.90) and *nebulo* (I. 1.104). This leaves only the glossary words *sicophanta*, *baburus* and *babbiger*; the everyday words *insipidus*, *monstrum* and *furibundus*; and the unknown form *silicernus* (see below note to line 16). It would seem that the poet had studied the *Satires* diligently. It is to be recalled that Wulfstan too seems to have known the *Satires* (see Campbell's notes to 1.884–5 and 2.791 in his edition of the *Narratio de S. Swithuno*). These references taken together may constitute evidence for the first direct knowledge of Horace in England in the late tenth century.

furcifer insipidus, monstrum, sicophanta baburus, 15
cerritus balatro, spurcus si non silicernus,
babbiger †agaffons†, epilenticus ac furibundus,
garrulus ac nebulo, barritor necne latrator,
finibus in patriis suetus seruare suillos
siue referre domum scapulis in nocte capellas; 20
qui lympham potare solens lacti sociatam
carnibus hyrcinis postquam satur atque butyro.
   ut fortunatos felix deuenit ad Anglos
(nomine mendoso quos nuncupat ipse 'tenaces')
insolito potus mero necnon hydromello, 25

Readings in C: 16 spurtus   25 hydri mello

15   *sicophanta*. A glossary word from Greek συκοφάντης, glossed as either *calumniator* (*CGL* v, 332.32, 394.4 and 658.11), *circumuentor* (*CGL* iv, 172.38) or *impostor* (*CGL* v, 557.50).

baburus. A word explained by Isidore (*Etym.* 10.31) as *stultus.ineptus*, whence it finds its way into the glossaries: see *CGL* iv, 589.4 and 599.1 and v, 493.17 and 591.54.

16   *silicernus*. This form is nowhere else attested. The word is correctly *silicernium*, as it occurs in Terence (*Ad.* iv. ii. 48). It is used in the form *silicernius* by Frithegodus, *Breuiloquium* 1302: 'optabatque grauem silicernius affore mortem'.

17   *babbiger*. A common glossary word (glossed invariably as *stultus*): see *CGL* iv, 24.16, 487.24 and 589.2 and v, 170.11 and 591.69; *The Harley Latin–Old English Glossary* (*Harley 3376*), ed. R. T. Oliphant, JL 20 (The Hague, 1966), B 1; *The Corpus Glossary*, ed. W. M. Lindsay (Cambridge, 1921), B 30.

agaffons. Very probably corrupt. There are two possibilities. First, that the initial *ag-* conceals *ac* and that *affons* conceals a Greek word, perhaps either ἄφωνος ('voiceless', 'dumb') or ἄφως ('without light'). One might compare the neologism *bradifonus* ('slow of speech') found in the exactly contemporary *Chronicon* of Æthelweard (ed. Campbell, p. 55). Possible too in this connection (though a bit more remote from the transmitted text) is that *affons* conceals ἄφρων ('foolish', 'silly'), a word which is found once in a glossary (*CGL* ii, 28.28) where it is glossed as *baburus*. More probable, however, is that the scribe has confused the rare word *agaso*, a word used as a term of abuse by Horace (*Serm.* ii, 8.72) and Persius (5.76). The word is also used by Abbo of St Germain-des-Prés, *Bella Parisiacae Urbis* 3.54: 'mulio strabo tuus neque sit neque agason inermis' (MGH, Poetae 4, 118). The third book of this work, which is charged with obscure Greek vocabulary, was circulated separately in England (there are several English manuscripts); so often was it used as a sourcebook of hermeneutic vocabulary that its poetic form was neglected and it was rewritten in simple prose. (It is published in this form by Stevenson, *Early Scholastic Colloquies*, pp. 103–12). Because it was known in England in this form, it is not improbable that the author of the *Altercatio* had read it. The

The cunning and unsavoury rascal bears a resemblance to [such a] monstrosity, the monster, the foolish slanderer, the crazy buffoon if not foul bag of bones, the sot, [? the horse-herd], idiotic and mad, the garrulous wretch, a howler as well as a whiner, accustomed in his own country to caring for pigs or to carrying goats back to the house at night on his shoulders, who, being accustomed to drinking water mixed with milk is thereafter satisfied with goat meat and butter (22).

But as the lucky fellow comes to the fortunate English (whom he himself designates by the false term 'tenacious'), drunk on unaccustomed wine as well as mead, now he praises his doctrine to the summits of the skies, seeking an empty name [for himself]. He dares to profess himself the greatest philosopher, accomplished in all learning, while at the same time he hardly knows what a philosopher is. (And from whence is this noun derived? Tell what gender it is!) What is more, he does not shrink from calling himself 'master in all arts', after the savage custom of the Greeks who, although

---

spelling *agason* as found here is not far removed from the transmitted *agaffons*, but it should be remarked that the quantity of the first syllable (*ăgāson*) would be false in the *Altercatio*.

epilenticus. Though the Greek is ἐπιληπτικός, the word is customarily spelled *epilenticus* in Anglo-Latin texts. See the *Vita Samsoni* (ed. R. Fawtier, Bibliothèque de l'École des Hautes Études 197 (Paris, 1912), p. 158): 'quis . . . enumerare queat quanti imbecilles, quanti caeci, quanti claudi, quanti epilentici . . .' Also Aldhelm, *de metris* (ed. E. Ehwald, MGH, Auct. Antiq. 15, 66.5).

18   *barritor*. Apparently a neologism, from *barritus*, 'the cry of an elephant', on the analogy of *latrator* from *latratus*.

19   *suillos*. The adjective is taken as substantive, 'swine'.

24   *tenaces*. This reference is obscure and may be irrecoverable at this remove. Since Ioruert in question here is a Welshman (see below, note to line 52), the word *tenax* may represent a personal witticism of Ioruert. The Welsh equivalent of *tenax* is *cadarn* ('strong', 'tenacious', 'mighty'). In the Middle Welsh prose story *Branwen uerch Lyr* (the second branch of the four Mabinogi) England is called twice *Ynys y Kedeyrn*, 'the Isle of the Mighty' (*Branwen uerch Lyr*, ed. I. Williams, *Pedeir Keinc y Mabinogi* (Cardiff, 1930), pp. 32 and 40). I suggest that Ioruert is here punning on the Welsh name for England. It should be noted that the *Mabinogion* as we have them are approximately two hundred years later than the *Altercatio*; the tradition of calling Britain *Ynys y Kedeyrn* could of course be older.

25   *hydromello* 'mead', after the Greek ὑδρόμελι. It is usually spelled with *o* (not *i*, as MS) in Anglo-Latin texts. Cf. a charter of Edmund dated 946 (Birch, *Cartularium Saxonicum*, no. 816); the *Vita Ethelwoldi*, probably by Wulfstan (PL 137, col. 89) and Ælfric Bata's difficult colloquy: 'et quid bibis?' – 'ceruisam uel medonem siue ydromellum, quod est mulsum. . .' (Stevenson, *Early Scholastic Colloquies*, p. 98).

nunc sintagma suum sublimat ad alta polorum
nomen inane petens. summum profiterier audet
se fore philosophum cunctoque sophismate comptum,
dum minime sciat hoc quid philosophus sit. (et unde est
hoc nomen tractum? cuius generis siet, ede).   30
insuper haud metu*i*t sese uocitare 'magistrum
artibus in cunctis' Graiorum more ferali

72r   qui, licet indocti, tamen omnia scire rogati
caris et primis persaepe fatentur amicis.
desinit haud talem nobis laudare poesim   35
qualem nec pueri dignantur cernere scolis.
hoc auet et bombis pompare poema superbis
gestit et hinc uanam – uentosus! – tollere famam.
abdicat et ueterum coluber documenta uirorum
scismate falsidico necnon et litigioso,   40
sinthecam uerbisque suam comit lutulentam.
dicit eam flamen secum cecinisse supernum
inmemor exempli diuini dogmatis almi,
quod monet ut laudes uitemus et ut populares

Readings in C: 31 metuet, *with a vertical stroke through the* e   36 dedignantur   40 necnon et sirmate litigioso

   26   *sintagma*. A word used by Jerome (*Ep.* 65.6) from Greek σύνταγμα, whence it is found frequently in the glossaries where it is glossed as *compositio* (*CGL* IV, 424.28), *documentum* (*CGL* V, 391.53) and *explanatio.ostensio.interpretatio* (*CGL* V, 558.37); see also *The Corpus Glossary*, ed. W. M. Lindsay, S 723–4, and P. Glogger, ed., *Das Leidener Glossar* (Augsburg, 1901), p. 39.17.

   28   *sophismate*. This word is used in classical Latin by Seneca, who suggests to Lucilius that *sophismata* should best be translated in Latin as *cavillationes* (*Ep.* 111.1). In the *Altercatio* here it does not mean 'sophistry' but rather 'learning'. The word is found only once in the glossaries (*CGL* V, 333.35) where it is explained as *graece generalis philosophia*; this is very close to the meaning it has here.

   29   *et unde est/hoc nomen tractum*. Does the student speak these lines, mimicking the master's class-room procedure? Or does the *magister* taunt the student to decline the very noun he has used contemptuously?

   30   *siet*. It is evident that the poet used this archaic form of *sit* for metrical reasons. Where he may have found such a form is a much more difficult problem. The form is frequent in Plautus and Terence; a list of such occurrences is given in Kühner–Holzweissig, *Ausführliche Grammatik* I, 803. It is improbable that the Anglo-Latin poet would have known Plautus, though he may just have known Terence. Terence was known at Fleury (Ebbo of Fleury had brought the codex Parisinus 7899 there at about this time) and it is quite possible that Winchester, because of its intimate connection with Fleury, may have had a copy of Terence as

untutored themselves, when asked usually say even to their best friends that they know everything (34). He does not desist from praising poetry to us such as not even schoolboys would deign to look at. He craves to praise his poetry in vain bragging and he longs to extend his fame – the wind-bag! – beyond here. And the snake-in-the-grass renounces the teachings of the ancients in false and contentious argumentation, and he glorifies his own muddy composition with the [following] words (41): he says that the celestial spirit has sung it [in collaboration] with him, forgetful of the gracious *exemplum* of divine doctrine which admonishes us to avoid praise and popular fame if we wish to enter the vales of heaven. What else do the precepts of the blessed Christ prohibit us frail mortals from, when he compares the holy kingdom to the ten virgins, than that we avoid human approbation? By which observance those inflated with rubbish and barren

---

well (see L. W. Jones, *The Miniatures of the Manuscripts of Terence* (Princeton, 1931), II, 101). Several late Latin poets – notably Juvencus – revived archaic forms (a thorough study of this conscious archaism in late Latin poetry would be useful!). Thus Juvencus at one point writes 'quae tanta siet permissa potestas' (2.40). Juvencus was a popular school author in England (to judge by the large number of English manuscripts alone), and it is possible that the Anglo-Latin poet found *siet* there.

40 *scismate.* A biblical word from Greek σχίσμα (John IX. 16; I Corinthians I. 10 and XII. 15), used frequently by patristic writers, and found in the glossaries where it is glossed as *diuisio..separatio* (*CGL* IV, 286.3) and as *dissensio* (*CGL* IV, 168.19 and 568.12).

I have deleted *sirmate* to restore the metre. *sirmate* may have been written above *litigioso* as a gloss and subsequently copied into the line. The word *syrma* is found in the glossaries where it is explained as *dictio longa* (*CGL* IV, 172.44 and V, 557.46).

41 *sinthecam.* A glossary word from Greek συνθήκη meaning *compositio* (*CGL* V, 389.50 and 557.4).

lutulentam. Horace likewise describes the poetry of Lucilius as *lutulentum* (*Serm.* I. 10.50) – another indication that the Anglo-Latin poet was familiar with the *Satires.*

rumores si caelica Tempe uelimus adire. 45
quid reliquum prohibent Christi praecepta beati
bis quinis ubi uirginibus pia regna coequat
nos fragiles quam humanos uitare fauores?
quo statim ritu uentosae quesquiliarum
fructibus et uacuae truduntur ab agmine regis 50
et flammis herebi cruciantur et igne perhenni.
his nisi desistas a prauo scismate, Ioruet,
72v incendere, miser, Plutoni consolidatus.
nomine, tuque piger, recto uocitaris 'Ioruet',
peruertens 'iornum' falso sintagmate uerum. 55
desine grandeuos iam iam uexare poetas!

⟨*magister*⟩

o male nate puer, centum ueterane dierum!
per uastum pelagus non te uehit alta triremis
uerum parua celox, fissuris undique fartis;
Thetidis undiuage glaucas iam suscipit undas. 60
Africus et uiolens spumosas uerrit harenas,
Iuppiter et pluuio caelum uelauit amictu –
cernis qua priuos celet sol nube colores.
idcirco noli, moneo, dare uela profundo,

Readings in C: 49 quesquiliarum .i. quisquiliarum   63 calores

---

45 *caelica Tempe*. This phrase would seem to mean the 'vales of heaven' or something of the sort; I have remarked above its extreme rarity. The only four occurrences of the phrase are Anglo-Latin and are late tenth century. It is worthwhile asking if this phrase too has been extracted from glossaries. Two glossaries (each about a century later than the present poem, and dependent the one on the other) give the following interesting gloss to the word *Tempe*: 'locus quidam. nebulis super tectis.in ualle cuius cacumina saxosa et alta multum.puto statuis [i.e. Statius] . . .' (*CGL* v, 157.27 and 248.6). And at this point each glossary quotes the following extract from Statius's *Thebaid*:

stat super occiduae nebulosa cubilia noctis
Aethiopasque alios, nulli penetrabilis astro,
lucus iners, subterque cavis grave rupibus antrum
it vacuum in montem, que desidis atria Somni
securumque larem segnis Natura locavit.
limen opaca Quies et pigra Oblivio servant
et numquam vigili torpens Ignavia vultu.
Otia vestibulo pressisque Silentia pinnis
muta sedent abiguntque truces a culmine ventos
et ramos errare vetant et murmura demunt

of fruit are expelled straightway from the company of the heavenly king and are tortured with the flames of hell and with eternal fire (51). With these flames, Iorvert, unless you desist from your depraved contentiousness, you'll burn, you poor wretch, given over to the possession of Pluto. And, you sluggard, you call yourself by the right name – Iorvert – in that you pervert the [?*iornum*] truth with false teaching. Stop abusing the ancient poets right now! (56)

⟨*magister*⟩

O ill-starred youngster, veteran of a hundred days! A lofty trireme does not carry you across the vast sea, but rather a small skiff with stopped-up cracks on every side; even now it takes in the grey waters of wave-wandering

> alitibus. non hic pelagi, licet omnia clament
> litora, non ullus caeli fragor; ipse profundis
> vallibus effugiens speluncae proximus amnis
> saxa inter scopulosque iacet: nigrantia circum
> armenta, omne solo recubat pecus, et nova marcent
> gramina, terrarumque inclinat spiritus herbas. (*Thebaid* 10.84–99)

I suspect that the poet may have coined the phrase *caelica Tempe* with just this Statian landscape in mind.

49 *quesquiliarum*. This word is not uncommon in Anglo-Latin of the tenth century. It is found in a series of charters of the reign of Edgar: 'qua de re infima quasi peripsima quisquiliarum abiciens ad instar praetiosorum monilium eligens animum sempiternis in gaudiis figens . . .' (Birch, *Cartularium Saxonicum*, nos. 635 and 695).

52 *Ioruet*. In the *Altercatio* and the *Responsio* the name occurs four times, twice spelled *Ioruet* and twice *Ioruert*. The name is Welsh. The first element of the name, *ior*, means 'lord'. In defence of the *Ioruet* spelling it is remotely possible that the second element is an Old Welsh form of *medd*, 'mead', the *m* becoming *u* by mutation (although it is unlikely that this mutation would have been represented orthographically as early as the tenth century). But the name *Ioruet* is nowhere attested in the Welsh genealogies, and the name 'lord of mead' would be highly inappropriate for one who was *insolito potus hydromello*. On the other hand the name *Iorwerth* (which could easily become *Ioruert* in Latin) is abundantly attested in the Welsh genealogies. See *Early Welsh Genealogical Tracts*, ed. P. C. Bartrum (Cardiff, 1966) and the index, pp. 198–9, in particular. Most of the genealogical material is from manuscripts that are later than the *Altercatio*. It is interesting that there should be this reference to a Welsh teacher – a successor to Asser – in Æthelwold's school at Winchester, lecturing on grammar and composing poetry.

55 *iornum*. The meaning of this pun eludes me. The first syllable (*ior*) is again the Welsh word for 'lord', but the suffix -*num* is not Welsh. Has the poet coined a word (meaning 'lordly' or something similar) by adding a Latin adjectival suffix to a Welsh stem?

ah, nimium ne naufragium patiaris iniquum;   65
optatum citius poteris nisi sumere litus
torrens praecipiti iam te submerserit amne.
⟨*discipulus*⟩
conquinisce, precor; foedum iam claude labellum!
si necdum cessare uelis, dic quod, rogo, siscis.
quid genus est distans species idionque colorans?   70
bis ternae que sint normae dialecticae, inqui;
inter quid genus et totum sit, si sapis, infi.

73r   quid pars a specie distet, te posco, profari,
quidque sit et rutilis proprium bis quinque loquelis
remis quae denis quicquid uersatur in orbe   75
sub ditione sua retinent. commune quid, ede.
et quia te modulatorem facis atque sophistam,
nobis dic pueris, sophiae rudibus documentis,
quid diatesseron, diapente sit ac diapason;
dic qu*i*d epogdous atque emiolius ast epytritus.   80
ritmi melodiam quo*t* possunt edere tantam?
partes simphoniae quot sint et nomina, dice;

Readings in C: 69 siscis .i. sciscis   71 inqui .i. inque   72 infi .i. infe   80 quod, uel
a[st] *in main hand above* est   81 quod

68   *conquinisce*. The *Thesaurus Linguae Latinae* (IV, 354.77 ff.) records only five
occurrences of the word: twice in Plautus (*Cist.* 657 and *Pseud.* 864), once each in
Priscian (*gramm.* II, 508.28), Nonius Marcellus (§84), and an atellan fragment of
Pomponius. The imperative form *conquinisce* is nowhere else recorded.

70   *idion*. From the Greek τὸ ἴδιον ('characteristic property', 'distinguishing
feature'), found frequently in the glossaries where it is glossed as *proprium*: *CGL* II,
330.40; III, 5.7, 147.17, 341.59 and 461.31; and V, 365.47.

71   The six norms of dialectic. Cf. Martianus Capella 4.336–8: 'ac prius illud
compertum uolo Romanos togatamque gentem uocabulum nondum nouare
potuisse, ac Dialecticen, sicut Athenis sum solita, nuncupari meique prorsum iuris
esse, quicquid Artes ceterae proloquuntur ... quippe in dicione mea iureque
consistunt sex normae, quis constant ceterae disciplinae. nam prima est de loquendo,
secunda de eloquendo, tertia de proloquendo, quarta de proloquiorum summa,
quinta de iudicando, quae pertinet ad iudicationem poetarum et carminum, sexta
de dicione, quae dicenda rhetoribus commodata est.' The various distinctions
genus, totum, pars, species (forma) are discussed in turn by Martianus 4.344–51.

inqui for *inque* (the orthographic variation of *i* and *e* is frequent in this manuscript;
see below, note to *de libero arbitrio* 30), the impv. of *inquam*. This form is attested only
in Plautus (*Bacch.* 883, *Merc.* 904 and *Pseud.* 538) and Terence (*Heaut.* 829 and
Phorm. 919).

Thetys. And the violent south-west wind sweeps along swirling sands and Jupiter has concealed the sky with a rainy garment: you see by what clouds the sun hides its own brilliance. For that reason do not, I warn you, set sail on the deep – alas! – lest you suffer a most terrible shipwreck. Unless you can reach the hoped-for shore quickly, the torrent will overwhelm you with its violent waters (67).

⟨*discipulus*⟩

Be humble, I pray you; close your foul mouth right now. And if you don't yet wish to cease, tell what you know, please. What is the *genus* which distinguishes the *species* and imparts the characteristic feature? Tell what are the six dialectical norms; say what is the difference between the *genus* and the whole, if you know it. I ask you to say how the individual part differs from the species, and what is particular to the ten resplendent predicates which keep the totality of expression under their control by means of ten subjects. Tell us what a common property is (76). And since you fancy yourself a musician and a sage, tell us boys, uncultivated in wisdom's doctrine, what is the *diatesseron*, what the *diapente* and what the *diapason*. Tell what is the *epogdous* and the *hemiolius* or the *epitritus*. How many harmonies can produce such a melodious sound? Tell how many parts of harmony there are and what are their names; make known now the [?essence ?substance] of the

---

72 *infi* for *infe* (*i* and *e* variation again), apparently the impv. of *infit*. Except for the present instance, this extremely rare form is attested only twice in all Latin, both times in a glossary. It occurs in a Greek–Latin glossary (*CGL* II, 82.2) where it is glossed as ἄρξε, and in the Parisinus lat. 11529–30 glossary, where the entry *infe.incipe dic narra* is found. The latter glossary is later than the composition of the poem.

75 *remis* from the Greek ῥῆμα, meaning here 'verb' or 'predicate'. It would seem that the ten 'verbs' or 'predicates' (ῥήματα) in conjunction with the ten 'subjects of speech' (*loquelae*) together constitute the totality of expression. The meaning of *loquela*, however, is virtually identical to that of ῥῆμα. For the ten ῥήματα see Martianus Capella 3.310.

79–82 The elements of musical theory: Censorinus, *de die natali* 10.6 ff.; Martianus Capella, *de nuptiis* 7.761 and 9.950–9; Favonius Eulogius, *Disputatio de somnio Scipionis* 22–4; Macrobius, *in somn. Scip.* 2.1.14–25; Calcidius, *in Timaeum* 45–8; Fulgentius, *Mitologiae* 3.9.127–8; and Boethius, *de musica* 1.10 ff.

80 *ast*. At the scribe's suggestion I have preferred the reading *ast* to *est*. If the reading *est* be preferred, the difference between direct and indirect speech must be accounted for, and the lines must be punctuated as follows:

> quid diatesseron, diapente sit ac diapason,
> dic. quid epogdous atque emiolius est epytritus?

artis et eximiae †lisina† nunc indice prode,
materiemque repertor*u*m patri*u*mque locellum.
hac ratione uales ferulis nos subdere priuis   85

. . . .

ad suam calcis poterint si dogmate duci,
optime praeceptor, uerax et habebere doctor.
omnia si sa*p*ere *et* narrare nequibis, adelphe,
spulpus eris, spulcus fueris, spulsusque manebis.
et quoniam nullum nos credis fingere metrum   90
(quod scelus est, iuras) sine menda posse, maligne,
ut scis falsidicus, stolidus, periurus, ineptus,
ter decies denos uersus cape, postque sileto!

73ᵛ   dicis adhuc, peruerse senex, nostros bene uersus
haud fore compactos uerum compage solutos –   95
†lempiris cruttonempiris et utique lillo†
⟨*magister*⟩
quin etiam nescire (nefas!) me dicis ymeras
per quas discurrens solidum sol conficit annum,
ni fallor, breuiter ueris sermonibus edam.
sunt ter centenae decies et denique senae   100

Readings in *C*: 84 repertorem, patriamque   88 sisabere

83   *lisina*. This word is corrupt, no doubt, but what it conceals is not readily discernible. Perhaps *usian* (*li* and *u* are often confused; *na* from *an* by transposition), which would preserve the true quantity of the Greek οὐσίαν. Against this is the fact that this poet generally avoids elision (note the hiatus between *quam* and *humanos* in 48 and between *dialecticae* and *inqui* in 71).

84   *repertorum*. G.pl. of *reperta*, 'discoveries'.

85   To resolve the conflict between *uales* (85) and *poterint* (86) I have posited a lacuna.

86   *calcis*. As it stands, this line makes no sense. Some sense may be made out of it by emending to *calcem* ('if through instruction they may be led to their goal'). But if, as I believe, some lines have been dropped out after 85, it is not possible to interpret 86 securely.

89   *spulpus eris* ... etc. There is no need for emendation here. This is sheer foolery. The words are formed on the analogy of *spurcus, stultus, spretus* and others.

95   *compage solutos*. An amusing reminiscence of Lucan 1.72.

96   *lempiris* etc. The line as transmitted is corrupt; the scribe would seem to have confused Greek words which were unfamiliar to him. The line might be tentatively restored as follows:

†lempiris	cruttonempiris	et utique	lillo†
[l]ἔμπειρος	κρύπτων ἐμπείροις	et utique	[κ]ίλλο[s]

'an expert concealing [his knowledge] from experts, and assuredly an ass'

most excellent art by some indication, and both the matter of your discoveries and your native treasure chest. By this procedure you will be able to subject us to your birch-rods (85) . . . if they may be led by instruction to their [?goal], O best of teachers, you will truly be considered a 'doctor'. If you don't know and can't explain all these things, brother, *spulpus* you'll be, *spulcus* you will have been, and *spulsus* you'll remain. And since you believe maliciously that we can compose no poetry without errors (which is a crime, you swear) – as you well know, you liar, dolt, perjuror, fool – take three hundred verses yourself, then be silent! (93) You still say, you perverse old man, that our verses are not well composed but rather give way at the seams – [you're an expert concealing his knowledge from experts, and assuredly an ass!] (96)

⟨*magister*⟩

Since you even say (O the horror of it!) that I don't know the days through which the sun in passing makes up the complete year, I shall tell you in true words (unless I err!). There are three hundred and then sixty to which are added five, not to mention a quarter which is joined on, which consists in six hours and thirty points, if you will, and I wish [to stress] that there are

---

It is noteworthy that both ἔμπειρος and κρύπτω are found in a seventh-century Greek–Latin glossary (BM Harley 5792, ptd *CGL* II, 214–483); ἔμπειρος is glossed as *expertus.peritus.sollers* (*CGL* II, 296.22) and κρύπτω as *celo.occulto.condo* (*CGL* II, 355.54). Many problems remain, however. First, κρύπτω has no direct object. The word κίλλος is extremely rare (as is the word μιλλός, 'slow of mind', 'dull'), but 1 can propose no suitable alternative. Finally, *ŭtique* has here a false quantity. The quantity may present no problem; cf. *de libero arbitrio* 123 ('sed pandit geminos mortalibus utique calles'), where the syllable is taken as long.

97   *ymeras*. This false quantity is well sanctioned by Anglo-Latin poetic practice; e.g. Wulfstan, *Narratio de S. Swithuno* 1.1082: 'illius ad tumulum, tres dum sol uertit ymeras'.

100   The numbers are slightly confusing: 300 (*ter centenae*) and then 60 (*decies denique senae*) and then 5 (*quinque superpositis*).

100–3   This material may conveniently be read in Bede, *de temporibus* 10 (PL 90, col. 284) or *de temporum ratione* 16 (PL 90, cols. 358–61); in Hrabanus Maurus, *de computo* (PL 107, cols. 670ff.); in Helperic, *de computo* (PL 137, cols. 17ff.); in the anonymous *de computo dialogus* (PL 90, cols. 650ff.); in Ælfric's *de temporibus anni*, which is in English and is very nearly contemporary with the poem's composition (ed. H Henel, EETS 213 (London, 1940), 30 and 52–6); or in Byrhtferth's *Manual* which is only slightly later (1011) (ed. S. J. Crawford, EETS 177 (London, 1928) 2 ff.). The poet of the *Altercatio* departs somewhat from received opinion in making an hour consist in five *puncti* rather than four (hence his statement in 103); perhaps he has confused the solar hour (which has four *puncti*) with the lunar hour (which has five).

quinque superpositis necnon quadrante iugato,
conficitur qui sex horis punctisque triginta,
si libet, et uolumus quinos horae fore punctos.
si*c*que quaternos bis denis mox adde quaternis.
quattuor annorum circis idcirco peractis   105
una dies interseritur quae iure 'bisextus'
(sextis quod Martis prisco de more kalendis
interponatur) recto uocitamine fatur.
nemo catus priscas audebit uertere normas.
nempe scio; brut*os* quapropter rite monebo   110
conentur ueterem ne uertere conditionem,

74r   ne post perniciem nigram transire paludem
cogantur miseri monstrumque uidere triforme.
desine praua loqui, rogo, seditiosa †camena†
inferni tenebras ne post patiaris amaras.   115
⟨*discipulus*⟩
infelix mortale genus quod talia curat
stultorum dictis et perturbatur iniquis!
nonne foret dominum satius tibi poscere Christum
crimina qu*i* tibimet laxet, post praemia donet
caelestis patriae, cuneis societque supernis?   120
conditione, pater, tali, te flagito, Ioruert:
hinc reprimas linguam nimium quo*d* seditiosam,
rursus stultiloquam ne cogas sumere pennam
me, qui mox actus, mores patriosque notabo.
sordes parce; precorque iterum mihi talia scribe.   125

Readings in C: 104 sique   110 bruttis   119 quo   122 quo

106   *bisextus* (misspelled *metri gratia*), cf. Bede, *de temporum ratione* 36 (PL 90, col. 463): 'item solis est annus, cum ad eadem loca siderum rediit, peractis CCCLXV diebus et VI horis, id est, quadrante totius diei, quae pars quater ducta cogit interponi diem unum quod Romani bissextum vocant . . .'

114   *seditiosa camena.* If the line is to be allowed to stand as transmitted, it must be assumed that the poet took *camena* to be n.pl., 'poems'. Though a mistake of this sort is possible for a poet drawing a great share of his vocabulary from glossaries, I can produce no parallel for this particular mistake. It is also possible that *camena* conceals *carmina*; *carmina* would be metrically intolerable in this position, but one could further assume a transposition of *seditiosa* and *carmina*. Accordingly the original line may have been:

desine praua loqui, rogo, carmina seditiosa

120   *cuneis supernis* 'heavenly hosts'. The phrase also occurs in a hymn to Æthelwold by Wulfstan, preserved in a Rouen manuscript (formerly at Jumièges

five points to the hour. Accordingly you add four at a time to the twenty fours [you already have]. Therefore once four revolutions of years have been completed, one day is inserted which is justly called the 'bissextus' by its proper name (because, following ancient custom, it was interposed at the sixth kalends of March [i.e. between 24 and 25 February]) (108). No one who is wise will dare to overthrow these ancient customs. I know, to be sure; for that reason I shall duly instruct brutes lest they attempt to overthrow the established tradition, so that after death they won't be compelled (the poor wretches!) to cross the black swamp and see the three-headed monster [i.e. Cerberus]. Stop writing foul, quarrelsome [?poems] lest you undergo afterwards the bitter shadow of hell (115).

⟨*discipulus*⟩

Unhappy mortal race that cares for such [nonsense] and is disturbed by the injurious words of fools! Will it not be sufficient for you to seek Christ who shall absolve your sins, who afterwards shall grant the rewards of the heavenly homeland, and enlist you in the heavenly hosts? I beseech you, Iorvert, my father, on such a condition: henceforth you repress your excessively quarrelsome tongue lest you compel me to take up again my foolish-speaking pen, me, who at once will delineate your deeds and native customs. Spare your filth; and, I pray you, write such poetry to me again (125).

---

but written at Winchester). The hymn is edited by C. Blume, 'Wolstan von Winchester und Vital von Saint-Evroult', *Sitzungsberichte der k. Akad. d. Wiss. in Wien* 146, 3 (1903), 6. (See also the comments by L. Delisle, *Journal des Savants* 1 (1903), 429 ff.) It is interesting to note that a later redaction of the poem by a Norman author (in an Alençon manuscript) deletes this curious phrase. Wulfstan writes 'nos super aethra poli cuneis adiunge supernis' which the Norman poet changes to 'nomina nostra notet quo Christus in arce polorum' (Blume, p. 6). Apparently the preciosity of the Anglo-Latin phrase was offensive to Norman taste. It is at any rate a curious phrase, and may indicate once more that Wulfstan was familiar with the *Altercatio*.

125   *parce*. The ante-classical use of *parco* with accusative is also found (but rarely) in late Latin; see Leumann–Hofmann–Szantyr, *Lateinische Grammatik* II, 32–3.

Responsio discipuli

74v

Gaudia dicto
iure magistro
necne salutem!
legat usia
prima secundam   5
pandere cunctis
quae ualet omne.
  nonne pudicum
ueridicumque
te fore iactas,   10
optime Ioruert?
cur mea falso
carmina blasmas,
dum neque uersum
rite queas nunc   15
pandere falsum?
aut mihi mendas
dice nefandas,
aut resipisce
atque fatere   20
non fore uerum
ore scelesto
teque locutum.
feceris hocni?
follis eris hic   25
ac furibundus,
stultiloquaxue,
siue malignus!
nempe, pater, scis
quod rationem   30
reddere debes –
Christus ut infit
de male gestis
necne profatis
ore loquelis   35
– luce sub illa
ualde tremenda,
qua manifesta
crimina cunctis

Responsio discipuli

I justly express my joy to my master as well as [my wishes for his] health.
First substance, which is in good health, appoints second to make known
everything to all (7).

Don't you vaunt yourself to be modest and truthful, excellent Iorvert?
Why do you falsely slander my poems, while you can't even compose a
verse that is faulty? Either show me my terrible mistakes, or else come to
your senses and confess it is not true and that you spoke with villainous
tongue (23). Won't you have done that then? You'll be a bellows in this
affair, and insane, or foolish, or else spiteful. For you know, father, that
you must render account – as Christ says of evil deeds as well as words

---

This poem is written in adonics (dactylic dimeter acatalectic); I know of no other
Anglo-Latin poetry in this metre. This metre was known to the Middle Ages
chiefly through Martianus Capella (*de nuptiis* 2.125) and Boethius (*de consolatione
philosophiae* 1, met. 8). To judge from the content of the present poems alone, each
of these authors was quite well known in tenth-century England (see above, note
to *Altercatio* 71 and pp. 103–4), and either of them may have provided the poet with
a model for his adonics.

13   *blasmas*. This form is attested nowhere else in Latin. There can be little
doubt that it derives in syncopated form from Greek βλασ[φη]μέω, 'to slander', a
word which is found frequently in the Vulgate in the Latinized form *blasphemare*.

iure patebunt   40
quae, quasi non sint,
corde latent nunc.
  hoc ideo te
posco benigne:
seditiosam   45
comprime linguam.
de reliquo nec
talia cures
uerba profari:
te fore comptum   50
artibus, et nos
posse poesim
fingere nullam.
desipis. atqui
credere ni uis   55
quod pueri sic
edere metrum
(improbe!) possunt
hic resident qui
dogmate docti   60
pontificali,
ut neque sensum
prodere murcum
siue poema
non fore rectum: 65
indice quibus
rite loquel*is*,
temet adhortor.
  conditione
denique tali,   70
frater amice,
desine iam nos
rodere uerbis.
ira recedat,
pace sequestra.   75
foedus et almum
consolidemus,
ne patiamur
demonis atras

75r (left margin, at line 55)

Reading in C: 67 loquela

spoken by the mouth – under that light greatly to be feared whereby all sins shall be manifest to all which, as though they didn't exist, now lie hidden in the heart (42).

For that reason I kindly beseech you: restrain your quarrelsome tongue. For the rest, may you not care to say such words: that you are accomplished in the arts and that we can compose no poetry. You're being foolish (54). And unless you wish to believe (you scoundrel!) that we boys who live here and are taught by the bishop's teaching can compose verse in such a way as neither to give a mutilated sense nor an incorrect poem, show us properly by what words [we err], I urge you (68).

Accordingly, under such a condition, my friend and brother, stop slandering us with your words. Let your anger abate, with peace in its wake. And

---

66   *indice.* False quantity here (*indīce*), as perhaps also at *Altercatio* 83.

inde catenas. 80
  conditor almus,
trinus et unus,
crimina nobis
cuncta relaxet,
  coetibus atque 85
consociatis,
poscimus, almis,
praebeat omne
cernere nobis
lumen in aeuum. 90

Carmen de libero arbitrio

75v Cuncta creans, natura triplex in usiade simpla,
  est natura deus, quicquid et ipse creat.
mentes insipidas sancto qui pneumate purgas
  me modo ueridica, posco, doce sophia
quid series fati, quid porrouidentia cosmi, 5
  liber et effectus antesciens animus,
gratia quid regis, praedestiuenatio quid sit,
  omnia qui uerbo condidit ex nihilo.
mens diuina cubum tria tempora nectit in unum;
  haec uidet in praesens, praeteritumque, sequens, 10
cuius ab intuitu nequeunt res flectere cursus.
  fatalis series ordinat omne quod est:
omnipotentis heri quicquid prouincia cernit
  actus per uarios digerit haec series.
dicimus haud aliud fatum uarios nisi rerum 15
  successus. taceat, flagito, stultiloquax!
notio, credo, quod est rerum qua prescius auctor
  quos nouit iustos conuocat ad superos,
uerbis quod sanctis exponit apostolus. inquit:
  'praesciuit famulos omnipotens proprios, 20
76r destinat, amplificat hos, iustificatque coronat,
  saluat, sanctificat, protegit atque fouet.'
arbitrii quoque libertas est priua uoluntas;
  haec mortem miseris praebet et astra probis.
partes in geminas dirimit genuina potestas: 25
  his reserat caelum, pandit et his herebum.
cognitio domini ne*c* uult abolere superni

Reading in C: 27 ne

let us establish a gentle treaty, lest we thereafter undergo the black chains of the demon (80).

May the benign creator, the three and one, forgive all our sins and, joined with the gentle heavenly host, we pray, may he grant to us that we see the light in all eternity (90).

Carmen de libero arbitrio

All-creating, threefold nature in uniform substance, God is nature and whatsoever he creates. You who purify our feeble minds through the agency of the Holy Ghost, teach me now with true wisdom, I pray, what be the series of fate, what the providence of the cosmos, what the unrestricted mind foreknowing [future] events, what the grace of the [heavenly] king, who created all things out of nothing by means of the Word, [and] what be predestination (8).

The divine mind binds the three times together into one cube; it sees into the present, the past and the future, from whose inspection created things may not bend their course. The fatal series ordains everything which exists: whatsoever the office of the omnipotent Lord regards, this series orders through various acts. I say that fate is nothing other than the various successive occurrences of things. Let any foolish objector be silent, I earnestly request! (16) I think that it is a conception of the world whereby the

---

This poem is written in elegiac couplets.

1 *usiade*. I have not found this form elsewhere. One wonders whether the poet (or his source) had misunderstood Greek οὐσία δέ or οὐσία δή. Or perhaps the *-de* is added to satisfy the metrical requirement, as *-or* is added to *prouidentia* in line 5.

2 *est, creat*. The transition to *purgas* in 3 would be less abrupt if one were to read *es* and *creas* in 2, though the transmitted text makes some sense.

5 *porrouidentia*. The poet clearly means *prouidentia*, but that word would not satisfy the exigencies of metre (*prōuĭdentĭa*). So the poet added an extra syllable, after the manner of Ennius, *induperator* (*Ann.* 1.27) and Lucretius, *indugredi* (1.82).

7 *praedestiuenatio*. Neither would *praedestĭnātĭo* scan. The enclitic *-ue* is inserted in the stem of the word to provide an extra syllable; this by a respectable practice called tmesis.

16 *laceat . . . stultiloquax*. The outburst against the imagined interlocutor is a device found frequently in Anglo-Latin poetry.

20 Cf. Romans VIII. 29.

arbitrium per quod comprobat ipsa suos.
o diuina dei pietas quae cuncta gubernas,
    legibus aeternis cosmica nexa l*i*gas;   30
pande tuis rigidum famulis rimantibus aequum:
    hoc genus humanum cur habet arbitrium
quod uehit a! poenas miseras barathrique ruinas,
    pro dolor! unde nefas promeruere iuge?
fraudibus anguinis postquam periere perempti   35
    ah! patria pulsi primigenae miseri
a quibus omne scelus uastum defluxit in orbem
    (quot natura creat sors homin*i*sque necat!)
effectum libertatis habuere malignum,
    corrupti uitiis criminibusque feris,   40

  76v   nec meritis uitam possent sperare beatam
    adiuti domini ni pietate forent
sanguine qui geniti lauit contagia mundi.
    felix culpa fuit talia quae meruit!
nam nesciret homo quantum se diligit auctor   45
    ni factura pius fieret ille deus,
qui nobis cupiens praebere suam deitatem
    artus humanos horruit haud fragiles.
hinc tamen effectus sileat, rogo, seditiosus:
    nullam uim patitur cognitione dei.   50
hoc propter poenis reprobi cruciantur amaris
    atque diem nequeunt cernere luciferum;
caelica Tempe probos facitis penetrare cluentes
    *u*t capiti Christo membra uenusta iug*ent*.

Readings in C: 30 legas   38 hominesque   54 et, iugat

30   *ligas* for MS *legas*. It will be noticed that the variation of *i* and *e* is frequent
in this manuscript; cf. *Altercatio* 14 (*atqui* for *atque*), 31 (*metuet* for *metuit*), 49
(*quesquiliarum*), 71 (*inqui* for *inque*) and 72 (*infi* for *infe*), as well as *de libero arbitrio*
38 and 181. Thus *legas* for *ligas* is to be considered rather as a variant spelling than
as a scribal error.

38   *hominisque* for MS *hominesque*. See above, note to line 30.

44   This line is from the Blessing of the Paschal Candle (*The Gregorian Sacramentary*, ed. H. A. Wilson. Henry Bradshaw Society (London, 1915)): 'o felix culpa
quae talem ac tantum meruit habere Redemptorem.'

53   *Tempe*. Here, as at *Altercatio* 45, the quantity of *Tempe* is false.
facitis is apparently a 'majestic' plural and addresses God.

54   It is not easy to see what MS *iugat* might refer to here. I conjecture *ut . . .
iugent*: 'that they may join their beautiful members to Christ, the head'. The line is

prescient creator summons those whom he knows to be just to him on high, which the apostle (Paul) expounds in holy words. He says: 'the omnipotent Father knew his own servants beforehand, he destines and strengthens these, vindicates and crowns, saves, sanctifies, protects and cherishes them.' Also, freedom of will is a personal choice; it grants death to the miserable and [life beyond the] stars to the good. This inborn power divides [mankind] into two halves: to these it opens heaven, to others it throws open hell (26). The understanding of our heavenly Lord does not wish to do away with this free will through which it proves who are its own [i.e. God's own]. O divine mercy of God which governs all things, tying together cosmic bonds with eternal laws: explain your stern justice to your inquiring servants – why does the human race have this free will which brings about (alas!) miserable punishments and the catastrophe of hell, from whence (how sad!) they deserved this perpetual wretchedness? (34)

After the wretched first men (Adam and Eve) perished, brought to ruin by the deceptions of the serpent and expelled (alas!) from their first home, from whom all sin poured into the vast world (how many things nature creates and the fate of man destroys!), they possessed the wicked effect of [their] free will, corrupt in vice and bestial sins, nor could they by their own merits hope for the blessed [eternal] life unless they had been assisted by the mercy of the Lord who, with the blood of his only-begotten Son washed away the sins of the world (43). A happy guilt it was which merited such [a redemption]! For man would not know how much his creator loves him unless that merciful God had become a creature himself, who, desiring to offer his godhead to us, did not scorn fragile human limbs. Hence let the quarrelsome creature be silent, I pray: it suffers no violence through the understanding of God's ways. For this reason sinners are tormented with bitter pains and cannot see the light-bringing day; but you [God] make your virtuous followers penetrate to the vales of heaven that they may join their beautiful limbs to the head, Christ (54).

That our doctrine may resound more clearly, we put in a few words some examples in the middle [of the poem] (56).

---

thus a conflation of two Pauline passages: I Corinthians XII.12 – 'sicut enim corpus unum est, et membra habet multa, omnia autem membra corporis cum sint multa, unum tamen corpus sunt: ita et Christus' (cf. I Corinthians VI. 15) together with Ephesians IV. 15–16 – 'per omnia, qui est caput Christus: ex quo totum corpus compactum, et connexum per omnem iuncturam subministrationis' (cf. Ephesians I. 22–3).

sermones nostri paucis paradigmata uerbis 55
ponimus in medium clarius ut resonent.
praesul et insigni clarissime dignus honore,
uates clariuidens, doctor et egregie,
augustam regi sedem qui corde parasti
expertem neui, criminis ac uitii, 60

77r   rex quia quem celsi nequeunt concludere caeli,
mentibus in sanctis is manet ac nitidis.
dogmate quodque mones claris prius actibus imples,
solamen, uirtus, pastor et exulibus.
claret hoc a domino quod ce*l*sa talenta benigno 65
sint tibi, summe pater: te decus omne decet.
mente meos sensus stolidos tu conspice, rector,
quod male dico loquens, corrige, posco cliens.
rex sapiens residet specula sublimis in alta
prouidus ac pugnax, praep*e*te mente sagax, 70
militibus multis circumdatus ac pretiosis,
bis seno procerum septus honore ducum,
†sarranis† recubans ostris sericisque tapetis:
is iubet in stadio currere mille uiros.
uestes purpureas centum totidemque coronas 75
imperat eximio ponere pro titulo
ante suos uisus, ac tali uoce profatur:
'uelox miles erit qui meus esse cupit,
qui celer optatam poterit contingere palmam
mox sertum capiat condicione mea, 80

77v   in numero satrapumque merebitur esse meorum
stemmate regali comptus et exuuiis;
qui piger et metam non quibit adire fugacem
inmunis redeat et titulis careat.
hic caesus diris uibicibus atque flagellis 85
nexus compedibus carceribus dabitur.
coetibus ille meis sociabitur atque cateruis;
cleptibus iste feris, ridiculus populis.'
rex deus est genitor, cuius sapientia proles,
spiritus et sanctus sp*l*endida sit specula; 90

Readings in C: 61 uel circumdare *written above* concludere *in main hand*   65 cessa
70 praepote   85 uel multis *written above* diris *in main hand*   90 spendida

55–6 The syntax is difficult: 'ut sermones nostri resonent clarius, ponimus paucis uerbis paradigmata in medium [carminis].'

Most distinguished bishop, worthy of extraordinary esteem, far-seeing poet, excellent man of learning, who prepared a mighty seat for the king with your heart free of blemish, sin and vice, a king who, since the high heavens could not contain him, yet remains in our holy and shining minds. Whatsoever you preach, you first practise in noble deeds; you are a solace, [a source of] virtue and a good shepherd to exiles. It is clear from the beneficent Lord that heavenly rewards are to be yours, greatest father: all glory is appropriate for you. Supervise with your mind my stolid faculties, master; what I express poorly correct, I your follower beseech you (68).

A wise king sits elevated on a high watch-tower, provident and militant, sagacious because of his alert mind, surrounded by many splendidly arrayed soldiers, enclosed by the dignity of twelve elders [or] leaders, reclining in purple [garments] on silk coverlets: this king commands a thousand men to run a race in the stadium. He orders a hundred purple robes and as many crowns to be placed before him as the highest possible reward, and speaks as follows (77): 'that soldier who wishes to be mine shall be swift; [he] who can attain to the desired victor's palm, let him capture the wreath according to my conditions, and he will deserve to be among the number of my viceroys, adorned with regal garlands and clothing; he who is sluggish and cannot attain the elusive goal, let him return unrewarded and lack recognition. Carved up with weals and lashes, and bound with shackles, he shall be committed to prison. The one will be associated with my followers and flock; the other with savage thieves, a laughing-stock to the people' (88).

---

61 *concludere.* The alternative reading which the scribe has added here in superscript (*circumdare*), as he has done at 85 and 101, presents some problem. For in each case the proposed alternatives cannot be construed simply as glosses, and in each case there seems to be little reason for deciding in favour of either reading. One is inclined to assume that the scribe was copying from the poet's working manuscript, and that the alternative readings were jotted down by the poet himself.

72 *bis seno.* The use of singular distributives is not common in Latin poetry of any period. This line is possibly modelled on Juvencus 2.430–1: 'haec fatus populo ex omni delecta seorsum/fortia conglomerat bisseno pectora coetu.'

73 *sarranis.* This word is found nowhere else. It is perhaps a corrupt form of either *saracis* ('a sort of tunic', see Du Cange *s.u. sarica*) or perhaps *sarapis*, a Latinized form of Greek σάραπις, 'a Persian robe with purple stripes'.

88 *cleptibus. Cleptes* is a common glossary word from Greek κλέπτης; see *CGL* II, 74.36, 350.28, 507.18 and 556.42 and III, 5.17, 14.7, 86.76, 147.47, 179.32, 251.41, 406.61 and 449.49; in each of these instances it is glossed as *fur*.

pallade ceu proprios sapiens rex ordinat actus,
   sic pater omnipotens omnia per sobolem;
sicut hic a solio certamina conspicit alto,
   omne quod hic gerimus flamine sicque deus.
prospectusque ducum sit contemplatio rerum;   95
   quod fuit, est, et erit haec uidet atque regit.
gratia sit domini pietas regisue uoluntas
   militibus dignis praemia quae tribuit.
arbitrii libertatem nam scammata signant;
   praesens uita gerit sic spatium stadii   100

78r   ut cursus alios dampnant aliosque coronant:
   uictus supplicium, uictor adit pretium.
liber hic effectus nostros sic dirigit actus;
   hunc uehit ad caelum, destinat hunc barathro.
sponsio sic regis praedestiuenatio: caelo   105
   promittit sanctis quae bona pro meritis,
inferni miseros et cogit adire tenebras
   arbitrio proprio qui periere mali.
rebus in humanis reor antescientia non sit;
   cunctisator rerum possidet hoc proprium.   110
in quantum fragilis hominum natura creantem
   aequiperare potest? esse quid hoc specimen
dicere nemo ualet; sed quantum res periturae
   distant a stabili simplicitate dei!
intuitus regis certantibus haud nocet illis;   115
   praesidium nulli ferre potest homini;
rex etiam uastis interstitiis segregatus
   nec solum uisu, sed neque uoce, manu.
actus praeteritos, praesentes, necne futuros
   auctor sic hominum prospicit intuitu,   120

78v   et quamuis ualeat mentes peruertere sontes
   ad meliora, tamen nil nocet arbitrio;
sed pandit geminos mortalibus utique calles:
   sentosus dexter, leuus ubique patet.
uix iter angustum raris comeantibus idem   125

Readings in C: 101 uel [dampn]e[nt] uel [coron]e[nt] *written in main hand above* dampnant *and* coronant   114 distent   120 autor

91   *pallade*. This word is unknown elsewhere and would seem to mean 'wisely' or something of the sort. It is perhaps a coinage from Pallas the goddess of wisdom, meaning 'after the manner of Pallas', that is, 'wisely'.

The king represents God the creator, whose wisdom is his Son, and let the splendid watch-tower be the Holy Ghost; as the king ordains his particular actions providently, so the omnipotent Father ordains everything through the agency of the Son; as the king observes the competition from his lofty throne, so God [observes] everything we do on earth through the agency of the Holy Ghost. Let the inspection of the leaders represent the [cosmic] contemplation of things; this [contemplation] sees and governs everything that was, is and shall be. Let the mercy or will of the king which grants rewards to worthy soldiers be the grace of the Lord (98). For the racecourse signifies free will; as the length of the racecourse represents this present life, so the racecourse damns some and crowns others: the conquered gets punishment, the conqueror reward. Here on earth free action thus directs our deeds: it takes one man to heaven, destines another to hell. Similarly the promise of the king [represents] predestination, which promises bounties to the saints in heaven according to their merits, and compels those miserable wretches to go to the shadows of hell who perished by their own will (108). I reckon that there is no foreknowledge in the human condition; the all-creator alone possesses this. In what way may the fragile nature of men equal [their] creator? What the difference is, no one is able to say; but how greatly do ephemeral things differ from the stable simplicity of God! The inspection of the king does not harm those who are in the contest; it may offer no assistance to any man. The king is even separated by vast distances, cut off not only by sight, but by voice and touch as well (118). Likewise the creator of men observes with his understanding our past, present and future deeds, and although he could turn our evil minds to better things yet he does not interfere with our will; but he does provide as it were two paths for mortals: the one on the right is thorny, the one on the left is completely open. He scarcely draws the narrow path to the attention of those few who follow it,

---

94 *flamine* 'through the agency of the Holy Ghost'. *flamen* in this sense (translating πνεῦμα) is frequently found in Anglo-Latin. e.g. Lantfridus, *Translatio et miracula S. Swithuni* (ed. E. P. Sauvage, *AB* 4 (1885), 400):

> alme Deus atque clemens,
> qui coelum, terram ac mare
> sancto gubernas flamine. . .

Also Frithegodus, *Breuiloquium* 491: 'in Patris et Nati, necnon et Flaminis Almi'.

110 *cunctisator*. This word is not attested anywhere in Latin, to my knowledge, and is perhaps a neologism here. Anglo-Latin authors are particularly fond of compound words in *cuncti-*, such as *cunctipotens* and *cunctitonans*.

118 *neque* after *sed* is slightly awkward. A small change to *quoque* would afford a more elegant expression.

signat, et is uitam ducit ad aetheriam;
alter adest spatio diffusus denique uasto:
    omne uehit barathrum pene genus hominum.
nosque sequi dextrum iubet ac uitare sinistrum
    cunctorum dominus lucifer atque salus   130
Christus cunctipotens qui cum patre regnat ubique,
    dogmatibus sanctis infit ubi populis.
semita stricta polum poterit reserare supernum,
    illam neruosus siquis adire cupit;
perniciemque parant sinuosi competa callis.   135
    mentis nunc oculis cernite uos, socii.
credo quod hoc domini demonstrent dogmata Christi:
    nemo labore carens percipiet requiem.
quapropter uitam si uultis habere perhennem
    ut sitis, fratres, uos moneo, celeres,   140
79r   ne torpore graui perdatis praemia caeli
    miles ut ille piger brauia tripudii.
currere nosque monent domini sintagmata Christi
    militis ac Pauli currere nosque docent,
scamatis in specie nostros ubi significauit   145
    actus humanos scamatis in specie.
pergite, posco, uiri, capiatis ut astra tonantis
    atque superna poli: pergite, posco, uiri.
his patet exemplis quod contemplatio uiri
    haud uertat proprium iudicis arbitrium,   150
uota, preces domino nisi quis pro flagitioso
    fuderit, omne scelus uertat ut in melius.
proles *at* aetherii splendorque sophia parentis
    laxat dira suis crimina tortoribus.
plures inde polum meruerunt scandere clarum   155
    consortes facti coetibus angelicis.

Readings in C: 131 patere   134 neuosis   148 tes qua   153 ut

123–4 The image of the *bivium* is common in medieval literature of all periods;
see the recent and extensive study by W. Harms, *Homo Viator in Bivio: Studien zur
Bildlichkeit des Weges*, Medium Aevum, Philologische Studien 21 (Munich, 1970).

134 *neruosus*. This emendation was suggested to me by Dr D. B. Gain of the
University of the Witwatersrand. I am very grateful to Dr Gain for reading the
text of these poems carefully and for making many helpful suggestions.

142 *brauium*. A biblical word from Greek βραβεῖον meaning 'prize' or 'reward';
cf. I Corinthians IX. 24 and Philippians III. 14.

and it leads to eternal life. The other is spread out over a wide space: it takes nearly the whole human race to hell (128). The lord of all things, the light-bringer and salvation, admonishes us to follow the right and avoid the left [path], Christ the all-powerful who reigns everywhere with his Father, in those places where he speaks to the peoples through his holy teaching. The straight and narrow path will open [the way to] the skies above, if anyone is energetic enough to follow it. The crossways of the winding path prepare destruction. Now, my friends, look with the eyes of your spirit (136). I believe that the teachings of Christ the Lord demonstrate this: [that] no one who fails to work will receive rest. Wherefore, if you wish to have eternal life, brothers, I advise you to be swift, lest you lose the rewards of heaven through heavy-footed sluggishness, as that lazy runner lost the prize of the race (142).

The teachings of Christ the Lord advise us to run, and those of Paul his soldier advise us to run [as well], where he signified our human actions with the likeness of the arena. Press on, men, I beseech you, that you may acquire the stars of the thunderer [i.e. God] and the lofty realms of the heavens: press on, men, I beseech you (148).

It is clear from these examples that the contemplation of man does not alter the will of the judge, unless one will have poured prayers and supplications to the Lord for one's sins, in order that one may turn all one's sin into something better. But the Son, the splendour and wisdom of the aetherial parent, forgives the dire sins of his tormentors. Therefore many have deserved to ascend the bright heaven, made consorts to the angelic hosts (156). The pious Stephen the Levite, moved by this virtue, made the illustrious Paul proceed to God. Thus let us too beseech the lord of heaven,

---

tripudii. A word of biblical origin meaning 'joy' (Esther VIII. 16), but known from the glossaries to mean specifically the joy of winning (*CGL* IV, 425.10 and V, 487.5 and 541.38).

143–8 These verses are epanaleptic. Epanaleptic verses seem to have been popular at Winchester at this time. There are three hymns to St Swithhun in a manuscript at Rouen (formerly at Jumièges but written at Winchester) which are both epanaleptic and abecedarii (ed. E. P. Sauvage, *AB* 5 (1886), 53–8), as well as a hymn to St Æthelwold and one to St Birin (ed. C. Blume, *Sitzungsberichte d. Akad. d. Wiss. in Wien* 146, 3 (1903), 3–12) which are also both epanaleptic and abecedarii. As Blume has shown (*ibid.* pp. 14 ff.), these hymns are to be attributed to Wulfstan.

144 I Corinthians IX. 24.

153 *at.* There are two possibilities here: either the transmitted *ut* may be retained, in which case *laxat* of 154 must be emended to *laxet* and the full stop after 152 removed. The reading *at* in 153 allows *laxat* in 154 to stand.

hac Stephanus Leuita pius uirtute coactus,
   illustrem Paulum fecit adire deum.
sic quoque nos caeli dominum rogitemus, adhelphi,
   pellat ut a famulis arbitrium sceleris,   160
quatinus a uitiis et neui crimine mundi

79v   conciues Petri simus in arce poli,
clauibus inmensi reserat qui limen Olimphi,
   cui mandauit oues altitonans niueas.
omnibus hoc nobis concedat gratia Christi   165
   sanguine quos proprio traxit ab hoste fero.
o dee cunctipotens cosmi qui regmina flectis,
   parce meo fluxit quicquid ab ore nequam.
te sine nil rectum nil iustum nilque pudicum
   scire potest miser et praeuaricatus homo;   170
quapropter toto mentis conamine poscens
   deprecor, ac numen flagito teque tuum,
dirige sic actus hominum, rector, ualeant quo
   post finem uitae denarium capere,
pontificemque pium meritis et honore colendum   175
   insignemque humilem protege, Christe, libens,
quem deus omnipotens cathedra subuexit in alta,
   dogmate mellifluo uerteret ut scelera.
gentes Anglorum felices praesule tanto
   ritus qui prauos corrigit ut genitor,   180
extorresque superuenientes uosque beati:

80r   cunctis his tribuit quicquid opus fuerit.
quis numerare queat bona nobis quae bonus ille
   contulit hanc postquam uenimus ad patriam?
idcirco dominum rogitemus corde fideli   185
   praebeat ut famulo gaudia pro merito.

Readings in C: 173 dirie   181 uos qui, *with* e *written above the* i *of* qui

157 Acts VI. 5 and VII. 55.

167 *regmina.* A syncopated form of *regimina,* it would seem, *metri gratia.*

174 Matthew XX. 10: 'venientes autem et primi arbitrati sunt quod plus essent accepturi: acceperunt autem et ipsi singulos denarios.' Cf. Augustine, *de genesi ad litteram* 9.6 (PL 34, col. 396): 'erunt sancti, quando peracto operis die denarium pariter accepturi sunt.' Note that the quantity of *dēnārĭum* here is false; this, with *uenĭmus* in 184, is one of the very few examples of false quantity in this poem that cannot be paralleled elsewhere in Anglo-Latin verse.

brothers, that he may drive away from his servants the will to sin, so that, clean from sin and the evil of stain, we may be compatriots of Peter in the summit of heaven, Peter who unlocks the threshold of Olympus with huge keys, to whom God the thunderer entrusted his snowy-white flocks. Let the grace of Christ grant this to all of us whom he drew away from the savage fiend with his own blood (166).

O God omnipotent, you who control the governance of the cosmos, have mercy on whatever worthless proceeds from my mouth. Without your assistance miserable and sinful man may not know anything that is right or just or modest. Wherefore, striving with the total effort of my spirit I beseech you, and entreat you and your divinity: so direct the deeds of men, master, that they may be able to get the *denarius* after the end of their life. And willingly protect, Christ, the merciful, renowned and humble bishop, who is to be respected for his merits and his honour, whom the omnipotent God elevated to the lofty *cathedra* so that he would alter our sins by his mellifluous doctrine (178). Happy the English with such a bishop, who corrects the depraved practices of the church like a father; and you foreigners lately arriving are blessed as well: to all these he has granted whatsoever was necessary. Who could count all the bounties which that good man has conferred on us since we came to this land? For that reason let us beseech the Lord with faithful heart that he grant happiness to his servant as he [i.e. the servant or bishop] well deserves (186).

Beowulf the headstrong

KEMP MALONE

The *Beowulf* poet tells us (194–201) that when his hero heard about Grendel's doings he had a good ship made ready for himself, saying he was minded to seek overseas the war-king (i.e. join Hrothgar), who stood in need of men. We learn further (202–4) that the wise men made no objection, though he was dear to them; they urged him on, saw (good) omens. These compatriots, presumably elders or councillors, come up again a little later, when the hero tells the Danish king:

> Þa me þæt gelærdon   leode mine,
> þa selestan,   snotere ceorlas,
> þeoden Hroðgar,   þæt ic þe sohte,
> forþan hie mægenes cræft   mine cuþon.[1]

King Hygelac himself was of another mind if we go by his words of welcome when Beowulf came home from Denmark:

> Hu lomp eow on lade,   leofa Biowulf,
> þa ðu færinga   feorr gehogodest
> sæcce secean   ofer sealt wæter,
> hilde, to Hiorote?   Ac ðu Hroðgare
> wi*d*cuðne wean   wihte gebettest,
> mærum ðeodne?   Ic ðæs modceare
> sorhwylmum seað,   siðe ne truwode
> leofes mannes.   Ic ðe lange bæd
> þæt ðu þone wælgæst   wihte ne grette,
> lete Suððene   sylfe geweorðan
> guðe wið Grendel.   Gode ic þanc secge
> þæsðe ic ðe gesundne   geseon moste.[2]

On the face of it, then, king and council were at odds in the counsel they gave Beowulf, who chose to follow the bold rather than the safe course, despite his lord's pleas. A headstrong hero he.

---

[1] 'Then my people, the best ones, the wise men, advised me to seek you, lord Hrothgar, because they knew my endowment of strength' (415–18).

[2] 'How went it with you men abroad, dear Beowulf, when you suddenly made up your mind to seek fighting, battle, far away, over salt water, at Heorot? Did you give Hrothgar, the illustrious lord, any relief at all from his widely known woe? Because of that [i.e. on your account] I heated myself into a distressful state of mind [lit. I made mood-care boiling hot with sorrow-surges]; I lacked faith in the dear man's course. I long urged you to have nothing to do with that deadly demon, to let the South Danes themselves settle the feud with Grendel. I say thanks to God for seeing you safe' (1987–98).

The event showed that the wise men had given good, the king bad counsel. This contrast may reflect the traditional association of wisdom with old age and bad judgement with youth; certainly Hygelac is said to be young (1969a) and his raid on the Low Countries proved disastrous (note the poet's characterizing *wlenco* 1206a). But Hrothgar characterizes Beowulf as wise (1841–3) despite his youth; that is, he reckons him a most exceptional if not indeed unique young man. It is odd to find the conflicting counsels so far apart in our text: lines 202–4 and 415–18 give not the slightest hint that anybody opposed Beowulf's plan and we hear nothing of Hygelac's opposition till his nephew's return from Denmark. We can reconcile the later passage with the earlier ones on the theory that Beowulf's *leode mine* (415b) excludes the king but this way of taking *leode* is hardly tenable. Alternatively we can explain the conflicting counsels as a case of traditional variants: the poet knew this trait in two forms and used both. Such discrepancies seldom disturb an audience if they come far apart in the narrative flow, as do the *Beowulf* passages quoted above. Each belongs to its scene, and listeners, unlike readers, cannot stop proceedings at will to compare mental notes.

We may make yet another approach, leaving the poet's hypothetical source(s) in the background and looking at the counsel simply as an artistic device. As such it serves to make the hero bigger than life. This function is obvious in the earlier passages. The men of wisdom at court whetted Beowulf (204a) because they knew how strong he was (418–24a) and deemed him more than a match for Grendel himself. In bringing out this well-weighed judgement of theirs the poet was heightening the stature of his hero. He was indirectly doing the same thing in the trait whereby Hygelac, despite his temperamental daring, feared for his beloved nephew's life and begged him not to seek out *þone wælgæst* (1995a). This magnification of Grendel heightened the stature of the man who overcame him. We may compare what the poet says about the feelings of Beowulf's followers when he and they had made their beds in Heorot and awaited the coming of Grendel. Their conviction that they were doomed arose from what they had come to realize that very day in Denmark. As the poet puts it:

> Nænig heora þohte   þæt he þanon scolde
> eft eardlufan   æfre gesecean,
> folc oþðe freoburh   þær he afeded wæs;
> ac hie hæfdon gefrunen   þæt hie ær to fela micles
> in þæm winsele   wældeað fornam,
> Denigea leode.[1]

[1] 'None of them thought that he was destined ever to go thence, seek again the dear home, people or court where he was reared; but they had learned that slaughter-death had taken men of the Danes, too many of them by far, in that wine-hall' (691–6a).

They had been aware of this from the start, of course, but only by hearsay from abroad, and now that they were lying abed in the very hall which Grendel haunted by night the fate of the Danes who had lain there before them was up in their thoughts. Both Hygelac and the champions that made up Beowulf's following (206a) knew as well as anybody how strong Beowulf was and if nevertheless they felt or feared he would prove no match for Grendel their misgivings made the hero all the greater in his victory.

Klaeber in his note on lines 1994 ff. says 'It has not been mentioned before that Hygelac tried to dissuade Beowulf from his undertaking ... The same motive, equally unfounded, appears in the last part, 3079 ff.'[1] By 'equally unfounded' Klaeber doubtless means that in the story of the dragon fight too we find no mention of an attempt at dissuasion till after the event. But though the motif of the headstrong hero is the same in both passages the circumstances are markedly different. Let us first take a look at the opening of Wiglaf's speech to the Geats who, after learning from Wiglaf's messenger that the fight is over, have come to the scene, where they see the dead bodies of king and dragon:

> Oft sceall eorl monig   annes willan
> wræc adreog*an*,   swa us geworden is.
> Ne meahton we gelæran   leofne þeoden,
> rices hyrde,   ræd ænigne,
> þæt he ne grette   goldweard þone,
> lete hyne licgean   þær he longe wæs,
> wicum wunian   oð woruldende.[2]

Wiglaf's *we* (3079a) tells us that he made one of a group in giving the king advice but otherwise we hear nothing of his fellows.

If now we compare the circumstances that led to advice-giving, we see that the devilry of the two monsters (human and reptile) may be contrasted as chronic (troll) *v.* acute (dragon). The troll was a cannibal who preyed on the Danes for twelve years (147a), making many visits to the king's hall, where he ate up or carried off the men he found, whereas the dragon was a hoard-keeper who lay on his hoard for 300 years (2278b) without harming anybody, so far as we are told, but when he found that a thief (2219a) had taken a cup (2282a) from the hoard he grew angry and as soon as night fell

---

[1] *Beowulf*, ed. F. Klaeber, 3rd ed. (Boston, 1950), p. 201.
[2] 'Often many a man by the will [i.e. wilfulness] of one must suffer distress, as has happened to us. We could not make the dear lord, the kingdom's keeper, listen to reason, see that he had better leave that gold-holder alone, let him lie where he long was, dwelling in his abode to the end of the world' (3077–83).

(like the troll, he left his hold only by night) he took stern vengeance on the whole Geatish tribe:

> Ða se gæst ongan   gledum spiwan,
> beorht hofu bærnan.   Bryneleoma stod
> eldum on andan;   no ðær aht cwices
> lað lyftfloga   læfan wolde.
> Wæs þæs wyrmes wig   wide gesyne,
> nearofages nið   nean ond feorran,
> hu se guðsceaða   Geata leode
> hatode ond hynde.   Hord eft gesceat,
> dryhtsele dyrnne,   ær dæges hwile.[1]

We learn further that Beowulf's hall (2325b–7a) and a Geatish fort (2333–5a) were among the buildings burnt down.

The approach of day brought a lull but the Geats had reason to think the attack would be renewed when night fell, since, as we are told (2314b–15), the dragon was unwilling to leave anything alive there. The tribe was clearly facing destruction and the king had to strike. Invincible aloft, the dragon could be fought by day on the ground and Beowulf, scorning (2345a) to gather a large force, sought the dragon's hold with eleven men (2401a), fewer than the fourteen (207b) he had taken with him to Denmark. These could not help him in the fight with Grendel, though they went through the motions (794b–7), and before the dragon fight Beowulf ordered his eleven to stand by and leave it to him to do the fighting (2529–32a). Here he took the view that monster-fighting was too much to ask or expect of anybody but himself (2532b–5a). The retainers at first obeyed orders but when they saw that their lord was hard pressed one of them, Wiglaf, came to the rescue; the other ten fled (2596–9a). With the help of the faithful retainer Beowulf killed the monster but at the cost of his own life.

What now of the advice that Beowulf got from Wiglaf and his fellows? If the king had agreed to do nothing would his subjects have been better off? Obviously he would be leaving them (and himself) at the mercy of the dragon, and the dragon was not merciful. Looked at rationally the advice makes sense only if the advisers hoped that the dragon in one night had done his all and would thenceforth let the Geats be. But if we go by the poet's words (2314b–15) the dragon's motto was 'thorough' and a counter-attack was the tribe's only hope of survival. Beowulf got bad advice from Wiglaf and his fellows and in rejecting it he showed wisdom as well as courage. His

---

[1] 'Then that guest began to spew flames, burn handsome houses. The blazing fires stood out, to the fright of men; the hateful sky-flier was not at all willing to leave anything alive there. The reptile's war-waging, the battling of the bitter foe, how that doer of harm in fight hated and brought low the men of the Geats, was widely seen, from near and far. [But] he shot back to hoard, hidden hall, before daybreak' (2312–20).

advisers by their advice showed that they had not thought things through.
Youth is hasty.

But though Beowulf had to counter-attack, was it wise of him to make the
fight single-handed? Certainly he proved unable to win without help. Yet
how well he took the measure of his retainers! When put to the test, all but
one fled the field, hardly to their lord's surprise. And our text makes it clear
enough that the hero was not over-confident. The poet here uses a technique
of alternation. The news of the hall-burning threw Beowulf into a deep
depression (2328–32), followed by a burst of confidence as he reviewed his
heroic past (2345–96). On the headland, when he made his long speech
(2425–515) to the eleven retainers, he was sad at heart, near death and ready
to die, as the poet tells us (2419b–20a), and in the speech itself he dwells on
death and grief (2435–89) but goes on to find reassurance in his service under
Hygelac, and he ends the speech with what the poet calls his last vow:

> Ic geneðde fela
> guða on geogoðe; gyt ic wylle,
> frod folces weard, fæhðe secan,
> mærðu fremman, gif mec se mansceaða
> of eorðsele ut geseceð.[1]

The epithet *folces weard* which the hero gives to himself at this crisis in his
people's story shows what he is doing when he takes his stand against the
dragon. As Klaeber puts it, Beowulf 'undertakes the venture primarily to
save his people'.[2] And it is worthy of note that he vows to fight only if the
monster leaves the cave to seek him out; he will not beard the dragon in his
den. This conditional vow of his in old age makes a striking contrast with
the vow he made in young manhood to seek out Grendel's mother wherever
she might be (1392–6). The actions that follow the vows likewise make a
contrast. Since the dragon would prove impregnable in his lair even as he had
proved invincible on the wing, the old hero makes him vulnerable for the
fight by luring him outside with a war-whoop (2550–2a), whereas the young
hero simply dived into the mere and fell into the clutches of the merewife
(1492–1502a).

Glory and booty will come to the hero if he wins the dragon fight and he
is mindful of both (2514a and 2536a); hence Klaeber's 'primarily'. One
must agree with Klaeber that these fruits of victory are secondary for
Beowulf, who is first of all the king, the *folces weard*. They are of course
conventional rewards for the hero of a dragon fight in popular story and it
would have been remiss of the poet to make his hero indifferent to either one.
The poet uses another conventional trait, the curse laid on the hoard (3051–7

---

[1] 'I dared many fights in youth; I am minded still, aged keeper of the nation, to seek battle, do a
famous deed, if the evil-doer seeks me out from [his] cave' (2511b–15).   [2] *Beowulf*, p. xxii.

and 3069–75), to explain the hero's death and seemingly the dragon's too (3058–62a). Since the hero was unaware of the curse (3067b–8) he could say with a whole heart his dying prayer of thanksgiving:

> Ic ðara frætwa   Frean ealles ðanc,
> wuldurcyninge   wordum secge,
> ecum Dryhtne,   þe ic her on starie,
> þæsðe ic moste   minum leodum
> ær swyltdæge   swylc gestrynan.[1]

To those of the poet's hearers who knew the course of events the hero's words would have a strong undertone of irony; to those who were hearing the tale of Beowulf for the first time the irony would be there, if at all, only in retrospect: they would know nothing of the curse for some time longer (3051–7) and not until nearly the end would they learn that Beowulf's people buried the hoard in his grave-mound, where it still lies, as useless to men as it was before (3167b–8).

We have seen that the headstrong hero motif in the first part of the action serves to magnify Grendel and thereby the hero who overcomes him. But Hygelac's speech brings out, besides, the narrowness of his nationalism: since it was the Danish hall that Grendel was haunting, the Geatish king thought it should be left to the Danes to deal with the troll. Again, the speech plays up Hygelac's love for his nephew, a love that made him unwilling to let the dear kinsman risk his life in a needless cause. In virtue of these traits the poet characterizes not only Hygelac but (indirectly) Beowulf as well. Love likewise had much to do with the stand that Wiglaf and his fellows took: they were loath to see their aged lord risking his precious life in a fight with a fire-drake, a fight which they felt sure he could not win.

Wiglaf in his speech did not mention dangers from abroad (*wræc adreogan* 3078a goes with *wollenteare* 3032a) but his messenger to the *eorlweorod* (2893b) had spoken at length about attacks that might be expected from the Franks and Frisians and from the Swedes, once they heard that Beowulf was dead. Beowulf himself in his first speech after the dragon fight had said

> Ic ðas leode heold
> fiftig wintra;   næs se folccyning
> ymbesittendra,   ænig ðara,
> þe mec guðwinum   gretan dorste,
> egesan ðeon.[2]

---

[1] 'To the lord of all, king of glory, everlasting God I say thanks for those treasures that I am looking at here; [I say thanks] because I was allowed to gain such for my people before I died' (2794–8).

[2] 'I have kept this nation for fifty years; that folk-king of dwellers round about did not exist, [not] any of those [folk-kings existed], who dared come near me with weapons, press me hard' (2732b–6a).

This speech and that of the messenger make a consistent pattern, on the principle of contrast which the poet follows, composing after the event: under Beowulf the Geats lived in peace and freedom; after his death the Geatish state fell, victim of attacks from abroad. The contrast serves, of course, to exalt the hero, whose greatness alone upheld the fortunes of his people. But this contrast can hardly be historical, and in any case it would hold good whether Beowulf died of a dragon's bite a little earlier or of old age a little later. The effect of the aged king's death on the international situation is one thing; the manner of his death, something else again.

Many great men have died in bed but for heroic story Beowulf's way of dying is as it should be: fighting to the utmost against an evil foe of his people, a foe stronger than he. And the help of his faithful retainer brings it about that the hero can slay the foe even though taking a wound that proves mortal. Beowulf dies as he had lived, a *folces weard* indeed.

The diet and digestion of allegory
in *Andreas*

DAVID HAMILTON

As a narrative poem, *Andreas* usually suffers from comparison with *Beowulf*. Stanley, for example, writes that the *Andreas* poet 'can do the big bow-wow like any man going', but also that the versified saint's legend is to *Beowulf* roughly as Cowley's *Davideis* is to *Paradise Lost*.[1] Such comparisons are of long standing, and the reasons for them are apparent. Further, the common emphasis in both poems on the language of war and seafaring and the similarities in the larger patterns of their plots – both heroes cleanse foreign lands – imply a degree of dependence.[2] Despite our knowledge, therefore, of *Andreas*'s Greek and Latin sources and of the traditional character of Old English poetic diction, most readers would agree generally, I suppose, with Brodeur's observation that the *Andreas* poet was familiar with *Beowulf* and sometimes reproduced its phrasing.[3]

But Brodeur argues also against seeing *Beowulf* as a model for *Andreas*, and I wish to stress even more firmly the later poet's originality. Discussions of dependence have inhibited our seeing the ways in which the *Andreas* poet is original and sometimes daring. His seafaring passages, for example, may remind us of *Beowulf*,[4] but they are developed further and to a different purpose. I believe, therefore, that we can best get at both the differences

---

[1] E. G. Stanley, 'Beowulf', *Continuations and Beginnings*, ed. E. G. Stanley (London, 1966), pp. 138 and 113.

[2] *Andreas and the Fates of the Apostles*, ed. George Philip Krapp (Boston, 1906); Krapp discusses the similarity of plot structure and lists 146 verbal parallels between *Andreas* and *Beowulf*, pp. li–lviii; see also Claes Schaar, *Critical Studies in the Cynewulf Group* (Lund, 1949). L. J. Peters, 'The Relationship of the Old English *Andreas* to *Beowulf*', *PMLA* 66 (1951), 844–63, explores *Andreas*'s independence from *Beowulf*; see also R. M. Lumiansky, 'The Contexts of the Old English *Ealuscerwen* and *Meoduscerwen*', *JEGP* 48 (1949), 116–26. The more recent studies have been more moderate. See *Andreas and the Fates of the Apostles*, ed. Kenneth R. Brooks (Oxford, 1961), p. xxvi; Brooks quotes Dorothy Whitelock approvingly: 'one can make a case for the influence of *Beowulf* on *Andreas*, . . . but it stops short of proof.' Hans Schrabram ('*Andreas* und *Beowulf*', *Nachrichten der Giessener Hochschulgesellschaft* 34 (1965), 201–18) also agrees that the *Andreas* poet knew *Beowulf* well but was not dependent on it.

[3] Arthur G. Brodeur, 'A Study of Diction and Style in Three Anglo-Saxon Narrative Poems', *Nordica et Anglica: Studies in Honor of Stefán Einarsson*, ed. Allan H. Orrick (The Hague, 1968), pp. 97–114, esp. 97–105.

[4] George K. Anderson, *The Literature of the Anglo-Saxons*, rev. ed. (Princeton, 1966), pp. 135–6.

between *Beowulf* and *Andreas* and the originality of the latter poem by isolating two elements fundamental to the narrative structure of the saint's legend, yet foreign, and quite likely beyond the concerns of the earlier epic. These are, first, a forceful repetition of a few words and phrases that unfold metaphorically as the poem progresses, and, second, an extended structure of dramatic irony that conveys and highlights the figurative language. The *Andreas* poet uses both of these devices more insistently and to more decisive effect than any other Old English poet. The ironic structure is especially important because it is often strongest in passages that are close, verbally, to *Beowulf*; and by giving those passages a fresh cast, the irony continually calls into question the poet's dependence either on *Beowulf* or on traditional heroic diction. Together, moreover, these devices organize *Andreas* as a unified narrative. They turn it from the diverse, encyclopaedic range of the epic and nourish instead the more exclusive concerns of continuous allegory.

Of the two devices, verbal repetition and dramatic irony, a simple example of the former is the frequent assertion that Mermedonia is a joyless land.[1] Another is the statement that Andreas shall venture his life there. The poet expresses this second idea formulaically four times. First, God instructs Andreas, saying 'Ðu scealt feran ond frið lædan' (174); then, after Andreas hesitates, God repeats 'Ðu scealt þa fore geferan ond þin feorh beran' (216). Later, speaking as the ship's pilot, God warns that men who travel to Mermedonia venture their lives:

> ... in þære ceastre   cwealm þrowiað,
> þa ðe feorran þyder   feorh gelædaþ. (281–2)

And Andreas, finally, tells his followers 'ge on fara folc feorh gelæddon' (430). The phrases *frið lædan* and *feorh beran* are the nucleus of this formula, and they acquire force from their likeness to *sweord beran, garholt bere, helmberend* and similar martial expressions in *Beowulf*.[2] In the epic, these phrases are metaphors for warriors and their advance on the enemy; but instead of

---

1 Matthew's lot fell so that he went to that island 'þær ænig þa git/ellþeodigra eðles ne mihte,/ blædes brucan' (15b–17a); also 21b–3a, 279–82 and 1155–60. All quotations from *Andreas* are from Brooks's edition.
2 In *Beowulf* 2516–21 the first term occurs in collocation with the last:

> Gegrette ða   gumena gehwylcne,
> hwate helmberend   hindeman siðe,
> swæse gesiðas: 'Nolde ic sweord beran,
> wæpen to wyrme,   gif ic wiste hu
> wið ðam aglæcean   elles meahte
> gylpe wiðgripan,   swa ic gio wið Grendle dyde.'

Helmberend occurs again (2642a), and one might compare these passages with 'þæt ic sweord bere oþðe sidne scyld' (437), and 'þæt we rondas beren' (2653b). A shift of emphasis in the metaphor occurs with the word *sawlberendra* (1004b). I am indebted to Donald Fry for first suggesting the direction of this comparison.

All citations from *Beowulf* are from F. Klaeber's 3rd ed. (Boston, 1950), but I have omitted the macrons.

bearing arms, Andreas risks his safety and his life, which thus become his weapons. In Mermedonia, the expression is made almost ludicrously concrete as the heathens drag Andreas about bodily. This kind of change in traditional metaphor shows that the *Andreas* poet was in partial control of heroic conventions; and thus, if we may change the emphasis in a remark of Kenneth Sisam's, it suggests that the poet was at least 'half weaned from heathen epic forms'.[1]

The most weighty example of verbal repetition in *Andreas*, though, grows from the many variations on the motif of food and drink. From the opening lines of the poem we hear that the Mermedonians starve and that they feed on strangers:

> Swelc wæs þeaw hira
> þæt hie æghwylcne ellðeodigra
> dydan him to mose meteþearfendum,
> þara þe þæt ealand utan sohte. (25b–8)

This fact accounts, naturally enough, for the joylessness of Mermedonia. It finds an echo in the poisonous drink given to prisoners and in the Mermedonians' intention of eating Matthew. When God summons Andreas, he describes the heathens as *sylfætan*, and thematically related language informs much of the long dialogue between Andreas and his pilot. Andreas complains that, having neither riches nor sustenance, he cannot pay the fare; the pilot insists that food and drink are necessary on a voyage, and Andreas observes that the pilot enjoys large stores of both. Once the boat is under way, the pilot offers meat to everyone. This meal refreshes Andreas, who then praises God; and with an awareness that, here as elsewhere, fails to trace accidentals to their source, he hopes God will sustain the pilot with a heavenly loaf. Later, while recounting Christ's miracles, Andreas quickly mentions the division of the five loaves and two fishes.[2]

Repeated so frequently, sustenance, be it heavenly or infernal, becomes the poem's most prominent motif. As the poem progresses, it occurs more sparingly, but always so as to reinforce a thematic design. When Andreas arrives in Mermedonia, he finds that the people there are suffering from famine, and he quickly prevents the starving heathens from eating a boy (1078–154). Finally, at the climax of the poem, the same motif animates the difficult images of the deprival of mead (*meoduscerwen*) and the bitter beer-drinking (*biter beorþegu*, 1526b–33a).[3]

---

[1] K. Sisam, 'Cynewulf and his Poetry', *Studies in the History of Old English Literature* (Oxford, 1953), p. 16. Sisam says 'only half weaned'.

[2] The relevant lines are 33–4, 53, 129–37, 153–4, 160, 175, 302, 312–13, 317–18, 365–7, 386–90 and 589–90.

[3] Lumiansky ('The Contexts') cites most of the passages referred to in this paragraph; the translation 'deprival of mead' is Brodeur's ('Diction and Style', p. 100).

Such frequency and consistency of repetition is quite different from the methods of *Beowulf*, and the difference points up, I believe, the special achievement of the *Andreas* poet. As a contrast, we might turn for a moment to an abbreviated repetition in the epic. Beowulf's arrival in Denmark inspires, among other reactions, some play on the idea that he comes in kindness. Hrothgar, for example, while speaking of Beowulf for the first time, says that 'hine halig God/for arstafum us onsende' (381b–2); then he repeats this hopeful note when he begins his welcoming address to the hero:

> For gewyrhtum þu,   wine min Beowulf,
> ond for arstafum   usic sohtest. (457–8)

An earlier remark of the coast-guard's, moreover, may be seen in relation to Hrothgar's thoughts, for the coast-guard, having sensed the strength and promise of Beowulf, hopes that God will hold him in kindness throughout his adventures:

> Fæder alwalda
> mid arstafum   eowic gehealde
> siðe gesunde! (316b–18a)

In other words, mercy should attend the man who comes on an errand of kindness.

The *Beowulf* poet repeats *arstafum* just frequently enough in the brief compass of 130 lines to give it some slight emphasis; yet, because it is an abstraction, the word is difficult to translate precisely. Klaeber defines it as 'kindness', 'favor', 'grace' or 'help'. As an abstraction, it points only generally to what the speaker expects of Beowulf, and we interpret the word finally in the light of his deeds. *Andreas* reverses this pattern. From the first we know that the Mermedonians lack food and drink. Whenever the poet brings up this idea or a related one, his diction is concrete and specific:

hlafes wist (21b), wæteres drync (22b), dydan him to mose meteþearfendum (27), drync unheorne (34b), atres drync (53a), hwylcne hie to æte ærest mihton (132), hwænne hie to mose meteþearfendum (136), werum to wiste ond to wilþege, / fæges flæschoman (153–4a), þæt hie tobrugdon blodigum ceaflum / fira flæschoman him to foddorþege (159–60), sylfætan (175b), welan ne wiste (302a), Nafast . . . / hlafes wiste, ne hlutterne / drync to dugoðe (311–13a), weland ond wiste ond woruldspede (318), ond mete syllan (366b), þa he gereordod wæs (385b), ond þe wist gife, / heofonlicne hlaf (388b–9a), Swylce he afedde of fixum twam / ond of fif hlafum (589–90a), wiste þegon (593b), þæt hie on elþeodigum æt geworhton,/ weotude wiste (1073–4a), to foddurþege feores ongyldan (1101), Þeod wæs oflysted / metes modgeomre (1112b–13a), Meoduscerwen wearð . . . biter beorþegu (1526b and 1533a).

We may say that this diction is the staple diet, the meat and potatoes of allegory in *Andreas*. Under such consistent usage, moreover, these concrete terms take on a peculiar vibrancy so that they become increasingly more suggestive of abstract and allegorical meanings. Phrases such as 'heavenly loaf', Andreas's benighted observation of the pilot's wealth and provisions, and the highly unrealistic account of how, amid a rising storm, Andreas sits calmly and refreshes himself on meat the pilot offers, force broader, metaphorical interpretations on this language. It makes no sense for Andreas to eat while his thegns despair unless his ability to relieve them depends upon the nourishment he receives. Later, then, when the Mermedonians choose one of their youths to eat, we understand the futility of their intended sacrifice and their need of more than flesh to sustain them. Whereas in *Beowulf* the poet repeats an abstraction for which we imaginatively interpolate a more concrete meaning, in *Andreas* the repetition of key concrete terms leads us gradually into the framework of allegory and to the kind of abstract conceptualization that the allegorical framework implies.

Arstafum, however, is but a slender point of balance for what approaches a generic distinction between epic and allegory, and a more telling comparison to the use of the motifs of food and cannibalism in *Andreas* would be Grendel's rôle as scourge of the Danes. As Brooks points out, Andreas's mission parallels that of Beowulf.[1] Grendel's plundering, moreover, is a thoroughly concrete event; its continuation through a dozen years and the reminders that Grendel bore God's anger imply a significance beyond wanton slaughter. Thus it is natural to associate Grendel with God's justice, and Hrothgar's sermon points the way to that interpretation. Nevertheless, the two poets characterize their antagonists quite differently, and, as a result, the allegorical impact of Grendel is less forceful than that of the motifs we have examined in *Andreas*. The Mermedonians are little more than a vehicle for the idea of spiritual hunger; their deprivation is unnaturally strained and can be understood only by recourse to an imposed, allegorical meaning. They embody spiritual privation, and their cannibalism, though basically a sympton of their inner nature, quickly becomes their total characterization. Grendel, on the other hand, though likewise a cannibal, is something more than that too. Although he can be seen as a manifestation of the Danes' spiritual weakness, Grendel is so rooted in folklore that he comes across as an independent figure, a monster of some sensitivity, and an outsider who threatens the Danish people. He is neither simply a sign of internal being nor characterized solely by deprivation. Thus it is not necessary to conceptualize Grendel's thematic significance in order to respond to his menace. The Mermedonians, on the contrary, enjoy none of his colour and fullness; and it is in response to their allegorized deprivation that God, appearing first as a disembodied voice, sends Andreas to refresh them. This journey requires three days, and

---

[1] *Andreas*, p. xxiii.

Andreas cannot accomplish it alone. Christ, however, as a young and marvellously skilful pilot, brings Andreas across the Water of Life aboard the Vessel of the Eucharist to the land where redemption proves possible and Christ may be recognized, at last, as a child. Though this much exegesis is too glib, I suggest that the action of *Andreas* cannot be assimilated without recourse to an extrapolated, allegorical reading, and that the steady repetition of specific words and phrases throughout the poem requires such analysis.[1]

The allegorical intentions of the *Andreas* poet, moreover, justify his indifference to ordinary realism: to the transformations of God as he appears to Andreas, to the protagonist's rapid and unmotivated acceptance of the mission after hesitating initially, to Andreas's dining calmly while the storm threatens, and to the tortures he endures and recovers from while flowers bloom from his spilled blood. *Beowulf* is a tale of fantastic adventure, of course, but if we grant some lee-way to heroes and monsters, we find that the actions in *Beowulf* are larger than life, but not radically different from it. The action of *Andreas*, however, is supernatural, and we accept it only in a controlled, didactic frame of reference. By accepting, then, blatantly unrealistic action as a convention, we recognize allegory as a reductive mode of narration that is indifferent to mimetic report.[2]

My argument so far has avoided two scholars whose work bears most directly on the kinds of allegorical intention that we may attribute to the poets of *Beowulf* and *Andreas*. Kaske's reading of *sapientia et fortitudo* as the controlling theme of *Beowulf* begins also with a demonstration of the poet's repetitive use of a selective thematic vocabulary as he figures forth an allegorical design.[3] Those key terms, however, are less insistently used than I have shown the motif of food to be in *Andreas*; furthermore, words and phrases such as *snotor ond swyðferhð*, *mid cræfte*, *lara liðe*, *mægen mid modes snyttrum*, *snotorlicor*, *mægenes strang* and so on are abstractions similar to *arstafum* that attract concrete characterization in Beowulf, Grendel and the other characters in the poem. In Kaske's reading, *Beowulf* becomes a rich counterpointing of persons and monsters with the abstract natures they

---

[1] I am indebted to discussions with my colleague Robert Lucas for being able to state the possibilities of allegory this forcefully.

[2] See Angus Fletcher, *Allegory: the Theory of a Symbolic Mode* (Ithaca, 1964), pp. 150–1. Fletcher argues that allegory is 'less diverse and more simple in contour' than are more mimetic plots. Graham Hough, similarly, distinguishes between 'naive allegory' and 'realism' according to the dominance of 'theme' in the former kind of narrative and 'image' in the latter. Hough would say, I trust, that the figure of Beowulf is an image but that the Mermedonian cannibals convey only a theme; G. Hough, *An Essay on Criticism* (London, 1966), pp. 123–4. Both critics probably take their cue from T. S. Eliot who, when writing on Dante, proclaimed him 'easy to read' because of the 'lucidity of style' that obtains in allegory; T. S. Eliot, *Selected Essays* (New York, 1950), pp. 201–4.

[3] R. E. Kaske, '*Sapientia et Fortitudo* as the Controlling Theme of *Beowulf*', *SP* 55 (1958), 423–56; repr. *An Anthology of Beowulf Criticism*, ed. Lewis E. Nicholson (Notre Dame, 1963), pp. 269–310.

personify, and Kaske warns that the poem builds towards allegory only tentatively, modulating from the adventure story in Denmark through the didactic model of Hrothgar's sermon and then into the encounter with the dragon which Kaske regards as *Beowulf*'s most certain allegorical figure. Thus *Beowulf*, rather than being a continuous allegory as a specialized narrative form, behaves as most stories behave; that is, it gradually asserts a thematic and controlling meaning. For many readers, *Beowulf* suggests more than it asserts; *Andreas*, however, asserts its allegorical intention straightaway and more continuously.

In three more recent articles devoted wholly or partially to *Andreas*, Thomas Hill has shown that several of its motifs are grounded in the Christian Latin tradition of patristic exegesis. In lines 761–72, for example, Andreas characterizes the Jews' anger towards Christ as a dragon stained in spirit that surges in their minds, and Hill relates this image – 'brandhata nið/weoll on gewitte, weorm blædum fag' – to the *draco malitiae* of patristic tradition and to Kaske's reading of the dragon in *Beowulf*.[1] In the same article, he also relates Andreas's praise of the young pilot's wisdom (505b–9) to the *topos* of *puer senex* as described by Curtius.[2] In another paper, he suggests that the Mermedonians' cold-heartedness towards Matthew (138a) may be related to the patristic use of heat and cold imagery in which heat represents the affirmative passion of charity and coldness its opposite.[3] And most recently, Hill discusses the conversion of the Mermedonians, especially the motifs of the flood rushing from the pillar and of the fire-bearing angel, as the mystery of baptism, expressed in terms of typological narrative.[4]

Each of these identifications of allegorical motifs seems certain, and the poem, I feel sure, may be mined much more extensively in these terms. The fact remains though that allegoresis of this kind is necessarily piecemeal, and by depending completely upon patristic sources it underplays the original work of the narrative poet. Hill worries about this point himself. In his last article, he reminds us that the Old English poet is necessarily independent in some degree from his sources and that his freedom allows for individual artistry:

The point I am attempting to make is that the Old English poem *Andreas* is rather more like the liturgy or a cathedral (to use a well worn simile) than a romantic poem, in that it is not entirely the original creation of a specific individual at a given moment of history; but at the same time this fact does not invalidate the esthetic and intellectual achievement which the poem represents.[5]

---

[1] 'Two Notes on Patristic Allusion in *Andreas*', *Anglia* 84 (1966), 156–62.
[2] *Ibid.* pp. 161–2; Hill cites Ernst R. Curtius, *European Literature and the Latin Middle Ages*, trans. Willard Trask (New York, 1953), pp. 98–101.
[3] 'The Tropological Context of Heat and Cold Imagery in Anglo-Saxon Poetry', *NM* 69 (1968), 522–32, esp. 531–2.
[4] 'Figural Narrative in *Andreas*', *NM* 70 (1969), 261–73, esp. 269.　　　　[5] *Ibid.* pp. 270–1.

And my point, likewise, is that the *Andreas* poet's achievement should not be measured only by his rearrangement of Christian Latin material, for it also involves patterns of imagery, word-play and related literary devices that are not peculiarly romantic at all but are the common properties of literary art in all eras. The skill of this poet may be observed within the narrative design of the poem itself and deserves examination in the poem's own terms.

Thus to return to the poem, the repetitious imagery of food and drink is, as we have seen, a major factor of the poem's design; but, although this diction is obviously suggestive when lifted from its narrative context, it would be much less forceful were it not for the carefully structured and extended dramatic irony that highlights its figurative use. When, for example, Andreas negotiates for passage and the pilot rebukes his poverty, Andreas becomes angry and accuses the pilot of pride:

> Ne gedafenað þe,   nu þe dryhten geaf
> welan ond wiste   ond woruldspede,
> ðæt ðu ondsware   mid oferhygdum,
> sece sarcwide. (317–20a)

Dramatic irony tightens this speech, for by calling attention to Andreas's ignorance it urges our consideration of the theme of spiritual refreshment. This theme, conveyed chiefly by the figurative language – 'welan ond wiste' – becomes the kernel of the poem to which the irony repeatedly directs our attention. If food be the stuff of this allegory, dramatic irony is its alimentary canal.

Nearly half of *Andreas* conforms to the pattern of this passage. The irony begins with the apostle's arrival on the beach and ends with Christ's departure from him on the Mermedonian roadside. This long section, a dialogue for the most part, serves to test the hero. Andreas's task is to recognize the pilot, that is to accept his revelation and to renew the faith that had wavered when God first announced his mission. The steadily ironic focus on Andreas is a strong unifying force throughout this section. The passage just discussed sets up the conditions of the voyage; then once the ship is under way, Andreas's ignorance allows further opportunities for ironic instruction. Some of these passages interest us especially as echoes of *Beowulf*, but the *Andreas* poet is seldom credited with being in control of the allusions he makes. There is ample reason, though, to believe that he was.

For example, as the voyage begins, the poet's praise of the ship echoes the ship-burial in *Beowulf*:

> Gesæt him þa se halga   holmwearde neah,
> æðele be æðelum;   æfre ic ne hyrde
> þon cymlicor   ceol gehladenne
> heahgestreonum.   Hæleð in sæton,
> þeodnas þrymfulle,   þegnas wlitige. (359–63)

Brodeur argues that here the *Andreas* poet had the passage from *Beowulf* 'in mind', and Brooks thinks the motif of praising the ship is used absurdly since there is no reason to describe this ship as *gehladene heahgestreonum*.[1] But Andreas is rich in spirit, and if we respond to the figurative language, we can see how freshly the poet uses this passage. He surrounds the troublesome phrase with *halga*, *holmwearde* and *hæleð*; and the continuing alliteration on *h*, varied and strengthened semantically through the phrase *æðele be æðelum*, enforces the metaphorical identity. The passage also foreshadows the pilot's subsequent comment that God must have calmed the seas because he valued the ship's cargo (526–36).

Moments later, amid the rising storm, the narrator says of Andreas's men that

> ænig ne wende
> þæt he lifgende   land begete,
> þara þe mid Andreas   on eagorstream
> ceol gesohte. (377b–80a)

These lines echo the Geats' fear as they prepared for bed and battle on their first night at Heorot (*Beowulf*, 691–3), but the *Andreas* poet also, and pointedly, makes his allusion ironic by adding 'Næs him cuð þa gyt/hwa þam sæflotan sund wisode' (380b–1). In *Beowulf*, of course, God's safe-keeping of the heroes is also made known. There the narrator observes that God gave the Weders good fortune and allowed the strength of one to overcome the enemy (696b–702a). God, however, is not physically present but unrecognized at Heorot. Consequently, the ironic dimension is active only in *Andreas*. His presence makes the limited awareness of Andreas's followers more apparent and underscores the inadequacy of their point of view.

The famous speech in which Andreas's followers pledge their loyalty and exalt the values of the *comitatus* offers another example of the poet's alert manipulation of heroic conventions. These lines compare with Wiglaf's rebuke of Beowulf's disloyal retainers and with passages in *Maldon*. In the final lines of the passage in *Andreas*, moreover, the poet refers awkwardly and inappropriately to weapons and war-play. Still he subordinates the traditional diction to his Christian theme. The line that precedes the disciples' speech says that these men objected to leaving their *leofne lareow* (404a). By identifying Andreas as a teacher, the poet modifies the traditional characterization of the leader as a military hero. The tag 'beloved teacher', furthermore, describes the pilot better than Andreas; therefore this comment and the expression of traditional loyalty that follows from it continue the ironic design. The particular use of this speech is more important, finally, than its traditional familiarity, for again it highlights central thematic considerations.

---

[1] 'Diction and Style', p. 98; *Andreas*, p. xxiv.

These men must weather the storm and remain with their teacher; they must learn, though, who their teacher is.

The irony is equally influential moments later when Andreas tries to encourage his followers by recalling for them the example of Christ's calming the storm on Galilee. This passage is twice reminiscent of *Beowulf*. The first few lines parallel the opening of Beowulf's speech just after Wealhtheow passes the beerhorn.

> Ic þæt hogode, þa ic on holm gestah,
> sæbat gesæt mid minra secga gedriht,
> þæt ic anunga eowra leoda
> willan geworhte, oþðe on wæl crunge
> feondgrapum fæst. (632–6a)

In *Andreas*, however, remembrance of these lines becomes an occasion for one of the repeated phrases that we have already discussed.

> Ge þæt gehogodon, þa ge on holm stigon,
> þæt ge on fara folc feorh gelæddon,
> ond for dryhtnes lufan deað þrowodon,
> on Ælmyrcna eðelrice
> sawle gesealdon. (429–33a)

The syntax of these passages indicates their varying usage. The *Beowulf* poet mentions going to sea, but then he lingers for one line that elaborates on the voyage. Thus for a moment the poem eddies about the conditions of the journey before it passes on to express the boldness of Beowulf's challenge. The *Andreas* poet, on the other hand, fuses these two elements so that undertaking the journey becomes a metaphor for venturing one's life. The separate acts in *Beowulf* are made identical in *Andreas*, and the latter poet develops his point forcefully. He constructs an extended progression through a series of discrete clauses, each of which ends in a verb phrase that becomes metaphorically related to *feorh gelæddon*. The sequence progresses steadily to the last, climactic clause, and the metaphorical language turns the speech away from its association with *Beowulf*. Again the semantic progress is from concrete to abstract usage: the men take to the sea, venture their lives, suffer death and bestow their souls. Thus the thematic point is most skilfully conveyed.

The ironic aspect of the speech appears then at its conclusion. Whereas Beowulf rebukes Unferth in part by observing that 'Wyrd oft nereð/ unfægne eorl, þonne his ellen deah' (572b–3), Andreas, with Christ the pilot still unrecognized beside him, comforts his followers by saying:

> Forþan ic eow to soðe secgan wille,
> þæt næfre forlæteð lifgende god
> eorl on eorðan, gif his ellen deah. (458–60)

The diet and digestion of allegory in 'Andreas'

The irony informing this long dialogue vanishes finally when Andreas recognizes Christ. Beforehand though, Andreas praises Christ's seamanship, assures him of a heavenly reward and repeatedly admires his youth and wisdom. Andreas's last speech recapitulates at length, and to some tastes laboriously, many of Christ's miracles. He calls them the signs by which Christ made himself known to the world; yet all the while Christ stands listening patiently, though unrecognized. By this time Andreas threatens to become a comic figure.[1] Nevertheless, the excessiveness of this passage must be seen, finally, to have its point: Andreas's inability to identify his Lord despite all the knowledge he is able to summon brings the ironic structure to its highest pitch and dramatizes the profound mystery of revelation.[2]

Thus far, then, the ironic frame of reference has informed our understanding of *Andreas* by emphasizing its chief thematic element – the motif of refreshment – and by fully dramatizing a religious mystery. Moreover, since any ironic passage must be interpreted so that first it contradicts and then it transcends its surface meaning, irony urges us past the literal sense of the text and directs us towards allegory. Traditional rhetorics defined irony as an allegorical trope,[3] and once we begin to read this narrative figuratively, we are prepared to follow Andreas's fantastic adventures in Mermedonia. One of the several pleasures that awaits us there is a reversal of the ironic design as the devil, while arguing with Andreas, assumes the burden of irony and warns that grim punishment is ordained for the apostle's deeds 1362–74). But by this time, Andreas has emerged into much of the awareness and power of his pilot.

Brief comparison with *Beowulf* will emphasize, I think, the extent to which the irony and figurative language unify *Andreas* and our reading of it. In broad terms, Beowulf's journey to Heorot and his successive encounters with the coast-guard, Wulfgar, Hrothgar and Unferth parallel the portion of *Andreas* that we have examined. Those encounters test Beowulf and prepare him for heroic action. That section of *Beowulf*, however, is more fragmented than Andreas's voyage, and, though only half as long,[4] encompasses a greater range of interests. An action such as Unferth's and Beowulf's

[1] George A. Smithson remarks that the 'author's zeal for religion was too strong, his regard for the art of narration too conditional' (*The Old English Christian Epic: a Study of the Plot Technique of the Juliana, the Elene, the Andreas and the Christ in comparison with the Beowulf and with the Latin Literature of the Middle Ages* (Berkeley, 1910), p. 331).

[2] Cf. Hill ('Two Notes', p. 162), who finds that the 'puer senex' *topos* portrays Andreas's perceptivity.

[3] For example, Bede, *De Schematis et Tropis Sacrae Scripturae Liber*: 'Eironeia est tropus per contrarium quod conatur ostendens: ut, Clamate voce majore, Deus est enim Baal, et forsitan loquitur, aut in diversorio est, aut in itinere, aut dormit, ut excitetur. Hanc enim nisi gravitas pronunciationis adjuverit, confiteri videbitur quod negare contendit' (*Venerabilis Bedae Opera quae Supersunt*, ed. J. A. Giles (London, 1843–4) VI, 94).

[4] The portion of *Beowulf* I refer to is from about line 229 to line 610; in *Andreas*, lines 174–976.

flyting, for example, attracts and conveys several widely varying modes of thought. Matters of geography, history and genealogy, the echoes of myth and legend, a close, psychological analysis of motivation and a discursive interest in ethical values all blossom from this single motif. Any subject in *Beowulf* is likely to accommodate interests as various as these, and the poem, therefore, is always opening into a multiform of possibilities, few of which are necessarily allegorical. Its directions of association are manifold; the *Beowulf* poet invites us to attend to the periphery of his poem and to look there for explanations that the narrative does not explicitly frame for us.[1] For these reasons, we find it digressive. *Andreas*, on the other hand, progresses within narrower limits. Its development of the sea-voyage is not especially close to the treatment of voyages in *Beowulf*. Instead, its closest analogue in Old English is *The Seafarer*, where a voyage also unfolds into an allegorical design. In *Andreas*, the hero journeys towards understanding, and the voyage and storm are physical manifestations of the apostle's spiritual progress. Throughout the voyage and all the later adventures history and geography intrude. The poet minimizes psychological motivation; witness the easy shift Andreas makes from rejecting God's command to following it eagerly. Patterns of remote myth and legend only faintly underlie the plot, as all the action adheres to an open and consistent allegorical progression. Repetition enhances this design by isolating the dominant motif. The narrow and frequently intense frame of dramatic irony 'digests' what repetition selects. Together these devices nourish the allegory of *Andreas*.

[1] I am indebted, of course, to J. R. R. Tolkien's complaint about the belief that the important matters in *Beowulf* are at its 'outer edges'; '*Beowulf*: the Monsters and the Critics', *Beowulf Criticism*, ed. Nicholson, p. 53, and also to the discussion of the 'epic synthesis' by Robert Kellogg and Robert Scholes, *The Nature of Narrative* (New York, 1966), *passim*.

Exodus and the treasure of Pharaoh

JOHN F. VICKREY

Some years ago Professor Fred C. Robinson advised retention of the usually emended manuscript reading *afrisc meowle* in line 580b of the Old English *Exodus* poem.[1] His argument was that *afrisc meowle*, 'African woman', alluded to the wife of Moses, who is mentioned elsewhere in the biblical Exodus though not in the passage to which the last lines of the *Exodus* poem correspond. Moreover, Robinson maintains, Moses's wife might have been familiar otherwise to an early medieval audience, for among the commentators she was identified as a type or figure of 'the church gathered out of the nations'.[2] In explaining why Moses's wife might be alluded to at this point, Robinson considers the suitability of such an allusion as an amplifying, even though extra-biblical, detail. His reasons are of weight. They concern, however, only the literal identity of the *afrisc meowle* as the wife of Moses; they make nothing of her significance as a type of the church. But another compelling reason for retaining the manuscript reading here may be found if the phrase *afrisc meowle* and also the following lines 582–9a are considered from the figural point of view. The passage as a whole has never been so considered.[3] The Israelites plunder the Egyptian treasure washed up on the shore, and that is that.

It seems clear that the *afrisc meowle* shares in this plundering. If it is not her hands which 'hofon halswurðunge' (582) she is at the least 'on geofones staðe golde geweorðod' (581). Professor Neil Isaacs, in a recent essay, finds

---

[1] My line numbers are those of G. P. Krapp's text, *The Junius Manuscript*, The Anglo-Saxon Poetic Records 1 (1931).

[2] Isidore, 'Ecclesiam ex gentibus Christo conjunctam', *Allegoriæ Quædam Scripturæ Sacræ*, Migne, Patrologia Latina 83, col. 109; see especially the references cited on pp. 375–6 in Fred C. Robinson, 'Notes on the Old English *Exodus*', *Anglia* 80 (1962), 373–8. The present interpretation would question Robinson's view that 'the poet leaned more toward the Josephan than toward the Christian-exegetical explanation of the *uxor Aethiopissa*' (p. 377).

[3] Bernard F. Huppé (*Doctrine and Poetry* (New York, 1959), p. 223) takes *afrisc meowle* as an allusion to the Bride in the Song of Songs. He does not discuss lines 582–9a. Edward Burroughs Irving, Jr (*The Old English Exodus*, ed. E. B. Irving (New Haven, 1953), p. 30) seems to take lines 580–9a literally, remarking that 'the battle ends traditionally and satisfyingly with the looting of the fallen enemy'. Neil D. Isaacs ('*Exodus* and the Essential Digression', *Structural Principles in Old English Poetry* (Knoxville, 1968), p. 156) concludes that they 'deal more specifically with the literal exodus . . .' Robert T. Farrell ('A Reading of Old English *Exodus*', *RES* 20 (1969), 416) speaks only of 'the despoiling of the Egyptian host'.

in the last line and a half (589b–90) 'a final doubling of the focus where "the place of death" is both the Red Sea and hell';[1] I suggest that we have another 'double focus' as the *afrisc meowle* shares in the spoils.

In the synoptic gospels Christ speaks of the strong man who is despoiled of his goods by the stronger man who enters his house: 'Cum fortis armatus custodit atrium suum, in pace sunt ea quae possidet. Si autem fortior eo superveniens vicerit eum, universa arma eius auferet, in quibus confidebat, et spolia eius distribuet.' This is Luke XI. 21–2; the wording in Matthew XII. 29 and Mark III. 27 is somewhat different, but the idea is much the same. The context is Christ as exorcist; hence the stronger man is Christ, the strong man is the devil and his goods are humankind, whom he holds in captivity. As Bede explained in his commentary on Mark III. 27, 'Alligavit autem fortem Dominus, hoc est ab electorum seductione compescuit diabolum, et tunc domum ejus diripuit, quia ereptos a diaboli laqueis eos quos suos esse prævidit, Ecclesiæ suæ membris adunavit, ac per distinctas in ea graduum variorum dignitates ordinavit.'[2] The metaphor of mankind as goods is implied elsewhere in the New Testament, as in Romans IX. 22–3, where Paul speaks of vessels of wrath become vessels of mercy, or Colossians II. 15, where Paul says that by his crucifixion Christ despoiled principalities and powers. The commentators did not hesitate to apply to phrases like *dividere spolia* which they found in the Old Testament the significance so plain in the New:[3] thus ps. LXVII (LXVIII). 13, in the Vulgate 'Rex virtutum dilecti dilecti; Et speciei domus dividere spolia', is understood by the commentators to prophesy Christ's despoiling the devil of his treasure, humankind, and giving that treasure to his church. Augustine, for example, says that 'speciosam quippe domum, id est Ecclesiam Christus fecit, dividendo illi spolia'.[4] Comments on Isaiah XLIX. 24–5 or LIII. 12 were to the same effect;

---

[1] '*Exodus* and the Essential Digression', p. 156.

[2] *In Marci Evangelium Expositio* I. iii (PL 92, col. 164). Cf. *In Lucæ Evangelium Expositio* IV. xi (on Luke XI. 22): 'Spolia vero ejus, ipsi homines sunt ab eo decepti. Quæ victor Christus distribuit, quod est insigne triumphantis, quia captivam ducens captivitatem . . . [Ephesians IV. 8 and 11]' (PL 92, cols. 477–8).

[3] Cf. Bede, *In Marci Evangelium Expositio* I. iii: 'parabolam . . . manifestissimam' (PL 92, col. 164).

[4] *Enarratio in Psalmum LXVII*. He continues 'sicut speciosum est corpus distributione membrorum. Spolia porro dicuntur quæ victis hostibus detrahuntur. Hoc quid sit Evangelium nos admonet, ubi legimus: Nemo intrat in domum fortis, ut vasa ejus diripiat, nisi prius alligaverit fortem [cf. Matthew XII. 29 and Mark III. 27]. Alligavit ergo diabolum Christus spiritualibus vinculis; superando mortem, et super cœlos ab inferis ascendendo: alligavit eum sacramento incarnationis suæ, quod nihil in eo reperiens morte dignum, tamen est permissus occidere; ac sic alligato abstulit tanquam spolia vasa ejus. Operabatur quippe in filiis diffidentiæ [Ephesians II. 2], quorum infidelitate utebatur ad voluntatem suam. Hæc vasa Dominus mundans remissione peccatorum, hæc spolia sanctificans hosti erepta prostrato atque alligato, divisit ea speciei domus suæ; alios constituens apostolos, alios prophetas, alios pastores et doctores in opus ministerii, in ædificationem corporis Christi [Ephesians IV. 11–12]' (PL 36, cols. 821–2). See also these commentaries on ps. LXVII. 13 and 19: pseudo-Jerome, PL 26, cols. 1075–6; Cassiodorus, PL 70, cols. 466 and 469; and *Glossa Ordinaria*, PL 113, col. 942.

Jerome remarks 'quod scilicet captæ prius gentes a gigante tollantur, et omnis illius suppellex, universaque familia apostolis dividatur'.[1] It is such passages and their interpretations that Augustine bears in mind when he says in *De Civitate Dei* xx. 8 'ut prius alligaretur fortis, ereptisque vasis ejus, longe lateque in omnibus gentibus ex firmis et infirmis ita multiplicaretur Ecclesia …'[2]

We can guess then why the *afrisc meowle*, 'the church gathered out of the nations', shares in the spoils, *herereaf* as they are called in the poem (584a) just as in the West Saxon version of Luke xi. 22.[3] The inference bears in turn on the lines which follow. *Hæft wæs onsæled* (584b) can be seen to be no mere parenthesis (it is so punctuated in a number of editions)[4] but a highly pertinent and summarizing comment: the despoiling of Pharaoh *is* the delivering of mankind. *Segnum dælan* (585b), 'to divide according to standards', literally the just division of the spoils among the tribes, is typologically the division of the nations, *gentes*, to the church or churches or among the apostles and other ministers of the church.[5] The poet's identification here was furthered by there being twelve apostles and twelve tribes, and, although there does not seem to have been a systematic identification of tribes with apostles, by there being one such identification very well established: that of Benjamin as a type of Paul on the basis of Genesis xlix. 27: 'Beniamin lupus rapax, Mane comedit praedam, Et vespere dividet spolia.'[6]

Further on, the phrases 'Iosepes gestreon,/wera wuldorgesteald' (588b–9a) suggest word-play and deliberate ambiguity. Joseph was a well-known type of Christ,[7] and it is obvious how mankind redeemed from the devil might be

---

[1] *Commentaria in Isaiam Prophetam* xiii. xlix (PL 24, cols. 491–2; also cols. 531–2 on Isaiah liii. 12). Cf. Remigius of Auxerre, *Commentaria in Isaiam* ii, on Isaiah liii. 12 (PL 116, cols. 993–4; also col. 970 on Isaiah xlix. 24–5).

[2] PL 41, col. 672.

[3] *The Gospel According to Saint Luke*, ed. Walter W. Skeat (Cambridge, 1874), p. 118; or *The West-Saxon Gospels*, ed. M. Grünberg (Amsterdam, 1967), p. 185.

[4] *Bibl. d. ags. Poesie*, ed. C. W. M. Grein i (Göttingen, 1857), 93; *Cædmon's Exodus and Daniel*, ed. Theodore W. Hunt, 4th ed. (Boston, 1889), p. 36; *Grein's Bibl. d. ags. Poesie*, rev. R. P. Wülcker ii (Leipzig, 1894), 475; and Irving, *Old English Exodus*, p. 65. I think the best punctuation would be a colon after *herereafes*.

[5] Common variants on this interpretation were that the *spolia* were distributed *as* apostles and other ministers or that the apostles themselves divide the spoils; see the references to Augustine and pseudo-Jerome, above, p. 160, n. 4.

[6] See, e.g., pseudo-Bede, *In Pentateuchum Commentarii – Genesis*, on Genesis xlix. 27, *Beniamin lupus rapax* … : 'Quod de Paulo manifestissima sit prophetia, patet omnibus, quod in adolescentia persecutus Ecclesiam, in senectute prædicator Evangelii fuit' (PL 91, col. 276). Commentaries on ps. lxvii. 28, *Ibi Beniamin*, make the same point.

[7] See, e.g., Augustine, *Contra Faustum* xii. xxviii: 'Ipse [Christus] mihi in Ioseph innuitur, qui persequentibus et vendentibus fratribus, in Ægypto post labores honoratur [Genesis xxxvii–xlvii]. Didicimus enim labores Christi in orbe gentium, quem significabat Ægyptus, per varias passiones martyrum; et nunc videmus honorem Christi in eodem orbe terrarum, erogatione frumenti sui sibi omnia subjugantis' (PL 42, col. 269).

thought of as Christ's treasure.[1] *Gestreon* can mean not merely 'treasure' but 'gain, acquisition'; compare the verbs (*ge-*)*streonan/-strynan*, 'to gain, get, obtain, acquire'.[2] Now the name 'Joseph' was understood to mean 'augmentation, increase';[3] and sure enough some commentators explained Genesis XLIX. 22 'Filius accrescens Ioseph' as prophesying Christ's acquisition of mankind.[4] *Wera wuldorgesteald* may be a deliberately ambiguous construction. Elsewhere in the poem *weras* is used indifferently of the Egyptians and of the Israelites.[5] *Wera wuldorgesteald* then can mean 'glorious possession of men', i.e. belonging to men (the Egyptians); it can also mean 'glorious possession of men', i.e. consisting of men, the dependent genitive now being taken to express a relationship seen also, for example, in *Beowulf* 2799a and 3011b *maðma hord*, 'hoard (consisting) of precious objects'.

Finally, *werigend* (589b) becomes more meaningful in the light of this figure. Literally, *werigend*, though not entirely inappropriate, is certainly not highly appropriate: the Egyptians have hardly been viewed as 'defenders, protectors' either of their adornments or of anything else. Figuratively, however, *werigend* is exact and alludes to the devils' attempt to defend and protect their treasure.

At first, this interpretation of the passage might suggest that the poet had lost control of his metaphors. What we would seem to have, in the sharing of the spoils, is the curious, indeed absurd, spectacle of mankind rescuing itself; for the Israelites on the safe shore and the spoils to be shared are the same thing: they both are mankind redeemed from the devil. It should be considered, however, that quite possibly in this poem, as Professor Cross and

[1] See the interpretations of ps. LXVII. 19, *cepisti captivitatem, accepisti dona in hominibus*, and Ephesians IV. 8, *captivam duxit captivitatem: dedit dona hominibus*. So, e.g., Manegold of Lautenbach alternatively explains ps. LXVII. 19: '*cepisti captivitatem*: id est, nos homines qui prius captivati . . . sub jugo peccati et mortis fuimus, et ita captivitas diaboli eramus: nos inquam cepisti hæreditatem tuam, quia principe illo devicto, felici et libera captivitate nos captivasti . . .' (PL 93, col. 836).

[2] J. Bosworth and T. N. Toller, *An Anglo-Saxon Dictionary* (Oxford, 1898), pp. 446–7 and 928, and T. N. Toller, *Supplement* (Oxford, 1921), p. 418. (*Ge-*)*streonan/-strynan* is also used elsewhere to describe the bringing of souls to Christ. See, e.g., *Andreas* 331 or *The Homilies of Wulfstan*, ed. Dorothy Bethurum (Oxford, 1957), p. 182.

[3] So Jerome, *Liber de Nominibus Hebraicis*: 'Joseph, augmentum' (PL 23, col. 781); Isidore, *Quæstiones in Vetus Testamentum – In Genesin* xxx. 22: 'Nisi enim Joseph fratres vendidissent, defecerat Ægyptus. Nisi Christum Judæi crucifixissent, perierat mundus. Joseph interpretatur augmentatio, sive ampliatio. Sed in illo Joseph ampliationem non habuit, nisi sola Ægyptus; in nostro vero Joseph augmentum habere meruit universus mundus. Ille erogavit triticum, noster erogavit Dei verbum' (PL 83, col. 274). So too pseudo-Bede (PL 91, col. 269 and 93, col. 352) and Hrabanus (PL 107, col. 637; cf. PL 111, col. 47).

[4] E.g. pseudo-Bede: '*Filius accrescens Joseph*. Hæc prophetia post passionem Domini paternæ vocis imaginem tenuit, quo redeunti in cœlum post victoriam Pater alloquitur dicens: *Filius accrescens Joseph*; filius accrescens utique in gentibus, quia cum ob incredulitatem Synagoga populum reliquisset, innumeram sibi plebem Ecclesiæ ex omnibus gentibus ampliavit' (PL 93, col. 362). See also pseudo-Bede (PL 91, col. 283) and Hrabanus (PL 107, col. 663 and 111, col. 47).

[5] Of the Egyptians, lines 149, 515 and 572; of the Israelites, lines 3, 236 and 577.

Miss Tucker have asserted, events 'are not presented to be recognised as one consistent allegory, but symbolic pictures would occur naturally to a learned Christian's mind'.[1] Dividing the treasure follows crossing the Red Sea, but these literal events, separate in time, may figure the same thing: the redemption of mankind.[2] The point should not be belaboured, but possibly it was our expectation of consistency which, given our knowing the significance of the *transitus*, delayed our perceiving that the division of the spoils meant much the same thing.

The same signification may in fact be seen much earlier in the poem. For the redemption of man is not, I suggest, figured only for the second time by the sharing of the spoils, but for the third time (at the least). The first figure was not the Red Sea crossing, but the tenth plague, the killing of the first-born. The treatment of this event in lines 33–53 has seemed to be marked by much obscurity of phrasing.[3] But we can throw some light on several points at least of this obscurity if we bear in mind first an interpretation, well-known to the commentators, of the killing of the first-born as the overcoming of devils,[4] hence the killing of sin in ourselves; and second the figure we have just examined, that of mankind as the devil's treasure of which he is deprived.

The phrases in question are 'hordwearda hryre' (35a), 'since berofene' (36b) and 'freond wæs bereafod' (45b). They have generally puzzled editors. Professor Irving, for example, remarks of 'since berofene' that 'the Israelites also "spoiled the Egyptians" before departing (Exodus XI. 2 and XII. 35–6);

---

[1] J. E. Cross and S. I. Tucker, 'Allegorical Tradition and the Old English Exodus', *Neophilologus* 44 (1960), 123.

[2] Other interpretations might relate these figures a little more consistently. Perhaps the poet adapted a suggestion such as that of Augustine that the treasure taken from the Egyptians before departure (Exodus XI. 2 and XII. 35–6) meant those Gentiles who 'adjungunt se populo Dei, ut simul de hoc sæculo tanquam de Ægypto liberentur' (*Contra Faustum* XXII. xci (PL 42, cols. 461–2), where he also repeats the interpretation given in *De Doctrina Christiana* II. xl (PL 34, col. 63). Isidore, PL 83, col. 295; Bede, PL 91, col. 308; pseudo-Bede, PL 93, col. 370; Hrabanus, PL 108, col. 56; and the *Glossa Ordinaria*, PL 113, cols. 220–1 also give both interpretations). Or perhaps the tribes crossing the Red Sea meant the twelve apostles (as well as the *fideles* more broadly), who now 'divide the spoils'. Hereby the grammatical ambiguity of *sælafe*, line 585 (nom./acc. pl.), is curiously apposite. It seems fairly clear that the *transitus* as a type may have had more than one anti-type. Isaacs ('*Exodus* and the Essential Digression', p. 155) concludes that it is a type of Judgement. Traditionally it meant baptism, and Cross and Tucker ('Allegorical Tradition', pp. 125–6) explain some details of the narrative to support this interpretation. Probably *geofon* in 'on geofones staðe golde geweorðod' (581) alludes to the Red Sea as baptism, for it is through baptism that the church is adorned, i.e. acquires new members. Baptism in turn signifies the Redemption; Augustine's commentary on ps. LXVII. 13 (see above, p. 160, n. 4) only spells out the obvious when he interprets the *vasa* as taken from the devil *remissione peccatorum*.

[3] Irving, *Old English Exodus*, p. 68, n. to lines 33–53, comments that the passage 'is in some ways a miracle of compression, but it raises great problems in interpretation'.

[4] E.g. Origen, *In Exodum Homilia* IV. 7: 'Delentur interim primogenita Ægyptiorum, sive hos principatus et potestates, et mundi hujus rectores tenebrarum [cf. Ephesians VI. 12] dicamus, quos in adventu suo Christus dicitur traduxisse [cf. Colossians II. 15] ...' (Migne, Patrologia Græca 12, col. 323). So too Isidore, PL 83, col. 294; Bede, PL 91, col. 303; and pseudo-Bede, PL 93, col. 369.

but to see a reference to that in this one phrase is perhaps basing too much on slender evidence. The phrase seems rather to be an elegiac cliché, not to be pinned down too exactly'.[1] 'Freond wæs bereafod' has seemed so hopeless that all editors except Irving have emended *freond* to *feond*. All these half-lines may be readily understood, however, once it is seen that the poet is representing humankind as the treasure of the devil. Take these lines:

> hordwearda hryre   heaf wæs geniwad,
> swæfon seledreamas,   since berofene. (35–6)

The first-born *are* our sins, and our sins hold us captive as the devil's treasure, 'facientes voluntatem carnis et cogitationum'; therefore the first-born are *hordweardas*, 'treasure-guardians'. The idea of 'hordwearda hryre' is essentially repeated in 'since berofene'; the two phrases look, so to speak, at two sides of an equation. For to kill sin *is* to deprive the devil of what had been his; therefore 'by the fall of the treasure-guardians' the devil, or at any rate his hall-joys, are at the same time 'deprived of treasure'.[2]

In 'freond wæs bereafod' this equation is simply fused. Pharaoh is the *freond* of the first-born; the devil is the *freond* of principalities and powers, i.e. of sin. For the lord or chief may be called *freond* when his rôle as comforter or protector is important in the context.[3] Here of course *freond* ironically emphasizes Pharaoh's, the devil's, utter inability to comfort and protect. The devil is deprived at once of his principalities and powers and of his treasure, humankind: as we have seen, to kill sin *is* to take away the treasure. The relationship fuses in *bereafod*.

It has long been thought that the poet's source for the plundering of the treasure was Josephus's statement that after the Egyptians had been drowned the Israelites seized their arms and equipment washed up on the shore.[4] But several commentators alluded to the parable of the strong man despoiled of his goods by the stronger in their interpretations both of the tenth plague (Exodus XI and XII) and of the canticle of Moses (Exodus XV);[5] again, as we have noted,[6] Augustine, followed by others, explained Exodus XI. 2 and XII. 35–6, the despoiling of the Egyptians before the departure, in a way which

---

[1] *Old English Exodus*, p. 69, n. to line 36.
[2] 'Hordwearda hryre' (512) perhaps makes the same point. In baptism our previous sins, i.e. the Egyptians 'a tergo insequentes', are wiped out. The death of sin is *ipso facto* the loss of the devil's treasure.
[3] *Beowulf* 2393, *Christ* 912, *The Dream of the Rood* 144, *Genesis* 2315 (also 2820?), *Psalms* LXXVII. 34 and XC. 2 and perhaps *The Panther* 15; cf. *The Wanderer*, 'oþþe mec freondleas[n]e frefran wolde' (28).
[4] Ferdinand Holthausen, 'Zur Quellenkunde und Textkritik der altenglischen Exodus', *ASNSL* 115 (1905), 162–3.
[5] Of the tenth plague: Origen, *In Exodum Homilia* IV. 9 (PG 12, col. 325); cf. Hrabanus, *Commentaria in Exodum* I. xxi (PL 108, col. 45). Of the canticle: Origen, *In Exodum Homilia* VI. 8 (PG 12, cols. 336–7); cf. Bede, *In Pentateuchum Commentarii – Exodus* XV (PL 91, col. 312) and Hrabanus, *Commentaria in Exodum* II. iv (PL 108, col. 69).   [6] See above, p. 163, n. 2.

lent itself to ready adaptation. It is quite possible that the poet's source was one such commentary rather than Josephus, or one of them as well as Josephus, so that the literal treasure spoken of by Josephus became identified as the figural treasure of the devil, the *vasa eius* of Matthew XII. 29.

Whatever his source, the poet made good use of the figure. From time to time he hints cryptically that the devil's treasure is mankind. He concludes the poem by adverting once again to the figure but in more detail. This time, in revealing the disposition of that treasure, he dramatizes the major theme of the poem, God's covenant with his chosen people.[1] When this is understood, the manuscript position of lines 580-9 – part of a focus of no little debate[2] – is perceived to be not merely defensible but splendidly appropriate and climactic. By this covenant, mankind, the treasure of Pharaoh, the chattels and very adornments of the devil's body, becomes the adornments of the church, which is the body of Christ.[3]

[1] Isaacs ('*Exodus* and the Essential Digression', p. 157) speaks of 'the Hebrews' covenant with God which is the explicit theme throughout this uniquely unified long Old English poem'. The 'major' theme would seem to be the figurative equivalent of the 'explicit' theme. See also Farrell, 'A Reading', p. 406.

[2] The problem of the ordering of lines 516-90 is discussed in Irving, *Old English Exodus*, pp. 11-12, Isaacs, '*Exodus* and the Essential Digression', pp. 153-7, and Farrell, 'A Reading', pp. 413-17.

[3] Ephesians I. 22-3: '. . . Ecclesiam, quae est corpus ipsius . . .'; cf. IV. 12 and v. 23 and 30, Romans XII. 5 and Colossians I. 18.

It may be noted that the figure of mankind as the devil's treasure possibly occurs at one other place in the poem:

> Þa wearð yrfeweard   ingefolca,
> manna æfter maðmum,   þæt he swa miceles geðah. (142-3)

I do not discuss this for two reasons: first because the manuscript here is damaged, two whole leaves having been lost between lines 141 and 142 (see discussion, Irving, *Old English Exodus*, pp. 6-7), and therefore any conclusions must be tentative; and second because, even apart from the condition of the manuscript, lines 135-53 present such numerous and complex problems that the whole passage is best considered in detail and by itself. (Irving (*Old English Exodus*, pp. 33-4) includes lines 141-53, 'containing an allusive and complicated description of the origins of the Egyptians' hostility', among those passages he considers 'tortuous and ambiguous in construction, long-winded and involved'.) I am now engaged in a study of this passage.

The vision of paradise: a symbolic reading of the Old English *Phoenix*

DANIEL G. CALDER

The classification of *The Phoenix* as a Christian allegory has obscured the perception that the poem may contain a single symbolic vision, for the attention given the poem has always centred on the apparent allegorizations drawn from the Lactantian *De Ave Phoenice*.[1] The long description of paradise at the beginning, the phoenix's journey from paradise, its fiery death and resurrection – elements derived from Lactantius and expanded by a clearly Christian reading – invite the exegete to untangle a carefully woven allegorical web. The exegetical approaches are, in some ways, justified. Even Lactantius's poem, which at no time refers to a system of Christian theology, is legitimately subject to this kind of inquiry, for the phoenix, standing by itself, had been a symbol charged with Christian meaning since the earliest patristic writers. Augustine's words may be taken as a summary statement for the Christian interpretation: 'Quod enim de phoenice loqueris ... Resurrectionem quippe illa significat corporum.'[2] In practice, however, strict allegorical readings of *The Phoenix* have not proved very helpful. An ever-changing perspective in the poem makes it difficult to discover a logically coherent and consistent pattern of allegorical meaning, and attempts to find such a pattern have led either to disappointment with the poem or to an exegetical system so rigid that it falsifies the poem itself.[3]

---

[1] See Arturo Graf (*Miti, Leggende e Superstizioni del Medio Evo* (1892–3; repr. Bologna, 1965) I, 40–1) who discounts the Lactantian authorship of *De Ave Phoenice*. See also *Lactanti De Ave Phoenice*, ed. Mary C. Fitzpatrick (Philadelphia, 1933). (All quotations are taken from this edition.) For various interpretations of what the Old English poet has done with his source one should also consult Oliver F. Emerson, 'Originality in Old English Poetry', *RES* 2 (1926), 18–31; N. F. Blake, 'Some Problems of Interpretation and Translation of the Old English *Phoenix*', *Anglia* 80 (1962), 50; and J. E. Cross, 'The Conception of the Old English *Phoenix*', *Old English Poetry: Fifteen Essays*, ed. Robert P. Creed (Providence, R.I., 1967), p. 45.

[2] *De Anima et ejus Origine*, Migne, Patrologia Latina 44, col. 543. 'What indeed you say about the phoenix ... it certainly signifies the resurrection of the body.' See also Fitzpatrick, *De Ave Phoenice*, pp. 27–30, and the introduction to '*The Phoenix*: a Critical Edition', ed. Joseph B. Trahern, Jr (unpub. thesis, Princeton, 1963), for a complete account of the patristic sources.

[3] Blake (*The Phoenix*, ed. N. F. Blake (Manchester, 1964), pp. 33–5) expresses disappointment with the poem. (All quotations are taken from this edition.) Those who would insist upon an overly

Daniel G. Calder

The allegorical confusion centres on two identifications: the phoenix is a dual symbol that in its ambivalence represents both the redeemer and mankind, fallen and then redeemed. Its journey out of paradise symbolizes the exile of the sinful from God's grace, but its return to Eden is both the coming of Christ to earth to redeem man and, as an extension of this, the Ascension of Christ and of those whom he has redeemed. The meaning of the bird shifts with the change in direction; its fable incorporates both the journey out and the return home. And the blessed, too, have a dual symbolism. They are at times identified with the phoenix, and then again they are the birds who follow the phoenix in its flight back to Eden.[1] In searching through the constantly shifting, fading and merging perspectives for the one allegorical key to the poem, we stumble instead upon a kaleidoscopic technique, not a logically systematic allegory, and this discovery reveals a many-faceted symbolic statement. The association of the phoenix with paradise offers details capable of several simultaneous allegorical extensions;[2] the accumulation of all these points of view finally defines the total symbolic vision. Perhaps we err when we discuss the poem as falling into two halves – the fable and its allegorization. For the symbols of the phoenix and the paradise to which it belongs are unitive. They provide the threads of a complex fabric that is nonetheless single and whole. *The Phoenix* is not a formal Christian allegory; rather, as an examination of the major symbols will show, it is a rendering of the relationship between beauty and salvation that unites all differing allegorical perspectives in one symbolic vision.

Paradise stands at the centre of this symbolic world and, in contrast to the *anhaga* who journeys exiled on the *hrimceald sæ* in *The Wanderer*, the *anhaga* (87a and 346b) in *The Phoenix* inhabits a world of lasting and exquisite beauty. As Arturo Graf has shown, the entire patristic tradition of paradise emphasized the beauty of Eden above all: 'Il Paradiso terrestre doveva essere di tale bellezza e magnificenza da vincere ogni più ardita e fervita

schematic interpretation of the poem include Cross ('Conception of the Old English *Phoenix*'), whose analysis, while illuminating in many respects, falls prey to the urgency of logical explication. Cross concludes that the poet wrote *The Phoenix* with an exegetical purpose in mind and embodied in the poem a fourfold meaning based on scriptural examples. Here (pp. 135–6) 'the representation of the Phoenix as the good Christian in his earthly nest is a *moral* or *tropological* interpretation, the bird as Christian in his heavenly dwelling is an *anagogical* interpretation, and the bird as Christ is a *typical* or *allegorical* interpretation'. See also Joanne S. Kantrowitz, 'The Anglo-Saxon *Phoenix* and Tradition', *PQ* 43 (1964), 1–13; Kantrowitz attempts to erect an allegory based on traditional meanings of the worm, the apple and the eagle.

[1] See Robert B. Burlin, *The Old English 'Advent': a Typological Commentary* (New Haven and London, 1968), p. 34; Burlin makes some very pertinent remarks on the flexibility of the medieval imagination in regard to the symbol of the phoenix.

[2] The moment when the phoenix came to be associated with paradise is lost in our mythic memory, though Blake (ed., p. 16) offers some tentative suggestions.

fantasia . . .; il Paradiso terrestre diventava un prototipo di bellezza.'[1] Certainly Augustine includes this deliberate emphasis in his discussion of paradise (Genesis II. 8–10): 'Non dixit, Et ejecit de terra Deus aliud lignum vel cæterum lignum; sed, *Ejecit*, inquit, *adhuc de terra omne lignum pulchrum ad aspectum, et bonum ad escam.*'[2] This beauty has its religious implications, both in the tradition as a whole and in *The Phoenix*. The beauty of the earthly paradise is most importantly a reflection of the beauty of the heavenly city in Revelation and as such adumbrates a world of sanctity.[3]

Augustine unequivocally equates paradise with blessedness and grace: 'Nemo itaque prohibet intelligere paradisum, vitam beatorum.'[4] And John Scotus Erigena reiterates much the same idea: 'Plantationem Dei, hoc est, paradisum in Eden, in deliciis æternæ ac beatæ felicitatis, humanam naturam esse diximus ad imaginem Dei factam.'[5] Such views embody the neoplatonic bias of early medieval theology which sees the world's beauty as evidence that it was created by God, the supreme artist. Augustine writes 'Deus autem ita est artifex magnus in magnis, ut minor non sit in parvis: quæ parva non sua granditate (nam nulla est), sed artificis sapientia metienda sunt.'[6] As Augustine further explains, the universe is a hierarchy: 'a terrenis usque ad coelestia, et a visibilibus usque ad invisibilia sunt aliis alia bona meliora; ad hoc inæqualia, ut essent omnia.'[7] Thus structured, it can be graded in three tiers – earth, paradise and heaven – in relation to an ascending order of beauty. So early manuscript illuminations often depicted it,[8] and so it exists in *The Phoenix*. To be sure, the Old English poet was writing a religious poem, not a tract on aesthetic theory. But the vision of paradise contains implicitly the foundation for a Christian aesthetic in the importance given to beauty, and this importance relates directly to the contemplation of the divine being, himself the source of all beauty.

[1] Graf, *Miti* I, 40 and 42. Interestingly, this emphasis on beauty in the descriptions of paradise and of the phoenix is the dominant tone in the twelfth-century 'Phoenix homily'; see *Early English Homilies from the Twelfth Century MS. Vesp. D. xiv*, ed. Rubie D-N. Warner, Early English Text Society o.s. 152 (London, 1917), 146–7.

[2] 'He did not say, and God threw forth [caused to grow] from the earth one tree or another, but he said, "He threw forth every tree that was beautiful to look at and good to eat"' (*De Genesi ad Litteram*, PL 34, col. 374).   [3] See Graf, *Miti* I, 19.

[4] 'No one keeps us from understanding paradise as the life of the blessed' (*De Civitate Dei*, PL 41, col. 394).

[5] 'We have said that the plantation of God, that is, paradise in Eden, in the delights of eternal and blessed happiness, is human nature created in the image of God' (*De Divisione Naturæ*, PL 122, col. 829).

[6] 'For God is a great artisan in great things in such a way that he is not less in small things: these small things are to be measured not by their own greatness (for there is none), but by the wisdom of their maker' (*De Civitate Dei*, PL 41, col. 335).

[7] '. . . from earthly things to heavenly things and from visible to invisible, some good things are better than others; and for this end they are unequal, in order that they might all exist' (*ibid.*).

[8] See Lars-Ivar Ringbom, *Paradisus Terrestris: Myt, Bild och Verklighet* (Helsingfors, 1958), p. 57, pl. 19. Here in an enlarged detail from a fourth-century mosaic one can see most clearly the three worlds of earth, paradise and heaven juxtaposed in tiers that illustrate the ascending order of beauty.

Let us begin our analysis of *The Phoenix* by examining paradise and then continue by comparing paradise with the phoenix itself. In this way we shall establish a frame of reference for the symbolic meaning of the poem. Yet it should be understood that this frame, however valid both within the general tradition and within the poem, is not the poet's explicit concern as he concentrates on narrating events in the life of the phoenix and delineating theological nuances. While the poet pursues his task, nevertheless, he weaves a visionary world into the texture of his narration; by tracing our way through this texture, we in turn discover what that visionary world is and how it clarifies the ambiguities in the narrative.

That the Old English poet exploits, intentionally or not, the Christian tradition of paradise becomes manifest when we compare his description with the Lactantian version. For in *The Phoenix* Eden is *torhte lond* (28a); it is noble, fruitful and joyous: 'se æþela feld/wridað under wolcnum wynnum geblo-wen' (26b–7). Bright light and joy characterize Eden; everywhere the poet stresses the beauty of the field. Water-streams are *wundrum wrætlice* (63a) and there is 'joy of water-floods' (70b). The effect is strongly visual; the poet evokes not the taste of the fruits in paradise but rather their beauty: 'Sindon þa bearwas bledum gehongne,/wlitigum wæstmum' (71–2a). These fruits are *holtes frætwe* (73b), a term combining the concept of 'ornamentation' with that of 'fruits'.[1] In fact, its wide distribution[2] makes *frætwe* the leitmotif of the description of paradise and, beyond that, the key image of the poem. By contrast, these images of beauty are not to be found in the *De Ave Phoenice*. This is not surprising, for Lactantius, as Graf has made clear, painted not the biblical Eden, but rather a garden from another tradition, the Wood of the Sun.[3] The Christian paradise of the Old English poet, on the other hand, is not simply a world of elemental nature, nor even the natural world from which all that is deleterious has been removed; it is a world of beauty crafted by God and imagined in terms of human adornment: its trees are 'gehroden hyhtlice Haliges meahtum/beorhtast bearwa' (79–80a).[4]

---

[1] Blake ('Some Problems of Interpretation', p. 58) writes: 'the correspondence between good works and the fruits of the earth (here *frætwe*) shows that at lines 609–10 we ought to translate *fægrum frætwum* by "good works". Just as the phoenix sits in its nest surrounded by the fairest fruits and spices (204–7), so also the blessed in heaven are girt with their own good works.' In omitting any reference to 'ornaments' he allows his gloss of *frætwe* to be governed too narrowly by his own allegorical interpretation.

[2] The poet uses *frætwe* in several contexts. He uses the word concerning both paradise (73b, 116b and 150b) and the phoenix (239a, 274a, 309a, 330a and 335a); he also uses it with reference to the sun (95b), the phoenix's nest (200b) and the blessed souls (585a and 610a). Twice he applies it to the earth (257a and 508a), but these are special cases; see below, p. 177.

[3] Graf, *Miti* 1, 40–1.

[4] C. L. Wrenn (*A Study of Old English Literature* (London and Toronto, 1967), p. 132) mentions that in the description of paradise there is 'more colour than usual', but he does not notice how specific images of beauty predominate.

The ornamental adornment of this garden does not remove it from the natural sphere. We are to take the fruits on one level as fruits indeed, though this display of divine artistry transforms them into the ornaments that mirror a divine grace through the agency of nature. Paradise contains within itself the possibilities of this double view and the tradition has always placed it midway between earth and heaven; hence its position on top of the highest mountain imaginable (28–30). Eden is both earth and heaven; it is the middle ground in which the mind of man can create a vision of the celestial out of natural materials. That which most closely resembles the heavenly in man's eye is the world of immutable beauty, and the poet of *The Phoenix* carefully distinguishes between nature with its frost and hail (14b–19a) and the beautiful artifact that is paradise. To each of the three settings in the poem will accrue its proper association and value in the hierarchy. In fine, the poem suggests the neoplatonic and Christian truth that heaven is a world of pure beauty, uncontaminated by nature, that paradise is a natural world where the divine presence transmutes the fruits into ornaments, and that the earth outside paradise is a desert waste (161a and 169b) which belongs to fallen nature.

The poet goes further: he associates jewels, in the figure of the sun, with paradise. He calls the sun rising from the night not only God's candle, but *glædum gimme* (92a). As a divine emissary of light the sun is a *torht tacen Godes* (96a); as a jewel, the sun shines ornamentally through paradise: *frætwum hlican* (95b). So the sun becomes identified with the world of paradisaical beauty. The poet maintains this image when describing the sun shining upon the natural world:

> Đonne wind ligeð,   weder bið fæger,
> hluttor heofones gim   halig scineð. (182–3)

The jewel signifies beauty as well as the holiness with which it is imbued. In *swegles gim* (208b) the image recurs; and in its last occurrence it receives further expansion by association with the phoenix as symbol of life's renewal:

> Bið him edniwe
> þære sunnan þegn   þonne swegles leoht,
> gimma gladost,   ofer garsecg up
> æþeltungla wyn   eastan lixeð. (287b–90)

All the connections are present here: the rising sun, both gem and joy, as emblem of renewal of life, and the phoenix as thegn of the sun (anticipating the later identification of the sun with Christ and the phoenix with the souls of the blessed). These images give structure and meaning to *The Phoenix*; they make paradise and the bird who lives there one.

This is what we see in the account of the phoenix's actions, even if a full description of the bird does not appear until well into the middle section. A comparison with the Latin makes this self-evident. The bird's ritual bathing is a simple act of devotion in the source:

> lutea cum primum surgens Aurora rubescit,
> cum primum rosea sidera luce fugat,
> ter quater illa pias immergit corpus in undas,
> ter quater e vivo gurgite libat aquam.[1]

The Old English strikes a quite different note:

> Swa se æþela fugel   æt þam æspringe
> wlitigfæst wunað   wyllestreamas.
> Þær se tireadga   twelf siþum hine
> bibaþað in þam burnan   ær þæs beacnes cyme,
> sweglcondelle. (104–8a)

In the Old English poem images of beauty accompany the act, and this difference has far-reaching ramifications. As an agent of beauty sent from God (96a), the sun breaks with rays of light through the morning, turning paradise into a world of divine art:

> Lond beoð gefrætwad,
> woruld gewlitegad,   siþþan wuldres gim,
> ofer geofones gong   grund gescineþ. (116b–18)

Nothing in Lactantius's poem suggests such a picture.

The song of the phoenix, however, can be found in the *De Ave Phoenice*, and Lactantius even relates the beauty of this song to the world of sanctity:

> incipit illa sacri modulamina fundere cantus
> et mira lucem voce ciere novam.[2]

But the Old English poet, expanding his source, develops the chant into a rich description where the phoenix's song rings out as a sound more beautiful than anything ever heard by man since God created the world (127–31a). The poet continues with his rhapsodic strain:

> Biþ þæs hleoðres sweg
> eallum songcræftum   swetra ond wlitigra
> ond wynsumra   wrenca gehwylcum. (131b–3)

---

[1] 'As soon as yellow Aurora rising turns red, as soon as she puts to flight the stars with her rosy light, twelve times [the phoenix] immerses her body into the holy water, twelve times [the phoenix] drinks water from the living flood' (35–9).

[2] 'She begins to pour forth the harmony of sacred song and to arouse new light with her wonderful voice' (45–6).

This sense of the bird's near timelessness has no counterpart in the Latin, and the hold that the knowledge of sin and mutability has on the Old English poet in his attempt to create a poetic landscape of safety and redemption affects the song of the phoenix too: its song is more beautiful than any of the instruments 'þe Dryhten gescop/gumum to gliwe in þas geomran woruld' (138b–9). The poet renders simply the sacred motif from the Latin into Old English:

> Singeð swa ond swinsað   sælum geblissad
> oþþæt seo sunne   on suðrodor
> sæged weorþeð. (140–2a)

Its song is at one with both the heavenly harmonies that float down from the open door of heaven into paradise (11–12) and the song of praise that the blessed sing at the end (622–31).[1] And as thegn of the sun that later becomes Christ – *seo soþfæste sunne* (587) – the phoenix represents the order of nature through which shines the order of grace as expressed in the incarnation. Thus its song far transcends purely mortal art. The phoenix occupies an ambiguous position which this particular passage illustrates very well. The bird is, first of all, quite removed from *þas geomran woruld*, since it dwells in paradise, the world of joy and gladness blessed by grace; yet, like man, it participates in the natural cycle of death and rebirth.

Not until well after the immolation and rebirth of the new phoenix does the poet offer a description of the bird (291–319).[2] In his picture of this new bird the Old English poet has created one of the great descriptive passages in the corpus, though some critics have raised their voices in objection. Blake maintains:

The phoenix was for [the poet] nothing more than a symbol and the phoenix story was of little interest to him in itself. It seems to me wrong therefore to stress the great beauty of the descriptions of the phoenix as some critics do. For the poet the phoenix was merely a means to an end, and to praise the poetic descriptions of the phoenix in their own right is likely to lead to a distorted view of the poem. It all too quickly degenerates into seeing the poem as a beautiful natural description to which an allegory was unfortunately appended. But for the poet the allegory was the most important feature of the poem and the phoenix myth was merely used as a garment to clothe the real essence of the poem.[3]

---

[1] Trahern ('*The Phoenix*', p. 146) writes: 'The song sung by the blessed souls here is a paraphrase of biblical quotations and liturgy. The beginning is an adaptation of Apocalypse VII. 12, "Benediction, and glory, and wisdom, and thanksgiving, and honour, and power, and strength to our God for ever and ever." The poet combines this with a paraphrase of the Tersanctus, which in turn rests upon Isaiah VI. 3, "Holy, holy, holy, the Lord God of hosts, all the earth is full of His glory."'

[2] Since Lactantius employs the same order, we may question Cross's contention ('Conception of the Old English *Phoenix*', p. 145) that the Old English poet went to the *De Ave Phoenice* simply for the best description available. If that were the case, there would seem to be no necessity to follow the order of the Latin as well. Also the actual description of the phoenix hardly corresponds to Lactantius's, as we shall see.   [3] 'Some Problems of Interpretation', pp. 56–7.

These are very strange words from one who later faults the poem for its bad and inconsistent allegory; they seem even stranger once one examines the poet's description of the phoenix. Blake seems unsure whether the phoenix is only a symbol or a real bird; he misses entirely the point of the phoenix's beauty.

  The poet's description is his own. Besides those elements taken from the Latin, he provides much that he did not find in Lactantius. Lactantius does mention the beauty of the bird and includes as details the gems of the phoenix's beak and eyes, as well as the yellow of the bird's feet. And both descriptions share a gleaming purple brightness. Here, however, the similarity ends. Arranging the variegated elements of his portrait, the Old English poet has made the phoenix into a work of art, hardly born of the natural world at all. First:

> Is se fugel fæger   forweard hiwe,
> bleobrygdum fag   ymb þa breost foran.
> Is him þæt heafod   hindan grene
> wrætlice wrixleð   wurman geblonden.
> Þonne is se finta   fægre gedæled,
> sum brun sum basu   sum blacum splottum
> searolice beseted. (291–7a)

The pattern of these and the following details is both too constant and too consistent to be fortuitous. From the poet's point of view, the phoenix is an object created by art; even the spots on his feathers have been 'artistically' arranged. In its rich colouring (more ostentatious and more vivid than in the Latin description), the bird is likened to an object fashioned by the hands of man:

>   Is seo eaggebyrd
> stearc ond hiwe   stane gelicast,
> gladum gimme,   þonne in goldfate
> smiþa orþoncum   biseted weorþeð. (301b–4)

Its beak also shines 'swa glæs oþþe gim' (300a). The connection of the phoenix with the gold vessel crafted by smiths reveals unmistakably the way in which we should take the description: the bird is akin to a work of man's creative imagination made tangible in the jewels and gold of the artist. This motif continues:

> Is ymb þone sweoran,   swylce sunnan hring,
> beaga beorhtast   brogden feðrum.
> Wrætlic is seo womb neoþan   wundrum fæger
> scir ond scyne.   Is se scyld ufan
> frætwum gefeged   ofer þæs fugles bæc. (305–9)

What was a simple and undeveloped metaphor in the Latin source has become a complex pattern, not only in the picture of the phoenix, but also in the entire poem. The poet creates a texture and emphasis quite different from those that many critics have allowed; he compares his phoenix with an object crafted by goldsmiths, adding a woven neck and an ornamented back. In this way the poet makes the phoenix one with its home in paradise, crafted by divine artistry. He also associates the sun, which was the divine source for the ornamented world of Eden, even more strongly with the phoenix in this passage: the woven ring on the phoenix's neck is like the ring of the sun, and suggests in addition the ring formed by the worshipping birds around the holy phoenix after its resurrection (339). This ring will also multiply and become the crowns on the heads of the blessed once they attain heaven (602). The phoenix is *wuldre gemearcad* (318b) and the poet leaves no doubt about the source of the glory: 'Ece is se Æþeling se þe him þæt ead gefeð' (319).

The basic problem which confronts interpreters may be illuminated by remembering the confusion into which Blake fell. For if we are to understand the integral relationship of the setting and the bird, we must keep in mind the place of beauty in the achievement of grace. God is the fountain of bliss and the artisan of paradise whose wondrous works are similar to the arts of man. Paradise, then, is a natural world made beautiful (and therefore nearly immutable) through the art of God. It is a vision of nature transformed by God's grace and radiance into a world of ornaments and gladness: the phoenix shares this position. It, too, is a natural creature transformed by the artistry that went into its creation. Like Eden, the phoenix inhabits an ambiguous middle level between the purely divine and the purely natural. The vision of paradise in *The Phoenix* thus forms the *locus* from which we can derive the meaning of the poem.

The vision implies a profound understanding of Adam's fall. It is in relation to sin and mutability that paradise is both a memory and a hope. The poet conveys his trust in the prospect of redemption by depicting a symbolic world where redemption becomes possible. Within this visionary world the poet creates a paradise that attracts man through its beauty to participate in an activity that imitates the art of God. And in this imitation, in creating an art for himself patterned on the divine fusion of nature and grace (the art of paradise), man begins to achieve salvation. This salvation, at least in some of its aspects, is a cooperative effort; if God creates a middle world between earth and heaven as a vision of what the beauty of the heavenly city will be, it is also incumbent upon man to transform the natural world that surrounds him into a thing of beauty, so that in his effort to achieve this transformation he may participate in God's grace. Thus in preparation for the fire that is to consume it, the phoenix builds its nest. The building of the nest is the only act of creation that occurs within the poem, and its ultimate intention is revealed when the poet points out that the phoenix constructs his new home because he desires to exchange old life for new:

> Bið him neod micel
> þæt he þa yldu   ofestum mote
> þurh gewittes wylm   wendan to life,
> feorg geong onfon. (189b–92a)

In order to make this transformation possible, the phoenix creates a nest out of the earth's fruits:

> Þonne feor ond neah
> þa swetestan   somnað ond gædrað
> wyrta wynsume   ond wudubleda
> to þam eardstede,   æþelstenca gehwone,
> wyrta wynsumra. (192b–6a)

These fruits, once gathered, become *torhte frætwe* (200b). The range of significances is now complete. From the world of unredeemed nature, still noble in its own right as part of God's creation (196b–9), the phoenix has gathered the fruits of the earth with which to make its nest. The nest itself then becomes a symbol of brightness and radiance because it, too, is transformed through the art of the phoenix. The moralization of the nest only reinforces the intimate relationship between the aesthetic and moral realms, for the poet identifies the nest with the good deeds of man:

> Þær him nest wyrceð   wið niþa gehwam
> dædum domlicum   Dryhtnes cempa. (451–2)

Schematically rendered, the elements of nature, which the phoenix takes from the earth, once formed into art, compose the 'brightest of nests' (227a). A moral reading then follows logically; in its desire to exchange old life for new (i.e. to achieve salvation) the phoenix reflects the art of paradise of which it is itself a part. The *frætwe* then become the 'good works' of men, who can pursue their own salvation, so the poet seems to tell us, by imitating the art of the phoenix. We are to deduce from this equation that man, inhabiting the realm of sin and nature where moral concerns are more important than aesthetic ones, can find redemption by using the fruits of the earth. Nevertheless this activity transcends the natural world rooted in mutability and reaches out toward the exemplary art of paradise with its resplendent vision of grace. Unless all three meanings of *frætwe* – fruits, ornaments and good works – are allowed within the scope of *The Phoenix*, the poem's full significance – even on the strictly moral level – is lost. We move in the poem from fallen nature to beauty and from beauty, through good works, to grace. At least that is the lesson as it applies to humanity. To skip directly, in the fashion of mechanical allegory, from the fruits themselves to their significa-tion as good works is to miss the whole point of the bird's beauty and the meaning of paradise.

Even in moments when the poet describes the purely natural, he still conveys an urgency to transmute the natural world of base metal into the golden world of beauty. We find this to be true when we examine the famous seed-grain metaphor, which replaces the life of a butterfly described by Lactantius. The metaphor is, as has often been pointed out, a superb natural parallel to the death and resurrection of the phoenix. New life arises from the seed planted in the ground. This process of death and rebirth in the world of nature reminds us that the phoenix, too, despite its semi-immortal status, has only a cyclical assurance of resurrection and must eventually perish in the all-consuming fire on Judgement Day. The ultimate subjection of the phoenix to the earth's demands enables the bird to represent humanity enmeshed in the web of mutable existence.

It follows that even the natural world, like the phoenix, may offer the promise of salvation through transformation:

> on lenctenne   lifes tacen
> weceð woruldgestreon   þæt þa wæstmas beoð
> þurh agne gecynd   eft acende
> foldan frætwe. (254–7a)

Eden may be a vision of nature crystallized into art, but earth itself has its *frætwe*. The dichotomy sets up a moral tension that can be resolved only through redemption and a return of the human soul to the celestial city. There are, then, a good art and a bad. The ornaments of the earth may direct the soul towards the idea of paradise and heaven or they may seduce that soul into the belief that their art is 'all it needs to know' on earth.[1] Nature possesses examples to lead the fallen to the visionary art of paradise, but she does not lack others to lure the sinful back to the dust of mortality. However, the enticements of the world, like paradise and the phoenix, will end in the apocalyptic fire:

> Weorþeð anra gehwylc
> forht on ferþþe   þonne fyr briceð
> læne londwelan,   lig eal þigeð
> eorðan æhtgestreon,   æpplede gold
> gifre forgripeð,   grædig swelgeð
> londes frætwe. (503b–8a)

[1] See Augustine, *De Doctrina Christiana* i, for his commentary on the use and abuse of nature.

The importance of paradise is its supreme position within the realm of the created universe. Before the Fall the distinction that now exists between the adornments of the earth and the adornments of paradise did not exist. We have learned, the poet writes,

>   þæt se Ælmihtiga
> worhte wer ond wif   þurh his wundra sped
> ond hi þa gesette   on þone selestan
> foldan sceates,   þone fira bearn
> nemnað neorxnawong. (393b–7a)

In this post-lapsarian world we realize that man has only his memory of a paradise lost and his ability to recreate that paradise in a vision of beauty. And now too the risen phoenix, returning home to paradise after its immolation and rebirth, exemplifies to man those attributes that make the bird a part of the best of 'earth regions' and give it a share in the beauty that mirrors heaven itself. The flight of the phoenix elicits a powerful response from humanity:

> Ðonne wundriað   weras ofer eorþan
> wlite and wæstma,   ond gewritu cyþað
> mundum mearciað   on marmstane
> hwonne se dæg ond seo tid   dryhtum geeawe
> frætwe flyhthwates. (331–5a)

This initial response is from art to art. The intervening moral thrust is a later development, coming after man responds to the sheer beauty of the bird and seeks to express that beauty through art of his own. When man learns that the phoenix has a significance that incorporates and then transcends sensuous splendour, the redemptive value and purpose of the bird are fulfilled. But once again it is important to see that the movement toward salvation begins in the perception of adorned beauty. Man's art in making a copy of the phoenix marks the starting point toward his own salvation. Beauty is the form of truth; splendour and adornment so signify a more perfect world, one not only to be emulated and adorned, but to be achieved. The distinction between the aesthetic and moral aspects of these devotional acts is that between adoration and discipline. Adoration, response to the beauty of the phoenix, is the beginning of hope; the achievement of the salvation this beauty promises comes in making the art moral, that is, in making the world itself and human life within it worthy of the highest art that can be envisioned – the grace of God.

That the poet associates the moral and the aesthetic closely in his view of salvation is clear in his allegorization of the nest where he invokes the 'wonder' of the nest as a defence against every evil:

> Þis þa wyrta sind,
> wæstma blede   þa se wilda fugel
> somnað under swegle   side ond wide
> to his wicstowe,   þær he wundrum fæst
> wið niþa gehwam   nest gewyrceð. (465b–9)

The building of the nest involves the moving of the plants of the earth to another level – a level that does indeed partake of the wondrous beauty of paradise. And from this vantage point the corresponding 'wonder' of the heavenly city is assured to those who merit that reward for their art of transforming nature:

> Beoð him of þam wyrtum   wic gestaþelad
> in wuldres byrig   weorca to leane. (474–5)

Whenever we choose earthly objects, no matter how beautiful, to represent the reality of heaven, the edges of the symbol inevitably tend to blur as if in negation or denial of the very realities they supposedly symbolize. The epistemological difficulty is inherent in the very method. Such is the case with both paradise and the phoenix. They both are and are not symbols of a heavenly world; they are the best in terms of the world that the human mind can find to carry man's hopes and notions of a perfect dwelling. Thus paradise is the heavenly city on earth; yet again it is not. Finally it will be destroyed. So the phoenix is man redeemed, and yet it is not redeemed and, like paradise, will be burned in the fire of Judgement. The idea of paradise with its dual relation to heaven above and earth below necessitates a symbol that serves a correspondingly dual rôle: paradise is a mirror reflecting two opposite worlds in one surface. And the phoenix functions in precisely the same way – as symbol of the divine and of the human in one adorned and risen bird.

Neither paradise nor the phoenix, then, achieves its total symbolic value until it has been imaginatively transmuted into the transcendent reality which it reflects – until the end comes and only the pure beauty of heaven exists, serene, unambiguous and immutable. Adumbrations of redemption through nature made art in paradise and the phoenix become salvation through God's grace in the vision of beauty that defines heaven at the poem's conclusion. Paradise itself is transformed through grace from a world of nature made art into a world of art without nature, namely heaven. Heaven is the apotheosis of the art of paradise. The imagery of the poem is basically analogous to the patristic identification of paradise with the church. As Bede, citing Isidore, briefly reports: 'Paradisus Ecclesia est; sic enim de illa legitur in Canticis canticorum: *Hortus conclusus est soror mea.*[1] In both the poem and the allegorical tradition, paradise serves as the symbol of how mankind can achieve salvation.

The closing section of the poem, the assumption into heaven of the blessed after Judgement, parallels the opening description of paradise in many respects. God replaces the sun which irradiated Eden and gave it beauty. As the sun was God's jewel, now God himself shines upon the blessed from his high throne, *wlitig wuldres gim* (516a). This recalls the relation between the sun and the phoenix at the opening of the poem, and helps to explain the dual nature of the bird. The phoenix represents man, fallen and then redeemed. But as the created and adorned bird the phoenix becomes Christ, for the redemptive power of grace as manifested in beauty transforms the phoenix into Christ himself. As a symbol, the phoenix contains in its own enigma the whole paradox of the incarnation: the phoenix is man and Christ just as Christ himself was both man and God. By interposing a symbolic layer between the two poles of the incarnational paradox, the poet illustrates the place of beauty in the achievement of the salvation that Christ's death and resurrection established for all mankind.

The coronation of the blessed in heaven completes the transformation of earth into glory and of men into blessed souls. Paradise and the phoenix, as intermediate symbols, have faded into the background as the poet presses the final connection of man to heaven, though these symbols have served their function of uniting the disparate and complex elements contained in the several allegorical perspectives. The passage that describes this corona-tion is so appropriate to the theme that it must be quoted in full:

> Þær se beorhta beag   brogden wundrum
> eorcnanstanum   eadigra gehwam
> hlifað ofer heafde.   Heafelan lixað
> þrymme biþeahte.   Ðeodnes cynegold
> soðfæstra gehwone   sellic glengeð
> leohte in life,   þær se longa gefea
> ece ond edgeong   æfre ne sweþrað,
> ac hy in wlite wuniað   wuldre bitolden
> fægrum frætwum   mid Fæder engla. (602–10)

The crowns of the blessed resemble the sun's bright ring, the bright ring around the phoenix's neck and the ring of adoring birds that surrounded the risen phoenix. In the true radiance of heavenly glory the souls have taken on a permanent gem-adorned beauty that is itself a part of the eternal bliss

---

1 'Paradise is the church; so indeed we read concerning that in the Song of Songs: "The enclosed garden is my sister"' (*Quæstiones super Genesim*, PL 93, col. 269). For an interesting discussion of the symbolism of paradise and the church in another Old English poem, see Richard L. Hoffman, 'Structure, Symbolism and Theme in *The Judgment Day II*', *Neophilologus* 52 (1968), 170–8.

of the glorious king, the *wlitig wuldres gim*. As good works were the beginning of a moral art in the natural world, so now these same works shine radiantly like heaven's divine gem, the sun:

Weorc anra gehwæs
beorhte bliceð   in þam bliþan ham
fore onsyne   ecan Dryhtnes,
symle in sibbe   sunnan gelice. (598 b–601)

Such, in outline, is the symbolic vision that *The Phoenix* presents. To the Old English poet this vision justifies his task and applies metaphorically to the salvation of his own soul and the souls of all mankind. Ambrose's belief in the resurrection symbolized by the phoenix draws on the hope that the phoenix offers to man: he asks 'Si ergo caro avis de cineribus suis resurgit, caro hominis de cineribus suis non resurget?'[1] For the poet, the hope is the one offered by the paradise to which the phoenix belongs – the world of grace that mirrors the art of God to man, so that man may be redeemed through the art of his own works and days, arriving, crowned at last, in the city of art, which is heaven itself.

---

[1] 'If therefore the flesh of the bird rises from its own ashes, will not the flesh of man rise from his own ashes?' (*De Trinitate Tractatus*, PL 17, col. 575).

Three versions of the Jonah story:
an investigation of narrative technique in
Old English homilies

PAUL E. SZARMACH

As Professor Clemoes has demonstrated, Ælfric treats a wide variety of subjects with both felicity and facility.[1] While Clemoes makes his case by presenting passages differing in intellectual content but displaying the same flexibility of style, it is noteworthy that first among his selections is a narrative excerpt from the Life of St Swithhun. Generally students of Old English prose have not chosen to pursue the implicit connections between narrative and intellectual prose, preferring, it appears, to keep generic guidelines clear and distinct. At least one significant exception is C. E. Wright's search for saga in histories and chronicles.[2] Clemoes's suggestion of a 'narrative style', however, merits a wider application to Old English homiletic literature. Obviously homilies are not stories, but one can find in the use of *exemplum*, anecdote and history a narrative style at work, or at least a narrative consciousness.

A good example of this concern for narrative in homiletic prose is the differing treatment given to the story of Jonah in certain Rogationtide homilies. These homilies are: (1) Vercelli, Biblioteca Capitolare CXVII, 106v–9v, homily XIX, untitled (referred to below as V), also extant as Cambridge, Corpus Christi College 162, pp. 403–12, *Feria .ii. in Letania Maiore* (referred to below as A) and Cambridge, Corpus Christi College 303, pp. 215–19, *Sermo in Letania Maiore* (referred to below as B); (2) Ælfric's homily *In Letania Maiore*, the eighteenth item in his First Series of *Catholic Homilies*, extant in several manuscripts; and (3) BM Cotton Cleopatra B. xiii, 44r–55v, *Dominica ante Rogationum* (referred to below as C), a redaction of VAB that incorporates several passages from Ælfric's homily.[3] The

---

[1] Peter Clemoes, 'Ælfric', *Continuations and Beginnings*, ed. E. G. Stanley (London, 1966), pp. 176–209. I wish to express my thanks to Professor Clemoes and Professor Fred C. Robinson for many helpful suggestions in the preparation of this article. A version of it was read at the Sixth Conference on Medieval Studies at Western Michigan University, May 1971.
[2] C. E. Wright, *The Cultivation of Saga in Anglo-Saxon England* (Edinburgh, 1939). Cf. Arthur G. Brodeur's review, *Jnl of Amer. Folklore* 54 (1941), 88–90.
[3] For information on the manuscripts see N. R. Ker, *Catalogue of Manuscripts Containing Anglo-Saxon* (Oxford, 1957), (1) pp. 460–4, 51–6 and 99–105, (2) pp. 512–13 and (3) pp. 182–5.

Paul E. Szarmach

Vercelli manuscript was written during the second half of the tenth century, CCCC 162 at the beginning of the eleventh, probably at St Augustine's, Canterbury, and CCCC 303 during the first half of the twelfth century, almost certainly at Rochester; Cleopatra B. xiii was written during the third quarter of the eleventh century, almost certainly at Exeter.[1] To compare the three versions, VAB, Ælfric's and C, is to observe not only how two Old English homilists, the author of VAB and Ælfric, saw different possibilities in the same narrative material but also how a third, the redactor of C, had his own point of view in adapting the work of the other two.

By specifying, without biblical authority, that the Ninevites' fast was a three-day one, all three Old English homilists show that their central concern with this narrative material is the relationship to Rogationtide that they see in it.[2] With this in view they focus on incidents from *Jonas* I (Jonah's attempted escape), *Jonas* II (his journey in the great fish) and *Jonas* III (his conversion of the Ninevites). Jonah's reaction to the conversion of the city, which is narrated in *Jonas* IV, is omitted. So too is the prophet's prayer in the belly of the great fish, which takes up eight of the eleven verses in the second biblical chapter, only its frame being kept, i.e. the fish's seizure of the prophet (all three homilists call the great fish a whale) and his subsequent release. Ælfric even goes further and eliminates any reference to the typologically important 'erat Ionas in ventre piscis tribus diebus et tribus noctibus' (*Jonas* II. 2). Thus it is clear enough that the homilists' common interest is in adapting their source for their Rogationtide theme. But in this they have not been as austere as, for example, Maximus of Turin had been in his *De Ieiuniis Ninivitarum*.[3] In this homily, presumably known to Ælfric and the Anglo-Saxon church through the homiliary of Paul the Deacon, Maximus confines himself to details from *Jonas* III to make his point about fasting and moral conversion.[4] He avoids any mention of the episode of Jonah and the whale. None of the Old English homilists, on the other hand, could forgo the narrative value of this story.

In VAB the Jonah story, forming nearly a quarter of the homily, comes past the midpoint of the whole exposition. The structure of the homily indicates that the homilist is using the story thematically. After beginning

---

[1] *Ibid.* pp. 460, 51 and 56, 99 and 105, and 182 and 184. Max Förster (*Die Vercelli-Homilien* (Hamburg, 1932; repr. Darmstadt, 1964), p. 1) gives 'about 1020' and 'about 1120' for CCCC 162 and CCCC 303 respectively.

[2] Similar adaptation occurs concerning the repentant Ninevite king sitting in ashes (*Jonas* III. 6). This is omitted in VAB, while Ælfric, with the C redactor following him, substitutes 'dyde . . . axan uppan his heafod'.

[3] Ed. A. Mutzenbecher, Corpus Christianorum Series Latina 23, pp. 332–4.

[4] Maximus's work is in the homiliary of Alain de Farfa and the supplement to the homiliary of Toledo as well as in the homiliary of Paul. See Réginald Grégoire, *Les Homéliaires du Moyen Âge* (Rome, 1966), pp. 52, 95 and 184. For the importance of the homiliary of Paul see Cyril L. Smetana, 'Aelfric and the Early Medieval Homiliary', *Traditio* 15 (1959), 163–204.

with a confession of faith in the Trinity, he relates the creation, the fall of Lucifer and the 'old story' of the fall of man. Having thus described the origin of sin and man's sinful nature, he makes a general plea for moral conversion, 'utan us wendan men þa leofestan to beterum þingum', and then tells his audience more specifically 'Us ys georne to witenne 7 to gehlystenne for hwylcum þingum we ðas gangdagas healdað . . . 7 mid hwylcum þingum we hie healdan sceolon.' The repentance that Rogationtide demands of us is thus set in a universal perspective. The homilist then describes Rogationtide's spiritual combat against the devil in dramatic dualistic terms, the devil contending with vices and the faithful shielding themselves with virtues.[1] Holy books, he continues, say that those faithfully and religiously observing these three days will protect themselves before God, gaining his forgiveness despite the number of sins they have committed. The story of Jonah is then introduced as a biblical precedent showing that a change of heart towards God during Rogationtide will result in divine forgiveness. After his account of this biblical tale the homilist gives the corresponding historical precedent of Mamertus of Vienne and closes with a further exhortation to choose 'the better'.

Since VAB has not been published except in Max Förster's facsimile of the Vercelli manuscript,[2] I give here the relevant portion of V:[3]

> (108r24) Uton nu gehealdan georne þis fæsten neah þam þe hit awriten is on haligum bocum þæt þa fæston þe þurh þæs witigan lare to Gode gecyrdon 7 þæt fæsten swa fæston swa [he] him wisode se wæs haten Ionas. Be ðam is on bocum awriten þæt God þurh haligne gast hine het faran to sumere mærre ceastre seo wæs   5 Ninive haten 7 þær sceolde bodigean Godes bebodu. Ac forþam þe ðæt folc wæs awyrged 7 æbreca, he him swiðe ondred 7 þæder faran ne (108v) dorste. Forðam þe God wæs swiðe yrre þære ceasterleode, ða wolde [he] forþi Godes bebodu forfleon. Ac him com to cyððe þæt [he] hie forfleon ne meahte. He þeah on fleame wæs oð   10 he to sæ becwom 7 him þær scip gebohte 7 mid þam scipmannum

3 *Supply* he *with ABC*   9 *Supply* he *with ABC*   10 *Supply* he *with ABC*

[1] The theme of spiritual combat is borrowed from Caesarius of Arles, *Sermo 207* (ed. G. Morin, CCSL 104, p. 829). See Paul E. Szarmach, 'Caesarius of Arles and the Vercelli Homilies', *Traditio* 26 (1970), 319.
[2] *Il Codice Vercellese* (Rome, 1913).
[3] 108r24–109r9. I supply my own punctuation, capitals and word-division and omit manuscript accents.

There are three main manuscript traditions of this homily: V, B and C. Originally A was very close to V but subsequently was corrected by superscription and addition under the influence of an ancestor of B. Never sharing an error with C against V and B, A almost always agrees with either V or B. See Paul E. Szarmach, 'Selected Vercelli Homilies' (unpub. thesis, Harvard, 1968), pp. 193–5.

him þohte ofer sæ to seglgenne. Ac he ne mihte swa he gemynt
hæfde Godes willan forfleon. Ac sona swa he wæs inagan on þæt
scyp, þa gereste he hine on anum ende. 7 þa sona swa þa menn þe
on þam scipe wæron ut on þære sæs dypan gesegled hæfdon, þa 15
onsende God mycelne ren 7 strangne wind 7 grimme yste on þa
sæ, swa þæt þæt scip ne mihte naþer ne forð swymman ne under-
bæc for unhyrsumnesse þæs witigan þe Ionas wæs haten. Þa forþam
þa ondredon þa scipmen him swiðe þearle, hluton him þa betwynan
for hwylces hiera gyltum him swa getimod wære. 7 þa behluton 20
hie hit sona to Iona[m] þam witigan, 7 he his nan þing nyste. Ða
wundrodon hie sona þæt se hlyt ofer þone Godes þegn gefeoll.
Awrehton hine þa of slæpe 7 rehton hit him eall. 7 he þafode þæt
hine man wearp ut on þa sæ, þa he ongiten hæfde þæt he nahwar God
forfleon meahte. 7 hie him fore gebædon. 7 hine sona an mycel 25
hwæll forswealh. 7 he wæs on him þry dagas 7 .iii. niht 7 syððan,
eal swa hit God wolde, seo sæ þone fisc ferede oð he com to þam
ilcan eðle þe he ær onbodian sceolde se witega 7 hine þær ut of him
aspaw ofer þære sæstaðe. 7 he ða sona on þreora daga fyrste
þurhfor þa mæran 7 þa myclan burh 7 bodode on þære Godes be- 30
bodu swa þæt se cyng mid þære ceasterware on God gelyfde on
eallre heortan. 7 he bebead þæt hie ealle fram þam yldestan oð þone
gingestan þreora daga fæsten healdan sceoldon. 7 he aras of his
cynesetle 7 him fram his cynereaf of awearp 7 hine mid hæran
ymbscrydde 7 to Gode georne cleopode mid eallre þære burhware. 35
7 he bebead ærest þæt ægðer ge (109r) þa menn ge ealle þa nytenu þe
hie ahton sceoldon þry dagas 7 þreo niht on an fæstan. 7 hie ða
swa dydon. 7 him ða God his mildheortnesse geaf 7 him fram þæt
fyrene clyne adyde, þe ofer þa ceastre wæs on þam genipe hangiende,
þæt sceolde forniman ealle þa burhware 7 forbærnan binnan 40
feowertigum dagum, butan hie to Gode gecyrran woldon. Ac hie
dydon swa him to donne wæs: gecyrdon to Gode ælmihtigum, 7
he him sona his mildheortnesse forgeaf, swa he symle deð ælcum
þara þe he ongyt þæt him on eallum mode to gecyrreð.

17 *After* sæ *C adds from* Ælfric swa þæt hi wæron orwene heora lifes *and substitutes* 7 þæt *for* swa
þæt þæt. *See below*, p. 191   21 *ABC* ionam   23–37 7 he ... fæstan: *the equivalent passage in*
C is influenced by Ælfric's *version. I print it below*, pp. 190–1   31 *V* cyng þære ceasterware mid hire

This is a treatment that is to a considerable extent independent of the
bible. At the outset the homilist establishes the premises of the story in short
order. God has given the prophet a command to preach to a cursed and
lawless people; no such characterization of the Ninevites occurs in *Jonas* I,
but it is the obvious implication of *Jonas* III. Though God's command puts

Jonah under a moral obligation (*sceolde bodigean*), he is fearful of the Ninevites and of God's anger with the city-dwellers. The narrative tension that is at the heart of the story is made plain: Jonah's fear leads to his plan to flee. But instead of proceeding directly to a description of the flight itself the homilist makes the forward-looking observation 'ac him com to cyððe þæt he hie forfleon ne meahte', thus calling attention to God's power and the binding force of his command. With *þeah* narration is reintroduced – a quick series of actions in Jonah's flight – but again the homilist interrupts after mentioning Jonah's intention to sail over the sea: 'ac he ne mihte swa he gemynt hæfde Godes willan forfleon'. The audience is told again that divine will will overcome human intention. The repeated moral message disregards narrative suspense in order to call attention to the thematic meaning of the story. The narrative then resumes. The prophet on board and at rest, the ship's company sails out on to the deep, only to encounter a fierce storm sent by God. Here the homilist adds a thematically significant dramatic touch, apparently derived from his own imagination, when he relates that the ship was checked on all sides by the divinely commanded elements:[1] a ship motionless during a raging storm, manned by a terror-stricken crew, is a perfect emblem for human futility in opposition to divine power. Yet this image is not enough to convey the moral in the eyes of the homilist, for he states explicitly that the ship's plight is the result of Jonah's disobedience. Then the crew casts lots with the obvious result. In the bible the shipmen have a dramatic existence and a fate of their own: they cry out to their various gods; they attempt to lighten the ship; they have a leader who wakes the sleeping Jonah and exhorts him; they decide among themselves to cast lots and they fire questions at Jonah when the lot falls on him; they reproach him for fleeing from God; until it proves hopeless, they try to avoid throwing Jonah overboard by rowing the ship to safety; they cry out to God for mercy; and when they have cast Jonah into the sea and the storm has subsided they become worshippers of the true God. But the homilist does not even mention that the storm dies down; in his version the shipmen serve only to direct attention away from themselves to Jonah; they wonder that a man whom they regard as God's *þegn* should have been responsible for the storm and they pray for Jonah when they cast him overboard. Confronted, Jonah consents to being thrown overboard 'þa he ongiten hæfde þæt he nahwar God forfleon meahte'. With this clause moral message and narrative action come together. The prophet acknowledges in his heart what the homilist has repeatedly stated to his audience. Jonah becomes the passive instrument of God and his ride in the whale begins. To the telling of this event the homilist adds a further thematically significant image, 'seo sæ

---

[1] See further, below, p. 189, n. 2.

þone fisc ferede', its significance underlined by an interpretative parenthesis, 'eal swa hit God wolde'. The fish carried by the current recalls in contrast the ship's motionlessness. It symbolizes the newly won accord between God and the prophet. When he turns to Jonah's preaching in Nineveh the homilist continues in the same manner. He graphically symbolizes God's anger with the unrepentant Ninevites by the *fyrene clyne* ('ball of fire') which, he says, hung over the city threatening to destroy it, shrouded in darkness; and tersely, but pregnantly, he makes explicit the citizens' response to the king's call for a three-day fast: '7 hie ða swa dydon'. This last addition, in itself, might seem insignificant, but forms of *don* echo throughout the homily to signify resolute moral action: the same thematic word is used when the moral of God's merciful response to the Ninevites' conversion is made explicit and extended to all who truly repent ('ac hie dydon swa him to donne wæs'); and it is used again with reference to the compliance of all Vienne with Mamertus's order of fasting ('7 hie ða ealle swa dydon') and in the homily's final exhortation ('do gehwa swa him sylfum for Gode gebeorhlicost þince').[1] Clearly this homilist's method is to invest his narrative with moral meaning both directly through thematic comment and indirectly through dramatic emblem.

Ælfric's aim is a more modest one. His version of the Jonah story[2] is part of a section that serves only to preface the quite separate main subject of his homily. The purpose of this prelude is to state what the principal liturgical practices proper to Rogationtide are and to place them in a historical perspective. Beginning with a short explanation of the term *litaniae*, Ælfric says that the observances of *gebed-dagas* were established in the days of Mamertus of Vienne when his people faced earthquake, ravenous beasts and heavenly fire. They, in turn, 'took example of the fast from the people of Nineveh'. Briefly and clearly Ælfric has made a historical link between his audience's observance of Rogationtide and the days of Jonah; by contrast the VAB homilist merely cites one bookish example, *Jonas*, and adds another, 'eac we ræddon on halegum bocum', when he gives his version of the observances at Vienne. With the historical chain thus brought to mind Ælfric is able to conclude his preface with a simple, effective exhortation concerning the present-day: 'We sceolon *eac* on ðissum dagum . . .'

The virtues of Ælfric's version are those of fidelity to the bible and a mastery of literary style. At the outset he gives the point of the whole story:

---

[1] The use of *don* to emphasize right moral action recalls in contrast the actions of Adam and Eve: 'Be ðam treowe Crist sylf forewarnode ægðer ge Adam ge Evan, 7 him sæde bam þæt swa hwylcum dæge swa hie ðæs treowes bleda æton, hie sceoldon forweorðan. 7 hie eac swa dydon' (107r8–12).

[2] *The Homilies of the Anglo-Saxon Church*, ... *the Sermones Catholici, or Homilies of Ælfric*, ed. B. Thorpe (London, 1844–6) I, 244–7. (Thorpe in his translation incorrectly makes Mamertus bishop of Vienna.)

'Þæt folc wæs swiðe fyrenful: þa wolde God hi fordon, ac hi gegladodon hine mid heora behreowsunge.' By beginning each of the two main episodes with God's command directly addressed to Jonah he places divine will in the forefront of his narrative and by the same means marks a two-part structure. Henceforth there is little need for interpretative comment in the manner of the VAB homilist: firm narrative outline by itself is enough. What is inessential to this outline is pared away: for instance, he does not mention that the seamen at first worshipped various gods and that they were converted to the true God only when they realized that it was he who had sent the storm on Jonah's account; nor does he mention that they tried to row the ship to safety so as to avoid throwing Jonah overboard. His most effective use of discourse occurs in the interchange between Jonah and the shipmen: 'Hi axodon hine hwæt he wære oððe hu he faran wolde. He cwæð þæt he wære Godes ðeow, se ðe gesceop sæ and land, and þæt he fleon wolde of Godes gesihðe. Hi cwædon: "Hu do we ymbe ðe?" He andwyrde: "Weorpað me oforbord, þonne geswicð þeos gedreccednys." Hi ða swa dydon, and seo hreohnys wearð gestilled . . .'[1] Ælfric has shortened the Vulgate. The passage moves swiftly from question and answer in indirect discourse to question and answer in direct discourse as Ælfric moves from narrator to dramatic reader. This progression creates a striking immediacy that makes Jonah's 'Weorpað me oforbord' all the more effective. The tension is immediately resolved, however, by the resolute action of the shipmen and its immediate consequence expressed simply by 'seo hreohnys wearð gestilled'. Ælfric's concern for economy and directness apparently explains his treatment of the storm. He avoids entirely such florid amplification as is found in patristic writers and even the comparatively modest efflorescence of the VAB homilist.[2] There are no rhetorical pyrotechnics in his simple 'þa sende him God to micelne wind and hreohnysse, swa þæt hi wæron orwene heora lifes'. Nor is there 'artfulness' in 'Hi ða wurpon heora waru oforbord, and se witega læg and slep.' A fine example of syndetic parataxis, this sentence brilliantly contrasts the shipmen's act of desperation with the 'wise one's' insouciance. Inversion and the syntactic position of *upp* heighten the drama when the lots are cast: 'Þa com ðæs witegan ta upp.' The reliance on writing that is simple in form and restrained in effect continues in the account of Jonah's second mission. Successive simple verbs impart energy to the episode, e.g. 'God ða gegearcode ænne hwæl, and he forswealh þone witegan, and abær hine to ðam lande þe he to sceolde, and hine ðær ut-aspaw.' And like-

---

[1] I have altered Thorpe's punctuation.
[2] Clemoes, 'Ælfric', pp. 196–7 discusses Ælfric's avoidance of elaborate detail. In the *De Jona* pseudo-Fulgentius gives an elaborate and detailed description of the storm (Migne, Patrologia Latina 65, cols. 878–80). Zeno of Verona amplifies the storm extravagantly and gives a lengthy allegorical interpretation of it (PL 11, cols. 444–50).

wise: 'Ða aras se cyning of his cynesetle, and awearp his deorwyrðe reaf, and dyde hæran to his lice, and axan uppan his heafod . . .' In this last example Ælfric preserves the effect of '. . . et surrexit de solio suo, et abiecit vestimentum suum a se, et indutus est sacco, et sedit in cinere' (*Jonas* III. 6). He adds a detail, the fasting of *sucendan cild*, and, when giving his moral summary, alludes to Sodom and Gomorrah as examples of unconverted cities. Smooth, direct, pertinent and controlled, Ælfric's account of *Jonas* is a model introduction to his homily. The skilful summary of his source is 'pure' narration. Like Aldhelm before him, but in quite another way, Ælfric understands the importance of an opening that captures the attention, and here the imagination, of his audience.

The quality of Ælfric's treatment was not unnoticed by the redactor of C when, at some later time,[1] he went to the trouble of conflating it with the VAB version. He inserts Ælfric's mention of the shipmen's despair at the proper point (see above, p. 186, VAB, line 17), returns briefly to the VAB account and then follows Ælfric more regularly after the prophet's awakening (VAB, line 23):

> . . . (51v12) 7 axodon hine hwæt he wære oððe hu he faran wolde.
> He cwæð þæt he wære Godes þeow, se þe gesceop heofenas 7
> eorðan, sæ 7 land, 7 ealle gesceaftu, 7 þæt he wolde of Godes gesyhðe
> fleon. Ac he hæfde þa ongyten þæt he nahwar God forfleon (52r) ne
> mihte. Hi cwædon, 'Hu do we embe þe?' He andwerde, 'Wurpað   5
> me ut oferbord; þonne geswicð þeos gedræcednyss.' Hi þa swa
> dydon 7 him fore gebædon. 7 seo hreohnys wearð þa sona gestilled.
> 7 hi ofrodon heora lac Gode 7 tugon þa forð. God þa sona asende
> ænne mycelne hwæl 7 se forswealh þone witegan 7 he wæs on him
> þry dagas 7 þreo niht and abær hyne to þam ylcan lande þe he ær   10
> to faran sceolde 7 hine þar ut aspau ofer þære sæstaðe. Þa com
> eft Godes word to þam witegan Ionam 7 cwæð, 'Aris nu 7 ga to þære
> mycclan byrig Nini (52v) ven 7 boda swa swa ic þe ær sæde.' He ferde 7
> bodode 7 sæde þæt heom wæs Godes grama onsigende, gyf hi
> to Gode bugan noldon. 7 he þa sona on þreora daga fyrste þurhfor   15
> þa mæran 7 þa micclan burh Niniven 7 bodude on þære Godes
> bebodu swa þæt se cyning mid ealre þære burhware on God gelyfde
> on eallre heortan. 7 he bebead þæt hi ealle fram þam yldestan oð
> þone gingestan þreora daga fæsten healdan sceoldon. 7 he aras of
> his cynesetle 7 him fram his cynereaf awearp 7 hyne mid hæran   20

8 *MS* tungan

---

[1] As has been mentioned above, the third quarter of the eleventh century is the date of the extant manuscript; the date of the redaction is unknown. Ker, *Catalogue*, pp. 183–4, was the first to point out C's debt to Ælfric. He gives a shorthand account of the relationship.

ymbscrydde to his lice 7 dyde axan uppon his (53r) heafod 7 bebead
þæt ælc mann swa don sceolde 7 to Gode georne clypode mid
ealre þære burhware. 7 he bead ærost þæt ægðer ge þa menn ge þa
sucendan cild ge furðon ealle þa nytenu þe hi ahton sceoldon þry
dagas 7 þreo niht on an fæstan.   25

In adopting material from Ælfric the redactor has remained essentially
faithful to the character of VAB. For instance, he retains its emblem of the
helpless ship in the face of Ælfric's more subdued treatment. And when he
adopts Ælfric's dialogue between Jonah and the shipmen he takes care to
keep and adapt to this fresh context VAB's reference to the prophet's newly
gained understanding. Indeed he goes in for a little thematic writing on his
own account when he expands Ælfric's reference to God as creator of the
world. His only diminution of VAB's thematic concerns is his omission of
the symbol of the sea carrying the whale along on its current 'eal swa hit
God wolde'. At the same time he has partly introduced into the narrative
Ælfric's sense of a two-part structure. The VAB homilist avoids this structure entirely by mentioning God's first command but passing over the
second. The C redactor does not alter the VAB treatment of the first command, but inserts Ælfric's translation of the second. While the structure in
C is thus not as symmetrical as in Ælfric's version, it is preserved; in fact the
direct discourse of the second command in contrast to the indirect narration
of the first gives an effect of increasing emphasis.

The main result of the redactor's choices is to strengthen the narrative
effect of VAB. Instead of the thematic but lacklustre '7 he þafode þæt hine
man wearp ut on þa sæ' he substitutes Ælfric's lively dramatization of the
exchange between Jonah and the shipmen. While the VAB homilist is
content with a summary '7 rehton hit him eall', the C redactor sees in
Ælfric's version a ready way to flesh out the confrontation. His earlier
insertion of Ælfric's clause, 'swa þæt hi wæron orwene heora lifes', before
the emblem of the ship is given, heightens interest in the plight of the shipmen and prepares for the dialogue. With these borrowings the redactor
develops and carries on the emphasis on narrative present in the description
of the stationary storm-tossed ship. That he does not follow Ælfric in the
details of the *waru* and the *tan* indicates his satisfaction with his major source
in this respect. The casting of lots is adequately handled there, the repetitive
hluton . . . behluton building to the contrast '7 he his nan þing nyste'; and with
the outright mention of despair and the description of the storm he sees no
need to add the detail of the cargo. He is in fact alert to retain whatever makes
for effective narrative in VAB: for instance, he transfers to a new, Ælfrician
context VAB's motif of the shipmen praying for Jonah when they have cast

him overboard, and, with reference to the whale's disgorging of the prophet, he adds to Ælfric's '7 hine þar ut aspau' VAB's 'ofer þære sæstaðe'. And sometimes he adds a touch of his own, as when he intensifies Ælfric's '7 seo hreohnys wearð gestilled' by inserting 'þa sona'. Clearly doctrinal or pastoral considerations do not enter into these choices: no pertinent moral content is added to the expressed theme of repentance by fasting.[1] Nor is the bible returned to as a source. It is simply a wish to dramatize and to heighten narrative tension that is at work.[2] Seeing the narrative potential of his material, the redactor is attempting to rework VAB to make it a better narrative. He is a narrator as well as a homilist.

This group of homilies treating the Jonah story suggests that Old English writers did react with literary imagination to the narrative potential of the homiletic material before them. VAB's version represents an ambitious, if only half successful, attempt at narrative writing for thematic purposes. What Wright says of the Cynewulf and Cyneheard episode in the *Anglo-Saxon Chronicle* can be applied to Ælfric's rounded narrative, *mutatis mutandis*: 'There is no waste; the saga is economical in words, presents the scene vividly, and with an unexpected change into *oratio recta* in the parley of the retainers gives an added dramatic interest to the whole scene.'[3] The C redactor takes inspiration from Ælfric's narrative skill to enliven the VAB account: he may not be fully aware of the VAB homilist's deeper purposes, but his choices bring out further the tendency towards narrative that is checked in VAB by the necessity for moral meaning. By implication he sees no conflict between moral and narrative elements; his alert use of Ælfric is the reaction of a critic who knows of something that is better narrative than what he already has. These three pieces, each in its own way, attest to the existence of a narrative consciousness in expository prose. While they are not 'vernacular' in any connotations of 'semi-pagan' and 'without Latin influence', they indicate a native gift that contributes to the achievement and variety of late Old English prose. Homiletic narrative is worthy of appreciation on its own terms.

[1] Cf. Haymo of Halberstadt (PL 117, cols. 127ff.) and Jerome (PL 25, cols. 1145ff.).

[2] The same tendency is evident in the redactor's version of the Mamertus story. Here he inserts Ælfric's summary of the calamities at Vienne: 'Eac wearð on þære ylcan byrig mycel eorðstyrung 7 feollon cyrcan 7 hus, 7 comon wilde bæran 7 wulfas 7 abiton þæs folces mycelne dæl 7 þæs cinges botl wearð mid heofenlicum fyre eall forbærned.' And he ends with Ælfric's *coda*: '7 seo gedrecednys þa sona geswac þe heom onsæt; se gewuna nu þæs fæstenes þurhwunað gehwar on geleaffulre gesomnunge.' The first borrowing combines with the excellent VAB account of the plague to produce a frightening picture. The heightening of action and the resultant appeal to the emotions of the audience are in line with the redactor's work on the Jonah story. The second borrowing, which makes the connection between Mamertus and Rogation Days quite explicit, results in a sharpening of focus similar to that in the redactor's use of the second divine command to Jonah. [3] *The Cultivation of Saga*, p. 80.

Conceivable clues to twelve Old English words

HERBERT DEAN MERITT

The queried compound ' ælhȳd'

In Cambridge, Corpus Christi College 383, on pp. 102–7, there are instructions for the tasks of a reeve, followed by several long lists of necessary tools and appurtenances.[1] The closing list is preceded by mention of some particular kinds of craftsmen – *mylewerde, sutere, leadgotan*, contains some sixty terms of tools and equipment and concludes with the entries *sapbox, camb, yrfebinne, fodderhec, fyrgebeorh, meluhudern, ælhyde, ofnrace, mexscofle*.[2] From the entry *ælhyde* BT *Suppl*[3] enters with a query *ælhȳd*, 'an eel-skin', and Hall enters *ælhyd*[4] queryingly defined as 'eel receptacle', 'eel-skin'. Perhaps *ælhyde* is not a compound and perhaps *æl* does not mean 'eel'.

One of the craftsmen mentioned just before the long list of equipment is the *sutere*, 'shoemaker'. Two kinds of equipment that he particularly needed were *æl*, 'an awl', and *hȳd*, 'hide'. In Ælfric's *Colloquy* the *sutor* states 'ego emo cutes, ic bicge hyda',[5] and the smith later asks where but from him would the shoemaker get his awl – 'aut sutori subula, oþþe sceowyrhton æl'. In a Middle English passage the mention of shoemakers is accompanied by mention of hides and awls.[6]

While the interpretation of *ælhyde* as eel receptacle or eel-skin leaves some query as to the utility of such equipment, the interpretation of *ælhyde* as

---

[1] Ptd F. Liebermann, *Anglia* 9 (1886), 259–65 and *Die Gesetze der Angelsachsen* (Halle, 1903–16; repr. Aalen, 1960) I, 453–5. [2] The punctuation is as printed by Liebermann.

[3] The following abbreviations are used: BT = J. Bosworth and T. N. Toller, *An Anglo-Saxon Dictionary* (Oxford, 1898); BT *Suppl* = T. N. Toller, *Supplement* to BT (Oxford, 1921); Hall = J. R. Clark Hall, *A Concise Anglo-Saxon Dictionary*, 4th ed. with suppl. by H. D. Meritt (Cambridge, 1960); *MED* = *Middle English Dictionary*, ed. H. Kurath and S. M. Kuhn (Ann Arbor, 1952–); Napier = *Old English Glosses*, ed. A. S. Napier (Oxford, 1900); WW = *Anglo-Saxon and Old English Vocabularies*, ed. T. Wright and R. P. Wülcker (London, 1884).

[4] No mark over *y*. For the definition 'eel-skin' one is referred to BT *Suppl*; for 'eel receptacle' one is referred to Liebermann, *Gesetze*, where the definition 'Aalbehälter' is given.

[5] WW, p. 97.

[6] '3e sutlers wiþ 3our blote hides ... and alles', cited in *MED*, s.v. *al*. Awl and hide are referred to side by side in a list in a Middle English metrical glossary, *sunt ansoria, solie, sibula, cordibanumque* (WW 628, 34), where *sibula* is glossed *nalle*, meaning 'an awl', and *cordibanum* is glossed *corduane*, which is ME *cordewane*, defined in *MED* as 'Cordovan leather, or a skin of it', and documented in such a context as 'in 12 pellibus de Cordewan'.

two words in a list, namely *æl*, 'awl' and *hyde*, 'hide',[1] brings into juxta-position two words that would understandably be mentioned together and that definitely belong to a trade, that of *sutor*, a craftsman mentioned just before the list of equipment.

The source of the lemma 'aidoneæ' and the meaning of its gloss 'hearpen'

In the Cleopatra Glossary (BM Cotton Cleopatra A. iii, 5r–75v) *aidoneæ* is glossed *hearpen*.[2] BT enters from Cot. 19, Lye, *hearpene*, 'a nightingale', but BT *Suppl* deletes this, noting that the Cleopatra Glossary is the source and querying if the entry is intelligible.[3] It is very possible that the lemma comes from the *Carmen de Ave Phoenice* of Lactantius.[4]

In most of the alphabetical sections of the Cleopatra Glossary, which extends from A up to and including P,[5] there is a batch of lemmata from Aldhelm ending with words from the final Riddle and followed by a batch of lemmata from Gildas, and between these batches occurs a usually small batch of unidentified lemmata. It is noticeable that in the A, C, E, I, L, M, N and O sections the concluding part of the unidentified batch contains a lemma or several lemmata documentable in the *Carmen* of Lactantius. In the A section a batch of eight concludes with the entry *aidoneæ* glossed *hearpen*. This lemma occurs at line 47 of the *Carmen*.[6] In the C section at the close of a batch of nineteen lemmata the next to the last entry is *cyllineæ* glossed *cillinescum*.[7] This lemma occurs in line 50 of the *Carmen*.[8] In the E section at the close of a batch of five lemmata the last entry is *exsangues* glossed *orblede*.[9] This lemma occurs at line 15 of the *Carmen*.[10] In the I section at the close of a batch of fourteen lemmata the last four entries[11] are *iuga* glossed *duna swioran*, *infandum* glossed *sio godwræce*, *insomnes* glossed *unslæpige* and *inplumen* glossed *ungefeþeredne*. These lemmata occur in the same order in the *Carmen*.[12] In the L section in a batch of seven lemmata the last two entries[13] are *libat* glossed *byrgeþ* and *legit* glossed *ceoseþ*. These two lemmata are found in the *Carmen* respectively at line 38 and line 69.[14] In the M section in a batch of eight lemmata the last entry is *modis* glossed *wrencum*.[15] This lemma occurs

[1] In its context *ælhyde* is accusative; the documented acc. s. of *hȳd* is *hȳde*.
[2] WW 355, 32.
[3] In *Fact and Lore about Old English Words* (Stanford, 1954), p. 26, I suggested that in *hearpen* might lie *earpen*, 'dark', and in *aidoneæ* a garbled Aἰθιοπία.
[4] Ed. S. Brandt in Corpus Scriptorum Ecclesiasticorum Latinorum 27, 135–47.
[5] WW 338–473.   [6] 'Quam nec aedoniae voces nec tibia possit'.
[7] WW 379, 4.   [8] 'Nec Cylleneae fila canora lyrae'.
[9] WW 397, 29.   [10] 'Non huc exsangues morbi non aegra senectus'.
[11] WW 427, 13–16.
[12] 'Sed nostros montes quorum iuga celsa putantur' (line 7); 'Nec scelus infandum nec opum vesana cupido' (17); 'Et curae insomnes et violenta fames' (20); 'Nec cuiquam inplumem pascere cura subest' (110).   [13] WW 438, 8–9.
[14] 'Ter quater e vivo gurgite libat aquam' (38); 'Tum legit aerio sublimen vertice palmam' (69).
[15] WW 447, 23.

in the *Carmen* at line 48.[1] In the N section in a batch of nine lemmata the last two entries[2] are *nemoris* glossed *bearwes* and *nothus* glossed *suðan wind oððe dooc hornungsunu*. These two lemmata are found in the *Carmen* respectively at line 62 and line 75.[3] In the O section in a batch of four lemmata the last entry is *obsequitur* glossed *folgað*.[4] This lemma occurs in line 33 of the *Carmen*.[5]

It seems reasonable to believe that the lemma *aidoneæ* comes from Lactantius's line 'Quam nec aedoniae voces nec tibia possit' (47),[6] the following lines (48–50) being 'Musica Cirrhaeis adsimulare modis,/Sed neque olor moriens imitari posse putetur/Nec Cylleneae fila canora lyrae', from which the lemmata *modis* and *cyllineæ* were probably taken. This context contains the word *lyrae*, for which an acceptable Old English gloss would be *hearpan*.[7] A gloss *hearpan* to *lyrae* would seem to be too far removed from *aedoniae voces* ever to become attached to *aedoniae*, although the Old English *Phoenix* brings the equivalents of *lyrae* and *voces* together in one line: 'ne hearpan hlyn ne hæleþa stefn' (135), where *hearpan* reflects *lyrae* and *stefn* reflects *voces*. In the *Durham Ritual, stefn*, glossing *vocem*, is compared to the sound of harping: 'stefn þæt ic giherde suae hearpara hearpandra in hearpum'.[8] Such association of sound and harp may have led a glossator to take *aedoniae voces* as *hearpende stefne*, an expression similar to the documented *bymendre stefne*,[9] in which case the gloss *hearpen* to *aidoneæ* is incomplete for *hearpende*.[10]

The gloss 'bærfisce' to 'nudapes'

In the Cleopatra Glossary in a small batch of nine lemmata of undetermined origin all beginning with the letter N, *nudapes* is glossed *bærfisce*.[11] In his *Vocabularium Saxonicum* Laurence Nowell took this gloss in stride, entered

---

[1] 'Musica Cirrhaeis adsimulare modis'.   [2] WW 456, 8–9.

[3] 'Adsuetum nemoris dulce cubile fugit' (62); 'Neu concreta noto [*v.l.* nothus] nubes per inania caeli' (75).   [4] WW 462, 23.

[5] 'Paret et obsequitur Phoebo memoranda satelles'.

[6] The *Thesaurus Linguae Latinae* documents the word only once elsewhere, from *incerti laus Pisonis*.

[7] Cf. *liram hearpan*, WW 437, 22.

[8] *Rituale Ecclesiae Dunelmensis*, ed. A. H. Thompson and U. Lindelöf, Surtees Society 140 (1927), 47, line 19.   [9] See BT *Suppl, s.v. biman*.

[10] The glosses in Napier are replete with instances of incompletions like *trahnie* for *trahniende* and *stærbl* for *stærblinde*. For many instances of the present participle ending *-end* in 2nd cl. wk vbs see Napier 1, 1003 n.

Although it has no discernible bearing on the interpretation of *hearpen*, some curiosity deserves mention about *hæleþa stefn* in the Old English *Phoenix*. Since *stefn* there reflects *voces* in the group *aedoniae voces*, one must wonder if *hæleþa* has anything to do with *aedoniae*. Perhaps the poet paid no attention to *aedoniae* and used a suitably alliterative word which occurs in such poetic groups as *hæleþa helpend*, *hæleþa scyppend* and *hæleþa hyhtgifa*. On the other hand he may have taken *aedoniae*, 'nightingale-like', to be a proper adjective like the accompanying *Cirrhaeis* and *Cylleneae* and thought that it referred to a particular race of men, *hæleþa*. In the Old English *Genesis* the Vulgate *rex Sodomorum* is reflected both by *Sodoma aldor* (2124) and *hæleþa waldend* (2139). Remarkably in the edition of Lactantius's *Carmen* in Migne, Patrologia Latina 7, the spelling is *Ædoniae*, capitalized.   [11] WW 456, 30.

bærfisc and defined it as *barefote*. As printed in WW, *bærfisce* is accompanied by Wülcker's note that one should read *bærfot*, and this is the queried interpretation of the gloss in BT *Suppl*, *s.v. bærfōt*. Such an interpretation certainly seems in order, but it may not be the whole story.

The batch of nine lemmata in which *nudapes* occurs contains at least three lemmata for which there is some likelihood that they come from Vergil. The first of the batch is *nubigenu*. Vergil used *nubigenae* at *Aeneid* VII. 674 and *nubigenas* at VIII. 293 in the context 'tu nubigenas . . . manu tu Cresia mactas' where the presence of three words ending in *u* may have induced a glossary compiler to write down the lemma in the odd form *nubigenu*. The entry but one above *nudapes* is *numine, leso*, as if lemma and gloss; the group *numine laeso* occurs at *Aeneid* I. 8. The lemma following *nudapes* is *nidore*, which occurs at *Georgics* III. 415, and its entry in the Corpus Glossary (CCCC 144) is assigned by the editor, Lindsay, to that source. There is no *nudapes* in Vergil's works, but something rather similar to it occurs at *Eclogue* I. 61: 'et freta destituent nudos in litore pisces'. From this passage *nudos* is glossed *bare* in Old High German,[1] and a quite acceptable Old English gloss to *nudos . . . pisces* would be *bære fiscas*, just as a quite acceptable gloss to *nudapes* would be *bærfot*. It seems possible that the compiler of the Cleopatra Glossary had two lemmata before him, one *nudos pisces* from Vergil and the other *nudapes* from some other source, and that he entered the lemma *nudapes*, confused its gloss *bærfot* with a gloss *bære fiscas* to *nudos pisces* and made the delightful entry *bærfisce*.

The apparent lemma 'baista'

On 2v of the Harleian Glossary (BM Harley 3376) the entry *badius . spadis* is followed by the entry *baista ḡ* above which is written *glasin*.[2] The *ḡ* is an abbreviation for *græce*. The entries are not independent of each other, and they are illuminated by a passage in Isidore's *Etymologies*: 'Badium . . . Ipse est et spadix, quem phoenicatum vocant: et dictus spadix a colore palmae quam Siculi spadicam vocant. Glaucus vero est veluti pictos oculos habens . . .'[3] It is Isidore's *badium* and *spadix* which correspond to the glossary entry *badius . spadis*. It is Isidore's *glaucus* which probably corresponds to *glasin*, since *glæseneage* is a known gloss to *glaucus*.[4] It is Isidore's *phoenicatum* and *palmae* which correspond to the part *bais* of *baista*, for φοῖνιξ and *palma* are glossary

---

[1] *Die althochdeutschen Glossen*, ed. E. Steinmeyer and E. Sievers (Berlin, 1879–98) II, 719, 50.
[2] WW 192, 3.
[3] Ed. W. M. Lindsay (Oxford, 1911), XII. i. 49–50. Here *badium* is accusative; the nominative *badius* occurs two sentences earlier.
[4] WW 416, 1. The possibility has been pointed out by R. Oliphant, *The Harley Latin–Old English Glossary* (The Hague, 1966), p. 23. He did not understand *baista*; nor does BT *Suppl s.v. glasin*.

equivalents of βαΐς.[1] The part *ta* of *baista* is a gloss to *bais*, a Latinized βαΐς, the equivalent of *palma*, for which the Old English gloss is *palmtwig*,[2] the part *twig* being an equivalent of OE *tā* as may be seen in the paired plurals *tan* and *twiga* glossing *vimina*.[3]

A glossary entry *bais* .ḡ. with *ta* above it would be readily understandable as βαΐς glossed by OE *tā*, but *ta* has confusingly been put after *bais* and between *bais* and .ḡ., leaving an apparent lemma *baista* in need of a gloss, this need being satisfied at least spatially by a superscript *glasin* corresponding to *glaucus*[4] in a context that accounts for the entries *badius . spadis* and *bais* glossed *ta* and signalled as Greek.

The origin of 'burgrūn', 'burgrūne'

In the Épinal (Bibl. Mun. 72), Erfurt (Bibl. der Stadt Amploniana Fol. 42, 1r–14r) and Corpus Glossaries *Parcas* is glossed respectively *burgrunae*, *burgrunae*, *burgrune*, and that this early interpretation of *Parcas* obtained for some time is indicated by a gloss *burgrunan* to *parcas* dating from about the year 1000.[5] In the Cleopatra Glossary in a batch of lemmata stemming from Isidore's *Etymologies*, *Furiae* is glossed *burgrunan*,[6] and in the Harleian Glossary *Furie* is glossed *burhrunan*.[7] These glosses are the only documentations of the word.

Since *Furiae* and *Parcae* are not the same thing, one may inquire about the origin of the Old English glossary tradition which took them as equivalent, and the answer may lie in the fact that a passage in Isidore's *Etymologies* admits of such equivalence. As an example of *antiphrasis* he cites 'Parcas et Eumenides, Furiae quod nulli parcant vel benefaciant'.[8]

As there are many compounds starting with *burg* meaning 'city, fortress, town', this seems to be the meaning in the glosses here concerned, and one may inquire further about how such a meaning applies to *Parcae* and *Furiae*.[9] Possibly it applies only to what Isidore and glossaries say about these words.

---

[1] *Glossaria Latina*, ed. W. M. Lindsay *et al.* (Paris, 1926–31) II, 239, 35: *palma . χεὶρ καὶ βαὶς καὶ φοῖνιξ*. Granted this equivalence, one still must inquire why a glossator should use a Greek gloss in this Isidore passage, and some answer may lie in the fact that Isidore himself, in discussing *palma*, uses a Greek word: 'Palma . . . Hanc Graeci phoenicem dicunt' (*Etymologies* XVII. vii. 1), a term which could lead a glossator to its equivalent βαΐς.

[2] WW 138, 10. [3] Napier 1, 922.

[4] A now missing lemma *glaucus* may once have accompanied the entry *badius . spadis*, for at least one glossary enters 'glaucus spadix equus qui oculos habet glauci coloris' (*Corpus Glossariorum Latinorum*, ed. G. Goetz (Leipzig, 1888–1923) V, 245, 13). This entry also stems from Isidore.

[5] Napier 38, 2 and p. xx, no. 38. [6] WW 410, 30. [7] WW 245, 16.

[8] *Etymologies*, I. xxxvii. 24.

[9] BT *Suppl*, *s.v. burgrūne*, compares *hægtesse*, which also glosses *Furia* and of which the part *hæg* is probably related to *hæg*, 'enclosure', in which case *hæg-* in *hægtesse* could be analogous to *burg-* in *burgrune*.

In mentioning *Parcas* and *Furiae* Isidore uses, as just noted, the word *parcant*, and again at *Etymologies* VIII. xi. 93 he states 'Parcas . . . quod minime parcant',[1] and this information was carried on in glossaries[2] and at times given a reverse twist as in 'Parcis servatricibus a parcendo servandoque dictis'.[3] Forms and derivatives of *parcere* are rendered in Old English by forms and derivatives of *beorgan*;[4] a documented variant of *gebeorgan* is *geburgan*;[5] and glossary interchange between *beorg* and *burg* is noticeable in the rendering of *popularibus* by *beorhleodum*,[6] the equivalent of *burhleodum*, and by the rendering of Aldhelm's *municeps* by *buruhleod* in one manuscript[7] and by *beorhleod* in another.[8] Influenced by Isidore's reference to *Parcas* as *Furiae* and by his and glossators' explanation of *Parcas* as *quod nulli parcant, quod minime parcant, a parcendo*, a glossary tradition for the interpretation of these words was started which reflected *parcant* and *parcendo* by a form of *beorgan* spelled *burg* in *burgrune* and *burgrunan*.

The etymology and meaning of 'kylu', 'cylew'

At WW 163, 26 *guttatus* is glossed *cylu*[9] and in the Cleopatra Glossary it is glossed *cylew*.[10] Dictionaries agree that *cylu* and *cylew* mean 'spotted, speckled'. Holthausen's *Altenglisches etymologisches Wörterbuch* enters *cylu*, 'gefleckt, gesprenkelt', as of unknown origin.

The glosses *kylu* and *cylew* probably have a source in common. The lemma for *kylu* occurs in a batch of lemmata taken largely from Isidore's *Etymologies* XII. i describing various colours of horses, and the same lemmata with approximately the same glosses occur, though alphabetically separated, in the alphabetized glossary containing the entry *guttatus . cylew*.

Isidore describes *guttatus* as 'albus nigris intervenientibus punctis', and in reference to horses *guttatus* means 'dappled';[11] but these facts shed no detectable light on the glosses. What Isidore says about *gutta*, however, may have influenced the glosses. At *Etymologies* XIII. xx. 5 he states: 'Gutta est quae stat, stilla quae cadit. Hinc stillicidium, quasi stilla cadens. Stiria enim Graecum est, id est gutta.' From this passage *stiria vel stillicidia* is glossed *ises gicel*,[12] which means 'icicle'. Another Old English word for

---

[1] This is followed by a remark about *Furiae* which is the source of the lemma *Furiae* in the Cleopatra Glossary. [2] E.g. *Corpus Glossariorum Latinorum* VII, 48.
[3] *Glossaria Latina* I, 424, 439. [4] See BT *Suppl, s.vv. beorgan* and *gebeorglic*.
[5] See BT *Suppl, s.v. gebeorgan*. [6] WW 178, 41. [7] Napier 8, 221.
[8] Napier 7, 293. After submission of the present article my attention was called to the mention in *JBAA* 3rd ser. 27 (1964), 21, n. 10, that Professor Whitelock suggested that *burgrune* as applied to *parcae* might be connected with 'to spare', OE *beorgan*.
[9] The spelling *cylu* is that of the Junius transcript (Oxford, Bodleian Library, Junius 71) from which the WW entry was made, but on 15r of BM Add. 32246, thought to be the source of the Junius transcript, the spelling is *kylu*. [10] WW 415, 29.
[11] *Guttatus . pomeled, ut equus*, WW 587, 28.
[12] WW 117, 14, which omits *vel* of the transcript and BM Add. 32246.

Conceivable clues to twelve Old English words

'icicle' is *cylegicel*.[1] Since the lemma *guttatus* is obviously related to *gutta*, a word equated by Isidore with *styria*, for which the Old English term is both *ises gicel* and *cylegicel*, a gloss to *guttatus* might contain the word *cyle* with adjectival formation like that in other colour adjectives such as *basu, fealu, geolu, hasu*.[2] Derived from *cyle*, the adjectives *kylu*[3] and *cylew* could mean 'chill' referring to a cold colour, somewhat as 'frosty' means both 'cold' and 'hoary'. As OE *hār* is used to describe both frost and the colour of a wolf, so *cyle* which described an icicle in *cylegicel*, might be used adjectivally to describe the colour of a horse, particularly one whose descriptive term *guttatus* could lead a glossator to think of *īs* and *cyle*.

The Harleian Glossary entry 'dodrante' . 'dreariende'

On 60v of the Harleian Glossary *dodrante* is glossed *dreariende*, and from this gloss BT *Suppl* and Hall enter *drēariend* queryingly defined as 'inrushing tide'. This suggested meaning is not at all without reason, for the glossary entry immediately preceding *dodrante* . *dreariende* is *dodrans .i. malina . egur*, the gloss *egur* is a known word meaning 'flood, high tide', *dodrans* is a Hisperic Latin word used by Aldhelm, among others, referring to surgings of the sea, and *malina* too is a Hisperic Latin word explained in Old English as *heahflod*.[4] But *dodrans* is also a usual Latin word, derived from *de* and *quadrans*, meaning 'a quarter off, three fourths',[5] and occurring noticeably in the legal term *heres ex dodrante*[6] referring to one who inherits three fourths of an estate. The following interpretation of *dreariende* is based on the assumption that it renders *dodrante* in this legal term, that the cross stroke on the first *d* of *dreariende* has been omitted either through sheer scribal oversight[7] or through attraction to the other *d*s in lemma and gloss, and that the gloss is to be read *ðre ariende*. In the manuscript the *e* and the *a* of *dreariende* are written tightly together, and probably the compiler thought that he was accurately entering a word *dreariende*, but he could have been wrong; for example, on Brussels, Royal Library 1828-30, 50v, a closely written *strupiar* is followed by a period mark and then by the gloss *midlu*, but the *ar* belongs with *midlu*. On 2v of the

---

1 *Andreas* 1260 and *The Phoenix* 59.

2 Somewhere a glossator seems to have been partial to this formation, for in the batch along with *kylu* are not only *fealu, dunfalu* and *geolu* but also the peculiar entry *avidius . grinu*.

3 This spelling with *k* only indicates an occasional velar pronunciation of *cyle*, as may also the eME spelling *cule* (see *MED*, *s.v. chele*).

4 WW 182, 39.

5 On BM Add. 32246, 12r, in a glossary containing some Old English glosses, is the entry 'dodrans est ubi deest quadrans'.

6 The term is familiar enough to find a place in Harper's *Dictionary of Classical Literature and Antiquities, s.v. dodrans*.

7 No idle assumption. The apparatus criticus of any edited Old English text is likely to contain several instances of MS *d* to be read as *ð*; there are fourteen such in *The Exeter Book*, ed. G. P. Krapp and E. V. K. Dobbie, The Anglo-Saxon Poetic Records 3 (1936).

Herbert Dean Meritt

Harleian Glossary the entry *baista* is written as one word with the *s* and *t* joined, but *bais* is a Greek word and *ta* is an Old English word.[1]

The word *ðre*, direct object of *ariende*, is a documented form of the Old English word for 'three',[2] and emphasis on 'three' in the lemma *dodrante* may be seen in 'in dodrante, id est in tribus hereditatis portionibus'[3] and in the entry '*dodrans* þridde del' in Ælfric's *Grammar*.[4]

The word *ariende* is the present participle of *ārian*, 'to honour', related to *ārigend*, 'benefactor', and to the past participles *geārad* and *geārod* documented in the contexts 'He wæs gearad mid freodome fram his hlaforde' and 'Mid welum geweorþod and mid deorwyrþum æhtum gearod',[5] where the meaning of the participles is 'endowed, presented'. In the glossing of *dodrante* which has to do with inheritance as in *heres ex dodrante*, the use of a form of *ārian* derived from *ār* is appropriate since *ār* means 'property', noticeably inherited property, as in 'Gemunde ða ða are, þe he him forgeaf,/wicstede weligne Wægmundinga,/folcrihta gehwylc, swa his fæder ahte',[6] and 'Ic geswutelige on ðisum gewrite hu ic mine are and mine æhta geunnen hæbbe',[7] and also 'Minra yldrena ðe me min ar of com and mine æhta'.[8] In the last two citations *ar* is grouped with *æht*, an Old English term for *hereditas*.[9] The gloss *ariende* mistakenly takes *dodrante* as a participle while 'þridde del' correctly takes *dodrans* as a noun, but *dodrante* looks very much like a participle; in the passage containing '*dodrans* þridde del' there is the entry '*amans* lufigende is ægðer ge nama ge participium'.

Read as *ðre ariende*, the gloss *dreariende* to *dodrante* means 'granting three' and refers to *dodrante* in the legal term *heres ex dodrante* applied to one who is granted three fourths of an estate as inheritance.

The origin of the term 'eaggebyrd' in 'The Phoenix' 301

It is generally agreed that in line 301 of *The Phoenix*, 'Is seo eaggebyrd stearc ond hiwe stane gelicast', the word *eaggebyrd* means 'the nature of the eye',[10] but the inducement for the formation of a compound with this mean-

---

[1] See the discussion above, p. 196.

[2] In *þre fæmnan*, *The Blickling Homilies*, ed. R. Morris, Early English Text Society o.s. 58, 63 and 73 (London, 1874–80), p. 145, line 31. Here *þre* is nominative, the same form as accusative in cardinal numbers, in which there is often no distinction of gender. For the accusative with *ārian*, cf. 'He araþ ða godan', cited in BT, *s.v. ārian*.

[3] Cited in *Thesaurus Linguae Latinae*, *s.v. dodrans*, from *Lex Burgundorum*.

[4] *Aelfrics Grammatik und Glossar*, ed. J. Zupitza (Berlin, 1880; repr. Berlin etc., 1966, with contr. by H. Gneuss), p. 61, n. 6.   [5] Cited in BT *Suppl s.v. ge-ārian*, 'to endow, present'.

[6] *Beowulf* 2606–8.   [7] Cited in BT *Suppl s.v. ār*, 'property'.

[8] Cited in BT *Suppl s.v. æht*, 'a possession'.

[9] *Hereditas* is glossed *æht* at Luke xx. 14 in the West Saxon Gospels (ed. W. W. Skeat, *The Holy Gospels in Anglo-Saxon, Northumbrian, and Old Mercian Versions* (Cambridge, 1871–87)).

[10] Not without some hesitation, however. The most recent editor of *The Phoenix*, after mentioning such interpretations as 'eye', 'eyeball', 'das Funkeln der Augen', states that one must admit that *eaggebyrd* is more likely to mean 'eye's nature' (*The Phoenix*, ed. N. F. Blake (Manchester, 1964), p. 77).

ing is open to inquiry. Various inflexional forms of *gebyrd* are documented renderings of *natos, natalium* and *natu*.[1] In a manuscript containing many Old English and some Latin glosses, *natam* is entered as equivalent of *ingenitam*.[2] In describing the eyes of the phoenix, Lactantius used the expression *ingentes oculi*.[3] Confusing *ingentes* with *ingenitus*, the translator would have had reason to come up with *eaggebyrd*.

The Old English gloss 'forceps'

On 8v of the Harleian Glossary *bullatere* is glossed *forceps*. The Old English glosses from this glossary are printed in WW, but the gloss *forceps* is not included, probably because *forceps* is a common Latin word.[4]

In the lemma *bullatere* lies *buleuterion*, a Latinized form of βουλευτήριον, 'a curia'. A usual glossary equivalent of βουλευτήριον is *curia*,[5] and *curia* is glossed *advocatio iuridica*.[6] In King Alfred's version of the *Cura Pastoralis* the rendering of *advocatione* is *forespræce*.[7] Under *forespræc* BT *Suppl* documents the forms *foresprec, forespec, forspæc*. The gloss *forceps* is an unusual spelling of OE *forspec*.

The lemmata 'Grues' and 'Cnues' and their Old English glosses

On 84r of Cleopatra A. iii, in a section headed *Incipit de Frugibus*, the lemma *Grues* is glossed *gryt*,[8] and from this gloss BT enters *gryt* defined only as 'grues'. BT *Suppl* enters this gloss under *grytt*, 'dust, meal', notes that an identical glossary entry, *Grues . gryt*, occurs at WW 414, 8[9] and suggests that in this latter instance one may compare the lemma *Grues*, glossed *yeldo*, at WW 521, 17, where *grues*, it states, is written for *caries*, since preceding and following lemmata indicate that the context from which the entry was made is Aldhelm's line 'Quae quassat caries et frangit fessa vetustas'.[10] This interpretation of *Grues* in the WW entry *Grues . yeldo* is repeated by BT *Suppl*, *s.v. ildu*, along with reference to the entry *Cnues . eldo* at WW 374, 4,[11] where the lemma *Cnues* is also taken by BT *Suppl* as a miswriting of *caries*.

[1] See BT *Suppl, s.v. gebyrd*.   [2] *Ingenitam .i. natam . ongeborene*, Napier, 2, 360.
[3] *Carmen de Ave Phoenice*, ed. Brandt, line 137.
[4] The recent editor of the Harleian Glossary, R. Oliphant, notes that he does not understand the gloss *forceps*.   [5] See, e.g., *Corpus Glossariorum Latinorum* VI, 297 *s.v. curia*.
[6] *Glossaria Latina* I, 158, 303.   [7] See BT *Suppl, s.v. forespræc*.
[8] WW 273, 26. The first letter of a lemma in a glossary is usually capitalized, but in a printed discussion it is customary to use lower case; the capitalization has here been kept for reasons that will appear.   [9] From 45v of the Cleopatra Glossary.
[10] The reason for this suggested comparison lies in the fact that the entry at WW 414, 8 is in a glossary that has drawn heavily from Aldhelm and the entry at WW 521, 17 (from Cleopatra A. iii, 111r) is definitely in an Aldhelm batch. Also in a note to *Grues* at WW 521, 17 Wülcker stated that *Grues* is miswritten for *caries* and referred one, unenlighteningly, to the entry *Cnues . eldo* at WW 374, 4, from 22v of the Cleopatra Glossary.
[11] See preceding note. The entry reproduces the manuscript correctly.

The entries *Grues.gryt* at WW 273, 26 and WW 414, 8 are correctly made from their manuscript documentations. J. Quinn pointed out that in the first of these entries *Grues* is equivalent to γῦρις, 'fine meal'.[1] It is assumable that in the second of these entries *Grues* is also equivalent to γῦρις.[2] But in these two entries the lemma *Grues* may have nothing at all to do with the lemma *Grues* in the entry *Grues.yeldo* at WW 521, 17.

In the manuscript from which was made the WW entry *Grues . yeldo* the lemma is not *Grues*; it is *Gnues*. The compiler of this glossary made his *C*s and *G*s at times very much alike and at times confusedly – back of what certainly seems to read *Groceos* on 112r lies surely *Croceos*. The glossary section containing the entry *Cnues . eldo* is in an alphabetized section that has drawn its lemmata from an unalphabetized glossary like that containing the entry *Gnues . yeldo*. In view of the documented *Cnues . eldo* and in view of the propensity to confuse *C* and *G* by the compiler who entered *Gnues . yeldo*, one may take *Gnues* there to be read as *Cnues*.

The manuscript entry *Gnues . yeldo* occurs in a large batch of glosses to lemmata from Aldhelm which are to be found one after another in the same order in an edited text of Aldhelm. The lemma immediately preceding the entry *Gnues . yeldo* is *Gymnica*, found at line 620 of Aldhelm's metrical *De Virginitate*.[3] The lemma immediately following the entry *Gnues.yeldo* is *Scobem*, found at line 643. Between these lines a line containing words to which the gloss *yeldo*, 'old age' might very likely apply is line 640: 'Quae quassat caries et frangit fessa vetustas',[4] and BT *Suppl* unhesitatingly takes *Grues* in the misprinted entry *Grues . yeldo* and *Cnues* in the correctly printed entry *Cnues . eldo* to be miswritings of Aldhelm's *caries*. Such miswritings are not wholly credible, nor do the glosses *yeldo* and *eldo* necessarily apply to *caries* – they might apply equally well to *vetustas*. Something other than *caries* in Aldhelm's line may have given glossary compilers, coming upon that line in their culling, some reason to enter in their glossaries a word *Cnues* and, mistakenly, a word *Gnues*.

There are documented variants to several words in the line 'Quae quassat caries et frangit fessa vetustas'. One variant of *caries* is *aries*[5] and from this line *aries* was glossed *wænðoll* (for *wæhðoll*), 'battering ram'.[6] One variant

---

[1] 'The Minor Latin–Old English Glossaries in MS Cotton Cleopatra A. iii' (unpub. Ph.D. thesis, Stanford, 1956), p. 45. He noted that γῦρις is a glossary equivalent of *pollis*, a word glossed by Old English *grytt*.
[2] It is in fact provable, for the entry *Grues . gryt* at WW 414, 8 is in an alphabetized batch of lemmata drawn from an unalphabetized glossary like that containing the entry *Grues . gryt* at WW 273, 26.
[3] *Aldhelmi Opera*, ed. R. Ehwald, Monumenta Germaniae Historica, Auct. ant. 15. 3.
[4] The same determination of context applies, though less closely, to the entry *Cnues . eldo* in the alphabetized glossary. The lemma immediately preceding *Cnues* is *Conglobatur*, found at line 619 of the metrical *De Virginitate*, and the immediately following lemma is *Cuderet* found in line 745.
[5] Ed. Ehwald, p. 379.   [6] WW 343, 39.

of *frangit* is *frangis*.[1] An Old English verb with meaning like that of *frangere* is *cnūian*, 'to pound, crush', and suiting the 2nd pers. s. *frangis* would be a 2nd pers. s. gloss *cnues* with ending -*es* like the 2nd pers. s. *spones*[2] on 107r of the glossary here concerned.[3]

It was a gloss *cnues* to *frangis* that was picked up by a glossary compiler along with a gloss *eldo* to the neighbouring *caries* or *vetustas*. This is the source of the glossary entry *Cnues . eldo*.

The entry *Cnues . eldo* is an error – an Old English word has been entered as a lemma. Such an error is not confined to the words here concerned. On 116v the compiler who wrote *Gnues . yeldo* entered *flanas* apparently as gloss to *tessa*, but *flanas* belongs to a preceding *Contos* and *tessa* is part of *hægtessa* which glossed a following *allecto*. On 84v the same compiler glossed the lemma *Unfer* by *grighund*, but both of these words are Old English.

Compared with the entry *Cnues . eldo*, the entry *Gnues . yeldo* shows a *G* miswritten for *C*, and the misprinting of this *Gnues* as *Grues* has caused lexicographers to associate it with *Grues* in the entry *Grues . gryt*, where *Grues* is written for *γῦρις*.

The meaning of 'scyld' in 'The Phoenix' 308

At line 308 of *The Phoenix* the word *scyld* occurs in the context 'Is se scyld ufan/frætwum gefeged ofer þæs fugles bæc.' Dictionaries are uncertain about the interpretation of *scyld* in this line.[4] N. F. Blake, the most recent editor of *The Phoenix*, finds the meaning of *scyld* here uncertain, mentions some previous suggestions and suggests himself that the word refers to a crest on the head.[5] He cites as the corresponding line in Lactantius's *Carmen* 'Hoc caput, hoc cervix summaque terga nitent'.[6]

The head of the bird is also described in lines 139–40: 'aptata est rutilo capiti radiata corona/Phoebei referens verticis alta decus',[7] and possibly it is *aptata* that is reflected by *gefeged* since on 12v of the Cleopatra Glossary *apta* is glossed *gefeged*.[8] In the two Latin passages just cited occur the words *cervix*, *corona* and *verticis*. In Old English *cervix* is rendered by *hnoll*,[9] 'crown of the head'. In Medieval Latin *corona* means 'crown of the head'.[10] In Old

---

[1] Ed. Ehwald, p. 379. He documents the reading *frangis* in Codex Gothanus I 75, eighth-century in insular script, and assigns first place to the manuscript in his edition.
[2] It glosses *inlicias* in Aldhelm's quotation from Cyprian: 'tu . . . oculos in te iuvenum illicias' (ed. Ehwald, p. 315, line 15). [3] WW 513, 7.
[4] BT, *s.v. scild* III, takes the word as being used of a bird's back and suggests something like 'shield-shaped' or 'shoulder-blade'. Hall, *s.v. scield*, queries 'part of a bird's plumage?'.
[5] Ed. Blake, pp. 77–8. [6] Ed. Brandt, line 130. [7] *Ibid.*
[8] WW 355, 27, where the lemma is given as *arta*, but this is a misprinting of *apta* in the manuscript. It should be noted that in the edited text of the *Carmen*, *aptata* is an edited reading, but it should also be noted that in the glossary entry *apta . gefeged*, the lemma *apta* is in a small batch of lemmata the last one of which, *Aidoneæ*, almost surely comes from the *Carmen*.
[9] See BT *Suppl*, *s.v. hnol*, and Hall, *s.v. hnoll*.
[10] See *Revised Medieval Latin Word-List*, ed. R. E. Latham (London, 1965), *s.v. corona*.

High German *vertex* is frequently rendered by *skeitila*,[1] 'parting of the hair, crown of the head' and in Old English *verticem capilli* is glossed *feaxes scadan*,[2] 'parting of the hair, crown of the head'. In Lactantius's description of the head of the bird there are three words, *cervix, corona* and *verticis*, documentably interpreted as 'crown of the head', and two of these interpretations, namely *skeitila* and *scadan*, are etymologically related to German *Scheitel*, 'parting of the hair, crown of the head', ME *schodynge* (and *scheydinge*) *of the heede*[3] and *shode* as in the Chaucerian 'joly shode' of Absalon which 'lay ful streight and evene'.[4] Reflecting Lactantius's *cervix, corona* and *verticis*, the word *scyld* in the *Phoenix* passage may mean 'crown of the head'. In an early text of *The Phoenix* this word *scyld* was, I suggest, spelled *scidl*, cognate with OHG *skeitila*, 'crown of the head', and in manuscript transmission transposed to *scild*,[5] orthographically identical with *scild*, 'shield', spelled *scyld* at line 463 of *The Phoenix*. Taking *scyld* at line 308 as originating in *scidl*, one may interpret 'Is se scyld ufan/frætwum gefeged ofer þæs fugles bæc' as 'the crown at the top is splendidly composed above the back of the bird'. If in *scyld* lies *scidl* meaning 'crown of the head' as does *hnoll*, the contiguous words *scyld ufan* are analogous to the documented 'fram ðam hnolle ufan'.[6]

OE '*sicettað*' rendering '*conticescent*'

An attested meaning of OE *sicettan* is 'to sigh, groan',[7] but in King Alfred's version of the *Cura Pastoralis* the word *sicettað* reflects Gregory's *conticescent*,[8] 'they shall be silent', and on 39v of the Harleian Glossary *conticiscent* is glossed *silebant vel siccitan*.[9] These words *sicettað* and *siccitan* are entered in BT *s.v. sicettan*, 'to sigh, groan', with the queried suggestion 'as opposed to expressing grief by speech'. There is another possible explanation.

The context of *conticescent* in the *Cura Pastoralis* is a passage from I *Regum* II. 9: 'impii in tenebris conticescent', rendered in Old English as 'ða unryhtwisan sicettað on ðam ðiestrum'. A reason for *sicettað*, 'they sigh', as a rendering of *conticescent* in this context is to be found in biblical commentary which associates *conticescent* at I *Regum* II. 9 with 'lamentation'. For example, Hrabanus: 'et impie in tenebris conticescent . . . ibi erit fletus',[10] and Rupertus: 'et impii in tenebris conticescent . . . in tenebris inferni conquiescent,

---

[1] E. G. Graff, *Althochdeutscher Sprachschatz* (Berlin, 1834–42) VI, 439–40.
[2] See BT, *s.v. scēada*.
[3] See *Promptorium Parvulorum*, ed. A. Way (London, 1843–65), *s.v. schodynge*.
[4] They are also etymologically related to Old English *scīd*, 'shide, split of wood'.
[5] Like *mild* for *midl* in the glossary entry *chamus . bridles mild* on BM Add. 32246, 9v; the Junius transcript has *bridles midl*, whence *bridles midl* at WW 120, 7.   [6] See BT, *s.v. hnol*.
[7] E.g. 'Ða begann se ealda incuðlice siccetan 7 mid wope wearð witodlice ofergoten', 'Ælfric: On the Old and New Testament', ed. S. J. Crawford, *The Old English Version of the Heptateuch* etc., EETS o.s. 160 (London, 1922; repr. 1969), p. 65, line 1104 – p. 66, line 1105.
[8] See BT, *s.v. sicettan*.   [9] WW 211, 42.   [10] PL 109, col. 19.

imo et ululantes dentibus stridebunt et flebunt'.[1] It is assumable that in the Harleian Glossary entry *conticiscent . silebant vel siccitan* the lemma comes from the same biblical context and reflects the same biblical commentary – in the Cleopatra Glossary *conticiscent*,[2] glossed only by *swigiað*, 'they are silent', comes definitely from I *Regum* II. 9.[3]

[1] PL 167, col. 1068.
[2] WW 364, 33.
[3] It is followed by lemmata from I *Regum* X. 22 and XIII. 12 and II *Regum* VI. 19. Known sources of batches of lemmata in this glossary are detailed in 'The Latin–Old English Glossary in MS Cotton Cleopatra A. iii', ed. W. G. Stryker (unpub. diss., Stanford, 1951).

The manuscript of the Leiden Riddle

M. B. PARKES

In April 1970 I was fortunate enough to have the opportunity to examine Leiden, Bibliotheek der Rijksuniversiteit, Vossius Lat. 4° 106, 25v, the page containing the text of the Leiden Riddle (see pl. I),[1] under extremely strong early morning sunlight. Strong sunlight combines the advantage of ordinary light with, to a much lesser degree, the advantages of both infra-red and ultra-violet light whilst permitting a prolonged and close scrutiny of the manuscript. In sunlight some of the applications of reagent appear as opaque white, whereas in a photograph they appear as dark stains because the opaque white does not register adequately on the negative.[2] In these conditions I was able to distinguish in the damaged parts of the text of the Leiden Riddle between traces of ink left upon the surface and stains left by the various reagents as well as other marks in the substance of the parchment itself. The following day I made an independent examination of the manuscript under ultra-violet light. Later by way of experiment a series of very hard prints was produced from photographs taken in ordinary light.[3] Subsequently I compared the various readings and as a result of these examinations I offer a new transcription and notes on the more difficult passages.

In the following transcription expanded abbreviations are indicated by means of italics. Square brackets [ ] enclose letters which have been deleted by the scribe, and angle brackets ⟨ ⟩ enclose letters which have been damaged: where traces of ink are still visible and the traces are sufficient to identify the letters beyond

[1] I am indebted to Mr C. J. E. Ball (who initiated this investigation) and to Dr N. R. Ker both of whom have read earlier drafts of this paper and have contributed valuable criticisms and suggestions. I am also indebted to Professor B. Bischoff for help on various points and to him and to Mons. F. Hauchecorne for references. However, I am alone responsible for the views expressed. I owe the opportunity to examine the manuscript to Dr P. J. F. Obbema, the Keeper of Western Manuscripts, who accorded me special facilities and many other kindnesses. He drew my attention to the stimulating article by Professor Gerritsen (discussed below), thus enabling me to read it with the manuscript in front of me, and also discussed various readings with me. I am indebted to the Librarian at Leiden for permission to reproduce the photograph of the manuscript.
[2] See the facsimiles in R. W. Zandvoort, 'The Leiden Riddle', *Collected Papers* (Groningen, 1954).
[3] This experiment was undertaken by Mr A. Austin from a photograph available in Oxford. The effect of such prints is to heighten the contrasts, thus emphasizing very faint traces obscured beneath only a light film of reagent.

question the letters have been printed in roman type; where the identification is based upon reconstruction the letters have been printed in italic; where it is not possible to determine the nature of missing letters from traces on the page I have supplied dots to indicate the number of letters which would fit into the space available. Insertions above the line are enclosed within half-square brackets. The suprascript numbers in round brackets refer to the notes which follow.

Mec seueta[. .]⁽¹⁾ uong uundrumfreorig o⟨bhis⟩ innaðae ⌐ ꟾaer⟨e⟩st⁽²⁾ ⟨cend. .⟩⁽³⁾⌐
Uaat icmecbiuorthæ uullanfliusu*m* heru*m*. ðerhheh craeft ⟨hy⟩gið⟨on⟩⁽⁴⁾ ⌐⟨c.m⟩⌐
Uundnae. menibiað. ueflæ niic uar ph⟨a⟩fæ⁽⁵⁾ niðerih ðrea⟨.⟩ungi ð⟨ræ.⟩⁽⁶⁾
   ðr&. me hlimmit⟨h⟩. Neme hrutendohrisil scel⟨ʄ⟩a⟨th⟩n⟨e⟩mec⁽⁷⁾ ou⟨an⟩a⁽⁸⁾
aam sceal cnyssa Uyrmas mecni au⟨e⟩fun uy⟨rd⟩icraeftum⁽⁹⁾
   ðaði goelu ⟨g⟩o⟨d⟩.u⟨e⟩bgeatu*m* fraetuath. ꟾ heliðum hyhtlicgiuæ⟨. .⟩
Uilm⟨e⟩c huc⌐⟨h⟩⌐trae suaeðehuidæ ofaer eorðu ⟨h⟩atan / mith
Nianoegun icme aeri⟨g⟩ faera⟨e⟩ egsanbrogum ð⟨e⟩hði ni⟨. . .⟩⁽¹⁰⁾
   ⟨niu⟩dlicae⁽¹¹⁾ obcocrum

1 *Mec seueta*[. .] The texture of the surface at this point is quite different from that at other points of difficulty. It appears as though the surface has been scraped with a knife and I suspect an erasure by the scribe. Prolonged scrutiny under strong sunlight suggested that the erased letters were possibly **th**, but nothing is visible under ultra-violet light.

2 *aer*⟨e⟩*st* The second **e** seems certain. Traces of ink left on the page which are visible when magnified under ordinary light and confirmed under ultra-violet light can only be interpreted as forming the letter **e**. The interpretation is based on three traces of the pen:

(*a*) The duct and direction of the down stroke visible in ordinary light differ from those of the minim stroke used elsewhere in the text for the letter **i**.

(*b*) This mainstroke has been crossed almost half-way down by a diagonal hair stroke. This hair stroke occurs at the point where one would expect the scribe to begin the tongue of the letter **e** and extends a little to the right of the mainstroke.

(*c*) There is a trace to the left of the following **s** which extends too far to the left and is of too unusual a shape to be interpreted convincingly as part of that letter (i.e. as an approach stroke either to the stem or the headstroke).

The hair stroke (*b*) when extended would connect with the trace (*c*) in precisely the right place for the two to form the head and tongue of the letter *e*. From this it would appear that the scribe wrote the **st** ligature close up to the letter **e** and on top of the point where the head and tongue joined.¹

3. ⟨*cend.* .⟩ In addition to the damage there are three sources of difficulty presented by this word: first the alignment of it – the sequence of letters slopes downwards from left to right; secondly there is a larger gap between the second and third

---

¹ My observations were checked by Dr P. J. F. Obbema when he examined the manuscript with me.

letters than between the other letters; thirdly the traces of the pen are difficult to distinguish from marks left by stains.

c is visible to the unaided eye.

e When magnified under strong sunlight three pen traces are visible, and they emerge more clearly under ultra-violet light. At the top there is a very long curve which comes well to the left and touches the headstroke of the letter **c**. Below this trace there is a straight diagonal trace. Attached to the left end of this diagonal trace there is a short curved downward stroke like a 'tail'.

In identifying the letter the crucial trace is the top one. The trace is too long to be regarded as the headstroke of the letter **a**. None of the other as in the text has a headstroke which trails as far to the left as this. The only possible interpretation of this trace is as the head of the letter **e**. The other two traces then fall into a recognizable pattern as respectively the tongue of the letter and the base of the mainstroke.

Since this is a radical departure from previous readings it is necessary to describe the phenomenon which may have given rise to such readings. To the right of the letter there appears to be a thin vertical line. Taken in conjunction with the three pen traces just described it could have been mistaken for the stem of the letter **a** (the other strokes forming the trailing head and the lobe of the letter). There are three objections to such an interpretation of this vertical line. First the shape of the line is unsuitable; secondly it protrudes above and beyond the top curve which cannot therefore be a continuation of it, and thus cannot form the trailing head of the stroke; thirdly close examination under a magnifying glass in strong sunlight convinced me that the vertical line is the edge of a stain: it seems to me to be *in* the page and not laid *on* it. I am convinced that this stain has confused earlier scholars and is the cause of the misinterpretation of this group of traces as **a**. In the last analysis trailing-headed **a** is a palaeographical anachronism.

n is clearly visible under ultra-violet light. The first minim of the letter has a pronounced (perhaps blotted) head, and only part of the bottom of this minim is visible. The 'arch' of the letter has been lost, but traces of the head and also the bottom of the next minim are visible when magnified under ultra-violet light.

Although there is more space between **e** and **n** than between **c** and **e**, I am convinced that this space is insufficient to accommodate a fourth letter.

d In strong sunlight and with the aid of a magnifying glass I saw faint traces identifiable as the round back of the letter **d**, a form which occurs also in ⟨*niu*⟩*dlicae* in line 9. These traces are also visible under ultra-violet light. However because of the alignment of the word the position of the traces is lower than one might have expected: the top of the ascender is only just above the level of the top of the letter **n**. Although the trace is much fainter than those of the other letters I am convinced that it *is* a trace and not the edge of a stain.

It is possible that other letters followed the **d** but prolonged scrutiny failed to reveal any traces whatsoever. There is certainly sufficient space to accommodate other letters.[1]

---

[1] My observations were checked by Dr P. J. F. Obbema when he examined the manuscript with me.

The following is a sketch of the traces I have described, much enlarged:

4 ⟨*hy*⟩*gið*⟨*on*⟩ Between **h** and **g** there appear under ultra-violet light traces which resemble the descender of **y**. The letters **on** are visible in a very hard print based on a photograph taken in ordinary light.

5 *h*⟨*a*⟩*fæ* **a** is certain under ultra-violet light.

6 *ð*⟨*ræ*⟩ Two traces which are recognizable as the stem and approach stroke to the shoulder of the letter **r** are clearly visible. **æ** is certain. Identification of the letter following **æ** is not possible because the traces are too indistinct.

7 *scel*⟨*f*⟩*a*⟨*th*⟩ The crossbar of **f** is visible by ultra-violet light.

8 *ou*⟨*an*⟩*a* Two traces, one recognizable as the bottom of the lobe of the letter **a** and the other as the second minim of **n**, are clear when magnified under ultra-violet light.

9 *uy*⟨*rd*⟩*icraeftum* The traces here interpreted as **d** are closely similar to those of the **d** in ⟨*cend*. .⟩ above.

10 *ni*⟨. . .⟩ **n** is followed by a minim stroke, here recorded as **i** for typographical convenience. After this it is possible to trace the extent of the word but not to identify the letters. There is a distinct 'shadow' which follows the line of writing up to a certain point. I calculate that after **ni** there is room for three letters, and possibly a fourth, but only if one of the letters were **l** or **i**. There is no trace of the *siæ* which Smith claims to have read.[1]

11 ⟨*niu*⟩*dlicae* There are five traces, the first three of which are recognizable as minim strokes. In a very hard print based on a photograph taken in ordinary light the last two traces are joined together at the bottom. There also appears to be a mark joining the top of these two traces (which suggests that they should be interpreted as the letter **a** and would give the reading *niadlicae*), but I am unable to determine whether this mark is a trace on the surface or a mark in it. Moreover the direction of the first trace differs from that of **a**. I have therefore transcribed as **u**.

Much discussion of the manuscript of the Leiden Riddle has centred round the date and the peculiar lay-out of the text. However even the best of these discussions (that of Gerritsen)[2] has omitted to take into account the full significance of two important features – the present state of the text and the lay-out of the text in relation to the rest of the page.

The principal causes of damage noted by both Ker[3] and Gerritsen[4] are rubbing and the applications of reagents by Pluygers in 1864. As is to be expected when a manuscript has been preserved for some time in a parchment wrapper, the principal damage by rubbing occurs along the inner edge

---

[1] *Three Northumbrian Poems*, ed. A. H. Smith (London, 1933), p. 47, n. 14.
[2] J. Gerritsen, 'The Text of the Leiden Riddle', *ESts* 6 (1969), 529.
[3] N. R. Ker, *Catalogue of Manuscripts containing Anglo-Saxon* (Oxford, 1957), App., no. 19.
[4] Gerritsen, 'The Text of the Leiden Riddle', p. 534.

of the leaf. As Gerritsen observed, both the Latin and Old English texts are affected, but since the Old English text extends further into the inner margin, the ends of the lines of the English text have been more affected by rubbing than those of the Latin.

However the damage to the Leiden Riddle text is more widespread than that suffered by the Latin text. When Bethmann examined the manuscript in 1845 and Dietrich in 1860 it is clear that the text was already difficult to read.[1] These two witnesses are important because they suggest that the text of the Leiden Riddle was added to the manuscript in a different ink from that used on the rest of the page, an ink which was more susceptible to fading or wear than that used for the main text and that used for the pen trials of letters and neums. It was because of the fading of the ink that in 1864 Pluygers applied reagents. Moreover, as the stains indicate, the applications of reagent were selective: they were applied to the text of the riddle and to the pen trials below, but *not* to the pen trials alongside the text. As a result these pen trials are undamaged by reagent and look fresher than the text of the riddle, obscured as it is both by the stain and by what seems to me from close examination to be a thin film of reagent.

It seems to me that because of the damage to the text of the riddle discussions of lay-out and date by Gerritsen and others (especially Smith) have proceeded on the assumption that the text must have been added to the page earlier than the undamaged pen trials, an assumption which could easily be induced by the fact that the language of the text preserves features of the Old English Northumbrian dialect of an early date. I wish to question this assumption, and to raise again the problems of lay-out and date.

The lay-out of the text on the page is discussed by Gerritsen, whose main concern is to demonstrate that the scribe tried to follow the arrangement of his exemplar. I wish to discuss the lay-out in relation to the pen trials of neums and letter forms which occur above the text of the riddle and alongside it in the outer margin. There were two vertical bounding lines ruled in drypoint by the ninth-century scribe who copied the main text on this quire. The scribe of the riddle, who has set the first three and last two lines against the outer vertical bounding line, has inset the beginning of the fourth, fifth and sixth lines: the fourth line is set against the inner bounding line and the fifth and sixth begin in the space between the two bounding lines. The significance of this insetting, if we follow Gerritsen's view that the scribe is following the lay-out of his exemplar, is not immediately obvious, especially since the fourth line is inset further than the other two; although Gerritsen scrupulously observes this fact, he does not discuss it. But if we

---

[1] L. C. Bethmann, *ZDA* 5 (1845), 199; F. Dietrich, *Commentatio de Kynewulfi Poetae Aetas Aenigmatum Fragmento e Codice Lugdunensi Editio Illustrata* (Marburg, 1860).

ignore the possibility of a relationship with the exemplar at this point and concentrate upon the immediate context – the lay-out of this particular part of the text at this particular point on the page – the reason for the insetting becomes obvious: the relationship between the pen trials and the text seems to me to indicate that the pen trials were already on the page when the scribe added the text. He inset the fourth line against the inner bounding line to avoid them, and he inset it further than the fifth and sixth because he was aware of the **ge**, the pen trial which intruded furthest into his written space. He inset the fifth and sixth lines less than the fourth because he found that he could tuck them in under the **e**, but nevertheless he had to inset the fifth line to avoid the tail of the **g** and could not return to the outer vertical bounding line with the sixth line because the last neum of the descending row of four neums was in the way. By contrast the three rows of neums below seem to me to be separate from these four and to be in a different relationship to the text.[1] This second group looks as though it has been written around the **U** of *Uil* in line 7 and therefore added after the text.

Furthermore a close inspection of the first line of the text suggests that it was written after the neums which stand above it. The neums touch the letters of the Latin verse above, but they do not come into contact with the Old English. The scribe of the riddle has used the existing ruling of the manuscript, but he has had to adapt his letter forms in order to avoid the neums. The headstroke of the **s** in *se* seems to illustrate this. When compared with the other **ss** in the text (for example, those in *hrisil* in line 4 and *suae* in line 7) the top of the curved headstroke of this letter is lower in relation to the beginning of the stroke (represented by the protrusion on the left hand side of the letter). Moreover, the **u** in *ueta* seems to have been dropped slightly to avoid the descending neum above.

The only plausible explanation of these features is that the text of the Leiden Riddle was added *after* at least some of the pen trials, but before the group of neums alongside line 7.

To appreciate the significance of this observation it is necessary first to outline the evidence for the origin and provenance of the manuscript. Professor Bischoff considers that the original manuscript, containing the riddles of Symphosius and Aldhelm, was copied in western France (in which region he would include the Loire basin and Orléans).[2] Dr K. A. de Meyier has demonstrated that the manuscript was probably at Fleury in the sixteenth century, when along with many other Fleury manuscripts it passed into the possession of Pierre Daniel (1530–1603), an Orléans lawyer who was bailiff

---

[1] In the present state of our knowledge it is not possible to identify the music represented by the neums.   [2] Personal communication.

of Fleury.[1] The original parchment wrapper of the manuscript (now Leiden, Bibliotheek der Rijksuniversiteit, Fragment Vossius Lat. 2° 122) is a fragment of a copy of Macrobius, other fragments of which are now Vossius Lat. 2° 12β² and London, British Museum, Royal 15 B. xii (1). The second Vossius fragment is also from Fleury.[3]

Numerous pen trials and in particular pen trials of neums are a characteristic feature of manuscripts which, according to the evidence of *ex libris* inscriptions, were at Fleury in the ninth and tenth centuries.[4] The most common position for such trials in these Fleury manuscripts is on the last page of the manuscript or on the following endleaves. 25v is the last page of Vossius Lat. 4° 106, and the pen trials on it are closely similar to those in Fleury manuscripts which I have examined. Not only the neums but also the series of small letters **bcd**[5] and names[6] (compare those of *Otgerius* and *Aglesardus*(?) on this page) are characteristic additions in Fleury manuscripts. From this comparison with other Fleury manuscripts it appears that Vossius Lat. 4° 106 was already at Fleury in the ninth century or the tenth.

The lay-out of the last page of Vossius Lat. 4° 106 suggests that the text of the Leiden Riddle was added after pen trials had been inserted at Fleury, and it must have been added before the manuscript left Fleury in the sixteenth century. Therefore the text was almost certainly added at Fleury. Several manuscripts now at Orléans offer supporting evidence in that they attest to the Fleury habit of using the last page for the addition of short texts as well as of pen trials and neums. In three manuscripts, Orléans 16 (p. 250), 84 (p. 288) and 174 (p. 209), these texts added on the last page have been copied in a pale brown ink which has proved more susceptible to fading or wear than that of the main text. In Orléans 14 the lay-out of the last page (p. 260) suggests that a short text was added after pen trials. This might help to explain a puzzling feature of the Leiden manuscript: why the scribe did not bother to erase the intrusive pen trials. He regarded the Old English text as something in the nature of an annotation or memorandum,

---

[1] K. A. de Meyier, *Paul en Alexandre Petau* (Leiden, 1947), p. 64. On Daniel see H. Hagen, *Zur Geschichte der Philologie* (Berlin, 1879), pp. 1–52, and the brief mention in L. V. Delisle, *Le Cabinet des Manuscrits* (Paris, 1868–81) II, 364.

[2] E. Pellegrin, *Bibliothèque de l'Ecole des Chartes* 115 (1957), 14–15.

[3] de Meyier, *Paul en Alexandre Petau*, p. 62.

[4] E.g. E. A. Lowe, *Codices Latini Antiquiores*, nos. 563, 796 and 802; and the following manuscripts in the Bibliothèque Municipale at Orléans (the dates given are those assigned to the hands of the main contents by Professor Bischoff): 184 (s. ix in.); 70 and 270 (s. ix¹); 14 and 147 (s. ix); 297 (s. x¹); 16 (s. x); 14 (s. x²): other examples are given below. There are a number of other manuscripts at Orléans with similar pen trials, but they do not contain the *ex libris* inscriptions. Some Fleury manuscripts with neumatic notation and now in the Vatican are illustrated by H. M. Bannister, *Monumenti Vaticani di Paleografia Musicale Latina* (Leipzig, 1913), pls. 15–17, nos. 122–33 (see also the review by E. K. Rand, *Amer. Jnl of Philol.* 35 (1914), 470).

[5] Cf., e.g., Orléans 84, p. 289; 14, p. 260; 270, p. 320; and 16, pp. 250–1.

[6] Cf., e.g., Orléans 343 (*bis*), p. 104; 159, p. i; 14, p. 11; and 192, p. 45.

transcribed from an annotation in one of the numerous copies of Aldhelm which must have found their way into such a renowned centre of the liberal arts at this time.

My explanation of the insetting, however, does not account for all the peculiarities of the lay-out of the text. The scribe wrote the first line and completed it by adding two words above. The same procedure of 'turning up' the line occurs at the end of the second line. The seventh line was completed in the space at the end of the sixth and is separated from the end of it by means of a paragraph mark. The eighth line is completed by insetting the remainder of the line below it. Gerritsen is particularly interesting on this point:

> The normal arrangement throughout the Latin riddles is for there to be a line-initial capital and no other, a new line of writing being started for each new line of verse. The Old English riddle, if written on the same principles, should have been fourteen capitalized lines. If written to agree with the Latin, each line of which is translated by two alliterative lines, it should have been seven capitalized long lines. What we actually find is seven capitals, in the places of the text where they would go according to the latter system, but we do not find that arrangement.[1]

The fact that the riddle was not set out in fourteen capitalized lines need not detain us: such an arrangement would presuppose that a scribe would have been familiar with a modern editor's way of setting out Old English verse. The statement that it is written with seven capitals and the fact that each of these introduces a pair of alliterative lines needs some clarification lest this too should lead us to fall into the trap of thinking that this scribe, or his exemplar, was conscious of the metrical form of the English poem and tried to indicate it in some way.

First let us examine the use of 'capital' letters. I think the scribe here is following the practice of punctuation in which a *littera notabilior* marks the beginning of a new *periodus*. Since five of the 'capitals' stand at the beginning of a line we would expect in each case to find the *punctus* at the end of the preceding line, but with the exception of line 6, the ends of the lines have been damaged and the *puncti* (if they existed) have been lost. However, in the case of line 6 a *punctus* does occur after *fraetuath* where we should expect to find it. In the case of the two 'capital' letters which occur in the middle of a line, there is a *punctus* at the end of the *periodus* before *Ne* in line 4, but I cannot see one before *Uyrmas* in line 5. Although not conclusive, it seems to me that the weight of the evidence, light as it is, points to the use of a 'capital' as a means of punctuation to indicate the beginning of a new *periodus*. According to the grammatical theory current during the early Middle Ages,

[1] Gerritsen, 'The Text of the Leiden Riddle', p. 538.

in Latin verse a *periodus* fell at the end of each line.[1] If the English text is a translation of Aldhelm's Latin, then the *periodi* must fall at those points in the translation which are each equivalent to a line of the Latin original. This is precisely what the punctuation of the Leiden Riddle indicates. Hence the arrangement of the lines. As Gerritsen points out, when the scribe set out to copy the text there were seven ruled lines left on the page.[2] The coincidence is remarkable; seven *periodi*, seven lines. The scribe started to copy each *periodus* on a line of its own, turning up the ends of *periodi* which would not fit the lines. From the way he treats the word-division it is obvious that the scribe knew no Old English; therefore he must have been following his exemplar. The arrangement indicates that somebody before him recognized the relationship of this text to its Latin original and punctuated it and laid it out accordingly, but in doing so need not have recognized the translation as English verse. The scribe here must have tried to follow the lay-out of his exemplar but had to abandon the attempt at the end of line 3 when he looked ahead and realized that he was faced with the necessity of avoiding the intrusive pen trials. He resumed his attempt to follow the lay-out at line 7 when the pen trials were no longer in the way.

Finally there is the question of when the Leiden Riddle was added. If it was added at Fleury, after some of the pen trials and before others, then a date for the pen trials will provide a clue to the date of the text. Pen trials are notoriously difficult to date. It is generally agreed that the main hands of Vossius Lat. 4° 106 are not later than the first half of the ninth century and this provides a *terminus post quem* for the pen trials. However, this can be narrowed down further by examining the way in which the neums were formed. The calligraphy of the neums on 25v is the same as that of neums which were added to two other Fleury manuscripts, Orléans 16 and 174, the main hands of which belong to the tenth century, and the neums in them cannot be earlier than that. Historically this is the most probable period for the addition of the neums, because from the mid tenth century onwards Fleury was acquiring a reputation as a school of music.[3] A *terminus ante quem* for the pen trials is provided by a change in the character of the calligraphy of neums added to Fleury manuscripts. This new calligraphy is characteristic of neums added to manuscripts whose main contents were copied at the end of the tenth century or in the eleventh.[4] All the neums on

---

[1] Cf. Isidore of Seville, *Etymologiae* I. xx, 'Totus autem versus periodus est' (Migne, Patrologia Latina 82, col. 96).   [2] Gerritsen, 'The Text of the Leiden Riddle', p. 539.

[3] See especially E. Lesne, *Les Livres 'Scriptoria' et Bibliothèques* (*Histoire de la Propriété ecclésiastique en France* IV, Lille, 1938), p. 136, and *Les Écoles* (*ibid.* V, Lille, 1940), p. 191; and Ch. Cuissard, *L'École de Fleury à la Fin du Xe Siècle* (Orléans, 1875).

[4] Orléans 342 contains both the earlier and the later neums. The main hand of this manuscript is dated s. x–xi by Professor Bischoff, but the manuscript does not contain an *ex libris* inscription. The calligraphy of the later neums is illustrated from an eleventh-century addition to a Fleury

Vossius Lat. 4° 106, 25v are of the earlier type and this suggests that they belong to the tenth century. If, as the lay-out of the page suggests, the text of the riddle was added after some of the neums but before others, then this would indicate that it too was copied in the tenth century.

Turning to the hand of the riddle itself we find a conflict of opinions as to the date. This is hardly surprising. To date a hand on palaeographical criteria alone, when the text is as damaged as this one, is a hazardous undertaking. Ker thinks that the handwriting of the riddle is 'contemporary' with the two hands of the manuscript.[1] Bischoff thinks that the hand of the riddle is later than those of the manuscript and would assign it to the end of the ninth century at the earliest or to the tenth.[2] Gerritsen thinks that the riddle was copied by the second scribe of the manuscript and bases his opinion on a detailed analysis of the shapes rather than the formation of the letters. His comparison of the hand of the riddle and that of the second scribe on this basis is hampered by his conviction that in the riddle the scribe is consciously imitating his Anglo-Saxon exemplar, and he explains away obvious differences of detail in this way. As a result his identification is not convincing.

My own opinion is that the riddle was copied by a third scribe. I think that this hand is tenth-century. My attribution is based primarily upon the general impression afforded by the duct of the hand, its proportions and its regularity in the formation of letters, and the treatment of ascenders, all of which differ from the hand above. One detail in this short piece seems to support this general impression. In the first a of the word *Uaat* at the beginning of the second line of the text the scribe has used the insular form of a which is not unlike a u with a hairline joining the top of the two main-strokes.[3] I have not found this form in Anglo-Saxon manuscripts before the turn of the ninth century to the tenth.[4]

This form presents a major obstacle to Gerritsen's attempt to identify the hand of the riddle with the early-ninth-century hand of scribe 2. His arguments in an effort to get round this obstacle are not convincing. He states that the hairline is not continuous and does not join the two main strokes. I cannot agree. Not only is it continuous in both ordinary and ultra-violet light, but its continuity is visible in photographs. He argues further:

> For an interpretation as a to be admissible it would in fact have to be shown that graphs of this shape occur elsewhere in the stint of scribe 2, and that they there have

manuscript now in the Vatican Library by Bannister, *Monumenti Vaticani*, pl. 17(b), no. 132. Compare especially the formation of the *clivis* and the *quilismata* in this plate with those alongside the text of the riddle.   [1] *Catalogue*, p. 479.

[2] 'Das "Leiden Riddle" . . . schien mir *c*. ix–x oder x zu sein' (personal communication).

[3] If in the last line of the text the reading *niadlicae* is preferred (see n. 11 to the transcription above), the first a would be a second example of the use of this particular insular form.

[4] See T. A. M. Bishop, 'An Early Example of the Square Minuscule', *Trans. of the Cambridge Bibliographical Soc.* 4 (1964–8), 246.

the value **a**. And not only is this impossible – scribe 2, we saw, employs only caroline **a**, open-headed **a**, and double-c **a** – but it is impossible for a very good reason: square-headed **a** does not make its appearance till almost a century after our MS. Therefore, however one interprets the cross-stroke, the character admits of only one interpretation, viz. **u**.[1]

In my opinion the more obvious explanation is correct. The letter *is* an **a**: the formation of the first main stroke is different from that of the first minim of **u** as can be seen by comparing this form with the two **us** in *uullan* in the same line. The first stroke of **a** is less vertical.[2] It follows that the hand of the riddle is unlikely to be earlier than the tenth century. It also follows on Gerritsen's own argument that the hand cannot be the hand of scribe 2 of the manuscript.

Further slight evidence for a tenth-century date is afforded by the fact that the riddle was copied in a different ink, a much paler ink than that of the rest of the manuscript and one which was more susceptible to fading and wear. In my argument above I cited three other Fleury manuscripts now at Orléans in which texts were added on the last page in a similar kind of ink. In two of these, Orléans 16 and 174, the main texts of the books were copied in the tenth century, and the additions cannot therefore be earlier than that.

Although each of these points is inconclusive in itself, together they acquire a cumulative force. In my opinion the Leiden Riddle was copied at Fleury in the tenth century. I believe that this may provide a further clue to those complex relationships which existed at that time between Fleury on the one hand and Brittany and the British Isles on the other, and which were outlined by Dom Louis Gougaud.[3] These relationships would repay further investigation.

[1] Gerritsen, 'The Text of the Leiden Riddle', p. 541.
[2] Compare the difference between **a** and **u** in pl. xix (*b*) of T. A. M. Bishop, 'An Early Example of the Square Minuscule'.
[3] L. Gougaud, 'Les Relations de l'Abbaye de Fleury-sur-Loire avec la Bretagne armoricaine et les Iles Britanniques', *Mémoires de la Société d'Histoire et d'Archéologie de Bretagne* 4, 2 (1923). Since this article was written the late Professor Wormald has drawn attention to the work of an English illuminator in a Fleury manuscript; see *England Before the Conquest: Studies in Primary Sources presented to Dorothy Whitelock*, ed. Peter Clemoes and Kathleen Hughes (Cambridge, 1971), p. 311.

Northumbria and the Book of Kells

T. J. BROWN

with an appendix by C. D. VEREY

It is a century and a half since the Book of Kells began to be revered as the supreme work of Irish calligraphy and art in the Early Christian period, and a quarter of a century since Monsieur François Masai challenged that traditional opinion, arguing that the Book was in fact made in Northumbria, apparently at Lindisfarne, or at least in some centre influenced both by Lindisfarne and Wearmouth–Jarrow – a definition which, he thought, could well apply to Iona. Masai's *Essai sur les Origines de la Miniature dite irlandaise*,[1] completed in Brussels in 1944, makes no pretence to be based on research at first hand; it was written as a critique of traditional beliefs about the origins of Hiberno-Saxon illumination, with particular reference to works by Mlle Françoise Henry and Mrs Geneviève Marsh-Micheli.[2] As such, it strikes me as a brilliant success, although some of its conclusions are false and some are not as well founded as they could have been, if Masai had revised his war-time text on the basis of a post-war examination of the manuscripts themselves. It was as a follower of Masai – his was the first book I read on Hiberno-Saxon art – that I persuaded Dr E. A. Lowe to consider, shortly before his death in August 1969, the attribution of the Book of Kells which will appear in the second edition of *Codices Latini Antiquiores*, part II;[3] and since Dr Lowe cited me as 'an expert in this field', I am under an obligation to publish the arguments that I advanced in 1968 and 1969, partly in letters and partly through reports which he received from his successive assistants Dr Braxton Ross and Dr Virginia Brown. The core of what I have to say is a reconsideration of a group of manuscripts, described in *CLA*, in the history of which Wearmouth–Jarrow had an important part to play. Lowe's devotion to the Venerable Bede and to the manuscripts produced at Wearmouth–Jarrow is well known,[4] and I should like my lecture to count as a tribute not

---

[1] Publications de Scriptorium 1 (Brussels and Antwerp, 1947).
[2] Françoise Henry, *La Sculpture irlandaise pendant les douze premiers Siècles de l'Ère Chrétienne*, 2 vols. (Paris, 1933); Geneviève L. Micheli, *L'Enluminure du Haut Moyen Âge et les Influences irlandaises* (Brussels, 1939); but not Françoise Henry, *Irish Art* (London, 1940).
[3] *Codices Latini Antiquiores: a Palaeographical Guide to Latin Manuscripts Prior to the Ninth Century*, 12 pts (Oxford, 1934–71). The second edition of pt II is to appear in 1972.
[4] 'A Key to Bede's Scriptorium', *Scriptorium* 12 (1958), 182–90; *English Uncial* (Oxford, 1960).

only to Bede's memory but to the memory of the palaeographer whose work has thrown such a bright light on the intellectual history of Bede's monastery.[1]

If the Book of Kells[2] is one of the masterpieces of an Hiberno-Saxon art that was common to Ireland, Scotland and Northern England in the seventh, eighth and ninth centuries, is its precise origin a matter of historical importance? Indeed it is: to be wrong about Kells – in itself a complete gallery of Hiberno-Saxon art – is to be wrong about insular palaeography and Hiberno-Saxon archaeology in general. I shall begin with a short account of the traditional attribution of Kells to Ireland and of Masai's counter-attribution to Northumbria. I shall then explain what I believe about the origin and date of the manuscript, on the evidence of its design, script and basic decoration, up to the level of its minor initials – all of which fall within the province of palaeography. Finally, to emphasize that any full solution of the Kells problem will be a matter for archaeology, I shall offer some archaeological and historical suggestions as examples of the kind of approach that liberation from an ancient palaeographical dogma seems to authorize.

I

The Book of Kells – I shall call it K from now on – was given to Trinity College Dublin between 1661 and 1681. It had belonged to the monastery of Kells, co. Meath, in 1007, when, say the Irish annals, it was stolen but found again after the loss of its precious binding. The monastery at Kells was suppressed in 1539 and in 1568 K was in Dublin. In 1621 it was back at Kells, where Archbishop Ussher collated its text, recording that it was said to have belonged to St Columba (d. 597).[3]

Ussher's contemporaries, the English Camden and the Irish Ware, knew their Bede and knew that the Irish had taught most of the English to write; but in 1681 the founder of Latin palaeography gave to all insular script that

---

[1] This paper is a revised version of the Jarrow Lecture delivered in St Paul's Church at Jarrow on Ascension Day 1971. Parts of the Book of Kells, the Durham Gospels and the Lindisfarne Gospels are reproduced by kind permission of, respectively, the Board of Trinity College, Dublin, the Dean and Chapter of Durham Cathedral and the Trustees of the British Museum. Of the many friends who have helped me in various ways, some by reading part of the text, I am most in debt to Gerald Bonner, Virginia Brown, Rosemary Cramp, Ian Doyle, Isabel Henderson, Kathleen Hughes, Braxton Ross, Robert Stevenson, Christopher Verey (especially for the Appendix) and David Wilson. My wife has been generous with indispensable advice and encouragement over many years. The following important paper reached me just too late for mention at the appropriate points: R. B. K. Stevenson, 'Sculpture in Scotland in the Sixth–Ninth Centuries A.D.', *Kolloquium über spätantike und frühmittelalterliche Skulptur* II (Mainz, 1971), 65–74. See also the additional notes, below, pp. 245–6.

[2] *CLA* II, no. 274; *Evangeliorum Quattuor Codex Cenannensis*, ed. E. H. Alton and Peter Meyer, 3 vols. (Berne, 1950–1).

[3] Aubrey Gwynn, 'Some Notes on the History of the Book of Kells', *Irish Historical Studies* 9 (1954–5), 131–61; William O'Sullivan, 'The Donor of the Book of Kells', *ibid.* 11 (1958–9), 5–7.

he recognized as such – whether Irish or English – the name of *scriptura saxonica*, taken from Archbishop Parker's publications of texts in Anglo-Saxon. Jean Mabillon's *saxonica* was insular minuscule; failing to recognize the corresponding majuscule, or half-uncial, as insular, he classed it with his *scriptura Romana secundae aetatis*.[1] In 1703 Humfrey Wanley, rejecting the sound old view that the English had learned from the Irish, claimed that all insular majuscule was Anglo-Saxon, and failed to notice that the majuscule of the Rushworth Gospels[2] in the Bodleian was signed by a scribe with the Irish name of Macregol.[3] The misunderstandings of Mabillon and Wanley were perpetuated by the two Benedictines and by Astle.[4]

It was Charles O'Conor, the Irish historian, who in 1814 set out to redress the balance by publishing a list of twelve early Irish manuscripts, including the minuscule Bangor Antiphonary,[5] of 680–91, and the majuscule Gospels of Macregol.[6] Having found Macregol's death, as abbot of Birr, in the Annals of Tigernach, *s.a.* 822, O'Conor turned the tables on Wanley and argued that since Macregol's Gospels was proved to be Irish, so were all other manuscripts in insular majuscule, including the Lindisfarne Gospels:[7] insular majuscule was in fact an exclusively Irish script. The Book of Durrow[8] and K were both mislaid when O'Conor first made his list, but Durrow came to light in time for him to give an excellent description of it in an appendix, under the erroneous belief that it was K.[9] The real K was rediscovered too late for O'Conor himself to comment; but the earliest modern accounts of it, beginning with J. O. Westwood's,[10] are all grounded in his version of insular palaeography. K was ascribed to Ireland partly for the good reason that it had been there since at least 1007, and partly for the bad reason that its majuscule script was specifically Irish. It was dated in the sixth century because of the tradition, recorded by Ussher, that it had belonged to St Columba, which was in line with a like tradition about Durrow, also recorded by Ussher and based on the altered wording of the colophon, and with the tradition about the psalter called the Cathach of St Columba.[11] Sixty years ago palaeographers were still dating K before the Lindisfarne Gospels,[12]

---

[1] *De Re Diplomatica Libri VI* (Paris, 1681), pp. 45–53 and 350–9.　　[2] *CLA* ii, no. 231.
[3] *Librorum Vett. Septentrionalium . . . Catalogus* (Oxford, 1705), sig. *c*v–*c*2r, pp. 81–2.
[4] [Tassin and Toustain], *Nouveau Traité de Diplomatique*, 6 vols. (Paris, 1750–65); Thomas Astle, *The Origin and Progress of Writing* (London, 1784 and 1803).　　[5] *CLA* iii, no. 311.
[6] *Rerum Hibernicarum Scriptores Veteres* (Buckingham and London, 1814) i, cxxix–ccxxxvii.
[7] *CLA* ii, no. 187; *Evangeliorum Quattuor Codex Lindisfarnensis*, ed. T. D. Kendrick, T. J. Brown, R. L. S. Bruce-Mitford, Heinz Roosen-Runge, A. S. C. Ross, E. G. Stanley and A. E. A. Werner, 2 vols. (Olten and Lausanne, 1956–60). Vol. ii, bk 1 cited henceforth as *Cod. Lind.*
[8] *CLA* ii, no. 273; *Evangeliorum Quattuor Codex Durmachensis*, ed. A. A. Luce, G. O. Simms, Peter Meyer and Ludwig Bieler, 2 vols. (Olten and Lausanne, 1960).
[9] *Rerum Hibernicarum Scriptores*, pp. ccxxxvii–ccxli.
[10] *Palæographia Sacra Pictoria* (London, 1843–5), pls. 16–17.　　[11] *CLA* ii, no. 266.
[12] Franz Steffens, *Lateinische Paläographie*, 2nd ed. (Trier, 1909), nos. 30 and 31; E. M. Thompson, *An Introduction to Greek and Latin Palaeography* (Oxford, 1912), pp. 374 and 385.

and the problem of distinguishing Irish from Anglo-Saxon manuscripts of the seventh and eighth centuries was still acute. It was Ludwig Traube who opened the way towards a solution by adopting the word 'insular' to cover both Irish and Anglo-Saxon script and to distinguish them from the contemporary scripts of the continent; his discovery allowed him to diagnose for the first time the confusions of Mabillon and of O'Conor.[1] Between 1910 and 1915 W. M. Lindsay inaugurated the modern period of early insular palaeography,[2] which has culminated in Lowe's descriptions of the insular manuscripts in *CLA*.

It was the archaeologists who began to lower the date of K. Margaret Stokes,[3] linking it with the Book of Armagh[4] and the Gospels of Macdurnan,[5] placed it in the ninth century. Bernhard Salin put Durrow, Lindisfarne and K in their right order, at long intervals: Durrow *c.* 600, Lindisfarne *c.* 700, K *c.* 800.[6] E. H. Zimmermann derived all three manuscripts from an earlier generation of Irish manuscripts, none of which had survived: Durrow was Irish, *c.* 700; English Lindisfarne and Irish K both belonged to the beginning of the eighth century. Furthermore, whereas Durrow had no descendants in Ireland, K was apparently ancestral to all Irish manuscripts of later date.[7] Having demoted both Durrow and K from their traditional role as the sixth-century patriarchs of Irish illumination, Zimmermann filled the gap with an imaginary generation of seventh-century Irish manuscripts: a precarious foundation for the artistic priority of Ireland which was soon to be undermined from several directions.

A. W. Clapham, in 1934, was the first to suggest that the main components of the Hiberno-Saxon style were not of Irish origin, and had been put together – perhaps by the Irish – in Northumbria, whence the style spread to Ireland itself and to the continent.[8] Lindisfarne, which he dated *c.* 710, was the best representative of the style, and Durrow – a little later and probably from Iona – marked a stage in the transmission of the style to Ireland. In 1935 F. C. Burkitt[9] looked at the texts of those three manuscripts, and of the Echternach Gospels.[10] Following Wordsworth and White and Clapham, he recalled that Lindisfarne (Y) had a so-called 'Italo-Northum-

1 *Vorlesungen und Abhandlungen* III (Munich, 1920), 95–100 (from 'Perrona Scottorum', first published in 1900).
2 *Early Irish Minuscule Script* (Oxford, 1910); *Early Welsh Script* (Oxford, 1912); *Notae Latinae* (Cambridge, 1915).
3 George Petrie, *Christian Inscriptions in the Irish Language*, ed. Margaret Stokes II (Dublin, 1878), 168–9.   4 *CLA* II, no. 270.
5 E. G. Millar, in *Bulletin de la Société française de Reproductions de Manuscrits à Peinture*, 8e année (1924), 7–15; Françoise Henry, *Irish Art During the Viking Invasions* (London, 1967), pp. 102–5.
6 *Die altgermanische Thierornamentik* (Stockholm, 1904), pp. 341–7.
7 *Vorkarolingische Miniaturen* (Berlin, 1916), pp. 21–37 and 231–310.
8 'Notes on the Origins of Hiberno-Saxon Art', *Antiquity* 8 (1934), 43–57.
9 'Kells, Durrow and Lindisfarne', *Antiquity* 9 (1935), 33–7.   10 *CLA* V, no. 578.

brian' text that was 'almost identical' with the text of the gospels in the Codex Amiatinus (A),[1] and that while the marginal readings and spellings of Echternach were 'Irish', the first hand of the manuscript generally supported A and Y. Durrow, he said, had many readings in common with AY and presented 'a text half-way between the pure Northumbrian of AY and the much more characteristically Irish form of Q [i.e. Kells]'. Burkitt concluded that Durrow took its non-Irish readings from the same south Italian source as AY and was therefore to be associated with Northumbria. Even if Durrow and Echternach are not directly connected with A and Y themselves, their texts still have more in common with that of a type of Italian gospel book known in England in the seventh and eighth centuries[2] than with the text normally found in manuscripts ascribed to Ireland. Of Kells (Q), Burkitt claimed that although it was predominantly Irish in text, it showed traces of Northumbrian influence best explained on the assumption that it was written at Iona. In 1932[3] Burkitt had already said of Durrow that 'the presence of this almost pure Northumbrian text with its Celtic decoration in Ireland raises a problem that calls for some sort of answer'; and this is the reference that Lowe took up in 1935, when he said this of Durrow: 'I confess that the Book of Durrow has always seemed to me a book apart among the group of early Irish manuscripts now at Dublin, and gradually the suspicion woke in me that perhaps English workmanship accounted for the orderliness of its script and the balance and sobriety of its ornamentation.'[4] Supported by Burkitt's view of the text, and by Zimmermann's observation that while it had no descendants in Ireland, it influenced the English Echternach Gospels, Lowe concluded that Durrow was 'written in Northumbria by a hand trained in the Irish manner'. He dated it 'saec. VIII' and explained the colophon, in which it is attributed to St Columba, as copied from the exemplar. For K, on the other hand, Lowe still accepted an Irish origin, probably at Kells itself, and a date of 'saec. VIII–IX'.[5]

It is on Clapham, Burkitt and Lowe that Masai's radical attack on the logic of the traditional 'Irish' view of Hiberno-Saxon illumination is based. First, he argues on historical grounds that Anglo-Saxon England was a more likely home for Hiberno-Saxon illumination than Ireland. Then he looks at the colophons in early Irish manuscripts and shows that the one which ascribes Durrow to St Columba has been too badly tampered with to be used as evidence of Irish origin; and he dismisses as illusion the view that Ireland had a long tradition of illumination before the eighth century. Like Clapham, he judges the repertoire of 'Irish' ornament to be more at home in England than in Ireland, adding that England was the true source of most so-called

---

[1] *CLA* III, no. 299.
[2] *CLA* II, nos. 126 (X) and 230 (O).
[3] '"As we have forgiven" (Matthew VI. 12)', *JTS* 33 (1931–2), 253–5.
[4] *CLA* II, xiv–xv.
[5] *CLA* II, nos. 273 and 274.

'Irish' influence on the continent. Accepting Lowe's attribution of Durrow to Northumbria, he agrees that since it is clearly at the beginning of the series of Hiberno-Saxon gospel books, and since the design of their monogram pages shows that the whole series has a common origin, the whole series must derive from Northumbria.[1] Within the series, Masai sees one major difference – between manuscripts in which the decoration is extremely precise or, as he puts it, 'metallic', and manuscripts in which the drawing is weak and imitative. Durrow, Lindisfarne and K are in the 'metallic' group; Macregol's Gospels is in the other.[2] He adds that Lindisfarne and K are very alike in script;[3] that Burkitt detected a Northumbrian element in K's text; and that T. K. Abbott found the prefaces in Durrow and those in K to be so close to each other that it seemed as if the writer of K had actually handled Durrow.[4] For Zimmermann, only the artist of Lindisfarne understood the palette of K; for Masai, only the painters of K understood the palette of Lindisfarne.[5] Iona, by the late eighth century, might perhaps have been exposed enough to Northumbrian influence to produce K; but his final conclusion is that Durrow, Echternach, Lindisfarne, the Durham Gospels (Durham, Cathedral Library, A. II. 17, part 1)[6] and K were all made in the scriptorium of Lindisfarne. He dates K at the end of the eighth century.[7]

Two of Masai's conclusions provoked especially sharp reactions: that insular majuscule was invented by the Anglo-Saxons; and that book decoration was unknown to the Irish before Durrow, which he dated *c.* 700.[8] Papers by Dr Carl Nordenfalk and by Mlle Henry soon put matters straight again for the seventh century;[9] but Masai's ascription of K to Lindisfarne has been cold-shouldered rather than refuted.[10] I hope to persuade you that detailed palaeographical comparisons – which Masai could not make between 1939 and 1944 – indicate a close relationship between K and a group of four manuscripts which Masai also ascribed to Lindisfarne: the Book of Durrow, and in particular the Lindisfarne, Echternach and Durham Gospels, which I shall call Durrow, L, E and D from now on.

[1] *Essai*, pp. 29–110.   [2] *Ibid.* pp. 120–3.
[3] *Ibid.* p. 210; Steffens, *Lateinische Paläographie*, no. 31.
[4] *Evangeliorum Versio Antehieronymiana* (Dublin, 1884) I, xxvi, 'fully endorsed' by Luce, *Codex Durmachensis*, pp. 32–7. Cf. Bieler, *ibid.* pp. 94–5.
[5] *Vorkarolingische Miniaturen*, p. 35; *Essai*, p. 124.
[6] *CLA* II, no. 149.   [7] *Essai*, pp. 126–7 and 128–34.
[8] *Essai*, pp. 137–9 and 101–10.
[9] Carl Nordenfalk, 'Before the Book of Durrow', *Acta Archaeologica* 18 (1947), 141–74; Françoise Henry, 'Les Débuts de la Miniature irlandaise', *Gazette des Beaux-Arts* 6th ser. 37 (1950), 5–34. Reviews by Françoise Henry and S. P. Ó Riordáin in *Studies* 37 (1948), 267–82; by Ludwig Bieler in *Speculum* 23 (1948), 495–502; and by Meyer Schapiro in *Gazette des Beaux-Arts* 6th ser. 37 (1950), 134–8.
[10] Although he ascribes K to Iona, Mr Walter Oakeshott, *The Sequence of English Medieval Art* (London, 1950), pp. 32–41, is fully in agreement with Masai when he concludes (p. 37) that 'in matters of art ... the main stream flows ... from Monkwearmouth and Lindisfarne to Kells'.

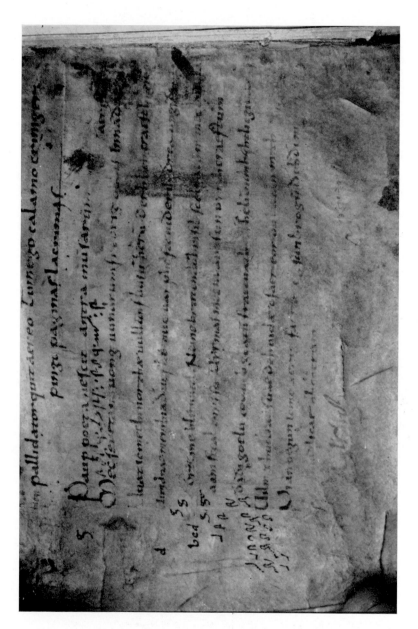

I   Leiden, Bibl. der Rijksuniversiteit, Vossius Lat. 4° 106, 25v, lower half (see pp. 211–12)

israhel accus secundum carnem leuita con
uersus a dño docmxpi euangelium inicalia con
scribsit ostendens illoquod accesserisuo de
bera xpo uiam inicium principiiuoce pro
phetice exclamationis · instruens ordinem
leuitace lectiones ostendit utpredicans pre
disignatum iohannem filium zachariae inuo
cen angeli euangelizantis emissum nonsolumuer
bum caro factam secorpus dni peruenibu
diuinae uocis animatum inicio euangelicae
Predicationis ostendens utquihaec legens
sciat cuiustatum carnis introno dm conuen
eras habitaculum caro debena agnoscere
atq illse uerbum uocas quao inconsonatab
perfecto erat inuentina deniq epenfeca euan
gelii opus inicians etalibapasmo dni predica
us dni inchoans pollabonabit praedicatem
carnis quam inpnionib · uicerat dicere sed
totus exprimicus expossicionem deserta ieiuni
numeri temptacionem diaboli concnecacioue
bestiarum pnociulit angelorum utdisitiueps
nos adintellegendum singula hebreu compnigisn Nec

IIa   D, 39v

ois putez:
R̄ spihs
ae iterio·

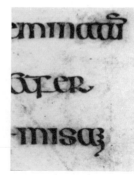

emmatiu
ater
misat

b   D, 8r, detail

c   K, 10r, detail

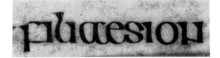

...cationis corruptabile· principium ingeniss
Incorruptibilis finis per unigenitum inapo
...ipsi redderetur dicentae xpo ego sum alpha
...ud hic est iohannis quisciens superuenis
se diem recessus sui cognouerat discipulis
suis inpresso permultae signorum experimē
ta comprobauit uiā discendens inde possum
sepulturae suae locum parauit oratione
copositus etiam patres suos tam extraneus
a dolore mortis quam a corruptione carnis
alienus inueniatur. qui etsi post omnes euā
gelium scribsi sed tamen dispositione
cationis ordinati post matheum ponitur
quoniam in dno quaecaeno issimus sunt non
uelut extrema. Subicetur numero sed
plenitudinis opere perfectus sunt et hoc
uirgini debebatur quorum tamen uel scri
torum in tempore dispositio uel librorum
ordin eratio·bus persingula a nobis non

19

IIIa   K, 19r

b   L, 95r, detail

c   K, 90v, detail

filium ioseph anaxanath acciac eruachahel
ana xanath potat aliquro bonisse dicit ei
philippus uau douoe uioe ihs nachanahel
uemcuem adse acciac deeo eccuniska heuia
inquodolus nouec dicit ei nachanael uiroe
menosa R sp ihs acciac ei prius quantae phi
lippus uocane cumessa subpiau uidiae R sp
ei nachahel auit rabbi cuesphusoicuesrex
isrl R sp ihs acciac ei quiachcrabi uidiae sub
pcu crcois maius hus uidebis Goiac eis ameuacmu
dicouebis uidebras aulum apercum Gauigelos
di ascacuoeuas acdisccuoeuas supraphiumhoin

ie uxca nupaae faecaeiuac nuchau
naungahiocae Geracc mauemhu ibi
uocauus ec ibi cuhs acdisapuli eius achuipuus
Gdepaeuac uiuo diac maucmhu adeum uiuum
nouhabenc Gdicic ei ihs quidmihi eebiea mu
lien nouroui ueuc honamca Dicic macen euq
miniscris quodocumq dixerit uobis faace
Geauc hr ibi lapidac hrdiae sexpossicae
secudum purupcacaoriem nudaeonum capien

of

IVa   D, 4v

b D, 7r, detail   c K, 93v, detail

oiat eis amen amen dico uobis · Uidebitis cae
lum apertum Et angelos di ascendentes
Et discendentes supra filium hominis · · ·
Die tertia nuptiae factae sunt
In channan galileae · Et erat mater
ihu ibi uocatus est autem ibi ihs Et disci
puli eius conuiptas Et deficiente uino dicit
mater ihu ad eum uinum non habent · Et
dicit ei ihs quid mihi Et tibi est mulier non
dum uenit hora mea · Dicit mater eius
ministris quodcumque dixerit uobis facite
Erant autem ibi lapideae hydriae sex
possitae secundum purificationem iude
orum capientes singulae metretas binas
uel ternas · Dicit eis ihs inplete hydrias a
quam Et impleuerunt eas usque ad sum
mum Et dicit eis ihs aurite nunc Et ferte
architriclino Et tulerunt · Ut autem

Va K, 295v

b D, 14v, detail

c K, 338r, detail

VI*a*   L, 135vb14

b   L, 236ra7

c   D, 211r16

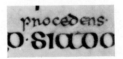

d   D, 75v8

e   D, 67r, lower margin

VII*a* Reconstructed sunken hut under construction at the Weald and Downland Open Air Museum, Singleton, Sussex. The reconstruction is based mainly on the middle Saxon hut excavated at Old Erringham, Sussex. *Photo: J. R. Armstrong*

VII*b* Buildings of an eighth-century mill at Tamworth, Staffordshire. The timbers have been preserved by permanently waterlogged conditions and show various constructional details normally only guessed at in excavated buildings. *Photo: P. A. Rahtz*

VIII   Chalton, Hampshire

a   Soil marks of superimposed early Saxon houses showing in the surface of the natural chalk before excavation.   *Photo: T. Hurst*

b   Post-holes and trenches of several partly superimposed early Saxon huts and houses after excavation.   *Photo: D. Leigh*

II

Since *CLA* contains most of what is known about early insular manuscripts, we may begin our detailed examination of Durrow, L, E, D and K by quoting Lowe's evaluations of them.

Durrow (*CLA* II, no. 273). 'Script is an expert calligraphic majuscule. . . Written in Northumbria by a hand trained in the Irish manner, and copied from an exemplar in the hand of St Columba . . . to judge by the two sub-scriptions on fol. 12v: "Rogo beatitudinem tuam. . ." . . . The Gospel text is of the Northumbrian family (A and Y). Palaeographically there is kinship with the Codex Epternacensis. . .' In 1935 Lowe's date was 'saec. VIII'; but in 1953 (*CLA* VI, x) he changed it to 'saec. VII²'.

Lindisfarne (*CLA* II, no. 187). 'Script is a handsome and graceful Anglo-Saxon majuscule – one of the noblest examples of Insular calligraphy by an English pen, despite inequalities in execution. . . Origin Lindisfarne; according to the tenth-century colophon . . . written by Eadfrith, Bishop of Lindisfarne (698–721). . . Palaeographically this tradition is perfectly accept-able. Text agrees closely with Amiatinus, even in errors. Lists of Neapolitan feasts are found before Mark and Luke. . .' Lowe's date in the description is 'saec. VIII in.'; at p. xiii he gives 'the end of the seventh century' 'if this engrossing work was accomplished, as may be presumed, before [Eadfrith] became Bishop'; in *CLA* II, 2nd ed., he gives 'saec. VII–VIII'.

Echternach (*CLA* V, no. 578). 'Script is a superb example of Anglo-Saxon calligraphy. Jerome's Prologue (fol. 1) is in stately majuscule. . . Written in Northumbria, or possibly in a Continental centre with close Anglo-Saxon connexions such as Echternach, where the volume was preserved for centuries. The subscription at the end of fol. 222v reads: "+ proemendaui ut potui. . ."' Date: 'saec. VII–VIII'. At *CLA* II, x, E and L alike are ascribed to Lindisfarne.

Durham (*CLA* II, no. 149). 'Script is a bold and very expert insular majuscule. . . Written probably in Northumbria, in a great centre of calli-graphy in the direct line of Irish tradition, or else in Ireland itself. Its text is not Northumbrian but Irish. Was at Chester-le-Street in the tenth century.' Date: 'saec. VII–VIII'; in *CLA* II, 2nd ed., 'saec. VIII'.

Kells (*CLA* II, no. 274). 'Script is a bold, very expert Irish majuscule – a veritable masterpiece of calligraphy. . . Written in a great Irish centre, probably in the monastery of Cenannus or Kells in co. Meath: was at Kells throughout the middle ages. . .' Date: 'saec. VIII–IX'.

These evaluations must be considered in the light of Lowe's remarks on insular palaeography in *CLA* II, x–xvi, and of the seven methodological

'Assumptions' that he set out in *CLA* iv, xii-xiv. He ascribed Durrow to Northumbria because of its supposedly Northumbrian text, its influence on Echternach and 'the orderliness of its script and the balance and sobriety of its ornamentation' – to be accounted for by 'English workmanship'.[1] Where L and E are concerned, Lowe emphasizes their textual and liturgical links with Naples and, through the Codex Amiatinus and the Burchard Gospels,[2] with Wearmouth–Jarrow. In each case he gives weight to the medieval provenance, in accordance with the first of his Assumptions. With St Willibrord's Martyrology, his Kalendar and the Moore Bede,[3] L and E are for Lowe at once 'examples of authentic English performance' and 'criteria for Northumbrian calligraphy'. Of D, as of Cambridge, Corpus Christi College 197,[4] he says in the preface that it exemplifies that strength of Irish influence in England which makes it hard to say whether an insular manuscript of the late seventh or early eighth century was written by an English or an Irish scribe, 'since at that period the English were still imitators, following closely the methods of their Irish masters'. In attributing D to Northumbria in preference to Ireland, Lowe gave more weight to provenance than to text. In the preface, he goes on to say that 'with the departure of the Irish from Northumbria their influence wanes; the English pupils begin to find their feet and English genius for sobriety and orderliness asserts itself. It now becomes possible to distinguish an English from an Irish manuscript.' The Irish scribe's 'whim and fancy' is contrasted with the English scribe's 'balance' and 'discipline'. 'One need only place side by side the Book of Kells and the Lindisfarne Gospels, or the Book of Mulling[5] and the Moore Bede, to see the force of these observations.' The contrast extends to the quality of the membrane and the way it was made up into quires, to the regularity of the ruling, to the use of critical marks and abbreviations. 'It is by paying attention to the temperamental differences between the two nations, which existed even then', that we can ascribe the St Paul at Trinity College Cambridge[6] to an Irish hand and Durrow to an English one.[7]

In ascribing K to Ireland, Lowe was doubtless moved by its Irish provenance and perhaps also by the 'Irishness' of its text. That K and L really exemplify the contrast drawn by Lowe between the Irish and the English temperaments may be doubted. First, the standard of book production in K is far higher than the dismal level cited as symptomatic of Irish origin, and although the handwriting is often exuberant, it is never weak or careless: indeed, 'veritable masterpiece of calligraphy' is high praise, from Lowe, for

[1] See above, p. 223.   [2] *CLA* iii, no. 299 and ix, no. 1423a and b.
[3] *CLA* v, nos. 605 and 606a and ii, no. 139.   [4] *CLA* ii, no. 125.
[5] *CLA* ii, no. 276.   [6] *CLA* ii, no. 133.
[7] 'The pure milk of Irish calligraphy' was to be found in *CLA* ii, no. 266; iii, no. 311, vii, no. 998 and ii, nos. 275 and 276; and ii, nos. 286 and 270.

any Irish manuscript. Secondly, to use one of Masai's criteria, the decoration of K is crisply 'metallic' throughout. Thirdly, the most conspicuous difference between K and L is in the lay-out and decoration of the text-pages: K is in one column, with lavish use of decorative initials; L is in two columns, with punctuation *per cola et commata*, and the decoration of the initials is severely restricted. L is laid out like an Italian gospel book of the sixth century, and K is laid out like Durrow; but then Lowe himself considered that Durrow was Northumbrian. L is Italianate and K is not;[1] but K is well up to the technical standards of Lowe's 'criteria for Northumbrian calligraphy'. Compared to the astonishingly close imitations of Italian gospel books made at Wearmouth–Jarrow in and soon after Ceolfrith's time (689–716) – books in which uncials replaced insular script and even the simplest insular decoration was studiously avoided – even L could be said, and often has been said, to look extremely 'Irish' by virtue of its script and decoration. In dealing with K in 1935 Lowe apparently bowed to tradition at the expense of his own criteria; and if he had not been so sure that K was Irish, he would perhaps not have seen such strong Irish influence in the two Northumbrian books that are most like it, namely D and CCCC 197.

In the course of our work on L, published in 1960, Dr Rupert Bruce-Mitford and I concluded that the man – we named him the 'Durham–Echternach Calligrapher' – who wrote, decorated and illustrated E also wrote, decorated and illustrated D.[2] It was their various scripts that first suggested to me that the two books were by the same hand, and in due course Bruce-Mitford came to the same conclusion about their decoration. I am as sure as ever I was that we were right. Like L and K, E and D differ in many ways. E is Italianate – two columns, punctuation *per cola et commata*, like L; D is not – one column, like Durrow and K. E is written in two kinds of rapid but expert minuscule, excepting the majuscule first page; D is all in majuscule, excepting the last lines of some pages. But the decorative minuscule, the majuscule, the display script, the decorative drawing and the figure drawing in E and D show a degree of likeness better explained by identity of hand than by mere community of training.

The majuscule of E and D is very close in style and quality to L's, and the three books share a notable group of scribal tricks designed to improve the justification at line-ends – among them a summary, stemless version of *t* in monograms, also found in Durrow but not in K.[3] The traces of uncial or half-uncial influence detectable in these devices confirm one's suspicion that the greater stateliness of the majuscule, by comparison with that of Durrow

---

[1] For Italian and insular gospel books, Patrick McGurk, *Latin Gospel Books from A.D. 400 to A.D. 800*, Publications de Scriptorium 5 (Brussels and Antwerp, 1961), 7–15.

[2] *Cod. Lind.*, pp. 100–2 and 246–50.

[3] *CLA* II, nos. 149 and 187; *Cod. Lind.*, pp. 70 and 98, pl. 3 (E, 1r).

and the earliest Irish manuscripts, is due to the influence of Italian models written in uncials and half-uncials.[1] Temperament apart, English scribes of about 700 had better models to follow than had Irish scribes of the same period. Travellers like Benedict Biscop, Ceolfrith and Wilfrid had endowed Northumbrian libraries with a rich stock of Italian exemplars; Benedict, for one, had spent long enough abroad to learn whatever the scriptoria of Gaul and Italy had to teach; and in John the Archchanter of St Peter's a Roman scholar came to Wearmouth–Jarrow as visiting professor.[2] In spite of the existence of Bobbio, Iona and the Irish monasteries apparently did not enjoy the sustained personal contact, as between pupils and masters, that linked the English church of the late seventh century and the early eighth to Italy and in particular to Rome.[3]

In the course of his work on the textual history of the gospels in early Northumbria, Mr C. D. Verey has recognized – for reasons which he kindly sets out in an appendix, below, pp. 243–5 – that the chief corrector of D also made a few corrections in L. He was evidently a contemporary of Eadfrith and of the Durham–Echternach Calligrapher; and in accordance with the fourth of Lowe's seven Assumptions,[4] we may reasonably invoke his contribution to D as evidence that D was written at Lindisfarne, where we know that L was written. Verey's important discovery confirms what Bruce-Mitford and I believed on more general grounds: that within a few years of 698, when the elevation of St Cuthbert called forth a major artistic effort at Lindisfarne, the scriptorium there produced L, E and D.[5]

A word about the dates of L, E and D. We have seen that Lowe, in effect, dated all three of them 'saec. VII–VIII'. Bruce-Mitford and I found no difficulty in staying within those limits: we put L *c.* 696–8 because of its close connections with objects made to celebrate the elevation of 698; we put E *c.* 690–700, since text and lay-out associate it with L, but the decoration seems to be more primitive; we put D *c.* 710, since some of the ornament is more evolved than L's, although script and especially lay-out look more primitive.[6] For L, E and D as a group I now prefer *c.* 698. The primitive air of E may be no more than an aspect of the deliberate simplicity of decoration which, like the uniquely rapid script of the main text, persuaded me that this strange and unfinished book was executed with remarkable speed; and if it was intended as a foundation gift for Willibrord's new monastery at Echternach, it cannot be earlier than 697 and is unlikely to be later than 706. E influenced some of the earliest products of the Echternach scriptorium.[7] If certain decorative motifs in D are more advanced than any in L, the

---

[1] *Cod. Lind.*, p. 94.   [2] Lowe, *English Uncial*, pp. 5–13.   [3] See below, p. 245, n.1.
[4] *CLA* IV, xiii.   [5] *Cod. Lind.*, pp. 5–16, 104–6, 246–50 and 288–9.
[6] *Cod. Lind.*, pp. xxiii–xxiv, 11–16, 102–6, 245–9 and 256.
[7] *Cod. Lind.*, pp. 96–7, 103–4 and 283.

unframed design of its one surviving monogram page (2r) seems to stand about half-way between the design of the first, unframed, monogram page in L and that of the other five, which are framed.[1] Further, we can now see that D is linked to L by the hand of Verey's corrector.

In 1960 I noted some 'Northumbrian symptoms' in K which persuaded me that 'Kells, wherever it may have been written, owes even more to the work of the Durham–Echternach Calligrapher and Eadfrith than they themselves owed to early Irish manuscripts such as the Cathach of St Columba and the Milan Orosius'.[2] I ought to have mentioned Durrow in the same breath as L, E and D, since it has enough connections with them – whether textual, palaeographical or archaeological – to rouse a strong suspicion that it too is a Lindisfarne manuscript.[3] What are these Northumbrian symptoms in K?

The striking likeness between the prefaces in Durrow and those in K has been mentioned;[4] and although the prefaces in E are better arranged, some of them are textually very close to Durrow and to K.[5] Of the fragmentary set of canon tables in BM Royal 7 C. xii, Dr Patrick McGurk has shown that its arcades stopped at the same point as the arcades in K,[6] and Bruce-Mitford that there are artistic links between the design of the remaining arcade (it survives only as an offset) and the canon tables in both L and K.[7] The Royal fragment is apparently Northumbrian, seventh- to eighth-century.[8] McGurk rightly concluded that K's canon tables derive from an exemplar which was available in Northumbria about 700. The gospel text in K shares 'some peculiar readings' with the text of D;[9] and Verey has established that D's text is not 'Irish', but basically akin to the OX family of Italian texts current in southern England in our period.[10]

The insular membrane used in Durrow, D and K is of similar quality; and in all three manuscripts quires of ten leaves are the rule.[11] E too has quires of ten, but the membrane is not prepared in the insular way. L has

---

[1] *Cod. Lind.*, pp. 104–6 and 246–50; but note Bruce-Mitford's opinion on D, 2r (p. 249).
[2] *Cod. Lind.*, pp. 105, n. 3 and 283. The Orosius is *CLA* iii, no. 328.
[3] Cf. Bruce-Mitford, *Cod. Lind.*, pp. 255–7.
[4] See above, p. 224; McGurk, *Latin Gospel Books*, nos. 86 and 87.   [5] *Cod. Lind.*, pp. 95–6.
[6] Patrick McGurk, 'Two Notes on the Book of Kells and its Relation to Other Insular Gospel Books', *Scriptorium* 9 (1955), 105–6.
[7] *Cod. Lind.*, pp. 190–2.   [8] *CLA* ii, 2nd ed., no. 217.
[9] R. A. B. Mynors, *Durham Cathedral Manuscripts* (Oxford, 1939), p. 16. Verey confirms this.
[10] C. D. Verey, 'A collation of the Gospel texts contained in Durham Cathedral MSS. A.II.10, A.II.16 and A.II.17 and some provisional conclusions therefrom regarding the type of Vulgate text employed in Northumbria in the eighth century together with a full description of each MS.' (unpubl. M.A. thesis, Durham, 1969), pp. 276–80.
[11] Roger Powell, 'The Book of Kells, the Book of Durrow: Comments on the Vellum, the Make-Up and other Aspects', *Scriptorium* 10 (1956), 3–21. For D, Mynors, *Durham Cathedral Manuscripts*, p. 16 and McGurk, *Latin Gospel Books*, p. 29. For the few non-insular leaves in D, which resemble the membrane of E, *Cod. Lind.*, p. 102.

quires of eight, and the insular membrane is of better quality. Since the Moore Bede is also in tens, the quiring of K is not an argument against Northumbrian origin. The odd man out is Eadfrith, who in L adopted the Italian fashion of eights, which was the rule at Wearmouth–Jarrow from the time of the Codex Amiatinus onwards, and became the general rule in England in the course of the eighth century.

Bruce-Mitford's analysis of the meticulously accurate geometrical construction that underlies the ornament of L[1] makes it hard to believe that the equally precise and even more intricate 'metallic' ornament of K derives from an independent tradition; and if Eadfrith invented the 'panelled' style of decoration[2] (not found in Durrow, E or D), it is in K, even more than in the undoubtedly Northumbrian *Cassiodorus in Psalmos* at Durham,[3] that the style reaches its apogee. To Zimmermann's and Masai's observations on the close relationship between the pigments in L and in K we can now add a scientific appreciation by Dr Heinz Roosen-Runge and Dr A. E. A. Werner.[4] They find that 'the range and nature of the pigments [in K] are almost identical with those [in L]', but that the two books differ in their use of those pigments. L, like Durrow, uses a 'single layer technique', while K generally uses 'a rather elaborate and sophisticated double layer technique in which one layer of paint is superimposed on another'. The upper layer has often flaked off, and 'there are other technical defects in [K] which indicate that the illuminator was not as skilled in the preparations of his colours as the illuminator of [L]'. In taste and technique alike the painter(s) of K apparently sought to outdo whatever had been achieved in L; but in spite of some technical and artistic accidents, the bond between stylistic ends and technical means is as intimate in K as in L. K is no mere imitation of L; it is an extension of the tradition which L established. There was undoubtedly some sort of personal contact between the Lindisfarne scriptorium and the scriptorium that made K.

In lay-out, scripts, scribal ornament and minor initials, it is D, and to a lesser extent E, that furnish the closest parallels to K. D and K arrange their texts in one column on a large page: D has twenty-two lines and a written space of about 257 × 195 mm (see pls. IIa and IVa); as a rule, K has seventeen lines in the gospels (see pl. Va) and nineteen in the prefaces (see pl. IIIa), and a written space of 250 × 170 mm. K distinguishes prefaces from gospels by something more than the number of lines to a page. The gospels are mostly in a large, somewhat exuberant majuscule, but 29v–31v and 292v–339v are in a plainer, slightly smaller majuscule (see pl. Va). Plainer

---

[1] *Cod. Lind.*, pp. 221–31.   [2] *Cod. Lind.*, pp. 250 and 255.
[3] *CLA* II, no. 152; Mynors, *Durham Cathedral Manuscripts*, pp. 21–2 and pls. 8–10.
[4] *Cod. Lind.*, pp. 273–4; see above, p. 224, n. 5.

and smaller still is the majuscule of the opening pages of the prefaces (8v–20v; see pls. III*a* and II*b*), while the rest of them is in a highly decorative script best described as minuscule (20v–26v) – majuscule **a** is used, but the angle of the pen is slanted, not straight. The same script recurs in the gospels at 127v–129v. L writes prefaces in a compressed majuscule, and E writes them in a small decorative minuscule quite distinct from the minuscule of the gospels.[1] McGurk has shown that to distinguish prefaces by a less imposing script was characteristic of early Italian gospel books;[2] and the uncial manuscripts of Wearmouth-Jarrow use so-called 'capitular' uncial for chapter-lists, the same script or a smaller size of 'text' uncial for prefaces and a larger size of 'text' uncial for the biblical text.[3] In its prefaces, K follows now L and now E, within a general framework of Italian influence. In 1935 Lowe attributed K to 'several scribes', but the obvious differences in script, which are fully comparable to the differences in the handwriting of the Durham–Echternach Calligrapher, occur against a background of impressive consistency in minor details, of which the following, found at line-ends, are a small sample: the many variant forms of **a** designed to save space; the tall, narrow form of uncial **d**; the curled final stroke of **m**; the compressed forms of uncial **r** and of uncial **s**; the flourished final strokes of **a**, **e**, half-uncial **r** and **s**, and **t**; the various vertical, current forms of **m** and **n**; supra-script letters (especially **u**) and subscript letters (especially **i**); the **s**-like stroke used for final **m**; and the **mo** ligature (see pl. II*c*).

In the larger majuscule used by K in the gospels, the thinner strokes usually have elaborate serifs (as at the top of majuscule **a**) and all the thicker strokes tend to be splayed out at the end (see **m**, **n** and **p** for straight strokes and **c** and **s** for curved strokes; pl. III*c*). This imposing script is to be found in L as display script (19r, 27r, 29r, 90r, 95r and 139r; see pl. III*b*) and throughout both L and D as minor initials. K uses it for the gospels in much the same way as the 'display' uncial – used only for the dedication in the Codex Amiatinus (Iv), and for the title page in the fragmentary Utrecht Gospels (101v) – is used for the main text in Durham A. II. 17, part II, another fragmentary gospels from Wearmouth-Jarrow.[4] When like is compared with like – the prefatory majuscule (8v–20r) and some of the text majuscule (292r–339v) in K with the text majuscule in L and D – the kinship between the three manuscripts is apparent (see pls. II*b* and *c* and V).

Again, the constellation of scribal tricks freely practised at line-ends in L, E and D includes some found in Durrow, others found in K, and others

---

[1] *Cod. Lind.*, pp. 73–4 and 96.

[2] *Latin Gospel Books*, pp. 10 and 14–15.

[3] Lowe, *English Uncial*, pls. vii–xiv; D. H. Wright, 'Some Notes on English Uncial', *Traditio* 17 (1961), 441–56, esp. 453–6.

[4] *CLA* III, no. 299; x, no. 1587; and II, no. 150. Lowe, *English Uncial*, pls. viii, xi and xiii.

found in both Durrow and K (see pls. II*b* and *c*).[1] In other single-column gospel books, and notably in the Lichfield, Rawlinson and Macregol manuscripts,[2] they are conspicuously rare. D and K both use a decorative, basically minuscule, script for the last lines of some pages (see pl. II*a*), and many of their decorative letter forms are the same.[3] E uses a modification of this script for its prefaces; and traces of it occur in two lines of the soberly Italianate L.[4] All other examples of the script, including the oldest (Durham, Cathedral Library, A. II. 10, 3v),[5] are apparently Northumbrian. The line of 'broken' script in K (11v) can be matched by odd words written in the same way in L (205r), E (10r) and D (47v).[6] K's display script, when not smothered and transformed by ornament, is very like E's and D's.[7]

In 1935 Lowe noted 'marginal arabesques' (see pl. III*a*) in the following: L, D, K, CCCC 197 and part of Durham A. II. 16.[8] The motif occurs once in E (110v); and in L, D and K it grows steadily more elaborate.[9] Bruce-Mitford's suggestion, based on a rudimentary form found in the Codex Amiatinus (972v), that it is of Italian origin[10] is confirmed by an example in the Codex Valeriani, an early-seventh-century gospels probably from north Italy,[11] which is already more advanced than the one in the Amiatinus. Spiral space-fillers in red are another feature of K that can be traced back to a simpler stage in Northumbrian manuscripts of about 700, and indeed beyond that to Durrow.[12]

The minor initials in the gospels in D and K bear much the same relation to each other as the scripts. In D, as in L, Ammonian sections begin with modestly enlarged initials, filled in one or two colours and modestly decorated with, for example, internal trumpet patterns and/or external spirals.[13] L, with its Late Antique norm of moderation, is the more restrained of the two: it goes no further than that, except in its display script (e.g. 3r, 27r, 95r and 211r) and in the initials to minor prefaces.[14] In D, however, when

---

[1] Bieler, *Codex Durmachensis*, p. 89; Brown, *Cod. Lind.*, pp. 72–3 and 97–101. In K, note supra- and subscript letters, the several forms of **a**, current **m** and **n** written vertically and the ligature of the former with suprascript **u**, ligatures, expanded letters, uncial **m** and the monograms of **u** with uncial **r** and half-uncial **n** and **s**.   [2] *CLA* II, nos. 159, 256 and 231.
[3] K, 12v and 20r; for D, *Cod. Lind.*, pp. 100–1 and pls. 4 and 11.
[4] For E, *Cod. Lind.*, pp. 96–7 and pls. 5 and 12–13; L, 133r and v.
[5] *CLA* II, no. 147.   [6] *Cod. Lind.*, pls. 10 and 12.
[7] E.g. K, 8r–18r *passim* and 188v. For E and D, *Cod. Lind.*, pp. 99–100 and pls. 6–7 and 9–14.
[8] *CLA* II, nos. 125, 148b, 149, 187 and 274. Durham A.II.16, fols. 24–33 and 87–101 is *CLA* II, no. 148b.   [9] *Cod. Lind.*, pp. 99, 218, 260 and 287 and fig. 50.
[10] *Ibid.* pp. 260 and 287; 'The Art of the Codex Amiatinus: Jarrow Lecture 1967', *JBAA* 32 (1969), 21 and fig. 3 (including examples from K).
[11] *CLA* IX, no. 1249; Carl Nordenfalk, *Die spätantiken Zierbuchstaben* (Stockholm, 1970), p. 175 and pl. 49c.
[12] Oakeshott, *Sequence*, pp. 35–6 on spiral space-fillers, and the 'gut' filling in initials, in Durrow, E, D and K. A spiral filler occurs at L, 57v.
[13] *Cod. Lind.*, pp. 77–8.   [14] *Ibid.* pls. 42–3.

the liturgical importance of a passage warrants it, larger and more elaborate
initials are inserted into the gospels (see pl. IV*a*);[1] and McGurk has shown
that in K some of the corresponding passages receive an illustration or a
whole page of decoration.[2] In parts of K every Ammonian section has an
initial on the same scale as the 'liturgical' initials in D;[3] and in these passages
K looks very unlike D. But in the parts of the gospels in K that are more
modestly decorated (29v–31v and 292r–339v), as also in the prefaces (8v–19v),
the contrast is far less striking (see pls. II*a*, III*a*, IV*a* and V*a*). Indeed, the
simplest initials in K are often no more elaborate than D's; and as in L, so
in K the descent in size from initial letter to text script (or to display script)
is usually an abrupt step, not the gradual diminuendo of the oldest Irish
manuscripts, of Durham A. II. 10 and of Durrow. Some of the 'liturgical'
initials in D are no less Irish than anything in K (see pl. IV*a*).[4] The internal
'tassels' so common in K's initials are as old, and as Irish in origin, as the
Cathach; but the differentiation of the motif into the two derivative forms
found in K had already taken place in D (see pls. IV*b* and *c*).[5] Professor
D. H. Wright has shown that the simplest initials in Durrow reveal most
clearly its Irish ancestry.[6] The simplest initials in K reveal not only distant
Irish, but also more recent Northumbrian ancestry. The slightly more elaborate initials in K that bear the heads of birds, animals and men can also be
matched in D, and in the display script etc. of L (see pls. V*b* and *c*).[7] D and K
seem especially close; but designs that are common in D may be rare in K,
and *vice versa*, and K often develops a design further than D. A few examples
must suffice. The ascender of **h**, often ending in a head, bends to left – a
link with some early Irish manuscripts and with Durham A. II. 10: L, 137r;
D, e.g. 14r, 25v, 74r and 92r; and K, 120v. The same **h** contains lozenge-
shaped **O**: D, 92r and K, 90v (**h** is an animal). The same **h** contains **a**, sometimes in a monogram or a ligature: D, 9r and 65r and K, e.g. 121r, 335v and
338r (see pl. V*c*). In the **&** ligature, the head of the **e** and crossbar of **t**
both penetrate the lower loop of **e**: D, 4v, 30r, 38*v, 40r, 54r and 66r; and
K, e.g. 163r–167r *passim* (see pls. IV*a* and V*a*). With serpentine **S** and **I** at
K, 274v, compare D, e.g. 31v and 79v.[8] Where K goes far beyond L and D is

---

[1] D, 4v, 38₂v, 66r, 69r, 70*v, 72r, 72v, 73v and 102v; cf. the initials for prefaces, 39r and 40r.

[2] 'Two Notes', pp. 106–7.

[3] E.g. K, 253v–84v (Luke xvi. 13–xxiii. 56).

[4] D, 4v, 38₂v, 66r, 69r, 70*v, 72v, 73v and 102v. For smaller initials with diminuendo, e.g. D, 17r, 34v, 35v, 52r and 69r. Cf. Nordenfalk, 'Before the Book of Durrow', pp. 156–7.

[5] Multiple tassels occur in the Cathach, 11r and 43r (*ibid.* figs. 8c and 15b); in D, 7r and 28r; and in K, e.g. 93v. Single, enlarged tassels occur in D, 21r and 36r; and in K, e.g. 94r. The single tassels in K have been simplified into triangles.

[6] *Das irische Palimpsestsakramentar im CLM 14429*, ed. Alban Dold and Leo Eizenhöfer, with D. H. Wright, Texte und Arbeiten 53–4 (Beuron, 1964), 37*–38* and pl. viii.

[7] D, 14r, 24v, 38r, 38₄r and 71v; for L, see above, p. 232, n. 14.

[8] Cf. Isabel Henderson, *The Picts* (London, 1967), figs. 26 and 29k.

in constructing initials from the twisted bodies of one or more living creatures (see pl. V*a*).[1]

More could easily be said; but until the facsimile of D projected by Early English Manuscripts in Facsimile has appeared, this will do. I conclude that in lay-out, scripts, scribal ornament and minor initials K descends from L, E and D, and in particular from D. It often goes far beyond them, not only in the more imposing, but also in the simpler aspects of its decoration; but when it does so, it is unique, and no other Hiberno-Saxon manuscript can be invoked to explain it. The palaeographer's Book of Kells may be less spectacular than the archaeologist's Book of Kells, but it is the same book; and in phylogenetics bones come before feathers. When Dr Lowe sent me, in May 1969, a copy of the revisions that he wished to make in the second edition of *CLA* ii, he had changed the date of K from 'saec. viii–ix' to 'saec. viii²' and had proposed the following attribution: 'Written in a great Celtic [*for* Irish] centre, possibly [*for* probably] in the monastery of Kells. . ., or, as some authorities prefer, at Iona before the early ninth century invasions by the Norse'. He later altered his definition of the script from 'Irish' to 'insular' and adopted the following attribution: 'The origin of this magnificent MS. is still in dispute. Professor T. J. Brown, an expert in this field, writes: "Written in a great Insular centre, as yet unidentified, but subject to Northumbrian influence, in script and decoration alike. The possibilities include Northumbria itself, Eastern Scotland, and the Columban community at Iona, for which a new headquarters was constructed at Kells in A.D. 807–814. In view of the apparent date of the manuscript, Kells itself seems improbable on historical grounds."' Kells, co. Meath, was apparently negligible as an ecclesiastical centre before it was taken over by Iona.[2] Neither Lowe nor I wished to exclude the possibility that 'the great insular centre' could have been elsewhere in Ireland.

If *c.* 698 is the right date for L, E and D as a group,[3] then 'saec. viii²' seems to me quite late enough for K on purely palaeographical grounds. Even the elaborate majuscule of K was already to hand in L and D, in minor initials and display script (see pls. III*b* and *c*). In decoration, the gap between the Lindisfarne trio and K is evidently greater; but K still looks like the child of an earlier, more meticulous, less eclectic age than manuscripts like the Stockholm Codex Aureus, the Leningrad Gospels or the Barberini Gospels, which belong in the second half of the eighth century.[4] In relation to Durrow, L, E and D, a date of 'saec. viii med.' strikes me as possible for K on any grounds; but archaeological reasons for dating it later may well be discovered

[1] E.g. Meyer, *Codex Cenannensis*, pl. vi.
[2] *The Life of St Columba by Adamnan*, ed. William Reeves (Dublin, 1857), pp. 278 and 388; Aubrey Gwynn and R. N. Hadcock, *Medieval Religious Houses: Ireland* (London, 1970), pp. 82 and 388.
[3] See above, p. 228.   [4] *CLA* xi, nos. 1642 and 1605 and i, no. 63.

in the future. A. M. Friend's belief that the canon tables and portraits in K derive from a manuscript made in Charlemagne's Palace School about 800 has been discredited by Albert Boeckler;[1] and his further belief that the canon tables were left unfinished when the Iona community moved to Kells has been undermined by what McGurk and Bruce-Mitford have noticed about the unfinished tables in Royal 7 C. xii.[2] The second set of tables in the Maaseik Gospels suggests that the idea of 'beast canons' was known in Northumbrian circles on the continent, if not in Northumbria itself, in the first half of the eighth century.[3] Of great importance both for the date and for the origin of K are two comparisons drawn by Professor Meyer Schapiro.[4] Some of the foliate ornament in K is very like the foliate ornament in the Leningrad Bede, a Wearmouth–Jarrow manuscript written in 746 or soon afterwards, and in the Leningrad Gospels, a manuscript of the second half of the eighth century which is – *pace* Lowe – Northumbrian.[5] The 'diagonal banding' used to fill initials in K (see pl. IIIa) is used both as filling and as background to initials in the Leningrad Bede and its slightly later offspring, BM Cotton Tiberius A. xiv.[6] K, in fact, had links not only with Lindisfarne but with Wearmouth–Jarrow. Schapiro puts K after the Leningrad Bede, since it contains more elaborate versions of the foliate patterns and of the banding; but while K is *codex ad pompam descriptus*,[7] the two Bedes are normal library books, and the discrepancy may be due less to a difference in date than to a difference in intention.[8]

III

To accept a Northumbrian ancestry for K on palaeographical grounds is to accept that the search for its home must start from Lindisfarne and run from east to west. How does this palaeographical conclusion fit into the historical and archaeological context of Hiberno-Saxon culture between about 700 and about 850? Three cases in our period counsel caution. The Codex Amiatinus, made at Wearmouth–Jarrow after 689, is such an excellent imitation of an Italian book that it is only recently that a majority of palaeographers have accepted the correct view, as argued by Lowe, that it was

---

[1] A. M. Friend, 'The Canon Tables of the Book of Kells', *Medieval Studies in Memory of A. Kingsley Porter*, ed. W. R. W. Koehler (Cambridge, Mass., 1939) II, 611–66. Albert Boeckler, 'Die Evangelistenbilder der Adagruppe', *Münchener Jahrbuch der bildenden Kunst* 3rd ser. 3–4 (1952–3), 121–44; 'Die Kanonbogen der Adagruppe und ihre Vorlagen', *ibid.* 5 (1954), 7–22.

[2] See above, p. 229.

[3] *CLA* x, nos. 1558 and 1559; Bruce-Mitford, *Cod. Lind.*, pp. 193–4.

[4] 'The Decoration of the Leningrad Manuscript of Bede', *Scriptorium* 12 (1958), 191–207.

[5] *CLA* xi, nos. 1621 and 1605.

[6] *CLA* S., no. 1703; R. A. B. Mynors in *Bede's Ecclesiastical History of the English People*, ed. Bertram Colgrave and Mynors (Oxford, 1969), pp. xliv and xlvi–xlvii.

[7] A term used of other books by Mabillon, *De Re Diplomatica*, p. 46.   [8] See below, p. 245, n.2.

written by English and not Italian scribes.[1] Some manuscripts written at
Salzburg under Bishop Arno after 785 are practically indistinguishable from
manuscripts written at St Amand, of which Arno had been abbot since 782:
he transplanted scribes from his old to his new seat.[2] Æthelwulf tells us that
in his monastery, a daughter of Lindisfarne, a priest called Ultan – *Scottorum
gente*: a Scot either from Ireland itself or from Scottish Dál Riada – wrote and
decorated books better than any *scriptor modernus*.[3] Did Ultan come to
Northumbria as master or as pupil? The general tenor of Æthelwulf's
account of him suggests the former. The scribe of K may have been a
brilliant mimic, who had never set foot in Northumbria or encountered a
Northumbrian teacher; but my conviction is that he was properly, indeed
lovingly, trained by a master or masters who were working in, or who had
once worked in, the Lindisfarne scriptorium. If he was Northumbrian by
birth, he may have stayed in his native land or migrated. If he was not a
Northumbrian, he may have visited Northumbria to learn and then gone
home again (or indeed *not* gone home again); or else he may have been trained
in his own country by a visitor from Lindisfarne.

In K we have to reckon not only with one great scribe but – it seems –
with more than one great illuminator:[4] which seems to rule out all
but a few major scriptoria. The easiest solution would be to follow Masai
and ascribe K to Lindisfarne. Professor Dorothy Whitelock has shown
that some aspects of Northumbrian culture in the second half of the
eighth century were far from dead.[5] Two archaeological features of K
associate it with Northumbria. It is unique among insular manuscripts for
the number and excellence of its foliate patterns, and especially its vine
scrolls;[6] and Northumbria is the home of the vine scroll *par excellence*. Again,
its picture of the Virgin and Child has been shown by Professor Ernst
Kitzinger to be very like the drawing of that subject on St Cuthbert's coffin.[7]
And yet there are other archaeological aspects of K that cannot be matched
in Northumbria.[8]

For palaeographers, the only recognized halt on the road between Northumbria and Ireland has always been Iona. Aidan, Adamnan, Iona's submission to Rome in 716 – all were part of Northumbrian history. Later
evidence for contact is rare, but Abbot Sléibíne of Iona did visit Ripon

[1] *English Uncial*, pp. 10–13.
[2] *CLA* x, viii–xviii.
[3] Alistair Campbell, *Æthelwulf de Abbatibus* (Oxford, 1967), lines 206–15.
[4] Henry, *Irish Art during the Viking Invasions*, pp. 73–7.
[5] *The Audience of Beowulf* (Oxford, 1951), pp. 99–104.
[6] Esp. K, 19v, 114r, 202r and 285r; Meyer, *Codex Cenannensis*, p. 36; Bruce-Mitford, *Cod. Lind.*, p.
    254 and fig. 63, comparing scrolls in K and on the Ormside bowl.
[7] 'The Coffin-Reliquary', *The Relics of St Cuthbert*, ed. C. F. Battiscombe (Oxford, 1956), pp. 248–64
    and pls. iv, fig. 4*a*, and x.   [8] See below, p. 246, n.3.

between 752 and 767.[1] The simple but handsome copy of Adamnan's *Vita Columbae* written by Abbot Dorbbene of Iona (d. 713)[2] is very unlike K – minuscule script and no decoration; but since one of the pair is a gospel book and the other only a *Vita*, the comparison is not between like and like. The Virgin and Child occurs on the stone crosses of Iona,[3] but not in Ireland itself. Mr R. B. K. Stevenson tells me that he sees the ornament of the St John's Cross at Iona as the closest sculptural parallel to the ornament of Kells, and he regards Northumbria as one of the two sources from which the forms of the Iona crosses are derived.[4] The next easiest solution would be to ascribe K to a phase in the life of Iona when the personnel of the scriptorium included Northumbrian scribes, or else Scottish scribes of Northumbrian formation. The archaeological and palaeographical evidence together would then indicate close personal links between Iona and Lindisfarne, perhaps during the half-century before the onset of the Vikings. Lindisfarne was raided as well as Iona; and if the crosses depend on Northumbria, it seems easier to imagine the necessary contacts in the period when north Britain as a whole was as yet untroubled by the raiders.

Even in peaceful times, the journey from Northumbria to Iona must have been laborious, involving a long journey over land and a very long voyage by sea. The journey from Northumbria to the country of the Picts was no more than a crossing of the Forth in a small boat, as by St Cuthbert and his two companions when they went from Melrose 'ad terram Pictorum, ubi dicitur Niuduera regio'.[5] After the early eighth century, the historical evidence for contacts between Northumbria and the Picts seems to be better than the evidence for contacts with the Scots. In the Jarrow Lecture for 1970[6] Dr Kathleen Hughes argued that although St Columba is usually regarded as the apostle of the northern Picts, the evidence suggests that Christianity in that area made quite a slow start. Before 710 the evidence for Latin learning in Pictland is, she claims, surprisingly negative. The only early Pictish text extant in later manuscripts is a Pictish king-list. Latin ecclesiastical culture seems to have thrived there only after King Nehton had made contact with Wearmouth–Jarrow in about 710, when he sought Ceolfrith's

---

[1] Kathleen Hughes, 'Evidence for Contacts between the Churches of the Irish and English from the Synod of Whitby to the Viking Age', *England Before the Conquest: Studies in Primary Sources presented to Dorothy Whitelock*, ed. Peter Clemoes and Kathleen Hughes (Cambridge, 1971), p. 55.

[2] *CLA* VII, no. 998.

[3] J. Romilly Allen, with Joseph Anderson, *The Early Christian Monuments of Scotland* (Edinburgh, 1903) III, 381–2 and 389; also 391–3 (cross at Kildalton, Islay), 249–50 and 363–4 (crosses in eastern Scotland).

[4] 'The Chronology and Relationships of some Irish and Scottish Crosses', *Jnl of the R. Soc. of Ant. of Ireland* 86 (1956), 84–96, esp. 86.

[5] *Two Lives of St Cuthbert*, ed. Bertram Colgrave (Cambridge, 1940), p. 82 (*Vita Anonyma* II. iv); also p. 192 (Bedae *Vita* xi).

[6] *Early Christianity in Pictland* (Jarrow, n.d.), esp. pp. 12–16.

advice on the Easter question and asked him for architects to build a stone church 'iuxta morem Romanorum'.[1] Bede says that the English and the Picts were at peace in 731;[2] and of the three Pictish kings who feature in the Lindisfarne *Liber vitae*,[3] the first, Oengus (d. 761), was allied to Eadberht of Northumbria against Strathclyde in 756.[4] The Northumbrian annals also record that in 774 and 796 two deposed Northumbrian rulers took refuge with the king of the Picts: Alhred went via Bamburgh; Osbald 'ad insulam Lindisfarnensem cum paucis secessit, et inde ad regem Pictorum cum quibusdam e fratribus navigio pervenit'.[5] Before we consider archaeological relations between Northumbria and the Picts, we may note that the hostility between Northumbria and Strathclyde instanced above and the total want of antiquities from that area before the tenth century seem to disqualify the Britons as possible makers of K.

The archaeologists who first studied the 'sculptured stones of Scotland' all compared one or another aspect of their decoration with 'Irish' manuscripts, and notably with Durrow, Lindisfarne and Kells: evidence, they considered, of Irish influence at Iona and among the Picts. I am speaking of John Stuart,[6] Joseph Anderson and Romilly Allen[7] – some of the first and greatest names in Hiberno-Saxon archaeology. Their contemporary successors, on the other hand – I mean Mrs Cecil L. Mowbray Curle,[8] Mr Stevenson,[9] Dr Isabel Henderson[10] and Professor D. M. Wilson[11] – have emphasized the Northumbrian element in Pictish sculpture and metal-work. Mrs Curle recognized it in the cross slabs of class II;[12] Stevenson and Mrs Henderson also recognize it in the symbol- and animal-stones of class I.[13] We recall that for part of the time between about 658 and the catastrophic defeat of Eadfrith in 685, some of southern Pictland was occupied by the Northumbrians; that soon after 669 Wilfrid could be described as bishop of the Picts; and that in 681 a bishopric for the occupied zone was founded at Abercorn, south

---

[1] Bede, *Historia Ecclesiastica*, ed. Colgrave and Mynors, p. 532.   [2] *Ibid.* p. 560.

[3] BM Cotton Domitian vii, 15r and v, ptd in *Catalogue of Ancient Manuscripts in the British Museum*, pt II, Latin (London, 1884), p. 81. The other two kings were Constantine (789–820) and Eoganan (d. 839).

[4] Dorothy Whitelock, *English Historical Documents*, c. *500–1042* (London, 1955), p. 241; *Symeonis Monachi Opera Omnia*, ed. Thomas Arnold, Rolls Series (1882–5), II, 40–1.

[5] Whitelock, *EHD*, pp. 243–4 and 248; ed. Arnold, pp. 45 and 57.

[6] *Sculptured Stones of Scotland*, 2 vols., Spalding Club (Aberdeen, 1856–67), esp. II, 14–15.

[7] See above, p. 237, n. 3.

[8] Cecil L. Mowbray, 'Eastern Influence on Carvings at St Andrews and Nigg, Scotland', *Antiquity* 10 (1936), 428–40; Cecil L. Curle, 'The Chronology of the Early Christian Monuments of Scotland', *Proc. of the Soc. of Ant. of Scotland* 74 (1939–40), 60–116.

[9] R. B. K. Stevenson, 'Pictish Art', *The Problem of the Picts*, ed. F. T. Wainwright (Edinburgh, 1955), pp. 97–128.   [10] *The Picts* (London, 1967), pp. 104–60.

[11] *Reflections on the St Ninian's Isle Treasure*, Jarrow Lecture 1969 (Jarrow, 1970).

[12] 'Eastern Influences', pp. 433–4; 'Chronology', pp. 80–2, 89–90 and 97–104. Also Stevenson, 'Pictish Art', pp. 112–23; Henderson, *The Picts*, pp. 127–34. The manuscripts most often cited are L and K.   [13] 'Pictish Art', pp. 106–10; *The Picts*, pp. 115–27.

of the Forth, under Bishop Trumwine.[1] Wilson, in his Jarrow Lecture on the St Ninian's Isle treasure, which he can show to be part of the small but impressive corpus of Pictish metal-work, connects the dotted animals on the bowls with like animals in L, and the 'extended' animals on the 'buttons' with like animals in K.[2] Pictish sculpture can show a few excellent vine scrolls,[3] well up to Northumbrian standards and better than any in Ireland.[4] The David on the St Andrews shrine is as remarkable as any of the figures in K;[5] and Mrs Henderson sees a particular likeness between the figure styles of K and of the cross slab at Nigg.[6] Three important elements in the art of K that are wanting in Northumbria are found in Pictish sculpture: naturalistic animal and human figures;[7] human figures interlaced;[8] and what Mrs Henderson calls 'fantastic animals' – creatures whose conformation and behaviour often recall the more sophisticated but no less fantastic fauna of K's initials.[9] Mrs Henderson tells me that the monuments that speak most clearly to her of K are the group from the Tarbat peninsula in Easter Ross, and especially the famous cross slab at Nigg.[10]

In Stevenson's ingenious and convincing explanation of the form of the Iona crosses, the part played by Northumbrian crosses counts for rather less than the part played by Pictish cross slabs.[11] Are we to see K as the work of an Iona under strong Pictish as well as Northumbrian influence? Or are we to see it as the work of a Pictish centre from which some or all of that influence passed to Iona? Geography, history and archaeology all indicate that if the Picts had a scriptorium capable of making K, it would have been likely to produce manuscripts in the Northumbrian manner. Of any book as magnificent as K, which among insular manuscripts recognizes as its peers only the Codex Amiatinus, the Lindisfarne Gospels and the Stockholm Codex Aureus, and which can hold up its head beside the manuscripts illuminated for the

---

[1] *Ibid.* pp. 51–9 and 81–2. [2] *Reflections*, pp. 5–12.

[3] Notably the Hilton of Cadboll cross slab (Allen, *ECMS*, pp. 61–3) and a fragment from Tarbat, apparently by the same hand, now in Edinburgh (*ibid.* pp. 73–5).

[4] Henry, *Sculpture irlandaise*, pp. 109–11 and pls. 54.4 (Tower Cross, Kells), 54.5 (Muiredach's Cross, Monasterboice) and 56 (Cross of the Scriptures, Clonmacnoise). The Kells example recalls Hilton of Cadboll; but Mlle Henry derives the Irish scrolls, which she dates in the ninth and tenth centuries, from Carolingian models. [5] Allen, *ECMS*, pp. 351–3.

[6] *Ibid.* pp. 75–83; Henderson, *The Picts*, pp. 147–9 and 154–7.

[7] K, 124v and 174v (eagle), 71r and 188v (fish), 76v (wolf) and 89r (horse-and-rider). Cf. Henderson, *The Picts*, pp. 117–27.

[8] Meyer, *Codex Cenannensis*, pls. xi–xii. Cf. Allen, *ECMS*, pp. 303–5 (Meigle, no. 26). For hunting and war scenes and for interlaced men on the Irish crosses, Henry, *Sculpture irlandaise*, pp. 117–27 and 82–7. [9] *The Picts*, pp. 137–40.

[10] Letter of 14 October 1971; and see above, n. 6. Mrs Henderson also quotes Romilly Allen, *Proc. of the Soc. of Ant. of Scotland* 25 (1890–1), 426: 'in the arrangement of the design [Nigg] approaches more nearly to the ornamental pages of the Irish books of the Gospels than any other [sculpture]'.

[11] 'Chronology and Relationships', pp. 86–91, suggesting that the ring in the crosses of Iona and of Ireland derives from Pictish cross slabs.

Carolingian and Ottonian emperors, it is as necessary to ask which king or kings subsidized the work, as which group of clergy did the work. Mrs Henderson argues that for most of the century between 741, when Pictish Oengus overcame Dál Riada, and 849, when Scottish Kenneth put an end to Pictish independence, the Picts were the dominant power north of Forth and Clyde.[1] In sculpture, expensive and often discriminating patronage was exercised during this period: at St Andrews; at Meigle and Aberlemno, in Strathmore, and at nearby St Vigeans; and in Easter Ross, especially in the Tarbat peninsula.[2] Where the portable St Ninian's objects came from, we do not know; but they are first-class work.[3]

If King Nehton begged architects from Wearmouth–Jarrow, and if the patrons who paid for the sculpture and the metal-work approved of the Northumbrian patterns so often followed by their craftsmen, some Pictish king may well have asked Bishop Æthelwald, who bound the Lindisfarne Gospels and ruled the monastery until his death in 740,[4] or one of his successors, for help in the production of books. A Northumbrian master or masters may have been sent on a temporary, or even a permanent mission to the Pictish court; or else a Pictish scribe or scribes may have served an apprenticeship in the Lindisfarne scriptorium. Books were undoubtedly among the objects which carried Northumbrian art along the eastern coast of Scotland[5] (the sites mentioned above are all on or near the sea);[6] and we need not doubt that, between Cuthbert's voyage and that of the *fratres* who went with Osbald, other Northumbrian clergy sailed northwards. If they were not great scholars, neither were the Picts illiterate.[7] Even intellectual stagnation is compatible with the production of fine books – for St Jerome, fine books positively indicated that condition: 'onera magis exarata quam codices'.[8] The will to turn out handsome gospels, psalters and the like may survive the will to copy texts for the library. Mr T. A. M. Bishop detects in eleventh-century England the 'formalism' that E. K. Rand detected at Tours in the mid ninth century.[9] The two inscriptions on opposite sides of one of the

[1] *The Picts*, pp. 62–6 and 91–103.
[2] Allen, *ECMS*, pp. 351–63, 373–4 and 511–13 (St Andrews); 296–305 and 329–40 (Meigle); 209–15 (Aberlemno); 234–42, 267–80 and 281 (St Vigeans); and 61–83 (Easter Ross).
[3] See below, p. 246, n. 4.　　　　　　　　　　　[4] *Cod. Lind.*, pp. 18–19.
[5] See above, p. 238, n. 12. Henderson, *The Picts*, pp. 124–6 and pls. 37–8, derives the eagle of St John in CCCC 197, p. 245, from Pictish carvings such as the symbol stone from Knowe of Burrian, Birsay, Orkney; but I believe that the books inspired the greater naturalism of the carvings, which would otherwise have had to develop *ex nihilo*.
[6] *Ordnance Survey Map of Britain in the Dark Ages*, ed. C. W. Phillips, 2nd ed. (Southampton, 1966), shows that the Northumbrian, and especially the Pictish sites are basically coastal, with landward extensions up river valleys.
[7] Hughes, *Early Christianity in Pictland*, p. 8.
[8] Donatien de Bruyne, *Les Préfaces de la Bible latine* (Namur, 1920), p. 39.
[9] Bishop, *English Caroline Minuscule* (Oxford, 1971), p. xviii; Rand, *A Survey of the Manuscripts of Tours* (Cambridge, Mass., 1929), p. 63.

chapes from St Ninian's Isle satisfy me that insular minuscule as well as insular majuscule was known among the Picts, and indeed by some Picts: the names on the 'minuscule' side are Pictish.[1] The stone at St Vigeans which bears the Pictish name *Drosten* is inscribed in a very respectable script in which the angular form of 'half-uncial' **r** suggests that the model was a formalized minuscule.[2] The beautiful Latin inscription in raised letters on a fragment of stone from Tarbat, Easter Ross[3] – an area which has already attracted our attention on archaeological grounds – proves familiarity with the solemn, capital type of insular display script which makes its first appearance in L, E and D, and recurs in K.[4] The inscriptions, in fact, testify not only to literacy but also to knowledge of the same range of insular scripts as we find in England. Whatever books the Pictish church may have lacked, it could not have existed without the gospels and the psalter.[5] One or more court monasteries or churches must have existed among the Picts; and if we cannot say where they were, the groups of stones from St Andrews, Meigle, Aberlemno, St Vigeans and the Tarbat–Nigg area, with the St Ninian's Isle treasure, show what sort of work they were able to do. The Pictish cross slabs make just as good a monumental background for a manuscript of the quality of K as the crosses of Northumbria or Iona. There is, in fact, nothing whatever to be astonished about in the suggestion that the only surviving manuscript from the hey-day of political power and artistic achievement among the Picts should be an illuminated gospel book of conspicuous originality and magnificence. The survival-rate of such books is, in any case, comparatively high.

Let us move on westwards from Scotland to Ireland. If K was made before 807–14, then the monastery of Kells itself can hardly be its home: the place was of no account before the arrival of the Iona community.[6] Against the possibility that K was made elsewhere in Ireland is the fact that K is far better explained by L, E and D, and the Leningrad Bede than by the certainly Irish manuscripts of the period down to about 750 – the Cathach, the manuscripts from Bobbio,[7] the palimpsest sacramentary in Munich,[8] the

---

[1] T. J. Brown in 'The St Ninian's Isle Silver Hoard', *Antiquity* 33 (1959), 250–2; A. C. O'Dell and Alexander Cain, *St Ninian's Isle Treasure*, Aberdeen University Studies 141 (Edinburgh, 1960), 46; Kenneth Jackson, 'The St Ninian's Isle Inscription: a Re-appraisal', *Antiquity* 34 (1960), 38–42.

[2] Allen, *ECMS*, pp. 235–9; cf. *CLA* II, nos. 121, 129, 157 and 214, none of which appears to be earlier than the late eighth century.

[3] Allen, *ECMS*, pp. 94–5; cf. the stone from Lethnott, Forfarshire, *ibid.* pp. 262–3.

[4] See above, p. 232, n. 7.

[5] John Stuart, *The Book of Deer*, Spalding Club (Edinburgh, 1869), pp. xxi–xxiv, sets out the all-too-inconclusive evidence for the late survival of ancient manuscripts in the Pictish area. The Book of Deer itself (Cambridge, University Library, Ii.6.32) contains marginal arabesques (*ibid.* pls. xxi–xxii); but the script looks Irish, and arabesques occur in Ireland as early as the Book of Armagh (*c.* 807).

[6] See above, p. 234, n. 2.

[7] *CLA* IV, xxiii.

[8] *CLA* IX, no. 1298; and see above, p. 233, n. 6.

Bangor Antiphonary (680–91), the Schaffhausen Adamnan (before 713) and the Cadmug Gospels (before 754).[1] The last-named, with its simple little portraits of evangelists, is the only one of these manuscripts to attempt anything more ambitious than simple initials, or the rudimentary carpet-page of the Milan Orosius.[2] If Durrow were Irish, it would be another matter; but even if it were, it would still be hard to deny that the line of descent from it to K passed through the Lindisfarne scriptorium. If we are to share Mlle Henry's belief that 'all which has been traditionally attributed to Ireland, does in fact belong to her', we must also share her belief that 'the problem of the metal-work can now be said to be solved' – solved, she says, because scientifically conducted excavations during the past few years have in almost every case led to the discovery of objects similar to those already known, of workshops and of objects only half finished.[3] Whether or not the Irish manuscripts before about 750 make a credible background for K, there is much to be said for Zimmermann's statement that all Irish manuscripts that are later than K depend on it.[4] For Zimmermann, K's date was early-eighth-century, which allows its Irish 'descendants' to link up with, indeed to include, the Cadmug Gospels, which was surely written before St Boniface's death in 754. If K belongs in the second half of the eighth century, as Lowe finally believed, it can still be the ancestor of the only members of the 750–850 group to which dates can be attached: the Stowe Missal (792–811 or 812), the Book of Armagh (c. 807) and Macregol's Gospels (before 822). K's descent from Northumbrian manuscripts is plain to see, and in seeking the origins of anything or anybody, we usually pay more heed to ancestry than to posterity, where information about both is available. Stevenson sees the Iona crosses as a necessary transitional stage between the Northumbrian crosses and the Pictish cross slabs on the one hand and the Irish high crosses on the other hand. I see Kells as the link that joins the Lindisfarne manuscripts of about 700, and the art of the Pictish cross slabs, to the Irish manuscripts of our later period. Dr Hughes has recently rounded up the evidence for direct contacts between England and Ireland during the eighth century.[5] It is considerable, but it does not explain the elements in K that appear to be Pictish rather than pure Northumbrian. That K itself, and not another book or books from the same centre, is responsible for the character of the later Irish manuscripts cannot, I think, be proved. Given that K was carried to Ireland by the Iona–Kells community, this may have happened during the half-century and more, after 807–14, during which the community temporarily reoccupied Iona and apparently, about 850–65, was associated

---

[1] CLA VIII, no. 1198. [2] CLA III, no. 328; Cod. Lind., pl. 20a.

[3] Early Christian Irish Art (Dublin, 1954), pp. 14–15.

[4] Vorkarolingische Miniaturen, pp. 22–3. [5] See above, p. 237, n. 1.

by the victorious Kenneth mac Alpin with the monastery at Dunkeld, founded by the Pictish king Constantine between 789 and 820.[1] The Columban clergy may indeed have acquired K in eastern Scotland, not produced it themselves. Furthermore, if K reached Ireland from Scotland, it is possible that some of the 'Irish' manuscripts that resemble it came from the same place; and this could be as true of manuscripts preserved on the continent as of manuscripts preserved in Ireland itself.

The Book of Kells is the most complex and the greatest work of Hiberno-Saxon art. If its date is between the 746 of the Leningrad Bede and the 822 of the Macregol Gospels, then Northumbria, Pictland, Iona and Ireland are all possible homes for it. It is for archaeology to settle the question. Palaeography can do little more than tell her sister where and when to start looking : at Lindisfarne, in the middle years of the eighth century. We can certainly apply to K Mrs Henderson's words about Pictish sculpture: 'it was . . . the creation of artists freely participating in the evolution of [the Hiberno-Saxon] style and contributing to it some of its most daring and magnificent monuments.'[2] My own archaeological answer to the question of origin is this: 'a great insular centre . . . subject to Northumbrian influence . . . in eastern Scotland'. Because of the vigour and freshness of the Lindisfarne elements that they include, I cannot easily believe that either K or the related antiquities from the Pictish area were made after the end of the eighth century. If K were of the ninth century, I should wonder how the style and technique of Eadfrith's scriptorium at Lindisfarne could have been so brilliantly revived after an interval of a century.

APPENDIX
The Lindisfarne Gospels and Durham Cathedral A.II.17
C. D. VEREY

The majority of corrections in the text of the Lindisfarne Gospels are by either the first hand or the rubricator or, later, by the glossator.[3] There is, however, a small number of contemporary corrections by another hand (hereafter called L corr.): these are found at 135vb14, *ponit seruorum accipientium* (see pl. VI*a*) and 236ra7, *prendere* (see pl. VI*b*) – these two clearly connected by the character of **p** – and at 255r, the two marginal notes *in exodo* and *in zacharia* – obviously by the same hand and linked to *prendere* at 236ra7 by the **d** of *exodo*. The variant on 220r, *bethesda*, appears to be in the same hand as the notes on 255r; and other minor, one-letter corrections, e.g. the frequent addition of *t* to *cotidiana* in the Neapolitan Lection lists and the *r* on *scibtione* (*sic*) at 136ra13, can probably be ascribed to L corr.[4] If

---

[1] Henderson, *The Picts*, pp. 88–9.   [2] *Ibid.* p. 157.   [3] *Cod. Lind.*, pp. 81–3.
[4] The unity of this group is discussed by Brown, *Cod. Lind.*, p. 82, but he there connected them with the work of the rubricator.

we take the corrections at 135vb14 and 236ra7 as a basis for comparison, there are certain features of L corr. which distinguish it from both the first hand (L) and the rubricator (R): L corr. is written with a thinner pen and the letters are made with a sloping pen, which gives them a more elongated appearance in contrast to the squarer, straight-pen letters of L and R; the bow of **p** springs from below the top of the descender (in L and R it leaves the top), and the bows of both **p** and **t** end in a square 'serif'[1] made by extending a straight third stroke below the curve, whereas in L and R the third stroke neatly closes the curve.

A comparison between L corr. and the hand of the main corrector in the Durham Gospels (hereafter called D corr.; see pls. VI*c, d* and *e*) shows a great similarity between the two hands, sufficient, upon consideration of detail, to suggest that these two sets of corrections were written by the same scribe. The pen angle is the same, and the features of **p** and **t** mentioned above are identical in both. In **p** the descender bends to the left at the top and the bow springs from the base of the serif; the bow is formed by the pen drawing first a hair-line upwards and then turning angularly, a square 'serif' across the line of the bow completing it. **t** has no serif on the bar, which is slightly sinuous and turns upwards to the right, while the bow ends in a square 'serif' drawn across, as in **p**. Both half-uncial and uncial **d** are found in D corr. but only the uncial form is found in L corr.: a comparison of pls. VI*b* and *d* shows that in both examples the second stroke of uncial **d** starts well above the bow of the letter and is sinuous, beginning with a slight downward pull before turning to the right at an angle of about forty-five degrees (in L and R and the Durham main hand the second stroke of uncial **d** starts with a horizontal hair-line, which is usually quite short). There is no serif on uncial **d** in either D corr. or L corr. The form of **u** is a little erratic, but a comparison between the serifs on the second *u* of *nudus* (see pl. VI*e*) with those on the first *u* of *seruorum* (see pl. VI*a*) confirms the similarity. If to the above we add a comparison of the other letters (which have less distinctive features), it is reasonable to conclude that both sets of corrections are by the same hand.

The identification of the same hand as a corrector in the Durham Gospels and in the Lindisfarne Gospels does not in itself prove that these manuscripts were originally written in the same scriptorium. However, strong palaeographical and artistic links between them have already led Professor Brown and Dr Bruce-Mitford to this conclusion;[2] therefore, the natural interpretation of the evidence above must surely be confirmation of the idea that they were produced in the Lindisfarne scriptorium at the same period.

A second point of connection between the Durham Gospels and the Lindisfarne Gospels is that D corr. almost always follows the Italo-Northumbrian gospel text-type found in the Lindisfarne Gospels.[3] Among the many instances where D corr. follows distinct Italo-Northumbrian readings are: Mark XIV. 44, the order

---

[1] The word 'serif' is in inverted commas because the stroke in question is not properly a serif, as is explained in the text.

[2] *Cod. Lind.*, pp. 89–100 and 246–50.

[3] On the Italo-Northumbrian text, see *Novum Testamentum Latine – pars prior, Quattuor Evangelia*, ed. J. Wordsworth and H. J. White (Oxford, 1889–98), pp. 780–1.

caute ducite; Luke IV. 7, the addition of *procedens* after *tu ergo* (see pl. VId); Luke V. 3, the addition of *autem* after *rogauit*; and Luke XIII. 28, the addition of *introire* after *prophetas*. If one accepts, on the palaeographical evidence cited above, that D corr. was working at Lindisfarne, the source of the text used by him must have been the exemplar of the Lindisfarne Gospels or another copy of the exemplar no longer extant. (It is most unlikely that a codex as sumptuous as the Lindisfarne Gospels, which was probably made for the translation of the body of St Cuthbert in 698, was itself used as an exemplar in the Lindisfarne scriptorium.)

ADDITIONAL NOTES

The following notes refer to publications which reached me after the above went to the printer

1 [See p. 228, para. 1.] Armando Petrucci, 'L'onciale Romana', *Studi Medievali* 3rd ser. 12. 1 (1971), 75–134, esp. 121–7, argues that the uncial models followed at Wearmouth–Jarrow were written in Rome itself.

2 [See p. 235, para. 1.] A selection of notes on early insular manuscripts made by Wilhelm Koehler mostly between 1954 and his death in 1959 has been published in Wilhelm Koehler, *Buchmalerei des frühen Mittelalters: Fragmente und Entwürfe aus dem Nachlass*, ed. Ernst Kitzinger and Florentine Mütherich (Munich, 1972), pp. 3–88. The notes printed by Professor Kitzinger, who was mainly responsible for editing this part of the book, deal in particular with Durrow, E, D, L, K, the Durham Cassiodorus (*CLA* II, no. 152), the Gospels of St Chad (*CLA* II, no. 159), St Gallen 51 (*CLA* VII, no. 901) and the Stockholm Codex Aureus (*CLA* XI, no. 1642). Koehler's main concern was with the stylistic relationships between these manuscripts; he had next to nothing to say as yet about their absolute as opposed to their relative chronology and ignored as untenable the traditional distinction between 'Irish' (Durrow and K) and 'Anglo-Saxon' (L). See Kitzinger's comment at p. 187, n. 5. At p. 188, n. 11 Kitzinger summarizes the progress of Koehler's ideas about the place of K in insular illumination. Although he changed his mind more than once and reached no final conclusion, Koehler never doubted that K was later than Durrow and L. What puzzled him was its relationship to St Gallen 51. Until the mid 1950s he placed K before St Gallen and immediately after L, as a product of the same creative period that had produced L itself; and he regarded St Gallen as the beginning of a decline which was intensified in those manuscripts of the late eighth century which followed the Lindisfarne tradition. His work on the initials, especially in 1954, persuaded him that K and St Gallen were parallel phenomena, about equally removed from L, the former marking a further development and the latter a decline (*Buchmalerei des frühen Mittelalters*, pp. 41–6). During the next few years his work on the human figures in the manuscripts led him to the conclusion that K presupposed St Gallen and so must be the later of the two (*ibid.* pp. 24 and 73–6). In 1958, in a general note on the relationship between Mediterranean and northern art, he dated K 'gegen Ende s. VIII' (*ibid.* p. 5).

In 1959, in a draft arrangement of all the major manuscripts in groups (*ibid.* pp. 12–17), Koehler went back – however tentatively – to his earlier belief that K belonged immediately after L. He associated it with the Codex Amiatinus, with L and in particular with the Durham Cassiodorus as the product of a short period during which a humanistic style broke in upon the native insular tradition represented by the Cathach, Durham A. II. 10, Durrow, E, D and CCCC 197. In K itself the humanistic and insular elements fused, with the latter in the ascendant. The Chad Gospels and St Gallen are put in his next group, under the heading of 'The victory of the insular tradition'. Macregol, with ornament derived from K and evangelists derived from another source, is put into a 'Retrospective group', which is not chronologically arranged, along with the Macdurnan Gospels (Lambeth Palace 771), the Cadmug Gospels, St Gallen 60 (*CLA* VII, no. 902), the Book of Dimma and TCD 56 (*CLA* II, nos. 275 and 272). Into Koehler's fifth and last group, headed 'The victory of the second humanistic invasion', go the Vespasian Psalter (*CLA* II, no. 193), the Stockholm Codex Aureus, BM Royal 1 E. vi with BM Tiberius C. ii (*CLA* II, nos. 214 and 191), the Barberini Gospels, the Book of Cerne (Zimmermann, *Vorkarolingische Miniaturen*, pls. 293–6) and the Maaseik evangelist.

Koehler's conclusions of 1959 were based on long and profound study of the most elaborate elements in the decoration of the manuscripts – the full pages of ornament and the figure subjects. His association of K with a trio of Northumbrian manuscripts, of which Amiatinus and L are securely localized, seems to me to support the conclusions about K's origin reached by Masai on more general grounds (see above, pp. 219 and 223–4) and by myself in this paper on the evidence of its handwriting and of the least elaborate elements in its decoration (see above, pp. 227–34). As to date, Koehler's archaeological conclusion seems perfectly consistent with my own palaeographical conclusion that 'saec. VIII med.' is not at all too early for K (see above, pp. 234–5). I have long thought that there are no palaeographical objections to 'saec. VIII[1]'; there is unbroken, indeed close continuity between the handwritings of L, E and D and that of K.

3 [See p. 236, para. 2.] In 'The *Madonna and Child* Miniature in the Book of Kells, pt 1', *Art Bulletin* 54.1 (March 1972), 1–23, Dr Martin Werner endorses and elaborates Kitzinger's conclusion about the Virgin and Child pictures in K and on the foot of St Cuthbert's coffin and argues that the evangelist symbols and the Christ in Majesty in K (1r and 32v) bear a similar relationship to the figures on the lid of the coffin. He cites Coptic examples of iconographical schemes in which all these elements are combined and suggests that something of the sort may have been used by Benedict Biscop to decorate his church at Wearmouth. He also illustrates a Virgin and Child with angels on an inscribed slab in Brechin Cathedral in eastern Scotland, which he tentatively dates in the second half of the eighth century. The second part of Werner's paper is to appear in *Art Bulletin*, June 1972.

4 [See p. 240, para. 1.] Kenneth Jackson, *The Gaelic Notes in the Book of Deer* (Cambridge, 1972), p. 17: 'One would be anxious to avoid the imputation of "Pictomania", but we should remember that Pictland had presumably been an agriculturally much richer, and doubtless on the whole a more populous and powerful country, than the old Dál Riada...'   T.J.B.

The Icelandic saga of Edward the Confessor: the hagiographic sources

CHRISTINE FELL

The author or compiler of the saga of Edward the Confessor *Saga Játvarðar konungs hins helga*[1] frequently refers to his sources. Sometimes he does this in vague terms such as 'svá segja sannfróðir menn' (ch. 1) and 'segja menn' (ch. 6). At other times he seems to be bringing together two sources as in the phrases 'Þat er ok sumra manna sögn' (ch. 6) and 'Ok er þat margra manna sögn' (ch. 8). Two references indicate English provenance for part of his material: 'Svá segja Enskir menn' (ch. 5) and 'Þat er sögn Enskra manna' (ch. 8). He also mentions Scandinavian sources, indicating awareness of Danish tradition in 'Ok þat hafa Danir til þess' (ch. 9) and alluding to a history of the kings of Norway in 'Sem sagt er í Æfi Noregs-konunga' (ch. 7). But he does not always find Scandinavian scholarship well-informed: 'Þá þykkjaz fróðir menn í Noregskonungs veldi eigi (víst) vita hverr þessi konungr hefir verit.' Fortunately Icelandic learning can supply the missing detail: 'þat er sagt frá orðum Gizurar Hallz sonar, eins hins vitrasta mannz á Íslandi' (ch. 2). This is his only reference to an authority by name.

The author's negative indications can also be useful. He tells us on two occasions that he cannot supply a detail because it is not in his source, and we can dismiss therefore any sources that contain it. He tells us of his difficulties in finding material on Edward: 'þótt vér kunnum fátt frá at segja sakir fáfræði ok fjarlægðar' (ch. 2). This may be only a conventional apology, but it is probably true that the sparsity of the saga's information on Edward results, not from the author's selectivity, but from the limited material available to him. In the *Flateyjarbók* version of the saga this complaint is fuller, drawing attention to the difficulty of chronology: 'en fyrir fáfræði vitum vér varla hvat fyrr eða síðar hefir verit á hans dögum, ok því segjum vér þat fyrst er oss þykkir mestrar frásagnar vert.' This suggests that the author was faced with the problem of linking material from various sources since the question of chronology would not have arisen if he were copying material from one source and could accept a given order. But it is also true

---

[1] *Icelandic Sagas*, ed. Gudbrand Vigfusson, Rolls Series (1887–94) I, 388–400. Subsequent chapter references are to this edition. For a bibliography of manuscripts, editions and comment see Ole Widding, Hans Bekker-Nielsen and L. K. Shook, 'The Lives of the Saints in Old Norse Prose, a Handlist', *MS* 25 (1963), 308–9.

that Edward's hagiographies provide remarkably little in the way of an historical framework for his visions and miracles.

The author tells us that he has a number of sources but that his material on Edward himself is limited, and if we look at the saga's structure we can see for ourselves that it is complex compilation, not simple translation. Only about half of it centres on Edward. The rest is legend and history connected with other outstanding personalities of the eleventh century. But the divisions of subject matter are not linked with the change from one source to another. The saga is divisible into four main sections, each one containing material from more than one source.

The first section deals briefly with Edward's genealogy and saintly characteristics, then moves on to legends about William of Normandy's parentage and marriage. The saga writer's link is the family one connecting kings of England with dukes of Normandy, but it is very tenuous and the Norman material is awkwardly introduced. The second section contains material on Edward ultimately from four separate sources. It opens with details of Edward's government and moves on to his vision of a Danish king being drowned as he was about to invade England. Then follows a miracle in which Edward gives a ring to a pilgrim who turns out to have been St John the Evangelist. Edward has two more visions, one of the seven sleepers of Ephesus, one of the sacrament as the body of Christ. The section ends with two of his healing miracles. The third section centres on English history, starting with Edward's accusation that Godwine caused the death of his young brother Alfred. Godwine tries to clear himself by oath but dies in the process. Harold Godwineson's oath to William, Edward's death and the battles of Stamford Bridge and Hastings come next, and these are all in parallel Scandinavian sources. But the Godwine story is not found there in the form in which the saga has it, and an English source for some of this material is likely. The fourth section deals with post-Conquest events in England, especially with the Anglo-Saxon emigration to Byzantium. This also could be from English sources, but on the other hand ex-Varangians seem to have been common enough in Iceland, and traditions may have filtered back from Byzantium itself.

The relation of *Játvarðar saga* to its sources has already been examined by H. L. Rogers.[1] Unfortunately it is not possible to accept Rogers's conclusions. His theory that the Icelandic life is based, not on a Latin *Vita*, but on an Anglo-Norman translation of the Latin, can be disproved fairly easily by a close examination of the texts.

---

[1] H. L. Rogers, 'An Icelandic Life of St Edward the Confessor', *SBVS* 14 (1956–7), 249–72. Rogers has also a complicated theory about the saga writer's use of the *scedulae* at Westminster. This is to some extent based on Bloch's arguments which have since been attacked by Barlow; see below, p. 249, n. 1.

The Icelandic saga of Edward the Confessor: the hagiographic sources

There are three Latin *Vitae Sancti Edwardi*, one by an anonymous bio-grapher, one by Osbert of Clare and one by Ailred of Rievaulx.[1] The first of these need not concern us. It is not the source of any part of the saga, contains very little parallel material and nowhere shows similarities of vocabulary or sentence structure. But both Osbert's work and Ailred's are among the sources of the saga.

Ailred's *Vita*, written between 1161 and 1163 after Edward's canonization, is filled with traditional hagiographic material about visions and miracles. It was the most popular of the three Lives and was translated and quoted freely by later writers. Chronicle and liturgy borrow from it and there are two Anglo-Norman translations of it and one in Middle English extant.[2]

The saga opens with material on Edward which is not exclusively from Ailred but contains two sentences which are direct translations from him. The first enumerates Edward's early signs of holiness:

Játvarðar saga, ch. 1: Hinn helgi Játvarðr elskaði þegar á unga aldri helga kirkju ok tíða-gerð, klaustra at vitja, ok þá munka at elska er hónum þóttu helgastir ok siðsamastir, svá ok ágætar ölmusur at gjöra þeim er vóru fátækir ok þurftugir.

Ailred, col. 742: Jam in illa aetate frequentare ecclesiam dulce habuit, crebrius orationi incumbere, sacris missarum interesse solemniis, visitandis monasteriis operam dare, quos sanctiores sciebat monachos in amicitiam copulare.

The second describes Edward's devotion to God, God's mother, St Peter and St John:

Játvarðar saga, ch. 1: Hann hafði jafnan ákall til almáttigs Guðs í sínum bænum, ok hans heilagra manna. En þó tignaði hann framast næst guði vára Frú, sanctam Mariam; þar næst Pétr postula sem sinn einkanligan fóstr-föður, ok Johannem ewangelistam svá sem gæzlu-mann þess hreina lifnaðar er hann hélt alla sína æfi.

Ailred, col. 769: Interea rex sanctus ævo jam gravis militiae suae stipendiis para-batur, augebatur ei in dies circa Deum et Dei matrem affectio, circa sanctos Dei devotio, inter quos beatissimum Petrum ut specialem patronum suum venerabatur, discipulum illum quem diligebat Jesus, ob singulare privilegium castitatis mira mentis dulcedine amplectebatur.

These two sentences from Ailred are close together in the opening chapter of the saga, but widely separated in the Latin. The significance of this I discuss later; here I wish only to show the closeness of the translation. These passages have no equivalent in the other Latin Lives and alone are enough to disprove Rogers's theory that the saga writer used Ailred in Anglo-Norman translation. The Anglo-Norman version edited by Luard and the Middle

---

[1] *Vita Ædwardi Regis*, ed. Frank Barlow (London, 1962); 'La Vie de S. Édouard le Confesseur par Osbert de Clare', ed. Marc Bloch, *AB* 41 (1923), 5–131; and 'Vita S. Edwardi Regis et Con-fessoris auctore Beato Aelredo', Migne, Patrologia Latina 195, cols. 737–90.

[2] *Lives of Edward the Confessor*, ed. H. R. Luard, RS (1858), pp. 25–157; *La Vie d'Edouard le Con-fesseur*, ed. Östen Södergård (Uppsala, 1948); and *The Middle English Verse Life of Edward the Confessor*, ed. G. E. Moore (Philadelphia, 1942).

English translation paraphrase rather than translate. The other Anglo-Norman version translates the Latin fairly closely, but even here it is possible to see that the Icelandic is consistently closer to the Latin than to the French. In the first passage Latin and Icelandic include the detail of Edward's visits to monasteries, but the Anglo-Norman does not. In the second it is clear that the saga's 'einkanligan fóstr-föður' is a precise translation of the Latin 'specialem patronum', not of the Anglo-Norman 'Qu'il pur sun avué teneit'.[1]

The author digresses on William of Normandy for the rest of chapter one and returns to Edward abruptly at the beginning of the next chapter: 'Nú er at segja frá hinum helga Játvarði.' He begins with a general account of England's delight at Edward's return and most of the *Vitae Edwardi* have something similar. But again there is one sentence which is direct translation from Ailred, a sentence which is neither in the other Latin Lives nor in the other vernacular translations:

Játvarðar saga, ch. 2: þvíat í hans kóronan fékk heilög kirkja frjálsi, ok höfðingjar framgang, en alþýðan frið ok frelsi.

Ailred, col. 745: amissam reciperet in Edwardo populus pacem, proceres gloriam, ecclesia libertatem.

Rearrangement in order of precedence may indicate the saga writer's different priorities, but still he is following the Latin closely. Yet the three sentences that I have quoted represent the full extent of the saga's demonstrable borrowing from Ailred. When he goes on to describe two visions and a miracle (the drowned king, the seven sleepers and the ring), all of which are in Ailred, he goes to other sources. This is perhaps why Rogers asserts so confidently that though *Játvarðar saga* has some affinity to Ailred's *Vita* it cannot be based directly on it. The saga writer then records Edward's vision of the sacrament followed by two healing miracles. These also are in Ailred, but the saga has no close similarities to Ailred's text.

The account of the vision in which Edward saw a Danish king drown is demonstrably from Osbert's *Vita*. Both saga and Osbert begin the story by saying that the feast was Pentecost and the church St Peter's, Westminster. Ailred does not mention the church till later and then does not say that it was at Westminster. The saga gives the climax of the story in words that are a close translation of Osbert's Latin:

Játvarðar saga, ch. 2: ok svá sem hann skyldi stíga upp í skip af báti, þá féll hann á kaf ok druknaði eptir réttum Guðs dómi.

Osbert, p. 76: Cumque de prora ad nauem in quam ingredi debebat pedem extenderet, iusto Dei iudicio, elapsus corruit, et demersus in mare miserabiliter exspirauit.

[1] *Vie*, ed. Södergård, line 4174.

Since 'iusto Dei iudicio', translated as 'eptir réttum Guðs dómi', does not occur in any other account of the incident there can be no doubt that Osbert is the saga's source here.

Edward's next vision, that of the seven sleepers of Ephesus, is translated by the saga writer from yet another source, this time the *Gesta Regum Anglorum* by William of Malmesbury.[1] William tells us that Edward's description of the sleepers could not have been derived from his reading since he included details 'quas nulla docet littera'. The story is told by both Osbert and Ailred but they do not have this detail. It is however in *Játvarðar saga*: 'ok flest þat sem í öngum bókum stendr áðr af þeim ritað'. All accounts of the vision say that after it Edward sent messengers with letters to the emperor, but in the version shared by William of Malmesbury and the saga writer they carry gifts as well. On their next journey the messengers carry letters from the Byzantine emperor to the bishop of Ephesus. William describes these letters as those 'quem sacram vocant', which the saga writer translates 'er Girkir kalla sakram'.

Scholars have already pointed out the saga's debt to Osbert and to William of Malmesbury, but the nature of the borrowing gives rise to a number of questions which have not been answered. Why if the saga writer knew the works of Ailred, Osbert and William did he restrict himself to translating so little from each? More curiously, why when each of the sources he used contains the incidents he borrows from elsewhere does he borrow them from elsewhere? The episode taken from Osbert contains an even more puzzling problem. In Osbert the name of the drowned king is given. In the saga, though the same name is given, the author attributes his knowledge of it to Gizurr Hallsson. If the author had access to Osbert's *Vita* the name should have been there; if he had access to the *Vita* only via Gizurr, why should Gizurr have been given the credit for supplying the name?

The obvious answer to the first of these problems is that the saga writer knew the works of Ailred, Osbert and William only in some exceedingly abbreviated form. The first place to look therefore is among the chronicles and encyclopaedic collections where excerpts from these writers might be quoted. This method provides one answer. The saga writer probably knew William of Malmesbury through the *Speculum Historiale* by Vincent of Beauvais.[2] There is plenty of evidence that the *Speculum* was well-known and widely used in Iceland and many writers of sagas acknowledge their debt to it. The author of *Játvarðar saga* does not acknowledge his debt, but his text is almost a word for word translation of the *Speculum*'s shortened version of

[1] William of Malmesbury, *De Gestis Regum Anglorum*, ed. William Stubbs, RS (1887–9), I, 274–6.
[2] Vincent of Beauvais, *Speculum Historiale* (Venice, 1494); cf. the editions of [Strasbourg] 1474, Venice 1591 and Douai 1624.

this episode. William's narrative is a lengthy one, and not only do the *Speculum* and the saga make the same cuts in it, they also stop at the same point. The *Gesta Regum* explains that the turning of the seven sleepers in their sleep presages many disasters about to overtake the world. The list is a long one and it is unlikely that the authors of saga and *Speculum* should independently weary of it in the middle of the same sentence. It is more reasonable to suppose that the *Gesta Regum* was known to the saga writer only through the *Speculum* and that this is why he makes no further use of William on Edward.

The difference between the full version and the shortened one can easily be demonstrated:

Játvarðar saga, ch. 3: Eptir þetta kom þat fram skjótt sem hinn helgi Játvarðr konungr hafði fyrir sagt um ófrið ok önnur veraldar-áfelli; þvíat Agarene, Arabes, ok Tyrkir, gerðu mykinn úfrið í Siria, Licia, ok Minni Asia, ok eyddu þar margar borgir, Effesum, Jerusalem, sjau ár; ok eptir þat næst á öðrum sjau árum andaðizt (þrír) páfar, – Victor, Stephanus, Nicholaus.

Speculum Historiale, bk 25, ch. 20: Nec mora omnia illa secuta sunt quae praedixerat. Agareni & arabes & turci syriam & liciam & minorem asiam & maioris multas vrbes inter quas ephesum & hierosolymam depopulati sunt. vij annis: postea proximis tres pape idest Victor, Stephanus. & Nicolaus mortui sunt.

Gesta Regum, p. 276: Nec moram festinatio malorum fecit, quin Agareni et Arabes, et Turchi, alienae scilicet a Christo gentes, Syriam, et Liciam, et Minorem Asiam omnino, et Majoris urbes multas, inter quas et Ephesum, ipsam etiam Jerosolimam, depopulati, super Christianos invaderent. Tunc etiam, mortuo Manichete Constantinopolis imperatore, Diogenes, et Michaelius, ac Bucinacius, et Alexius vicissim se de imperio praecipitarunt: quorum ultimus, ad nostra tempora usque durans, Johannem filium reliquit heredem, astutia et fraudibus quam probitate notior, multa noxia in peregrinos sacri itineris machinatus; Anglorum tamen fidem suspiciens, praecipuis familiaritatibus suis eos applicabat, amorem eorum filio transcribens. His septem annis proximis tres papae, Victor, Stephanus, Nicolaus, apostolatus vigorem continuis mortibus labefactarunt: e vestigio quoque Henricus, pius Romanorum imperator, defunctus, successorem Henricum filium habuit, qui multas oppressiones orbi Romano fatuitate nequitiaque sua intulit.

The general similarity between the *Speculum* and saga summaries is obvious, but there is one point which establishes the link between them. In William's account the words 'His septem annis proximis' refer to the deaths of three popes and the emperor. The *Speculum*'s summary is ambiguous. Depending on punctuation, 'vij annis' could be taken with the preceding account of destruction in the Middle East, and the phrase 'postea proximis' ('vij annis' understood) to the following report of papal deaths. This is how the saga writer has taken it and he could not have made this mistake had he been using William's full text and not Vincent's summary. Early printed editions of the

Speculum have differing punctuations at this point, and the 1494 edition quoted above demonstrates a punctuation which would encourage mistranslation. The Old Norse translator must have used a manuscript with equally misleading punctuation.[1]

The *Speculum* does not contain the excerpts from Ailred and Osbert that the saga writer knows and they are not commonly found in the chronicles. Certainly no chronicle compiler, as far as I can ascertain, makes use of the same details from Ailred as those that the saga has. In the liturgy on the other hand we find excerpts from the *Vitae* which are closely connected with the saga material. There are lessons for St Edward's day in the Westminster missal and in the Exeter, Salisbury and Hereford breviaries. The ones in Westminster are unconnected with the others and not comparable with the saga. The other three all have lessons derived mainly from Osbert but including occasional sentences from Ailred.[2] They are obviously related texts though they diverge in detail. Exeter is very close to the saga. Something similar to lection 1 in Exeter must be the source for the first part of the saga's opening chapter:[3]

Játvarðar saga, ch. 1: Hinn helgi Játvarðr konungr í Englandi var son Aðalráðs konungs Etgeirs sonar, er fyrstr var einn konungr yfir Englandi. [Af honum heyrði hinn helgi Dunstanus biskup engla-söng í lopti á hans burðar-tíma, meðr þeim hætti, at á hans dögum mundi heilög kristni fá frið ok framgang í Englandi.] Móðir hins heilaga Játvarðar var Emma dróttning, dóttir Ríkarðar hertoga af Norðmandí; [hón var systir Roðbertz er kallaðr var *diabolus*; hann lét hertogadóm, ok gékk í heremíta-líf.] Hinn helgi Játvarðr elskaði þegar á unga aldri helga kirkju ok tíða-gerð, klaustra at vitja, ok þá múnka at elska er hónum þóttu helgastir ok siðsamastir, svá ok ágætar ölmusur at gjöra þeim er váru fátækir ok þurftugir. Hann hafði jafnan ákall til almáttigs Guðs í sínum bænum, ok hans heilagra manna. En þó tignaði hann framast næst guði vára Frú, sanctam Mariam; þar næst Pétr postula sem sinn einkanligan fóstr-föður, ok Johannem ewangelistam svá sem gæzlu-mann þess hreina lifnaðar er hann hélt alla sína æfi.

Ordinale Exon. III, 375 (lesson 1, St Edward's Translation): Preciosus confessor domini, et rex insignis edwardus, ex antiquis anglorum regibus prodijt oriundus. Cuius pater, athelredus, filius edgari primi anglorum monarche, [frater beati edwardi martyris et sancte edithe uirginis] extitit. Emma uero, ricardi ducis normannorum

---

[1] For another example where Icelandic translates a passage from William of Malmesbury via the *Speculum Historiale* see H. Gering, *Íslenzk Æventyri* (Halle, 1882), no. XCVI, pp. 305–7 and 347–8. On the textual history of the *Speculum* see B. L. Ullman, 'A Project for a New Edition of Vincent of Beauvais', *Speculum* 8 (1933), 312–26.

[2] *Ordinale Exon.*, ed. J. N. Dalton, Henry Bradshaw Society 37–8, 63 and 69 (1909–40), III, 375–80; *Breviarium ad usum insignis ecclesiae Sarum*, ed. Francis Procter and Christopher Wordsworth (Cambridge, 1886) III, cols. 909–14; and *The Hereford Breviary*, ed. W. H. Frere, HBS 26, 40 and 46 (1904–15), II, 370–1. Why the liturgy should have this curious jumble of material from Ailred and Osbert is not clear. Further work on the manuscripts of Ailred might be enlightening.

[3] My brackets indicate what is *not* parallel in the two texts.

filia, mater fuit. [Uerum, ingruente in anglia danorum tempestate, ad auos suos in normanniam puer transducitur, ne procella seuiencium cicius absorberetur.] Iam tunc, in illa tenera etate, dulce habuit frequentare ecclesiam, crebrius oracioni insistere, sacris missarum interesse solempnijs, uisitandis monasterijs, operam dare. Augebatur in dies, circa deum et matrem dei affectio, circa sanctos dei deuocio. Inter quos, beatissimum petrum ut specialem patronum uenerabatur, iohannem uero euangelistam ob singulare castitatis priuilegium amplectabatur. Quorum munitus patrocinio, mente integer et carne permansit.

That is the whole of the first lesson. The opening sentences are from Osbert, and then follow the two which we have already cited from Ailred, widely separated in the *Vita*, but linked here, as they are linked in the saga. The saga and the lesson have the same genealogical information, except that the saga omits the bit about Edward the martyr and St Edith in favour of Dunstan's prophecy at the birth of Edgar. Lives of Dunstan were known in Iceland, but that particular detail could have been noted from the lesson for St Dunstan's day. The saga's genealogical addition on the Norman side may have come from Scandinavian sources. That Emma was sister of Robert, father of William the Bastard, is not true, but the error occurs in *Heimskringla*[1] as well as in *Játvarðar saga*.

The other lessons in the Exeter breviary cover the visions of the Danish king, the seven sleepers and the sacrament as Christ, the story of St John's ring and the two miracles that are in the saga. It will readily be seen that this catalogue of material corresponds almost exactly to what the saga has on Edward. The other breviaries do not include the miracles, nor is their first lection so closely parallel to the saga. Nevertheless I do not wish to press the correspondence between saga and Exeter breviary too closely. For though it is true that all the incidents in the Exeter lessons are the same as those in the saga there are differences in detail. Exeter's second lesson contains a sentence which is not too far removed from the one of Ailred's quoted in the saga, 'Recepit populus pacem, proceres gloriam, ecclesia libertatem', but for an exact quotation of this sentence we have to go to lesson one for Edward's day in the Hereford breviary. Secondly in the account of the vision of the Danish king's death the saga translates Osbert's 'iusto Dei iudicio'. This is not in Exeter, but it is in Salisbury. On the other hand the name of the king which the saga writer claims to know only through Gizurr Hallsson is in Salisbury, but not in Exeter. The evidence demonstrates I think quite clearly that the saga writer's source for his material on Edward is a service-book. The saga is closest to Exeter, but even in the details where it differs from Exeter the other breviaries show that the material is to be

---

[1] Snorri Sturluson, *Heimskringla*, ed. Bjarni Aðalbjarnarson, Íslenzk Fornrit 26–8 (Reykjavík, 1951), III, 168.

found in the liturgy and that, although the precise nature of lectionary borrowing from Ailred varies from redaction to redaction, the general pattern of borrowing is similar. Use of the liturgy explains why the saga writer translates closely material from both Ailred and Osbert and yet evidently has not access to the complete *Vita* of either. In this way his complaints about shortage of material become comprehensible.

It seems sensible at this point to look at the external evidence for the use of service-books in Iceland, and we are in a particularly favourable position to do this. There are two important church registers extant both dating from the fourteenth century, one for the diocese of Hólar, the other for that of Skálaholt.[1] Between them they cover Iceland. Not all the entries are explicit and we cannot always distinguish exactly which books a church possessed, but still they give much useful information.

The following is a random selection of material from the register of Bishop Auðun of Hólar *c.* 1318. The church of Skinnastaðir owned a 'martyrologium' and 'suffragium sanctorum'. Garðr had a 'lesturbok vm sumarid'. Skútustaðir possessed a splendid set of liturgical books including 'lesbok god. tekur til ad jola faustu og til paska. ad dominicum. aspiciens bok god de sanctis. tekur til ad Jonsmessu. og framm vm allra heilagra messu. . . lesbok. tekur til ad paskum ok til jolafostu. oc fram til paska. oc ad skipudu. lesbok a veturinn de sanctis.' Grenjastaðir was equipped with 'saungbækur oc lesbækur og ad aullu per anni circulum'. Múli had in its fairly large library 'legendu bækur per anni circulum, legenda de sanctis ä ij selskinns bokum, forn bok de sanctis a sumarid'. Illugastaðir had both a 'messubok per anni circulum' and 'legendu bækur per anni circulum'. Flatey's collection showed limitations: 'lesbok per anni circulum ad dominicum enn til Columba messu de sanctis'. Grímsey owned a comprehensive collection of liturgical books including several 'de sanctis'. Grytubakki had only one 'bok de sanctis'. Höfði at first appears only to have had the saints 'fra Jonsmessu baptistæ og framm vm Andres messu', but 'kyrckiann ä enn þessar bækur Sanctorum bok med lesi oc saung . . .' At Laufás there was a 'sogubok oc ä margar heilagra manna sogur'. The wording suggests a vernacular text, but the church also owned 'lesbækur ij per anni circulum'. At Svalbarð there was a 'lesbok de sanctis a sumarid', at Möðruvellir a 'lesbok de sanctis'. At Saurbær the books included 'legendu bækur per anni circulum', while Mikligarðr had 'lesbækur ij per anni circulum' and Grund a single 'lesbok per anni circulum'. Hrafnagil possessed a 'historia bok de sanctis' and another 'bok de sanctis inter paska et pentecosten'.

It would be tedious to continue the list for there are ninety-eight churches in the Hólar register and 298 in the Skálaholt one. The examples quoted,

---

[1] *Diplomatarium Islandicum* (Copenhagen and Reykjavík, 1857–) II, 423–89 and IV, 27–240.

taken from the first forty inventories in the Hólar catalogue, are sufficiently revealing. Scarcely any church was entirely without books. Indeed Lilli Gjerløw has pointed out that 'the early church charters stipulate services which presuppose a full set of liturgical books'.[1] The books almost invariably include 'lesbok de sanctis' or 'lesbok per anni circulum'. It is not possible to count the references because not enough are precise and some churches do not specify their books but simply give the number or the value. We cannot always be sure whether references are to the common or proper of saints, to lessons from the gospels or lessons from saints' lives. But we can be sure that there must have been dozens of lectionaries and sanctorales in the Icelandic church libraries, even the poorest containing one or maybe part of one.

Some of the service-books were from England, though this is specified only in the Hólar register, not in that for Skálaholt. Múli had an 'enskur gradull' and an 'enskur psaltare'. At Háls in Fnjóskadalr there was an 'enskur gradall' and two books 'j spiolldum enskar'. At Laufás they owned a 'messubok ensk'. Perhaps, as the editor of the *Diplomatarium Islandicum* suggests, the word *reddingabækur* found in the inventory of Hrafnagil church is the English word 'reading-book', and the books too may have been English. The word *enskr* could indicate either language or provenance, but either way England evidently provided Iceland with some of her religious texts.[2] Most of these books must have been in the churches long before the inventories were compiled. The internal evidence that the Edward material in *Játvarðar saga* comes from the lessons for St Edward's day is fully supported by the external evidence for the prevalence of lectionary material in Icelandic libraries.

The suggestion that the author of *Játvarðar saga* was using liturgy may help us a little with the critical question of the date of the saga. The compilation as it stands is in late-fourteenth-century manuscripts, but several scholars have wished to see a twelfth-century layer of writing present.[3] It is very likely that the lessons themselves were early translated for actual use and that when the fourteenth-century compiler started work on his saga of Edward he had already a set of vernacular lections to hand. Hans Bekker-Nielsen has pointed out that certain Icelandic manuscript fragments might be described as parts of 'homiletic handbooks'[4] and such vernacular collections of liturgical material may have been the author's starting-point. This

1 Lilli Gjerløw, *Ordo Nidrosiensis Ecclesiae* (Oslo, 1968), p. 40.
2 Lilli Gjerløw, *Adoratio Crucis* (Oslo, 1961), demonstrates the use of English service-books in Norway.
3 Rogers, 'Icelandic Life of St Edward', pp. 266–7 and 271; and Lars Lönnroth, 'Studier i Olaf Tryggvasons saga', *Samlaren* 84 (1963), 74 ff. But see P. Hallberg's criticism of Lönnroth's position, *Samlaren* 86 (1965), 163.
4 Hans Bekker-Nielsen, 'Fra ordbogens værksted. 3. Homiletisk haandbog?', *Opuscula I*, Bibliotheca Arnamagnæana 20 (Copenhagen, 1960), 343–4.

might also explain the curious reference to Gizurr Hallsson. Most probably the name of the king occurred in the lections and Gizurr provided not the name but the identification 'son Knútz konungs hins ríka ok Alfifu' (ch. 2), but the later compiler, knowing that this incident was not recorded in the kings' sagas, thought Gizurr must have provided both name and parentage. Alternatively the specific service-book may not have supplied the name, but Gizurr may have been able to give it from his fuller knowledge of the material. It is possible that we ought to associate Gizurr not just with providing a name but with translation of service-books for common use.

If a fourteenth-century compiler were revising an early set of vernacular lections he would be responsible for rewriting the seven sleepers legend as found in the *Speculum* and presumably he added all the material not concerned with Edward. But there is one other Edward story which he must have tampered with, and that is the flamboyant one of St John and the ring. This story is reputedly in Ailred and not in Osbert, but in fact it is appended to the Cambridge, Corpus Christi College 161 text of Osbert's work, though in a form slightly different from Ailred's. The versions in the liturgy are closer to the Corpus Christi manuscript of Osbert than to Ailred. *Játvarðar saga* is close to neither. In the Latin King Edward gives his ring to a pilgrim, who turns out to be St John the Evangelist. John gives the ring to two pilgrims and tells them to go and see King Edward when they get back to England. The first part of this is the same in the saga. But in the second part the saga introduces a knight, prisoner of the Saracens, instead of the two pilgrims, and St John not only hands the ring over to him but miraculously releases him from captivity and transports him back to England.

There are no parallels to this in the Middle English or Anglo-Norman translations, but we find the story in St John's *Miracula* as well as in Edward's. The Middle English version in the *South English Legendary*[1] and the Icelandic version in two sagas of St John, *Jóns saga postola IV* and *Tveggia postola saga Jóns ok Jacobs*,[2] have some affinities with *Játvarðar saga*. In the *South English Legendary* there is no life of Edward the Confessor, but this one story about him turns up among the miracles of St John. It is not quite as in Ailred, Osbert or the saga, but it contains one detail which links it with the saga. The recipient of the ring is one knight, not two pilgrims, though admittedly this knight is no prisoner of the Saracens but is abroad 'auntres forto fonde' (line 512). In the two Icelandic sagas of St John the text is so close to the one in *Játvarðar saga* that either any one of them is a source for the other two or they are all taken from the same source. We are not sure enough about the

---

[1] *The South English Legendary*, ed. Charlotte d'Evelyn and Anna J. Mill, Early English Text Society 235–6 and 244 (London, 1956–9) II, 609–10.

[2] *Postola Sögur*, ed. C. R. Unger (Christiania, 1874), pp. 507–9 and 710–11.

dates of these three sagas to say that one is earlier than the others. They are all probably from the first half of the fourteenth century. There are slight indications in the retention of Latin words that the three are independent translations. All three have *in processione* and *ewangelista*, but only *Játvarðar saga* has *á einni momentu*, only *Jóns saga* has *resignera* and only *Jóns ok Jacobs saga* has *Anglia* and *curiam*. It seems probable that the story of the knight imprisoned by Saracens, a post-Crusade recension, came to Iceland among the *miracula* of St John. A further indication that the author of *Jóns saga* must have been using a collection of this kind, not Edward material, is his inclusion of another English miracle by St John, this time concerning that splendid man Edmund who later became archbishop of Canterbury: 'virðuligan mann Ethmundum, er siðan varð Cantuariensis erchibyskup i Englandi'. A collection of St John's miracles including the Edward one may well have been the source for all three sagas and have been translated independently in each case.

Játvarðar saga is found in fourteenth-century manuscripts and is almost certainly a fourteenth-century compilation. The *Speculum Historiale*, for example, could scarcely have reached Iceland much before the end of the thirteenth century. But some of the material must have been available in Iceland earlier. The lectionary passages from Osbert, known to Gizurr Hallsson, must have been in Iceland before 1206, the date of Gizurr's death. It is possible that the lessons for Edward's day were translated about this time and that these lessons were later used as the basis for a saga when hagiographical saga writing increased in popularity. But Edward the Confessor's life lacks the dramatic impact of a martyr's or reformer's or even an eccentric hermit's. His cult never became intensive in England, and it is not surprising that an Icelandic saga writer should have found himself at a loss for material. He solved his problem by fitting his picture of Edward into a picture of England at the time of the Norman Conquest. For this he turned away from hagiography and explored the resources of chronicle, history and legend.

Structural criticism:
a plea for more systematic study of
Anglo-Saxon buildings

H. M. TAYLOR

From the Norman Conquest onward, the architectural history of England has been put on a firm basis by the work of nineteenth-century writers who were able to associate precise dates, and even named builders, with a considerable number of buildings as a result of the survival of contemporary written records which could be unequivocally linked to the surviving buildings. For the period before 1066 the position is very different: the studies of the last century have indeed established firmly the principal distinctive features of Anglo-Saxon workmanship; but for only a handful of buildings is there any written record that allows a firm assignment of date;[1] and there is consequently a wide divergence of opinion between scholars in the dates which they assign to individual buildings or particular architectural features.

When we bear in mind the strictly limited amount of written evidence that is available for the buildings of Anglo-Saxon England, it follows that further progress towards determining a more precise architectural history must depend largely upon our using more fully the evidence that is latent in the buildings themselves, and in associating that evidence as closely as possible with such written history as is available, in ways that will be elaborated below. Sometimes, as is indicated below, the evidence latent in the buildings can be supplemented from written records or by excavation; but it is important to realize that as a general rule it is only from standing fabric that we can get information about the structural details which are so important in enabling us to recognize other buildings of similar date.

In order to make fresh progress in a systematic manner, it seems desirable as a first step to list all the known surviving buildings of the Anglo-Saxon period for which there is contemporary or nearly contemporary recorded history. A first tentative list of such buildings is accordingly published as appendix 1 to this essay. Its first object is to point the way to the buildings

---

[1] See H. M. Taylor, *Why Should We Study the Anglo-Saxons?* (Cambridge, 1966), pp. 43–5. The list there given has, on more mature reflection, been amended in appendix 1 of this article, list (1), by deletion of St Martin's church at Canterbury and by the addition of the ruins at Glastonbury.

which are most immediately worthy of fresh detailed study, because such studies are most likely to be able to be associated with historical records and thus to yield positive evidence about dates. But since any such list is unlikely at first to be complete, its second object is to encourage other workers in this field or allied ones to fill any gaps that they may notice in it.

As a second step towards better use of the evidence that is available, it seems desirable to draw up a further list, namely that of known surviving buildings which contain fabric of more than one Anglo-Saxon period. Such buildings are clearly also worthy of further detailed study, because the relationship of the fabric of different periods can establish a sequence in time, and a listing of the sequences derived from a number of such buildings may then serve to show that certain features always occur in the later phases while other features always occur earlier. A tentative list of buildings which show more than one phase of Anglo-Saxon workmanship is accordingly published as appendix II, in the hope that its publication will serve the same two objects as those mentioned for appendix I.

Lists, however, will not in themselves lead to any material advance in knowledge. Progress will depend upon more careful study of the evidence that can be yielded by each of the buildings; and, in particular, by association of evidence from the buildings with evidence from the written records that are available. Moreover, systematic recording of this evidence can do much to point the way to results that would otherwise be quite beyond our reach.

It is well known in other fields of study that closer and more systematic use of basic material has yielded fruitful results from evidence that has long been available but has not previously been fully used. Two simple examples may serve to illustrate this assertion. In the field of archaeology, a modern excavation with its insistence on careful sections and accurate recording can provide much more evidence than came from the haphazard methods of the past. Similarly, in the field of written history, a modern scholar may have at his disposal many published texts, each of which is based upon careful comparison of all the available sources, whereas earlier scholars often had to seek out the individual manuscripts and then labour to interpret them and assess their reliability. The basic material was the same in both but the modern scholar can make much more fruitful use of it because of the work done by others to put it conveniently at his disposal and to discriminate between reliable and unreliable records.

I have coined the phrase 'structural criticism' to denote in the field of architectural history a similar kind of work to that which in general history is associated with the title 'textual criticism'. This similarity of nomenclature is meant to emphasize my belief that the basic evidence which is latent in our early buildings needs to be made much more generally and reliably available to scholars by means of the publication of definitive studies on all the important buildings, each such study being based upon a thorough examination of the building itself and a careful review of whatever contemporary or later medieval history may be available. Moreover each study should be accompanied by detailed and accurate plans, elevations and sections, which will serve as the basis for further discussion about the building concerned. In addition each study should include all available records of restorations and modifications of the building in post-medieval times, with particular reference to contemporary accounts of modification or destruction of ancient fabric. Finally, each study should, of course, give full reference to any similar recent studies and should show clearly the extent to which their findings are confirmed or rendered doubtful.

In many ways it is easier to explain the methods that are involved by applying them to specific examples; but, since I have published elsewhere some such studies without any enunciation of general principles, it will now be best to make an attempt to describe the principles, and to refer to the published studies for illustrative examples.[1]

THE PROCEDURES OF STRUCTURAL CRITICISM

The study and recording of the buildings

The main purpose of this essay is to describe not only why the buildings themselves need much closer study than has yet been given to them but also how such study should be organized and published.

In the first place it should be noted that the buildings of most interest in this search for architectural history are usually those that have been most often modified throughout the Anglo-Saxon period; because only these will contain the richest assortment of early and later features, and only in these will there be the best chance that the later features will unambiguously demonstrate their lateness by proclaiming their relation to earlier ones. Buildings of this sort are necessarily complicated, and their secrets will not be disclosed by cursory examination. Detailed study and measurement are necessary, as well as carefully drawn plans, sections and elevations. Every feature needs study, for example to see whether it shows signs of later modification, or whether it proves that another feature is earlier by resting on it or by partially cutting it away.

If such study of a building leads to a hypothesis that it has developed in a number of separate building phases, it is important as a next step to make outline plans and elevations to illustrate the building at each of the

---

[1] See H. M. Taylor, 'Repton Reconsidered', *England Before the Conquest: Studies in Primary Sources presented to Dorothy Whitelock*, ed. P. Clemoes and K. Hughes (Cambridge, 1971), pp. 351–89; and 'St Giles' Church, Barrow, Shropshire', *ArchJ* 127 (1970), 211–21.

phases concerned. In the first place these drawings will serve to test the internal consistency of the tentative architectural history and to reject any obviously false step; and in the second place they will serve as an enduring record of the early features and the later ones when the time comes to collate evidence from many different buildings.

If a wall contains a feature which is thought to have been inserted later, or two features of which one cuts away part of another, it is important to make measured drawings which show clearly the relation of the individual stones. It is also important to support these drawings by photographs. It may be asked why both drawings and photographs should be necessary. The importance of the photographs is perhaps obvious since they are less open to criticism on the ground of personal error or prejudice. The importance of the drawings is, nevertheless, at least equally great: for example some details will escape even the most careful photograph, and sometimes in a photograph lines of weathering will look surprisingly like joints in the stonework; moreover the making of a careful measured drawing will often bring home facts which otherwise would completely escape observation. Finally it is only by the combination of plan, elevation and section (all drawn to the same scale) that the results in their full detail can be made available to others who do not have the opportunity to visit the building itself.

Whenever possible, drawings of this sort to record the details of individual features should show the jointing of the separate stones of the masonry, both those that form the outline of the feature itself and those of the main fabric of the adjoining area of wall. Only by making drawings in such detail will the evidence recorded be sufficient to answer questions about the relation of the feature to the wall in which it stands and to serve to classify the feature in relation to others of similar general outline in other buildings.

If a building is of more than one storey, a proper appreciation of its structure is usually difficult without the help of a series of measured drawings to show how the separate parts are related. For simple buildings like rectangular towers the preparation of the necessary drawings usually presents little difficulty, because changes in exterior dimensions can usually be seen from outside, while interior dimensions can be determined at each floor and wall thicknesses can be measured through the openings. Heights may present some difficulty, but can usually be determined by lowering a weighted measuring-tape from the parapet.

In more complicated buildings there may be difficulty in linking levels inside a building with those outside, especially if the part of the building under consideration is remote from any doorway. Windows often provide a convenient solution to such a problem: the height of a corner of one pane of glass can be measured in relation to the base-levels for all observations both inside and outside the buildings and thus the two base-levels can be linked together. Similarly the thicknesses of walls are often most conveniently determined by direct measurement through a window or by measuring up to the glass on either side.

The most acute difficulties are likely to be presented by a complicated building like an irregularly planned crypt below a chancel of somewhat similar shape. The best method of proceeding may then be to establish a set of rectangular axes for all measurements in the crypt and an independent set of axes for measurements in the chancel above. As a final operation the two sets of axes can then be linked together both in plan and in elevation by two sets of measurements through windows, in the way described above.

In all operations which involve elaborate measurements it is most important to carry out independent checking of the observations before ending a day's work on the site, in order to bring to light the errors which can then so easily be set right but which could render useless the whole set of observations if they were not discovered until later.

Written evidence

Early

Contemporary written records are almost always the most important single group of sources for architectural history, because as a rule only they can provide precise dates for the fabric. Therefore the study of a building, as described above, should go hand in hand with a search through all known written evidence about it for every crumb of historical evidence. Unfortunately it is very seldom that early records about a site provide enough architectural detail to make it certain that they relate to the building which survives on the site at the present day, or to any particular phase of its development.[1] Sometimes, however, structural criticism may help to associate the historical records more closely to the building, particularly if both the written records and the building itself show that there have been several separate successive phases of building activity. It may then become clear that there is a probable way in which the phases recorded in the written history can be associated with the phases that are shown by the fabric itself. It is, however, important to appreciate that any such linking of written history with a building can, at best, be only tentative: not only may there

---

[1] A notable exception is St Augustine's abbey at Canterbury. Bede's account of the church of St Peter and St Paul shows beyond doubt that the area now preserved under cover in the grounds of the abbey is the north *porticus* of St Gregory where the archbishops were buried. Goscelin's later account of the rebuilding by abbots Wulfric and Scotland not only fixes the identity of the tombs of Archbishops Laurentius, Mellitus, and Justus in the *porticus* of St Gregory but also serves to identify the octagonal building east of the early church as the work of Abbot Wulfric (1047–59). See, for example, H. M. Taylor and Joan Taylor, *Anglo-Saxon Architecture* (Cambridge, 1965), pp. 135–9.

be other possible ways of linking the history to the building, but it may even be the case that an essential link is missing from either or both of the historical and structural chains of evidence so that no direct association is possible between them. Finally, it is important to discriminate between contemporary records and records that were made long after the events concerned. In view of the fallibility of human memory the latter kind of record must as a rule be treated with considerable reserve.

Modern

A quite different category of written evidence is that which may be provided by the observations of architects and antiquaries of the last few centuries, particularly such records as illustrate or describe buildings before or during restorations or demolitions of that period.[1] Evidence of this type needs to be used with care, because not all drawings are accurate and others can be shown to relate to proposals for restoration rather than to original features; but even after allowing for all these difficulties there is an important store of evidence in the writings and drawings of the past few centuries. When evidence of this type is used to provide information about features which have been subsequently destroyed, the reliability of the information is, of course, greatly increased if the features are confirmed by drawings by two or more independent observers or if a description in words is available as confirmation of a drawing.[2]

Evidence from excavation

In recent years, popular fancy has been much more attracted by archaeological excavation than by close study of standing fabric. It is indeed true that archaeological excavation can often produce important information which cannot be obtained in any other way, particularly about buildings which have been completely or almost completely destroyed. But this should not be allowed to distract attention from the special importance of standing fabric. It should be borne in mind that only standing fabric can provide information about the details of windows, doorways, upper floors and all the special features which are so important in distinguishing between buildings of different dates. There is, therefore, a continuing need for the most careful study of the early buildings which have survived to the present day.

Sometimes evidence about the history of a building is concealed by plaster

---

[1] Faculties authorizing alterations to the fabric sometimes give useful information, particularly if they are accompanied by plans or specifications.

[2] See, for example, Haigh's description and Gorham's drawing of the arches that no longer exist in the side walls of the church at Repton; Taylor and Taylor, *Anglo-Saxon Architecture*, p. 514 and fig. 555.

on its walls or by earth which has accumulated about them. If structural examination indicates that this is so, a special note should be included in the published report so that the necessary steps can be taken, when possible, to investigate the matter further. It is particularly important that any such work should be carried out only by persons properly trained in the techniques involved, because of the very real risk that evidence will otherwise be destroyed rather than brought to light. Investigations recently carried out at Kornelimünster on the site of the ninth-century abbey of Inda provide a splendid example of the way in which excavation can be used in conjunction with detailed study of standing walls, to provide information which neither method could have yielded had it been used alone.[1] Opportunity was taken in connection with structural works in the church to enable a comprehensive excavation to settle the position, nature, and extent of the earliest and all subsequent buildings on the site. This evidence was then used to indicate where early fabric might still survive above ground, hidden beneath modern plaster on the walls of the present church. Such plaster was then stripped from the walls to allow careful examination of their construction; and, finally, wherever necessary the mortar joints were raked out to clear them of modern repointing and so to make possible a comparison of the internal mortar with that in the foundations.

These investigations point the way to steps which need to be taken in a number of the more important English churches where there is substantial standing fabric from the Anglo-Saxon era. For example, at Deerhurst and Wing almost all the structural details within the churches are covered by Victorian plaster, the removal of which would almost certainly show whether or not certain doorways and windows are contemporary with the walls in which they stand. Similarly, at these and other churches there is urgent need for excavation within and beside the church to settle whether or not the present fabric represents the earliest building on the site. Detailed examination of the fabric by these two methods in conjunction would almost certainly allow the architectural history of these important early buildings to be placed on a much more secure footing than is possible at present.

FEATURES WHICH INDICATE THE DEVELOPMENT
AND ADAPTATION OF BUILDINGS

It is probably true to say that one of the greatest recent advances in our understanding of Anglo-Saxon architectural history has sprung from a fuller appreciation that many of the buildings show clear signs of their development and adaptation by successive generations of users, and that they are not

[1] Leo Hugot, *Kornelimünster*, Beihefte der Bonner Jahrbücher 26 (Cologne, 1968).

simple structures arising from a single phase of building, as was often supposed. But, conversely, there is a risk that reliable discoveries of this sort concerning one building may lead to ill-considered claims that a similar complicated history of development can be seen in another. Such claims must, of course, be carefully examined; but they should be accepted only if the available evidence clearly supports the proposed history.

It may help to clarify the methods of structural criticism if next we consider some classes of features which are of particular importance in giving indications about the history of buildings and which should therefore be looked for and recorded in detail.

Straight vertical joints

In building a wall, or a junction between two walls, care is usually taken to provide good bonding of the stones or bricks and to avoid continuous straight vertical joints which would obviously tend to weaken the structure. If therefore a straight vertical joint is seen, without any bonding or with only very occasional bonding units, it can generally be taken as an indication that the wall on one side of the joint is a later addition.

Perhaps the most striking examples of straight vertical joints are provided by some later Anglo-Saxon west towers whose side walls were built against the west walls of earlier naves without any bonding into them. Sometimes the masonry of the tower is quite differently coursed from that of the nave, thus emphasizing that the two buildings are of different date; but in other examples the masonry of the tower is similar to that of the nave and it is less easy to be certain whether or not the two walls are bonded. In difficult cases it may be possible to get supporting evidence from other features. Sometimes, as at Branston in Lincolnshire, a plinth running round the nave may settle the matter by continuing along the west front under the later side walls of the tower;[1] or sometimes, as at Kirk Hammerton in Yorkshire, the deciding factor may be old plaster which has been sealed in place on the west wall of the nave by the later side walls of the tower even though plaster has everywhere else long since disappeared from the main walls of the nave.[2]

The round towers of Norfolk and Suffolk are often claimed as having been originally built as isolated defensive structures against which churches were later built; but when there is any difference in date, careful inspection will usually show that the round tower was in fact built later against the west wall of the nave. A particularly clear example is at Little Bradley in Suffolk.[3]

A straight vertical joint of unusual interest occurs at the chapel of St Pancras in the grounds of St Augustine's Abbey at Canterbury, where the lower courses of the west porch are not in bond with the west wall of the

---

[1] Taylor and Taylor, *Anglo-Saxon Architecture*, pp. 93–4 and fig. 404.
[2] *Ibid.* p. 362.　　　　　　　　　　　　　　　[3] *Ibid.* p. 90 and fig. 39.

nave, but where proper bonding begins a few feet above the ground. After considering supporting evidence from a change in the character of the mortar at about the same level, Sir William St John Hope deduced that the nave was begun without a west porch and that, when its walls had been built only a few feet high, there was a change of plan whereby the west porch was then laid out and thereafter the nave and porch were built up as a unit.[1]

Evidence of this type always needs careful study, because bonding is not necessarily made course by course even when walls are built simultaneously. For instance at Brixworth in Northamptonshire the Rev. C. F. Watkins reported as long ago as 1867 that the walls of the west porch were not bonded course by course into the west wall of the nave but had nevertheless certainly been built simultaneously because they were bonded in sections of several courses at a time up their whole height.[2]

In considering the architectural history that is implied by a straight-forward unbonded vertical joint it is also important to bear in mind that even the subsequent addition of a feature such as a porch or a tower may not necessarily mean either the lapse of a great many years or the onset of a new phase of planning. It may, by contrast, simply mean the continued execution of a plan that was envisaged from the beginning but was in part deferred either to limit the initial effort and expenditure or to secure that the functionally most important parts of the church were completed more rapidly than would otherwise have been possible.

Changes of quoining

One of the most distinctive features of many stone buildings is the treatment of the quoins or salient angles. Sometimes these quoins are formed of the same fabric as that of the walls themselves; but more often in medieval buildings they are formed of larger stones, no doubt with a view to greater strength as well as some degree of decorative effect.[3]

As a general rule it will be found that any single phase of a building employs a uniform type of quoining, or conversely that a change in the character of quoining in a single building implies that the parts with different quoining belong to different phases of erection. For example, in Lincolnshire, several churches have long-and-short quoining on their naves and chancels but, by contrast, the towers have side-alternate quoining and can clearly be seen to have been added later because they are built against the west wall of the nave without bonding.

[1] *Ibid.* p. 147.
[2] C. F. Watkins, *The Basilica and the Basilical Church of Brixworth* (London, 1867), pp. 31 and 50.
[3] For an explanation of the names used to describe the several different types of quoining used in Anglo-Saxon buildings and for illustrations of the principal types see Taylor and Taylor, *Anglo-Saxon Architecture*, pp. 6–7 and figs. 4–5.

H. M. Taylor

It is always worth while to record the type of quoining on each part of a building and to note whether the type remains constant throughout the whole height of each quoin. If so, there is a strong indication either that the building is of a single period or that any successive phases in its erection followed without any appreciable lapse of time.[1] Conversely, if the type of quoining changes within the height of a single quoin, there is an indication of building periods separated by appreciable amounts of time that allowed for a change in fashion of this distinctive feature. A good example of this latter point is to be seen in the tower of St Peter's church at Barton-on-Humber, where the lower two stages, including the original belfry, have well defined long-and-short quoining, whereas the third stage, which is of obviously different workmanship throughout, has side-alternate quoining in stones the same in size as those used in the main fabric of its walls.[2]

Changes of fabric in the walls

The fabric of which a wall is built probably gives rather less clear indication of date than does the distinctive character of the quoining; but it is nevertheless well worth while to note changes in the fabric of the wall, particularly if they occur within a single structural unit. Sometimes it seems that changes of fabric were used to differentiate between parts of a building so as to give a decorative effect or to emphasize the greater importance of the sanctuary; but if a change of fabric occurs within a single unit such as the nave then it seems likely that it indicates a division between an original building and a later addition. Any such indication is, of course, strengthened if there is found to be a clearly defined straight joint (whether vertical or horizontal) between the two areas of different fabric.

Inserted features

It is important to appreciate the skill with which, throughout the Middle Ages, features such as windows, doorways and even wide arches leading to towers, side-chapels or aisles were inserted into previously existing walls. Sometimes the workmanship is so skilful that only the most careful inspection will decide whether or not a feature is contemporary with the wall in which it now stands; and this difficulty becomes particularly acute if the surrounding wall is of rough rubble. On the other hand if the wall is carefully coursed, whether of only roughly squared rubble or of ashlar, then the later insertion of a feature usually becomes more easy to determine, because there is almost always some clue such as broken faces of adjoining stones,

[1] I first saw an enunciation of this and the converse principle by E. Gilbert, 'New Views on Warden, Bywell and Heddon-on-the-Wall Churches', *Archaeologia Aeliana*, 4th ser., 24 (1946), 167–74.
[2] Taylor and Taylor, *Anglo-Saxon Architecture*, pp. 52–6 and fig. 379.

small intrusive stones used to make good the gaps beside the feature, or even more subtle indications such as a lack of careful bonding between the courses of the original wall and such important structural elements as the jambs or imposts of the inserted feature.[1] In this connection it is important to examine carefully both faces of the wall beside any feature which is suspected of having been inserted later, since one side of the wall may show its nature more clearly than the other. Careful study of the wall in different conditions of lighting may help; and so also will the execution of a careful drawing of the feature with an appreciable area of the adjoining wall, showing all the jointing of the stonework.

The insertion of a long horizontal feature such as a string-course or plinth is almost certain to leave fairly obvious disturbance unless the wall is built of irregular rubble or was carefully coursed in a way which allowed the insertion to be made along the line of one of the courses. Similarly the insertion of a vertical linear feature such as a pilaster-strip would almost certainly leave traces of disturbance such as broken stones or irregular patching.

The removal of a long linear feature is also likely to leave clear evidence; and in this case the evidence may be as clear in a rubble fabric as in ashlar, or perhaps even clearer because of the general absence of straight alignments in rubble fabric.

As a general principle I believe it is wise to regard the features in a wall as being parts of the original fabric unless clear evidence is available to the contrary, whether from reliable records or from the fabric itself. This may sound self-evident; but there is often a very real temptation to regard a feature as a later insertion if we have been led to believe that a wall is early and if we see that it contains a feature which we believe to be late. In such a circumstance it will usually be best to reconsider all the evidence for the divergent dating of the wall and the feature rather than to accept too readily that the feature is a later insertion.

SUMMARY

A scheme has been outlined above, in general terms, for initiating a systematic review of the evidence for the dating of Anglo-Saxon buildings; and suggestions have been made about methods that should be followed and features to which special attention should be given. In addition, reasons have been given for believing that attention should be directed, in the first instance, to the churches listed in appendices I and II and to such other churches as may be added later to these lists.

[1] See, for example, my argument that the great western arch in the tower of the church of St Regulus at St Andrews in Scotland is a later insertion: Taylor, *Why Should We Study the Anglo-Saxons?*, p. 36 and fig. 8.

H. M. Taylor

Examples of the application of these methods to two churches have recently been published, and similar studies are in progress for Bradford-on-Avon, Brixworth, Deerhurst and Wing. These studies represent the first steps towards the goal referred to in the preface to *Anglo-Saxon Architecture*, namely 'a more precise system of dating than has hitherto been possible for pre-Conquest churches'.

APPENDIX I

Historical references to Anglo-Saxon churches

The early records which relate to the sites where Anglo-Saxon fabric exists at the present day can be divided into the three classes which are named below, together with the churches which belong to each class. Brief details of the historical evidence will be found in the entries for each church in *Anglo-Saxon Architecture*.

1. *Records which with certainty allow the assignment of a precise date or period to the erection of surviving Anglo-Saxon fabric*

These are records which fix the date or period of the erection or dedication of a church on the site concerned and which give enough architectural or other evidence to identify the record as applying to the existing fabric. In the cases of the churches marked with an asterisk it is possible further to associate separate phases of building described in the records with parts of the building which can be seen to be of different building periods.

Churches in class 1

Canterbury	Hexham, St Andrew
*St Peter and St Paul	Kirkdale, St Gregory
St Mary	Monkwearmouth, St Peter
Deerhurst, Odda's chapel	*Winchester, Old Minster
*Glastonbury abbey	

2. *Records which give a precise date or period for the erection of a church on the site but do not of themselves provide enough evidence to allow this to be associated certainly with the surviving fabric*

For the purpose of this study this list is the most important, because additional historical evidence or additional evidence from the fabric of the churches may allow us with reasonable certainty to associate the historical record with the surviving fabric.

The churches which are marked with an asterisk will be found also in appendix II as churches in which the fabric itself declares more than one building date. If the historical records relate to several successive phases of development (as is the case for Jarrow, Lyminge and Repton), there is some hope of associating the historical phases with the building phases, provided always it is borne in mind that such an association is never likely to be proved with certainty.

Churches in class 2

*Bradford-on-Avon	Peterborough
Bradwell-on-Sea	*Reculver
Breedon-on-the-Hill	*Repton
*Brixworth	Ripon
Burgh Castle	Rochester
*Jarrow	*Stow
*Lyminge (two churches)	Wareham
Minster-in-Sheppey	York

3. Records which mention an Anglo-Saxon church on the site but give no information to date its erection or to associate the surviving fabric with the record

This list is given for the sake of completeness; unless additional historical evidence can be found it is unlikely that additional structural evidence will provide any secure association with the historical records. The churches marked with an asterisk are those in which the fabric itself proclaims more than one building period.

Churches in class 3

Alkborough	Melton Magna
Bakewell	Mersea, West
Bosham	Muchelney
Britford	Norton
Bywell	Notley, White
Canterbury:	Romsey
*St Martin	St Albans
St Mildred	Sherborne
St Pancras	Staindrop
Corbridge	Stonegrave
*Deerhurst, St Mary	Tredington
Hackness	Wharram-le-Street
Hadstock	Whitfield
Hart	Whittingham
Lastingham	*Wing
Lyminster	Yeavering

Within the buildings listed in this appendix, not only does the architectural material available for study vary widely, from a mere fragment to an almost complete church, but also the historical records vary from a single cursory mention of a site to detailed records such as those for St Augustine's abbey at Canterbury which allow precise and secure dating of more than one phase of the surviving fabric. The buildings most worthy of further study will usually be those for which the most complete information is available.

APPENDIX II

Buildings which appear to contain Anglo-Saxon fabric of two or more dates

Appleton-le-Street
Bardsey
Barton-on-Humber
Bedford, St Peter
Billingham
Bracebridge
Bradford-on-Avon
Branston
Brigstock
Brixworth
Canterbury:
  St Martin
  St Peter and St Paul
Carlton-in-Lindrick
Colchester
Corbridge
Deerhurst, St Mary
Elmham, North
Geddington
Glastonbury
Haddiscoe Thorpe
Hough-on-the-Hill

Jarrow
Kirkdale
Kirk Hammerton
Ledsham
Lincoln:
  St Mary
  St Peter
Lydd
Lyminge (two churches)
Marton
Middleton-by-Pickering
Monkwearmouth
Reculver
Repton
Skipwith
Stafford
Staindrop
Stow
Whitfield
Whittingham
Winchester
Wing

Like those listed in appendix 1, these buildings differ widely in the extent of the architectural material which they offer for further study.

The Anglo-Saxon house:
a new review

P. V. ADDYMAN

The past two decades have witnessed an almost complete revision of ideas about the character of Anglo-Saxon settlements. The advances have come in the main from a series of archaeological excavations in which techniques commonly used in prehistoric archaeology have been applied to sites of the period in the light of results from contemporary settlements on the continent. The excavations have in effect produced entire new categories of evidence about the domestic accommodation, service buildings and general planning of settlements of all levels of Anglo-Saxon society, in most of England and in all parts of the Anglo-Saxon period. In 1950 almost no domestic buildings were known other than the sunken huts found first by Leeds at Sutton Courtenay and subsequently by others in various parts of the country. Leeds's conclusions, accepted albeit with reluctance by scholars, were that 'the bulk of the people, we can now be assured, were content with something that hardly deserves a better title than hovel, only varying in its greater or lesser simplicity'.[1] Such buildings stood in stark and suspect contrast to the relatively sophisticated stone churches from the earliest days of Christianity found in various parts of the country. Radford, moreover, in a seminal paper in the first volume of *Medieval Archaeology* demonstrated that they stood in some considerable contrast to the settlements and to the standards of domestic accommodation enjoyed by the ancestors and contemporaries of the Anglo-Saxons on the continent.[2] Indeed Miss Cramp showed in the same volume that literary evidence for far more sumptuous buildings, long known from *Beowulf* and other sources, had with the excavation of the Sutton Hoo ship burial become archaeologically acceptable, for it was clear that much of the circumstantial detail in *Beowulf* must have been closely based on observation.[3] The same auspicious inaugural volume contained the first archaeological notice of the discovery of the Northumbrian royal palace at Yeavering, near Wooler in Northumberland, where such buildings were found.[4] Since

[1] E. T. Leeds, *Early Anglo-Saxon Art and Archaeology* (Oxford, 1936), p. 21.
[2] C. A. Ralegh Radford, 'The Saxon House: a Review and some Parallels', *MA* 1 (1957), 27–38.
[3] Rosemary J. Cramp, '*Beowulf* and Archaeology', *ibid.* pp. 57–77.
[4] *Ibid.* pp. 148–9.

that time some 150 secular timber buildings have been excavated in various parts of England, two or more palaces have been investigated and others located, and many more sunken huts have been discovered. A number of archaeological excavation reports have been published and an appreciable body of data has otherwise been made available. There is now evidence enough for some tentative conclusions to be reached on the character of Anglo-Saxon domestic building. This paper takes the opportunity afforded by the inauguration of another periodical to review the evidence and to present some of these conclusions. It is something of a tribute to Radford's paper for its rôle in coaxing forth the new evidence and to the enlightened excavation policy of the Ancient Monuments Inspectorate of the Department of the Environment which has sponsored most of the work. Nor would the paper have been possible without the generous cooperation of the various excavators who have permitted reference to be made to their finds, often in advance of definitive publication.

The main burden of Radford's paper was that a wealth of excavated evidence from various parts of Germanic Europe spelled out inescapable conclusions on the nature of the Anglo-Saxon house. The idea of small pit dwellings would have to be abandoned for 'the picture of the wooden long-house with its ancillary buildings'. 'Only houses on this scale', he further suggested, 'fit the picture of the Anglo-Saxon ceorl, the social equivalent of the continental freeman . . ., the peasant farmer tilling his hide (*terra unius familae*, the land of one household) of some 120 acres of arable with pasture and other common rights.' It is no aim of this paper to review once again the continental evidence, even though excavation of relevant sites continued unabated. It will suffice to note that the recent work has if anything strengthened the general conclusion that most north European migration period settlements consisted of one or more large halls, often of the so-called 'three-aisled' form and often of 'long-house' type[1] or of the Warendorf type,[2] each with appropriate ancillary buildings. The extensive excavations at Wijster, near Beilen in central Drenthe, in particular have produced a series of variant buildings within the long-house tradition and have revealed in remarkable detail the lay-out and development of settlement and cemetery on an extensive inland site, in contrast to the intensive terp and warft sites better known to archaeology.[3] Wijster is another of the many settlements deserted at the very period of migration which should have seen the transfer of traditions of settlement lay-out, building design and, above all, traditions of

[1] W. Haarnagel, 'Das nordwesteuropäische dreischiffige Hallenhaus und seine Entwicklung im Küstengebiet der Nordsee', *Neues Archiv für Niedersachsen* 15 (1950), 79–91.

[2] W. Winkelmann, 'Die Ausgrabungen in der frühmittelalterlichen Siedlung bei Warendorf (Westfalen)', *Neue Ausgrabungen in Deutschland* (Berlin, 1958), pp. 492–517.

[3] W. A. Van Es, *Wijster, a Native Village beyond the Imperial Frontier* (Groningen, 1967).

carpentry, from the Dutch and north German littoral to England. The forthcoming reports on the great excavations at the Federseen Wierde, in the heart of that area where cemetery evidence indicates intimate insular contact and inspiration in the fourth and fifth centuries, will also be of particularly critical relevance in understanding the nature of the early Anglo-Saxon village.[1]

The earliest Germanic settlements in England must belong, as an increasing and varied body of evidence indicates, to a period well before the traditional date of the *adventus Saxonum*. Most of these early settlements were closely connected with Romano-British towns and settlements. 'Romano-Saxon' pottery, the early Germanic cremation urns from cemeteries near various Romano-British towns in eastern England and the distribution of various items of Germanic metal-work considered to indicate the presence of *laeti* in late Roman Britain all suggest that the earliest Germanic buildings in England are likely to be found within or near places occupied in late Roman times. Myres, however, has recently identified extremely early Germanic pots in long-lived cremation cemeteries in eastern England that are not necessarily connected with Roman settlements.[2] There is little enough evidence at present about the settlements of this earliest Anglo-Saxon presence, but what there is tends to confirm its dual nature. The settlement at Bishopstone, Sussex, if it is contemporary with the adjacent cemetery, may belong to this initial settlement phase.[3] Neither it nor the Mucking/Linford site in Essex, nor the important site at West Stow, Suffolk, seems to have been on contemporary Roman settlements, whatever the relationship of the occupants may have been to Romano-British people nearby.[4] They seem to be *de novo* villages. On the other hand early buildings, equally clearly Germanic, have been found within late Roman towns. They have usually been seen as dwellings of the *laeti* or *foederati*. Canterbury and the Saxon Shore fort at Portchester, Hampshire, have produced sunken huts to which a fifth-century date must be given, and pottery of this date from Winchester suggests that it is only a matter of time before such buildings are found there. Doubtless any of those Romano-British towns whose extra-mural cemeteries have produced Germanic objects or with which early Anglo-Saxon cemeteries are associated might be expected to contain such buildings, though site finds tend to suggest that *laeti*, if they have any reality, may equally well be found in conventional late Roman buildings. As the practice of extensive

---

[1] In the meantime interim reports can be found in *Germania* 35 (1957), 275–317; 39 (1961), 42–69; and 41 (1963), 280–317.
[2] J. N. L. Myres, *Anglo-Saxon Pottery and the Settlement of England* (Oxford, 1969), pp. 73–4.
[3] *MA* 13 (1969), 240.
[4] S. E. West, 'The Anglo-Saxon Village of West Stow: an Interim Report of the Excavations 1965–8', *ibid.* pp. 15–18.

area excavation is progressively adopted by urban archaeologists, the relationships of these early mercenaries and settlers to the indigenous population may become clear, as will the extent to which, in their new environment, they favoured buildings reflecting their own traditions.

Such fourth- or fifth-century Germanic buildings as have been found in late Roman towns are of the sunken or *Grubenhaus* type (see pl. VII*a*). They have been found in some of the *insulae* of Roman Canterbury, apparently honouring the existing street lay-out. In one case there was a line of six huts. No evidence for larger buildings was found and Professor Frere tends to the conclusion that the huts may under certain circumstances have been self-sufficing.[1] The two huts so far located at Portchester were also clearly set out in relation to the Roman street.[2] The Portchester huts enjoyed an organized water supply from a wood-lined well. The lining of this well, preserved intact by waterlogging, demonstrates the high standards of carpentry to be expected in early Anglo-Saxon England. Small objects from the well-filling testify also to the finest traditions of woodworking. In the light of these finds it is surprising that no more ambitious timber buildings have been found. The fourth-century buildings at Portchester are very imperfectly known since the method of construction employed leaves very little archaeological trace and later disturbance has been extensive. It may be possible that the sunken huts were built while the Roman buildings were still standing, perhaps in the spaces between them. They might thus be just as much ancillary buildings in these contexts as they are in later Saxon villages. Equally, larger buildings may have been destroyed by later disturbance.

In other late Roman towns where there are indications of *laeti* or other early Germanic settlers there is evidence of late-fourth- or early-fifth-century buildings more closely akin to Roman traditions. At Catterick, Yorkshire, the *laeti*-horizon buckles come from a stone building; and more recent excavations have shown that reconstruction of parts of the town occurring in the late fourth century was followed by at least one more building phase. At Dorchester, Oxfordshire, there is evidence to suggest that simple rectangular buildings, perhaps half-timbered, with unmortared stone footings, may have accommodated the troops whose presence is suggested by the well-known Dorchester burials.[3] It is possible that sunken huts of the early fifth century may yet be found at Dorchester. A scatter of Anglo-Frisian pottery was found, and such a hut was built there in the mid sixth century (see fig. 2*a*), still, it appears, set out in relation to the Roman street.[4]

[1] S. S. Frere, 'The End of Towns in Roman Britain', *The Civitas Capitals of Roman Britain*, ed. J. S. Wacher (Leicester, 1966), pp. 91–3.

[2] Barry Cunliffe, 'Excavations at Portchester Castle, Hants 1966–1968', *AntJ* 49 (1969), 65–7, and 'The Saxon Culture-Sequence at Portchester Castle', *ibid.* 50 (1970), 67–70.

[3] Sheppard Frere, 'Excavations at Dorchester on Thames, 1962', *ArchJ* 119 (1962), 121–3 and 130–1.   [4] *Ibid.* pp. 123–31.

The survival and use of Romano-British buildings may thus explain the lack of timber buildings of Germanic type in these contexts. Equally the oft-quoted excuse for their absence, later disturbance, may indeed have destroyed much of the evidence. The reason, however, may be that excavations on a scale large enough to locate timber buildings, possibly with hardly any occupation material or recognizable floors and perhaps few artifacts that are culturally distinctive, are only just beginning. Barker's excavations at Wroxeter have revealed that patience and sophisticated excavation techniques involving wide stripping over very large areas can reveal vestiges of late or post-Roman timber buildings in a site long thought to have had a terminal

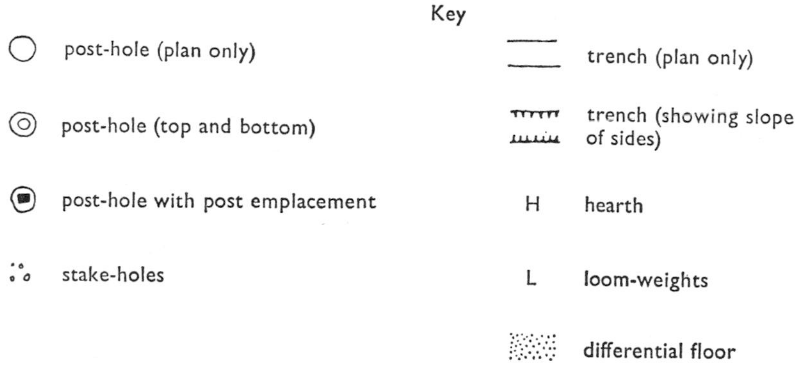

Key

○	post-hole (plan only)	———	trench (plan only)
◎	post-hole (top and bottom)	⊤⊤⊤⊤⊤ ⊥⊥⊥⊥⊥	trench (showing slope of sides)
⬤	post-hole with post emplacement	H	hearth
∴∘	stake-holes	L	loom-weights
		▨	differential floor

FIG. I   Key to figs. 2–8

occupation of quite a different sort.[1] There is no certainty that the long-house built into the latest levels of the town was in fact Germanic, but there is equally no reason why it and the various other late buildings should not have been the dwellings of federates of Germanic extraction in the fourth century or the fifth; this at least seems to be their date.

The *de novo* Anglo-Saxon villages of the fifth and sixth centuries, though few enough of them have been excavated, appear to correspond far more closely to the continental pattern. West's excavations at West Stow have provided the type site.[2] Here an entire settlement in occupation throughout much of the fifth and sixth centuries has been meticulously revealed in excavations of the highest standard. Some six halls were occupied at one time or another during this period, each apparently with one or more sunken huts nearby. Other buildings and structures seem to have been common to the village as a whole. The lay-out of the buildings, apparently in discrete units related to a much used central area, accords well with the picture

---

[1] Philip Barker, 'Some Aspects of the Excavation of Timber Buildings', *World Archaeology* 1 (1969), 228–33.   [2] West, 'West Stow', *MA* 13 (1969), 1–20.

which might be expected on comparative, historical and anthropological grounds. The West Stow halls (see fig. 3), substantial post-built rectangular structures, do not appear to have the division into living and stock quarters so well known on continental sites. This may reflect a difference in economy;

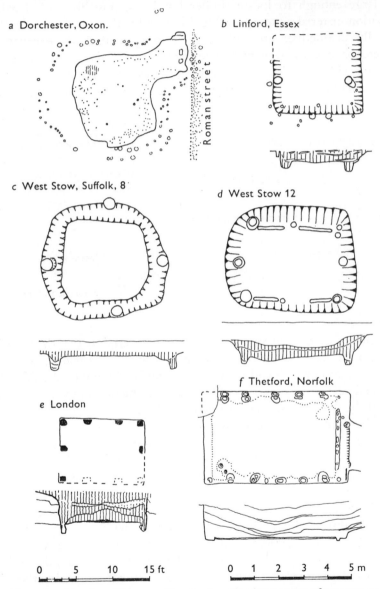

FIG. 2   The main types of small huts: *a* without main posts; *b* two posts; *c* four posts set in sides; *d* six posts; *e* and *f* multiple posts. (Another type, with four posts set in the corners, is not shown.) All these examples have sunken floors except West Stow 8. Scale about 1:120

or perhaps no more than a difference in environment, a factor already stressed in attempts to account for regional differences in the continental settlements themselves.[1] Provision of winter shelter for cattle, though desirable, is not essential in southern and eastern England.[2] It seems, however, that sheep raising and wool working formed an important part of the economy of the West Stow villages, and the buildings and village lay-out may simply reflect this. West's definitive report is eagerly awaited for the light it will throw on

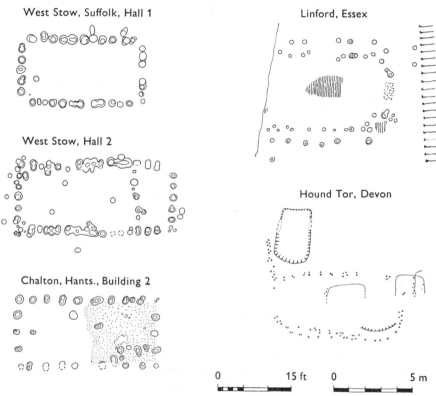

West Stow, Suffolk, Hall 1

Linford, Essex

West Stow, Hall 2

Hound Tor, Devon

Chalton, Hants., Building 2

0   15 ft   0   5 m

FIG. 3   Small post-built or stake-built houses. Early Saxon
except Hound Tor (late). Scale about 1:240

these and a host of other points crucial to the understanding of village life and rural economy in early Anglo-Saxon England. In the meantime his interim report provides important insights and forms the basis from which all discussion of the development of Anglo-Saxon building must begin.[3]

[1] Helen Parker, 'Feddersen Wierde and Vallhagar: a Contrast in Settlements', *MA* 9 (1965), 1–10, esp. 10.
[2] J. E. Grundy, 'Notes on the Relationship between Climate and Cattle Housing', *Vernacular Architecture* 1 (1970), 3–5. In Norfolk today 24% of cattle-herds lie out throughout the year and in Suffolk 14%.   [3] See below, p. 302.

At none of the other sites of the earliest phases of Anglo-Saxon settlement has enough been adequately excavated to allow generalizations about the overall plan of the settlement. At Bishopstone there are only a few sunken huts and one larger house. The Linford/Mucking settlements and cemeteries, near Stanford-le-Hope, Essex, though extensively excavated, pose considerable problems of interpretation. Barton's excavations on one side of the settlement revealed post-built rectangular houses (see fig. 3) somewhat reminiscent of those at West Stow, together with sunken huts and ditches apparently defining areas of occupation.[1] The more recent excavations undertaken by Mr and Mrs Jones on adjacent parts of the Thames gravel terrace upon which the site lies have revealed two early Anglo-Saxon cemeteries and numerous sunken huts, some eighty-one or more, but no traces of post-built or other larger structures.[2] Mr and Mrs Jones believe that the huts formed the main buildings at least in the part of the site they have examined, though they do not exclude the possibility, in view of Barton's evidence, that there were larger buildings elsewhere. If this is so it raises severe problems in the interpretation of villages examined before excavation techniques involving wide-spread stripping were adopted. The early and perhaps middle Saxon site at Sutton Courtenay, for instance, was excavated piecemeal, as sunken huts were discovered in quarrying, and it has been assumed in recent years that it was only because of inadequate excavation technique that larger timber buildings were not found.[3] The Mucking evidence renders this easy assumption at least open to question. It remains possible that the sunken huts at Mucking are an area of specialized buildings attached to the more normal series nearby. It is also possible that larger timber buildings were not built in a technique which necessitated the digging of deep post-holes or other substantial footings through the topsoil into the subsoil where alone they would have been recognized. Professor Jope's Cassington excavations are another instance in which large timber buildings failed to be found, though sunken huts and other traces were found.[4] Professor Jope believes, however, if the traces had been as shallow or as ephemeral as, for instance, those in the Maxey settlement, he would not have found them.[5] That Mucking stands apart from other early Saxon settlements is also suggested by the extensive excavations at New Wintles Farm near

[1] K. J. Barton, 'Settlements of the Iron Age and Pagan Saxon Periods at Linford, Essex', *Trans. of the Essex Archaeol. Soc.* 3rd ser. 1 (1961–5), 88–93.

[2] M. U. Jones *et al.*, 'Crop-Mark Sites at Mucking, Essex', *AntJ* 48 (1968), 215–17, and *MA* 13 (1969), 231–2.

[3] Radford, 'The Saxon House', pp. 28–30. For the original reports see *Archaeologia* 73 (1923), 147–92; 76 (1927), 59–80; and 92 (1947), 79–83.

[4] Brian V. Arthur and E. M. Jope, 'Early Saxon Pottery Kilns at Purwell Farm, Cassington, Oxfordshire', *MA* 6–7 (1962–3), 1–4.

[5] Post-holes in structure B at Maxey, for instance, were noticed only after three careful cleaning operations: *MA* 8 (1964), 25–8.

Eynsham, Oxfordshire. Here three rectangular post-built structures (see fig. 5) and ten sunken huts were found sparsely distributed over an area of some 46 acres (18·65 hectares), together with other structures and possibly trackways and palisades. The general plan[1] almost demands the presence of larger timber buildings in the many extensive spaces, unless the settlement was very widely spaced indeed. The New Wintles Farm site nevertheless provides a basis for the reinterpretation of the many early Saxon occupations known in the Thames valley,[2] and it must be suspected that similar larger buildings could have been found at the two Cassington sites, at Sutton Courtenay and at many other places.

The Anglo-Saxon villages from which sunken huts are known now number over a hundred and have recently been listed by Hurst.[3] They have been found in most areas of early Saxon settlement, wherever, in fact, there are pagan Anglo-Saxon cemeteries. The various types represented are shown in figs. 2 and 4. Two examples, however, in particular are relevant here for the light they throw on the presence of larger timber buildings. Emergency excavations at Upton, Northamptonshire (see fig. 4),[4] revealed remarkably complete evidence of a hut with a dug out floor combined with post walls and evidence for looms and superstructure, preserved by burning. This large hut, some 30 ft by 18 ft (9·15 m by 5·5 m), approaches in size a small hall, and gives a rare glimpse of the internal fittings of an Anglo-Saxon house, with looms leaning against the gabled end walls. The remarkable buildings found at Puddle Hill, Dunstable, Bedfordshire,[5] combine post construction with the dug out floor in a rather different way (see fig. 4), having the sunken portion enclosed within a longish house built of posts or posts in trenches. It is a clear hint that extensive clearance of the many chalkland areas near the Puddle Hill site where sunken huts are found would produce evidence of larger timber buildings. The relationship of the Anglo-Saxon sites on Puddle Hill to the remarkable timber building for which a Dark Age date has been hinted at, recently found at Dunstable itself, would be of extreme interest, but must await clear demonstration of the date of the Dunstable structure.[6]

Excavations at present in progress at Chalton, Hampshire (see pls. VIII*a*

[1] Sonia C. Hawkes and Margaret Gray, 'Preliminary Note on the Early Anglo-Saxon Settlement at New Wintles Farm, Eynsham', *Oxoniensia* 34 (1969), 1–4.

[2] The settlement pattern and economy of the area is at present being studied by Miss Freda Beresford under the auspices of the Institute of Archaeology at Oxford.

[3] *Deserted Medieval Villages: Studies*, ed. Maurice Beresford and John G. Hurst (London, 1971), pp. 145–68.

[4] D. A. Jackson *et al.*, 'The Iron Age and Anglo-Saxon Site at Upton, Northants', *AntJ* 49 (1969), 202–21.

[5] C. L. Matthews, 'Saxon Remains on Puddlehill, Dunstable', *Bedfordshire Archaeol. Jnl* 1 (1962), 48–57.

[6] Mr Matthews's excavations are to be followed by further work by the Department of the Environment.

and *b*), have located a village, sited high on an exposed down-top overlooking the valleys where throughout the ages occupation has more normally taken place. Early Saxon pottery can be picked up after ploughing over some 14

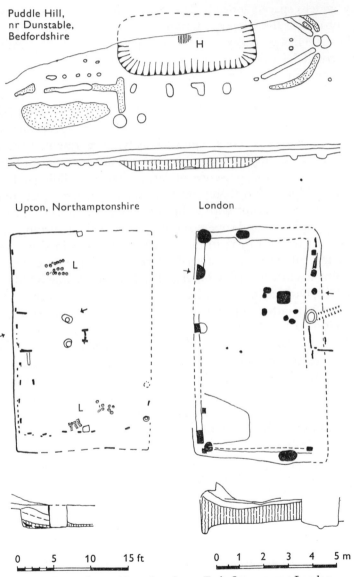

FIG. 4 Larger huts with sunken floors. Early Saxon except London (middle). Scale about 1:120

acres (5 to 6 hectares) and there is much other occupation material. A trial excavation has revealed two houses set end to end, built of posts set in continuous trenches, both succeeding structures built of posts set in individual post-holes (see figs. 3 and 6). The two later buildings, 38 ft by 21 ft and 36 ft by 21 ft (11·5 m by 6·25 m and 11 m by 6·25 m), are remarkably similar

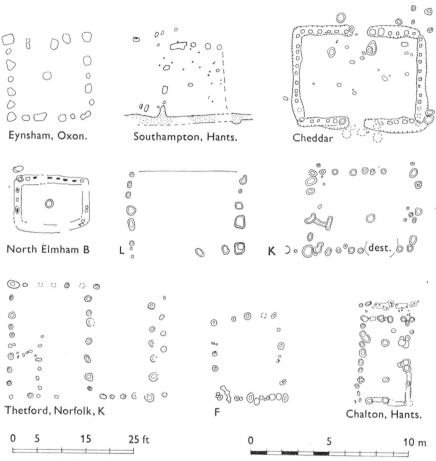

Eynsham, Oxon. Southampton, Hants. Cheddar

North Elmham B L K (dest.)

Thetford, Norfolk, K F Chalton, Hants.

0 5 15 25 ft   0 5 10 m

FIG. 5 Small post-built huts of various periods. The Eynsham hut is a sketch only; scale of the remainder about 1:240

in plan, with three doors, two in the mid-point of the side walls and one in an end wall. Both had an internal partition cutting off about one fifth of the building apparently into three small square rooms. Fences, smaller buildings and other structures nearby suggest that further excavation could reveal the full plan of the village throughout a long life in which many complicated revisions of plan took place. The excavation will do something to provide evidence for the settlements of the South and West Saxons, of whom little is known. In Kent, indeed, settlements are hardly known outside Canterbury. Yet the wealth and aspirations of the early kingdom of Kent in early Anglo-Saxon times suggest that here if anywhere we must expect villages closely reflecting the standards of the continent. Their jewellery and pottery reflect the diverse origins of the Kentish settlers and the varied influences which subsequently affected them. The carpentry traditions are likely to have been equally diverse, and it can be only a matter of time before a wealth of evidence is found in the county. The same, however, with little qualification could be said of all areas of early Anglo-Saxon settlement.

If our ideas of early Saxon settlements still rest on somewhat slender evidence, the general character of settlements in middle Saxon times is fast becoming clear. Villages, estates, royal townships and towns have all been excavated recently. Of consuming interest are Hope-Taylor's investigations at Yeavering and Dunbar, where the sprawling buildings of two Northumbrian royal vills have been examined.[1] The centre of such settlements, as historical and literary evidence would have led us to suppose, was the great hall. The series of such halls at Yeavering, repeatedly replaced as variously dictated by disaster or by improvements in design, shows evidence of considerable architectural sophistication. In each phase the hall was constructed in timber. Thus building A2 was an aisled hall with narrow end rooms, planked floors and heavy outer walls of posts in palisade construction set alternatively deeper and shallower in continuous trenches. There was an enclosure behind it. Its successor, A4, differed in having massive buttress posts, 8 ft deep in some cases, inclined inwards. There were also internal partitions producing two end rooms. The timbers were squared and of uniform dimensions. A burial associated with this remarkable and massive building was accompanied by an enigmatic artifact possibly identifiable as a relation of the Roman *groma* or surveyor's instrument. The building was certainly set out, as were many Anglo-Saxon buildings, and most at Yeavering, with an exact understanding of proportion. The latest reconstructions of the great hall at Yeavering show innovations in plan and construction. The wall construction was of post-holes with beam trenches between. In plan, A3 was a simple rectangle with an annex at either end. There were doors in the mid-point of the long sides, and, set off-centre, in the ends. There is a suggestion, because of the asymmetrical door settings, that the buildings had centre posts, somehow incorporated with aisle posts. Its successor, A1, possibly

---

[1] Both unpublished. For Yeavering see Brian Hope-Taylor, 'The Site of *ad Gerfrin*: an Investigation of its Archaeological and Historical Significance' (unpub. Ph.D. thesis, Cambridge, 1961). For a summary see *MA* 1 (1957), 148–9.

incomplete with only one annex, had end doors set symmetrically. Interestingly it compares closely in plan with the halls identified from aerial photographs at Yeavering's successor, Maelmin, some two miles away.[1] These buildings, of which A4 was over 80 ft long and over 50 ft wide, demonstrate a mastery of structural carpentry which must, on a less ambitious scale perhaps, have had its counterpart in the lesser vill. The remarkable correspondences in plan, if not in construction and size, between the A4 hall and the two later buildings at Chalton, Hampshire, at the other bound of Anglo-Saxon England, imply a distinctive and wide-spread architectural tradition.

Hope-Taylor has argued for a variety of influences in the Yeavering buildings and structures, with hints that the Northumbrian carpenters drew fruitfully on local native traditions, on Germanic ideas and on ideas derived apparently quite directly from a classical milieu. The unit of measurement, apparently of 11·05 ins, used to set out the buildings C1 to C4, seemingly a row of subsidiary halls or bowers set in echelon in relation to the great hall in the A3 phase, is but one amongst the host of new and potentially most important facts to have been established by this excavation of consummate skill. The release of Hope-Taylor's report will also present important data on contemporary construction methods. The evidence from the sunken hut C1, for instance, is crucial to the general intepretation of these frequently found structures.

Briefest examination of the historical sources indicates that considerable numbers of royal vills of middle or late Saxon date await discovery in all parts of England.[2] Rahtz has recently located and dated such a site at Hatton Rock, near Hampton Lucy, Warwickshire. Topographical study has pinpointed another, perhaps, at Rendlesham, Suffolk.[3] It is on sites such as these and their late Saxon successors that we may eventually expect to discover secular buildings of stone, attested indeed by Asser,[4] though even at Alfred's vill at Cheddar, Somerset, recently excavated by Rahtz, the main buildings were of timber until the twelfth century. It is an urgent need, moreover, that early or middle Saxon vills should be excavated in southern

[1] David Knowles and J. K. S. St Joseph, *Monastic Sites from the Air* (Cambridge, 1952), pp. 270–1; for Yeavering see also *The Uses of Air Photography*, ed. J. K. S. St Joseph (London, 1966), pp. 126–7.

[2] F. M. Stenton, *Anglo-Saxon England*, 2nd ed. (Oxford, 1947), pp. 345–7.

[3] Philip Rahtz, 'A Possible Saxon Palace near Stratford-upon-Avon', *Antiquity* 44 (1970), 137–43, and R. L. S. Bruce-Mitford, 'Saxon Rendlesham', *Proc. of the Suffolk Inst. of Archaeology and Nat. Hist.* 24 (1949), 228–51.

[4] 'What shall I say of the cities and town he restored, and of the others which he built where none had been before? Of the buildings marvellously wrought with gold and silver under his direction? Of the royal halls and chambers, wonderfully built of stone and of wood at his command? Of royal vills made of masonry removed from the old sites and most admirably rebuilt in more suitable places by the king's order?' (*Asser's Life of King Alfred*, ed. W. H. Stevenson (Oxford, 1904; repr. 1959 with contr. by D. Whitelock), p. 77.)

England. Bruce-Mitford's recent demonstration of the supreme skill of the East Anglian court blacksmith in the early seventh century, while emphasizing that we have long under-estimated general cultural standards, implies that the king's cauldron hung from the roof of a great hall of Yeavering proportions, for its suspension chains and hooks together with its own depth add up altogether to a height of 14 ft (4·25 m).[1] It implies that the East Anglian king sat in halls as lofty and fine as did his contemporary at Yeavering; as fine as Hrothgar's *Heorot*.

Prompt and detailed interim reports allow an initial assessment to be made of the excavations in progress at North Elmham, Norfolk.[2] There are sound reasons for believing that North Elmham was the seat of a bishopric after the subdivision of the East Anglian diocese in 673, and that it continued as such, with a gap in the ninth century and the early tenth, until the see was removed to Thetford in 1071. Dr Wade-Martins's excavations have uncovered a series of timber buildings, ditches and other features which by stratigraphic succession and associated finds can be shown to span this period and beyond. It seems not unreasonable to identify the settlement as part of the episcopal estate. In period I, attributed to the middle Saxon period, the site was divided up into rectangular areas by ditches. In three of the enclosed areas were found halls, built of posts set in continuous trenches. One of the halls, building S (see fig. 6*d*), apparently had internal posts, an annex at one end and a door in the mid-point of one side. There is evidence, therefore, for planned lay-out and for the scale and general character of the domestic accommodation. In the next period the whole area was planned afresh. A large hall (U) (see fig. 7), some 60 ft by 20 ft (18·3 m by 6·1 m), faced an L-shaped building (P) across a court-yard and there was a latrine building (O) nearby. Entry to the court-yard was gained between the two halls, apparently from an already existing street, the ancestor of one of the medieval streets of North Elmham. The large hall had one obvious doorway in the side wall near one end, and its walls, represented by continuous trenches, may reflect the same construction methods as those used in the first period. Earlier features and later disturbances make interpretation of its internal arrangements difficult, but, like its predecessors, it probably had a hipped roof. The enigmatic building P, defined by shallow flat-bottomed trenches, poses certain structural problems, as does the apparently open-sided building (Y) on the south side of the court-yard. This building has one straight wall and incurved side walls. Whatever the problems of structural interpretation, period II, tentatively considered by Wade-Martins to represent the tenth-century episcopal palace,

[1] Paper communicated to the Society of Antiquaries of London, 1971.
[2] Peter Wade-Martins, 'Excavations at North Elmham, 1967–8: an Interim Report', *Norfolk Archaeology* 34 (1969), 352–97, and 'Excavations at North Elmham, 1969: an Interim Report', *ibid.* 35 (1) (1970), 25–78.

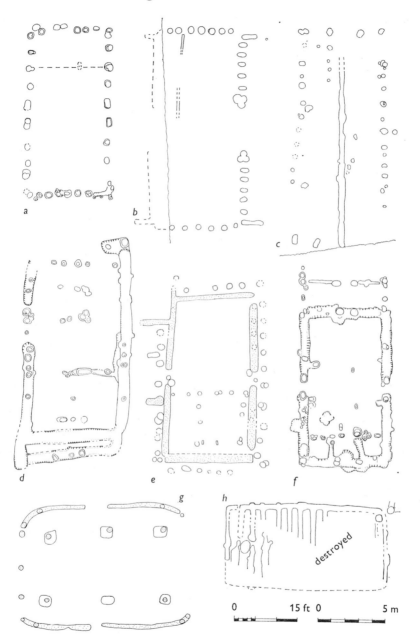

FIG. 6 Medium-sized post-built structures, possibly houses or halls: *a* and *f* Chalton, Hampshire (early); *b* and *c* Maxey, Northamptonshire (middle); *d* North Elmham, Norfolk (middle); *e* and *g* Portchester, Hampshire (late); *h* St Neots, Huntingdonshire (late). Scale about 1:240

provides an invaluable view of an estate quite different from that seen at Yeavering. The area was replanned once again in the late tenth century, when the cathedral cemetery was extended over part of the site and the

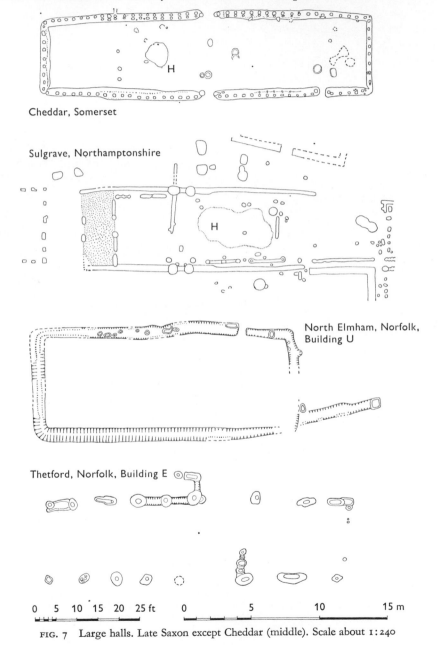

Cheddar, Somerset

Sulgrave, Northamptonshire

North Elmham, Norfolk, Building U

Thetford, Norfolk, Building E

0   5   10   15   20   25 ft   0   5   10   15 m

FIG. 7   Large halls. Late Saxon except Cheddar (middle). Scale about 1:240

remainder was occupied by smaller rectangular buildings built of posts in individual post-holes, reflecting the wider spacing of the posts, and by a few post-in-trench buildings. The roofs appear no longer to have been hipped, but to have involved a ridge-piece, reflected sometimes by internal supports; and there is evidence for trussing. These small houses stood in individual fenced areas, each with its own series of ancillary buildings. Clearly the character of occupation on the site had changed once again. In a final period of occupation in the late eleventh century a further building technique made its appearance, with the construction of a boat-shaped hall. Wade-Martins rightly stresses the importance of the North Elmham excavation in showing a continuous architectural development, based on some thirty-two buildings, as well as in demonstrating the character of an episcopal settlement, or at least of parts of it, at various times between the eighth century and the eleventh.

The middle Saxon settlement at Maxey, Northamptonshire, of which some 75,000 sq ft have been excavated, perhaps one eighth of the total area, may have been a village or an estate of another type.[1] The eight or so buildings uncovered were set around a relatively unoccupied central area. They seem, so far as is possible to guess, to have been occupied at the same time. Most were post-built, but one had elements consisting of posts joined by short sections of ground-sill, another had a short section of posts set in a continuous trench and one had a central element based on ground-sills (see fig. 6). Each structure was different in plan and construction, though most were fairly long and approximately rectangular. They varied in length from 35 to 50 ft (10·65 to 15·25 m) and in width from 16 to 22 ft (4·85 to 6·85 m). A main problem is whether the various plans and methods of construction reflect different functions: were the buildings peasant dwellings in a vill or the specialized structures of something that might more accurately be described as an estate? The dilemma illustrates well the limitations of archaeological evidence and the problems of identifying the various types of settlement to which contemporary documents refer. The Maxey settlement may, indeed, be one of the estates referred to there in the tenth century; or it may be something else altogether.[2] Such problems are unlikely to be answered until a complete parish is exhumed, as it is hoped will eventually happen at Chalton.

Even in those towns where early Anglo-Saxon occupation can be demonstrated it has been difficult to show an archaeological continuum into middle Saxon times. Where there is evidence at all, it seems – with the exceptions of the historically documented towns of Canterbury and York – to favour

[1] P. V. Addyman, 'A Dark-Age Settlement at Maxey, Northants.', *MA* 8 (1964), 20–73.
[2] *Ibid.* p. 22.

virtual desertion, with a renewal of urban life in the eighth century. Significant archaeological evidence has emerged in recent years to show that one town at least, the Saxon forerunner of Southampton, was founded at this time and flourished rapidly.[1] The coin finds indicate that the place, perhaps the *Hamwih* of early documents, was occupied between about 700 and 940. It covered 73 acres (29·55 hectares) or more and grew rich on the profits of international trade. Though excavations have been undertaken on the site for many years, only recently have they revealed timber buildings. There is evidence for post-built structures (see fig. 5) and for houses based on ground-sills or of posts with ground-sills. There is a clear likelihood that they were set out in relation to gravelled roads and that fences divided one property from another. Buildings, however, have often left little archaeological trace and their former presence can only be inferred from the blank spaces within areas otherwise riddled with pits, wells and the ubiquitous latrines, themselves often set within small wooden buildings. Nevertheless as excavation progresses a detailed picture is emerging of a heavily built-up and commercially prosperous community, by any physical criterion already a town. It is likely that the structures revealed represent only a proportion of the types formerly existing, but they give the impression that the constricted urban conditions gave rise to smaller buildings, some perhaps of specialized purpose.

Evidence of secular buildings in other towns known to have been occupied in middle Saxon times is slow in coming. The small building at Portchester, 16 ft by 20 ft (4·85 m by 6·1 m), built of posts set in post-holes, presumptively associated with a well, cesspit and rubbish pit of the eighth century, and possibly with boundary ditches, may be such a building, though Portchester was hardly a town at that time.[2] There are suggestions of timber buildings in the Brook Street site at Winchester which may belong to the period, for they supersede a seventh-century cemetery and are themselves superseded by late Saxon structures. Here too they have something of the aspect of a loosely planned estate, perhaps one of a number within the Roman city walls. At Dorchester on Thames too there were large timber buildings which, stratigraphically, could belong to this period, though the Badorf ware found nearby need no longer imply a ninth-century date. The buildings, of posts set in continuous trenches, are more in scale with what might now legitimately be expected in such towns.[3]

In addition to the various excavated buildings of middle Saxon date whose character can be guessed there is now an increasing body of structures,

1 P. V. Addyman and D. H. Hill, 'Saxon Southampton: a Review of the Evidence', *Proc. of the Hampshire Field Club and Archaeol. Soc.* 25 (1968), 61–93, and 26 (1969), 61–96.
2 Cunliffe, 'Excavations at Portchester Castle, Hants 1966–1968', pp. 65–7 and fig. 3.
3 Frere, 'Excavations at Dorchester on Thames, 1962', pp. 125–8.

usually individual buildings, whose status is not known. Such sites as
Fladbury, Worcestershire, or Sedgeford, Norfolk, were most probably
villages and a majority of the individual finds should probably so be classed.
They have also been listed by Hurst.[1] For the purpose of this paper they
provide useful corroboration of the development of Anglo-Saxon timber
architecture, but beyond this the value of the excavation of individual
buildings is limited.

The work of the late F. G. Wainwright indicated the power of archaeology
to settle long-lived academic controversies about the nature of late Saxon
towns, and a number of excavations have taken place in recent years in
towns throughout Wessex, Mercia, the Danelaw and East Anglia. Attention
has usually been directed towards the defences, but already much information is available about the internal lay-out of the towns[2] and about the
plans and general character of houses and other buildings. Already, too,
generalization is becoming possible about building traditions and standards
of domestic accommodation. Progress first came with the work of Jope and
others in Oxford.[3] The inferences to be drawn from late Saxon and Norman
historical sources about the character of Oxford's town-houses have been
recognized for some time and it is now possible to say that the houses lay
along streets more or less on the lines of later medieval streets, though it
appears they were at this time much narrower. Davison's work in Queen
Street has added the details of a series of timber-framed buildings to the
timber-lined cellars or, as Hope-Taylor would have it, latrines, recovered
on the site of the Clarendon Hotel in Cornmarket.[4] Oxford, despite its early
lead in medieval archaeology and the vigilance and strenuous labours of a
succession of distinguished workers, has been reluctant to yield up its late
Saxon buildings. One may suspect that most towns which have remained in
occupation to the present day will prove difficult for archaeological research.
In London, for instance, a town of the first importance, Professor Grimes's
extensive excavations have revealed only two occupation sites, one at the
site of the Financial Times Building in Cannon Street and the other at
Bucklersbury, off Cheapside.[5] In both places the huts were late variants on
the sunken type (see fig. 4), the larger of the two at Cannon Street being
some 16 ft by 30 ft (4·85 m by 9·15 m) with upright posts joined by trenches
for horizontal timbers, as in building C1 at Yeavering, West Stow and Upton.

[1] *Deserted Medieval Villages*, ed. Beresford and Hurst, pp. 149–68.
[2] Martin Biddle and David Hill, 'Late Saxon Planned Towns', *AntJ* 51 (1971), 70–85.
[3] E. M. Jope, 'Saxon Oxford and its Region', *Dark Age Britain*, ed. D. B. Harden (London, 1956),
pp. 234–45.
[4] E. M. Jope, 'The Clarendon Hotel, Oxford. Part I. The Site', *Oxoniensia* 23 (1958), 5–10.
Davison's work is unpublished.
[5] W. F. Grimes, *The Excavation of Roman and Medieval London* (London, 1968), pp. 155–60.

P. V. Addyman

It had a doorway in the centre of one side and seems to have had planked floors. The smaller hut, 12 ft by perhaps 9 ft (3·65 m by 2·75 m), had planked walls retained upright by posts. There were suggestions of larger buildings nearby. These are poor buildings to be the only ones known from a town of international importance. It is therefore something of a comfort that glimpses can be gained of the London of late Saxon times from documentary sources and of its palace area from other archaeological investigation.[1]

Most of the archaeological deposits of Saxon London have long since gone. The same irrevocable destruction faces such deposits in most of the other important Saxon towns in the present decade. It will mean the loss of the one source from which Anglo-Saxon urban history can be written. One of the many rescue operations launched in the face of this archaeological disaster has taken place at Brook Street, Winchester.[2] Here the varying fortunes of a Winchester street have been traced from the re-establishment of the place as a town in the ninth century throughout the Middle Ages. It is of particular interest to see the formation and eventual amalgamation of properties on the site. The long timber buildings which occupied the area in late Saxon times are a considerable addition to knowledge of the contemporary town-house. Biddle considers the two-doored building which preceded the church of St Mary in Tanner Street, on this site, to have been secular, perhaps a bower. If so, it is a rare example, though hardly unexpected, of a pre-Conquest domestic building in stone.[3] The early establishment of the property boundaries and of the types of land use and the remarkable persistence of properties through the town's subsequent history have significance for the topographical study of other towns.

Similar persistence of land boundaries has been found at Lydford, Devon.[4] Though small, remote and never particularly prosperous, this town also seems to have been laid out in formal plots in relation to a street grid and earth and timber defence. One property at Lydford proved to have a frontage of 80 ft (24·4 m) on the main street. The house on this property, set parallel to the street and some 10 ft or so back from it, had a sunken floor some 34 ft by 13 ft (10·35 m by 4 m). The great widths of the properties at Lydford contrast with those at Winchester and perhaps reflect the relative values of street frontage in the two towns. This clearly had its effect on both the lay-out and the plan of the houses. There seems every indication that the Lydford houses include substantial timber structures of post and of post-in-

[1] MA 6–7 (1962–3), 309.
[2] M. Biddle, 'Excavations at Winchester, 1970', AntJ 51 (1971).
[3] Personal communication from Mr Biddle; the building was discovered under St Mary's church in 1971.
[4] P. V. Addyman and A. D. Saunders, Lydford, Devon: Castle, Fort and Town, Royal Archaeological Institute, forthcoming.

292

trench construction, but there were certainly also less ambitious ones of timber with turf walls revetted internally and externally by wattle. The type is reminiscent of contemporary peasant houses on Dartmoor. In early Norman times such buildings were constructed, indeed, within the fort at Lydford.[1] They had been burnt down and the archaeological traces were thus well preserved. It seems clear enough that, for all their unity of planning, the *Burghal Hidage* towns contained houses in the local vernacular traditions. The little that is known of the internal buildings of Wallingford, for instance, shows different traditions again.[2]

Professor Cunliffe's extensive excavations at Portchester Castle have provided the most satisfactory evidence yet recovered for the buildings to be found within the defences of a late Saxon burh,[3] again apparently in the local vernacular. A picture is emerging of occupation complexes which contained halls, ancillary buildings, a stone-built tower with external plaster rendering, wells, cesspits and a boundary fence (see fig. 6). There were various reconstructions, changes in plan and alterations in land use. Cunliffe rightly points out that it would be premature at this stage to speculate on the functions of the various buildings, particularly as only part of the site has been excavated, and the main buildings may indeed not yet have been located. In the meantime, however, the preliminary accounts, as for instance of building M2,[4] are an excellent demonstration of what can be established from excavated evidence.

Far more extensive excavation at Thetford, Norfolk, has revealed a sample three acres of the very large late Saxon town there. For the present at least this will be the type site for eastern England and the point of reference for interpretation of the increasing number of contemporary buildings excavated in other parts of East Anglia. Even when Radford's paper appeared Thetford had already produced a large timber hall. Davison's recent excavations for the Department of the Environment have shown properly constructed roads, a maze of boundaries and an extraordinary sequence of timber buildings, some certainly houses, but others of quite uncertain function.[5] The sequence started with sunken huts which, significantly perhaps, were absent completely in later phases. Outstanding among the later buildings was a great aisled hall over 110 ft (33·5 m) long (see fig. 8), perhaps the largest building so far located in Anglo-Saxon England, and a cumulative building which eventually

[1] *MA* 10 (1966), 196–7, and Addyman and Saunders, *Lydford*, forthcoming.
[2] Nicholas P. Brooks, 'Excavations at Wallingford Castle, 1965: an Interim Report', *Berkshire Archaeol. Jnl* 62 (1965–6), 17–21, and personal communication on the results of the 1966 excavation.   [3] *AntJ* 49 (1969), 67–9.
[4] Barry Cunliffe, 'Excavations at Portchester Castle, 1963–5', *AntJ* 46 (1966), 45.
[5] Brian K. Davison, 'The Late Saxon Town of Thetford: an Interim Report on the 1964–6 Excavations', *MA* 11 (1967), 189–208.

reached a length of some 135 ft (41·15 m). In both buildings posts in separate post-holes were used. In a later phase there was a large hall of trussed couples. In another part of the excavation smaller post-built buildings were found; and in yet another there were detached buildings incorporating cellars, one

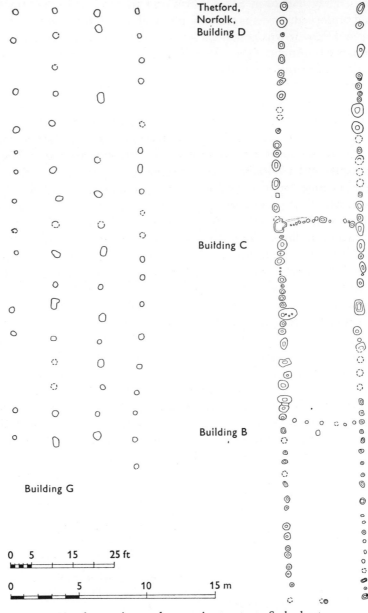

FIG. 8 Very large unitary and composite structures. Scale about 1:240

timber-lined. It became clear that earlier excavations had been concerned with a part of the site different again still, described by the excavator as an 'industrial slum'. The settlement, though exhibiting some elementary planning, does not have the regularity of contemporary Wessex towns. It may be more typical of areas of Scandinavian settlement and influence. The excavation has, anyway, produced a variety of structures of the highest interest and has provided an essential object lesson that 'the variation in form and lay-out shown within a relatively small area at Thetford makes it dangerous to generalize even about this one part of the town. In a town not conditioned by an inherited regular pattern of streets and walls, zoning may may well have resulted in differing patterns of settlement through the town.'[1] This having been said, it hardly seems worthwhile to discuss the very incomplete building traces from other eastern and northern towns – Norwich, Stamford, York and others. In York, where waterlogged conditions often mean preservation of timber and other organic remains, opportunities have been grasped at Hungate and recently in reconstruction work within certain York banks to see something of contemporary construction methods. At Barclays, for instance, sole-plates were observed in a late Saxon context.[2] The forthcoming spate of urban development in York will provide further opportunities. Such survivals are of the highest interest, as Rahtz's recent work on the Saxon mill at Tamworth has shown (see pl. VII*b*), adding superstructure and structural detail to the bare ground-plans normally available.[3]

The sites of various town palaces of the late Saxon kings can be pinpointed by historical and topographical study, but archaeological evidence of the physical characteristics exists for only one of them, at Westminster. Even here it is indirect. The walls of the Norman hall at Westminster Palace have a slight curvature in plan. The buttresses and arcading do not correspond from one side to the other. To explain these facts it has been suggested that the new hall of William II was built around an already standing hall which remained in use until its successor was complete. The curved walls of the new building reflect the curved walls of the old and indicate therefore that the old hall was of the 'boat-shaped' plan, common in northern Europe and apparently also in England.[4] Whatever the validity of this claim, and whatever the veracity in detail of the Bayeux Tapestry which shows various royal halls, the excavation of an urban palace is now clearly a major need. There are hints that the hall at Winchester, which is at least in part available for excavation, may well prove to be, in its various phases, an architectural

---

[1] *Ibid.* p. 195.   [2] Excavations by the late Jeffrey Radley, *MA* 15 (1971).
[3] Information from a duplicated interim report, 1971.
[4] R. Allen Brown, H. M. Colvin and A. J. Taylor, *The History of the King's Works* (London, 1963) I, 47.

achievement well in advance of what has in the past been thought likely in Anglo-Saxon royal palaces. A hint of the possibilities has been gained from the one late Saxon royal vill yet excavated, at Cheddar, Somerset, a rural establishment, and not necessarily a particularly important one.

Rahtz's excavations have traced the development of the Cheddar estate from the ninth century to the thirteenth. There are plans, apparently tolerably complete, representing the lay-out at a number of periods. The main accommodation and focus of the establishment was at all times the hall, as it had been at Yeavering and other earlier palaces. In the pre-tenth-century phase the hall was a remarkable bow-sided structure some 78 ft (23·75 m) long and 20 ft (6·1 m) wide at the mid-point (see fig. 7). There were two entrances set opposite each other in the mid-points of the sides and a subsidiary entrance near one end. The walls were of close-set posts in a continuous trench. There were inward sloping inner posts in the same trench in the middle part of the hall, which has suggested that there was a first floor in this part or that internal roof supports were needed. Also attributed to this phase were a smaller building in slighter post-in-trench construction with opposed entrances, 25 ft by 14 ft (7·65 m by 4·25 m) (see fig. 5), and a larger building, 30 ft by 24 ft (9·15 m by 7·6 m) built of posts in individual postholes and with various internal features. A published plan shows the existence of another subsidiary building and a drain running from the hall through an enclosure fence.[1] A broad storm-water ditch ran along one side of the entire establishment. Initial interpretations see the larger of the subsidiary structures as a *bur*, or bower, a private chamber of the king or the resident reeve, well known from historical sources. Though the hall itself is an outstanding structure, the small number and relative lack of pretension of the ancillary buildings have occasioned some surprise. It is possible that at this period the estate had not reached the pretensions of a royal palace and that the reference in Alfred's will is to the monastic establishment nearby.[2] Certainly when the witan met at Cheddar in the next century it was confronted by a new lay-out, with a timber hall – shorter but broader than its predecessor and having a separate latrine building – a chapel, a replacement bower and an enigmatic structure thought at least initially to have been a corn-mill, though curiously reminiscent of the structure assigned to chickens, geese and their caretaker on the St Gall monastery plan.[3] Cheddar at this period is doubtless the *villa celebris*, the *palatio regis*, of contemporary sources. The accommodation, still curiously limited though palatial, raises the problem of

---

[1] *Ibid.* p. 4.
[2] Philip Rahtz, 'The Saxon and Medieval Palaces at Cheddar, Somerset – an Interim Report of Excavations in 1960–62', *MA* 6–7 (1962–3), 53–66.
[3] H. Reinhardt, *Der karolingische Klosterplan von St Gallen (Schweiz). Der St Galler Klosterplan* (St Gall, 1952).

where the witan's members actually lived when they met at Cheddar – in temporary structures, in another part of the site or in an adjacent village? There is clearly still much to learn both about the specific use of such houses as the king's at Cheddar and about their relationship to the locality. Again the answer will come only with the detailed and long-term study of a particular establishment and its environment.

Hope-Taylor has established that the royal estate at Kingsbury, Old Windsor, Berkshire, seems to have been converted into a major establishment some time before there is specific evidence of its royal ownership. The construction of the mill and of the stone domestic building with glazed windows and possibly tiled roof which stood nearby took place in a phase which had begun by the mid eighth century. The buildings were destroyed in the late ninth century or the early tenth. Amongst structures from later phases Hope-Taylor mentions some built on sleeper beams, a technique which makes its appearance in the tenth century or the eleventh. Clearly the publication of this important site would add much to our understanding both of late Saxon estate management and of building construction.[1] It will be of interest to compare it with the buildings of a thegn's residence being revealed at Sulgrave, Northamptonshire. The ground-sill construction made its appearance here too in the early eleventh century, when the hall, more than 80 ft (24·4 m) long, was constructed (see fig. 7). This great house, of five square bays with an open cobbled porch at one end, seems to anticipate the traditional medieval arrangement, having a service end, separated by screen and cross-passage from the hall proper, with its central hearth and benches. There was an L-shaped chamber block at the other end, perhaps partly over-sailing the hall. Near the porch end, on the axis of the hall, was a detached timber building, perhaps a kitchen. There was a free-standing stone building set to one side of the hall, later incorporated into the post-Conquest defences to serve as a gateway.[2] There seems no reason to doubt the implications of this excavation that all the features of twelfth-century manorial lay-out were already known and used in England well before the Conquest. It can be only a matter of time, presumably, before comparable lay-outs are found. Sites such as Therfield, Hertfordshire, or Grantchester, Cambridgeshire, or Southoe, Huntingdonshire, all of which have produced evidence of pre-Conquest occupation in an apparently manorial situation, could well provide them, and investigation of the relationship between church tower and residence at Earls Barton, Northamptonshire, would be particularly interesting.[3] At Otley, Yorkshire, Mrs Le Patourel's excavations of the late Saxon arch-

[1] *MA* 2 (1958), 183–5.
[2] B. K. Davison, 'Excavations at Sulgrave, Northamptonshire, 1968', *ArchJ* 125 (1968), 305–7.
[3] Brian K. Davison, 'The Origins of the Castle in England', *ArchJ* 124 (1967), 202–11.

bishop's palace have shown that there, too, many features thought of as typically medieval were anticipated.

Such advances have come from the work of the Deserted Medieval Village Research Group on later medieval villages that it is surprising we still know so little of their late Saxon predecessors. Buildings earlier than the twelfth century are remarkably elusive in the various excavations, even though there may be Domesday or pre-Conquest documentation. At present knowledge rests on the excavation of individual buildings, usually on sites with an early desertion date. The North Elmham excavations probably give a point of reference for East Anglia, whatever the precise status of the excavated area at this period. There are in addition a string of individual structures from the area, at Langhale, at the pottery production site at Grimstone, and at Sedgeford, Norfolk, the latter originally attributed to the middle Saxon period.[1] Excavations under Waltham Abbey have revealed one, and yet another has been rescued in advance of road-works at Buckden, Huntingdonshire. The Buckden house, apparently of ground-sill construction and of 'boat-shaped' plan, is but one of a series of late Saxon settlements located in the St Neots area by the archaeological vigilance of Mr C. F. Tebbutt. Together the sites[2] provide a tolerably complete idea of local life and economy. The now damaged sites at and near Southoe seem to have been individual holdings typical of the dispersed units of this area. Salvage excavations at Little Paxton nearby produced the lay-out of fields and settlement enclosures, though the houses themselves were difficult to recognize. At Eaton Socon the plan of a long-lived post-built hall with wattle and daub walls was found, while nearby at St Neots new excavations have considerably expanded the oft-quoted evidence recovered in the 1929–32 excavations. The new work makes it clear that the sunken huts were restricted to part of the settlement only. The village is now seen as a site of 20 acres (8·1 hectares) or more, set on a gravel terrace overlooking a tributary of the Ouse. Large wooden houses, some post-built and some founded on ground-sills (see fig. 6), together with smaller post-built huts, stood in ditched or fenced areas, apparently with access ways between. The lay-out is reminiscent of the peasant holdings of a medieval village, though the houses seem in some ways more ambitious than those of later ages. The settlement seems to have had a boundary ditch.

[1] *MA* 3 (1959), 298. Pottery associated with the house is apparently not middle but late Saxon (information from Mr K. R. Wade).

[2] C. F. Tebbutt, 'An Eleventh-Century "Boat-Shaped" Building at Buckden, Huntingdonshire', *Proc. of the Cambridge Ant. Soc.* 55 (1962), 13–15; P. V. Addyman, 'Late Saxon Settlements in the St Neots Area, I: the Saxon Settlement and Norman Castle at Eaton Socon, Bedfordshire', *ibid.* 58 (1965), 38–73; 'St Neots Area II: the Little Paxton Settlement and Enclosures', *ibid.* 62 (1969), 59–93; and 'St Neots Area III: the Village or Township at St Neots', *ibid.* 64 (1972), forthcoming; and T. C. Lethbridge and C. F. Tebbutt, 'Southoe Manor', *ibid.* 38 (1938), 158–63.

The St Neots sites together provide some idea of the late Saxon village in the Ouse valley, and a similar composite story is being assembled for Dartmoor with the work of Mrs Minter at Hound Tor, Hutholes and other sites.[1] At Hound Tor a succession of buildings has been revealed whose walls are represented by double lines of stake-holes (see fig. 3). The houses, all earlier than their stone-built thirteenth-century successors, represent at least ten phases of construction and reconstruction. They are interpreted as constructions of turf with wattles supported on stakes. Some scholars consider such buildings would have had a relatively short life, though there seems no real reason to suppose that they were reconstructed more frequently than in each generation. The houses, as the Lydford town excavation has shown, were in the normal local tradition. The site has also produced sunken huts. Another part of the west has shown quite different house traditions. The hamlet at Mawgan Porth in Cornwall is a series of court-yard houses. The main accommodation in each was a 'long-house' with accommodation for cattle and people under the same roof-line. One excavated example was 33 ft by 15 ft (10·05 m by 4·55 m) and there were centre posts and internal partitions. There were doorways in the side walls and in one end wall. The end door led into the small court-yard, around which were smaller buildings, some also used for domestic accommodation. The hamlet seems to have been occupied between 900 and 1050. The houses are clearly a response to the particular building traditions and environmental circumstances of the area, but certain features, in particular the general arrangements in the main house, are strikingly reminiscent of houses in the heartland of Anglo-Saxon England. Any way Mawgan Porth and the south-western sites subsequently examined by Professor Thomas[2] provide a remarkably detailed story of contemporary life. They stress the essential variety of Anglo-Saxon England. Study of its villages will eventually be a series of local studies, reflecting varied responses to environment and local resources. There is no reason to doubt that the traditions of English vernacular building were any less varied in the eleventh century than they were in the sixteenth when we can first adequately study them from surviving remains.

Limited and patchy though it is, the new archaeological evidence is already allowing far more to be read into more conventional sources. The rare contemporary illustrations have in some cases proved to be more accurate than could have been supposed. The houses on the Bayeux Tapestry, recently

[1] *MA* 6–7 (1962–3), 341–3 and fig. 102; *ibid.* 8 (1964), 282–3 and fig. 91; and *ibid.* 10 (1966), 210 and fig. 86.

[2] The sites are Gwithian and Hellesvean; see A. C. Thomas, *Gwithian, Ten Years Work, 1949–1958*, West Cornwall Field Club (1958), and A. Guthrie, 'The Hellesvean Dark Age House', *Proc. of the West Cornwall Field Club* n.s. 2 (1956–61), 151–3. For Mawgan Porth see *Recent Archaeological Excavations in Britain*, ed. R. L. S Bruce-Mitford (London, 1956), pp. 167–96.

discussed by Urban Holmes, have been brilliantly related to the archaeological evidence by Allen Brown.[1] They purport to be buildings variously in England and Normandy, from all parts of the social spectrum. Valuable as much for the detail as for the general, they show construction methods and the tools employed and confirm the impression of a rich and varied architecture, at least in the secular work mostly achieved in timber. Manuscript illustrations are less dependable since they may copy non-local models; but a systematic study of them for their evidence of contemporary building traditions, whether ecclesiastical or secular, is long overdue. Another source of information is sculpture. It forms a particularly important source for the Danelaw, where excavation has been slow in coming. Here hog-backed tombstones, ostensibly in the form of houses, have long been recognized as evidence of a tradition of timber building involving 'boat-shaped' plans, bowed roofs, and well carpentered wall timbering. They have recently been the subject of detailed study which places their chronology and interpretation on a firm basis.[2] It is of some interest too that excavation has already corroborated the conclusions drawn from the hogbacks and indeed from house-shaped caskets which appear to tell the same story. The Cheddar hall, seemingly in a non-Viking context, and the houses at Buckden and St Neots are all of this form. The type has long been well known in Viking contexts in the Isle of Man, Orkneys, Shetlands and elsewhere in the British Isles.[3] Its north European distribution has recently been discussed in general,[4] and the rationale behind such buildings has been succinctly and sanely analysed in Hope-Taylor's discussion of the Buckden house, where precise suggestions are made for the terminology to be used in discussion of the subject.[5] The very clear links which 'boat-shaped' buildings seem to have with Denmark, recently reinforced by the excavations at Århus, have given rise to the speculation that such houses may have been a Viking introduction to the country. The evidence on the point is circumstantial, though the tendencies exhibited by early Anglo-Saxon buildings towards the bowed shape, as for instance in the Chalton buildings, may perhaps suggest a parallel development.[6]

[1] R. Allen Brown, 'The Architecture', *The Bayeux Tapestry*, ed. Sir Frank Stenton, 2nd ed. (London, 1965), pp. 76–87. [2] T. Lang in an unpub. Ph.D. thesis, Durham.

[3] H. J. Fleure and Margaret Dunlop, 'Glendarragh Circle and Alignments, The Braaid, I.O.M.', *AntJ* 22 (1942), 39–53; C. A. Ralegh Radford, *The Early Christian and Norse Settlements, Birsay* (Edinburgh, 1959), and Rousay, *MA* 8 (1964), 240.

[4] Torsten Capelle, '"Schiffsförmige" Hausgrundrisse in frühgeschichtlicher Zeit', *Frühmittelalterliche Studien* 3 (1969), 244–56.

[5] Brian Hope-Taylor, 'The "Boat-Shaped" House in Northern Europe', *Proc. of the Cambridge Ant. Soc.* 55 (1962), 16–22.

[6] For Århus see Ole Klindt-Jensen and Hellmuth Andersen, 'Det ældste Århus', *Kuml* 1963, 75–87. For speculation on the origins of British Dark Age houses in general see Lloyd R. Laing, 'Timber Halls in Dark Age Britain – some Problems', *Trans. of the Dumfriesshire and Galloway Nat. Hist. and Ant. Soc.* 46 (1969), 110–27.

The Anglo-Saxon house: a new review

Architectural historians have made considerable progress in recent decades in the understanding of later medieval building traditions. Clearly very few timber buildings, if any, survive from the Anglo-Saxon period, even though a remarkable antiquity has recently been claimed on the basis of radiocarbon dating for some Essex barns. It has seemed to successive workers, however, that the tradition of carpentry and lay-out seen in the earliest surviving buildings must reflect a considerable ancestry. In particular there has been much discussion of the origins of the 'long-house', examples of which are found in parts of western England and in Wales.[1] The cruck-building tradition, of which surviving examples too have a particular distribution, has given rise to discussion and speculation. Finally there is the suggestion that the 'king-post' tradition of roofing found in northern England might be the end-product of an age-old tradition of building with centre posts.[2] The various contributions to the subject are stimulating and of the greatest interest, but the basic validity of the approach is not beyond doubt. Smith's recent contribution to the cruck-building controversy, for instance, depends largely on the distribution of examples built in late medieval or post-medieval times.[3] Smith's researches have led him to reject the various theses which claimed for this distinctive roofing technique a Germanic or Scandinavian origin. He considers the distribution, with a preponderance in the midlands, the west, the north and Wales, has a Celtic flavour, and compares it with Jackson's map of surviving Celtic place-names, artifacts older by a millennium or more. Smith pleads special circumstances for his subject, the innate conservatism of the carpenter and the nature of the craft technique which is handed down by demonstration and whose products are not portable. The appearance of a new type of structure in any given place, he argues, bespeaks the arrival of a carpenter trained in the areas where the structural form evolved. To the archaeologist, well used to the concepts of invasion, diffusion and independent invention, conclusions of this sort are made difficult to accept not by their inherent unlikelihood but by the degree to which he is asked to stretch credulity. Traditions, laws and almost all aspects of material culture – ceramics, metal-work and art styles – show changes in the millennium in question which render the end utterly unrecognizable from the beginning. Perhaps the archaeologist is even more influenced by the way in which a few archaeological investigations of deserted medieval villages in lowland England have so thoroughly upset the speculations on the distribution of surviving long-houses; for they were formerly far more

[1] The current position is summarized and contributions to the discussion listed in *Deserted Medieval Villages*, ed. Beresford and Hurst, pp. 104–13.

[2] J. T. Smith, 'Appendix' to M. W. Thompson, 'Excavation of the Fortified Medieval Hall of Hutton Colswain at Huttons Ambo, near Malton, Yorkshire', *ArchJ* 114 (1957), 86–91.

[3] J. T. Smith, 'Cruck Construction: a Survey of the Problems', *MA* 8 (1964), 119–51.

extensive in their distribution. On the question of cruck origins archaeology may never provide the answer, since a cruck-building may well, as Innocent showed, leave little physical trace. Certainly, however, claims based on ambiguous evidence from individual sites are best avoided for the time being.

The evidence reviewed in this paper is enough to show that almost all inherited ideas about the standards of Anglo-Saxon domestic accommodation must be revised. Whether it is enough to permit new generalizations to replace the old is, however, doubtful. Perhaps it can be allowed that from the first the Anglo-Saxon immigrant favoured nucleated settlements; all that is known of the structure of contemporary society demands it. It is still not clear, however, whether the humble sunken hut did or did not constitute the main or most common dwelling in such settlements. Hurst, while leaving the question open, is clearly more inclined than some to accept that it did. What does emerge from the excavations is that sunken huts were far more common in early Saxon times than later. Many middle Saxon and later Saxon sites have none at all and in others they were often rather specialized and are best regarded as cellars (see fig. 2*f*, Thetford) or stores. Even the early ones have usually produced some evidence of industrial activity, often spinning or weaving. This having been said, it is striking to discover that a reconstruction of a sunken hut such as has recently been made at the Weald and Downland Open Air Museum (see pl. VII*a*) provides a convenient and relatively commodious building.

The sunken huts, whether two-post, four-post or framed (see figs 2 and 4), resemble closely the similar structures known throughout Germanic Europe.[1] It is thus surprising that the surface-built structures, which were undoubtedly present from the first in Anglo-Saxon England, do not have close continental parallels. Conversely the true Germanic long-house has yet to be found in England. Even the basic elements, the aisled lay-out and the accommodation for cattle and humans under the same roof-line, have not been found in early settlements, though both features do occur eventually. Conclusions are premature when only a handful of houses are known, whereas cemeteries of the early Saxon period can be numbered in hundreds. Nevertheless the way in which Anglo-Saxon building subsequently developed hardly suggests that such a tradition was ever strong. It rather suggests that roofs from the first were based not on aisle posts, but on load-bearing walls or possibly in some cases on crucks. The earliest buildings seem to have had posts in individual post-holes (see fig. 9). Some, for instance West Stow halls 1 and 2 and Chalton house 2, appear to have matched pairs of posts, which might

[1] W. U. Guyan, 'Einige Karten zur Verbreitung der Grubenhäuser in Mitteleuropa im ersten nachchristlichen Jahrtausend', *Jahrbuch der schweizerischen Gesellschaft für Urgeschichte* 42 (1952), 174–97.

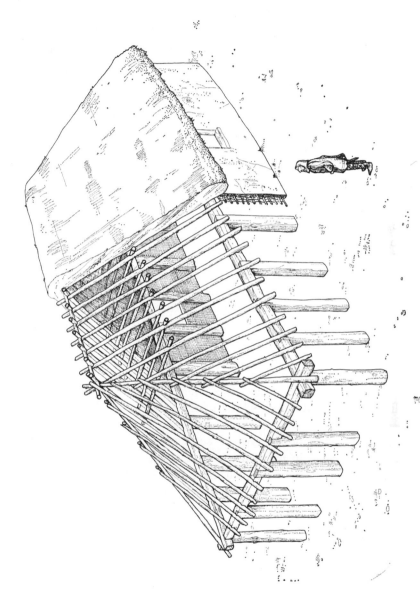

FIG. 9   Chalton, Hampshire. Hypothetical reconstruction of structure with individually set posts. The superstructure is entirely conjectural. *Drawing: R. Warmington*

303

indicate coupling (see fig. 3). There is a clear tendency towards a plan including opposed doors in the mid-point of the long sides and very often a door in one of the end walls (see pl. VIII*b*). This tradition runs intermittently throughout the Anglo-Saxon house series to emerge at Sulgrave as the well-known domestic plan. It was a tradition familiar to Bede's contemporaries, as a famous passage shows:

Thus, O king, the present life of men on earth, in comparison with that time which is unknown to us, appears to me to be as if, when you are sitting at supper with your ealdormen and thegns in the winter time, and a fire is lighted in the midst and the hall warmed, but everywhere outside the storms are raging, a sparrow should come and fly rapidly through the hall, coming in at one door, and immediately out at the other.[1]

Another intermittently recurrent feature is the partitioning of one or both ends of the house, presumably to provide private quarters. It is seen in simple form at West Stow, Chalton and North Elmham, as an evolution from partitions to annexed rooms in the Yeavering halls, and perhaps in the tripartite divisions of later buildings such as the long hall at Cheddar or the one at Sulgrave. Private quarters were also normally provided for the lord in a separate building, as the circumstantial account of the death of Cynewulf in 786 in the *Anglo-Saxon Chronicle*, *s.a.* 757, indicates. Such separate buildings may have been identified at Yeavering and at Cheddar, while the Brook Street stone building at Winchester may have had a similar function in an urban or quasi-urban estate.

Although recognizable themes are thus emerging as the corpus of excavated buildings grows and although the general character of Anglo-Saxon building is no longer in doubt, it is still too early to attempt any sort of classification either of buildings or of settlement types. Contemporary sources are clearly correct in implying a great variety of buildings and the treatises on estate management make it clear that many had quite specific functions.[2] Doubtless this will be reflected in plan and in construction, but at present it is only on a handful of excavated sites that specific functions can be assigned to various buildings. It is becoming clear too that at least by late Saxon times varied and distinctive local traditions of timber building had grown up. It will be surprising if the combined effects of environment, differing resources and varying inherited tradition had not produced wide regional variations at a much earlier date. The various plans illustrated in fig. 6 are therefore likely to be unrepresentative, though they may give an indication of the sort of settlement and building lay-out to be expected.

[1] Bede, *Ecclesiastical History of the English Nation* II. 13.
[2] Cambridge, Corpus Christi College 383, pp. 102–7: *Die Gesetze der Angelsachsen* (Halle, 1903–16; repr. Aalen, 1960) I, 453–5 (considered a twelfth-century copy of an eleventh-century original).

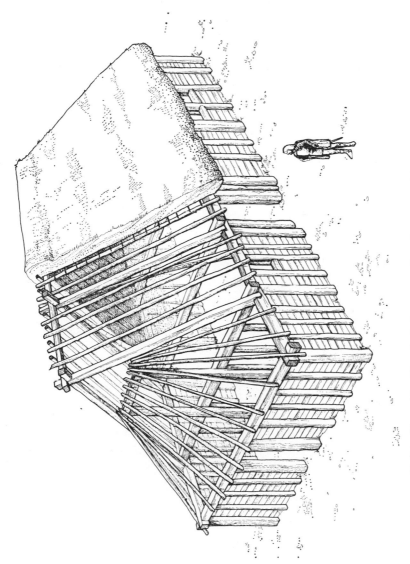

FIG. 10 Chalton, Hampshire. Hypothetical reconstruction of structure with posts set in continuous trenches. The superstructure is entirely conjectural. *Drawing: R. Warmington*

The distribution of excavated sites is uneven. There is hardly an excavated house from the whole of Yorkshire, for instance, if sunken huts be excepted. It is impossible, therefore, to suggest any general structural evolution. Nevertheless the Northumbrian royal sites have apparently produced an internally consistent evolution; and there is a similarly satisfactory sequence at North Elmham. The various Cheddar buildings, it is said, could represent a quite credible local unilinear development. Yet the trends are by no means consistent from area to area. If generalization is possible it is that the larger buildings in the early Saxon period were normally post-built, with posts set in individual post-holes. These were sometimes paired and thus probably coupled across the buildings; and there is a hint of cruck-framing. In some areas such buildings were replaced by structures of posts more or less closely set in continuous trenches (see figs. 6, 7 and 10). The new tradition seems to have been wide-spread in middle Saxon times. The change is perhaps a response to the closer spacing of posts and a desire to anchor the wall-cladding into the ground. In many cases the walls were clad with wattle, as Alfred, in his delightful vignette of house-building, seems to have considered a norm.[1] It is of interest to see a return to the use of individual posts in late Saxon times in East Anglia, doubtless reflecting some specific change in basic construction of the superstructure. One particular technique, the use of ground-sills and their integration to produce a rigid foundation, also appears widely in late Saxon times – though there is sporadic use of horizontal beams in middle Saxon times – and some of the later sunken huts seem to have walls based on sills or on posts with short sills between. The late Saxon version, however, is a sophisticated and important advance which appeared at Old Windsor in the late tenth century or the eleventh and was already present in the mill at Tamworth, with planking over joists and with a wide variety of joints and pegging apparently – according to C-14 dates – in the eighth century. Such structures come as a surprise to vernacular architects, who would not normally expect such a technique until the late Middle Ages. Even so, the technique is described in detail in *Byrhtferth's Manual*.[2] It was clearly of particular importance in those parts of England which favoured a house with 'boat-shaped' plan. The St Neots building, here shown in hypothetical reconstruction (fig. 11), demonstrates the structural implications.

Excavations now being undertaken by the Ancient Monuments Inspectorate of the Department of the Environment on Saxon settlement sites should

---

[1] In Alfred's preface to his translation of St Augustine's *Soliloquies*, trans. H. L. Hargrove, *Yale Studies in English* 22 (1904); repr. D. Whitelock, *English Historical Documents* c. *500–1042* (London, 1955), p. 884.

[2] *Byrhtferth's Manual*, ed. S. J. Crawford, Early English Text Society o.s. 177 (London, 1929), p. 142; for a commentary see Thompson, 'Excavation at Huttons Ambo', p. 80.

rapidly fill many of the gaps in our knowledge of Anglo-Saxon houses. It has been possible to select from the large number of sites threatened with destruction a representative series to provide sample complete village excavations in various parts of the country, examples of an archiepiscopal estate in late Saxon times and further sample excavations in middle and late

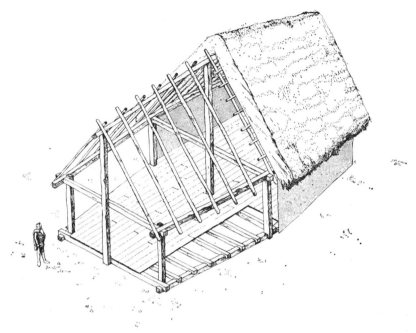

FIG. 11   St Neots, Huntingdonshire. Hypothetical reconstruction of structure with ground-sills. The superstructure is entirely conjectural. *Drawing: R. Warmington*

Saxon towns and to investigate specific buildings. Progress is likely to be even more rapid in the next fifteen years than it has been in the last, though it can scarcely have more fundamental effects. The real progress will have come, however, with publication of the excavations.

Bibliography for 1971

MARTIN BIDDLE, ALAN BROWN, T. J. BROWN

and PETER HUNTER BLAIR

This bibliography is meant to include all books, articles and significant reviews published in any branch of Anglo-Saxon studies during 1971. It excludes reprints unless they contain new material. It will be continued annually. A.B. has been mainly responsible for sections 2, 3 and 4, T.J.B. for section 5, P.H.B. for sections 6 and 7 and M.B. for section 8. Peter Clemoes has been coordinating editor.

The following abbreviations are used where relevant (not only in the bibliography but also throughout the volume):

AB	*Analecta Bollandiana*
ABR	*American Benedictine Review*
AHR	*American Historical Review*
AntJ	*Antiquaries Journal*
ArchJ	*Archaeological Journal*
ASE	*Anglo-Saxon England*
ASNSL	*Archiv für das Studium der neueren Sprachen und Literaturen*
BGDSL	*Beiträge zur Geschichte der deutschen Sprache und Literatur*
BNJ	*British Numismatic Journal*
BROB	*Berichten van de Rijksdienst voor het Oudheidkundig Bodemonderzoek*
CA	*Current Archaeology*
CCM	*Cahiers de Civilisation Médiévale*
CHR	*Catholic History Review*
DUJ	*Durham University Journal*
E&S	*Essays and Studies by Members of the English Association*
EC	*Essays in Criticism*
EconHR	*Economic History Review*
EEMF	Early English Manuscripts in Facsimile
EHR	*English Historical Review*
ELN	*English Language Notes*
EStn	*Englische Studien*
ESts	*English Studies*
IAF	*Issledovanija po Anglijskoj Filologii*
IF	*Indogermanische Forschungen*
JBAA	*Journal of the British Archaeological Association*
JEGP	*Journal of English and Germanic Philology*
JEH	*Journal of Ecclesiastical History*

JL   Janua Linguarum
JTS   Journal of Theological Studies
MA   Medieval Archaeology
MÆ   Medium Ævum
MLN   Modern Language Notes
MLQ   Modern Language Quarterly
MLR   Modern Language Review
MP   Modern Philology
MS   Mediaeval Studies
N&Q   Notes and Queries
NC   Numismatic Chronicle
NM   Neuphilologische Mitteilungen
PMLA   Publications of the Modern Language Association of America
PQ   Philological Quarterly
RB   Revue Bénédictine
RES   Review of English Studies
SAP   Studia Anglica Posnaniensia
SBVS   Saga-Book of the Viking Society for Northern Research
SN   Studia Neophilologica
SP   Studies in Philology
TLS   Times Literary Supplement
TPS   Transactions of the Philological Society
TRHS   Transactions of the Royal Historical Society
YES   Yearbook of English Studies
ZAA   Zeitschrift für Anglistik und Amerikanistik
ZDA   Zeitschrift für deutsches Altertum und deutsche Literatur
ZVS   Zeitschrift für vergleichende Sprachforschung

1. GENERAL

Bond, Donald F., *A Reference Guide to English Studies*, 2nd ed. (Chicago and London)

Clemoes, Peter, and Kathleen Hughes, ed., *England Before the Conquest: Studies in Primary Sources presented to Dorothy Whitelock* (Cambridge) [cited below as *Whitelock Studies*]

Davis, Norman, 'Kenneth Sisam', *NM* 72, 762

Gardner, John, *Grendel*, illustrations by Emil Antonucci (New York) [a novel]

Henderson, I., *A List of the Published Writings of Hector Munro Chadwick and of Nora Kershaw Chadwick* (Cambridge)

Käsmann, Hans, '[Nachruf auf] Bogislav von Lindheim †', *Anglia* 89, 161–3

McKisack, May, *Medieval History in the Tudor Age* (Oxford) [including essays on Leland and Parker]

Peppard, Murray B., *Paths through the Forest: a Biography of the Brothers Grimm* (New York)

Robinson, Fred C., 'Old English Bibliography 1970', *OE Newsletter* 4.2, 10–30
'Old English Research in Progress, 1970–1971', *NM* 72, 504–12

Stacpoole, Alberic, '*Regularis Concordia* Millennium Conference' (with appendices by D.H.F.) *Ampleforth Jnl* 76, 30–53

Whitelock, Dorothy, list of writings of, *Whitelock Studies*, pp. 1–4

Wiley, Raymond A., ed., *John Mitchell Kemble and Jacob Grimm, a Correspondence, 1832–1852* (Leiden)

2. OLD ENGLISH LANGUAGE

Anderson, John, '*Ablaut* in the Synchronic Phonology of the Old English Strong Verb', *IF* 75, 166–97

Awedyk, Wiesław, 'Some Remarks on the Phonology of Old English', *SAP* 3, 69–74

Bammesberger, Alfred, 'Urgermanisch **funsaʒ*', *Die Sprache* 17, 46–9

Baron, Naomi S., 'A Reanalysis of English Grammatical Gender', *Lingua* 27, 113–40, and *Stanford Occasional Papers in Linguistics* 1, 54–88

Benning, Helmut A., *Die Vorgeschichte von ne. 'duty': zur Ausformung der Pflichtidee im Substantivwortschatz des Englischen*, Linguistica et Litteraria 7 (Frankfurt am Main)

Brorström, Sverker, 'A Historical Survey of Prepositions Expressing the Sense "for the duration of"', *ESts* 52, 105–16

Cameron, Kenneth, see sect. 6

Campanile, Enrico, 'Elementi Lessicali di Origine Inglese nel *Vocabularium Cornicum*', *Studi e Saggi Linguistici* 10, 193–201

Cooke, W. G., '*Hronas* and *Hronfixas*', *N&Q* 18, 245–7

Cross, J. E., 'Lexicographical Notes on the Old English *Life of St Giles* and the *Life of St Nicholas*', *N&Q* 18, 369–72

Dodgson, J. McN., *The Place-Names of Cheshire, Part III, The Place-Names of Nantwich Hundred and Eddisbury Hundred*, English Place-Name Society 46 (Cambridge)

Feilitzen, Olof von, and Christopher Blunt, 'Personal Names on the Coinage of Edgar', *Whitelock Studies*, pp. 183–214

Fellows Jensen, Gillian, 'The Scribe of the Lindsey Survey', *Namn och Bygd* 57, 58–74

Forsberg, Rune, 'On Old English *ād* in English Place-Names', *Namn och Bygd* 58, 20–82

Gardner, F. F., *Syntactic Patterns of Old English, an Analysis*, JL, series practica 140 (The Hague)

Geipel, John, *The Viking Legacy: the Scandinavian Influence on the English and Gaelic Languages* (Newton Abbot)

Götz, Dieter, *Studien zu den verdunkelten Komposita im Englischen*, Erlanger Beiträge zur Sprach- und Kunstwissenschaft 40 (Nürnberg)

Green, Donald C., 'Formulas and Syntax in Old English Poetry: a Computer Study', *Computers and the Humanities* 6, 85–93

Gugeleva, O. V., 'Sravitel'nyj analiz drevneanglijskix intervokal'nyx konsonantnyx grupp i konsonantnyx sochetanij isxoda odnoslozhnovo slova [Comparative Analysis of Old English Intervocalic Consonant Groups and Final Consonants of a Monosyllabic Word]', *IAF* 4, 53–8

Halle, Morris, and Samuel Jay Keyser, *English Stress: its Form, its Growth, and its Role in Verse* (New York)

Hogg, Richard M., 'Gemination, Breaking, and Reordering in the Synchronic Phonology of Old English', *Lingua* 28, 48–69

Jacobs, Nicolas, 'OE *wered* "drink", *werod* "sweet"', *N&Q* 18, 404–7

Jones, Charles, 'Some Features of Determiner Usage in the Old English Glosses to the Lindisfarne Gospels and the Durham Ritual', *IF* 75, 198–219

Kabell, Aage, 'Mittelenglisch *bryniges*', *Anglia* 89, 117–18

Kastovsky, Dieter, 'The Old English Suffix *-er(e)*', *Anglia* 89, 285–325

Kim, Suksan, 'The Vowel Shift in Unstressed Syllables of Old English', *Lang. Research* 7, 1–10

Kispert, Robert J., *Old English: an Introduction* (New York)

Kristensson, Gillis, 'An Etymological Note: Old English *drȳgan* "to make dry"', *SN* 43, 257–9

Krupatkin, Ja. B., 'Fonologicheskij variant fonemy i nesmyslorazlichitel'nye oppozicii [Phonological Variant of a Phoneme and Non-Distinctive Oppositions]', *Voprosy Jazykoznanija* 1971, no. 3, 49–59

Lass, Roger, 'Boundaries as Obstruents: Old English Voicing Assimilation and Universal Strength Hierarchies', *Jnl of Ling.* 7, 15–30

Leyerle, John, '*The Dictionary of Old English*: a Progress Report', *Computers and the Humanities* 5, 279–83

'*The Dictionary of Old English*: a Report to Group 1, Old English, of the MLA made on December 29, 1970', *OE Newsletter* 4.2, 3–9

Maling, Joan M., 'Sentence Stress in Old English', *Linguistic Inquiry* 2, 379–99 [metrics]

Markey, Thomas L., 'The Germanic *-e/-a* Period', *NM* 72, 1–5

McGovern, John F., see sect. 6

Meid, Wolfgang, *Das germanische Präteritum: Indogermanische Grundlagen und Ausbreitung im Germanischen*, Innsbrucker Beiträge zur Sprachwissenschaft 3

Miedema, H. T. J., 'Noordzeegermaans en Vroegoudfries: De Niet-Friese Ingweonismen in Schönfeld's *Historische Grammatica*', *Leuvense Bijdragen* 60, 99–104

Millward, Celia M., *Imperative Constructions in Old English*, JL, series practica 124 (The Hague)

Novikov, D. P., 'Xarakteristika èlementov ob"ektno-predikativnovo sochetanija (na materiale drevneanglijskovo jazyka) [On the Elements of the Object-Objective Complement Construction (Using Old English Material)]', *IAF* 4, 114–21

Okasha, Elisabeth, see sect. 8*i*

Oxford English Dictionary: *The Compact Edition of the Oxford English Dictionary*, 2 vols. (Oxford)

Page, R. I., 'How Long Did the Scandinavian Language Survive in England? The Epigraphical Evidence', *Whitelock Studies*, pp. 165–81

Peltola, Niilo, 'Observations on Intensification in Old English Poetry', *NM* 72, 649–90

Piirainen, Elisabeth, *Germ. '*frōō-' und germ. '*klōk-':* Eine bedeutungsgeschichtliche Untersuchung zu Wörtern für "Klugheit" und "pflanzliches Wachstum", Mémoires de la Société Néophilologique de Helsinki 37

Pilch, Herbert, 'The Phonemic Interpretation of Old English Spelling Evidence', *Acta Linguistica Hafniensia* 12, 29–43

Pyles, Thomas, *The Origins and Development of the English Language*, 2nd ed. (New York)

Rauch, Irmengard, review article on G. Bech, *Das germanische reduplizierte Präteritum* (Copenhagen, 1969), *Lingua* 27, 367–81

Ross, Alan S. C., 'Two Vestigial Distinctions in the Late North Northumbrian Dialect of Anglo-Saxon', *Archivum Linguisticum* n.s. 2, 117–27

Schenker, Walter, '*Es/os*-Flexion und *es/os*-Stämme im Germanischen', *BGDSL* 93, 46–58

Seebold, Elmar, 'Das germanische Wort für den Heiden', *BGDSL* 93, 29–45

Shores, David L., *A Descriptive Syntax of the Peterborough Chronicle from 1122 to 1154*, JL, series practica 103 (The Hague)
'Morphosyntactic Relations in *The Peterborough Chronicle*, 1122–1154', *ESts* 52, 1–13

Snyder, William H., 'Zur Gemination in der dritten Ablautsreihe der starken Verben', *ZVS* 85, 70–83

Speedie, David C., 'A Note on Old English Diphthongization of Back Vowels after Initial *i*', *Archivum Linguisticum* n.s. 2, 147–50

Squires, Ann, 'Collation of the Anglo-Saxon Gloss to the Durham Ritual', *N&Q* 18, 362–6

Stanley, E. G., 'Studies in the Prosaic Vocabulary of Old English Verse', *NM* 72, 385–418

Steinberg [Shtejnberg], N. A., 'K probleme glagol'noj prefiksacii v drevneanglijskom jazyke [On the Problem of Verbal Prefixation in Old English]', *IAF* 4, 59–65

Wakelin, Martyn F., 'OE *bræzen, brazen*', *Neophilologus* 55, 108

Yamakawa, Kikuo, 'OE *þær* and *hwær*: a Study of *Where* Developing in the Subordinating Function (I)', *Hitotsubashi Jnl of Arts and Sciences* 12, 1–19

Zernoff [Zernov], B. E., 'O mestoimenii vtorovo lica v strukture imperativnovo predlozhenija drevneanglijskovo jazyka [The Occurrence of the Second Person Pronoun in the Old English Imperative Sentence]', *IAF* 4, 122–7

Zhirmunskij, V. M., 'Sushchestvoval li "protogermanskij" jazyk? [Did a "Proto-Germanic" Language Really Exist?]', *Voprosy Jazykoznanija* 1971, no. 3, 3–6

3. OLD ENGLISH LITERATURE

a. General

Cross, J. E., 'The Ethic of War in Old English', *Whitelock Studies*, pp. 269–82

Gatch, Milton McC., *Loyalties and Traditions: Man and his World in Old English Literature*, Pegasus Backgrounds in English Literature (New York)

Göller, Karl Heinz, *Geschichte der altenglischen Literatur*, Grundlagen der Anglistik und Amerikanistik 3 (Berlin)

Göttert, Karl-Heinz, 'Literaturgeschichte als germanische Philologie: Bemerkungen zu einer neuen Fachenzyklopädie', *Archiv für Kulturgeschichte* 53, 158–65 [review article on L. E. Schmitt, ed., *Kurzer Grundriss der germanischen Philologie bis 1500* II]

Schmitt, Ludwig Erich, ed., *Kurzer Grundriss der germanischen Philologie bis 1500* II, *Literaturgeschichte* (Berlin) [pp. 1–47, Georges Zink, 'Heldensage'; 117–63, Frederick Norman, 'Altenglische Literatur']

Scragg, D. G., see sect. 5

b. Poetry
i. General

Cable, Thomas, 'Constraints on Anacrusis in Old English Meter', *MP* 69, 97–104

Gradon, Pamela, *Form and Style in Early English Literature* (London)

Green, Donald C., see sect. 2

Kuhn, Hans, *Kleine Schriften, Aufsätze und Rezensionen aus den Gebieten der germanischen und nordischen Sprach-, Literatur- und Kulturgeschichte* II (Berlin) [including 'Finn Folcwalding' (1969), pp. 183–8; 'Zur Geschichte der Walthersage' (1963), pp. 126–34]

Maling, Joan M., see sect. 2

Mandel, Jerome, 'Contrast in Old English Poetry', *Chaucer Rev.* 6, 1–13

Opland, Jeffrey, '*Scop* and *Imbongi*: Anglo-Saxon and Bantu Oral Poets', *Eng. Stud. in Africa* 14, 161–78

Peltola, Niilo, see sect. 2

Raffel, Burton, *The Forked Tongue: a study of the Translation Process*, De Proprietatibus Litterarum series maior 14 (The Hague)

Rebsamen, Frederick, '*Beowulf is my Name*' *and Selected Translations of other Old English Poems* (San Francisco)

Stanley, E. G., see sect. 2

Taylor, Paul B., 'The Rhythm of *Völuspá*', *Neophilologus* 55, 45–57

Wienold, Götz, *Formulierungstheorie: Poetik: Strukturelle Literaturgeschichte: am Beispiel der altenglischen Literatur* (Frankfurt am Main)

ii. 'Beowulf'

Baird, Joseph L., 'The "Nor"-Clause of *Beowulf* 1084–85a', *MP* 69, 133–5

Ball, C. J. E., '*Beowulf* 99–101', *N&Q* 18, 163

Britton, G. C., 'Unferth, Grendel and the Christian Meaning of *Beowulf*', *NM* 72, 246–50

Cable, Thomas, 'Clashing Stress in the Meter of *Beowulf*', *NM* 72, 42–50

Campbell, Alistair, 'The Use in *Beowulf* of Earlier Heroic Verse', *Whitelock Studies*, pp. 283–92

Ciklamini, Marlene, 'The Problem of Starkaðr', *Scandinavian Stud.* 43, 169–88

Cox, Betty S., *Cruces of 'Beowulf'*, Stud. in Eng. Lit. 60 (The Hague)

Girvan, Ritchie, '*Beowulf*' *and the Seventh Century: Language and Content* (repr., London) [including a new chapter 'Sutton Hoo and the Background of the Poem' by Rupert Bruce-Mitford, pp. 85–98, and Select Bibliography by Christopher Ball, pp. 99–104]

Hill, Thomas D., '*Hwyrftum scriþað: Beowulf*, line 163', *MS* 33, 379–81

Kaske, R. E., '*Beowulf* and the Book of Enoch', *Speculum* 46, 421–31

Klegraf, Josef, '*Beowulf* 769: *ealuscerwēn*', *ASNSL* 208, 108–12

Lehmann, Ruth P. M., 'Six Notes on *Beowulf*', *NM* 72, 35–41

Lönnroth, Lars, 'Hjálmar's Death-Song and the Delivery of Eddic Poetry', *Speculum* 46, 1–20 [pp. 13–16 on *Beowulf* 2724–891]

McConchie, R. W., 'The Problem of Cremation in *Beowulf*', *ANZAMRS, Bull. of the Australian and New Zealand Assoc. for Med. and Renaissance Stud.* 6, 16–17 [summary]

Raffel, Burton '*Beowulf*', *Translated, with an Introduction and Afterword by Burton Raffel* (Amherst)

Ramsey, Lee C., 'The Sea Voyages in *Beowulf*', *NM* 72, 51–9

Smithers, G. V., 'The Geats in *Beowulf*', *DUJ* 63, 87–103

Tegethoff, Wilhelm, *Der altangelsächsische '*Beowulf*': ein Werk Adalberts von Bremen. Neuauslegung: Übersetzung und Kommentar* (Osnabrück)

Wentersdorf, Karl P., '*Beowulf*'s Withdrawal from Frisia: a Reconsideration', *SP* 68, 395–415

iii. Other poems

Benskin, Michael, 'An Argument for an Interpolation in the Old English *Later Genesis*', *NM* 72, 224–45

Bliss, A. J., 'Some Unnoticed Lines of Old English Verse', *N&Q* 18, 404 [captions to the illustrations in MS Junius 11]

Calder, Daniel G., 'Setting and Mode in *The Seafarer* and *The Wanderer*', *NM* 72, 264–75

'Perspective and Movement in *The Ruin*', *NM* 72, 442–5

Campbell, Jackson J., 'Schematic Technique in *Judith*', *ELH* 38, 155–72

Capek, Michael J., 'The Nationality of a Translator: some Notes on the Syntax of *Genesis B*', *Neophilologus* 55, 89–96

Clemoes, Peter, 'Cynewulf's Image of the Ascension', *Whitelock Studies*, pp. 293–304

Diekstra, F. N. M., '*The Wanderer* 65b–72: the Passions of the Mind and the Cardinal Virtues', *Neophilologus* 55, 73–88

'*The Seafarer* 58–66a: the Flight of the Exiled Soul to its Fatherland', *Neophilologus* 55, 433–46

Doubleday, James F., '*Ruin* 8b–9a', *N&Q* 18, 124

'The Principle of Contrast in *Judith*', *NM* 72, 436–41

Fry, Donald K., '*Wulf and Eadwacer*: a Wen Charm', *Chaucer Rev.* 5, 247–63

Halliman, Dorothy M., 'The Old Saxon Genesis Fragments' [a prose translation; typescript deposited in Dept of Western MSS, Bodleian Library, Oxford]

Hieatt, Constance B., 'Dream Frame and Verbal Echo in the *Dream of the Rood*', *NM* 72, 251–63

Hill, Thomas D., 'Two Notes on *Solomon and Saturn*', *MÆ* 40, 217–21

    'Further Notes on the Eschatology of the Old English *Christ III*', *NM* 72, 691–8

    'Sapiential Structure and Figural Narrative in the Old English *Elene*', *Traditio* 27, 159–77

Lipp, Frances Randall, '*Guthlac A*: an Interpretation', *MS* 33, 46–62

Lucas, Peter J., '*Exodus* 265: *Ægnian*', *N&Q* 18, 283–4

Marold, Edith, 'Hunwil', *Die Sprache* 17, 157–63 [Unwen in *Widsith*]

Osborn, Marijane, 'Two Inconsistent Letters in the Inscription on the Franks Casket, Right Side', *NM* 72, 30–4

Regeniter, W., *Sagenschichtung und Sagenmischung: Untersuchungen zur Hagengestalt und zur Geschichte der Hilde- und Walthersage* (Munich)

Remly, Lynn L., 'The Anglo-Saxon Gnomes as Sacred Poetry', *Folklore* 82, 147–58

Roberts, Jane, 'A Metrical Examination of the Poems *Guthlac A* and *Guthlac B*', *Proc. of the R. Irish Acad.* 71, sect. C, 91–137

Torkar, Roland, 'Textkritische Anmerkungen zum ae. Gedicht *Instructions for Christians*', *Anglia* 89, 164–77

Trask, Richard M., '*The Descent into Hell* of the Exeter Book', *NM* 72, 419–35

Tripp, Raymond P., Jr, '*The Dream of the Rood*: 9b and its Context', *MP* 69, 136–7

Vickrey, John F., 'The *Micel Wundor* of *Genesis B*', *SP* 68, 245–54

Whitman, F. H., 'Riddle 60 and its Source', *PQ* 50, 108–15

c. Prose

Bately, Janet, 'The Classical Additions in the Old English Orosius', *Whitelock Studies*, pp. 237–51

Clark, Cecily, 'The Narrative Mode of *The Anglo-Saxon Chronicle* before the Conquest', *Whitelock Studies*, pp. 215–35

Cross, J. E., 'Source and Analysis of some Ælfrician Passages', *NM* 72, 446–53

    '"De Signis et Prodigiis" in *Versus Sancti Patricii Episcopi de Mirabilibus Hibernie*', *Proc. of the R. Irish Acad.* 71, sect. C, 247–54 [concerns the Old English Martyrology etc.]

    see also sect. 2

Davis, R. H. C., see sect. 6

Derolez, René, 'The Orientation System in the Old English Orosius', *Whitelock Studies*, pp. 253–68

Harrison, Kenneth, see sect. 6

Heyworth, P. L., 'Alfred's "Pastoral Care": MS Cotton Tiberius B. xi', *N&Q* 18, 3–4

Jack, R. Ian, 'The Significance of the Alfredian Translations', *ANZAMRS, Bull. of the Australian and New Zealand Assoc. for Med. and Renaissance Stud.* 6, 25 [summary]

Liggins, E. M., 'The Authorship of the Alfredian Canon', *ANZAMRS, Bull. of the Australian and New Zealand Assoc. for Med. and Renaissance Stud.* 6, 23–4 [summary]

Loyn, Henry R., see sect. 5

Meaney, Audrey L., 'Alfred, the Patriarch and the White Stone', *ANZAMRS, Bull. of the Australian and New Zealand Assoc. for Med. and Renaissance Stud.* 6, 22–3 [summary]

Nichols, Ann Eljenholm, 'Ælfric and the Brief Style', *JEGP* 70, 1–12

Pope, John, 'Ælfric and the Old English Version of the Ely Privilege', *Whitelock Studies*, pp. 85–113

Shores, David L., see sect. 2

Torkar, Roland, 'Zu den Vorlagen der ae. Handschrift Cotton Julius E. vii', *NM* 72, 711–15

Tristram, Hildegard L. C., *Vier altenglische Predigten aus der heterodoxen Tradition, mit Kommentar, Übersetzung und Glossar sowie drei weiteren Texten im Anhang* (privately ptd, Freiburg im Breisgau)

4. ANGLO-LATIN, LITURGY AND OTHER LATIN ECCLESIASTICAL TEXTS

Bolton, W. F., 'Pre-Conquest Anglo-Latin: Perspectives and Prospects', *Comparative Lit.* 23, 151–66

Clemoes, Peter, see sect. *3biii*

Colker, M. L., 'Latin Verses Lamenting the Death of Saint Wulfstan of Worcester', *AB* 89, 319–22

Eckenrode, Thomas R., 'Venerable Bede as a Scientist', *ABR* 22, 486–507

Fransen, I., 'Fragments Épars du Commentaire Perdu d'Alcuin sur l'Épître aux Éphésiens', *RB* 81, 30–59

Gamber, K., 'Das Basler Fragment. Eine weitere Studie zum altkampanischen Sakramentar und zu dessen Präfationen', *RB* 81, 14–29 [relevant to the study of the liturgy in England]

Hamman, Adalbertus, ed., *Patrologiae Cursus Completus a J.-P. Migne Editus, Series Latina, Supplementum* 4 pt 4 (Paris) [cols. 2175–83, additions and corrections to works of Aldhelm, including *Epistola ad Acircium*, ed. after Ehwald; cols. 2183–91, similar material for Æthilwald; cols. 2215 ff., similar material for Bede, including *De Psalmo 41, De Psalmo 83, Oratio ad Deum, Hymni Tres, De Locis Sanctis, Nomina Locorum, De Gradibus Consanguinitatis*, after J. Fraipont, D. Hurst and L. Machielsen]

Hunter Blair, Peter, see sect. 6

Lagorio, Valerie M., 'Aldhelm's Aenigmata in Codex Vaticanus Palatinus Latinus 1719', *Manuscripta* 15, 23–7

Loyn, Henry R., see sect. 5

Meyvaert, Paul, see sect. 6

Offler, H. S., see sect. 6

Rosenthal, Joel T., see sect. 6

Schaller, D., 'Poetic Rivalries at the Court of Charlemagne', *Classical Influences on European Culture AD 500–1500*, ed. R. R. Bolgar (Cambridge), pp. 151–7 [concerns Alcuin]

Stallbaumer, Virgil R., see sect. 6

5. PALAEOGRAPHY, DIPLOMATIC AND ILLUMINATION

Bishop, T. A. M., *English Caroline Minuscule* (Oxford)

Dodwell, C. R., 'L'Originalité Iconographique de plusieurs Illustrations Anglo-Saxonnes de l'Ancien Testament', *CCM* 14, 319–28

Ker, Neil, 'The Handwriting of Archbishop Wulfstan', *Whitelock Studies*, pp. 315–31

Lowe, E. A., *Codices Latini Antiquiores*, Supplement (Oxford)

Loyn, Henry R., ed., *A Wulfstan Manuscript containing Institutes, Laws and Homilies: British Museum Cotton Nero A. i*, EEMF 17 (Copenhagen) [including plates of specimens of Wulfstan's handwriting in other manuscripts]

Scragg, D. G., 'Accent Marks in the Old English Vercelli Book', *NM* 72, 699–710

Wilson, David M., see sect. 8*a*

Wormald, Francis, 'The "Winchester School" before St Æthelwold', *Whitelock Studies*, pp. 305–13

6. HISTORY

Bachrach, Bernard S., 'The Feigned Retreat at Hastings', *MS* 33, 344–7

Biddle, Martin, see sect. 8*a*

Birkeli, Fridjov, 'The Earliest Missionary Activities from England to Norway', *Nottingham Med. Stud.* 15, 27–37

Braswell, Laurel, 'Saint Edburga of Winchester: a Study of her Cult, AD 950–1500, with an Edition of the Fourteenth-Century Middle English and Latin Lives', *MS* 33, 292–333

Brooks, Nicholas, 'The Development of Military Obligations in Eighth- and Ninth-Century England', *Whitelock Studies*, pp. 69–84

Cameron, Kenneth, 'Scandinavian Settlement in the Territory of the Five Boroughs: the Place-Name Evidence, Part II, Place-Names in Thorp', *Med. Scandinavia* 3, 35–49

'Scandinavian Settlement in the Territory of the Five Boroughs: the Place-Name Evidence, Part III, the Grimston-Hybrids', *Whitelock Studies*, pp. 147–63

Campbell, Alistair, *Skaldic Verse and Anglo-Saxon History* (1970 Dorothea Coke Memorial Lecture in Northern Studies, University College, London)

Campbell, James, 'The First Century of Christianity in England', *Ampleforth Jnl* 76, 12–29

Campbell, Miles W., 'Queen Emma and Ælfgifu of Northampton: Canute the Great's Women', *Med. Scandinavia* 4, 66–79

'A Pre-Conquest Norman Occupation of England?', *Speculum* 46, 21–31

Clark, Cecily, see sect. 3*c*

Davis, R. H. C., 'Alfred the Great: Propaganda and Truth', *History* 56, 169–82

Dodgson, J. McN., see sect. 2

Fellows Jensen, Gillian, see sect. 2

Forsberg, Rune, see sect. 2

Galbraith, V. H., 'Sir Frank Stenton (1880–1967)', *AHR* 76, 1116–23

Harrison, Kenneth, 'Early Wessex Annals in the Anglo-Saxon Chronicle', *EHR* 86, 527–33

Hart, Cyril, 'The Tribal Hidage', *TRHS* 5th ser. 21, 133–57

Harvey, Sally, 'Domesday Book and its Predecessors', *EHR* 86, 753–73

Hughes, Kathleen, *Early Christianity in Pictland* (1970 Jarrow Lecture) [concerns Bede's knowledge]

'Evidence for Contacts between the Churches of the Irish and English from the Synod of Whitby to the Viking Age', *Whitelock Studies*, pp. 49–67

Hunter Blair, Peter, 'The Battle at *Biedcanford* in 571', *Bedfordshire Mag.* 13, 27–30

'The Letters of Pope Boniface V and the Mission of Paulinus to Northumbria', *Whitelock Studies*, pp. 5–13

The World of Bede (New York ed.)

Kirby, David, 'Britons and Angles', *Who Are the Scots? A Search for the Origins of the Scottish Nation*, ed. G. Menzies (BBC Publications)

Loomis, Dorothy Bethurum, '*Regnum* and *Sacerdotium* in the Early Eleventh Century', *Whitelock Studies*, pp. 129–45

Loyn, Henry, 'Towns in Late Anglo-Saxon England: the Evidence and some Possible Lines of Enquiry', *Whitelock Studies*, pp. 115–28

see also sect. 5

Martin, Kevin M., 'Some Textual Evidence concerning the Continental Origins of the Invaders of Britain in the Fifth Century', *Latomus* 30, 83–104

Matthew, D. J. A., 'The New Confessor', *History* 56, 423–6 [review article on Frank Barlow, *Edward the Confessor*]

McGovern, John F., 'The Meaning of *Gesette Land* in Anglo-Saxon Land Tenure', *Speculum* 46, 589–96

Meyvaert, Paul, 'Bede's Text of the *Libellus Responsionum* of Gregory the Great to Augustine of Canterbury', *Whitelock Studies*, pp. 15–33

Myres, J. N. L., see sect. 8*a*

Offler, H S., 'Hexham and the *Historia Regum*', *Trans. of the Architectural and Archaeol. Soc. of Durham and Northumberland* n.s. 2, 51–62

Okasha, Elisabeth, see sect. 8*i*

Petersohn, Jürgen, 'Normannische Bildungsreform im hochmittelalterlichen England', *Historische Zeitschrift* 213, 265–95

Pope, John, see sect. 3*c*

Rosenthal, Joel T., 'Edward the Confessor and Robert the Pious: 11th Century Kingship and Biography', *MS* 33, 7–20

Sawyer, Peter, *The Age of the Vikings*, 2nd ed. (London)

Stallbaumer, Virgil R., 'The Canterbury School of Theodore and Hadrian', *ABR* 22, 46–63

'The York Cathedral School', *ABR* 22, 286–97

Stenton, F. M., *Anglo-Saxon England*, 3rd ed. rev. Doris Mary Stenton with Dorothy Whitelock (Oxford)

Thomas, Charles, *Britain and Ireland in Early Christian Times, AD 400–800*, Library of Medieval Civilization (London and New York)

Wallace-Hadrill, J. M., *Early Germanic Kingship in England and on the Continent* (Oxford)

'A Background to St Boniface's Mission', *Whitelock Studies*, pp. 35–48

'Sir Frank Stenton', *History* 56, 55–9

Welch, M. G., 'Late Romans and Saxons in Sussex', *Britannia* 2, 232–7

White, Donald A., 'Changing Views of the *Adventus Saxonum* in Nineteenth and Twentieth Century English Scholarship', *Jnl of the Hist. of Ideas* 32, 585–94

York, Ernest C., 'Isolt's Ordeal: English Legal Customs in the Medieval Tristan Legend', *SP* 68, 1–9

7. NUMISMATICS

Birkhan, Helmut, 'Pfennig', *Numismatische Zeitschrift* 86, 59–65

Blunt, C. E., and G. van der Meer, 'A New Coin Type for Offa', *BROB* 19, 213–14

Carson, R. A. G., ed., *Mints, Dies and Currency: Essays dedicated to the memory of Albert Baldwin* (London)

Dolley, Michael, see sect. 8*h*

Dolley, M., and J. K. Knight, 'Some Single Finds of Tenth- and Eleventh-Century English Coins from Wales', *Archaeologia Cambrensis* 119, 75–82

Elmore Jones, F., 'Southampton/Winchester Die-Links in Canute's Quatrefoil Type', *BNJ* 39, 6–11

Fearon, Daniel, 'The Re-discovery of a Group of Fifteen Pence from the Milton Street Hoard', *Numismatic Circular* 79, 54–6

Feilitzen, Olof von, and Christopher Blunt, see sect. 2

Glendining and Co., *Catalogue of the R. P. V. Brettell Collection of Coins of Exeter* [sale on 28 October 1970]

Catalogue of the Important Collection of Anglo-Saxon Silver Pennies formed by F. Elmore Jones Esq. [sale on 12 and 13 May]

Grinsell, L. V., 'A Sceatta from Portishead, Somerset', *BNJ* 39, 163–4

Harris, E. J., and P. F. Purvey, 'Eight Pennies of Aethelstan', *Seaby's Coin and Medal Bull.* 1971, 88–9

Jaanusson, Hille, 'Ett Estniskt Korsformat Hänge från Bjurhovda i Västerås', *Fornvännen* 66, 99–104 [with three pennies of Æthelred II]

Lyon, Stewart, 'Historical Problems of Anglo-Saxon Coinage – (4) The Viking Age', *BNJ* 39, 193–204

Metcalf, D. M., and F. Schweizer, 'The Metal Contents of Silver Pennies of William II and Henry I (1087–1135)', *Archaeometry* 13, 177–90 [including data back to 1050]

Morehart, Mary, 'Some Dangers of Dating Sceattas by Typological Sequences', *BNJ* 39, 1–5

Pagan, H. E., 'Robert Austen and the Bank of England Collection', *BNJ* 39, 12–18

Purvey, P. Frank, 'The F. Elmore Jones Collection of Anglo-Saxon Coins', *Seaby's Coin and Medal Bull.* 1971, 133

Seaby, W. A., 'An Æthelred/Sihtric Watchet Die-Link', *Seaby's Coin and Medal Bull.* 1971, 90–1

Bibliography for 1971

Stewart, B. H. I. H., 'The Early Coins of Ethelred II's Crux Issue with Right-Facing Bust', *NC* 7th ser. 11, 237–42

Walker, D. R., 'Another Early Saxon Coin from Shakenoak', *Oxoniensia* 35, 106–7

8. ARCHAEOLOGY

a. General

Biddle, Martin, 'Archaeology and the Beginnings of English Society', *Whitelock Studies*, pp. 391–408

Department of the Environment, *Archaeological Excavations 1970* [gives a summary of all sites, including Anglo-Saxon, excavated by the Department or with the aid of Department Funds]

Kennett, David, 'Bedfordshire Archaeology, 1970–71', *Bedfordshire Archaeol. Jnl* 6, 81–8 [including Anglo-Saxon discoveries of various periods and coin acquisitions by museums]

Myres, J. N. L., 'The Angles, the Saxons and the Jutes', *Proc. of the Brit. Acad.* 56, 145–74

Owles, Elizabeth, 'Archaeology in Suffolk, 1970', *Proc. of the Suffolk Inst. of Archaeology* 32, 92–107 [including Anglo-Saxon finds]

Rahtz, Philip, 'Medieval and Later Archaeology in England and Wales', *Kwartalnik Historii Kultury Materialnej* 18, 587–615

Wilson, David M., 'Art of the Viking Age: the Rosc Exhibition in Dublin', *Apollo* 94, 254–61

'Medieval Britain in 1969: I. Pre-Conquest', *MA* 14, 155–65 [survey of archaeological work]

b. Towns and other major settlements

Addyman, P. V., and D. H. Hill, 'Saxon Southampton: a Review of the Evidence. Part II. Industry, Trade and Everyday Life', *Proc. of the Hampshire Field Club and Archaeol. Soc.* 26, 61–96

Alcock, Leslie, 'Excavations at South Cadbury Castle, 1970: Summary Report', *AntJ* 51, 1–7

[Barker, Philip] 'Wroxeter', *CA* 25, 45–9 [recent excavations, sub-Roman to Saxon]

Biddle, Martin, 'Excavations at Winchester, 1969: Eighth Interim Report', *AntJ* 50, 277–326

Biddle, Martin, and David Hill, 'Late Saxon Planned Towns', *AntJ* 51, 70–85

Fowler, P. J., 'Hill-Forts, A.D. 400–700', *The Iron Age and its Hill-Forts*, ed. David Hill and Margaret Jesson (Southampton), pp. 203–13

Hassall, J. M., and David Hill, 'Pont de l'Arche: Frankish Influence on the West Saxon Burh?' *ArchJ* 127, 188–95

Hassall, T. G., 'Excavations at Oxford 1969', *Oxoniensia* 35, 5–18

'Oxford', *CA* 24, 22–7 [recent excavations, including Anglo-Saxon]

Hill, D., and J. Hassall, 'Viking Warfare – the Siege of Paris 885–6', *Ago* 1. 9, 16–22 [relevant to the study of fortifications in England]

[Hurst, Henry] 'Gloucester', *CA* 26, 77–83 [recent excavations, including Anglo-Saxon]

Loyn, Henry, see sect. 6

Radford, C. A. Ralegh, 'The Later Pre-Conquest Boroughs and their Defences', *MA* 14, 83–103

[Rahtz, Philip, and Ken Sheridan] 'Tamworth', *CA* 29, 164–8 [recent excavations, including Anglo-Saxon mill]

Wade-Martins, Peter, 'Excavations at North Elmham 1970: an Interim Note', *Norfolk Archaeology* 35, 263–8

West, S. E., 'The Excavation of the Town Defences at Tayfen Road, Bury St Edmunds, 1968', *Proc. of the Suffolk Inst. of Archaeology* 32, 17–24

c. Rural settlements

Beresford, Maurice, and John G. Hurst, ed., *Deserted Medieval Villages* (London) [containing important surveys of knowledge of Anglo-Saxon villages and structures]

Brodribb, A. C. C., A. R. Hands and D. R. Walker, *Excavations at Shakenoak, II: Sites B and H* (privately ptd, Oxford, 1971) [various Anglo-Saxon finds, including a sceatta of BMC Type 32(a)]

Ravenhill, W. L. D., 'The Form and Pattern of Post-Roman Settlement in Devon', *Proc. of the Devon Archaeol. Exploration Soc.* 28, 83–94

d. Pagan cemeteries

Evison, Vera I., 'Five Anglo-Saxon Inhumation Graves Containing Pots at Great Chesterford, Essex' (with a contribution by J. N. L. Myres), *BROB* 19, 157–73

Hagen, Richard, 'Anglo-Saxon Burials from the Vicinity of Biscot Mill, Luton', *Bedfordshire Archaeol. Jnl* 6, 23–6

Kennett, David H., 'Graves with Swords at Little Wilbraham and Linton Heath', *Proc. of the Cambridge Ant. Soc.* 63, 9–26

Moss-Eccardt, John, 'An Anglo-Saxon Cemetery at Blackhorse Road, Letchworth, Hertfordshire', *Bedfordshire Archaeol. Jnl* 6, 27–32

e. Churches, monastic sites and Christian cemeteries

Baker, David, 'Excavations at Elstow Abbey, Bedfordshire, 1968–70. Third Interim Report', *Bedfordshire Archaeol. Jnl* 6, 55–64 [Christian Anglo-Saxon cemetery]

Biddle, Martin, 'Winchester and Deerhurst' (with a rejoinder by Edward Gilbert), *Trans. of the Bristol and Gloucestershire Archaeol. Soc.* 89, 179–80

'The Buildings of New Minster: Excavations North of the Cathedral, 1970', *Winchester Cathedral Record*, 40, 48–56

Cramp, Rosemary, 'Decorated Window-Glass and Millefiori from Monkwearmouth', *AntJ* 50, 327–35

Gem, R. D. H., 'The Anglo-Saxon Cathedral Church at Canterbury: a Further Contribution', *ArchJ* 127, 196–201

Bibliography for 1971

Gilbert, E. C., 'The Date of the Late Saxon Cathedral at Canterbury', *ArchJ* 127, 202–10

Hare, Michael, 'Anglo-Saxon Work at Carlton and Other Bedfordshire Churches', *Bedfordshire Archaeol. Jnl* 6, 33–40

Pocock, Michael, and Hazel Wheeler, 'Excavations at Escomb Church, County Durham, 1968', *JBAA* 3rd ser. 34, 11–29

Rahtz, Philip, 'Excavations on Glastonbury Tor, Somerset, 1964–6', *ArchJ* 127, 1–81

'Deerhurst', *CA* 28, 135–9 [excavations at the church, 1971]

Smedley, Norman, and Elizabeth Owles, 'Excavations at the Old Minster, South Elmham', *Proc. of the Suffolk Inst. of Archaeology* 32, 1–16

Taylor, H. M., 'St Giles' Church, Barrow, Shropshire', *ArchJ* 127, 211–21

'The Chapel, Church and Carved Stones at Heysham', *ArchJ* 127, 285–7

'Repton Reconsidered: a Study in Structural Criticism', *Whitelock Studies*, pp. 351–89

Thomas, Charles, *The Early Christian Archaeology of North Britain* (Glasgow)

Wormald, Francis, see sect. 5 [discusses fragment of wall-painting from the foundations of the New Minster, Winchester]

f. Ships

Evans, Angela Care, and Valerie H. Fenwick, 'The Graveney Boat', *Antiquity* 45, 89–96

Greenhill, Basil, 'The Graveney Boat', *Antiquity* 45, 41–2

'Graveney Boat', *Mariner's Mirror* 57, 142

Jenkins, Frank, 'The Graveney Boat', *Cantium* 3, 15–17

g. Sculpture

Clemoes, Peter, see sect. 3*biii*

Cramp, Rosemary, 'The Position of the Otley Crosses in English Sculpture of the Eighth to Ninth Centuries', *Kolloquium über spätantike und frühmittelalterliche Skulptur* II (Mainz), 55–63

Radford, C. A. R., 'Stone Cross', in Philip Rahtz, 'Excavations on Glastonbury Tor, Somerset, 1964–6', *ArchJ* 127, 48–9

Ross, Margaret Clunies, 'A Suggested Interpretation of the Scene Depicted on the Right-Hand Side of the Franks Casket', *MA* 14, 148–52

Stevenson, R. B. K., 'Sculpture in Scotland in the 6th–9th Centuries A.D.', *Kolloquium über spätantike und frühmittelalterliche Skulptur* II (Mainz), 65–74

Taylor, H. M., 'Anglo-Saxon Sculpture of the West Coast', *ArchJ* 127, 245–7

'The Whalley Crosses', *ArchJ* 127, 281

'Halton Crosses', *ArchJ* 127, 287–8

Wilson, David M., 'Manx Memorial Stones of the Viking Period', *SBVS* 18, 1–18

Bibliography for 1971

h. Metal-work and other minor objects

Dolley, Michael, 'The Nummular Brooch from Sulgrave', *Whitelock Studies*, pp. 333–49

Graham-Campbell, James, 'An Anglo-Saxon Ornamented Silver Strip from the Cuerdale Hoard', *MA* 14, 152–3

Hinton, David A., 'Two Late Saxon Swords', *Oxoniensia* 35, 1–4

Kennett, David H., 'Applied Brooches of the Kempston Type at St John's, Cambridge', *Proc. of the Cambridge Ant. Soc.* 63, 27–9

Nerman, Birger, 'The "Standard" of Sutton Hoo – a Torchholder?', *AntJ* 50, 340–1

Okasha, Elisabeth, and Leslie Webster, 'An Anglo-Saxon Ring from Bodsham, Kent', *AntJ* 50, 102–4

Rigold, S. E., 'Six Copper-Alloy Objects from St Augustine's, Canterbury', *AntJ* 50, 345–7

Rigold, S. E., and Leslie E. Webster, 'Three Anglo-Saxon Disc Brooches', *Archaeologia Cantiana* 85, 1–18

Shaw, Muriel, and Lilian Thornhill, 'Coulsdon: Saxon Knives from Cane Hill Cemetery', *Bull. of the Surrey Archaeol. Soc.* 74, 4

Speake, George, 'A Seventh-Century Coin-Pendant from Bacton, Norfolk, and its Ornament', *MA* 14, 1–16

Tester, P. J., 'An Anglo-Saxon Spearhead from Bexley', *Archaeologia Cantiana* 85, 212–14

Wilson, D. M., 'An Anglo-Saxon Playing-Piece from Bawdsey', *Proc. of the Suffolk Inst. of Archaeology* 32, 38–42

Ypey, J., 'Zur Tragweise frühfränkischer Gürtelgarnituren auf Grund niederländischer Befunde', *BROB* 19, 89–127

i. Inscriptions

Düwel, Klaus, and Wolf-Dieter Tempel, 'Knochenkämme mit Runeninschriften aus Friesland. Mit einer Zusammenstellung aller bekannten Runenkämme und einem Beitrag zu den Friesischen Runeninschriften', *Palaeohistoria* 14, 353–91 [English examples listed and discussed]

Okasha, Elisabeth, *Hand-List of Anglo-Saxon Non-Runic Inscriptions* (Cambridge)
'A New Inscription from Ramsey Island', *Archaeologia Cambrensis* 119, 68–70
'Some Lost Anglo-Saxon Inscriptions from St Nicholas' Church, Ipswich', *Proc. of the Suffolk Inst. of Archaeology* 32, 80–4

Okasha, Elisabeth, and Leslie Webster, see sect. 8*h*

Osborn, Marijane, see sect. 3*biii*

Page, R. I., see sect. 2

Wilson, David M., see sect. 8*g*

j. Pottery

Addyman, P. V., and J. B. Whitwell, 'Some Middle Saxon Pottery Types in Lincolnshire', *AntJ* 50, 96–102

Cunliffe, Barry, 'The Saxon Culture-Sequence at Portchester Castle', *AntJ* 50, 67–85

Jones, M. V., 'Saxon Pottery from a Hut at Mucking, Essex' (with contributions by J. N. L. Myres and Vera I. Evison), *BROB* 19, 145–56

Kennett, David H., 'Pottery and Other Finds from the Anglo-Saxon Cemetery at Sandy, Bedfordshire', *MA* 14, 17–33

Myres, J. N. L., 'Two Anglo-Saxon Potters' Stamps', *AntJ* 50, 350

Rodwell, Warwick, 'Some Romano-Saxon Pottery from Essex', *AntJ* 50, 262–76

Schmid, P., 'Die Siedlungskeramik von Mucking (Essex) und Feddersen Wierde (Kr. Wesermünde) – ein Formenvergleich', *BROB* 19, 135–44

West, Stanley E., 'Pagan Saxon Pottery from West Stow, Suffolk', *BROB* 19, 175–81

9. REVIEWS

Arnold, Ralph, *A Social History of England from 55 BC to AD 1215* (New York, 1967): Rosalind Conklin Hays, *CHR* 56, 701–2

Bacquet, Paul, *La Structure de la Phrase Verbale à l'Époque Alfrédienne* (Paris, 1962): Alfred Reszkiewicz, *SAP* 3, 143–52

Barley, M. W., and R. P. C. Hanson, ed., *Christianity in Britain, 300–700* (Leicester, 1968): R. Gilyard-Beer, *MA* 14, 214; Kathleen Hughes, *EHR* 86, 342–3; C. E. Stevens, *AntJ* 50, 134–6

Barlow, Frank, *Edward the Confessor* (London and Berkeley and Los Angeles, 1970): H. R. Loyn, *EHR* 86, 790–2; Bryce Lyon, *AHR* 76, 1143–4; D. J. A. Matthew, see sect. 6; Colin Morris, *JEH* 22, 360–1

Bech, Gunnar, *Das germanische reduplizierte Präteritum* (Copenhagen, 1969): F. O. Lindeman, *Norsk Tidsskrift for Sprogvidenskap* 24, 329–35; Albert L. Lloyd, *Language* 47, 711–14; Irmengard Rauch, see sect. 2

Benton, John F., *Town Origins: the Evidence from Medieval England* (Boston, 1968): H. R. Loyn, *CCM* 14, 269–70

Bessinger, Jess B., Jr, and Stanley J. Kahrl, ed., *Essential Articles for the Study of Old English Poetry* (Hamden, 1968): Helmut Gneuss, *ASNSL* 208, 214; Martin Lehnert, *ZAA* 19, 72–3; T. A. Shippey, *YES* 1, 208–9

Bessinger, Jess B., Jr, and Philip H. Smith, Jr, *A Concordance to Beowulf* (Ithaca, New York, 1969): Gerhard Graband, *ASNSL* 208, 123–6; Martin Lehnert, *ZAA* 19, 73–5; L. Whitbread, *ESts* 52, 444–6

Blunt, C. E., and M. Dolley, with F. Elmore Jones and C. S. S. Lyon, *Sylloge of Coins of the British Isles. University Collection, Reading, Anglo-Saxon and Norman Coins; Royal Coin Cabinet, Stockholm, Anglo-Norman Pennies* (London, 1969): S. E. Rigold, *MA* 14, 219–20; W. A. Seaby, *AntJ* 50, 140–1

Brown, R. Allen, *The Normans and the Norman Conquest* (London, 1969): J. C. Holt, *History* 56, 436–7; Henry Loyn, *AntJ* 50, 143–4

Bruce-Mitford, R. L. S., *The Sutton Hoo Ship Burial, a Handbook* (London, 1968): D. P. Kirby, *EHR* 86, 153–4

Burlin, Robert B., *The Old English 'Advent': a Typological Commentary* (New Haven and London, 1968): Rosemary Woolf, *MÆ* 40, 60–1

Campbell, Alistair, ed., *Aethelwulf, 'De Abbatibus'* (London, 1967): C. van de Kieft, *Neophilologus* 55, 106–7

Carlton, Charles, *A Descriptive Syntax of the Old English Charters* (The Hague, 1970):
C. J. E. Ball, *RES* 22, 467–8; R. Bruce Mitchell, *MÆ* 40, 181–4

Carnicelli, Thomas A., ed., *King Alfred's Version of St Augustine's Soliloquies* (Cambridge, Massachusetts, 1969): Jackson J. Campbell, *JEGP* 70, 526–8

Chaney, William A., *The Cult of Kingship in Anglo-Saxon England* (Manchester, 1970):
Frank Barlow, *MÆ* 40, 179–81; Roberta Frank, *N&Q* 18, 265; Milton McC.
Gatch, *Church Hist.* 40, 210–11; John Godfrey, *JEH* 22, 281; H. R. Loyn,
History 56, 433–4; Ernst Werner, *Zeitschrift für Geschichtswissenschaft* 19, 697–8

Chibnall, Marjorie, ed. and transl., *The Ecclesiastical History of Orderic Vitalis,
Books III and IV*, II (Oxford, 1969): J. O. Prestwich, *EHR* 86, 382

Clark, Cecily, ed., *The Peterborough Chronicle 1070–1154*, 2nd ed. (Oxford, 1970):
Norman E. Eliason, *MLR* 66, 848–9; H. R. Loyn, *History* 56, 254; R. M.
Wilson, *MÆ* 40, 185

Colgrave, Bertram, ed. and transl., *The Earliest Life of Gregory the Great by an
Anonymous Monk of Whitby* (Lawrence, Kansas, 1968): Margaret Deanesly,
CHR 57, 472–3; Paul Meyvaert, *JTS* 22, 253–6

Colgrave, Bertram, and R. A. B. Mynors, ed., *Bede's Ecclesiastical History of the
English People* (Oxford, 1969): Ludwig Bieler, *Latomus* 30, 410–12; Gerald
Bonner, *JEH* 22, 132–4; Anthony G. Dyson, *Jnl of the Soc. of Archivists* 4,
341–2; Peter Hunter Blair, *MÆ* 40, 58–60; Paul Meyvaert, *Speculum* 46, 135–7;
J. N. L. Myres, *EHR* 86, 344–6; H. S. Offler, *DUJ* 63, 234–6; Hanna Vollrath-
Reichelt, *Historische Zeitschrift* 213, 404–5

Creed, Robert P., ed., *Old English Poetry: Fifteen Essays* (Providence, Rhode Island,
1967): P. M. Vermeer, *ESts* 52, 348–56

Diamond, Robert E., *Old English: Grammar and Reader* (Detroit, 1970): Marjory
Rigby, *MLR* 66, 654–5

Dodgson, J. McN., *The Place-Names of Cheshire* (Cambridge, 1970 and 1971): Basil
Cottle, *RES* 22, 463–5; Gillian Fellows Jensen, *SBVS* 18, 201–6; Margaret
Gelling, *N&Q* 18, 189–91

Douglas, David C., *The Norman Achievement, 1050–1100* (Berkeley and Los Angeles,
1969): Stuart E. Prall, *The Historian* 33, 679

William the Conqueror (London, 1969, paperback): D. J. A. Matthew, *EHR* 86, 561–3

Dunning, T. P., and A. J. Bliss, ed., *The Wanderer* (London, 1969): R. F. S. Hamer,
MÆ 40, 262–6; Martin Lehnert, *ZAA* 19, 75–6; Johanna Torringa, *ESts* 52,
55–7

Fellows Jensen, Gillian, *Scandinavian Personal Names in Lincolnshire and Yorkshire*
(Copenhagen, 1968): W. F. H. Nicolaisen, *EHR* 86, 602

Finberg, H. P. R., *West Country Historical Studies* (Newton Abbot, 1969): W. G.
Hoskins, *EHR* 86, 156; E. John, *Agricultural Hist. Rev.* 19, 99–101

Fisher, E. A., *Anglo-Saxon Towers* (Newton Abbot, 1969): F. W. Brooks, see
Fisher, E. A., *The Saxon Churches of Sussex*; H. M. Taylor, *AntJ* 50, 387–8

The Saxon Churches of Sussex (Newton Abbot, 1970): (and *Anglo-Saxon Towers*
(Newton Abbot, 1969)) F. W. Brooks, *History* 56, 434; Eric Fletcher, *JBAA*
3rd ser. 34, 95; David Parsons, *ArchJ* 127, 305–6; H. M. Taylor, *Antiquity* 45,
229

Foote, P. G., and D. M. Wilson, *The Viking Achievement* (London, 1970): Richard Bailey, *Antiquity* 45, 64–5; Régis Boyer, *Études Germaniques* 26, 552–5; D. Wyn Evans, *MLR* 66, 235–6; Christine Fell, *Scandinavica* 10, 67–8; J. T. Lang, *JBAA* 3rd ser. 34, 97–8; M. W. Thompson, *MA* 14, 218–19

Fry, Donald K., *'Beowulf' and 'The Fight at Finnsburh': a Bibliography* (Charlottesville, Virginia, 1969): Fred C. Robinson, *Speculum* 46, 367–9

Galster, Georg, *Sylloge of Coins of the British Isles. The Royal Collection of Coins and Medals, National Museum, Copenhagen.* Part III, Anglo-Saxon Coins: Cnut (London, 1970): V.J.S., *BNJ* 39, 180–1

Gardner, John, *Grendel* (New York, 1971): F. W. Bateson, *New York Rev. of Books* 17.11, 16–17

Geipel, John, *The Viking Legacy* (Newton Abbot, 1971): Bruce Dickins, *Antiquity* 45, 316

Gellinek, Christian, ed., *Festschrift für Konstantin Reichardt* (Bern and Munich, 1969): Ursula Dronke, *Scandinavica* 10, 64–5

Gillett, Edward, *A History of Grimsby* (London, 1970): F. D. Blackley, *The Historian* 33, 678–9

Ginsche, Gunhild, *Der junge Jacob Grimm 1805–1819* (Berlin, 1967): Rolf Hiersche, *IF* 75, 341–6

Girvan, Ritchie, *'Beowulf' and the Seventh Century* (repr., London, 1971): E.G.S., *N&Q* 18, 202

Godfrey, John, *The English Parish 600–1300* (SPCK, 1969): M. M. Harvey, *DUJ* 63, 145–6

Goldsmith, Margaret E., *The Mode and Meaning of 'Beowulf'* (London, 1970): W. F. Bolton, *RES* 22, 317–19; J. A. Burrow, *EC* 21, 280–8; Kemp Malone, *Speculum* 46, 369–71; T. A. Shippey, *MLR* 66, 655–6; R. M. Wilson, *English* 20, 22–3

Grimes, W. F., *The Excavation of Roman and Mediaeval London* (London, 1968): Graham Webster, *Archaeology* 24, 85–6

Grünberg, Madeleine, *The West-Saxon Gospels* (Amsterdam, 1967): E. G. Stanley, *ASNSL* 208, 135–6

Hart, Cyril, *The Hidation of Northamptonshire* (Leicester, 1970): I. Blanchard, *EconHR* 2nd ser. 24, 294; J. Campbell, *Northamptonshire Past and Present* 4, 326–7

Henry, P. L., *The Early English and Celtic Lyric* (London, 1966): Michael N. Nagler, *ESts* 52, 255–9

Herold, Curtis Paul, *The Morphology of King Alfred's Translation of the Orosius* (The Hague, 1968): E. M. Liggins, *MÆ* 40, 266–8

Hoffmann, Werner, *Altdeutsche Metrik* (Stuttgart, 1967): Peter Ochsenbein, *Wirkendes Wort* 21, 63; Helmut Tervooren, *Zeitschrift für deutsche Philologie* 90, 102–3

Holm, Gösta, ed., *En Diskussion om Stanamnen* (Lund, 1967): Hans Kuhn, *IF* 75, 346–51

[Hoops, Johannes], *Reallexikon der germanischen Altertumskunde*, 2nd ed. 1, 1 and 2 (Berlin, 1968 and 1970): A.P., *Deutsches Archiv für Erforschung des Mittelalters* 26, 570–1; Rudolph Schützeichel, *Beiträge zur Namenforschung* 6, 95; Matthias

Springer, *Zeitschrift für Geschichtswissenschaft* 19, 450; Norbert Wagner, *ZDA Anzeiger* 82, 145–8

Hoyt, Robert S., ed., *Life and Thought in the Early Middle Ages* (Minneapolis, 1967): William M. Daly, *CHR* 56, 705–7

Hubert, Jean, Jean Porcher and W. F. Volbach, *Europe in the Dark Ages* (London, 1969): C. A. Ralegh Radford, *AntJ* 50, 384

Hunter Blair, Peter, *The World of Bede* (London, 1970): M. Oldoni, *Studi Medievali* 11, 830–3; Richard W. Pfaff, *Church Hist.* 40, 477–8

Huppé, Bernard F., *The Web of Words: Structural Analyses of the Old English Poems 'Vainglory', 'The Wonder of Creation', 'The Dream of the Rood', and 'Judith'* (Albany, New York, 1970): W. F. Bolton, *CCM* 14, 284–5; Angus Cameron, *Speculum* 46, 383–4

Hurst, D., ed., *Bedae Venerabilis Opera, Pars II: Opera Exegetica, 2A: De Tabernaculo, De Templo, In Ezram et Neemiam*, Corpus Christianorum Series Latina 119a (Turnhout, 1969): Gerald Bonner, *JEH* 22, 132–3

Ilkow, Peter, *Die Nominalkomposita der altsächsischen Bibeldichtung* (Göttingen, 1968): Juw fon Wearinga, *JEGP* 70, 373–5

Irving, Edward B., Jr, *A Reading of 'Beowulf'* (New Haven, 1968): Martin Green, *Style* 5, 206–9; Josef Klegraf, *ASNSL* 208, 126–9

Introduction to '*Beowulf*' (Englewood Cliffs, New Jersey, 1969): Terence P. Logan, *Mod. Lang. Jnl* 55, 120

Jackson, K. H., ed., *The Gododdin* (Edinburgh, 1969): I. Ll. Foster, *Antiquity* 45, 73–5; J. R. C. Hamilton, *MA* 14, 214–15; J. Beverley Smith, *EHR* 86, 152–3

Jansson, Sven B. F., *Swedish Vikings in England: the Evidence of the Rune Stones* (London, 1966): Heinrich Beck, *ASNSL* 208, 196

Jones, Gwyn, *A History of the Vikings* (London, 1968): Régis Boyer, *Études Germaniques* 26, 550–2; H. R. Ellis Davidson, *AntJ* 50, 141–3; Elsebeth Sander-Jørgensen, *Archaeology* 24, 88–9; A. R. Taylor, *SBVS* 18, 200–1

Kastorsky, Dieter, *Old English Deverbal Substantives Derived by means of a Zero Morpheme* (Esslingen, 1968): Ewald Standop, *IF* 75, 356–9

Ker, N. R., *Medieval Manuscripts in British Libraries* 1 (London, 1969): F. Wormald, *MÆ* 39, 322–3

Kirby, D. P., *The Making of Early England* (London, 1967): J. Campbell, *EHR* 86, 826

Kivimaa, Kirsti, '*Þe*' and '*þat*' *as Clause Connectives in Early Middle English with Especial Consideration of the Emergence of the Pleonastic 'þat'* (Helsinki, 1966): K. C. Phillipps, *ESts* 52, 160–2

Klein, Ernest, *A Comprehensive Etymological Dictionary of the English Language* (Amsterdam, 1966–7): Hans Schabram, *IF* 75, 332–7

Klindt-Jensen, Ole, *The World of the Vikings* (London, 1970): Richard Bailey, *Antiquity* 45, 233–4

Koskenniemi, Inna, *Repetitive Word Pairs in Old and Early Middle English Prose* (Turku, 1968): Matti Kilpiö, *NM* 72, 373–5

Koziol, Herbert, *Grundzüge der Geschichte der englischen Sprache* (Darmstadt, 1967): Gerhard Nickel, *ASNSL* 207, 461–4

Krapp, George Philip, *Modern English: its Growth and Present Use*, rev. Albert H. Marckwardt (New York, 1969): John Algeo, *Jnl of Eng. Ling.* 5, 122–5

Kratz, Henry, *Frühes Mittelalter: Vor- und Frühgeschichte des deutschen Schrifttums* (Bern and Munich, 1970): Jochen Splett, *Beiträge zur Namenforschung* 6, 180–3

Krause, Wolfgang, *Runen* (Berlin, 1970): Karl Martin Nielsen, *Danske Studier* 1971, 132; Claiborne W. Thompson, *Scandinavian Stud.* 43, 437–9

Kristensson, Gillis, *Studies in Middle English Topographical Terms* (Lund, 1970): E. G. Stanley, *N&Q* 18, 188–9

Kühlwein, Wolfgang, *Die Verwendung der Feindseligkeitsbezeichnungen in der altenglischen Dichtersprache* (Neumünster, 1967): E. G. Stanley, *IF* 75, 352–6 *Modell einer operationellen lexikologischen Analyse: altenglisch 'Blut'* (Heidelberg, 1968): Hartmut Beckers, *ASNSL* 208, 122–3

Lagerqvist, L. O., *Svenska Mynt under Vikingatid och Medeltid* (Stockholm, 1970): M.D., *Numismatic Circular* 79, 105–6

Lampe, G. W. H., ed., *The Cambridge History of the Bible* II, *The West from the Fathers to the Reformation* (Cambridge, 1969): J. N. Bakhuizen van den Brink, *JEH* 22, 65–7

Leake, Jane Acomb, *The Geats of 'Beowulf'* (Madison, Milwaukee, and London, 1967): G. V. Smithers, *EHR* 86, 346–9

Leslie, R. F., ed., *The Wanderer* (Manchester, 1966): Johanna Torringa, *ESts* 52, 55–7

Lindsay, Jack, *Arthur and his Time: Britain in the Dark Ages* (New York, 1966): William A. Chaney, *Archaeology* 24, 86–8

Marsh, Henry, *Dark Age Britain: some Sources of History* (Newton Abbot, 1970): M. A. O'Donovan, *History* 56, 432

McLaughlin, John C., *Aspects of the History of English* (New York, 1970): John Algeo, *Jnl of Eng. Ling.* 5, 122–9; J. A. Johnson, *Language* 47, 703–9

Meaney, Audrey L., and Sonia Chadwick Hawkes, *Two Anglo-Saxon Cemeteries at Winnall, Winchester, Hampshire* (London, 1970): K. R. Fennell, *MA* 14, 215–16

Meritt, Herbert Dean, *Some of the Hardest Glosses in Old English* (Stanford, 1968): Sherman M. Kuhn, *JEGP* 70, 651–4

Müller, Gunter, *Studien zu den theriophoren Personennamen der Germanen* (Cologne and Vienna, 1970): Hartmut Knoch, *Archiv für Kulturgeschichte* 52, 173–5

Myres, J. N. L., *Anglo-Saxon Pottery and the Settlement of England* (Oxford, 1969): Michel de Bouard, *Revue Archéologique* 1971, 160–2; Vera I. Evison, *ArchJ* 127, 303–5; Peter Hunter Blair, *EHR* 86, 826–7; John G. Hurst, *MA* 14, 216–17; Wencke Slomann, *AntJ* 50, 385–6

Nickel, Gerhard, *Die Expanded Form im Altenglischen* (Neumünster, 1966): Thomas Gardner, *Anglia* 89, 121–5; Simeon Potter, *YES* 1, 202–3

Nicolaisen, W. F. H., ed., *The Names of Towns and Cities in Britain* (London, 1970): G. W. S. Barrow, *Scottish Hist. Rev.* 50, 79–80; Ian Fraser, *Scottish Stud.* 15, 82–3; Maurice A. Mook, *Names* 19, 147–9

Nist, John, *A Structural History of English* (New York, 1966): Alicja Wegner, *SAP* 3, 169–71

Ogilvy, J. D. A., *Books Known to the English 597–1066* (Cambridge, Massachusetts, 1967): Helmut Gneuss, *Anglia* 89, 129–34

Okasha, Elisabeth, *Hand-List of Anglo-Saxon Non-Runic Inscriptions* (Cambridge, 1971): *TLS* 6 August, p. 953; E. G. Stanley, *N&Q* 18, 305–8

Orrick, Allan H., ed., *Nordica et Anglica: Studies in Honor of Stefán Einarsson* (The Hague, 1968): Heinrich Beck, *Anglia* 89, 378–9 [Franks Casket]

Page, R. I., *Life in Anglo-Saxon England* (London, 1970): J. E. Cross, *Antiquity* 45, 67–8; D. P. Kirby, *History* 56, 252–3

Pearsall, D. A., and R. A. Waldron, ed., *Medieval Literature and Civilization: Studies in Memory of G. N. Garmonsway* (London, 1969): Morton W. Bloomfield, *Anglia* 89, 377–8; Ursula Dronke, *Scandinavica* 10, 64–6

Petersson, H. Bertil A., *Anglo-Saxon Currency: King Edgar's Reform to the Norman Conquest* (Lund, 1969): Brita Malmer, *BNJ* 39, 171–80

Pillsbury, Paul W., *Descriptive Analysis of Discourse in Late West Saxon Texts* (The Hague, 1967): Broder Carstensen, *Anglia* 89, 246–8; Mirosław Nowakowski, *SAP* 3, 165–8

Polomé, Edgar C., ed., *Old Norse Literature and Mythology: a Symposium* (Austin, Texas, and London, 1969): W. Edson Richmond, *Jnl of Amer. Folklore* 84, 247–8

Pope, John C., ed., *Homilies of Ælfric: a Supplementary Collection* (Early English Text Society, 1967–8): J. E. Cross, *SN* 43, 569–71; M. R. Godden, *Anglia* 89, 251–4

Raffel, Burton, *'Beowulf', Translated* (Amherst, 1971): F. W. Bateson, *New York Rev. of Books* 17.11, 16–17

Ramat, Paolo, *Grammatica dall'Antico Sassone* (Milan, 1969): Rolf Hiersche, *ZDA Anzeiger* 82, 1–4

Richardson, H. G., and G. O. Sayles, *Law and Legislation from Æthelberht to Magna Carta* (Chicago, 1967): Michael M. Sheehan, *CHR* 56, 715–17

Rissanen, Matti, *The Uses of 'One' in Old and Early Middle English* (Helsinki, 1967): Simeon Potter, *YES* 1, 203–4

Robinson, Fred C., *Old English Literature: a Select Bibliography* (Toronto, 1970): D. A. H. Evans, *SN* 42, 485–6

Sampson, George, *The Concise Cambridge History of English Literature*, 3rd rev. ed. (Cambridge, 1970): Basil Cottle, *RES* 22, 174–8

Sawyer, P. H., *Anglo-Saxon Charters: an Annotated List and Bibliography* (London, 1968): Claude Fagnen, *Bibliothèque de l'École des Chartes* 128, 436–9; H. P. R. Finberg, *AntJ* 50, 148–9

Schabram, Hans, *Superbia* I (Munich, 1965): C. A. Ladd, *N&Q* 18, 186–7

Schlauch, Margaret, *Medieval Literature and its Social Foundations* (Warsaw and London, 1967): Douglas Gray, *N&Q* 18, 40

Schmitt, Ludwig Erich, ed., *Kurzer Grundriss der germanischen Philologie bis 1500* I, *Sprachgeschichte* (Berlin, 1970): Paul Salmon, *MLR* 66, 698–9

    ed., *Kurzer Grundriss der germanischen Philologie bis 1500* II, *Literaturgeschichte* (Berlin, 1971): see Göttert, Karl-Heinz, sect. 3*a*

Schwab, Ute, ed., *Waldere: Testo e Commento* (Messina, 1967): Horst Dölvers, *ASNSL* 208, 141–2

See, Klaus von, *Germanische Verskunst* (Stuttgart, 1967): Peter Ochsenbein, *Wirkendes Wort* 21, 63

Seebold, Elmar, *Vergleichendes und etymologisches Wörterbuch der germanischen starken Verben* (The Hague, 1970): B. J. Koekkoek, *JEGP* 70, 715–16

Siebs, Benno Eide, *Die Personennamen der Germanen* (Wiesbaden, 1970): Geart B. Droege, *Names* 19, 57–8

Smith, A. H., *The Place-Names of Westmorland* (Cambridge, 1967): Gillis Kristensson, *ESts* 52, 466–70

ed., *Three Northumbrian Poems*, 2nd ed. (London, 1968): Helmut Gneuss, *ASNSL* 208, 214–15

Southern, R. W., *Medieval Humanism and Other Studies* (Oxford, 1970): Frank Barlow, *History* 56, 419–22; Giles Constable, *JEH* 22, 256–9; G.S., *Deutsches Archiv für Erforschung des Mittelalters* 26, 642

Stanley, Eric Gerald, *Continuations and Beginnings* (London, 1966): Fred C. Robinson, *ESts* 52, 252–5; Klaus Weimann, *Anglia* 89, 126–9

Stenton, F. M., *Preparatory to Anglo-Saxon England*, ed. Doris Mary Stenton (Oxford, 1970): Coburn V. Graves, *The Historian* 33, 464; R. H. Hilton, *EconHR* 2nd ser. 24, 141–2

Stevenson, Robert B. K., ed., *Sylloge of Coins of the British Isles. National Museum of Antiquities of Scotland*. Part I (London, 1966): John MacQueen, *Scottish Hist. Rev.* 50, 163–4

Stevick, Robert D., *Suprasegmentals, Meter, and the Manuscript of 'Beowulf'* (The Hague, 1968): G. Storms, *ESts* 52, 157–9

Strang, Barbara M. H., *A History of English* (London, 1970): R. M. Wilson, *English* 20, 22–3

Thirsk, Joan, ed., *Land, Church, and People: Essays presented to Professor H. P. R. Finberg* (supplement to *Agricultural Hist. Rev.* 18, 1970): W. G. Hoskins, *The Local Historian* 9, 362–3

Ullmann, Walter, *The Carolingian Renaissance and the Idea of Kingship* (London, 1969): D. A. Bullough, *History* 56, 82–3; P. McGurk, *JEH* 22, 62–3

Vinogradoff, Paul, *English Society in the Eleventh Century* (1908, repr. Oxford, 1968): Claude Fagnen, *Bibliothèque de l'École des Chartes* 128, 462–5

Visser, F. Th., *An Historical Syntax of the English Language* III, 1 (Leiden, 1969): Norman Davis, *RES* 22, 64–6; Torben Kisbye, *SN* 43, 329–31; Samuel R. Levin, *JEGP* 70, 649–51

Watts, Ann Chalmers, *The Lyre and the Harp* (New Haven, 1969): D. A. H. Evans, *SN* 42, 486–91; Alison I. Gyger, *MÆ* 40, 172–5; H. L. Rogers, *RES* 22, 465–6

Werckmeister, Otto-Karl, *Irische-northumbrische Buchmalerei des 8. Jahrhunderts und monastische Spiritualität* (Berlin, 1967): Paul Meyvaert, *Speculum* 46, 408–11

Westphalen, Tilman, *'Beowulf' 3150–55: Textkritik und Editionsgeschichte* (Munich, 1967): Gerhard Nickel, *ASNSL* 208, 129–35

Whallon, William, *Formula, Character, and Context* (Washington, D.C., and Cambridge, Massachusetts, 1969): Frederick M. Combellack, *Classical Philol.* 66, 41–3; D. A. H. Evans, *SN* 42, 486–91; R. M. Wilson, *MLR* 66, 846

Whitelock, Dorothy, ed., *The Will of Æthelgifu* (Oxford, 1968): H. R. Loyn, *Antiquity* 45, 228–9; J. N. L. Myres, *EHR* 86, 603; F. Wormald, *AntJ* 51, 119

Wilson, R. M., *The Lost Literature of Medieval England*, 2nd ed. (London, 1970): R. T. Davies, *MLR* 66, 849–50; Norman Davis, *RES* 22, 322–4

Zupke, Ronald Edward, *Dictionary of English Weights and Measures from Anglo-Saxon Times to the Nineteenth Century* (Madison, Milwaukee, and London, 1968): M.-J. Tits-Dieuaide, *Le Moyen Âge* 74, 170–4

DATE DUE